Cambridge Series on Judgment and Decision Making

Emerging Perspectives on Judgment and Decision Research

This volume offers answers by a top group of experts to the question "Where is judgment and decision research heading as we forge into the 21st century?" The chapters represent state-of-the-art perspectives developed by some of the most innovative thinkers in the field. The book is organized around five themes: fortifying traditional models of decision making – looking at traditional topics in new ways; elaborating cognitive processes in decision making – exploring the interplay between decision research and cognitive psychology; integrating affect and motivation in decision making – relating how affect and motivation interact with decision making; understanding social and cultural influences on decision making – recognizing the importance of social and cultural contexts for decisions; and facing the challenge of real-world complexity in decision research – seeing the challenges and rewards of research outside the laboratory. The book concludes with a commentary based on an analysis and synthesis of the new ideas presented here.

Sandra L. Schneider is Associate Dean of the College of Arts and Sciences and Professor of Cognitive and Neural Sciences in the Department of Psychology at the University of South Florida. She received her Ph.D. in experimental psychology from the University of Wisconsin–Madison.

James Shanteau is Professor of Psychology at Kansas State University. He received his Ph.D. in experimental psychology from the University of California, San Diego.

D0387969

Cambridge Series on Judgment and Decision Making

The purpose of the series is to convey the general principles of and findings about judgment and decision making to the many academic and professional fields to which these apply. The contributions are written by authorities in the field and supervised by highly qualified editors and the Publications Board. The series will attract readers from many different disciplines, largely among academics, advanced undergraduates, graduate students, and practicing professionals.

Emerging Perspectives on Judgment and Decision Research

Edited by

Sandra L. Schneider
University of South Florida

James Shanteau
Kansas State University

CAMBRIDGE
UNIVERSITY PRESS

PUBLISHED BY THE PRESS SYNDICATE OF THE UNIVERSITY OF CAMBRIDGE
The Pitt Building, Trumpington Street, Cambridge, United Kingdom

CAMBRIDGE UNIVERSITY PRESS
The Edinburgh Building, Cambridge CB2 2RU, UK
40 West 20th Street, New York, NY 10011-4211, USA
477 Williamstown Road, Port Melbourne, VIC 3207, Australia
Ruiz de Alarcón 13, 28014 Madrid, Spain
Dock House, The Waterfront, Cape Town 8001, South Africa

http://www.cambridge.org

First published 2003

Printed in the United States of America

Typeface Palatino 10/13 pt.   *System* LATEX 2_ε [TB]

A catalog record for this book is available from the British Library.

Library of Congress Cataloging in Publication Data
Emerging perspectives on judgment and decision research /
edited by Sandra L. Schneider, James Shanteau.
    p.   cm. – (Cambridge series on judgment and decision making)
Includes bibliographical references and index.
ISBN 0-521-80151-6 – ISBN 0-521-52718-X (pbk.)
1. Decision making.   2. Judgment.   I. Schneider, Sandra L.
II. Shanteau, James.   III. Series.
BF448 .E47   2002
153.8'3 – dc21   2002025618

ISBN 0 521 80151 6 hardback
ISBN 0 521 52718 X paperback

To Charles Gettys, N. John Castellan,
and Hillel Einhorn

Contents

Contributors

MONICA D. BARNES Cognitive and Neural Sciences, Department of Psychology, University of South Florida

MICHAEL H. BIRNBAUM Department of Psychology, California State University, Fullerton, and Decision Research Center, Fullerton

CHARLES J. BRAINERD Division of Learning, Technology, and Assessment, University of Arizona

JULIA M. CLANCY Department of Psychology, University of Melbourne

JAMES H. DAVIS Department of Psychology, University of Illinois, Urbana-Champaign

MICHAEL E. DOHERTY Department of Psychology, Bowling Green State University

MICHAEL R. P. DOUGHERTY Department of Psychology, University of Maryland, College Park

J. RICHARD EISER Centre for Research in Social Attitudes, Department of Psychology, University of Sheffield

GLENN C. ELLIOTT Swinburne Computer Human Interaction Laboratory, Swinburne University of Technology

MELISSA L. FINUCANE Kaiser Permanente Center for Health Research, Hawaii, and Decision Research, Eugene, Oregon

CHARLES F. GETTYS Department of Psychology, University of Oklahoma (deceased)

SCOTT D. GRONLUND Department of Psychology, University of Oklahoma

BETH A. HAINES Department of Psychology, Lawrence University

VALERIE M. HASKELL Department of Psychology, University of South Florida

REID HASTIE Graduate School of Business, University of Chicago

ALICE M. ISEN Department of Psychology and Johnson Graduate School of Management, Cornell University

TATSUYA KAMEDA Department of Behavioral Science, Hokkaido University

GARY KLEIN Klein Associates Inc.

STEFAN KRAUSS Center for Educational Sciences, Max Planck Institute for Human Development

APARNA A. LABROO Johnson Graduate School of Management, Cornell University

JENNIFER S. LERNER Department of Social and Decision Sciences, Carnegie Mellon University

TOBIAS LEY Know Center, University of Graz

FARRELL J. LLOYD Department of Internal Medicine, Mayo Clinic, Scottsdale

R. DUNCAN LUCE Department of Cognitive Science, Department of Economics, and the Institute for Mathematical Behavioral Sciences, University of California, Irvine

LAURA MARTIGNON Center for Adaptive Behavior and Cognition, Max Planck Institute for Human Development

TERESA MARTIN Department of Psychology, California State University, Fullerton, and Decision Research Center, Fullerton

JIM MCLENNAN Swinburne Computer Human Interaction Laboratory, Swinburne University of Technology

SHAILA M. MIRANDA Department of Information Technology and Operations Management, Florida Atlantic University

COLLEEN MOORE Department of Psychology, University of Wisconsin–Madison

MARY M. OMODEI School of Psychological Science, La Trobe University

ANDREA L. PATALANO Beckman Institute for Advanced Science and Technology, University of Illinois, Urbana-Champaign

ELLEN PETERS Decision Research, Eugene, Oregon, and Department of Psychology, University of Oregon

MARK F. PETERSON Department of Management, International Business, and Entrepreneurship, Florida Atlantic University

REBECCA PLISKE Department of Psychology, Dominican University

JULIA POUNDS Federal Aviation Administration, Oklahoma City

DAVID A. RETTINGER Department of Psychology, Yeshiva University

VALERIE F. REYNA Departments of Surgery and Medicine, University of Arizona, and Office of the Assistant Secretary for Educational Research and Improvement, U.S. Department of Education

SANDRA L. SCHNEIDER Cognitive and Neural Sciences, Department of Psychology, and Office of the Dean, College of Arts and Sciences, University of South Florida

JAMES SHANTEAU Department of Psychology, Kansas State University

PAUL SLOVIC Decision Research, Eugene, Oregon, and Department of Psychology, University of Oregon

PETER B. SMITH School of Social Sciences, University of Sussex

OLA SVENSON Risk Analysis, Social and Decision Research Unit, Department of Psychology, Stockholm University

PHILIP E. TETLOCK Haas School of Business, University of California at Berkeley

RICKEY P. THOMAS Department of Psychology, Kansas State University

EINAR B. THORSTEINSSON Department of Psychology, University of New England

R. SCOTT TINDALE Department of Psychology, Loyola University, Chicago

ELIZABETH S. VEINOTT Department of Psychology, The University of Michigan

ALEXANDER J. WEARING Department of Psychology, University of Melbourne

DAVID J. WEISS Department of Psychology, California State University, Los Angeles

J. FRANK YATES Department of Psychology and Business School, The University of Michigan

Preface

We dedicate this book to three now-deceased "giants" in the history and development of the Society for Judgment and Decision Making (SJDM). Each of these individuals contributed his time, effort, and even money to help the society succeed in the formative years. Without their collective efforts, SJDM would not exist today. Had they not become involved when they did, there would have been no annual JDM meetings, no forums to discuss questions such as "What is new in JDM?" no SJDM publication outlet, and ultimately no *Emerging Perspectives* book. We owe it all to these three.

The first is Charles Gettys (University of Oklahoma), who, along with James Shanteau, organized the first few JDM meetings. Chuck's view of what a good meeting should be established precedents that are reflected in JDM meetings today. For example, he always wanted one or two major figures from outside JDM to speak at every meeting. He also emphasized that sessions should provide extensive opportunities for feedback and discussion. Chuck's name will always be tied to the founding of JDM.

The second is N. John Castellan (Indiana University), who was not only an early supporter of the meetings, but also the "organizational brains" behind the group. He edited the *Newsletter* for many years, helped organize several of the meetings, and was the first secretary/treasurer. John's most lasting contribution may be the establishment of SJDM as a legal entity; for example, he wrote the original bylaws and drew up the incorporation papers. In large part, John's forward-looking efforts made the Society what it is today.

The third is Hillel Einhorn (University of Chicago), whose enthusiastic support of early JDM meetings ensured the success of a fledgling effort. Hilly spoke at most of the early meetings, either as a presenter or as a discussant. His presence on the program, as well as that of others from the Center for Decision Research at the University of Chicago, provided both intellectual substance and visibility to the early meetings. Hilly also recognized the importance of including international speakers and helped make JDM into a worldwide presence.

We dedicate the present volume to the memory of these three founders of SJDM; their contributions will be with us always.

The Genesis

It is not always easy to tell how a project will start or where (or when) it will end. In the case of the *Emerging Perspectives* project, we can trace the origin to a conversation overheard between two attendees at the 1996 meeting of SJDM in Chicago. The gist of the comment by the first person was that "JDM is in a crisis." And the reason for a crisis? "A lack of new ideas" came the reply from the second.

This conversation struck a nerve with J. S. (James Shanteau); he had been one of the founders of SJDM, along with Chuck Gettys, N. John Castellan, and Hillel Einhorn (to whom this book is dedicated). If JDM as a field is running out of new ideas, then indeed there is a crisis. So the heart of the matter is, "What is new in JDM?"

After thinking about this issue for a year, J. S. attempted a partial answer at the 1997 meeting in Philadelphia. He gave a talk on "Five New Perspectives on Judgment/Decision Making" in which he described what he thought were several new and exciting ideas for JDM. These ranged from research on affect and individual differences in decision making to incorporation of memory models and new variants of utility into decision theory. The response to the talk was immediate and vocal, with audience reactions flowing over into break time.

Sandra Schneider (S. S.) was at the presentation and approached J. S. about the possibility of jointly editing a book to highlight these emerging perspectives. At first, J. S. resisted due to prior commitments to work on two other book projects – a Festschrift to Ward Edwards (Shanteau, Mellers, & Schum, 1999) and an edited book on competence in decision making (Smith, Shanteau, & Johnson, in press). Nonetheless, S. S. persisted (it took at least 30 minutes) and ultimately persuaded J. S. to form a partnership to produce an edited volume.

S. S. and J. S. then spent considerable time formulating a plan for the book that is described in the next section. After seeing the plan, the SJDM Publications Committee, Cambridge University Press, and, most important, potential authors were enthusiastic about the prospects for a book that would explore some exciting recent advances in JDM research. We then moved ahead with implementing the plan.

In 1999, S. S. and J. S. organized a JDM symposium ("Emerging Perspectives in JDM Research") to provide a taste of what was to come in the volume. The symposium was well attended and positively received, providing continuing momentum for the project. Although there were the inevitable unanticipated delays (e.g., added administrative responsibilities for both S. S. and J. S.), the book continued moving forward. We believe the sustaining energy behind this project goes back to the importance of that original question, "What is new in JDM?" This book offers some partial answers to that question from some of the best minds in the JDM field today.

References

Shanteau, J., Mellers, B. A., & Schum, D. A. (1999). *Decision science and technology: Contributions of Ward Edwards*. Boston: Kluwer Academic Publishers.

Smith, C., Shanteau, J., & Johnson, P. (In press). *Psychological investigations of competent behavior*. New York: Cambridge University Press.

Acknowledgments

We are grateful for and would like to acknowledge the invaluable contributions of the many individuals without whom this book could not have been completed.

We would like to thank all of the reviewers of various portions of the book, including Carl-Martin Alwood, Jonathan Baron, Gwendolyn Campbell, Beth Crandall, Robyn Dawes, Michael Doherty (who reviewed the entire book and provided helpful comments to several chapter authors), Ward Edwards, Maj-Lene Hedenborg, Richard Jennings, Mark Pezzo, J. Edward Russo, and Sanny Shamoun, as well as all of the chapter authors who reviewed the chapters of others. We would also like to thank the Publications Committee of the Society for Judgment and Decision Making for their help and encouragement. In addition, many thanks are due to Philip Laughlin and his assistant Michael Green, for their helpfulness, responsiveness, and patience throughout the publication process.

At the University of South Florida, Florencia Stanley, Sharon Tuxhorn, and Nanette Fenelon were instrumental in providing organizational and secretarial support. Several students, both graduate and undergraduate, also deserve thanks for their input, including Monica Barnes, Christine Caffray, Stephanie Hart, Alex Jackson, Jason Read, Susan Reitmeyer, and Forrest Samnik.

Encouragement from National Science Foundation colleagues Ann Bostrom, William Butz, and Wanda Smith is also much appreciated.

At Kansas State University, Leah Pickett provided tremendous organizational help at the beginning. In the latter stages, Sharon Sterling offered her incredible secretarial services. Also, various graduate students at KSU (most notably Rickey Thomas, Brian Friel, Jan Crow, and John Raacke) offered comments on specific chapters.

Finally, we would like to extend a special thanks to our families for their continued support, patience, and understanding while this project was being completed.

Without the help of all of these individuals, the book would not have been possible. We are most grateful to all of them.

Introduction: Where to Decision Making?

Sandra L. Schneider and James Shanteau

The Plan

The overriding goal of this book is to provide a forum for fresh perspectives on decision making. The aim is to expose readers to a wide variety of promising perspectives for enhancing the scope of judgment and decision-making research. The specific purposes of the book are (a) to bridge the gap between traditional decision-making paradigms and newer lines of research and theory; (b) to expand awareness of these new theories and approaches; and (c) to demonstrate how these alternative approaches can enhance development of the judgment and decision-making field. The chapters in this volume illustrate how much richer the field is becoming through attention to a number of novel perspectives that have not been a part of traditional judgment and decision-making approaches.

Over the past several years, there has been a growing concern that the progress of decision-making research may be limited by focusing heavily on traditional schools of thought (e.g., approaches emphasizing deviations from rationality and utility theory). At the same time, there has been accumulating evidence to show that numerous unexplored factors are likely to impact judgment and choice. For example, many researchers have come to appreciate the vital roles that memory, context, and emotion play in determining decision strategies. This volume provides a forum for updating assumptions of traditional schools of thought as well as introducing new perspectives that push the envelope of judgment and decision-making paradigms.

By providing a richer context for thinking about decision making, this book is also relevant for cognitive and social scientists interested in judgment and choice behavior. Many chapters provide explicit bridges from the study of basic psychological processes (including memory, comprehension, attention, emotion, and motivation) to the analysis of decision making. Most chapters also reflect a sensitivity to decision contexts, for example, by exploring naturalistic situations, stages of development, and levels of expertise. In addition, much of the volume includes attention to social processes, such as group and team interactions, relationship goals, and cultural influences that shape decision making.

In selecting authors for the book, we prepared an A list of authors and topics. We are pleased to say that, with only a couple of exceptions due to medical problems or overwhelming previous commitments, virtually everyone on our A list participated in the volume. Thus, in the selection of authors and topics, we believe that we hit a "home run."

The Book

Our instruction to authors was to provide an overview of not only their own perspective, but also the overall stream of related research. We wanted authors to describe specific emerging perspectives within the broader context and to speculate on future directions/extensions of their research stream. In this way, the *Emerging Perspectives* volume offers an answer by a top group of experts to the question "Where is judgment and decision research heading as we forge into the 21st century?" Thus, the chapters here represent state-of-the-art work developed by some of the most innovative thinkers in the field.

We believe that this volume will be useful to established judgment and decision-making researchers as well as graduate students. In addition, the insights here may be helpful to scholars in related disciplines. The book is organized around five themes and concludes with a commentary. In what follows, we list major themes and provide a brief description for each of the chapters.

Fortifying Traditional Models of Decision Making

In this section, several traditional topics and issues are considered in new ways. New perspectives on expected utility theories come from examinations of the usefulness of traditional decision aids, the rationality assumptions of subjective expected utility theory, and the descriptive accuracy of rank-dependent utility models. Bayesian inference is also explored relative to a criterion for *ecological rationality,* which is defined as behavior adaptive to the current task environment.

The volume starts with one of the most central questions driving decision research: *What is a good decision?* J. Frank Yates, Elizabeth S. Veinott, and Andrea L. Patalano tackle this question in their effort to understand why people are so unreceptive to many decision aids. They report two empirical studies of subjectively "hard" and "bad" decisions and a review of major decision-aiding approaches. They show that in decision makers' eyes, *decision quality* is a coherent construct that extends far beyond the conception that is implicit in many decision aids and in much of decision scholarship generally. This analysis therefore provides a plausible account of people's indifference to those aids. It also highlights the need for a broader notion of a "good" decision than has been customary in decision research and suggests the shape that such a conception might take. The analyses of Yates et al. further indicate that people are subject to forces encouraging beliefs that their personal decision making is seldom problematic – beliefs that have far-reaching scholarly and practical significance.

R. Duncan Luce, one of the most notable names in choice theory, revisits the concepts underlying *subjective expected utility* (SEU) theory – the backbone of decision making under risk. Luce demonstrates that the rationality assumptions that have been so critical to SEU theory come into question when one adds two new features. These new features, *status quo* and *joint receipt*, are among the constructs that have been particularly salient in descriptive studies of decision making. If one accepts SEU theory with the additional concession that it is reasonable to distinguish gains from losses, then the representation of rational behavior in many situations is not uniquely determined. Luce suggests that researchers need to be cautious given that what seems rational may depend on how the domain of study is formulated.

In an examination of the descriptive value of variants of utility theory, Michael H. Birnbaum and Teresa Martin use a novel Web-based research tool to explore preferences for dominated options. Using a variety of new conditions, they replicate findings from previous experiments to show that altering a gamble's representation by splitting a single event (e.g., a 20% chance of gaining $12) into two equivalent but less probable events (e.g., two 10% chances of gaining $12) can systematically lead people to select an inferior option. These violations of the coalescing principle support the descriptive efficacy of *configural weighting* over *rank-dependent* utility models. The studies also suggest important methodological advances in the ability to generalize across participants and procedures and to extrapolate to new predictions.

In the final chapter of this section, Laura Martignon and Stefan Krauss examine the tension between *Bayesian* decision making and *fast-and-frugal* decision strategies. They present the results from several studies to explore the conditions under which fast-and-frugal decision strategies are more or less likely to be used. They suggest that strategy shifts can be predicted by how information is represented, the difference in validity between the best cue and other cues, and the number of cues in conflict with the best cue. The authors provide an empirical test to show that the selection of a fast-and-frugal (e.g., Take The Best) or Bayesian strategy is dictated by predictable ecological properties of the environment.

Elaborating Cognitive Processes in Decision Making

The chapters in this section illustrate the interplay between contemporary decision research and advances in cognitive psychology. These chapters show how decision making can be better understood by considering the role of memory, comprehension, and developmental processes.

To open this section, Michael R. P. Dougherty, Scott D. Gronlund, and Charles F. Gettys develop a theoretical framework for incorporating memory into the explanation of decision-making phenomena. They show what various memory models predict about how *representation, retrieval,* and *experience* can be expected to influence decisions. Dougherty et al. emphasize the implications of abstraction-based versus exemplar-based decision representations, memory order effects, and differential activation effects in decision making, as well as memory factors associated with expertise in a decision domain. The authors conclude that the need for an integrative theory of cognition might best be met by a concerted effort to gain an understanding of the relationships between memory and decision-making processes.

Like Dougherty et al., David A. Rettinger and Reid Hastie suggest that the cognitive representation of a decision situation influences decision outcomes. However, their emphasis is on exploring how the decision content influences the type of representation adopted for the decision. Based on a pilot study and a review of relevant decision factors, Rettinger and Hastie identify seven *representation strategies* for comprehending a decision situation. They then provide evidence, based on an empirical investigation and a computer simulation, that different representations are likely for different decision content areas. Narrative representations, for instance, tend to be more common for legal stories, whereas decision trees may be more common for gambles. Like the other authors in this section, Rettinger and Hastie conclude that a deeper understanding of decision making can be gained by combining decision processes with cognitive models that are typically applied to account for higher-order thinking.

Valerie F. Reyna, Farrell J. Lloyd, and Charles J. Brainerd return to the traditional JDM theme of rationality, but they address the issue through examination of phenomena linked to memory and development. They suggest that decision making in natural contexts can be explained by incorporating cognitive issues in an integrative approach such as *fuzzy-trace* theory. This approach identifies different levels of reasoning rather than simply categorizing decisions as either rational or irrational. They suggest that increasing reliance on the underlying *gist* of information often improves the rationality of behavior by avoiding the distractions of superficial variables that can lead to inconsistent choices.

Beth A. Haines and Colleen Moore complete this section with an extensive review of literature concerning children's decision making and identification of critical variables in the *development of decision-making skills*. First, the authors explore the advantages of a developmental perspective for gaining insights into decision-making processes. They then review the implications of cognitive and social-cognitive findings to identify how decision-making skills and biases are likely to vary as a function of development. The authors suggest that the study of decision making could be substantially improved by greater emphasis on (a) the interaction between internal and contextual variables in determining the *subjective representation* of decision problems and (b) the development of *metacognitive skills* that influence decision strategies.

Incorporating Affect and Motivation in Decision Making

The role of affect and motivation has become increasingly important in social and cognitive psychology, and judgment and decision-making researchers have been among the leaders in this exploration. All of the chapters in this section share a commitment to understanding how affective or motivational processes interact with cognitive processes to influence the ways in which decisions are made and evaluated.

To begin the section, Ola Svenson presents *differentiation and consolidation* (Diff Con) theory as a means of capturing the affective and evaluative processes that guide behavior before, during, and after decision making. In Diff Con theory, the predecision differentiation phase involves several processes aimed at finding or creating an alternative that is sufficiently superior to its competitor(s). The postdecision consolidation phase involves processes aimed at ensuring that the outcome of the decision comes as close as possible to what was desired. Svenson provides a detailed description of these *pre- and postdecision processes*, emphasizing how an option's attractiveness is a dynamic interaction of affect and value. Svenson describes how the theoretical advances of Diff Con theory hold the potential to both broaden and deepen our understanding of decision making.

Melissa L. Finucane, Ellen Peters, and Paul Slovic briefly review the long history of research on affect and offer a new account targeted to decision making. The authors describe an *affect heuristic* process wherein positive and negative feelings, attached to relevant images, guide decision making. Empirical support for the affect heuristic is presented, along with suggestions for applications in a number of areas such as attention, deliberative versus nondeliberative processes, information representation, and psychophysical numbing (depersonalization). Finucane et al. conclude with a call to incorporate context as well as affect in exploring the complex systems guiding judgment and decision making.

Going beyond the more general exploration of affect in decision making, Alice M. Isen and Aparna A. Labroo focus on the ways in which *positive affect* can improve decision making and choice. Their chapter emphasizes the *cognitive flexibility* afforded by positive affect in a number of domains, ranging from diagnostic assessment to product representation and consideration. Their review of the literature shows the facilitating effects of positive affect in areas such as problem solving, creative thinking, negotiation, and information integration. In addition, Isen and Labroo introduce a likely neuropsychological mechanism responsible for these facilitative effects. They suggest that findings in cognitive neuroscience are likely to provide key insights into how affect influences problem solving and decision making. They recommend that decision researchers take advantage of the opportunities to expand decision-making models by integrating behavioral and biological evidence with an understanding of other factors.

In the section's final chapter, Sandra L. Schneider and Monica D. Barnes consider the advantages of elaborating common goals that people have in decision making relative to relying solely on the traditional decision goal of maximizing expected utility. The authors describe a qualitative study in which people in varying age groups reported goals for decision making across three time frames. The results of this study, along with a brief overview of motivation and evolutionary theories, reveal a predominance of *relationship goals* and motives coupled with more *basic survival-related motives* and personal goals associated with *achievement* and *positive self-view*. Given these goals and motives, the authors emphasize the importance of temporal and situational contexts as fundamental to creating meaning in decision making. Schneider and Barnes conclude that theories of decision making are likely to be perceived as more useful if they incorporate the goals and motives that are responsible for the perceived need to decide.

Understanding Social and Cultural Influences on Decisions

Although almost everyone recognizes that decision making takes place in a social and cultural context, relatively few researchers until now have managed to incorporate such factors into decision research. This section of the volume presents some of the progress that is being made in this endeavor, along with insights for continuing development.

Jennifer S. Lerner and Philip E. Tetlock open this section with a demonstration of how the construct of *accountability* can bridge individual, interpersonal, and institutional levels of analysis. They start with the observation that decision theories typically consider individuals in isolation. Lerner and Tetlock go on to argue that accountability is a universal feature of social life, with multiple influences on judgment and decision making. Their chapter provides empirical evidence for the influence of accountability on the accuracy of the decision-making process, and provides a framework for identifying the key factors that moderate accountability's influence. The authors conclude that attention to accountability, as well as other aspects of the social context, is likely to lead to a reevaluation of what it means to be accurate or rational in judgments and decisions.

Nowhere is the importance of social context more obvious than in the area of group decision making. Tatsuya Kameda, R. Scott Tindale, and James H. Davis explore how individual preferences and cognitions are aggregated to generate group decisions. The authors focus on *social sharedness*, or the degree to which preferences and cognitions are shared by members of the group at the outset of their interaction. They discuss several models and empirical phenomena related to social sharedness to illustrate its explanatory value as a common thread in group decision making. Kameda et al. also consider the dual meanings of consensus, distinguishing the impact of shared preferences from shared information or knowledge.

J. Richard Eiser tackles an issue in social judgment, approaching the problem from a connectionist learning perspective. His chapter is concerned with the *accentuation principle*, wherein social categorization can lead to the accentuation of differences in judgments about members of different categories. He presents two studies using connectionist computer simulations to demonstrate how the accentuation principle might arise from a self-organizing interaction among diverse influences and tendencies (rather than as a result of the manipulation of cognitive concepts, as might be predicted by the more traditional symbolic view of categorization). Eiser suggests that these demonstrations may encourage researchers to reconsider the level at which judgment processes are described. By considering a more basic level, he suggests that researchers may avoid the tendency to produce explanatory constructs that do little more than redescribe the phenomena.

The final chapter in the section, by Mark F. Peterson, Shaila M. Miranda, Peter B. Smith, and Valerie M. Haskell, considers some of the implications of the cultural and social context in organizational decision making. The authors point out how sociocultural context influences several aspects of group decision-making processes, including the *reasons for participating* in the process, *assumptions about time* and temporal aspects of the process, and the *social function* of the process. They elaborate on how these factors can influence the decision stages of information acquisition, identification, development, selection, and changed understandings. They provide an example of how these sociocultural factors can be mapped onto particular contexts using studies of international virtual teams. Peterson et al. conclude that sociocultural variables go beyond simple individual differences and that decision making cannot be understood without serious attention to the cultural context within which decisions – and decision makers – are embedded.

Facing the Challenge of Real-World Complexity in Decisions

As the chapters in this section remind us, judgment and decision making cannot be divorced from the world outside the laboratory. However, operating outside the lab brings its own challenges – and its own rewards. A sampler of these challenges and rewards is provided here.

To begin the section, Rebecca Pliske and Gary Klein, pioneers in the study of *Naturalistic Decision Making* (NDM), explain how constraints in the real world lead to alternative perspectives on decision making. This chapter provides a broad overview of the NDM perspective, including the history and scope of the NDM "movement" and a brief description of several NDM models such as the *recognition-primed decision* model. The authors explain that the typical methods of NDM research include cognitive task analysis and simulations. Using examples from the military, firefighting, weather forecasting, and other applied domains, Pliske and Klein provide a comparison of NDM and more traditional decision research, concluding that both perspectives can benefit from an integration of findings.

The next chapter provides an interesting example and analysis of the complexity of real-world decision making. Julia M. Clancy, Glenn C. Elliott, Tobias Ley, Mary M. Omodei, Alexander J. Wearing, Jim McLennan, and Einar B. Thorsteinsson describe an in-depth study of command styles in a computer-simulated (microworld) forest firefighting task. After elaborating on the characteristics of *distributed dynamic decision-making tasks*, the authors introduce a study to test how decision effectiveness is influenced by whether the leader tends to convey intentions or tends to communicate which particular actions should be taken. Clancy et al. argue that there are several advantages to an *intention-based control style* for hierarchically structured teams, given the more equitable distribution of cognitive workload and decision-making responsibility. The authors' approach also demonstrates a method by which many variables critical to real-world performance can be investigated systematically by means of a laboratory-based experimental study.

To conclude the section, James Shanteau, David J. Weiss, Rickey P. Thomas, and Julia Pounds offer new insights and a new approach into the evaluation and assessment of *expertise* in decision tasks. The authors begin by reviewing typical approaches to assessing expertise, including measures such as experience, accreditation, peer identification, judgment reliability, and factual knowledge. They then introduce the *Cochran-Weiss-Shanteau* (CWS) approach, which combines a measure for *discrimination* with a measure for *consistency* to provide a descriptive index of level of expertise that is functionally superior to other measures. Shanteau et al. reanalyze existing data in the areas of medical diagnosis, livestock judging, and auditing to illustrate the advantages of the CWS approach. They recommend continued research to further elaborate the usefulness of such an evaluation tool in complex decision-making arenas.

Commentary

No effort of this magnitude should end without analysis and synthesis of the new ideas and concepts presented. For this book, we were fortunate to convince Michael Doherty to take on this task of providing integrative comments. His final chapter affords a unique perspective on the new approaches and paradigms proposed here and places them in a historical context. Doherty describes *optimistic* and *pessimistic* camps and an overarching *realistic* camp within the field of judgment and decision making, comparing these camps to the perspectives of authors in this volume. In addition, he extracts several themes that are interwoven throughout the book and identifies several other directions that might be included in future projects. He offers an insightful capstone in our quest to explore "What is new in judgment and decision-making research."

In looking back to the origins of this project and appreciating where the project has taken us, we are pleased to see all of these things that are new, exciting, and continually developing avenues in judgment and decision-making research. We are also pleased to acknowledge that there were far too many new trends and discoveries to be able to include them all in this volume. We look forward to hearing about additional breakthroughs and innovations as the judgment and decision-making field continues to evolve.

Part I

Fortifying Traditional Models of Decision Making

1   Hard Decisions, Bad Decisions: On Decision Quality and Decision Aiding

J. Frank Yates, Elizabeth S. Veinott, and Andrea L. Patalano

ABSTRACT

Behavior-focused decision aids have had little documented success. A proposed contributor is this: To most deciders, *decision quality* entails myriad diverse facets, with an emphasis on material welfare. Yet, the typical decision aid (and its theoretical underpinning) is predicated on a narrow conception of decision quality that has other emphases. Deciders therefore often ignore such aids because they appear irrelevant to significant decider concerns. And when deciders do try the aids, the results disappoint them because the aids leave untouched quality dimensions that matter to them. Two empirical studies and a critical review of the most popular aiding approaches (from decision analysis to expert systems) support this thesis. The chapter offers for consideration a new, comprehensive decision quality conception intended to facilitate both fundamental and practical scholarship. The analysis also argues for *decision attribution theories* that would explain how deciders think they decide and why they believe that their decisions sometimes fail.

CONTENTS

We are indebted to Cynthia Jaynes, Kyle Dupie, Arnie Isa, Jason Dixon, and Kenneth Kim for their expert and conscientious assistance in conducting the research described in this chapter. It is also our pleasure to acknowledge the University of Michigan Business School's support of part of the research described here. We greatly appreciate the comments of David Weiss, Sandra Schneider, and an anonymous reviewer on an earlier version of the chapter. We are also grateful for the suggestions of other members of Michigan's Judgment and Decision Laboratory, including John Godek, Jason Riis, Winston Sieck, and Michael Tschirhart.

How can we help people make better decisions? This question has in-spired the labors of virtually all decision behavior scholars, including those who focus their attention on *fundamentals* (e.g., whether, how, and why choices among gambles violate the axioms of expected utility theory). Unfortunately, in many practical situations, there is little hard evidence that the techniques and devices, that is, decision aids, grow-ing from these efforts have, in fact, yielded substantial, demonstrable improvements in how people decide (e.g., O'Connor et al., 1999). And consultants who have made valiant efforts to promote the application of behavior-focused aids in such settings privately acknowledge that prospective users of the aids have been increasingly indifferent – if not hostile – to those tools. Critics of traditional decision scholarship iden-tifying themselves with the *naturalistic decision-making* movement (cf. Klein, Orasanu, Calderwood, & Zsambok, 1993; Zsambok & Klein, 1997) have conveyed the same message, but more openly and bluntly. Many of these critics have actually tried the tools, found them wanting, and been left disillusioned.

Why have behavior-focused decision-aiding efforts so often met with minimal success? There are undoubtedly many reasons for this state of affairs; failure frequently has many parents. Here, however, we concen-trate on just one particular potential contributor, which turns on the concept of *decision quality*. The plan of this chapter is as follows: In the first section, we present and elaborate our focal proposition, that deci-sion quality is not a unitary construct in people's heads and that decision aids often fail because they do not address the dimensions of decision quality that people wish to improve. The second section describes two empirical studies that provide evidence bearing on the plausibility of that proposition. The third section sketches and characterizes a representative sample of leading behavior-focused decision-aiding strategies. We show how those characterizations, coupled with the results of the empirical studies, buttress the claim that problematic aspects of decision quality conceptions really do play a significant role in determining how well decision-aiding attempts fare. In the fourth and final section of the chapter, we discuss the implications of our analyses for decision aiding and for decision scholarship more generally.

The Decision Quality Thesis

The following definition of a *decision* is a synthesis of how the term is actually understood and used across the myriad disciplines that study decision making, not just psychology (cf. Yates & Estin, 1998; Yates & Patalano, 1999):

> **A decision is a commitment to a course of action that is intended to produce a satisfying state of affairs.**

Thus, quality is part and parcel of the very idea of a decision. Consider, for instance, a decision that yields a more satisfying state of affairs for the implied beneficiary (who may or may not be the person making the decision) than does some other decision. This is equivalent to saying that that first decision has higher quality than its competing alternative. Or consider the "better decisions" sought by decision scholars more generally. These are, implicitly, ones that have quality superior to that possessed by "worse decisions."

The decision idea further suggests that when a decision maker – a *decider* – is confronted with a decision problem, a metadecision process focusing on decision quality ensues. In the voice of the decider, the following kind of soliloquy can be expected on some occasions:

> Suppose I were to make this decision the way that I'm naturally inclined to make it. What measure of quality could I expect? . . . That bad, huh? It sure would be good if I had help assuring better quality.

Hence, on such an occasion, the decider would be receptive to a decision aid that appears to enhance the chances of making a decision with adequately high quality. But what, exactly, does the decider mean by *quality?* The thesis we entertain is this: In the mind of the typical person – be that person a decider or a decision scholar – decision quality is not a unitary construct. Instead, it consists of several distinct, imperfectly correlated facets. Moreover, the facets comprising one person's notion of decision quality are unlikely to correspond perfectly to those of another, and indeed may well surprise that other person. (*"That's* what you mean by a good decision?") Further, the facets that are – or are seen by deciders to be – most pertinent in some decision problems can be markedly different from those most relevant in other problems. And, finally and significantly, the quality conceptions implicitly assumed and addressed in any specific decision-aiding effort (or body of decision scholarship) are almost necessarily incomplete relative to the full range of facets that legitimately comprise any single person's notion of decision quality. These propositions, if true, would constitute a partial account for the apparently limited success of such aiding efforts. Suppose that the decider is concerned about, say, quality facets F1, F2, F3, F4, and F5. According to the present thesis, there is a good chance that any decision aid offered to the decider will appear to address only, say, quality facets F2 and F6, where the decider sees F6 as entirely irrelevant. Little wonder, then, that the decider would find that aid unappealing and would not even try it. Any actual potential of the aid for enhancing decision quality would be moot.

Empirical Studies: Decision Quality Facets for Personal Decisions

Our basic thesis was motivated by extensive study of the literatures on decision making in numerous disciplines. It was also grounded in qualitative observations and informal interviews of seemingly countless deciders discussing their real-life decision problems. Here we describe two empirical studies we performed in order to test the impressions originating in those less structured inquiries. In the best of circumstances, such studies would examine decisions made by people in a wide variety of contexts. But practical constraints precluded that. Thus, we focused on personal decisions made by convenience samples of college students. The specific considerations identified in our studies should in no sense be regarded as representative. Yet, there appears to be no reason to expect that the broad categories of decision quality facets implicated by those considerations do not apply to decision problems and deciders generally.

Study 1: Decision "Hardness" and "Easiness"

Two major classes of decision quality facets can be distinguished. The first class consists of aspects associated with the *products* of a decision per se. That is, they concern what the decision yields for the decision beneficiary. In contrast, the second class of decision quality aspects concerns the *process* by which a decision is made, more specifically, *decision process difficulty* as experienced by the decider. In other words, they pertain to what makes a given decision problem either "hard" or "easy" for the decider to solve. It is legitimate to regard difficulty as an element of decision quality for the same reason that people consider the difficulty of negotiating for a new car to be part of the overall adequacy of the transaction. Study 2 was designed to be enlightening about product aspects of decision quality. In contrast, Study 1 focused on decision process difficulty, a kind of decision-making *cost*, in the broad sense. One justification for using a decision aid would be the expectation that it would alleviate the difficulties associated with arriving at a satisfactory decision (cf. Clemen, 1991). The objective here was to discover the specific *kinds* of difficulty that people experience generally and hence plausibly would seek to avoid when they are in situations where they have to decide. That people would indeed welcome such relief is implicit in the following kind of remark often reported in news accounts of both heroic and tragic events: "Sadly, we had to make a very tough decision."

Method

Participants. Ninety-nine introductory psychology students at the University of Michigan participated in this study in exchange for course credit. Sixty-three percent were female.

Procedure. A questionnaire in booklet form was administered to participants in groups of 10–15 people. Participants were instructed to "imagine hard and easy decisions that you have made." Each participant was then asked to describe two or three hard decisions and two or three easy ones that "you have made in the past year." Since hard decisions had priority for us, out of concern for time constraints, all participants wrote about their hard decisions first. For both hard and easy decisions, participants were asked three key questions (among others). They were asked to first describe the circumstances that gave rise to each decision problem, then to explain why the decision was hard (easy) for them, and after that to indicate how they solved the given problem.

Further, for each decision, each participant was asked to report (a) how many options had been available; (b) how long it took to make the decision; (c) the degree to which the participant felt that he or she took either too little or too much time making the decision; (d) how satisfied the participant was with the decision's eventual outcome; and (e) the extent to which the participant felt that his or her decision was the best possible given the circumstances.

Results and Discussion

Basic hard/easy comparisons. In total, participants described 212 hard decisions and 200 easy ones. The topics of these decisions ran the gamut but tended to fall into three major categories: academic issues (e.g., which college to attend, what major to choose, which classes to take), relationships and social life (e.g., whom to date, which fraternity or sorority to join), and financial matters, such as consumer purchases (e.g., which car to buy). For both hard and easy decisions, participants typically reported choosing among three or four options. Several pertinent hard versus easy comparisons included the following:

- *Decision time:* Hard decisions took a median of 3 weeks to make, whereas easy decisions typically took only 2 days. Although participants spent more time making hard decisions than easy ones, there was no difference in their ratings of the appropriateness of the amount of time taken, $t(86) = -1.90$, *ns*. That is, participants appeared to feel that hard decision problems simply demanded more time to solve properly and that they gave those problems their due. Of course, it is possible that hard and easy problems tend to have different deadlines attached to them, too.

- *Satisfaction:* Participants' satisfaction with the outcomes of their decisions was rated on a 9-point scale, where 1 = "Not At All Satisfied" and 9 = "Extremely Satisfied." The mean satisfaction ratings for hard and easy decision outcomes were 7.6 and 8.1, respectively, $t(89) = 2.71$, $p < .01$, for a within-participants comparison on the first hard and the first easy decision cited by each participant with complete satisfaction data. That is, participants were significantly more pleased with the results of their easy decisions than their hard decisions. Note, however, that the magnitude of the difference in satisfaction ratings was small, only half a scale point. And it is

especially noteworthy that the mean rating for the hard decision outcomes was less than one and a half scale points from
the maximum possible. In other words, on average, no matter
what, participants were rather pleased with what their decisions
yielded.

- *Relative decision adequacy:* One defensible (and common) definition of a *good decision* is that it is the selection of the best
  alternative available at the time the decision is made. This
  conception of good decision making is useful because it acknowledges that, in some circumstances, all potential outcomes are unpleasant in an absolute sense (e.g., in medical situations where patients are already in irreversibly poor
  health). A measure of decision adequacy that focuses solely
  on absolute ratings of outcome satisfaction would neglect
  such possibilities. That is why participants here were also
  asked to rate the adequacy of their decisions relative to,
  in hindsight, the best available on a 9-point scale, where
  1 = "Not the Best" to 9 = "Definitely the Best." The mean ratings for hard and easy decisions were, respectively, 7.6 and 8.0,
  $t(91) = 2.06$, $p < .05$. Once again, although participants were
  less pleased with their hard decisions than with their easy ones,
  by no means did they regret either.

"Why hard/easy?" coding procedures. Our primary aim was to understand how people come to regard some decisions as hard but others
as easy. Implicit is the assumption that subjective hardness is simply
the lay characterization of a decision being difficult to make and that
hardness attributions are specifications of the different kinds of difficulty that weigh upon deciders. Recall that our data-collection procedure was to have participants bring to mind decisions that they
themselves had made and that they themselves classified as either
hard or easy. Participants then gave their own accounts of why they
made those classifications. The reported explanations constituted our
basic data. Consistent with our initial proposition, participants' explanations for what made decisions either hard or easy were remarkably
diverse. Nevertheless, it was obvious that there was structure within that
diversity.

Our strategy for discerning the structure underneath the data and
then encoding them for further analysis was the following: First, each
of the investigators independently read the protocol for every decision

described by every participant. Each investigator then developed his or her own scheme for classifying the participants' reasons for considering a decision to be either hard or easy. After that, the investigators reached a consensus about a common coding scheme for subjective hardness and another for subjective easiness. The hardness scheme contained 29 categories and the easiness scheme included 24.

With these coding schemes in hand, we then developed training materials and taught two naive coders to apply the respective schemes to the original data. The coding procedure required that the coder consider explicitly whether each category in the coding scheme was or was not present in a given protocol. Thus, it was entirely possible that a given decision might have been regarded as hard (or easy) for several reasons, not just one. (Ultimately, it turned out that the number of hard codes assigned to the typical hard decision was 1.9, and the average easy decision was given 1.6 easy codes.) The coders were instructed to be conservative, to encode only direct attributions for why a decision was hard or easy, not to infer what attribution "made sense" given the participant's remarks or the situation described. For example, buying a car might seem like a big expense for anyone. But unless the participant discussing a car-buying decision explicitly mentioned that expense was a reason the decision was hard, the coder was not to record the "expense" hardness category. After training, each coder independently encoded every protocol. At regular intervals as the coding activity proceeded, the coders met and compared their codes. When discrepancies arose, the coders discussed their disagreements and reached a final consensus about whether a given category was or was not represented in a particular protocol.

Emergent hardness categories. The hardness and easiness categories are most usefully interpreted when they are structured into a smaller number of *supercategories*. One particularly enlightening structure has seven supercategories for hardness. A parallel structure was recognized for easiness as well. Here we describe the supercategories encompassing the 29 hardness categories that emerged from the data in the kind of language a decider might use in characterizing a given form of hardness:

- *Hardness 1 – Outcomes: Serious: "This decision is hard because a serious loss of some kind can (or is likely to) result from it."* The specific loss categories commonly cited by participants included ones with long-term, possibly irreversible, effects, ones that entailed hurting another person, ones that required violating personal (e.g., moral) principles, ones that involved large, significant outcomes, and ones that held great risks.

- *Hardness 2 – Options: "This decision is hard because of burdens imposed by the number and/or character of the available options."* Thus, there might be too many or too few options among which to choose, or those options might require comparisons on too many factors.

- *Hardness 3 – Process: Onerous: "This decision is hard because the process of making it is onerous."* Among the specific kinds of onerousness cited by the participants were the amount of effort required, the presence of emotional circumstances, time pressure, uncertainty, and the decider's feeling that he or she lacks essential expertise.

- *Hardness 4 – Possibilities: "This decision is hard because it is difficult to imagine or predict what its possible outcomes might be."* One particular form this variety of hardness takes arises when the decider has had little or no experience with the kinds of alternatives under consideration.

- *Hardness 5 – Clarity: "This decision is hard because it is especially unclear which alternative is superior to its competitors with respect to the considerations on which they are being compared."* An important variant of clarity hardness is simply a lack of dominance, that is, there is no option that is at least as good as every other option with respect to every consideration and better with respect to at least one of those considerations. Cases of "tying" implicate another variant, where, in the aggregate, two or more options seem tied for first place in their overall appeal; for example, the decider would be inclined to say, "But I love them both!"

- *Hardness 6 – Value: "This decision is hard because I am unsure how I would feel about specific outcomes that might result from it."* For instance, the decider might have never experienced some particular outcome and is uncertain whether the experience would be pleasant or unpleasant and to what degree.

- *Hardness 7 – Advisors: "This decision is hard because of conflicting recommendations or advice."* In one kind of situation where this type of hardness occurs, the decider is faced with advisors who contradict one another. In another, an advisor who is important to the decider pushes views or actions that contradict the decider's own opinions.

Emergent easiness categories. The supercategories for easiness were essentially mirror images of the hardness supercategories. They can be characterized as follows:

- *Easiness 1 – Outcomes: Mild: "This decision is easy because its potential outcomes are insignificant, nothing to worry about."* Specific instances of problems involving this kind of easiness entailed considerations such as short-term effects, reversibility, minimal risk, and the existence of a win-win situation with options that precluded any sort of loss.
- *Easiness 2 – Options: "This decision is easy because the available options require minimal reflection."* One variant of this type of easiness occurs when a decision must be made in order to achieve a specific objective (e.g., satisfying a requirement that a student must complete an advanced laboratory course to earn a particular degree) and there is indeed an option available that clearly attains that goal. In a decision entailing another variant, the constraints are so exacting that otherwise appealing alternatives are eliminated out of hand, leaving only a small, manageable number to ponder.
- *Easiness 3 – Process: Benign: "This decision is easy because the process of making it is not unpleasant."* One common form of process easiness was identified when participants said that they "just knew" which option to pick. Others were indicated when participants said that their decisions took minimal effort, that they had had experience making similar decisions before, or when one option was favored with respect to some overriding consideration.
- *Easiness 4 – Possibilities: "This decision is easy because projecting its possible outcomes is straightforward."* Decisions involving alternatives that participants had experienced previously were often easy in the possibilities sense; the decider felt sure about what *could* happen, even if he or she did not know what *would* happen if any particular option were pursued.
- *Easiness 5 – Clarity: "This decision is easy because it is readily apparent which alternative is better than its competitors, taking into account all the pertinent considerations."* A common form of this kind of easiness arose when, for whatever reason, the available

option pool contained one dominating alternative, for example, it had all positive features and no negatives. In another form, one option was clearly closer to the decider's ideal than were its rivals.

- *Easiness 6 – Value: "This decision is easy because I know for sure how I would feel when experiencing each of its potential outcomes."* Such confidence generally arose among participants as a result of their prior experience with those outcomes, which made clear to them whether they liked or disliked those outcomes and to what extent.

- *Easiness 7 – Advisors: "This decision is easy because of the recommendations or encouragement of others."* One form such easiness can take entails essentially turning the decision problem over to others, letting them figure out what the decider ought to do.

Category incidence rates. Table 1.1 displays the percentages of decisions the participants classified as hard and easy for reasons belonging to the various hardness and easiness supercategories just described. Several conclusions are indicated by the findings summarized in the table. The first is that there are indeed many distinct kinds of decision difficulty that weigh upon deciders; there was considerable breadth and variety in the ways our participants saw their decisions as being hard or easy. A second conclusion implicit in the table is that hardness and easiness citations are not complementary. That is, even if a particular category was cited often as a reason hard decisions might be hard, this provided no assurance that the parallel category would be cited just as frequently as a reason for easy decisions being easy. And then there are the specific categories that were most commonly mentioned. Particularly notable is "Outcomes: Serious Loss Potential" for hardness. The data indicate that, by far, when people say that a decision is hard, they mean that they are concerned about things like the stakes involved – what the decision beneficiary could lose through the decision.

At least tentatively, the data have several implications for those seeking to provide decision-making assistance that would be well received by prospective clients. Most obviously, the description (and, ideally, the reality) of that assistance should convince the client that that assistance would reduce significantly the client's chances of experiencing a serious loss of any kind. (The implied hypersensitivity to losses is reminiscent of

Table 1.1. *Percentages of Decisions Classified by Participants at Least Once as Hard or Easy for Reasons Corresponding to Various Hardness and Easiness Supercategories*

Supercategory	Percentage
Outcomes	
Hard (Serious loss potential)	69.8%
Easy (Insignificant)	17.5%
Options	
Hard (Too many/few, Character)	10.8%
Easy (Minimal reflection required)	21.0%
Process	
Hard (Onerous)	22.1%
Easy (Benign)	31.0%
Possibilities	
Hard (Obscure)	8.0%
Easy (Apparent)	15.0%
Clarity	
Hard (Ambiguous superiority)	23.1%
Easy (Obvious superiority)	41.5%
Value	
Hard (Uncertain)	7.5%
Easy (Clear-cut)	21.5%
Advisors	
Hard (Disagree)	5.1%
Easy (Recommend, Encourage)	4.5%

Note: Hard and easy supercategory percentages sum to more than 100% because participants typically cited more than one reason that a given decision was hard or easy.

numerous assertions and results in the decision behavior literature, such as the steepness of value functions for losses postulated in Kahneman and Tversky's 1979 prospect theory.) The other supercategories with sizable incidence rates (e.g., 20% or more) contain advice that might well be wise, too. Thus, for instance, a decision aid developer and consultant would probably find it fruitful to build and promote aids that are transparently effortless and perhaps even fun to use (addressing deciders' process concerns). Those aids should also make one of the decider's options stand out as distinctly better than its competitors (addressing deciders' implicit demands for clarity). And, if at all possible, an aid should help the decider to clearly and, presumably, accurately anticipate how the decider would actually feel about the potential outcomes of the actions under consideration (speaking to deciders' sensitivity to value clarity).

Study 2: Decision "Badness" and "Goodness"

Recall that Study 1 was intended to shed light primarily on people's conceptions of decision quality most closely associated with the difficulty of the processes by which they arrive at their decisions. In contrast, Study 2 was designed to illuminate quality notions identified more strongly with the products of decisions. Our guiding assumption was that these notions are especially likely to be manifest when people reflect upon real decisions they have made and that they themselves regard as having been either good or bad. Thus the following approach, which paralleled the one used in Study 1.

Method

Participants. One hundred and ten introductory psychology students at the University of Michigan participated in this study in exchange for course credit. Fifty-four percent were female.

Procedure. Each participant completed a questionnaire that was administered by computer. The questionnaire first told the participant that our purpose was to understand what participants thought made a decision either good or bad. The participant was told that we would focus on decisions the participant had actually made, but only decisions about which the participant had had to "think hard." The computer then required the participant to bring to mind four such decisions made within the previous year, two good decisions and two bad ones. For each of those decisions, the participant first wrote a brief descriptive title. The participant then rated the goodness or badness of the decision "relative to all the important decisions you have ever made" on an 11-point scale ranging from −5 ("Extremely Bad") to 0 ("Neither Good Nor Bad"), to +5 ("Extremely Good"). Next, the participant rated the importance of the decision, again "relative to all the important decisions you have ever made," on an 11-point scale ranging from 0 ("Not Important At All") to 10 ("Extremely Important"). The product of these quality and importance ratings yielded an *impact score* for the decision. The computer then selected two of the participant's four decisions for further consideration, the "really bad" decision with the more negative impact score and the "really good" decision with the more positive impact score.

The computer next requested that the participant answer a series of questions about each of the focal good and bad decisions. (The good–bad and bad–good orders were counterbalanced across participants.) First, the computer asked the respondent to "explain why you classified the present decision as a bad (good) one." It then asked for specific details about how the decision was actually made, including when and how the decider came to realize that there was a decision to make and how long it took to make that decision.

Basic bad/good comparisons. As implied by the preceding procedure description, 110 bad and 110 good decisions were examined, one of each for every participant. The mean quality ratings of the focal good and bad decisions were, respectively, +3.6 and −2.4 (on the scale from +5 to −5), $t(109) = 28.99$, $p < .001$, thus providing something of a check on the manipulation. Observe, however, considering the distance of the ratings from the 0 neutral point, that the focal good decisions seemed to be better than the focal bad decisions were bad. The mean importance ratings of the focal good and bad decisions were 7.7 and 5.6, respectively, $t(109) = 7.22$, $p < .001$. That is, the participants' bad decisions did not seem as important to them as their good ones. Taken together, the quality and importance ratings suggest the same story indicated in Study 1: People are, on the whole, not greatly displeased with the real-life decisions they make. Perhaps substantively significantly (a point to which we return later), on average it took participants far less time to bring to mind their bad decisions (53 seconds) than their good ones (70 seconds), $t(109) = 4.78$, $p < .001$. Nevertheless, they required about the same amount of time to write about them, approximately 10.5 minutes, $t < 1$.

"Why bad/good?" coding procedures. We used basically the same approach as in Study 1 for developing and applying schemes for encoding participants' explanations for why their decisions were either bad or good. So there is no need for us to review the procedural details. We should note, however, that those procedures yielded 20 categories of decision badness and 24 of decision goodness. Further, on average, 2.3 distinct coding categories were assigned to each bad decision and 3.7 to each good decision. In and of itself, as was the case with perceptions of hardness and easiness, this constitutes evidence of the multifaceted character of people's subjective notions of decision quality. Decisions are not seen as simply good or bad to some degree; they excel or fall short with respect to a host of qualitatively distinct dimensions that capture people's attention.

Emergent badness categories. The supercategory structures for badness and goodness contained five parallel supercategories each. We first describe the supercategories for badness in the voice of a decider explaining why he or she regarded a particular decision as bad.

- *Badness 1 – Experienced Outcomes: Adverse: "This decision was bad because it resulted in bad outcomes."* Recognition of violating personal (e.g., moral) principles was one major form this kind of badness assumed. Another entailed any sort of bad outcome that had never even been contemplated at the time the decision was made, that is, *blindsiding.* A related but different variety was implied when there were bad outcomes that had been recognized as possible but were not actually *expected* to occur.

- *Badness 2 – Missed Outcomes: Favorable: "This decision was bad because it resulted in me missing out on good outcomes."* In one form of this kind of badness, the decision caused the decider to miss out on some good experience that would have occurred otherwise. In another, the decision led to the relinquishment of a good thing the decider already possessed, such as a satisfying relationship.

- *Badness 3 – Options: "This decision was bad because of its implications for my options, presently or in the future."* In one common form of this kind of badness, the decision limited the decider's future options, such as closing off certain career paths. When participants cited a second, "fuzzier" variety, they reported that they knew that there were better options than the ones they chose but, for no good reason, they rejected those options.

- *Badness 4 – Process: "This decision was bad because the process used to make it was bad."* This process category did not seem to be differentiated in any principled way. Participants who cited factors that fell into this category felt that, for miscellaneous reasons, such as minimal care or time devoted to the task, and independent of its actual outcomes, the process employed in making a decision was flawed.

- *Badness 5 – Affect: "This decision was bad because I felt bad while (or after) making it."* A sense that the decision exposed the decider to risk was reported for one variation of this kind of badness (e.g., the risk of contracting a sexually transmitted disease). The feeling of regretting an action defined another.

Emergent goodness categories. These were the supercategories for goodness, again as a decider might characterize them.

- *Goodness 1 – Experienced Outcomes: Favorable: "This decision was good because it yielded good outcomes."* For the most frequently cited version of this first form of goodness, participants indicated that the given decision had already produced good outcomes. In another, however, such outcomes were merely anticipated. A third variation acknowledged that, although not all decision outcomes were favorable, on balance, those outcomes *tended* to be good ones. In still another form, which we labeled *relative elation,* the decider believed that the decision's outcomes were better than those that would have resulted from another option the decider might have selected but did not.

- *Goodness 2 – Missed Outcomes: Adverse: "This decision was good because it prevented me from experiencing bad outcomes."* The first variety of this kind of goodness occurred when the decision precluded the decider from experiencing bad outcomes that otherwise would have taken place. The alternative form arose when the decision rescued the decider from a bad situation that already existed, such as a dysfunctional relationship.

- *Goodness 3 – Options: "This decision was good because of how it improved my options."* When this type of goodness was cited, making the pertinent decision opened up new (and presumably attractive) alternatives that either did not exist before or were at least unrecognized.

- *Goodness 4 – Process: "This decision was good because the process used to make it was good."* When participants reported this category of goodness, they mentioned that some aspect of how the decision was made – irrespective of its outcomes – contributed to its appraisal as a good decision.

- *Goodness 5 – Affect: "This decision was good because I felt good while (or after) making it."* One variation of affect goodness entailed a general sense of pleasure with the given decision's outcomes. The other most common form of this kind of goodness occurred when the decision made the decider feel good about him- or herself, for example, experience a sense of pride.

Category incidence rates. Table 1.2 presents the percentages of decisions the participants regarded as bad and good for reasons belonging to the badness and goodness supercategories just sketched. The table

Table 1.2. *Percentages of Decisions Classified by Participants at Least Once as Bad or Good for Reasons Corresponding to Various Badness and Goodness Supercategories*

Supercategory	Percentage
Experienced outcomes	
Bad (Adverse)	89.0%
Good (Favorable)	95.4%
Missed outcomes	
Bad (Favorable)	25.7%
Good (Adverse)	30.3%
Options	
Bad (Limiting)	44.0%
Good (Improved)	14.7%
Process	
Bad (Flawed – outcome independent)	20.2%
Good (Sound – outcome indpendent))	6.4%
Affect	
Bad (Risk exposure, Regret)	23.9%
Good (Pleasure, Self-esteem)	40.4%

Note: Bad and good supercategory percentages sum to more than 100% because participants typically cited more than one reason that a given decision was hard or easy.

clearly buttresses the conclusion that deciders' personal decision quality concepts are multifaceted, entailing constructs that are typically quite distinct from one another. Implicit in the data is also the conclusion that the acknowledged facets tend to differ from person to person and from one decision to the next. An especially striking feature of the results is that subjective notions of decision quality are overwhelmingly dominated by outcomes: Good decisions produce good outcomes and bad decisions yield bad ones, directly or in the opportunity cost sense. We are also struck by the extent to which people's appraisals of decisions are affected by abstractions, for example, the kind of counterfactual reasoning implicit in the "Missed Outcomes" supercategories.

As with Study 1, it is useful to consider the practical implications of the incidence rates in Table 1.2 for those who aspire to help people decide better. Again, but in even more dramatic fashion, the data (concerning the outcome supercategories) indicate that a decision aid developer or consultant simply *must* convince clients that his or her offerings have a good chance of improving clients' situations materially and even morally. The options responses suggest that it would be wise to speak to deciders' concerns about the long-term implications of their decisions as well. And the affect citations imply that decision aids and consultations ideally should seek to have deciders feel an undifferentiated "warm glow" about the decision-making experience and its aftermath as well. Further, at least some attention should be devoted to conveying the idea that an aid or consultation is sound in ways that do not translate immediately and directly into favorable outcomes for the decision beneficiary.

A Review: Quality Conceptions Implicit in Decision-Aiding Practice

There are many approaches to behavior-focused decision aiding as well as specific aids derived from those approaches. Nevertheless, they fall into a relatively small number of major classes. Here we briefly describe six of the most popular ones: decision analysis, debiasing techniques, social judgment theory (and its relatives), general decision support systems, group decision support systems, and expert systems. In each case, we attempt to discern the conceptions of decision quality that developers and practitioners have (implicitly or explicitly) sought to address and enhance with their techniques and devices. We then try to reconcile the foci of those aids with what our empirical studies suggest that deciders think that they *need* to address in order to make adequate decisions.

Decision Analysis

At one level, at least, decision analysis is an exceptionally broad and comprehensive approach to decision aiding. Applications have been reported in domains as diverse as the siting of public utilities (e.g., Keeney & Nair, 1977), capital investment in mining (e.g., Hax & Wiig, 1977), policies for treating intracranial aneurysms (Aoki et al., 1998), and mediation in legal trials (e.g., Aaron, 1995). Von Winterfeldt and Edwards (1986) wrote a book on decision analysis, which they introduced as "a set of formal models, semiformal techniques for interacting with people, and bits of lore and craft" (p. 2) used in the service of helping people to be rational in making inferences and decisions. They described the goal of decision analysis as structuring and simplifying the task of making hard decisions as well and as easily as the nature of those decisions permits. Decision analytic methods include such things as (a) ways to organize or structure a decision problem (e.g., with decision trees or influence diagrams), (b) techniques for assessing uncertainty (including the use of debiasing techniques, discussed subsequently), (c) procedures for measuring value and utility, (d) operations for combining information to arrive at a choice (e.g., expected utility theory and multiattribute utility theory), and (e) sensitivity analyses (discerning how much conclusions depend on the precise values used). Decision analysts are not greatly concerned with inherent bias in human strategies per se. The assumption is that, as long as time and effort are taken to elicit biases in multiple ways, various techniques (including debiasing procedures) can be applied to ensure that reasonable judgments are acquired to guide decisions properly. Furthermore, decision analysis uses tools such as sensitivity analysis to ensure that small judgment differences do not significantly affect the recommendations derived in an analysis.

As suggested by von Winterfeldt and Edwards's (1986) description of the field, typically, as far as decision analysts are concerned, decision quality is embodied in the rationality or logicalness of the process by which people decide. And the particular variety of rationality of interest is commonly referred to as *internal consistency* or *coherence* (cf. Yates, 1990, chapters 5 and 9). When a person is rational in the coherence sense, that person avoids endorsing principles that contradict one another. That person also seeks to avoid holding beliefs and making choices that conflict with principles he or she accepts as appropriate, for example, the axioms of probability theory, expected utility theory, or a particular variety of multiattribute utility theory. Implicitly – and sometimes explicitly – analysts assume that adherence to rationality is threatened by two recurrent features of decision situations: uncertainty and multiple conflicting objectives. Hence the character of the techniques described previously. Our empirical results suggest that real deciders rarely acknowledge a concern with the rationality of their decision processes and certainly not in the coherence sense. Instead, they are preoccupied with results – good outcomes of various kinds. Analysts sometimes imply that there is in fact a strong link between coherence and results (e.g., Morris, 1977, p. 13). And some appear to believe that the typical decider shares that faith, as suggested by the remarks of Matheson and Howard (1968, p. 12): "Most persons follow logical decision procedures because they believe that these procedures, speaking loosely, produce the best chance of obtaining good outcomes."

Our data do not prove the point, but they are consistent with the possibility that faith in a strong coherence–outcome link is *not* widely shared. If real, this lack of faith would constitute a potentially significant contributor to the relative unpopularity of decision analysis. As we will discuss, this is not to say that people think that decision rationality and outcomes are independent. Instead, people might simply believe that rationality, in the decision analytic, coherence sense, is far from sufficient for producing decisions that yield good outcomes. And the obvious demands and burdens imposed by those methods (e.g., time and tedium) lessen their appeal even more. Of course, analysts might well respond that decision analysis is simply inappropriate for the small-scale personal problems of students like our research participants; the stakes do not warrant the required investment. (On the other hand, at least some decision analysis advocates would probably disagree; cf. Baron & Brown, 1991.) Yet, the complaints of skeptics about decision analysis as applied in standard "serious" domains (e.g., Ubel & Loewenstein, 1997) are actually quite consistent with the perspectives of our participants. Now suppose that the proposed interpretation is correct. Then decision analysts would be wise to make a concerted effort to convince deciders that there is indeed a strong connection between coherence and decision outcomes.

Debiasing Techniques

Debiasing techniques focus on the role of judgment in decision making. The approach developed out of a series of experimental findings demonstrating that people make systematic errors in assessing probability or, more generally, likelihood. Two of the most well-known errors are *hindsight bias* and *overconfidence*. The first is the phenomenon whereby, in hindsight, people are overly optimistic about what could have been anticipated in foresight (e.g., Fischhoff, 1975). As a concrete example, when appraising a subordinate's failed hiring decisions, a manager might be inclined to say, "*Anybody* should have been able to predict that those employees wouldn't work out." The manager would therefore be inclined to fire the subordinate for exercising poor judgment. But hindsight research suggests that the manager's opinions about what anybody would have predicted are too generous to that anybody. Thus, firing the subordinate would be ill advised. Overconfidence refers to instances – which are extremely common, in the laboratory, at least – in which people believe that their judgments are more accurate than they really are. For example, suppose that a physician makes a series of pneumonia diagnoses and, for each case, reports a probability judgment that that diagnosis is correct. Then, if the physician is overconfident, the average probability judgment will exceed the proportion of correct diagnoses (cf. Yates, Lee, Shinotsuka, Patalano, & Sieck, 1998).

Debiasing techniques are applied in two ways. The first focuses on specific decision problems as they arise, the same way that decision analysis does. The goal is to prevent biases from injecting themselves into the judgments supporting the given, here-and-now decision. A concrete example is a set of author instructions that appears in every issue of the *International Journal of Forecasting*:

> [A]uthors of controversial papers are invited to attach a "Note to Referees." This note would describe the model (hypotheses) and possible outcomes, but *not the results*. The referees would be asked to evaluate the methodology and to predict the outcomes prior to reading the paper. They would then review the entire paper and complete the regular Referee's Rating Sheet.

Informed by research on the origins of the phenomenon, those instructions are intended to reduce the effects of hindsight bias on referees' appraisals of the manuscripts they are considering. Significantly, for the decision aid receptivity issues examined here, over the years very few authors have exercised this hindsight bias protection option (J. S. Armstrong, personal communication, May 4, 2000). The second debiasing approach entails encouraging or training deciders to alter permanently their basic judgment procedures. Their judgments would then be free of the focal biases when the decider confronts any decision problem that might present itself. Russo and Schoemaker's (1989) instructions for how managers can reduce their personal tendency to exhibit overconfidence are a good illustration (e.g., establishing a routine of seeking information that might contest one's initial opinions about any decision-related issue).

Interestingly, advocates of debiasing techniques seldom explicitly discuss why the techniques ought to be used, that is, what the advocates assume decision quality to be and why their methods should be expected to improve such quality. Perhaps that is because they consider the arguments self-evident. Such an argument could go something like the following: Most decisions are predicated at least partly on what the decider believes is likely to happen in the future, for example, that customers will respond positively to the introduction of a new product. Tendencies like hindsight bias and overconfidence amount to systematic discrepancies between deciders' judgments about what is going to occur and what really does occur. These biases impose a low ceiling on how good the outcomes of the decisions can possibly be. Consider, for instance, a decision to introduce a new product that rests on overly optimistic predictions about how much customers will like that product. One of the few ways this decision could turn out well would be for the profit margin on each unit to be astronomically high, which is, of course, unlikely. This argument for debiasing techniques is highly compelling. It is also compatible with our participants' explanations for why they thought that a good number of their bad decisions were bad, for example, that those decisions yielded bad outcomes that they had failed to anticipate. Nevertheless, we have seen little evidence that debiasing techniques are frequently employed in actual practice. Why? Five plausible explanations suggest themselves:

- *Surprise:* It is likely that (consistent with our data), in some instances, the bad outcomes that deciders fail to predict are total surprises (e.g., side effects of a medical treatment completely new to a patient). That is, those outcomes were not even envisioned as possibilities when the decisions were being deliberated. Hence, deciders never tried to predict them in the first place. The concept of judgmental bias would be moot in such situations because there are no judgments.
- *Predictability:* It is conceivable that deciders believe that some occurrences are due entirely to chance and are, therefore, inherently unpredictable. In such a case, deciders would consider it futile to even attempt to make accurate judgments. And, once again, debiasing techniques would be seen as pointless.
- *Relevance:* Even if a decider thinks that an event is predictable to some degree, the decider might not believe that failures to anticipate the event accurately have significant implications for eventual decision outcomes. Alternatively, the decider might believe that errors in judging that event are due mainly to factors other than the biases addressed by the debiasing methods a decision consultant happens to be offering. This third possibility is implicit in some scholars' skepticism about the true practical importance of many of the biases commonly discussed in the literature (e.g., Christensen-Szalanski, 1993).
- *Efficacy:* There might well be instances in which deciders are convinced that a particular bias significantly and adversely affects judgments that, in turn, greatly increase the chances of bad decision outcomes. Yet, they may have little faith that the specific

debiasing methods being offered to them would actually work, serving to reduce the bias enough to make an investment in those methods worthwhile.

- *Habit:* Suppose that, as bias researchers contend, the judgment processes that give rise to various biases are natural. Then, even when not "hard-wired" into our basic cognitive architecture, those processes could become firmly ingrained as habits, with all the common characteristics of automaticity (cf. Anderson, 1985). In particular, those processes would tend to be evoked without conscious control or even awareness. If this is indeed so, then merely telling a decider about a debiasing technique, as is the custom, is unlikely to have any lasting impact on judgment behavior as it actually occurs in daily life.

At the moment, no one knows which, if any, of these possible explanations for the limited use of debiasing techniques are valid. But debiasing advocates would do well to find out and then revise their approaches accordingly.

Social Judgment Theory (and Its Relatives)

As the name suggests, like debiasing techniques, social judgment theory concerns itself with the judgments that typically provide essential foundations for people's decisions. The perspectives on those judgments differ markedly in the two approaches, however. Unlike debiasing methods, social judgment theory emphasizes the assumption that, in real-life judgment situations, people necessarily derive their judgments from the presumed pertinent facts or *cues* they happen to perceive in that situation. Specifically, they use their assumptions about how cues and the events of interest tend to be associated with one another in the *natural ecology.* For instance, in trying to anticipate the performance of a prospective intern, assuming that such factors tend to be predictive, a supervising physician might pay attention to the applicant's medical school record, her recommendations, and various impressions she created in her interviews. The resulting forecast would be predicated on the supervisor's beliefs about how strongly and in what form those factors generally tend to be associated with internship performance (their validity) as well as how those factors tend to covary with one another (their redundancy). Thus, all else being the same, in predicting an intern's performance, the supervisor would place heavy emphasis on factors assumed to be strongly associated with performance and less emphasis on other, weaker (or redundant) predictors. The accuracy of the supervisor's predictions would depend on (among other things) the actual cue validities and redundancies, the correspondence between these facts and the supervisor's emphases, and how reliably the supervisor goes about the judgment task from one case to the next.

Social judgment theory traces its origins to the probabilistic functionalism espoused by Egon Brunswik and his colleagues from the 1930s to the 1950s (e.g., Tolman & Brunswik, 1935). But it has evolved over the years into a set of specific technologies and practices grounded in the spirit of Brunswik's views (cf. Brehmer & Joyce, 1988; Cooksey, 1996; Hammond, Stewart, Brehmer, & Steinmann, 1986). Social judgment theory methods provide specific means for assessing key elements of the ecology (e.g., cue validities) and of the person's judgment *policy* (e.g., the person's emphases on particular cues and his or her consistency). The theory also describes in quite precise ways how these factors lead to varying degrees of judgment accuracy. One way that social judgment theory can be "social" concerns the fact that different individuals faced with the same judgment tasks often disagree in their predictions, sometimes heatedly. Social judgment theory methods provide a means for explaining such disagreements in terms of the parties' different implicit assumptions about the ecology (e.g., about cue validities) and how they go about the judgment task (e.g., the emphases they put on particular cues and how reliably they execute their judgment policies). The isolated differences can then be examined and sometimes resolved, perhaps resulting in a collaborative judgment system that outperforms whatever existed before. Work by Cooksey, Freebody, and Davidson (1986) is illustrative. These authors derived models of the policies by which different elementary school teachers anticipated pupils' reading performance on the basis of factors such as socioeconomic status and early indices of cognitive functioning. Those models revealed significant differences in how the teachers went about this task, differences that might well have remained obscure otherwise, even to the teachers themselves. If they chose to, the teachers could then relatively easily arrive at a common consensual policy for, say, prescribing instructional interventions for students expected to have difficulty.

Important "relatives" of social judgment theory are various technologies that (a) assess the pertinent facts about a given case and then (b) use some sort of formal combination rule to synthesize those facts into a decision-relevant judgment for that case. In our internship application example, the pertinent residency program might, for instance, have a system whereby all the major facts known about a given candidate (e.g., medical school records, referee ratings, interviewer impressions) are encoded numerically and then a performance prediction is made according to a linear equation. In that equation, the weights applied to the various encoded facts would translate into the effective impact those facts will have on the predictions. Meehl (1954) was the first to bring significant attention to the potential of such systems. Meehl showed that, under specified conditions, the systems consistently yielded more accurate clinical psychological assessments than did human diagnosticians. Later work, especially that of Robyn Dawes and his associates (cf. Dawes, 1979), provided further evidence of the efficacy of such *actuarial* judgment procedures. Just as importantly, such work used methods deriving from social judgment theory to explain *why* those systems so often outperformed humans. For instance, it showed that the most important factor is that human consistency is so grossly inferior to system consistency that it wipes out any advantages humans might have over the systems in other respects.

To the best of our knowledge, no one has done a survey to settle the issue definitively. But informal observation suggests that decision-aiding methods that draw on the ideas underlying social judgment theory and its relatives, even if not their particulars, are more commonly employed than debiasing techniques. (And if we include the formal models used in standard business forecasting for financial and marketing purposes, this is surely true.) Nevertheless, certainly in the eyes of proponents, social judgment theory and related techniques are utilized far less often than might be expected, especially given the seemingly clear-cut statistical evidence of their efficacy (see, for example, McCauley, 1991). Again, why?

To a point, whatever explains indifference to debiasing methods (including possibly the hypotheses described earlier) is likely to contribute to coolness toward social judgment theory and similar methods as well. After all, both approaches focus on the judgments people use to inform their decisions. But there are significant differences in the approaches that are likely to implicate different accounts for people's reluctance to apply them, too. For one thing, social judgment theory entails a statistical perspective that emphasizes multiple repeated instances of virtually the same situation, for example, a long history of interns and internship applicants for a residency program or a large database of mental health patients, as in the Meehl (1954) studies. In contrast, at least superficially, for many of the biases addressed by debiasing methods (especially hindsight bias), the focus is on single cases. And the layperson deciders who participated in our studies were certainly concerned with single cases. The kinds of personally significant decision problems they discussed (e.g., what career to pursue) were in most cases one-of-a-kind problems for them as individuals, although they would not have that character for professionals seeing essentially similar cases over and over (e.g., counselors, internship admissions officials, or mental health diagnosticians). Regardless, though, the statistical-versus-single-case distinction might be significant in a fashion consistent with our data.

Recall that one thing that mattered greatly to our respondents was feeling good about the process by which they made their decisions, including the self-esteem, the pleasure, and even the sense of morality the process provided. Social judgment theory and related methods are likely to suffer on these grounds. Dawes (1979) and McCauley (1991) both convey some of the misgivings potential users have about the techniques. One is the seeming dehumanization entailed in treating all people (e.g., internship candidates) the same way, as required in a statistical approach. That approach ignores the uniqueness that is prized almost as a moral imperative in individualist cultures like that of the United States. Another is the seeming marginalization of human deciders themselves when, in the kinds of systems advocated by Dawes and Meehl, functions that were once performed by humans (e.g., clinical diagnosis) are instead performed by programmed machines. (Schoemaker & Russo, 1993, describe other interesting cases in banking.) Even worse, the machines essentially function as black boxes programmed to apply algorithms that are not rationalized in terms of the everyday causal models and language that real people prefer and use. Worse still, designed to encompass only a small number of predictive cues, the algorithms cannot accommodate the extenuating circumstances that human deciders feel compelled to take into account in individual cases (e.g., a family crisis during medical school).

The implied challenge for decision aid specialists adopting the approach of social judgment theory and related methods is to configure and present them in ways that do not ignite these negative associations. One approach would be to acknowledge explicitly people's potential misgivings and seek to dampen them (e.g., by emphasizing the fairness of treating all internship candidates the same way). Another would involve having judgments rendered by both humans and machines and then deriving a composite judgment from them, such as an average.

There are good arguments as well as evidence (e.g., McClish & Powell, 1989) that in many circumstances, such composite judgments should outperform both human and machine assessments.

General Decision Support Systems

Even among those who build, use, and study them, there is some disagreement about what exactly should and should not be considered a decision support system. Nevertheless, a definition consistent with most conceptions is that a decision support system is a computer-based system, typically interactive, that is intended to support people's normal decision-making activities (cf. Finlay, 1994; Silver, 1991). One key feature of the decision support system idea is the central role of computers. Another, which is perhaps more fundamental, is that decision support systems are not designed to alter fundamentally how the decider thinks about decision problems. And they are certainly not intended to replace the decider, making choices in his or her place. Instead, they are supposed to help (i.e., support) the decider do what he or she is inclined to do more or less naturally. Decision support systems are commonly recognized as having three basic components, configured as suggested in Figure 1.1 (cf. Carter, Murray, Walker, & Walker, 1992, p. 16):

- *Data component*: Provides substantive information the decider might request.
- *Model component:* Performs operations on information retrieved through the data component, according to models of virtually any degree of complexity.

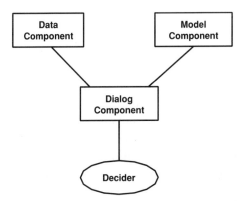

Figure 1.1 Configuration of a prototypical general decision support system.

- *Dialog component:* Allows the decider to interact with the system in particular ways, that is, constitutes the interface between the system and the decider, including things like search engines for exploring the system's databases.

We normally think of decision support systems only on the grand scale seen in large organizations such as public corporations and government agencies. But more familiar, personal-level technologies amount to decision support systems as well. Consider, for instance, an ordinary consumer (like any of us) using the on-line version of *Consumer Reports* magazine when shopping for a new refrigerator. The pertinent article on refrigerators, conveyed via the Internet, is output from the data component of the consumer's shopping decision support system, listing a host of refrigerators along with their specifications, test results, and repair statistics. The decider's personal computer, the network software, and the *Consumer Reports* displays (e.g., product × attribute tables or matrices) represent the dialog component. The typical *Consumer Reports* article provides an overall score for each of the products reviewed. These scores are a synthesis of assessments on the various features of the products – for example, temperature performance, noise – for the various refrigerators reviewed. The rules by which such scores are computed are typically weighted sums, where the weights operationalize relative feature importance. They are part of the model component of the decision support system. If the shopper wished to, he could rather easily import the data from the *Consumer Reports* refrigerator × feature matrix into his own spreadsheet. He could then perform any operations desired (e.g., compute weighted sums with importance weights different from those used by *Consumer Reports*), extending the model component of the system. It is noteworthy that the procedures commonly acknowledged as models within decision support systems include ones usually identified with decision analysis as well as social judgment theory–related tools.

A variety of aims for decision support system users are implicit in the criteria by which systems are evaluated. Generally, though, the aims fall into two broad classes, effectiveness and efficiency (cf. Finlay, 1994). *Effectiveness* refers largely to decision outcomes. Although decision support systems retain the decider's basic, natural logic, they can (and are expected to) improve outcomes because the systems' data components supply information the decider often will not have otherwise (e.g., about what refrigerators are on the market and what their specifications and performance records are). This point does not appear to be discussed explicitly or extensively in the decision support literature. But those data components can also be expected to bring attention to objectively important considerations that naive deciders would probably overlook entirely when left to their own devices (e.g., vacuum cleaner emissions of breathable particles that can aggravate asthma and other respiratory disorders). Decision support system *efficiency* pertains to things like decision-making time and other process costs. Besides effectiveness and efficiency, decision support system developers (and, perhaps more importantly, their purchasers in businesses) pay a great deal of attention to how users feel about their experiences with the systems.

Some observers (e.g., Adelman, 1992) note that decision support systems are far less common than their early proponents anticipated that they would be (and for reasons quite similar to those argued here, such as inattention to potential users' requirements). This seems to be especially so in governmental (including military) contexts. Nevertheless, it is clear that decision support systems are much more popular than the decision aids we discussed previously. Indeed, within the business world, some kinds of systems have become virtually mainstream (see, for example, Churchill's, 1999, discussion of decision support systems for marketing). The comparative success of decision support systems is understandable, given our results. The fact that decision support systems are normally evaluated along many different dimensions is an acknowledgment of the multifaceted nature of how people conceptualize decision quality, part of our primary thesis. And the breadth of the systems (i.e., their inclusion of three distinct components that themselves are often quite broad) is very likely a response to deciders' multifaceted quality demands. It seems that commercial decision support systems would *have* to have evolved to be responsive to many of the things that deciders regard as attractive in a decision aid. Otherwise, they would have simply disappeared from the marketplace.

Similar pressures have probably ensured that the decision support systems that have survived possess certain specific advantages, too, efficiency in particular. After all, decision time and other costs are easy to assess and hence to reduce. This is especially so when there is sufficient motivation, such as the ever-present demand in the business world to control operating expenses. In their self-acknowledged pursuit of effectiveness, decision support system developers undoubtedly convey to users their aspiration to facilitate the achievement of the good outcomes our data indicate that deciders crave above all else. The data components of decision support systems provide deciders with relevant facts that they obviously did not know before (e.g., product information from *Consumer Reports* and other databases). This surely nourishes the expectation that the systems lead to decisions with better outcomes. Whether decision support systems really do deliver all the benefits that users believe that they deliver is unclear (see, for example, Kottemann, Davis, & Remus, 1994). Yet, it *is* clear that the decision support system approach to decider receptivity has elements that the advocates of other decision aids would find worthwhile to adopt.

Group Decision Support Systems

Group decision support systems are decision support systems with one additional component beyond the three that characterize all such systems: a *group process component*. The purpose of this extra feature is to manage the interactions among several people participating in a decision-making effort. Group decision support systems acknowledge that individuals acting alone virtually never make significant decisions for organizations of any size. Instead, those decisions typically require the involvement of many people. Part of the reason is that such big decisions almost always involve political considerations. But the principle that two (or more) heads are better than one suggests that such collaboration ought to have inherent advantages for yielding objectively better decisions, too (cf. Hill, 1982). Yet, an empirically documented fact of life is that group interaction often leads to *process losses* whereby such potential goes unrealized. For instance, people sometimes withhold defensible but unconventional opinions because they fear public ridicule. Group process elements of group decision support systems seek to reduce such process losses.

In practice, group decision support tools put considerably less emphasis than other decision support systems on databases and on modeling tools and other complex information-manipulation aids. Instead, they concentrate on group process issues. This seems to be because in the kinds of decisions that are delegated to groups (e.g., corporate strategic decisions with unique circumstances and large stakes), there is often little clarity about the characteristics of the "right" decision. And, more often than not, there are fundamental differences that must be resolved concerning group members' values. Indeed, some have contended that *the* main goal of group decision support systems is to help groups work through such differences and arrive at a consensus more quickly (Olson

& Courtney, 1992). Group decision support systems usually try to do this by structuring the communication process in particular ways. For instance, they sometimes shape how input is given, when ideas are evaluated, how it is determined who speaks when, whether comments are anonymous or not, when and how voting takes place, and how individual opinions are elicited to create a climate that makes rapid consensus likely. PLEXSYS, developed by Nunamaker, Applegate, and Konsynski (1987), is a good example of a computerized group decision support tool that carries out many of the functions envisioned for such systems more generally.

Some evaluations of group decision support systems highlight group output, such as the number of new ideas generated via electronic brainstorming (e.g., Dennis & Valacich, 1993). More often, though, they tend to focus on various aspects of process, for example, how the systems change group interaction and confidence, consensus, and satisfaction of group members (cf. Dennis, George, Jessup, Nunamaker, & Vogel, 1988). Conclusions about the efficacy of group decision support systems are mixed. The systems appear to reliably yield some kinds of improvements. But they seem to pose notable challenges, too, such as increases in the social distance between group members induced by computer-mediated communications (cf. Watson, DeSanctis, & Poole, 1988). These challenges, as well as the expense, unnaturalness, and logistical difficulties associated with using computers to manage group decision making, undoubtedly help to explain why group decision support systems are far less common than more general systems (Lewis, Keleman, & Garcia, 1996). Our empirical studies did not examine participants' conceptions of group decision quality per se. Thus, our data do not speak directly to the group process aspects of group decision support systems. Nevertheless, they certainly do not disagree with anything that has been revealed in the group decision support system literature. For instance, users' negative reactions to system interference with comfortable aspects of normal, face-to-face group interaction accord well with our participants' concerns about decision process pleasantness, difficulty, and associated affect.

Expert Systems

The term *expert* in the expression *expert system* is intended to communicate either or both of two ideas. The first is that the computer program so described is supposed to perform a task, such as problem solving, to a high degree of proficiency, at the level an expert would achieve. The second is that the system is built to mimic more or less literally the details of how a specific acknowledged human expert goes about that task. Whether modeled on any particular human expert or not, expert systems execute operations that have the qualitative nature that commonly characterizes how real people reason. For instance, they typically rely mainly on production rules of the "if-then" form, for example, "If all of the applicant's referee ratings are 4 or better, then ... " This can be contrasted to the quantitative rules that are common in the model components of most decision support systems (e.g., the linear equations of multiattribute utility theory or typical social judgment theory–related schemes). Our concern here is with expert systems that perform tasks entailed in solving decision problems. King (1990) provides an excellent illustration of a system that performs a chore normally carried out by loan officers. Specifically, the system evaluates credit requests for small business ventures, rendering recommendations to either "Give credit," "Consult a superior for more advice," or "Deny credit."

An expert system has three basic components in addition to its interface with the user (cf. Durkin, 1994; Prerau, 1990):

- *Component 1 – Knowledge base:* A repository containing essential facts, rules of thumb, or *heuristics,* and conventions about when and how to apply those facts and rules for the given domain (e.g., what information is used for appraising loan applications and what recommendations should be offered for particular configurations of facts).
- *Component 2 – Working memory:* A register for the information the user provides about the given case under consideration (e.g., storage for the particulars on Jane Smith's application for a loan to support the establishment of her software business).
- *Component 3 – Inference engine:* A processor that applies the facts, rules, and conventions in the knowledge base to the case-specific contents of working memory to perform the task set for the system (e.g., to deliver a credit appraisal for Jane Smith's new venture).

The contents of the knowledge base are critical, hence the reason that expert systems are sometimes referred to as *knowledge-based systems* or simply *knowledge systems.* Normally, the knowledge base is acquired through systematic, intensive interviews and observations of one or more recognized human experts. More generally, though, its contents could also be collected from any source, including scholarly literature, as occurs often in medical informatics (van Bemmel & Musen, 1997). The entire process by which an expert system is built is commonly called *knowledge engineering*. Most expert systems are designed to function the way human experts behave when they serve as consultants. Conversations between experts and clients are a normal, essential element of consultations. Thus, expert systems typically contain one final feature:

- *Component 4 – Explanation module:* A set of routines that provide natural language-like explanations of how the system arrived at its conclusions for a given case (e.g., why it recommended denying a loan to Jane Smith's software company), essentially a recitation of the rules that were applied to the facts of the given case (e.g., collateral below the minimum required).

Expert systems are sometimes used as stand-alone decision aids, but there seems to be a consensus that usually they are most appropriately deployed in conjunction with decision support systems. Sometimes this amounts to simply making certain that a decider draws upon both the given decision support system and the available expert system. Alternatively (and preferably), the expert system is embedded in the larger decision support system, creating what is sometimes called a *hybrid* (Ignizio, 1991, p. 39) or *intelligent* decision support system (King, 1990, p. 53).

As in the case of decision support systems, some (e.g., Adelman, 1992) believe that expert systems have failed to live up to expectations for them or to their true potential. Nevertheless, it seems safe to say that a great many decision-related expert systems have been built and that many of them are actually in service. Durkin (1994) conducted a survey that yielded more than 600 actual expert systems for business and medical purposes, many of which we can assume to be used to assist in decision making (see also Liebowitz, 1998). Durkin estimated that his survey captured only about 20% of extant systems, which would imply more than 3,000 business and medical systems altogether. This suggests a level of popularity far beyond that of any of the decision aids we discussed previously. Why the difference?

The difference is partly due to the powerful contemporary cachet of anything that smacks of high technology. That is, businesspeople, in particular, want to at least *try* any innovation that conveys the image that their companies are on the cutting edge of the high-tech revolution (cf. Liebowitz, 1990, p. 3). In addition, however, expert systems are developed with an eye for precisely the kinds of considerations that our data suggest are likely to drive potential users' receptivity to any decision aid. Take the case of explanation. The participants in our studies indicated that the character of the decision process matters to them a great deal. For instance, they want the process to be comfortable. Discussion with other people who might be more experienced with a given class of decision problem (i.e., experts) is routine for deciders in real life. A usual and natural feature of such discussions is give-and-take. An advisor does not simply offer a recommendation that the decider then either blindly accepts or rejects, with no questions asked. Instead, the decider requests and receives arguments for that recommendation, which the decider can then scrutinize. Unlike what occurs with the decision aids we discussed previously, this capability exists (at least minimally) for expert systems. And then there is the dominant emphasis on outcomes. Developers go to great lengths to make certain that the tasks for which they develop expert systems are manageable, well-defined ones for which expertise is clearly defined, and they avoid other, more risky tasks. Further, the human experts they choose to mimic with their systems are people who are widely accepted as experts. Accordingly, deciders almost certainly expect that using the resulting systems would yield for them the same kinds of good outcomes that presumably justified the recognition of the modeled human experts as experts in the first place.

Themes

Implicit in our review of various decision-aiding approaches are several key themes. It is useful for us to be explicit about those themes and what they imply. As Table 1.3 suggests, the six decision-aiding approaches we have discussed seem to differ sharply in their popularity. Decision analysis, debiasing techniques, social judgment theory and its relatives, and group decision support systems constitute the less popular approaches. General decision support systems and expert systems comprise the more popular class. The themes we recognize are identified with the features indicated in the last four columns of Table 1.3:

Coverage. Our main thesis has been that the typical decider recognizes several distinct facets of decision quality, that is, dimensions of goodness and ease, and that the particular aspects that are significant to any two different deciders are unlikely to coincide perfectly. To the extent

Table 1.3. *Distinctive Features of Less Popular and More Popular Decision Aid Classes*

Decision Aid Class	Feature			
	Coverage[a]	Emphasis[b]	Natural?[c]	Outcome Effects "Obvious?"[d]
Less Popular				
Decision analysis	Narrow	Procedural	Harder	No
Debiasing techniques	Narrow	Procedural	Harder (?)	No
Social judgment theory and relatives	Narrow	Procedural	Harder (?)	No
Group decision support systems	Narrow	Procedural	Harder	No
More Popular				
General decision support systems	Broad	Substantive	Easier	Yes
Expert systems	Narrow (But)	Substantive	Easier	Yes

[a] Range of quality aspects targeted.
[b] Emphasis on improving the procedure used for deciding versus providing facts about the substance of the decision problem.
[c] Whether required activities are harder or easier than customary, natural routines for deciding.
[d] Intuitive obviousness of positive effects on likely outcomes for a given decision problem.

that this is true, a decision aid's popularity is enhanced when its coverage of quality aspects is broad, that is, when it improves the decider's chances of making decisions that shine with respect to many aspects rather than only a few. As suggested by Table 1.3, all of the less popular decision-aiding approaches we reviewed have narrow coverage. For instance, decision analysis concentrates almost exclusively on ensuring the rationality of how the decider does things like synthesize probability and value (e.g., via expected utility operators). In contrast, general decision support systems tend to have very broad coverage, often actually encompassing the other aids as options along with many others among which the decider is free to pick and choose at will. Any single expert system is typically, by design, quite narrowly focused. But, because they are modular that way, several different expert systems can be offered to a decider at any one time.

Emphasis. Two broad varieties of decision aids can be recognized. *Procedural* aids seek to improve the chances of making good decisions by improving (or replacing with better substitutes) the procedures the decider would be inclined to apply spontaneously. In contrast, *substantive* aids aim to increase the odds of achieving good outcomes by giving the decider information that is particular to the substance of the given decision problem. For instance, a substantive aid might provide the decider with previously unknown and significant facts about the options under consideration. It could even inform the decider of previously unknown options that would prove to be highly satisfactory. As indicated in the second feature column of Table 1.3, all of the less popular decision aids emphasize procedure, whereas the more popular ones highlight substance. The significance of the procedure-versus-substance distinction is likely mediated by the last two themes we discerned, which we consider next.

Naturalness. Our data indicate that deciders want their decision processes to "feel good" in several respects. For instance, they apparently feel strongly that a decision process should not be inordinately effortful or otherwise unpleasant. Thus, unless there is good reason, they would not want the process imposed by a decision aid to be more onerous than the natural ones they would apply on their own. And, ideally, the process demanded by the aid would make things easier than what is natural. Most often, the less popular decision aids we reviewed make the decision process unnatural and hard for deciders. In part, this is a necessary consequence of the fact that all those aids are procedural; their purpose is to *improve* on nature. In contrast, general decision support systems and expert systems are expressly designed to conflict as little as possible with how deciders customarily decide. Indeed, also by design, they typically make the decision process easier. For instance, via their databases, decision support systems afford ready access to decision-relevant information that deciders otherwise would find difficult, if not impossible, to acquire in a reasonable amount of time. And expert systems perform tasks that might take the decider a seeming eternity to perform, if the decider is capable of carrying out those tasks at all.

Outcome Effect Obviousness. The participants in our studies indicated that their overriding concern was that their decisions produce good outcomes for their beneficiaries. Our sense is that decision aids differ considerably in the impression that, for a given decision problem, those aids are likely to lead to a decision with better outcomes than any decision the decider would make on his or her own. As suggested in Table 1.3, in our view (which admittedly needs to be verified for generality), for the more popular aids, general decision support systems and expert systems, the likelihood of achieving better outcomes appears obvious, whether that is actually the case or not. Such impressions seem plausible if for no other reason than that, as substantive aids, these systems routinely draw upon or provide facts that are entirely new to deciders. It is therefore easy for deciders to then say things like "My! I had no idea that was the case. That changes my mind right there." In contrast, the positive effects on decision outcomes promised by the less popular aids probably seem much more "dicey" to deciders. When it exists at all, the empirical evidence for the outcome efficacy of the new procedures entailed by these aids is statistical. When a decider arrives at a decision after applying such an aid, the decider can readily say, "For all I know, I could just as easily have arrived at the same decision doing what I normally do – and with a lot less hassle."

The Bigger Picture

The research we have described had a sharply focused aim. But as the work proceeded, we came to realize that the issues we examined, as well as our findings, have wider implications than might be immediately obvious. In this last section, we bring attention to those implications, some of which are likely to be unsettling to some observers.

Recall that an important goal of all decision scholars, and especially decision aid developers and decision consultants, is to help people decide better. However, before they can begin even trying to do that, they must convince deciders to try their wares. Earlier in this chapter, we framed this focal problem in the voice of a decider who is confronted with a decision problem and eventually concludes that she would be receptive to a suitable decision aid. It is useful for us to revisit that scenario but to extend it, to imagine that the decider does indeed choose to adopt an aid that has been offered to her, on a trial basis at least:

> Suppose I were to make this decision the way that I'm naturally inclined to make it. What degree of quality could I expect? . . . That bad, huh? It sure would be good if I had help ensuring better quality. . . . Hmmm . . . here's a decision aid that looks interesting. Perhaps *it* would do the trick. Let me look at it more carefully. . . . Seems promising. I think I'll give it a whirl.

This is the kind of soliloquy a developer or consultant would love to see, of course. It actually entails several constituent assessments. It is instructive to examine each of those assessments carefully, considering what it actually involves, how likely it is that a real decider would make that assessment (and why), and what this implies for decision aiding and for decision scholarship more generally.

Assessment 1: Decision Quality

The decider's "degree of quality" phrase implicates our primary initial focus. Our thesis was that the typical decider uses expressions like *degree of quality* to refer to a host of different things, that, subjectively, decision quality is a multifaceted construct. Further, the specific facets that any particular decider has in mind are likely to correspond only imperfectly to those that define any other decider's quality conception. As we have argued, our data agree strongly with this proposition. A variety of practical conclusions follow from the thesis, some of which were implicit in our review of major decision-aiding approaches. But one of them seems paramount and bears repeating and generalizing: The adoption of a decision aid should be enhanced significantly if that aid is constructed (and sold) as one that addresses many different aspects of decision quality, not just one.

Our data and review also highlight the significance of the decision quality concept in fundamental decision scholarship. The decision literature contains surprisingly little discussion about what the term *decision quality* ought to mean. Nevertheless, there has been *some* treatment of the subject. Authors who favor the decision analytic perspective emphasize abstract rationality, such as consistency with the axioms of utility theory or probability theory (e.g., Baron, 1988; Dawes, 1988; Edwards, Kiss, Majone, & Toda, 1984). Other authors highlight some form of *accuracy.* One form, for instance, refers to the correspondence between a decider's evaluation of an alternative and an evaluation based on a rule that some people regard as normative, such as an additive value function (e.g., Payne, Bettman, & Johnson, 1988). Another form (e.g., Frisch & Jones, 1993) emphasizes the distinction between *decision utility* and *experience utility.* The former refers to the decider's anticipatory appraisal of an alternative at the time of the decision, before it is actually selected and enacted (e.g., the appraisal of a book being contemplated for purchase). The latter describes the decider's assessment of the actual experience with an alternative (e.g., the decider's degree of liking or disliking a book the decider actually reads). The pertinent decision quality conception emphasizes the correspondence between decision and experience utility; the higher the correspondence, the better. Yet another class of quality conceptions focuses on the decision process, highlighting process features that arguably ought to be expected to enhance the decider's satisfaction with chosen alternatives (e.g., Frisch & Clemen, 1994; Janis & Mann, 1977). Each of these definitions of decision quality can be (and has been) argued to be inadequate in some way. And there is clearly no universal agreement on which definition should be accepted.

Consensus on a suitable definition would be good for decision scholarship generally and certainly for decision aiding. After all, if we are uncertain about where we are trying to go (e.g., helping people achieve good decisions or understanding the nature of what deciders themselves consider to be decision making), how can we tell when we have arrived there? Moreover, consensus would probably allow for more productive and efficient scholarly discussions and collaborations. We hold no illusions that definitional consensus will occur any time soon. Achieving consensus on a decision quality conception that is not vacuously broad but nevertheless accommodates the multifaceted character implicit in everyday practical and scholarly usage is a formidable task. Nevertheless, we offer for initial consideration a set of quality definitions that we have employed for some time in our own work (cf. Yates & Estin, 1998; Yates & Patalano, 1999). These definitions appear to serve a useful focusing function. Importantly, they are also consistent with the responses of participants in the studies reported here and with decision-making practices in a variety of practical domains we have examined (e.g., business, medicine, personal counseling, aviation). The definitions:

Good Decision. A good decision is one that is strong with respect to one or more of the following five criteria:

1. *The aim criterion:* The decision meets the decider's explicitly formulated aim or aims (e.g., when a company sets out to hire a person who keeps good financial records and the chosen applicant does indeed keep good records).
2. *The need criterion:* The decision satisfies the actual needs of the beneficiary, needs that may or may not correspond to the decider's aim(s) (e.g., when a company needs someone to maintain

good financial controls, and in fact hires such a person, even if by accident, as when the company merely searched for a person who keeps good records).

3. *The aggregated outcomes criterion:* Collectively, all of the actual outcomes of the decision, including ones beyond particular aims and needs, are better than the active reference, such as the status quo or the beneficiary's aspiration level (e.g., when a company hires a candidate who keeps good records, meets its cost control needs, and moreover solves the company's morale problems, thereby leaving the company much better off than before).

4. *The rival options criterion:* In the aggregate, the outcomes of the decision are superior to those that would have resulted from any and all available competing alternatives (e.g., when, taking everything into account, a company is better off having hired Person X than it would have been hiring any other candidate on the market).

5. *The process costs criterion:* The costs of arriving at the decision are minimal (e.g., in money, time, effort, or aggravation) (e.g., when the process of searching for and reviewing job candidates not only causes little interference with normal work routines but is actually pleasant for all involved).

Good Decision Process. A good decision process is one that tends to yield good decisions.

With its emphasis on outcomes, our definition of a good decision differs sharply from the one that holds sway among decision analysts, and intentionally so. Those who practice decision analysis often pointedly seek to discourage deciders from their natural inclination to appraise decisions according to outcomes. For example, some urge deciders to recognize that "in an uncertain world where unforeseeable events are common, good decisions can sometimes lead to bad outcomes" (Hammond, Keeney, & Raiffa, 1998, p. 52). The present quality conceptions would discourage such statements; "good decision" and "bad outcomes" are inherently contradictory in that view, as our data suggest they are to the typical decider. The proposed notion of a good decision process, with its focus on what the process *tends* to produce, is statistical. Thus, it acknowledges the inescapable fact of sampling that not every decision made by a good real-life decision process will result in good outcomes (i.e., strength with respect to every quality criterion).

That conception therefore leads to the endorsement of statements like this: "Decisions that are made by a good *process* can sometimes lead to bad outcomes."

It is important to recall that, from the decision analytic perspective, a good decision is defined to be one that adheres to principles of rationality, such as expected utility maximization, which rest on notions of logical consistency or coherence. Our data suggest that most deciders would be content with pursuing this kind of decision goodness only if there were compelling evidence that doing so would, even if only on average, be rewarded by superior outcomes. As we noted previously, such evidence does not appear to have been reported. Instead, advocates of coherence conceptions of decision quality have relied on the plausibility of a strong coherence–outcomes link. In contrast, besides being statistical, the proposed alternative conception of decision quality is patently empirical. Decisions made according to a good process should be documented as typically yielding few serious shortcomings in terms of the various quality criteria, whether this is the result of adherence to principles of coherence or anything else.

Investigators have sometimes described to two different groups of research participants the circumstances surrounding some decision problem (e.g., a medical treatment dilemma) and the decision that was made in the pertinent situation. One group is then told that the decision turned out well (e.g., the patient recovered), but the other is told that the outcome was bad (e.g., the patient died). When asked for their opinion of the decision, participants in the former group tend to characterize that decision as better than do those in the latter group. Investigators who hold to the decision analytic conception of decision quality (e.g., Baron & Hershey, 1988) consider such results to be evidence of an error called *outcome bias*. In the convention proposed here, they are not. Rather, they are merely a reflection of people's customary semantic preferences. Studies of outcome bias have revealed useful facts about such preferences. Yet, in our view, such research could be even more revealing of fundamental principles if we simply acceded to those preferences, as in the proposed decision quality conception.

Assessment 2: Need

The second assessment made by the decision aid–receptive decider in our scenario is that she would welcome – she needs – a decision aid because she would expect her decision to have poor quality if she were left to her own devices. *("That bad, huh?")* This perception of need is clearly critical. After all, if there is no need, why bother with the very idea of a decision aid? For the moment, let us suppose that when she speaks of decision quality, our decider is referring to decision products rather than the decision process, for example, the costs of deciding. The uncomfortable conclusion suggested by our data as well as other evidence is this: People like the decider in our scenario are rare. Unlike her, typical deciders are likely to believe – rightly or wrongly – that they are perfectly capable of making most decisions well, with no assistance whatsoever. If true, this conclusion would, in and of itself, constitute an exceptionally compelling explanation for across-the-board indifference to decision aiding and a formidable hurdle for any decision aid developer or consultant to overcome.

So, what is the evidence? Recall that, in Study 1, participants were more satisfied with the outcomes of their easy decisions than those yielded by their hard decisions. Yet, in absolute terms, on average participants were highly pleased with how *all* their decisions turned out. Also recall that, in Study 2, participants regarded the badness and importance of their bad decisions as less extreme than the goodness and importance of their good decisions. Moreover, they were faster in bringing to mind their worst decisions than their best ones, plausibly because those decisions were especially distinctive in their unusualness. These data agree with the proposition that people generally think that their unaided decision making in the past was, for the most part, just fine. So why should they not expect that their future decisions will be just as good?

Results from a variety of other studies also suggest that people have high expectations that their decisions will turn out well. Those results further suggest that these expectations might well be too high, and for specific reasons. First are findings in the literature on *bolstering* (cf. Janis & Mann, 1977). This is the oft-documented phenomenon whereby, after a person has chosen some object (e.g., a work of art), the person's appraisal of that object, relative to the rejected competitors, becomes more favorable. Theories used to explain bolstering cite the tendency for deciders to enhance their perceptions of the attractiveness of those aspects of the chosen object that happen to be strong rather than weak. Thus, the possibility of bolstering should be facilitated for decisions involving ambiguous and multifaceted consequences as compared to those entailing simpler ones (e.g., complex paintings vs. sacks of flour). As our data have demonstrated, people are inclined to appraise typical real-life decisions with respect to several aspects rather than just one. This therefore implies an especially high likelihood that people will remember their decisions as good ones, perhaps even better than they had anticipated in the first place.

Another literature suggests that, even when a decision yields outcomes that are both objectively and subjectively bad at the moment they occur (e.g., disability from an accident), the decider will not indefinitely experience and remember them that way (cf. Kahneman, 1999). Instead, the experience will be effectively neutralized, plausibly through mechanisms such as the development of lower adaptation and aspiration levels (e.g., lower mobility goals than before the disability). The pertinent literature also invites a related and especially powerful speculation. It suggests that, no matter what their circumstances might be, people are highly likely to reason as follows: "I'm quite content with the way things are. So why do I need to make any radical decisions of any kind? And if I don't need to make any big decisions, then I certainly don't need any *help* with those decisions."

Attribution processes are yet another reason to expect deciders to recall their past decisions as good ones, no matter what. There is credible documentation of the tendency for people to attribute to their own actions (e.g., their own decisions) the good things that happen to them (cf. Ross & Fletcher, 1985), but when bad things occur, they are inclined to attribute them to other factors, such as chance, essentially explaining them away. Dispositions like these plausibly have surprising, far-reaching implications. For instance, even when people or organizations are in dire straits because of bad prior decisions, they are unlikely to acknowledge (or even recognize) that fact. Instead, they are inclined to say things like "Well, yes, we're in a bit of a bind here, but it's just a run of bad luck. It has nothing to do with how we make decisions. So there's no point in us even talking about things like decision aiding." Evidence for tendencies like these has not been limited to people's appraisals of their past decisions. It is probably manifest in reports of particular kinds of overconfidence, too. A good example is the tendency for trial lawyers to be overly optimistic that they will win the cases they choose to take to court (e.g., Loftus & Wagenaar, 1988).

Now suppose that people do, in fact, seldom perceive a need for help in making decisions that will turn out well for them. What should a decision aid developer or consultant do? Seek another vocation because the demand for his or her services simply does not exist? Several less extreme and more defensible alternatives suggest themselves.

Option 1 – Emphasize Ease. The first alternative is to abandon the aim of helping people make decisions with better outcomes and instead develop aids that help people make the same decisions they would make anyway, but more easily. As we saw before, this is effectively the goal that many decision support systems and expert systems pursue and achieve. And, as we also conjectured, prospective decision-aiding clients readily see the value of such assistance and hence welcome it.

Option 2 – Destroy Illusions. A second alternative is predicated on the assumption that people's belief in the adequacy of their own past and future decisions is at least partly illusory. That is, deciders could bene-fit from assistance but do not realize that fact. The tack that a decision aid developer or consultant could then take would be to enlighten the decider, to destroy the illusions. It seems that, if the opportunity exists, an especially effective way to do this is to have the decider keep accu-rate *decision logs*. That is, before major decisions are made, the decider would record things like the aims of those decisions. And then, imme-diately after the decisions are made and their outcomes are determined, the decider would record what those outcomes were. Periodically, those records would be reviewed. To the extent that the decider's quality ap-praisals are indeed illusory, outcomes should systematically fall short of expectations. And the decider should be convinced of the actual need for assistance. A derivative of this second approach would be especially appropriate, it seems, in organizations. Although the various mecha-nisms we have reviewed should serve to reinforce people's illusions about the efficacy of their own decisions, they should not influence ap-praisals by other people. That is, although we ourselves might think that our decisions are consistently outstanding, others would not evaluate them so generously. Thus, a good way to deflate self-appraisals would be to complement them with appraisals by others. In the typical orga-nization, it is those other appraisals that matter the most anyway. Of course, in business organizations, financial outcomes are unambiguous and typically have central significance. Nevertheless, even there, imme-diately assessable financial outcomes of decisions are almost never the sole concern.

An important prerequisite of this second option should not go un-noticed: The decider must be receptive to being exposed to arguments and evidence that his or her decisions are at greater risk than suspected. Our hunch is that this is an especially significant hurdle for decisions that any given person makes only a few times in life, such as career choices, home purchases, and the decision about whether to marry a current suitor. And because of emotional factors and a perception of the uniqueness of one's personal circumstances, arguments about the risks of marriage decisions are especially prone to fall on deaf ears, despite widespread awareness that the divorce rate is extremely high in many places, nearly 50% in the United States.

Option 3 – Frame Bad Decisions as Pathologies and Traumas. A final approach to the problem of deciders perceiving no need for assistance is radical. Even taking into account some measure of self-serving illusion in people's appraisals of their own decisions, this approach concedes the possibility that, on average, most people's decisions *do*, in fact, yield good outcomes for them. This view rests on an analogy with health care. The vast majority of the population is in decent if not good physical health. On the other hand, everyone occasionally gets sick, and some experience traumas of various kinds, such as injuries from car accidents. The health care system, which is clearly indispensable, is designed to deal with these unusual occurrences. The public health segment of the system seeks to reduce their incidence, whereas the medical segment treats them when they happen to occur. This *pathology/trauma model* could serve as a prototype for how to design a *decision care system.* We all realize that, although we might be in perfect health today, that situation could change dramatically in an instant. Part of the mission of a decision care system would be to convince people that they are at risk for rare but catastrophic decisions, too. Physical illness and trauma are obvious. A challenge for decision specialists is to make catastrophic decision failures obvious, too. A second challenge would be to design decision aids that perform preventive functions analogous to public health interventions. A third would be to create aids that yield decisions that minimize the damage when outcomes are bad (i.e., mitigate risks) or that allow for rapid recovery from failed decisions.

Assessment 3: Relevance and Efficacy

This was the third important assessment made by the decider in our scenario: *"Seems promising (as a means of ensuring better decision quality)."* The decider has actually made two distinct constituent assessments within this larger one. The first is that the focal decision aid is relevant to the decision problem at hand. That is, it addresses factors that, in turn, affect decision quality facets the decider cares about. The focus of our empirical studies about hard-versus-easy and good-versus-bad decisions was on this kind of assessment, identifying personally relevant quality dimensions. The second assessment is that the aid in question would actually work, that it really *would* improve the chances of making decisions that are good with respect to the particular aspects of decision quality deemed relevant by the decider. Our sense is that, as implicit in our review of major decision-aiding approaches, this kind of assessment must be critical to people's receptivity to a decision aid. After all, if a decider thinks that an aid addresses a personally significant aspect of decision quality (e.g., exposure to risk) but has little chance of actually delivering good quality, why bother with it?

Underneath the decider's judgment about an aid's odds of facilitating good decisions must be a personal *naive decision attribution theory* of the form illustrated in Figure 1.2(a). That theory is the decider's conception of how the process by which he or she decides yields a decision that, in turn, achieves or falls short of the decider's multifaceted standard of good decision quality. The theory also includes beliefs about the nature of any decision aid that is available. When pondering whether to adopt that aid, the decider speculates about how, if applied, it would affect various aspects of decision quality, both directly and indirectly through its effects on elements of the decider's process. For instance, suppose the decider believes that when decisions in the relevant class fail, it is mainly because the decider is ignorant of critical facts. Then the decider will adopt an aid only if it appears that it would supply those facts.

To the best of our knowledge, no one has actually studied naive decision attribution theories. But we speculate that these theories have interesting and important properties. It seems doubtful that, according to these theories, a significant contributor to failed decisions is that deciders synthesize facts in ways that disagree with, say, expected utility or multiattribute utility maximization. To the extent that this is true, this implicates a contributor to people's indifference to forms of decision analysis that emphasize such rules. Parallel to deciders' naive decision attribution theories are *valid decision attribution theories*, as sketched in Figure 1.2(b). Rather than deciders' speculations, these theories describe actual process and decision aid features and their true influences on decisions and decision quality. Thus, although deciders themselves might think that, say, expected utility or multiattribute utility rules are irrelevant to decision quality, that may or may not be the case in reality. An important part of the future agenda for decision research is the accurate depiction of both naive and valid decision attribution theories. In the

(a)

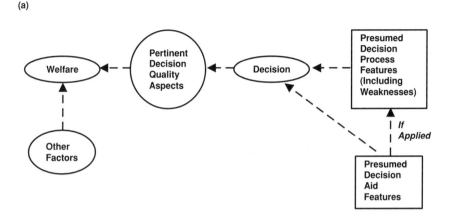

(b)

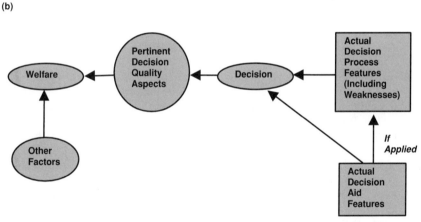

Figure 1.2 Schematic representation of decision attribute theories: (a) naive and (b) valid.

discussion thus far, we have limited ourselves to attributions for decision quality. We predict, though, that the most useful theories will be ones that go a step further and, as suggested in Figure 1.2, encompass the decision beneficiary's welfare as well. For instance, the data and ideas reviewed in this chapter suggest that it is not at all unlikely that many people believe that their personal welfare – what really matters to them – is largely a function of factors that have nothing to do with their decisions. People holding such beliefs would, understandably, have little interest in decision aids or, for that matter, decision making.

References

Aaron, M. C. (1995). The value of decision analysis in mediation practice. *Negotiation Journal, 11*(2), 123–133.

Adelman, L. (1992). *Evaluating decision support and expert systems*. New York: Wiley.

Anderson, J. R. (1985). *Cognitive psychology and its implications* (2nd ed.) New York: Freeman.

Aoki, N., Kitihara, T., Fukui, T., Beck, J. R., Soma, K., Yamamoto, W., Kamae, I., & Ohwada, T. (1998). Management of unruptured intracranial aneurysm in Japan: A Markovian decision analysis with utility measurements based on the Glasgow outcome scale. *Medical Decision Making, 18*, 357–364.

Baron, J. (1988). *Thinking and deciding*. New York: Cambridge University Press.

Baron, J., & Brown, R. V. (Eds.). (1991). *Teaching decision making to adolescents*. Hillsdale, NJ: Erlbaum.

Baron, J., & Hershey, J. C. (1988). Outcome bias in decision evaluation. *Journal of Personality and Social Psychology, 54*, 569–579.

Brehmer, B., & Joyce, C. R. B. (Eds.). (1988). *Human judgment: The SJT view*. Amsterdam: North-Holland.

Carter, G. M., Murray, M. P., Walker, R. G., & Walker, W. E. (1992). *Building organizational decision support systems*. Boston: Academic Press.

Christensen-Szalanski, J. J. J. (1993). A comment on applying experimental findings of cognitive biases to naturalistic environments. In G. A. Klein, J. Orasanu, R. Calderwood, & C. E. Zsambok (Eds.), *Decision making in action: Models and methods* (pp. 252–261). Norwood, NJ: Ablex.

Churchill, G. A., Jr. (1999). *Marketing research: Methodological foundations* (7th ed.). Fort Worth: Dryden.

Clemen, R. T. (1991). *Making hard decisions: An introduction to decision analysis*. Boston: PWS-Kent.

Cooksey, R. W. (1996). *Judgment analysis: Theory, methods, and applications*. San Diego: Academic Press.

Cooksey, R. W., Freebody, P., & Davidson, G. (1986). Teachers' predictions of children's early reading achievement: An application of social judgment theory. *American Educational Research Journal, 23*, 41–46.

Dawes, R. M. (1979). The robust beauty of improper linear models in decision making. *American Psychologist, 34*, 571–582.

Dawes, R. M. (1988). *Rational choice in an uncertain world*. San Diego: Harcourt Brace Jovanovich.

Dennis, A., George, J., Jessup, L., Nunamaker, J., & Vogel, D. (1988). Information technology to support electronic meetings. *MIS Quarterly, 12*, 591–624.

Dennis, A. R., & Valacich, J. S. (1993). Computer brainstorms: More heads are better than one. *Journal of Applied Psychology, 78*, 531–537.

Durkin, J. (1994). *Expert systems design and development*. New York: Macmillan.

Edwards, W., Kiss, I., Majone, G., & Toda, M. (1984). What constitutes "a good decision?" *Acta Psychologica, 56*, 5–27.

Finlay, P. (1994). *Introducing decision support systems.* Oxford: Blackwell.

Fischhoff, B. (1975). Hindsight ≠ foresight: The effect of outcome knowledge on judgment under uncertainty. *Journal of Experimental Psychology: Human Perception and Performance, 1*, 288–299.

Frisch, D., & Clemen, R. T. (1994). Beyond expected utility: Rethinking behavioral decision research. *Psychological Bulletin, 116*, 46–54.

Frisch, D., & Jones, S. K. (1993). Assessing the accuracy of decisions. *Theory and Psychology, 3*, 115–135.

Hammond, J. S., Keeney, R. L., & Raiffa, H. (1998). The hidden traps in decision making. *Harvard Business Review, 16*(5), 47–58.

Hammond, K. R., Stewart, T. R., Brehmer, B., & Steinmann, D. O. (1986). Social judgment theory. In H. R. Arkes & K. R. Hammond (Eds.), *Judgment and decision making* (pp. 56–76). Cambridge: Cambridge University Press.

Hax, A. C., & Wiig, K. M. (1977). The use of decision analysis in a capital investment problem. In D. E. Bell, R. L. Keeney, & H. Raiffa (Eds.), *Conflicting objectives in decisions* (pp. 277–297). New York: Wiley.

Hill, G. W. (1982). Group versus individual performance: Are $N + 1$ heads better than one? *Psychological Bulletin, 91*, 517–539.

Ignizio, J. P. (1991). *An introduction to expert systems: The development and implementation of rule-based expert systems.* New York: McGraw-Hill.

Janis, I., & Mann, L. (1977). *Decision making.* New York: Free Press.

Kahneman, D. (1999). Objective happiness. In D. Kahneman, E. Diener, & N. Schwarz (Eds.), *Well-being: The foundations of hedonic psychology* (pp. 3–25). New York: Russell Sage Foundation.

Kahneman, D., & Tversky, A. (1979). Prospect theory: An analysis of decision under risk. *Econometrica, 47*, 263–291.

Keeney, R. L., & Nair, K. (1977). Selecting nuclear power plant sites in the Pacific Northwest using decision analysis. In D. E. Bell, R. L. Keeney, & H. Raiffa (Eds.), *Conflicting objectives in decisions* (pp. 298–322). New York: Wiley.

King, D. (1990). Modeling and reasoning: Integrating decision support with expert systems. In J. Liebowitz (Ed.), *Expert systems for business and management* (pp. 51–76). Englewood Cliffs, NJ: Yourdon Press.

Klein, G. A., Orasanu, J., Calderwood, R., & Zsambok, C. E. (Eds.). (1993). *Decision making in action: Models and methods.* Norwood, NJ: Ablex.

Kottemann, J. E., Davis, F. D., & Remus, W. E. (1994). Computer-assisted decision making: Performance, beliefs, and the illusion of control. *Organizational Behavior and Human Decision Processes, 57*, 26–37.

Lewis, L. F., Keleman, K. S., & Garcia, J. E. (1996). Possible barriers and challenges to the adoption of group support systems. *Group Decision and Negotiation, 6*, 189–194.

Liebowitz, J. (Ed.). (1990). *Expert systems for business and management.* Englewood Cliffs, NJ: Yourdon Press.

Liebowitz, J. (Ed.). (1998). *The handbook of applied expert systems.* Boca Raton, FL: CRC Press.

Loftus, E. F., & Wagenaar, W. A. (1988). Lawyers' predictions of success. *Jurimetrics Journal, 16,* 437–453.

Matheson, J. E., & Howard, R. A. (1968). An introduction to decision analysis. In Decision Analysis Group (Eds.), *Readings in decision analysis* (pp. 7–43). Menlo Park, CA: Stanford Research Institute.

McCauley, C. (1991). Selection of National Science Foundation graduate fellows: A case study of psychologists failing to apply what they know about decision making. *American Psychologist, 46,* 1287–1291.

McClish, D. K., & Powell, S. H. (1989). How well can physicians estimate mortality in a medical intensive care unit? *Medical Decision Making, 9,* 125–132.

Meehl, P. W. (1954). *Clinical versus statistical prediction.* Minneapolis: University of Minnesota Press.

Morris, W. T. (1977). *Decision analysis.* Columbus, OH: Grid, Inc.

Nunamaker, J. F., Applegate, L. M., & Konsynski, B. R. (1987). Facilitating group creativity with GDSS. *Journal of Management Information Sciences, 3*(4), 5–19.

O'Connor, A. M., Rostom, A., Fiset, V., Tetroe, J., Entwistle, V., Llewellyn-Thomas, H., Holmes-Rovner, M., Barry, M., & Jones, J. (1999). Decision aids for patients facing health treatment or screening decisions: Systematic review. *British Medical Journal, 319,* 731–734.

Olson, D. L., & Courtney, J. F. (1992). *Decision support models and expert systems.* New York: Macmillan.

Payne, J. W., Bettman, J. R., & Johnson, E. J. (1988). Adaptive strategy selection in decision making. *Journal of Experimental Psychology: Learning, Memory, & Cognition, 14,* 534–552.

Prerau, D. S. (1990). *Developing and managing expert systems: Proven techniques for business and industry.* Reading, MA: Addison-Wesley.

Ross, M., & Fletcher, G. J. O. (1985). Attribution and social perception. In G. Lindzey & E. Aronson (Eds.), *Handbook of social psychology* (3rd ed., Vol. 2, pp. 73–122). New York: Random House.

Russo, J. E., & Schoemaker, P. J. H. (1989). *Decision traps: The ten barriers to brilliant decision-making and how to overcome them.* New York: Doubleday.

Schoemaker, P., & Russo, J. E. (1993). A pyramid of decision approaches. *California Management Review, 36* (1), 9–31.

Silver, M. S. (1991). *Systems that support decision makers: Description and analysis.* New York: Wiley.

Tolman, E., & Brunswik, E. (1935). The organism and the causal texture of the environment. *Psychological Review, 42,* 43–77.

Ubel, P. A., & Loewenstein, G. (1997). The role of decision analysis in informed consent: Choosing between intuition and systematicity. *Social Science and Medicine, 44,* 647–656.

van Bemmel, J. H., & Musen, M. A. (Eds.). (1997). *Handbook of medical informatics.* Houten, the Netherlands: Springer.

von Winterfeldt, D., & Edwards, W. (1986). *Decision analysis and behavioral research.* New York: Cambridge University Press.

Watson, R. T., DeSanctis, G., & Poole, M. S. (1988). Using a GDSS to facilitate group consensus: Some intended and unintended consequences. *MIS Quarterly, 12,* 463–478.

Yates, J. F. (1990). *Judgment and decision making.* Englewood Cliffs, NJ: Prentice Hall.

Yates, J. F., & Estin, P. A. (1998). Decision making. In W. Bechtel & G. Graham (Eds.), *A companion to cognitive science* (pp. 186–196). Malden, MA: Blackwell.

Yates, J. F., Lee, J.-W., Shinotsuka, H., Patalano, A. L., & Sieck, W. R. (1998). Cross-cultural variations in probability judgment accuracy: Beyond general knowledge overconfidence? *Organizational Behavior and Human Decision Processes, 74,* 89–117.

Yates, J. F., & Patalano, A. L. (1999). Decision making and aging. In D. C. Park, R. W. Morrell, & K. Shifren (Eds.), *Processing of medical information in aging patients: Cognitive and human factors perspectives* (pp. 31–54). Mahwah, NJ: Erlbaum.

Zsambok, C. E., & Klein, G. (Eds.). (1997). *Naturalistic decision making.* Mahwah, NJ: Erlbaum.

2 Rationality in Choice Under Certainty and Uncertainty

R. Duncan Luce

ABSTRACT

Since the time of Savage (1954) it has been accepted that subjective expected utility (SEU) embodies the concept of rational individual behavior under uncertainty. If, however, one alters the domain formulation in two ways, by distinguishing gains from losses and by adding a binary operation of joint receipt, then equally rational arguments lead in the case of binary mixed gambles to predictions quite different from those of SEU. A question, raised but not really answered, is whether there is a rational argument for choosing one domain formulation over the other.

CONTENTS

This research was supported in part by National Science Foundation Grants SBR-9520107 and SBR-9808057 to the University of California, Irvine. I thank Ward Edwards and an anonymous referee for useful, if sometimes challenging, comments.

The Conventional Wisdom: SEU

Among those who study individual decisions under risk or uncertainty, fairly wide agreement seems to exist that a rational person will abide by expected utility (EU) under risk and subjective expected utility (SEU) under uncertainty. Various axiomatizations of EU and SEU can be found that are all based on behavioral properties that are viewed as locally rational. Probably the one mentioned most often is Savage (1954). In one way or another, the representation arrived at is as follows. Suppose that $x_i, i = 1, \ldots, k$, are sure consequences and $\{E_1, \ldots, E_k\}$ forms an event partition of a universal set E arising from some chance experiment $\mathbf{E}$; then a gamble – which is brief for an uncertain alternative – can be represented as vector $(x_1, E_1; \ldots; x_k, E_k)$ of event–outcome pairs $(x_i, E_i), i = 1, \ldots, k$. This is interpreted to mean that the consequence is x_i if, when the experiment is run, the outcome lies in E_i. It is shown that preferences among such gambles can be represented by an order-preserving utility function U over consequences and gambles and a finitely additive probability function S over events such that

$$U(x_1, E_1; \ldots; x_k, E_k) = \sum_{i=1}^{k} U(x_i) S(E_i) \tag{1}$$

is order preserving of preferences.

A good place to see how widely this model is accepted as the normative rule for rational behavior is Edwards (1992). The model involves a number of locally rational behavioral features that I describe in this section. *Locally rational* simply means that the behavioral assertion meets some criterion of rationality. It is to be distinguished from the *global rationality* that some people associate with the EU or SEU representations and all of their behavioral implications.

Locally rational properties, which are of two major types (given in the following two subsections), are normative for decision making in much the same way that principles of logic are normative for reasoning and the postulates of probability theory are for characterizing risk.

SEU Implies Accounting Rationality

Because of its bilinear form, Eq. (1) has some strong behavioral implications. One example occurs when we look at compound gambles in which one or more of the x_i are themselves gambles whose underlying experiments are independent of E; then one can show for Eq. (1) that all that matters in evaluating the compound gamble is the set of certain consequences plus the listing of chance event combinations needed to give rise to each. Moreover, the order in which the events occur is immaterial. This is a form of unbounded rationality against which Simon (1956) warned.

I refer to assumptions of this type as *accounting indifferences* because they involve alternative formulations of situations that have the same "bottom line" for the decision maker, and so a rational person should be indifferent among the several formulations.

To keep the issues as focused as possible, let us confine attention to binary gambles, that is, those with just two consequences. For such a binary gamble g, let $C = E_1, \bar{C} = E \backslash C$, that is, all elements of E that are not in C, and $x_1 = x, x_2 = y$, so $g = (x, C; y, \bar{C})$. We also admit the possibility of one level of compound gambles. So, for example, if f and h are gambles, then so is $(f, C; h, \bar{C})$. We assume there is preference order $\succsim$ over such gambles, and preference indifference is denoted by $\sim$.

A few important special binary cases make the idea of accounting indifferences clear.

Some Elementary Accounting Equivalences
  Idempotence:

$$(f, C; f, \bar{C}) \sim f.$$

This simply says that if f occurs no matter what the outcome of experiment E is, then the gamble is indifferent to f.
  Certainty:

$$(f, E; h, \emptyset) \sim f,$$

where $\theta = \bar{E} = E \backslash E$. In this case, the gamble gives rise to f with certainty, so the gamble is indifferent to f.
  Complementarity:

$$(f, C; g, \bar{C}) \sim (g, \bar{C}; f, C).$$

Here the order in which the outcome–event pairs are written is immaterial.

These are viewed as so simple and transparent that they are little discussed in the literature. A slightly more complex accounting indifference involves a first-order compounding of binary gambles.

Event Commutativity. For all consequences x, y, independently run experiments **E**, **F**, and events $C \subseteq E$, and $D \subseteq F$,

$$((x, C; y, \bar{C}), D; y, \bar{D}) \sim ((x, D; y, \bar{D}), C; y, \bar{C}). \tag{2}$$

The argument for the rationality of event commutativity is that one receives x if both C and D occur, which in the formulation to the left of $\sim$ happens with the events arising in the order D, C and on the right side in the order C, D; otherwise, the consequence is y.

SEU Implies Preference Rationality

In addition to accounting indifferences, SEU corresponds to certain important patterns of preference that all seem highly rational in an intuitive sense. Recall that $f \succsim h$ symbolizes that gamble f is preferred or indifferent to gamble h.

Transitivity. For all gambles f, g, and h,

$$f \succsim g \quad \text{and} \quad g \succsim h \Longrightarrow f \succsim h.$$

Here one can think of replacing g in the preference inequality $g \succsim h$ by f, which is preferred to g, and so f should also be preferred to h. Some, most notably Fishburn (1982), have questioned the rationality of transitivity, but for the most part, decision analysts agree that a rational decision maker should be transitive. For strict preference, one argument is that an intransitive person can be made into a money pump in the following sense. Suppose g is owned and f is preferred to g; then for some sufficiently small amount of money $\varepsilon > 0$, the decision maker will trade ε and g to get f. But with an intransitive triple, money is extracted from each transaction, presumably, indefinitely or until the decision maker revises his or her preferences so as to be transitive. The most striking violation of transitivity, known as the *preference reversal phenomenon*, has been shown to arise from mixing judgment and choice procedures. This means not a violation of transitivity so much as the need for distinct theories of choice and judgment (see Luce, 2000, pp. 39–44).

Consequence Monotonicity. For all non-null events $C, \bar{C}$ and gambles f, g, h, then,

$$g \succsim h \iff (f, C; g, \bar{C}) \succsim (f, C; h, \bar{C}).$$

Both consequence monotonicity and transitivity are examples of a basic principle of rationality, namely, that it is desirable to replace something by something else that the decision maker prefers when all else is fixed.

Event Montonicity. For all experiments **E**, events $A, B, C \subseteq E$ with $A \cap C = B \cap C = \theta$, and gambles f, g, with $f \succ g$,

$$(f, A; g) \succsim (f, B; g) \iff (f, A \cup C; g) \succsim (f, B \cup C; g). \tag{3}$$

De Finetti (1931) first formulated this condition (called, in translation, *additivity in qualitative probability*) as a central feature of his qualitative probability theory (see Fine, 1973, and Fishburn, 1986). The rationality lying behind event monotonicity is clear. The decision maker prefers the gamble that makes the preferred gamble f more likely than g to be the consequence, and so we infer from $(f, A; g) \succsim (f, B; g)$ that A is perceived to be at least as likely to occur as B. But if that is true, then augmenting both events by the same disjoint C should maintain that likelihood order, and so the preference on the right should hold (Luce & Marley, 2000; Marley & Luce, 2002).

These Properties Go a Long Way Toward Implying Binary SEU

Although I do not state a precise theorem for deriving the binary SEU representation, the locally rational properties I have listed – idempotence, certainty, complementarity, event commutativity, transitivity, consequence monotonicity, and event monotonicity – play a very crucial role.

As would be expected, there has been extensive discussion of the degree to which these properties, and so SEU, is an adequate description of behavior. I do not attempt to describe the details of these somewhat complex, arcane, and controversial debates. My conclusion, based on a careful examination of the literature, is that a major source of descriptive failure in the binary case lies in two places: event monotonicity (Ellsberg, 1961) and the assumption of unlimited accounting indifferences (Luce, 1992, 2000).

Indeed, with respect to the latter, there seems to be a sharp separation between event commutativity, which seems to hold descriptively, and a slightly more complex accounting equivalence called *autodistributivity*, which does not seem to hold. This boundary corresponds to the distinction between SEU and what is called *rank-dependent utility* (RDU) (Luce & Fishburn, 1991, 1995; Luce & von Winterfeldt, 1994, appendix; Quiggin, 1993; Tversky & Kahneman, 1992). In the latter model the binary SEU expression is modified in two ways: The weights are not probabilities (i.e., are not finitely additive), and the weighted utility representation of $(x, C; y, \bar{C})$ depends on whether $x \succsim y$ or $x \prec y$. Adding the autodistributivity property forces RDU to become SEU. Thus, RDU exhibits a form of bounded rationality of the sort urged by Simon (1956).

Still, RDU, as typically stated for gambles with three or more alternatives, does not appear to be an adequate descriptive theory. Work by, among others, Birnbaum and Chavez (1997), Birnbaum and Navarrete (1998), and Wu (1994) makes it clear that RDU is not descriptive beyond the binary case (see Luce, 2000). And so those who wish to develop descriptive theories have additional work to do. But that is not my issue in this chapter.

A Peculiarity of the Conventional Wisdom

Everyone dances around an oddity of conventional SEU. That theory simply does not distinguish between what are perceived as incremental gains and as losses. One tack is to say that one decides among choices not in terms of the alternatives, as one usually thinks of them, but rather in terms of one's total asset position. In choosing among risky alternatives, such as stocks, one supposedly thinks not about the alternatives, but about one's total financial situation in each case.

A second tack is to say that the utility function is shaped differently for gains and for losses. Often utility is assumed to be concave for monetary gains and convex for losses. However, this way of treating it seems very artificial within the context of standard SEU theory because the representation is invariant under positive linear transformations of utility, and so the kink can occur at any numerical level. That means, for all but one choice of utility function, either that the utility of some gains is assigned negative values or that the utility of some losses is assigned positive ones. That seems counterintuitive.

When providing advice to decision makers, it must take skill to convince them to ignore the distinction between gains and losses. And I know of no experiment that is presented in terms other than incremental gains and losses.

From a descriptive point of view, there is something deeply wrong with SEU even in the binary case when applied to gambles with mixed gains and losses. Attempts to apply utility ideas in practical decision-making situations, including certain business decisions and medical diagnosis and treatment where there are decided gains and losses, have encountered inconsistencies of estimates of the utilities for the domains of gains, losses, and mixed gambles (Fishburn & Kochenberger, 1979; Hershey, Kunreuther, & Schoemaker, 1982; von Winterfeldt & Edwards, 1986).

These failures go far beyond those involving complex accounting equivalences, and they raise the question of whether SEU really does capture what most people mean by rationality. Serious reevaluation seems called for.

Additional Primitives

To clearly distinguish gains from losses, one needs to introduce certain new primitives that have not been a part of the traditional axiomatization.

Status Quo, Gains, and Losses

The first primitive is the concept of *no change from the status quo*, which I will abbreviate to *status quo*. One is tempted to call this the *zero consequence*, but that too readily suggests that the consequences are money, and the model is far more general than that. I use the traditional mathematical symbol, e, of abstract algebra for an identity element, which is what no change from the status quo turns out to be in a well-defined sense (see Axiom JR5 later). The structure that we provide forces $U(e) = 0$, and so the representation is no longer unique up to positive linear transformations but only up to positive similarity ones; that is, U and U' are utility functions for the same situation if and only if for some constant $\alpha > 0$, $U' = \alpha U$.

Any consequence or gamble with $g \succ e$ is said to be perceived as a *gain* and any with $g \prec e$ as a *loss*. Thus, the utility of a gain is always a positive number and that of a loss is always a negative number.

Joint Receipt

The second additional primitive is what I call *joint receipt*. Mathematically, it is simply a binary operation $\oplus$ over consequences and gambles. The behavioral interpretation of $f \oplus g$ is that one receives both f and

g. So, for example, in the gamble $(f \oplus g, C; h, \bar{C})$ the interpretation is that if event C occurs, the consequence is the receipt of both f and g, whereas if $\bar{C}$ occurs, the consequence is the singleton h. Clearly, joint receipt is a common occurrence of everyday life. Indeed, more often than not, one deals simultaneously, or nearly so, with two or more goods, two or more bads, or mixes of both goods and bads. As we shall see, the general case of the joint receipt of more than two entities devolves to the binary one under the assumptions made.

The traditional way to deal with joint receipts in economics has been as vectors called *commodity bundles*. That approach strikes me as somewhat more artificial than treating it as an operation. Which formulation is used matters because they lead to quite different mathematical structures – vector spaces versus ordered algebras.

Once one considers such an operation, it is clear that it can be studied without reference to uncertainty. It looks very much like a classical measurement situation from physics. The relevant structure is $\mathfrak{D} = \langle D, e, \succsim, \oplus \rangle$, where D is the domain of entities under consideration, which may or may not include gambles; e in D is the status quo; $\succsim$ is a preference order over D; and $\oplus$ is a binary operation over D. This looks a great deal like the kinds of structures that arose early on in physical measurement, for example, of mass except for the fact that we have elements of D both better than and worse than e. Nonetheless, the situation is very similar.

Additive Representation of Joint Receipt. The question is, what properties are reasonable to assume for $\mathfrak{D}$, and where do they lead in terms of a representation? We state the latter first. There will be sufficient axioms to prove the existence of $V : D \to \mathbb{R}$, that is the set of real numbers, such that for all f, g in D

$$f \succsim g \iff V(f) \geq V(g), \tag{4}$$

$$V(f \oplus g) = V(f) + V(g), \tag{5}$$

$$V(e) = 0. \tag{6}$$

Because of Eq. (5), this representation is called *additive* over $\oplus$.

It is usually dismissed as a theory of value as soon as it is stated. Among the arguments given are the following:

- *Complementary goods:* The claim is that some goods have value only together. Examples are shoes in pairs (for people with both feet), guns and appropriate bullets, pairs of earrings (at least prior to about 1968), and so on. This is easily bypassed simply by defining the elementary goods as consisting of those groupings that are relevant to the decision maker, which, of course, is what stores usually do. Note, however, that what one considers as unitary may differ whether one is a buyer or seller or even by the type of seller. For example, an automobile dealer typically treats vehicles as unitary goods, whereas a repair supply shop deals with parts of automobiles such as valves and brake drums.

- *Incompatible goods:* For well-known practical reasons, some valued goods should not be placed in close proximity if, for example, an explosion is to be avoided. This is no less a problem in mass measurement, and obvious precautions are taken.
- *Leads to utility that is proportional to money:* Consider the domain of money consequences. If one supposes that $x \oplus y = x + y$ and that V maps onto a real interval, then it is easy to show from Eqs. (4) and (5) that for some constant $\alpha > 0$, $V(x) = \alpha x$. But everyone knows that utility of money is not linear with money (e.g., the St. Petersburg paradox). This argument has two weaknesses. First, it is not at all clear that $x \oplus y = x + y$ is actually correct (Luce, 2000; Thaler, 1985). Second, and more important, no reason has been provided to suppose that V is actually proportional to U, where U is the utility function determined from gambles. This is explored more fully in the next section of this chapter.

Axioms Underlying the Additive Representation. We turn now to the assumptions that are well known to give rise to this representation (Hölder, 1901; Krantz, Luce, Suppes, & Tversky, 1971). I will simply list them and then discuss them from a rational perspective.

Definition. $\langle \mathcal{D}, e, \succsim, \oplus \rangle$ is said to form a *joint-receipt preference structure* if and only if the following five conditions holds for all f, g, h in $\mathcal{D}$:

Axiom JR1. Weak Order:

$\succsim$ is transitive and connected.

Axiom JR2. Weak Commutativity:

$f \oplus g \sim g \oplus f.$

Axiom JR3. Weak Associativity:

$f \oplus (g \oplus h) \sim (f \oplus g) \oplus h.$

Axiom JR4. Weak Monotonicity:

$$f \succsim g \Longleftrightarrow f \oplus h \succsim g \oplus h.$$

Axiom JR5. Weak Identity:

$$f \oplus e \sim f.$$

The adjective *weak* in each case refers to the fact that the property holds for indifference, $\sim$, not just for equality, $=$. (Given axiom JR1, we know that $\sim$ is an equivalence relation, and so if one works with the equivalence classes of $\sim$, all of these become transformed into the usual conditions involving $=$ rather than $\sim$.)

The rationality of weak transitivity is unchanged from the gambling context. The rationalities of weak commutativity and associativity are species of accounting indifference. Both simply require that neither the order in which joint receipt is written nor the grouping into binary pairs is material as far as preference is concerned. It is important not to misinterpret what this means. Preference for the goods can easily be confounded by other considerations. For example, suppose that you receive a shipment of three goods, x, y, z, but when you open them you find that x' is included instead of the x you ordered. Suppose further that they were packed in two cartons. Do you care if x' is in its own carton and y and z are in another or that x' and y are in one carton and z is in a separate one? Most of us do, because with x' in a separate container, it is easier to return it in exchange for x. This preference concerns not how you feel about the goods as such, but convenience in dealing with the error.

Weak monotonicity has the same compelling rational flavor it always has. However, the following example has been suggested (in a review of one of my grant proposals) as casting doubt upon it. Suppose that g is a lottery and x is a modest sum of money such that $x \succ g$ but $x < EV(g)$, where EV denotes expected value. Now suppose that z is a very large sum of money – $1 million ($1M) for most people will do. The claim is that $x \oplus z$ may be less preferred than $g \oplus z$ because with $1M in the bank, one need not be so risk averse as without it. I am not certain that people change their stance about gambles so easily, nor from a rational perspective do I see why they should.

Weak identity simply asserts that adding no change from the status quo to any valued alternative has no impact on the preference pattern. This has more to do with the meaning of terms than it does with anything that is empirically testable.

There are two additional axioms of a different character. The first is an Archimedean one that can be stated as follows. For any gamble f and any integer n, let $f(n)$ denote the joint receipt of n copies of f. Formally,

$$f(1) = f,$$

$$f(n) = f(n-1) \oplus f.$$

Axiom JR6. Archimedean. If $f \succ e$ and any g, there exists an integer n such that

$$f(n) \succ g.$$

This property says that enough of any one gain exceeds in preference any other gain (and certainly any loss). For this to make sense, one has to have trading of some sort as an implicit background postulate because most of us do not care to have huge amounts of one good.

The next axiom is a structural one that says that for each gain there is a compensating loss and for each loss there is a compensating gain. This assumption no doubt limits the applicability of the theory. For example, many of us think that there are personal disasters, among them death or total incapacitation, for which no gain can compensate. Accepting that limitation, we assume:

Axiom JR7. Inverse. For each $f \in \mathcal{D}$, there exists $f^{-1} \in \mathcal{D}$ such that

$$f \oplus f^{-1} \sim e. \tag{7}$$

These seven conditions are well known to be sufficient to yield the additive representation stated in Eqs. (4) to (6), and that representation implies that Axioms JR1 to JR6 must hold (Hölder, 1901).

Linking Joint Receipt and Gambles of Gains: Segregation

Now, given that we have some idea of how to derive utility U from gambles and value V from joint receipt, an immediate question is: How do these two structures relate, and in particular, how does U relate to V? Clearly, over the same domain, they must be strictly increasing functions of each other because they both preserve the same preference order. The issue is what other restrictions exist.

We continue to confine ourselves to gains for the moment. For this purpose, let $\mathcal{B}$ denote the set of binary gambles closed under joint receipt, and let $\mathcal{B}^+ \subset \mathcal{B}$ be such that $g \in \mathcal{B}^+$ if and only if both $g \in \mathcal{B}$ and $g \succsim e$. Consider the following possible link between the structures:

Definition. (Binary) segregation is said to hold if and only if for all f, g in B^+,

$$(f \oplus g, C; g, \bar{C}) \sim (f, C; e, \bar{C}) \oplus g. \tag{8}$$

The gamble to the left of $\sim$ yields $f \oplus g$ when the event C occurs and g otherwise, and the joint receipt on the right side yields g as well as f when C occurs and e otherwise. So, in reality, they are two different ways of expressing exactly the same situation, and it seems as locally rational as any of the other accounting indifferences we have encountered.

Segregation, weak commutativity, binary RDU (which, of course, includes binary SEU for gains as a special case), and assuming the utility function is onto an interval and the weighting function is onto $[0, 1]$, are sufficient to show that for some real constant δ (with the dimension $1/U$)

$$U(f \oplus g) = U(f) + U(g) - \delta U(f)U(g). \tag{9}$$

From this it follows that joint receipt has an additive representation V of the form shown in Eq. (5). We call V a *value function*. In fact, Eq. (9) is known to be the only polynomial form in the two variables $U(f)$ and $U(g)$ with $U(e) = 0$ that can be transformed into an additive one, and for that reason, I call this representation *p-additive*.

Depending on the sign of δ, there are three distinct relations between U and V:

$$\delta = 0 \implies \text{for some } \alpha > 0, \quad U = \alpha V, \tag{10}$$

$$\delta > 0 \implies \text{for some } \kappa > 0, \quad |\delta| U = 1 - e^{-\kappa V}, \tag{11}$$

$$\delta < 0 \implies \text{for some } \kappa > 0, \quad |\delta| U = e^{\kappa V} - 1. \tag{12}$$

Note that Eq. (11) is necessarily concave and bounded in V, whereas Eq. (12) is convex and unbounded in V.

A similar development holds for all losses, but with different constants, $\alpha' > 0$, $\delta' > 0$, and $\kappa' > 0$. For simplicity, and with very little real loss of generality, we will assume that $\kappa' = \kappa$.

In what follows, it is simpler to state things in terms of

$$U_+(x) = |\delta| U(x), \quad x \succsim e, \tag{13}$$

$$U_-(x) = |\delta'| U(x), \quad x \prec e. \tag{14}$$

Nonbilinear Utility of Mixed Gambles

Utility of Mixed Joint Receipt

I will not give the full details for the mixed case, which can be found in Luce (1997, 2000), but only for the basic ideas. We assume that V is additive throughout the entire domain of alternatives.

Consider mixed joint receipts. The results are described in detail only for the case where the joint receipt is seen as a gain, that is, $f_+ \succ e \succ g_-$ and $f_+ \oplus g_- \succsim e$. When U is proportional to V we have

$$U(f_+ \oplus g_-) = U(f_+) + \frac{\alpha}{\alpha'} U(g_-).$$

The more interesting cases are the two exponential cases, Eqs. (11) and (12). What is surprising about them is that from the additive representation of V and the p-additive representation of U over gains and separately over losses, we find that the U representation of mixed joint receipt is nonlinear. The key to deriving this is the very well known, indeed defining, property of exponentials, namely, $e^{V(x \oplus y)} = e^{V(x)+V(y)} = e^{V(x)} e^{V(y)}$. Taking into account the sign of V and Eqs. (11) and (12), one can show for concave gains that

$$U_+(f_+ \oplus g_-) = \frac{U_+(f_+) - U_+(g_-^{-1})}{1 - U_+(g_-^{-1})}. \tag{15}$$

When U_+ is convex in V for gains, the formula is the same except that the minus sign in the denominator is changed to a plus sign. Somewhat similar formulas arise when the joint receipt is seen as a loss (see Luce, 2000, pp. 240–241).

So, to this point, we see that locally rational assumptions about gambles and joint receipt lead to an unanticipated nonlinearity. The question is: What does this imply about the utility of mixed gambles? Recall that this is where the traditional bilinear theories seem to have encountered serious descriptive difficulties and their normative use has proved somewhat unsatisfactory.

Linking Joint Receipt and Gambles: General Segregation

The question now becomes: Given that we have the representation of the utility of mixed joint receipts, what can we say about the utility of mixed gambles? The most obvious, locally rational link between the two structures is a generalization of segregation. To that end, define the "subtraction" corresponding to $\oplus$:

$$f \ominus g \sim h \Longleftrightarrow f \sim g \oplus h.$$

We assume that the element h exists, which for money alternatives is no issue.

Definition. *General segregation* holds if for binary gambles f, g, with $f \succsim g$, and underlying experiment $\mathbf{E}$ with event C,

$$(f, C; g, \bar{C}) \sim \begin{cases} (f \ominus g, C; e, \bar{C}) \oplus g, & \text{if } (f, C; g, \bar{C}) \succ e \\ (e, C; g \ominus f, \bar{C}) \oplus f, & \text{if } (f, C; g, \bar{C}) \prec e \end{cases}. \quad (16)$$

As with segregation, this condition is entirely rational, provided that one is willing to accept the idea that one simplifies the given gamble differently, depending on whether it is seen as a gain or a loss.

We assume both general segregation and a separable representation in the following sense. There are weighting functions $W_{\mathbf{E}}^+$ and $W_{\mathbf{E}}^-$ and a utility function U such that for gambles of the form $(f_+, C; e, \bar{C})$, $U W_{\mathbf{E}}^+$ forms a separable representation in the sense that

$$(f_+, C; e, \bar{C}) \succsim (g_+, D; e, \bar{D}) \Longleftrightarrow U(f_+) W_{\mathbf{E}}^+(C) \geq U(g_+) W_{\mathbf{E}}^+(D),$$

and for gambles of the form $(e, C; g_-, \bar{C})$, $U W_{\mathbf{E}}^-$ forms a separable representation. Under these conditions and dropping the $\mathbf{E}$ subscript on the W's, we have the following conclusions:

- If U is proportional to V, then for $(f_+, C; g_-, \bar{C}) \succ e$,

$$U_+(f_+, C; g_-, \bar{C}) = U_+(f_+) W^+(C) + \frac{\alpha}{\alpha'} U_-(g_-)[1 - W^+(C)];$$

$$(17)$$

and for $(f_+, C; g_-, \bar{C}) \prec e$,

$$U_-(f_+, C; g_-, \bar{C}) = \frac{\alpha'}{\alpha} U_+(f_+)[1 - W^-(\bar{C})] + U_-(g_-) W^-(\bar{C}).$$

$$(18)$$

This, of course, is bilinear and so consistent with SEU.

- Suppose that U is exponentially related to V and is concave for gains and convex for losses (for the convex/concave case the signs are in parentheses). Then for $f_+ \succsim e \succsim g_-$ with $(f_+, C; g_-, \bar{C}) \succ e$,

$$U_+(f_+, C; g_-, \bar{C}) = U_+(f_+) W^+(C) + \frac{U_-(g_-)}{1 + (-)U_-(g_-)}[1 - W^+(C)]$$

$$(19)$$

and for $(f_+, C; g_-, \bar{C}) \prec e$,

$$U_-(f_+, C; g_-) = \frac{U_+(f_+)}{1 - (+)U_+(f_+)}[1 - W^-(\bar{C})] + U_-(g_-)W^-(\bar{C}).$$

(20)

- Suppose that U in terms of V is either concave for both gains and losses or convex for both. Then for $(f_+, C; g_-, \bar{C}) \succ e$,

$$U_+(f_+, C; g_-, \bar{C}) = U_+(f_+)W^+(C) + U_-(g_-)[1 - W^+(C)] \quad (21)$$

and for $(f_+, C; g_-, \bar{C}) \prec e$,

$$U_-(f_+, C; g_-, \bar{C}) = U_+(f_+)[1 - W^-(\bar{C})] + U_-(g_-)W^-(\bar{C}). \quad (22)$$

The last case, like the proportional one, is bilinear, similar to SEU. The most interesting case is the middle one, Eqs. (19) and (20), where the utility function is concave in one region and convex in the other. This leads to a nonbilinear form different from that of SEU. What happens is that for a gamble perceived as a gain, the weight assigned to the loss term is increased (decreased) by an amount dependent on the utility of the loss in the concave/convex (convex/concave) case. When the gamble is seen as a loss, the change is in the weight assigned to the gain term; it is increased (decreased) in the concave/convex (convex/concave) case.

Linking Joint Receipt and Gambles: Duplex Decomposition

Luce (1997) and Luce and Fishburn (1991, 1995) have studied another link – a nonrational one – between joint receipt and gambles that is called *duplex decomposition*. It first appeared in the empirical work of Slovic and Lichtenstein (1968). It asserts that for all f_+ a gain, g_- a loss, and C and event of experiment **E**

$$(f_+, C; g_-, \bar{C}) \sim (f_+, C'; e, \bar{C}') \oplus (e, C''; g_-, \bar{C}''), \quad (23)$$

where, on the right side of $\sim$, events C' and C'' mean occurrences of event C arising from two independent realizations of gambles.

There were three motives originally for studying duplex decomposition: its vague plausibility despite its nonrational character; the empirical data of Slovic and Lichtenstein (1968), which suggested it in the first place; and the mathematical fact that under certain assumptions it leads to the bilinear form of Kahneman and Tversky's (1979) and Tversky and Kahneman's (1992) cumulative prospect theory. Within

the context of an additive value representation, it leads to a somewhat different nonbilinear form than does general segregation for the
case of U concave with V in one region and convex in the other. For
$(f_+, C; g_-, \bar{C}) \succsim e$, then for the case of concave gains and convex losses
(convex gains and convex losses)

$$U_+(f_+, C; g_-, \bar{C}) = \frac{U_+(f_+)W^+(C) + U_-(g_-)W^-(\bar{C})}{1 + (-)U_-(g_-)W^-(\bar{C})}. \tag{24}$$

The result for $(f_+, C; g_-, \bar{C}) \prec e$ is similar with $1 - (+)U_+(f_+)W^+(C)$ in
the denominator.

The net effect is to take the standard expression for cumulative
prospect theory (CPT) and modify it. If the gamble is seen as a gain,
then the CPT form is increased (decreased) in the case of concave gains
and convex losses (convex/concave), whereas for a perceived loss it is
decreased (increased).

For some purposes, this form may be more descriptive than that derived from general segregation. For example, Sneddon and Luce (2001)
used certainty equivalence data from 144 respondents of Cho, Luce, and
von Winterfeldt (1994) to compare the models. Using a minimum least
squares measure, they found that the additive V models, where $\oplus$ is associative throughout the domain, do better than the additive U models
(basically, CPT) for about 84% of the respondents; that the nonbilinear
fits are better than the bilinear ones for about 67% of the respondents;
and that the nonrational duplex decomposition is favored over the rational general segregation by about 3 to 1.

But my concern here is with rationality, not description, so I will not
pursue duplex decomposition further. More details may be found in my
monograph (Luce, 2000).

Six Related Observations

1. Adding the concepts of (no change from) the status quo and joint
   receipt has at least two happy features. First, they capture some
   very common features of decision situations, namely, the distinction between gains and losses and the simple fact that consequences and alternatives often involve several unitary, valued
   entities. Second, they lead to a simple theory of how to evaluate
   preferences among certain consequences that is independent
   of our descriptions of behavior under uncertainty. Note, however, the cautious "how to evaluate preferences" rather than

"the utility of preferences" because one may not automatically assume that the value function V arising from joint receipts is necessarily proportional to the utility function U arising from binary gambles of all gains and all losses. The relation between U and V must be investigated, which is done by discovering a qualitative behavioral connection linking the gambling structure to the joint receipt one. The one proposed, called *segregation*, is a type of accounting rationality. Moreover, if the utility function U is rank dependent (including SEU as a special case), then U is one of three functions of V: proportional, negative exponential, or exponential.

2. Of course, the classical SEU theory applies to the mixed case because it fails to distinguish gains from losses. But making that distinction, which I claim virtually everyone does, and accepting that SEU is a suitable rational theory for binary gambles of gains and separately for binary gambles of losses, then the representation of rational behavior in the mixed case is neither uniquely determined nor necessarily bilinear. For example, assuming that V is additive over joint receipt, then with U concave relative to V for one region and convex for the other one, the predictions of the rational general segregation for the mixed case are not bilinear. This nonbilinearity holds also for the link called *duplex decomposition*, which, although not rational, appears to be somewhat more descriptively accurate than general segregation.

3. This is an odd impasse. At least since the work of Savage (1954), it has been widely held that SEU is *the* rational theory for individual decision making under uncertainty. Now we see that there can be two equally rationally based theories with quite different predictions (or prescriptions) in cases of mixed gains and losses. Or put another way, the union of Savage's assumptions and the rational ones for joint receipt and its relations to gambles are consistent only in two cases. The first is when U is proportional to V, and the weights satisfy both finite additivity and $W^+(C) + W^-(\bar{C}) = 1$; see Eqs. (17) and (18). These requirements are strong. For example, if the domain of sure consequences includes amounts x, y of money and if, as seems rational, $x \oplus y = x + y$, then it is easy to prove that $U(x)$ is proportional to x. Thus, over lotteries of money consequences with known probabilities, this rational case reduces to expected

value, not EU, and over more general gambles it is subjective expected certainty equivalents. The second case is when the same restriction holds for the weights and U is either exponential or negative exponential in V for both gains and losses; see Eqs. (21) and (22). These restrictions on U and W are fairly severe and not descriptive of many people.

4. A question immediately comes to mind: Is there some deeper sense of rationality that permits one to select between the two formulations? Because the major distinction between the approaches is whether or not one distinguishes between gains and losses and whether or not the operation of joint receipt is included among the primitives, the question becomes: Is there a rational argument for either excluding or including the status quo and joint receipts? I know of none. There is a pragmatic argument that says that since almost everyone makes the gain–loss distinction, it probably should not be ignored in a rational theory. And there is also the pragmatic argument that because joint receipt is ubiquitous, it too probably should not be ignored by theorists. But I do not see either of these as rationally compelling, merely plausible. But equally, I do not see any rational or otherwise compelling reason for excluding them.

5. What does this development say to a decision analyst? The discoveries described are too new and insufficiently absorbed and criticized by the field for anyone – even their author – to have full confidence about them. So, at the moment, the only reasonable stance is caution in basing prescriptive recommendations solely on EU or SEU. I would like to see systematic efforts comparing, including decision makers comparatively evaluating, the recommendations from SEU and the present nonbilinear forms for mixed gains and losses, in particular Eqs. (19) and (20). Probably such studies should also include the nonrational, but apparently often descriptive, theory based on duplex decomposition, Eq. (24). Because the estimates for gains and losses separately agree in all versions, the focus is entirely on the mixed gain–loss case, which of course is the case of usual interest.

6. What does it say to the scientist? Perhaps that we simply have to live with the fact that what seems rational depends more on the formulation of the domain of study than we had previously acknowledged. These observations certainly need additional discussion by the field.

References

Birnbaum, M. H., & Chavez, A. (1997). Tests of theories of decision making: Violations of branch independence and distribution independence. *Organizational Behavior and Human Decision Processes, 71*, 161–194.

Birnbaum, M. H., & Navarrete, J. (1998). Testing descriptive utility theories: Violations of stochastic dominance and cumulative independence. *Journal of Risk and Uncertainty, 17*, 49–78.

Cho, Y., Luce, R. D., & von Winterfeldt, D. (1994). Tests of assumptions about the joint receipt of gambles in rank- and sign-dependent utility theory. *Journal of Experimental Psychology: Human Perception and Performance, 20*, 931–943.

de Finetti, B. (1931). Sul Significato Soggettivo della Probabilità. *Fundamenta Mathematicae 17*, 298–329. Translated into English in P. Monari and D. Cocchi (Eds., 1993), On the Subjective Meaning of Probability, *Probabilitá e Induzione* (pp. 291–321). Bologna: Clueb.

Edwards, W. (Ed.). (1992). *Utility Theories: Measurements and Applications*. Boston: Kluwer.

Ellsberg, D. (1961). Risk, ambiguity and the Savage axioms. *Quarterly Journal of Economics, 75*, 643–669.

Fine, T. (1973). *Theories of Probability: An Examination of Foundations*. New York: Academic Press.

Fishburn, P. C. (1986). The axioms of subjective probability. *Statistical Science, 1*, 335–358.

Fishburn, P. C. (1982). Non-transitive measurable utility. *Journal of Mathematical Psychology, 26*, 31–67.

Fishburn, P. C., & Kochenberger, G. A. (1979). Two-piece von Neumann–Morgenstern utility functions. *Decision Sciences, 10*, 503–518.

Hershey, J., Kunreuther, H. C., & Schoemaker, P. (1982). Sources of bias in assessment procedures for utility functions. *Management Science, 28*, 936–954.

Hölder, O. (1901). Die Axiome der Quantität und die Lehre vom Mass. *Berichte der Sächsischan Gesellschaft der Wissenschafton, Mathematische-Physische Klasse, 53*, 1–64.

Kahneman, D., & Tversky, A. (1979). Prospect theory: An analysis of decision under risk. *Econometrica, 47*, 263–291.

Krantz, D. H., Luce, R. D., Suppes, P., & Tversky, A. (1971). *Foundations of Measurement*, Vol. I. New York: Academic Press.

Luce, R. D. (1992). Where does subjective expected utility fail descriptively? *Journal of Risk and Uncertainty, 5*, 5–27.

Luce, R. D. (1997). Associative joint receipts. *Mathematical Social Sciences, 34*, 51–74.

Luce, R. D. (2000). *Utility of Uncertain Gains and Losses: Measurement-Theoretic and Experimental Approaches*. Mahwah, NJ: Erlbaum. Errata: see Luce's web page at http:www.socsci.uci.edu.

Luce, R. D., & Fishburn, P. C. (1991). Rank- and sign-dependent linear utility models for finite first-order gambles. *Journal of Risk and Uncertainty, 4*, 25–59.

Luce, R. D., & Fishburn, P. C. (1995). A note on deriving rank-dependent utility using additive joint receipts. *Journal of Risk and Uncertainty, 11*, 5–16.

Luce, R. D., & Marley, A. A. J. (2000). Separable and additive representations of binary gambles of gains. *Mathematical Social Sciences, 40,* 277–295.

Luce, R. D., & von Winterfeldt, D. (1994). What common ground exists for descriptive, prescriptive, and normative utility theories? *Management Science, 40,* 263–279.

Marley, A. A. J., & Luce, R. D. (2002). A simple axiomatization of binary rank-dependent expected utility of gains (losses). *Journal of Mathematical Psychology, 46,* 40–55.

Quiggin, J. (1993). *Generalized Expected Utility Theory: The Rank-Dependent Model.* Boston: Kluwer.

Savage, L. J. (1954). *The Foundations of Statistics.* New York: Wiley.

Simon, H. A. (1956). Rational choice and the structure of the environment. *Psychological Review, 63,* 129–138.

Slovic, P., & Lichtenstein, S. (1968). Importance of variance preferences in gambling decisions. *Journal of Experimental Psychology, 78,* 646–654.

Sneddon, R., & Luce, R. D. (2001). Empirical comparisons of bilinear and non-bilinear utility theories. *Organizational Behavior and Human Decision Making, 84,* 71–94.

Thaler, R. H. (1985). Mental accounting and consumer choice. *Marketing Science, 36,* 199–214.

Tversky, A., & Kahneman, D. (1992). Advances in prospect theory: Cumulative representation of uncertainty. *Journal of Risk and Uncertainty, 5,* 204–217.

von Winterfeldt, D., & Edwards, W. (1986). *Decision Analysis and Behavioral Research.* Cambridge: Cambridge University Press.

Wu, G. (1994). An empirical test of ordinal independence. *Journal of Risk and Uncertainty, 9,* 39–60.

3 Generalization Across People, Procedures, and Predictions: Violations of Stochastic Dominance and Coalescing

Michael H. Birnbaum and Teresa Martin

ABSTRACT

Stochastic dominance is implied by certain normative and descriptive theories of decision making. However, significantly more than half of participants in laboratory studies chose dominated gambles over dominant gambles, despite knowing that some participants would play their chosen gambles for real money. Systematic event-splitting effects were also observed, as significantly more than half of the participants reversed preferences when choosing between the split versions of the same choices. Similar violations were found with five different ways of displaying the choices. Studies conducted via the Web show that the effects generalize beyond the laboratory, even to highly educated people who have studied decision making. Results are consistent with configural weight models, which predict violations of stochastic dominance and coalescing, but not with rank- and sign-dependent utility theories, including cumulative prospect theory, which must satisfy these properties. This research program illustrates three directions for testing the generality of theories – generality across people, procedures, and new predictions.

CONTENTS

Support was received from National Science Foundation Grants SBR-9410572 and SES 99-86436. Experiment 3 is from a master's thesis by the second author (Martin, 1998) under the direction of the first. We thank Sandra Schneider for suggesting the test of graphic displays (Experiments 4 and 5), Michele Underwood for her assistance during pilot testing of pie chart displays, and Christof Tatka for suggesting a reversal of the branch order (Experiment 5).

84

In choosing between risky gambles, it is eminently rational to obey stochastic dominance. If gamble *A* always gives at least as high a prize as gamble *B* and sometimes better, gamble *A* is said to dominate gamble *B*. Few deny that one should choose the dominant gamble over the dominated gamble once one comprehends dominance.

Stochastic dominance is not only a rational principle of decision making, it is also imposed by descriptive theories that are supposed to predict the empirical choices that people make. Kahneman and Tversky (1979) proposed that people detect and reject dominated gambles in an editing phase that precedes evaluation. Rank-dependent expected utility (RDEU) theory (Quiggin, 1982, 1993), rank- and sign-dependent utility (RSDU) theory (Luce, 2000; Luce & Fishburn, 1991, 1995), cumulative prospect theory (CPT) (Tversky & Kahneman, 1992; Wakker & Tversky, 1993), lottery-dependent utility theory (Becker & Sarin, 1987), and others (e.g., Camerer, 1992; Lopes & Oden, 1999; Machina, 1982) assume or imply that people obey stochastic dominance.

Therefore, the finding by Birnbaum and Navarrete (1998) that there are choices in which 70% of the people tested violate stochastic dominance is not only upsetting to the view that people are rational, but also disproves descriptive theories that retain stochastic dominance. This finding was not the result of happenstance. The choices tested by Birnbaum and Navarrete had been designed by Birnbaum (1997) to violate stochastic dominance, according to configural weight models and parameters fit to previous data involving choices that tested other properties.

Recipe for Violations of Stochastic Dominance

Birnbaum (1997) noted that configural weight models known as the *rank-affected multiplicative* (RAM) and *transfer of attention exchange* (TAX) models imply violations of stochastic dominance in a recipe that can be illustrated by the following example. Start with $G_0 = (\$12, .1; \$96, .9)$, a gamble with a .1 probability of winning \$12 and a .9 probability of winning $96. Now split the lower branch of G_0 (.1 to win $12) to create a slightly better gamble, $G+ = (\$12, .05; \$14, .05; \$96, .9)$. Next, split the higher branch of G_0 to create a slightly worse gamble, $G- = (\$12, .1; \$90, .05; \$96, .85)$. Clearly, $G+$ dominates G_0, which dominates $G-$.

The RAM model with parameters of Birnbaum and McIntosh (1996) and the TAX model with parameters of Birnbaum and Chavez (1997) both predict that people should prefer $G-$ to $G+$, violating stochastic dominance. The RAM and TAX models are configural weight models that represent the subjective values of gambles by their weighted averages, with weights that are affected by ranks. The theories allow a subjective function of prizes, $u(x)$, and a weighting function of probability, $S(p)$; in addition, they allow configural weighting that is affected by the ranks of the branches' consequences.

In the RAM and TAX models, each branch (each distinct probability–payoff combination) of a gamble carries some weight. When a fixed probability is split to create two branches from one, the sum of the weights of the two separate branches can exceed the weight of the coalesced branch, unlike the RDEU models. These configural weight models have some similarity to the RDEU models in that weights are affected by ranks, but the definition of *ranks* differs between the two approaches. In the RDEU models, cumulative weight is a monotonic function of cumulative probability (rank); however, in RAM and TAX, it is the distinct probability-consequence *branches* in the display that have "ranks" and are carriers of weight.

To illustrate the TAX model, assume that a gamble's utility is a weighted average of the utilities of its consequences. Suppose, for simplicity, that subjective probability is proportional to objective probability, and suppose that utilities are proportional to monetary consequences. So far, we have expected value. We now add the key idea: Suppose in three-branch gambles that any branch with a lower-valued consequence "taxes" (or "takes") one-fourth of the weight of any distinct branch with a higher-valued consequence. The configural weights of the lowest, middle, and highest outcomes of $G+ = (\$12, .05; \$14, .05; \$96, .9)$ are then, respectively, $w_L = .05 + (1/4)(.05) + (1/4)(.9) = .2875$; $w_M = .05 - (1/4)(.05) + (1/4)(.9) = .2625$; and $w_H = .9 - (1/4)(.9) - (1/4)(.9) = .45$. The average value of $G+$ is therefore $50.32. Similarly, for $G- = (\$12, .1; \$90, .05; \$96, .85)$, $w_L = .325$, $w_M = .25$, and $w_H = .425$, for an average of $67.2, which exceeds $50.32 for $G+$, violating dominance.

It is worth noting that this pattern of weighing was not fit to violations of stochastic dominance post hoc, but rather was estimated from violations of branch independence. Violations of branch independence are compatible with the RAM, TAX, and RDEU models. Thus, data that are compatible with all three models were used to make a new prediction that distinguishes the class of configural models (that violate stochastic dominance) from the class of models that satisfy this property.

The class of rank-dependent RDEU/RSDU/CPT models must satisfy stochastic dominance for any choices (Birnbaum & Navarrete, 1998, pp. 57–58; Luce, 1998, 2000). For example, with the CPT model and the parameters of Tversky and Kahneman (1992), the corresponding certainty equivalents of the gambles are $70.26 for $G+$ against 65.17 for $G-$.

Equations for the CPT, RAM, and TAX models are presented in Birnbaum and Navarrete (1998, pp. 54–57). Calculations for the CPT, RAM, and TAX models can be made in URL http://psych.fullerton.edu/mbirnbaum/taxcalculator.htm, and http://psych.fullerton.edu/mbirnbaum/cwtcalculator.htm, which are described in Birnbaum et al. (1999). These on-line, Netscape-compatible JavaScript calculators can be used to compute certainty equivalents according to the CPT model and parameters fit to Tversky and Kahneman (1992) and to the RAM and TAX models and parameters of Birnbaum (1997, 1999a). The calculators allow the user to compute certainty equivalents of gambles with two to five nonnegative consequences. The user can also change parameter values to explore their effects on predictions.

Birnbaum and Navarrete (1998) tested four variations of this recipe for $G-$ versus $G+$ with 100 undergraduates and found that about 70% violated dominance, averaged over the four variations.

Birnbaum, Patton, and Lott (1999) tested a new sample of 110 students with five new variations of the same recipe and found an average of 73% violations. These studies also tested two properties derived by Birnbaum (1997), which he named *lower cumulative independence* and *upper cumulative independence*. These properties are also implied by RSDU/RDEU/CPT theories, and they were also violated systematically.[1]

---

[1] Birnbaum (1997, p. 96) derived the following conditions (where $0 < z < x' < x < y < y' < z'$ and $p + q + r = 1$):

    Lower cumulative independence: If $S = (z, r; x, p; y, q)$ is preferred to $R = (z, r; x', p; y', q)$, then $S'' = (x', r; y, p + q)$ preferred to $R'' = (x', r + p; y', q)$.

    Upper cumulative independence: If $S' = (x, p; y, q; z', r)$ is not preferred to $R' = (x', p; y', q; z', r)$, then $S''' = (x, p + q; y', r)$ is not preferred to $R''' = (x', p; y', q + r)$.

    Any theory that satisfies comonotonic independence, monotonicity, transitivity, and coalescing must satisfy both lower and upper cumulative independence (Birnbaum &

Because violations of stochastic dominance contradict so many proposed descriptive theories, it is important to determine if the results are unique to the particular procedures used in previous research. Can the conclusions of these laboratory studies be generalized to predict the results with procedures and people other than those tested?

The experiments of Birnbaum and Navarrete (1998) and Birnbaum et al. (1999) required undergraduates to make more than 100 choices between gambles. Participants were not paid, so they had no financial incentive to choose wisely. In addition, people were asked not only to choose the gamble they preferred, but also to state the amount they would pay to receive their chosen gamble rather than the other gamble. If the results are unique to these procedures, such as the method of display of the gambles, the lack of financial incentives, or the instruction to judge strength of preference, then perhaps the RDEU class of models could be retained at least for certain types of experiments.

The purpose of this chapter is to review experiments that followed those of Birnbaum and Navarrete (1998) and Birnbaum et al. (1999) in order to examine more closely the conditions under which people violate stochastic dominance. Two of the studies were conducted via the World Wide Web in order to recruit participants who were demographically diverse in order to check the generality of the results to groups other than college students. Five studies featured here have not been previously published.

Changes in Procedures

The following changes in procedure were made: (1) Offer financial incentives; perhaps with financial incentives, people might conform to stochastic dominance. (2) Collect fewer choices per person; perhaps with many trials, people get bored, careless, or adopt simple strategies that have systematic errors. (3) Try other formats for displaying the gambles; if the violations of stochastic dominance are due to processes of choice (as opposed to evaluation of the gambles), changing the juxtaposition of the branches might affect the incidence of violations. (4) Put related

Navarrete, 1998, pp. 53–54), including the class of RDEU/RSDU/CPT models. Both cumulative independence properties were systematically violated, as predicted by the configural weight RAM (Birnbaum, 1999b) and TAX models (Birnbaum & Navarrete, 1998).

choices on the same page to allow judges to see the consistency of their choices more easily. (5) Remove instructions or feedback concerning violations of transparent dominance in the warm-ups used in previous research; perhaps this procedure somehow affects the strategies adopted. (6) Omit the procedure whereby judges were asked to evaluate the difference between the two gambles; perhaps the task of judging strength of preference alters the choice process.

In Experiments 1 and 2, all six of these variations of procedure were made, using two variations of the format of Kahneman and Tversky (1979) for presentation of each choice. In Experiment 3, we used the procedure of Birnbaum and Navarrete (1998), with extensions to include a greater variation of the recipe for stochastic dominance. Experiments 4 and 5 recruited participants via the World Wide Web. Such samples are demographically diverse and allow the investigator to check the generality of results across demographic groups. In Experiments 4 and 5, two other variations for presentation of the gambles were tried. In Experiment 4, either text or pie charts were used to display the probabilities (perhaps with pie charts, judges can "see" stochastic dominance more easily). In Experiment 5, the order of the consequences was reversed in order to see if this reversal would produce different results from those obtained with pie charts.

Test of Event Splitting/Coalescing

Coalescing is the assumption that if a gamble has two equal consequences, one can combine them by adding their probabilities without changing the utility of the gamble. For example, $GS = (\$12, .1; \$12, .1; \$96, .8)$ should be indifferent to $G = (\$12, .2; \$96, .8)$. Coalescing was assumed as an editing principle, *combination*, in the original prospect theory (Kahneman & Tversky, 1979). Coalescing is implied by RDEU/ RSDU/CPT theories but not by configural weight theories (Birnbaum & Navarrete, 1998; Luce, 1998). Luce (1998) showed that coalescing also distinguishes other decision-making theories and that coalescing and rank-dependent additivity can be used to deduce rank-dependent expected utility theory. Birnbaum (1999a) hypothesized that violations of coalescing might account for violations of stochastic dominance, cumulative independence, and also upper-tail independence (studied by Wu, 1994).

Note that event splitting was used as one ingredient of the recipe creating violations of stochastic dominance. Our present studies tested if event splitting can be used to also eliminate violations of stochastic dominance within the same gambles. Although there is no asymmetry in the mathematics between coalescing and event splitting, intuitively the two ways to convert gambles are different. There is only one way to coalesce equal consequences in a gamble (converting from gamble GS to G), but there are many ways to split events to convert a gamble into equivalent gambles (converting G to GS).

Luce (1998, p. 91) noted that previous tests of event splitting (Humphrey, 1995; Starmer & Sugden, 1993) were not optimal. He remarked, "data from the coalesced and uncoalesced cases were from two nonoverlapping sets of subjects, so it is not possible to do a two-by-two cross tabulation. . . . Given . . . [that] there are substantial individual preference differences among people, I view this as a decidedly weak test of the property." The present studies all use designs that support strong tests.

To test coalescing more directly, we split consequences in $G+$ and $G-$ to create four-outcome gambles, $GS+$ and $GS-$. The split versions of these examples are $GS+ = (\$12, .05; \$14, .05; \$96, .05; \$96, .85)$ versus $GS- = (\$12, .05; \$12, .05; \$90, .05; \$96, .85)$. The choice, $GS+$ versus $GS-$ is really the same choice as $G+$ versus $G-$, except for coalescing. In Table 3.1, $G+$ and $G-$ are I and J in row 5, respectively, and $GS+$ and $GS-$ are U and V in row 11.

The configural weight RAM model of Birnbaum and McIntosh (1996), with parameters estimated in previous research, predicts that judges should violate stochastic dominance by preferring $G-$ to $G+$. The TAX model of Birnbaum and Chavez (1997) makes the same prediction. These configural weight models also predict that judges should show an event-splitting effect by preferring $GS+$ to $GS-$.

Methods

In Experiment 1, 31 undergraduates (10 male and 21 female) were told that they would have a chance to play one gamble for real money. They were told that 2 people (out of 31) would be randomly selected to play one gamble for either the face amount, half the face amount, or twice the face amount, which might yield cash prizes as high as $220. This instruction appeared to produce considerable excitement among the participants. One trial would be selected, and each selected judge would play the gamble that she or he chose on that trial during the study. Judges were reminded that the trial selected might be any one of the

Table 3.1. *Choices, Predictions, Modal Choices, and Percentage Choices (Experiments 1 and 2)*

Row	Choice		Predictions			Results % Choice	
			TAX	CPT	Mode	Exp 1	Exp 2
1	A: .50 to win $0 .50 to win $100	B: .50 to win $25 .50 to win $35	A	A	B	52	52
2	C: .50 to win $0 .50 to win $100	D: .50 to win $45 .50 to win $50	D	D	D	81*	61
3	E: .50 to win $4 .30 to win $96 .20 to win $100	F: .50 to win $4 .30 to win $12 .20 to win $100	E	E	E	100*	88*
4	G: .40 to win $2 .50 to win $12 .10 to win $108	H: .40 to win $2 .50 to win $96 .10 to win $108	H	H	H	97*	100*
5	I: .05 to win $12 .05 to win $14 .90 to win $96	J: .10 to win $12 .05 to win $90 .85 to win $96	J	I	J	74*	82*
6	K: .80 to win $2 .10 to win $40 .10 to win $44	L: .80 to win $2 .10 to win $10 .10 to win $98	K	L	L	65	58
7	M: .06 to win $6 .03 to win $96 .91 to win $99	N: .03 to win $6 .03 to win $8 .94 to win $99	M	N	M	77*	55
8	O: .80 to win $10 .20 to win $44	P: .90 to win $10 .10 to win $98	P	P	P	77*	70*
9	Q. .20 to win $40 .80 to win $98	R: .10 to win $10 .90 to win $98	Q	Q	Q	65	46
10	S: .10 to win $40 .10 to win $44 .80 to win $110	T: .10 to win $10 .10 to win $98 .80 to win $110	T	S	T	74*	79*
11	U: .05 to win $12 .05 to win $14 .05 to win $96 .85 to win $96	V: .05 to win $12 .05 to win $12 .05 to win $90 .85 to win $96	U	U	U	94*	79*
12	W: .05 to win $10 .05 to win $98 .90 to win $106	X: .05 to win $44 .05 to win $49 .90 to win $106	W	X	W	68	
13	Y: .03 to win $6 .03 to win $6 .03 to win $96 .91 to win $99	Z: .03 to win $6 .03 to win $8 .03 to win $99 .91 to win $99	Z	Z	Z	90*	97*
14	A': .05 to win $10 .95 to win $98	B': .10 to win $44 .90 to win $98	B'	B'	B'	71*	

* Denotes a percentage significantly different from 50%. Choice percentages indicate agreement with the modal choice in Experiment 1, and are therefore all above 50%, except in row 9, where only 46% in Experiment 2 chose Q.

A. Format of Birnbaum and Navarrete (1998) and Experiment 3

```
 .05  .05  .90            .10  .05  .85
 $12  $14  $96            $12  $90  $96
```

B. Format in Experiment 1

```
I:   .05 to win $12        J:  .10 to win $12
     .05 to win $14            .05 to win $90
     .90 to win $96            .85 to win $96
```

C. Format in Experiment 2 (and Experiment 4)

```
●5. Which do you choose?

        ○I:   .05 probability to win $12
              .05 probability to win $14
              .90 probability to win $96
   OR
        ○J:   .10 probability to win $12
              .05 probability to win $90
              .85 probability to win $96
```

D. Reversed Text Format of Experiment 5

```
●5. Which do you choose?

        ○I:   .90 probability to win $96
              .05 probability to win $14
              .90 probability to win $12
   OR
        ○J:   .85 probability to win $96
              .05 probability to win $90
              .10 probability to win $12
```

Figure 3.1 Four formats for presentation of a choice between gambles.

choices, so they should make each choice carefully. Judges circled their preferred gamble in each choice. [Immediately after the choices were completed, games were played publicly as promised, and two students (who seemed quite animated) won cash by drawing slips randomly from urns.]

The 14 choices in Table 3.1 were printed on a single side of a page, using the format in Figure 3.1B. Figure 3.1A shows the format of Birnbaum and Navarrete (1998) and of Birnbaum et al. (1999), also used in Experiment 3, for comparison.

Two pairs of choices tested stochastic dominance and coalescing. Rows 5 and 11 included $G+ = (\$12, .05; \$14, .05; \$96, .90) = I$ versus $G- = (\$12, .10; \$90, .05; \$96, .85) = J$, and $GS+ = (\$12, .05; \$14, .05; \$96, .05; \$96, .85) = U$ versus $GS- = (\$12, .05; \$12, .05; \$90, .05; \$96, .85) = V$. $GS+$ versus $GS-$ is really the same choice as $G+$ versus $G-$, except for coalescing. Rows 7 and 13 created another variation of the same recipe, with the dominant gamble counterbalanced in the left–right position.

In Experiment 2, undergraduates (8 male and 24 female) viewed the gambles presented on a computer screen instead of on paper. Twelve of the choices in Table 3.1 were included (all except rows 12 and 14). The gamble printed on the left in the paper version was placed above the other gamble in the computer version, as illustrated in Figure 3.1C. Formats in Figures 3.1B and 3.1C differ in the juxtaposition of the branches.

In Experiment 2, choices were displayed on a computer screen by a browser, displaying a HyperText Markup Language form, which collected the data. Judges used the mouse to click a radio button next to the gamble they preferred. They were told that two participants would be selected randomly to play one of their chosen gambles for the face value. Experiment 2 was a laboratory pilot test of procedures later used by Birnbaum (1999b, 2000) and in Experiments 4 and 5.

Experiment 3 used 100 undergraduates, tested with procedures of Birnbaum and Navarrete (1998), in which choices were displayed as in Figure 3.1A.

Two choices for each set compared $G+$ versus $G-$ and $GS+$ versus $GS-$, where $GS+ = (x, s; x+, r; y, q; y, p)$, $GS- = (x, s; x, r; y^-, q; y, p)$, $G+ = (x, s; x+, r; y, p+q)$, and $G- = (x, s+r; y^-, q; y, p)$, where $s = 1 - p - q - r$. There were five sets with $(x, x+, y^-, y) = (\$4, \$10, \$92, \$98)$, $(\$6, \$12, \$93, \$99)$, $(\$6, \$9, \$91, \$97)$, $(\$7, \$10, \$84, \$90)$, and $(\$3, \$9, \$91, \$97)$, for rows 1 to 5 of Table 3.3, respectively. The values of (r, q, p) are given in Table 3.3. Note that choices in the first two rows resemble those used in previous research, but choices in the last three rows use smaller values of p and larger values of q. These 10 choices were included among 103 others (Martin, 1998). Instructions made it clear that in Experiment 3 the "financial incentives" were strictly hypothetical (as in Birnbaum and Navarrete, 1998).

Experiments 4 and 5 were conducted via the Web, using the general instructions and the 20 choices of Birnbaum (1999b). Experiment 4 compared choices displayed as in Figure 3.1C against those displayed by means of pie charts, as in Figure 3.2. Experiment 5 tested a reversal of the order of consequences, as shown in Figure 3.1D, against pie charts.

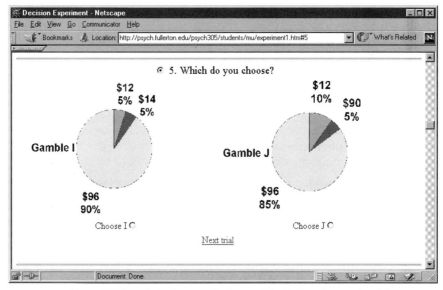

Figure 3.2 Use of pie charts to display gambles in Experiments 4 and 5.

The 999 participants (304 male and 689 female) were recruited via search engines, links in Web sites listing contests and games with prizes, and links in sites listing psychology experiments. This recruitment procedure is similar to that used in the Internet B study of Birnbaum (2000). Participants were assigned to conditions by clicking their birth months, which linked them to different variations of display procedures. Every third birth month was assigned to text and other months to the pie chart display. During the run of the study, the association of birth months with conditions was counterbalanced by Latin Square.

In text display formats, probability was described in terms of the number of equally likely tickets out of 100 in an urn, from which 1 ticket would be drawn to determine the prize. In the pie chart display format, the probability mechanism was described as a spinner device whose pointer was equally likely to stop in any equal-sized slice of the pie. The percentage of each slice was also displayed, as illustrated in Figure 3.2. Web participants were informed that three participants (in each study) would be selected to play one of their chosen gambles.

Results

Choices 1 and 2 of Table 3.1 form an indirect test of consequence monotonicity: $A = (\$0, .5; \$100, .5)$ versus $B = (\$25, .5; \$35, .5)$ and $C = A$ versus $D = (\$45, .5; \$55, .5)$. If a subject prefers B to A, then the same judge should prefer *D* to *A* because *D* strictly dominates *B*. There were no violations in Experiments 1 or 2. Rows 3 and 4 were transparent tests of consequence monotonicity in three-outcome gambles. They are termed *transparent* because everything is the same except the value of one consequence. There was 1 violation out of 62 choices in Experiment 1 and 4 out of 66 in Experiment 2. The overall rate of 3.9% violations of consequence monotonicity is similar to the figure of 4% reported by Birnbaum and Navarrete (1998) for similar tests.

The last three columns of Table 3.1 show modal choice and the percentages of judges who made the modal choice in Experiments 1 and 2, respectively. Modal choices are the same in both studies, except in choice 9; none of the choice percentages differ significantly between Experiments 1 and 2. Asterisks indicate choice percentages that deviate significantly from 50% by a two-tailed binomial sign test with $\alpha = .05$, tested separately in each experiment. Predicted choices in Table 3.1 were calculated for CPT and TAX models using previously published parameters.

We can ask how well these models predict the results. The prior CPT and TAX models make different predictions for 5 of the 14 choices (Choices 5, 6, 7, 10, and 12). In four of these five choices (except row 6), the majorities were consistent with the TAX model's predictions, using previously estimated parameters. Each judge was scored for these differential predictions, and it was found that 43* of the judges in Experiments 1 and 2 had more choices consistent with the prior TAX model than with the prior CPT model, compared to only 12 whose choices had a majority consistent with the CPT model. (Throughout this chapter, asterisks indicate statistical significance, tested against the binomial null hypothesis, with $p = 1/2$ and $\alpha = .05$. In this case, 43* indicates that significantly more than half of the 43 + 12 subjects had more choices correctly predicted by TAX.)

Although one might improve fits by estimating parameters from the data, violations of stochastic dominance in rows 5 and 7 refute CPT (RDEU/RSDU) with any parameters.

Cross-tabulations for the two tests of stochastic dominance and coalescing are shown in Table 3.2 for Experiments 1 and 2. In all four tests, the majority of participants violated stochastic dominance in the coalesced form *and* satisfied stochastic dominance in the split form.

In Experiment 1, 23* and 24* judges violated stochastic dominance in the choices of rows 5 and 7 of Table 3.1, respectively. In Experiment 1, 20 judges violated stochastic dominance on both of these choices, 7 violated it once, and 4 had no violations (76% violations overall).

Table 3.2. *Tests of Stochastic Dominance and Coalescing*[a]

	Rows 7 and 13		Rows 5 and 11	
Split	$G+ = N$	$G- = M$	$G+ = I$	$G- = J$
Experiment 1				
$GS+$	6	22*	8	21*
$GS-$	1	2	0	2
TOTAL	7	24*	8	23*
	Rows 7 and 13		Rows 5 and 11	
Split	$G+ = N$	$G- = M$	$G+ = I$	$G- = J$
Experiment 2				
$GS+$	14	18*	5	21*
$GS-$	1	0	1	6
TOTAL	15	18	6	27*

[a] Each entry shows the number of judges who had each conjunction of preferences in each pair of choice problems.
Note: Asterisks indicate frequencies significantly greater than 50% of participants.

In Experiment 2, 27 and 18 judges violated stochastic dominance in rows 5 and 7, respectively; there were 17 with two violations, 11 with one, and only 5 with no violations (68.2% violations overall). Averaged over studies and rows, the average rate of violation is 71.9%. These rates of violation are significantly greater than 50% but not significantly different from the rate of 70% violations reported by Birnbaum and Navarrete (1998).

In Experiment 1, there were 28* and 29* judges who satisfied stochastic dominance in the split form (rows 11 and 13 of Table 3.1) of the same two choices, which represents 92% satisfactions overall. According to any theory that satisfies coalescing and transitivity, there should have been no changes in preference due to event splitting, except by chance. Instead, the off-diagonal reversals of 21 to 0 and 22 to 1 each has a probability of less than 3 in 1 million, given the null hypothesis that either switch of preference is equally likely. In addition, the majority (19, or 61%) violated stochastic dominance on *both* comparisons of three-outcome gambles *and* satisfied it on *both* choices between four-outcome split variations of the same gambles. Results for Experiment 2 are similar, with 21–1 and 18–1 counts for preference reversals produced by event splitting and 88% satisfaction of stochastic dominance when split.

Table 3.3. *Tests of Event Splitting and Stochastic Dominance in Experiment 3*

Gambles				Choice Patterns			
r	q	p		$-+$	$--$	$+-$	z
.01	.02	.96	a	74*	3	3	8.09
.03	.03	.92		61*	3	1	7.62
.03	.74	.14	a	49	2	3	6.38
.30	.30	.30	a	43	1	1	6.33
.04	.59	.36		32*	3	6	4.22

Notes: $+$ indicates satisfaction of dominance, i.e., $G+$ preferred to $G-$ and $GS+$ preferred to $GS-$. The most common pattern, $-+$, represents a violation in the coalesced form and a satisfaction in the split form. In rows marked a, dominant gambles were presented on the right. Values of z test event splitting (all are significant). Asterisks indicate frequencies significantly different from 50 in $-+$ column only ($n = 100$).

Results for Experiment 3 are shown in Table 3.3. In all five variations, event-splitting effects are significant, because the $-+$ pattern ($G-$ preferred to $G+$ and $GS+$ preferred to $GS-$) occurs significantly more often than the opposite pattern of preferences ($+-$) in each row (z values are all significant). Summing over rows for each person, 91* of the 100 judges had more preference reversals of $-+$ than the opposite switch, 2 had more of the opposite, and 7 were tied.

The choices in the lower rows of Table 3.3 were designed on the basis of intuition to produce fewer violations (more satisfactions) of stochastic dominance. Table 3.3 shows that the frequency of violations of stochastic dominance (the sum of $-+$ and $--$) varies with the pattern of probabilities (p, q, r) used to construct the choices. The variations with large p and small q and r, like those used in previous research, give more violations of stochastic dominance (70.5% for the first two rows) than those with smaller values of p and larger q (43% for the last three rows). The frequencies of $-+$ in the first two rows are each significantly greater than 50%; however, the frequency in the last row is significantly less than 50%. (These row differences are also significant by tests of correlated proportions.) The prior TAX model does not predict this reversal of preference between rows in Table 3.3. It is not yet clear if this effect reveals a structural flaw in the TAX model or merely represents an error in specification of its functions or parameters.

Internet Research: Lab and Web

The Internet provides a new way to conduct judgment and decision-making research. It has several advantages, the most important being the reduced cost and effort required to test large numbers of participants. Because the study can run day or night without a laboratory assistant, and because the data are directly entered and organized by the software that controls the study, one can do in weeks what used to take half a year to complete (Birnbaum, 2000, 2001).

There are two obvious causes for concern with Web studies. The first is that there is less control in a Web study compared to that in the laboratory. For example, one can make sure that laboratory participants do not use calculators, but one could only instruct Web participants and ask them if they followed instructions; one cannot control conditions via the Web in the same way as in the laboratory. The second concern is that Web participants may have quite different demographic characteristics from those recruited from the usual college subject pool. Although heterogeneity is a concern for studies with small samples, the demographic variations in large samples of Web studies presents an opportunity to check the generality of laboratory results to a wider variety of people than are usually studied.

Birnbaum (1999b) wanted to recruit people highly expert in decision making. Members of the Society for Mathematical Psychology and the Society for Judgment and Decision Making were recruited to complete an experiment on-line. The recruitment method appears to have been successful, because there were 95 "experts," participants with doctorates who also indicated that they had read a scientific article or book on the theory of decision making. These 95 were among the 1,224 people from 44 nations who participated.

In order to compare the Web with the laboratory studies, a sample of 124 students from the usual subject pool were also tested in the laboratory using the same materials. It was found that the rate of violation of stochastic dominance varied significantly with demographic characteristics of gender, education, and experience reading an article on decision making. However, even among the 95 "experts" in the study, 46 violated stochastic dominance on the choice in row 5 of Table 3.1 *and* satisfied it in the split form, compared to only 7 with the opposite reversal of preference.

Following the recruitment of the highly educated sample, a "B" sample was recruited by methods designed to reach the general public

Table 3.4. *Violations of Stochastic Dominance (S. Dom.),*
Monotonicity (Mono.), and Coalescing (Experiments 4–5)

Group	Sample n	S. Dom. (%)	Mono (%)
Exp 4 and 5	999	63.5	9.8
Text	172	59.6	9.9
Text *Rev*	169	62.4	10.7
Pies	353	65.2	8.5
Pies*	305	64.4	8.2
Internet B	737	58.8	7.9

Notes: Experiment 4 compared Text with pies; Experiment 5 compared reversed text (Text *Rev*) with pies*. Internet B refers to the sample reported by Birnbaum (2000) recruited by the same methods as in Experiments 4–5. The procedures of Internet B matched those of the Text condition of Experiment 4.

Table 3.5. *Violations of Stochastic Dominance and Monotonicity in* *Experiments 4–5, by Demographic Characteristics*

Group	Sample n	S. Dom. (%)	Mono (%)
Females	689	65.8	9.4
Males	304	58.4	10.9
Read *DM*	219	56.2	9.8
Canada	41	58.5	7.3
U.K.	57	64.0	12.2
N. Europe	47	44.7	12.8

Note: N. Europe = Belgium, Switzerland, Estonia, Finland, Germany, Hungary, the Netherlands, Norway, and Sweden. Read *DM* indicates participants who claim to have read a scientific work on decision making.

(Birnbaum, 2000). These participants were recruited by links in sites advertising "free" games and contests with prizes.

The findings on the Web and in the laboratory yield much the same results: Violations of stochastic dominance can be markedly reduced by event splitting. In the Internet B sample ($n = 737$), it was found that 59% violated stochastic dominance in the coalesced form compared to only 8% in the split form.

Experiments 4 and 5 used samples recruited via the Web to assess two other formats for presentation of the gambles. Results of these studies are shown in Tables 3.4, 3.5, 3.6. Table 3.4 shows that gambles presented

Table 3.6. *Violations by Educational Level in Experiments 4–5*

Group	Sample n	S. Dom. (%)	Mono (%)
<12	49	61.2	12.2
12	214	68.2	11.2
13–15	364	63.6	8.1
16	244	62.7	11.5
17–19	73	60.3	12.3
20	55	54.5	1.8

Notes: Group education levels by year-equivalents of education; <12 = non–high school graduate; 12 = high school graduate, 13–15 = some college; 16 = college degree; 17–19 = graduate studies; 20 = doctorate. Violations of stochastic dominance (S. Dom.) and monotonicity (Mono) are given in percentages, averaged over two variations of $G+$ versus $G-$ and $GS+$ versus $GS-$.

as pie charts or with reversed order of branches yielded results quite comparable with those obtained previously. The text condition ($n = 172$) corresponds to that used in the Internet B in stimulus format, method of recruiting the sample, and rates of violation in coalesced and split forms. The reversed text (Figure 3.1D) and pie chart (Figure 3.2) formats of presentation yield very similar results that show slightly higher rates of violation of stochastic dominance in the coalesced form. Overall rates of violation are lower in the Internet than in the laboratory studies, but most Web participants are also better educated than the subject pool laboratory samples.

Tables 3.5 and 3.6 illustrate how one can partition the data from a Web study to analyze the results within different demographic groups. Consistent with previous results (Birnbaum, 1999b, 2000), we found that education, male gender, and having read a scientific work on decision making were correlated with lower rates of violation of stochastic dominance. Overall, the rate of violation in the coalesced form is 63.5%, but among those 219 who report having read a work on decision making, it is 56.2%. The rate among females is 65.8% and among males it is 58.4%, a gender difference observed in previous studies (Birnbaum, 1999b, 2000). The rate is lower among Northern and Central European participants compared to Americans, but this group is also more highly educated than the average U.S. participant. Table 3.6 shows that those with doctorates are less likely to violate stochastic dominance than those having only high school degrees.

Although there are differences between methods of presentation and among groups in Tables 3.4 to 3.6, the overall findings are that rates of violation are still quite high in all conditions and demographic groups, and that rates are much higher in the coalesced form than in the split form. Thus, the conclusions of the research regarding decision-making models are very much the same in the laboratory and on the Web.

The present studies found significant violations of stochastic dominance and coalescing despite changes in procedure that were hypothesized to possibly reduce or eliminate the effects. From a lack of difference between procedures, one cannot conclude that all variations of procedure have no effect. However, one can conclude from Experiments 1 and 2 that violations of stochastic dominance reported by Birnbaum and Navarrete (1998) are robust enough that they can be replicated with statistically significant results in small samples, even with six changes in procedure hypothesized to reduce or eliminate the effects. One can reject the hypothesis that these changes reduced violations of stochastic dominance to the minority. The rates of stochastic dominance violation are similar to those reported previously, when the participants and choices resemble those used in previous research.

Financial Incentives

The effects of financial incentives have been studied in a number of papers (see the review in Camerer & Hogarth, 1999). However, there does not yet seem to be a body of evidence showing that preferences among gambles with positive consequences are systematically affected by the difference between real and hypothetical financial incentives (Camerer, 1989; Camerer & Weber, 1992; Mellers, Weiss, & Birnbaum, 1992; Tversky & Kahneman, 1992). Experiment 3, like previous studies with strictly hypothetical incentives, found rates of violation similar to those of Experiments 1 and 2, which had real incentives. Experiments 4 and 5 also used real incentives, yet rates of violation significantly exceeded 50% in all experiments.

Perhaps the stakes were too low in these studies to produce majority conformance to stochastic dominance. Although some theorize that behavior would change if the stakes were high enough, it would be useful to have a theory that specifies exactly how and why behavior depends on the magnitude of the stakes. If a person systematically violates dominance on many small, repeated decisions, the global effect could be quite large, so it is hard to see why systematic violations in small decisions are compatible with global rationality. Furthermore, it is not clear that people who gamble with real and large stakes (e.g., those who play blackjack in Las Vegas casinos) are behaving any more rationally than those who make judgments of their likely behavior in hypothetical tasks.

Although it is possible that the modest prizes (actual prizes won varied from $50 to $120) caused people to violate stochastic dominance intentionally, the behavior of the students in Experiments 1 and 2 gave every appearance of enthusiastic interest. Because the same people who violate stochastic dominance in rows 5 and 7 largely satisfy consequence monotonicity in rows 3, 4, 11, and 13, we think it is more likely that violations of stochastic dominance are due to a lack of understanding rather than to a lack of motivation.

Framing of Choices Is Not Necessary

Tversky and Kahneman (1986) reported a violation of stochastic dominance that was produced by "masking" the dominance relation with framing. The framing was accomplished by making it seem that the dominated gamble always gave the same prize or a higher one for every possible "event" (color of a marble drawn from an urn). Because the numbers of marbles of a given color differed in the two gambles, the events were not really the same. Their manipulation produced 58% violations of stochastic dominance, which was not significantly greater than 50% in their study but was quite different from the results in another framing of the same choice, where the same color marble always gave the same or a higher prize for the dominant gamble. Results such as those of the present studies suggest that the event framing used by Tversky and Kahneman is not required to produce large violations.

Birnbaum, Yeary, Luce, and Zhou (submitted) asked participants to judge the buying and selling prices of the same gambles presented for choice by Birnbaum and Navarrete (1998) ($G+$ and $G-$ were judged on separate trials, separated by many others). They found that judgments showed the same violations of stochastic dominance as reviewed here for choices. Thus, choice is not required to produce the violations. Explanations that hinge on comparisons, contrasts, frames, or regrets between the components of gambles do not appear to explain why violations are observed in judgment as well as choice. Instead, it seems more plausible to attribute the effect to the evaluation of the gambles rather than to choice processes.

Event-Splitting Effects and Distribution Effects

All five experiments reported here find evidence of powerful event-splitting effects. Most judges (92%, 88%, 95%, and 90% in Experiments 1, 2, 3, and 4–5, respectively) satisfied stochastic dominance in the four-outcome split versions gambles $GS+$ and $GS-$. However, most judges (76%, 68%, 70%, and 64% in Experiments 1, 2, 3, and 4–5, respectively) violated stochastic dominance with choices between three-outcome gambles that resemble the original recipe for $G+$ and $G-$. The RAM and TAX models with prior parameters correctly predict this reversal between the coalesced and split forms of the same choices.

Experiment 3 (Table 3.3) also shows that rates of violation of stochastic dominance and coalescing depend on how the probability is split in the recipe. This finding indicates that the results cannot be explained by the idea that judges ignore probabilities and choose on the basis of consequences alone (the consequences are nearly identical in all rows of Table 3.3). The majority reversal between the first and last rows is not predicted by the prior parameters in the TAX model. This phenomenon deserves further theoretical and empirical investigation.

Martin (1998) tested for event-splitting effects in another design in which choices between two-outcome gambles, R and S, which were presented with either the higher or lower consequences of either R or S split or coalesced. This design was intended to test event-splitting independence, the assumption that event splitting should have the same directional effect whenever the same probability paired with a positive consequence is split (Birnbaum & Navarrete, 1998, p. 71). She found that splitting the higher branch produced a significant improvement of either gamble, but splitting the lower branch had nonsignificant effects. Independence would have required that splitting the lower (but positively valued) branch should also have improved the gamble, whereas configural weight averaging models with prior parameters predict that splitting the lower-valued branch makes the gamble worse. Thus, Martin's (1998) data with that design added evidence of event-splitting effects (for higher-valued consequences), but they neither clearly refuted nor conformed to event-splitting independence.

It is interesting to consider that event splitting can be used both to induce violations of stochastic dominance and to reduce them. Event splitting was used to produce $G-$ and $G+$ from G_0, which created the violations of stochastic dominance; and splitting again created $GS-$ and $GS+$, which reversed preferences by producing satisfaction of stochastic dominance. These results strengthen the case made by Birnbaum and Navarrete (1998) and Birnbaum et al. (1999) that coalescing is the property whose failure explains violations of RDEU/RSDU/CPT models.

Three Types of Generalization: Participants, Procedures, and Predictions

This program of research illustrates important directions for generalizing psychological research: generalization across participants, generalization across procedures, and generalization across novel predictions.

Generalization across groups of people can be facilitated greatly by recruiting participants from the Internet. By recruiting large and heterogeneous samples of participants, Internet research allows one to check if the results found with undergraduates generalize to those obtained in other groups. The ability to obtain large samples of high-quality data quickly, conveniently, and at low cost via the Web will likely accelerate the pace of empirical research. In the Internet studies reviewed here, violations of stochastic dominance were observed in the majority of all samples except those highly educated in decision making, among whom violations were still substantial. Although rates of violation depend on gender, education, and experience reading an article on decision making, the conclusions regarding theory would be essentially the same for all sub-samples tested.

Similarly, these results show that results can be generalized across a variety of different procedures. Although rates of violation appear slightly different with different methods for displaying the gambles, the same conclusions are reached with or without financial incentives and with five different ways to display the choices. The findings do not appear to hinge on certain other particulars of procedure used in the early laboratory studies of Birnbaum and Navarrete (1998) and Birnbaum et al. (1999), such as the stimulus display or the instruction used in those studies to judge the strength of preference.

Event splitting or coalescing might also be considered a variable of procedure because both represent different ways of displaying the same (objective) choices. This variable makes a very large, significant difference in every group studied and within every variation of display procedure tested so far. Event-splitting effects are not compatible with the RDEU/RSDU/CPT class of models, but the configural weight RAM and TAX models predict these effects. Clearly, this variable needs to be represented by theory.

The third type of generalization, extrapolation to new predictions, is probably the most important for the study of theory. This approach can hardly be considered a new direction in our field, because the derivation and empirical testing of new implications that distinguish classes of theories has long been recognized as a classic technique in empirical science. However, this concept may not have had as much success in psychology as in other fields of science because of the many variables of context and individual differences that affect small laboratory experiments.

Perhaps as a consequence of seeing results vary from one laboratory to another, there has been a tendency to look at behavior as the result of conflicting principles that are so numerous and complex that no theory will ever account for all data. Tversky and Kahneman (1992), for example, gave a "pessimistic assessment" that neither their CPT model nor any model will suffice to account for all choices between gambles. I do not share their view, as I think that as good theory is developed, what seemed exceptions and complexities fall out as implications of the new theory. What is an anomaly or a paradox to one theory is the prediction of another.

I think that many failures to replicate are due to imprecise descriptions of experimental paradigms in scientific publications. The use of Internet experiments has the advantage that all of the details of procedure are available to other scientists, facilitating clean replication and variation of procedure.

This chapter presents a case in which this classical approach of testing differential predictions to new situations leads to a clean result. One class of theories (including RDEU/RSDU/CPT models) cannot account for violations of stochastic dominance and coalescing, and another class (including TAX and RAM models) predicted them in advance of the experimental tests. In addition to these successful predictions, configural weight models correctly predicted violations of lower and upper cumulative independence, and they account for traditional Allais paradoxes with the same set of parameters (Birnbaum, 1999a). When a theory accounts for old data and continues to make successful new predictions, one begins by induction to believe that the next new prediction from the theory will hold. At the same time, induction applied to the history of science shows that all theories eventually fall as new implications are derived and tested. But as each new result becomes well established, it restricts possible theoretical representations and brings us closer to scientific understanding.

References

Becker, J., & Sarin, R. (1987). Lottery dependent utility. *Management Science, 33,* 1367–1382.

Birnbaum, M. H. (1997). Violations of monotonicity in judgment and decision making. In A. A. J. Marley (Ed.), *Choice, decision, and measurement: Essays in honor of R. Duncan Luce* (pp. 73–100). Mahwah, NJ: Erlbaum.

Birnbaum, M. H. (1999a). Paradoxes of Allais, stochastic dominance, and decision weights. In J. Shanteau, B. A. Mellers, & D. A. Schum (Eds.), *Decision science and technology: Reflections on the contributions of Ward Edwards* (pp. 27–52). Norwell, MA: Kluwer.

Birnbaum, M. H. (1999b). Testing critical properties of decision making on the Internet. *Psychological Science, 10,* 399–407.

Birnbaum, M. H. (2000). Decision making in the lab and on the Web. In M. H. Birnbaum (Ed.), *Psychological experiments on the Internet* (pp. 3–34). San Diego, CA: Academic Press.

Birnbaum, M. H. (2001). *Introduction to behavioral research on the Internet.* Upper Saddle River, NJ: Prentice Hall.

Birnbaum, M. H., & Chavez, A. (1997). Tests of theories of decision making: Violations of branch independence and distribution independence. *Organizational Behavior and Human Decision Processes, 71*(2), 161–194.

Birnbaum, M. H., & McIntosh, W. R. (1996). Violations of branch independence in choices between gambles. *Organizational Behavior and Human Decision Processes, 67,* 91–110.

Birnbaum, M. H., Luce, R. D., Yeary, S., & Zhou, L. (submitted). Contingent Valuation, Endowment, or Viewpoint Effects: Testing properties in judgments of buying and selling prices of lotteries. *Manuscript.*

Birnbaum, M. H., & Navarrete, J. B. (1998). Testing descriptive utility theories: Violations of stochastic dominance and cumulative independence. *Journal of Risk and Uncertainty, 17,* 49–78.

Birnbaum, M. H., Patton, J. N., & Lott, M. K. (1999). Evidence against rank-dependent utility theories: Violations of cumulative independence, interval independence, stochastic dominance, and transitivity. *Organizational Behavior and Human Decision Processes, 77,* 44–83.

Camerer, C. F. (1989). An experimental test of several generalized utility theories. *Journal of Risk and Uncertainty, 2,* 61–104.

Camerer, C. F. (1992). Recent tests of generalizations of expected utility theory. In W. Edwards (Eds.), *Utility theories: Measurements and applications* (pp. 207–251). Boston: Kluwer.

Camerer, C. F., & Hogarth, R. M. (1999). The effects of financial incentives in experiments: A review and capital-labor-production theory. *Journal of Risk and Uncertainty, 19,* 7–42.

Camerer, C., & Weber, M. (1992). Recent developments in modeling preferences: Uncertainty and ambiguity. *Journal of Risk and Uncertainty, 5,* 325–370.

Humphrey, S. J. (1995). Regret aversion or event-splitting effects? More evidence under risk and uncertainty. *Journal of Risk and Uncertainty, 11,* 263–274.

Kahneman, D., & Tversky, A. (1979). Prospect theory: An analysis of decision under risk. *Econometrica, 47,* 263–291.

Lopes, L. L., & Oden, G. C. (1999). The role of aspiration level in risky choice: A comparison of cumulative prospect theory and SP/A theory. *Journal of Mathematical Psychology, 43,* 286–313.

Luce, R. D. (1998). Coalescing, event commutativity, and theories of utility. *Journal of Risk and Uncertainty, 16,* 87–113.

Luce, R. D. (2000). *Utility of gains and losses: Measurement – theoretical and experimental approaches.* Mahwah, NJ: Erlbaum.

Luce, R. D., & Fishburn, P. C. (1991). Rank- and sign-dependent linear utility models for finite first order gambles. *Journal of Risk and Uncertainty, 4,* 29–59.

Luce, R. D., & Fishburn, P. C. (1995). A note on deriving rank-dependent utility using additive joint receipts. *Journal of Risk and Uncertainty, 11,* 5–16.

Machina, M. J. (1982). Expected utility analysis without the independence axiom. *Econometrica, 50,* 277–323.

Martin, T. (1998) *Comparing rank dependent, subjective weight, and configural weight utility models: Transitivity, monotonicity, coalescing, stochastic dominance, and event splitting independence.* Master's thesis, California State University, Fullerton.

Mellers, B. A., Weiss, R., & Birnbaum, M. H. (1992). Violations of dominance in pricing judgments. *Journal of Risk and Uncertainty, 5,* 73–90.

Quiggin, J. (1982). A theory of anticipated utility. *Journal of Economic Behavior and Organization, 3,* 324–345.

Quiggin, J. (1993). *Generalized expected utility theory: The rank-dependent model.* Boston: Kluwer.

Starmer, C., & Sugden, R. (1993). Testing for juxtaposition and event-splitting effects. *Journal of Risk and Uncertainty, 6,* 235–254.

Tversky, A., & Kahneman, D. (1986). Rational choice and the framing of decisions. *Journal of Business, 59,* S251–S278.

Tversky, A., & Kahneman, D. (1992). Advances in prospect theory: Cumulative representation of uncertainty. *Journal of Risk and Uncertainty, 5,* 297–323.

Wakker, P., & Tversky, A. (1993). An axiomatization of cumulative prospect theory. *Journal of Risk and Uncertainty, 7,* 147–176.

Wu, G. (1994). An empirical test of ordinal independence. *Journal of Risk and Uncertainty, 9,* 39–60.

4   Can L'Homme Eclaire Be Fast and Frugal?
     Reconciling Bayesianism and
     Bounded Rationality

Laura Martignon and Stefan Krauss

ABSTRACT

Gigerenzer and his ABC research group have developed two important yet
seemingly conflicting paradigms of inference. On the one hand, they have
shown empirically that people are Bayesians when information is given in
natural frequencies, even when more than one piece of information is provided. On the other hand, the same researchers state that, when confronted
with multiple cues, people apply fast and frugal strategies, for instance, by
relying only on the most valid piece of information (this strategy is called
take the best). Comparing both paradigms raises the question, Under which
circumstances are humans fast and frugal decision makers, and when do
they integrate multiple-cue information in a Bayesian manner? We analyze
the subtle tension between the two branches of ABC's research and present
experiments that are designed to resolve it. We detect crucial features of information that, when provided to participants, determine which decision
paradigms they follow. We propose new perspectives and a wide field of
possible experiments for the future.

CONTENTS

We thank Oliver Vitouch for important suggestions and Silke Atmaca for support in data
analysis.

Cognitive psychology and the theory of decision making are sciences of debate. In order to understand the justifications for the rising of a current, one has to become familiar with the currents before it that caused it, often as a response or even as an attack to them. Here we want to focus on the currents that followed the development of the Bayesian paradigm for decision making. The theoretical and experimental research line was started by Ward Edwards in the late 1940s and was guided by the Enlightenment's view that rationality in human thinking follows the laws of logic and probability. Most of Edwards's research from 1949 to 1962 was devoted to the subjective expected utility (SEU) maximization model as descriptive of human reasoning under uncertainty. The heuristics and biases program, initiated by Amos Tversky and Daniel Kahneman in the late 1960s, is to be seen as the dialectic answer of the next generation to Edwards's proposal. They provided an avalanche of studies reporting that people's reasoning does not follow the laws of logic and probability, in particular, that they do not reason the Bayesian way. Kahneman and Tversky (1972) made the by now famous statement: "In his evaluation of evidence, man is [. . .] not a Bayesian at all" (p. 450). Their program convinced most cognitive psychologists that humans are not apt to reason probabilistically. This conviction persisted until the early 1990s, as Steven Gould (1992) exemplifies: "Tversky and Kahneman argue, correctly I think, that our minds are not built (for whatever reason) to work by the rules of probability" (p. 469).

A famous inference task in the heuristics and biases program became known as the *mammography problem*, which asks for the probability that a patient has breast cancer, based on the positive mammogram and on the given prevalence of the disease (Eddy, 1982). Although the correct answer to Eddy's question was about 8%, most medical doctors gave an answer between 70% and 80%, which was close to the test's sensitivity of 80% but far from the actual base rate of the disease, namely, 1%. Some scientists endorse the view that illusions are hardwired in our brains (Piattelli-Palmarini, 1994). The further message of the heuristics and biases program was that rather than being rational in a classical sense, humans tend to use heuristics, or rules of thumb, that fall behind the normative paradigm.

A vigorous counterattack to these positions – that humans are not Bayesians (1) and that they use weak heuristics instead (2) – was undertaken in Gerd Gigerenzer's work of the 1990s, which challenged the main components of Tversky and Kahneman's program. Gigerenzer's counterattacks to (1) and (2) can be formulated as follows:

To (1): People are Bayesians if provided with adequate representations of information.
Gigerenzer and the ABC Group showed that replacing probabilities – common in the classical task wordings of Tversky and Kahneman – by natural frequencies increases people's reasoning skills dramatically (Gigerenzer & Hoffrage, 1995; Hoffrage, Lindsey, Hertwig, & Gigerenzer, 2000). For instance, instead of "the probability that a woman has breast cancer is 1%," Gigerenzer and Hoffrage (1995) used the formulation "10 out of 1,000 women have breast cancer."

These results have been extended to Bayesian situations with more than one piece of information (Krauss, Martignon & Hoffrage, 1999; Krauss, Martignon, Hoffrage & Gigerenzer, submitted). In these complex tasks, the probability has to be assessed that a patient suffers from a disease – such as breast cancer – provided with the outcomes of two or even more medical tests (for the task formulation, see the subsequent discussion). This means that people *integrate* the information given by different cues.

To (2): Heuristics used by humans are not necessarily weak.
The ABC Group also contested Tversky and Kahneman's claim that heuristics used by humans are weak substitutes for normative strategies. ABC analyzed simple, fast, and frugal heuristics used by humans for a variety of inference tasks and showed that these heuristics are in many ways fitter than their normative pendants. One class of these heuristics is *one-reason decision making* (see Part III of Gigerenzer, Todd, & the ABC Group, 1999). Here the inference to be made is based on one reason (the "best" cue), and the remaining cues are ignored. Thus, the fast and frugal paradigm claims that people *do not integrate* information.

The claim that people integrate several pieces of information in a Bayesian way when provided with natural frequencies (1), and the claim that people use fast and frugal heuristics for multiple-cue decision making (2), appear – at least at first glance – to be antagonistic. This tension is the focus of this chapter. In the first section we review the results concerning claim (1) of ABC on the general Bayesian task, which constitutes one side of the antagonism. In the second section we review the fast and frugal paradigm (2), concentrating on its prototype heuristic, namely, Take The Best. After both sides of the antagonism have been exposed we elucidate – in the third section – the exact nature of the tension in detail. First, empirical results will show that the ecological rationality argument, another cornerstone of the ABC program, can be seen as the reconciling element between the two views. In the fourth section, finally, we open up emerging perspectives for this new research area by proposing future experiments.

The ecological rationality argument states that those heuristics that smartly exploit information structure in the environment are fit. Using a philosophical metaphor, Gigerenzer's paradigm, supported by this ecological rationality argument, is a synthesis of classical rationality, as formulated by Laplace, and its antithesis, the heuristics and biases program of Tversky and Kahneman.

Generalizations of the Natural Frequency Approach

There is a lively discussion on the facilitating effect of frequency representations originally pointed out by Gigerenzer and Hoffrage (1995) and by Cosmides and Tooby (1996). Since 1998, most articles on Bayesian reasoning address this approach by confronting, replicating, or simply commenting on it. We list, among others, Mellers and McGraw (1999), Lewis and Keren (1999), Macchi (2000), Over (2000), Evans, Handley, and Perham (2000), and Fiedler, Brinkmann, Betsch, and Wild (2000). It should be noted that these debates are concerned with a very small part of the Bayesian reasoning paradigm. All these articles on Bayesian reasoning focus on Bayesian tasks structured like this: Knowledge on a *binary criterion* (on the states "breast cancer" or "no breast cancer") has to be updated on the basis of *one binary cue* (say, a mammogram with two possible values, positive or negative). Up to this point, there is no tension between the Bayesian paradigm and the fast and frugal paradigm: In the Bayesian paradigm only one cue is provided, so the question of whether participants integrate cues is irrelevant.

The tension arises the moment more than one cue is available. Krauss et al. (1999, submitted) showed that when the breast cancer task is enhanced to involve two cues (mammography test and ultrasound test), applying the Bayesian norm does not pose problems if information is presented in terms of natural frequencies. The natural frequency version is (two-cue situation):

> 100 out of every 10,000 women at age 40 who participate in routine screening have breast cancer.
>
> 80 of every 100 women with breast cancer will have a positive mammogram.
>
> 950 out of every 9,900 women without breast cancer will also have a positive mammogram.
>
> 76 out of 80 women who had a positive mammogram and have cancer also have a positive ultrasound test.
>
> 38 out of 950 women who had a positive mammogram, although they do not have cancer, also have a positive ultrasound test.
>
> How many of the women who get a positive mammogram and a positive ultrasound test do you expect to actually have breast cancer?

Krauss et al. provided students with this task in probabilities as well. The corresponding probability version was:

> The probability that a woman at age 40 has breast cancer (B) is 1%. The probability that the disease is detected by mammography (M) is 80%.
>
> The probability that mammography (M) erroneously detects the disease, although the patient does not have it, is 9.6%.
>
> The probability that the disease is detected by an ultrasound test (U) is 95%.
>
> The probability that the ultrasound test (U) erroneously detects the disease, although the patient does not have it, is 4%.
>
> What is the probability that a woman at age 40 has breast cancer, given that she has a positive mammogram and a positive ultrasound test?

Provided with this probability version, only 12.2% of the participants obtained the correct answer,[1] whereas 54.4% obtained the correct answer

---

[1] Note that the wording of the probability version does not refer to the question of conditional independence between both tests. Krauss et al. (1999) did not include any statement on this matter because the two tests obviously have no influence on each other.

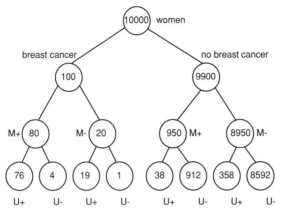

Figure 4.1 A natural frequency tree describing a Bayesian diagnosis involving two cues.

when provided with the natural frequency version (Krauss et al., 1999). This proves that when information on a two-cue task is presented in a fashion that maintains the features of Gigerenzer and Hoffrage's natural frequencies, Bayesian reasoning is akin to the workings of the human mind. Krauss et al. (submitted) showed that the facilitating effect of natural frequencies can even be generalized beyond the two-cue cases (e.g., to situations with three cues or to tasks where information is no longer binary).

For understanding the tension between these results and the fast and frugal paradigm (2), it is helpful, as we will see in Section 2, to structure the natural frequency information of the task into a tree consisting of nested subsets (Figure 4.1).

If more than two tests are available, we simply add branches downward, a new level for each new test. For n cues (i.e., medical tests) we will have 2^{n+1} nodes at the lowest level.

The Prototype of Fast and Frugal Heuristics: Take The Best

We will concentrate on one heuristic that embodies one-reason decision making called *Take The Best* and is a member of the adaptive toolbox (Gigerenzer et al., 1999). We consider a two-alternative choice task, such as which of two German cities has a larger population, which of two

---

Analyzing participants' protocols revealed that all participants implicitly made this assumption. This is in accordance with the finding of Waldmann and Martignon (1998) that people assume conditional independence between cues if there is no explicit evidence suggesting dependency.

American cities has a higher homelessness rate, or which of two stocks will yield a higher return. In general terms, the task is to predict which object, A or B, has a higher value on a criterion. This is actually a categorization task where a pair (A, B) is to be categorized as $X_A > X_B$ or $X_B > X_A$ (where X denotes the criterion, for instance, city population size). This inference is to be made on the basis of n binary cues. For instance, the population of an American city, A, tends to be larger than that of another city, B, if A has a university (cue value 1) and B does not (cue value 0).

The essence of the Take The Best heuristic is its lexicographic processing of information, as when deciding which of two numbers is larger. To establish that 110011 is larger than 101100, we compare the first digits on the left, and because they coincide, we move to the second digits, which differ. At this moment, we make the decision that the number with a 1 as the second digit is larger than the number with a 0. In this case, the second digit is "the best" cue. This is exactly how Take The Best operates. Observe that in our decimal system the ordering of digits corresponds to the decaying ordering of powers of 10, from left to right, so that the cue "which is the first digit from left to right?" is the one with the highest validity (see later). If this cue does not discriminate because both first digits are the same, the next best cue is "which is the second digit from left to right?", and so on. The validity of a cue is the probability of a correct inference when the cue discriminates. In the number example, cue validity is 100% for each cue (given that the previous cues did not discriminate). When comparing cities, cues do not necessarily provide such a perfect environment. For instance, the fact that one city has a university and the other does not might lead to a correct inference in only 80% of city comparisons.

If object A has a 1 on a cue and object B has a 0, we expect to have $X_A > X_B$, at least most of the time. The validity of the cue will establish whether a cue should be used as it is (positive correlation between cue and criterion) or whether it should be inverted (negative correlation between cue and criterion), that is, whether its 0's should be changed into 1's and vice versa. Formally, Take The Best can be described by means of the following rules:

- Compute the validity of the ith cue v_i by

$$v_i = \frac{R_i}{R_i + W_i}$$

where R_i is the number of right (correct) inferences and W_i is the number of wrong (incorrect) inferences based on cue i alone, when one object has the value 1 and the other has the value 0. If the cue has a validity of less than 0.5, then invert it, that is, change each 1 into a 0 and each 0 into a 1. Finally, rank the cues according to their validity. For every object, we define the *cue profile* as the vector of 0's and 1's ordered according to the ranking of cues.

- Pick the first cue, namely, the one with the highest validity and look up the cue values of the two objects to be compared. If one object has a cue value of 1 and the other has a value of 0, stop the search and make the inference that the object with a value of 1 has the largest value on the criterion.
- If the first cue does not discriminate, pick the second one, and so on. Stop the moment a cue discriminates between the objects. If no cue discriminates, guess (toss a coin).

Thus, the search for information stops when the first cue is found on which the two alternatives differ. This simple stopping rule demands no cost-benefit considerations: Its motto is "Take the best reason and ignore the rest." The accuracy of such a simple heuristic compared with that of normative, optimizing strategies has been surprising. A report of comparisons with benchmark models can be found in Gigerenzer et al. (1999).

The Tension Between the Bayesian and the Fast and Frugal Paradigms

Let us first summarize two directions of the ABC group's research:

1. *Bayesian paradigm:* Even when confronted with more than one cue, people are Bayesians (when provided with natural frequencies). This means that they *integrate* the information given by different cues in a Bayesian fashion (Krauss et al., 1999, submitted).
2. *Fast and frugal paradigm:* People use Take The Best. This means that they just rely on the cue with the highest validity (that discriminates between two alternatives). Thus, people *ignore* the information given by the remaining cues (Gigerenzer et al., 1999).

The natural question arises: If these two paradigms are part of *one* theory of decision making, is there a fundamental inconsistency? Our aim is to show that both paradigms can live together in peace within the same decision-making framework. We will show that there are certain features of the environment that determine the switch from one strategy to the other. Our objective here is to identify those crucial features and to clarify how they can lead to the use of one or the other strategy. We first show that the breast cancer task – when more medical tests (= cues) are provided – and the city-comparison task are equivalent in essential aspects. We do this first by shedding light on the apparent differences between both tasks and then by showing why they nevertheless are two instances within the same framework. Which are the apparent differences?

- Bayesian categorizations, as performed for the breast cancer task, usually include base rate information – as opposed to the city-comparison task. In the medical diagnosis task the prior probability, or base rate, of the patient's having the disease, $P(D)$, is usually not equal to the probability of the patient's not having the disease, $P(\neg D)$. In contrast, the probability that the first of two cities drawn randomly from a sample is larger than the second one is 50% because, for each chosen pair (A,B), we also could have chosen (B,A). Thus 50% is nothing but the base rate of picking a pair of cities in which the first one has the larger population.

- In the breast cancer task, for each cue (= medical test), two numbers are given in the instruction sheet, namely, the sensitivity and the specificity. The reason for this is that medical tests usually do not have just *one* validity; instead, their goodness depends on the actual state of disease (D or ¬D). This means that a medical test can make a correct decision in two ways: It can correctly detect a disease or it can correctly declare its absence. Both probabilities do not necessarily coincide; rather (with C = cue and D = disease):

$$\underbrace{P(C+ \mid D)}_{sensitivity} \neq \underbrace{P(C- \mid \neg D)}_{specificity}$$

In the city-comparison task, there is only one way to make a correct decision based on a cue, namely, going for the option with cue value 1. Thus sensitivity and specificity collapse into validity. Of course, one could also look at the overall validity of a medical test and express it in terms of its sensitivity and specificity:

$$P(C+ \cap D) + P(C- \cap \neg D)$$

$$= P(C+ \mid D)\, P(D) + P(C- \mid \neg D)\, P(\neg D) = \text{validity of C}$$

Observe that the validity of the test, namely, its overall probability of making a correct decision regardless of whether the patient has the disease (D) or not (¬D), integrates sensitivity and specificity along the corresponding base rate.

- In the city-comparison task the query is deterministic ("Is the population of A larger than the population of B?"), whereas in the breast cancer task, the query is probabilistic ("What is the probability ..."?). Yet, in general, the city-comparison task requires making inferences under uncertainty, and the probabilist would immediately convert the query into "What is the probability that $X_A > X_B$?". Clearly, assessing a probability allows for a deterministic attitude if required, depending on whether the obtained probability is higher or lower than 50%.

The issues just treated show that the city-comparison task can be viewed as a special case of a Bayesian task. The natural question is now: What are the crucial features of the task environment that trigger the use of Take the Best and what are the features that trigger a Bayesian strategy? In order to tackle this question empirically, one has to devise a task in which information is presented in such a way that both strategies, the Bayesian and the fast and frugal, can be used by the participant and verified by the experimenter.

Resolving the Conflict Empirically

The following variant of a stock-buying task was given to 41 participants recruited from Berlin's universities (in Table 4.1, which describes the design of Experiment 1, this task is labeled Task 2):

> The three stock-trade magazines A, B and C were evaluated on the reliability of their forecasts of market rates during the past year.
> It was found out that magazine A was correct in 80% of all cases, magazine B in 67% of all cases, and magazine C in 60% of all cases.
> The next issue of magazine A forecasts a rise in a certain stock, whereas the next issues of magazines B and C predict a fall in that same stock.
> What would be your attitude concerning this stock? Buy it or sell it?
> Please give detailed reasons for your decision.

Table 4.1. *Three Variants of the Experimentally Investigated Stock-Buying Task*

	Validity of Magazine			Bayesian Prediction (Likelihood Combination Rule)	Participants' Behavior
	A	B	C		
Task 1 ($N = 40$)	87%	65%	58%	72% that stock rises	75% buy
Task 2 ($N = 41$)	80%	67%	60%	57% that stock rises	61% buy
Task 3 ($N = 51$)	70%	67%	65%	38% that stock rises	20% buy

Note: The column on the left lists the validities of magazines A, B, and C. The middle column lists the Bayesian results of the likelihood combination rule, and the column on the right lists the percentages of participants who decided to buy. The task reported previously can be found in the middle row (Task 2).

Both strategies, Take The Best and Bayesian, are candidates for approaching this task.[2] If the Bayesian strategy is adopted, the missing base rate will be assumed to be 50% and the sensitivity and specificity will be assumed to coincide with the validity, that is, the given proportion of overall correct predictions of rising and falling stock prices for each magazine.[3] In our experiments (Experiments 1 and 2; see later), people were asked to make a decision *and* formulate a justification. From these justifications, it was possible to detect which strategy they used. Let us see which prediction each strategy would make.

Take The Best (TTB)

Because the validity of magazine A is the highest, TTB would just rely on A, and this, in turn, would lead to the decision to buy the stock in question.

Bayesian Strategy

In the case of more cues, Bayes' formula can be extended to the likelihood-combination rule. Multiplying the likelihoods for each magazine yields:

$$\frac{80}{20} \cdot \frac{33}{67} \cdot \frac{40}{60} = \frac{105600}{80400} \quad \Rightarrow$$

[2] Note that TTB actually involves searching for cues and ordering them according to their validity. In this paradigm we only focus on the decision stage of TTB.

[3] In general, a stock-trade magazine is equally good at predicting rising and falling prices of stocks.

$$P(\text{share will rise}) = \frac{105{,}600}{105{,}600 + 80{,}400} = 57\%$$

Therefore, a Bayesian also would buy the stock in the described situation. In this case, both strategies predict the same behavior. Here the policy adopted has to be captured from participants' justifications of their decisions. Analyzing our participants' protocols yielded the following: In the described task, 61% of participants decided to buy. In the protocols, many of them gave clear hints for their use of TTB (e.g., "I prefer to base my decision on *one* reliable source"). Very few participants tried to integrate all cues (in either a mathematical or an intuitive way). If they did, they did not do it in a Bayesian way. Given this evidence, such a task does not seem to trigger a Bayesian strategy. Thus the interesting question is: Which features of the provided information might influence people's behavior in such a task? We investigated empirically two crucial features of the preceding task, namely, the difference between validities of cues (Experiment 1) and the number of cues contradicting the best cue (Experiment 2).

Experiment 1: Difference Between the Validities of the Cues

In order to investigate the impact of varying validities, we constructed three decision tasks by manipulating the differences between validities in the preceding task as follows. In this between-subject design, 40 participants were assigned Task 1, 41 participants were assigned Task 2, and 51 participants were assigned Task 3. The results reveal that the use of Take The Best is indeed sensitive to the differences in the validities. If the validities of magazine A and B are similar (Task 3), most people refuse to rely on A alone (Task 3).

Experiment 2: Number of Cues Contradicting the Best Cue

For the following experiment, we asked participants to imagine that *one* magazine with a validity of 90% recommends buying a certain stock. In addition, we asked them to imagine that one, two, or three magazines, all with a validity of 70%, contradict magazine A. In this within-subject design, every participant was assigned all tasks (4a, 4b, and 4c; see Table 4.2). If participants in Task 4c were still prone to rely on magazine A, they were asked how many magazines with a validity of 70% it would take to make them change their minds.

Table 4.2. *Another Three Variants of the Experimentally Investigated Stock-Buying Task*

(N = 41)	Validity of Magazine				Bayesian Prediction (Likelihood Combination Rule)	Participants' Behavior
	A	B	C	D		
Task 4a	90%	70%			79% that share rises	86% buy
Task 4b	90%	70%	70%		62% that share rises	49% buy
Task 4c	90%	70%	70%	70%	41% that share rises	15% buy

Note: The column on the left lists the validities of magazines A, B, C, and D. The middle column lists the Bayesian results of the likelihood combination rule, and the column on the right lists the percentages of participants who decided to buy.

Here the protocols revealed the same result: People tend to use Take The Best, but not under all circumstances. The use of Take The Best can be exemplified by the protocols of two participants who claimed that they trusted magazine A, regardless of the number of other magazines with 70% validity that gave the opposite advice. One of them wrote: "Just because a few stupid people believe something it must not be true. The professional knows best." Yet, if the number of contradicting cues is too large, many people switch to other strategies that integrate information in some way. It is important to note that in our paradigm (providing no base rate, etc.), we found no instances of explicit Bayesian strategies. This suggests that when natural frequencies are not provided (or not naturally sampled), people tend to adopt non-Bayesian strategies for integration.

One crucial environmental feature that seems to trigger switching the decision strategy is whether cues are compensatory or non-compensatory (Gigerenzer et al., 1999). A set of cues ordered according to the ranking by validity v is called *noncompensatory* if the rescaled Goodman–Kruskal validities ($\gamma = 2v - 1$) satisfy the condition that no cue is overridden by the combination of the following cues. Note that in Experiment 2, participants were extremely sensitive to the compensatoriness of cues: For instance, in Task 4b, the rescaled validities are 80, 40, and 40, and since $80 = 40 + 40$, the second and third cues together have the same effect as the first one. The fact that half of the participants voted for buying and the other half for selling shows their sensitivity to noncompensatoriness.

In summary, if information is presented by sequentially partitioning a set in to nested sets according to the natural frequency scheme, then, as has been shown, humans are Bayesians, whereas if validities of cues are provided, people tend to use Take The Best – if the most valid cue is not compensated for by the remaining ones. Other important factors that influence the chosen strategies, like time pressure and search costs, have been analyzed by Payne, Bettman, and Johnson (1993) and by Rieskamp and Hoffrage (in Gigerenzer et al. 1999).

Outlook

Clearly, the investigated tasks are just one possible way of empirically approaching the present research question. We want to point out the wide field of future research that is opened by our first attempt to capture policy in cases with more than one available cue. Our planned research concentrates on the "emerging perspective" resolving the tension between Bayesian and fast and frugal strategies: It is the adaptation between environment and decision strategies that matters. Our first results show that whether or not people use fast and frugal heuristics has to do with the ecological properties of the environment.

References

Cosmides, L., & Tooby, J. (1996). Are humans good intuitive statisticians after all? Rethinking some conclusions from from the literature on judgment under uncertainty. *Cognition, 58*, 1–73.

Eddy, D. M. (1982). Probabilistic reasoning in clinical medicine: Problems and opportunities. In D. Kahneman, P. Slovic & A. Tversky (Eds.), *Judgment under uncertainty: Heuristics and biases*, (pp. 249–267). Cambridge: Cambridge University Press.

Evans, J. S. B. T., Handley, S. J., & Perham, N. (2000). Frequency versus probability formats in statistical word problems. *Cognition, 77*, 197–213.

Fiedler, K., Brinkmann, B., Betsch, T., & Wild, B. (2000). A sampling approach to biases in conditional probability judgments: Beyond base rate neglect and statistical format. *Journal of Experimental Psychology: General, 129*, 399–418.

Gigerenzer, G., & Hoffrage, U. (1995). How to improve Bayesian reasoning without instruction: Frequency formats. *Psychological Review, 102*, 684–704.

Gigerenzer, G., Todd, P., & the ABC Research Group (1999). *Simple heuristics that make us smart*. New York: Oxford University Press.

Gould, S. J. (1992). *Bully for brontosaurus: Further reflections in natural history*. New York: Norton.

Hoffrage, U., Lindsey, S., Hertwig, R., & Gigerenzer, G. (2000). Communicating statistical information. *Science, 290*, 2261–2262.

Kahneman, D., & Tversky, A. (1972). Subjective probability: A judgment of representativeness. *Cognitive Psychology, 3*, 430–454.

Krauss, S., Martignon, L., & Hoffrage, U. (1999). Simplifying Bayesian inference: The general case. In L. Magnani, N. Nersessian, & P. Thagard (Eds.). *Model-based reasoning in Scientific discovery* (pp. 165–179). New York: Plenum Press.

Krauss, S., Martignon, L., Hoffrage, U. & Gigerenzer, G. (submitted). Bayesian reasoning and natural frequencies: A generalization to complex situations. *Manuscript*.

Lewis, C., & Keren, G. (1999). On the difficulties underlying Bayesian reasoning: A comment on Gigerenzer and Hoffrage. *Psychological Review, 106*, 411–416.

Macchi, L. (2000). Partitive formulation of information in probabilistic problems: Beyond heuristics and frequency format explanations. *Organizational Behavior and Human Decision Processes, 82*, 217–236.

Mellers, B. A., & McGraw, A. P. (1999). How to improve Bayesian reasoning: Comment on Gigerenzer and Hoffrage. *Psychological Review, 106*, 417–424.

Over, D. E. (2000). Ecological rationality and its heuristics. *Thinking and Reasoning, 6*, 182–192.

Payne, J. W., Bettman, J. R., & Johnson, E. J. (1993). *The adaptive decision maker*. New York: Cambridge University Press.

Piattelli-Palmarini, M. (1994). *Inevitable illusions: How mistakes of reason rule our minds*. New York: Wiley.

Waldmann, M. R., & Martignon, L. (1998). A Bayesian network model of causal learning. In M. A. Gernsbacher & S. J. Derry (Eds.). *Proceedings of the twentieth annual conference of the cognitive science society* (pp. 1102–1107). Mahwah, NJ: Erlbaum.

Part II

Elaborating Cognitive Processes in Decision Making

5 Memory as a Fundamental Heuristic for Decision Making

Michael R. P. Dougherty, Scott D. Gronlund, and Charles F. Gettys

ABSTRACT

Research in behavioral decision theory has largely failed to address the memory processes underlying judgment and decision making. With a few notable exceptions (e.g., Brainerd & Reyna, 1990b; Dougherty, Gettys, & Ogden, 1999; Pennington & Hastie, 1993), most research on memory and decision making has been piecemeal, with no overarching theoretical framework to unify the empirical results. In this chapter, we propose a broad theoretical framework for studying memory and decision making consisting of three parts: (1) representation, (2) retrieval, and (3) experience and domain knowledge. We propose this framework as an organizing theme for both past and future research and show how existing memory models (fuzzy-trace theory, MINERVA-DM, and TODAM) have been, and can be, applied to study decision behavior. We also briefly discuss the relationship among various memory and decision-making models.

CONTENTS

The authors would like to thank Marlys Lipe, Danko Nikolic, and Jennifer Perry for their many valuable comments on an earlier draft of this chapter.

Research on memory and decision making dates back to the heuristics and biases paradigm popularized by Tversky and Kahneman in the 1970s and 1980s (see Kahneman, Slovic, & Tversky, 1982). During this period, research focused on describing the cognitive processes underlying judgment and decision making, and many of the proposed heuristic mechanisms were based on memory theory. For example, the availability heuristic (Tversky & Kahneman, 1973; see also Sedlmeier, Hertwig, & Gigerenzer, 1998) was proposed as a mechanism for frequency and probability judgments; judgments were assumed to be based on the *ease* with which instances could be retrieved from memory. Likewise, the representativeness heuristic (Kahneman & Tversky, 1973) proposed that probability judgments were based on the *similarity* between the to-be-judged event and a prototype stored in memory. Unfortunately, most of the research on heuristics and biases was directed at cataloging the situations in which people were *biased*, and little attention was devoted to the development and refinement of theories that described the underlying cognitive processes.

The lack of theoretical development during the heuristics and biases period has not gone unnoticed, as several decision theorists have expressed dissatisfaction with the general approach (Gigerenzer, 1991, 1996; Goldstein & Hogarth, 1997). This dissatisfaction, in turn, has motivated theorists to develop broader theories of decision behavior, many of which are based on memory theory. For example, Arkes (1991) argues that several judgment and decision-making phenomena are the result of association-based (i.e., memory-based) processes. Gigerenzer, Hoffrage, and Kleinbölting's (1991) theory of Probabilistic Mental Models (PMM) proposes that simple memory processes are central to frequency judgments and choice. Pennington and Hastie's (1993) Story Model is based on text-comprehension models and has been used to study jury decision making. Brainerd and Reyna's (1990b) fuzzy-trace theory (FTT) is a memory-based model in which various reasoning errors arise from people's tendency to rely, to different degrees, on abstracted, gist-like, or specific, verbatim memory representations. Finally, Dougherty et al.'s (1999) MINERVA-DM (MDM) model is an extension of Hintzman's (1988) MINERVA II memory model, and is able to account for a wide variety of likelihood and frequency estimation phenomena. Although these theories represent different approaches to studying decision making, all propose that simple memory mechanisms are central.

In this chapter, we present a broad theoretical framework for studying memory and decision making. Our thesis is that memory processes are a fundamental heuristic for decision making and that many judgmental phenomena can be better understood by examining how information is represented in and retrieved from memory. We review evidence and theoretical work suggesting that memory should receive a larger role in judgment and decision-making models. As we will show, a small number of simple memory mechanisms is sufficient to account for a wide array of judgment and decision-making phenomena.

The remainder of this chapter is divided into three sections. In the first section, we discuss historical differences between memory research and traditional behavioral decision theory. We discuss why decision theorists have been slow to adopt cognitive process models, as well as the pros and cons of using mathematical models of memory to describe judgment and decision-making behavior. In the second section, we present a broad theoretical framework based on memory theory that can be used to explain a wide range of judgment phenomena. How is judgment affected by encoding and retrieval operations, representational assumptions, and experience? Finally, we conclude by discussing the relationship among various memory and decision models and examining several directions for future theoretical development.

Why Use Memory Theory to Explain Judgment and Decision Making?

Cognitive versus Decision Theory

Historically, research in cognitive psychology has been split between researchers with a theoretical emphasis and those with an empirical or hypothesis-testing emphasis (Ratcliff, 1998). Although decision researchers have tended to take a more quantitative/theoretical approach, this split nonetheless exists in our field as well. More importantly, even those decision researchers who emphasize the theoretical over the empirical have approached their theorizing differently than most cognitive theorists.

Perhaps the most striking difference between decision theorists and cognitive theorists is the focus of their theories and models. Decision theorists tend to focus on developing mathematical models that describe *data*. In so doing, some of the models have become psychologically unrealistic, incorporating algorithms that are likely beyond the cognitive capabilities of humans (for similar criticisms see Gigerenzer & Goldstein, 1996). Moreover, many of these models assume normative rationality – an assumption that is increasingly at odds with what we know about human cognition. In contrast, cognitive theorists often develop quantitative models that describe *processes*. Although the mimicking of the data is of primary concern, it is an emergent property of the process model. In contrast to the traditional decision theory approach, these models often assume bounded rationality: Although people make errors in memory retrieval, these errors arise from a system that is actually quite accurate in most circumstances (Anderson, 1989, 1991; Simon, 1956).

The differences in focus are due, in part, to differences in approach. Decision theorists tend to be *task oriented*, concentrating on the decision task without acknowledging that it shares psychological processes with other tasks. In contrast, cognitive theorists tend to be *process oriented*, concentrating on understanding psychological processes without recognizing that processes are modified by tasks. Consequently, many decision models do not adequately specify the processes that underlie judgment, and many cognitive models apply only to a small range of laboratory tasks. The ideal process model would explain, and integrate, a range of experimental findings across a range of cognitive paradigms.

Sometimes decision theorists *do* develop theories that explicitly model cognitive processes, but often they do not. Instead, decision theorists often postulate several possible cognitive processes that underlie behavior without specifying the nature of the processes or attempting to distinguish among the various possibilities. This is particularly true of research on heuristics and biases (for a discussion of this and related criticisms see Gigerenzer, 1991, 1996; Kahneman & Tversky, 1996). A good example of this is the availability heuristic. In their original paper, Tversky and Kahneman (1973) proposed two possible processes to describe how people make intuitive frequency judgments: (1) the *ease* with which instances can be retrieved from memory and (2) a metacognitive mechanism such as a feeling of knowing. The first of these mechanisms can be operationalized in several ways: time to retrieve the first instance, number of instances retrieved in a short period of time, or a feeling of familiarity as determined by a global matching process (see Dougherty et al., 1999; Sedlmeier et al. 1998). Availability, therefore, is necessarily a vague-descriptive theory, as any one of several process models could be applied.

Proposing vague or ill-specified theories is not necessarily bad, and in many cases these vague propositions serve as motivation for future research. However, at some point it becomes necessary to narrow the set of possibilities for progress to continue. Arguably, the prominence of ill-specified theories in the judgment and decision-making literature has slowed theoretical progress and forestalled the integration of decision research into the broader domain of cognitive psychology. Unless fundamental changes in approach are made, advances in judgment and decision making will continue to be slow.

Shifting Levels of Analysis: Memory Process Models as a New Approach

We propose dropping decision-making theorizing to a lower level of analysis. Instead of developing vague, ill-specified theories of decision phenomena, we propose studying decision making as a function of the underlying properties of memory.

Memory process models are an alternative approach to studying decision making. The memory models approach involves the processing of stored representations of the decision maker's past environment. Most current memory theories assume that environmental stimuli are encoded into memory, but as traces that are less than perfect replicas of the environmental stimuli that created them. Because of various encoding factors, such as attention to the stimulus, memory traces are assumed to be degraded copies of the stimulus. This property of memory contributes to less than perfect retrieval, which in turn can lead to systematic biases in judgment.

The memory models approach has several advantages over the vague-explanation approach. First, memory models typically are formalized mathematically, requiring that explicit assumptions be made about the representation and the processes of memory. This allows for direct tests of the model, which in turn facilitates the refinement, or all-out rejection, of the model (Hintzman, 1991). A second advantage of using mathematical memory models is that it allows researchers to study decision behavior as a natural consequence of the underlying properties of memory rather than as an isolated process (Weber, Goldstein, & Busemeyer, 1991). To the extent that we can capitalize on existing theories of cognition, we can begin to develop integrative theories that link decision making to the broader context of memory and cognition. Third, mathematical models can provide insight when intuition fails. As Hintzman (1991) has pointed out, formal models "can help one to develop new intuitions about behavior of systems having properties such as variability, parallelism, and nonlinearity" (p. 47). Thus, formal models themselves have heuristic value: They are tools to aid thinking.

This is not to say that mathematical models are infallible and always advance scientific thought. On the contrary, one possible problem with building math models is that they can exaggerate the confirmation bias. Because math modelers have invested a considerable amount of intellectual effort in their enterprise, empirical tests of models may focus on predictions that have a low probability of disconfirming the model, rather than on more risky tests that have a *high* probability of disconfirmation (Hintzman, 1991). A second problem concerns the assumptions of the model. Often, to implement a model at the mathematical level, many assumptions must be made. Some of these assumptions are central to the modeling enterprise, but others are arbitrary. For example, for mathematical convenience, MINERVA II assumes that events are represented in memory as vectors with a tertiary code (e.g., $+1$'s, -1's, and 0's). This is an arbitrary assumption; we could just as well assume a continuous code with vectors having any real number between 1 and 100. Nevertheless, these arbitrary assumptions impact how well the model will account for the data. Thus, we might choose to reject a model whose core assumptions are fundamentally correct but whose arbitrary assumptions lead to poor data fits. Alternatively, it is possible for a model to provide good data fits even if its core assumptions are incorrect (as is the case with Bower's (1961) one-element model, which assumed all-or-none learning). A third problem with mathematical models concerns identifiability. It is possible to develop models that differ substantially in either their core or arbitrary assumptions but that make essentially the same predictions. This has been found to be true of several of the global matching models of memory, despite very different assumptions about representation and retrieval (for a review see Clark & Gronlund, 1996).

Despite the aforementioned problems, the integration of memory theory into decision models arguably will lead to greater insight into the processes underlying judgment and decision making. The level of analysis afforded by this approach will allow decision researchers to go beyond ill-defined, vague heuristics, leading to a fuller understanding of decision processes. In what follows, we present a general framework for studying memory and decision making that capitalizes on several mathematical models of memory. We hope to convince you that these models are a valuable resource for decision theorists, as they provide a powerful explanatory framework for past decision-making research and a generator for future research.

A Theoretical Framework for Studying Memory and Decision Making

Memory is important for decision making in a variety of ways. For example, memory structures support decision making by enabling people to build representations of decision problems (Pennington & Hastie, 1993). Additionally, in many cases, the data on which decisions are based are not provided by the decision task, but instead must be retrieved from memory. Thus, memory serves as the database of information that is used as input for making decisions, and the extent of this database (i.e., one's expertise) may, to some extent, determine the accuracy of those decisions.

In this section, we describe three aspects of memory that we believe are fundamental to judgment and decision making: (1) representational properties, (2) retrieval from memory, and (3) experience and domain knowledge. We propose this framework as an organizing theme for both past and future research and show how existing memory models (e.g., fuzzy trace theory, MINERVA-DM, and TODAM) have been, and can be, applied to study decisional behavior. We will end by discussing the relationships among these models and propose a few possible directions for future research.

Representational Properties

Two general classes of theories describe how information is represented in memory: instance-based and abstraction-based theories (Anderson, 1995). Instance-based theories assume a relatively simple memory representation: Environmental stimuli are assumed to be stored in memory as specific instances, often with each experience represented by a separate memory trace. Abstraction-based theories assume a relatively complex representation in which an abstract or summary of the stimulus event is stored rather than a verbatim copy. For example, when one reads a text, only the information necessary for understanding the text is encoded; the specific details (i.e., the specific sentence structures) are lost (Bransford & Franks, 1971; Sachs, 1967). Thus, encoding of the gist results in the loss of details but the retention of meaningful information.

Instance-based and abstraction-based theories assume two fundamentally different types of memory representation, and each representation has different implications for judgment and decision making. As will become apparent, neither class of theory is sufficient to account for the full range of experimental results, differing in the types of decision problems to which they can be applied. Thus, these two classes of theories are complementary, rather than competing, and both can be used to gain insights into the memory processes underlying judgment and decision making.

Instance-Based Theories. One example of an instance-based theory is Hintzman's (1988) MINERVA II memory model. MINERVA II assumes that memory consists of a database of instances (i.e., memory traces) representing the participant's past experiences. Thus, for each experienced event, a separate trace is assumed to be encoded in memory. Due to various factors that affect encoding (e.g., perceptual acuity, attention to the stimulus), traces are assumed to be less than perfect copies of the environmental events that created them. The encoding parameter (L) signals how well the traces are encoded in memory.

Traces can represent anything of theoretical importance: words, diseases, symptoms, faces, and so on. In an extension to the MINERVA II model (MINERVA-DM (MDM), Dougherty et al. (1999) assumed that traces contain the components necessary to model decision making. To allow for a high degree of generality, it is assumed that traces consist of three concatenated components: a hypothesis component (H), a data component (D), and an environmental context component (E). These components form the basis of MDM's inference process and enable it to model a variety of judgment situations, including P(H | D), P(D | H), and P(H) and several of the heuristics and biases (e.g., representativeness, availability, hindsight, validity effect, overconfidence, and conservatism). Several factors affect MDM's predictions, most notably quality of encoding.

Encoding quality. Encoding quality in instance-based theories refers to how well individual events are encoded in memory. For example, encoding quality may be high for events to which we attend and low for events that receive little or no attention (cf. Boronat & Logan, 1997; Craik, Govoni, Naveh-Benjamin, & Anderson, 1996; but see Mitchell & Hunt, 1989, for discussion of the effect of *effort* on encoding). Encoding quality has an obvious effect on how well people can recall or recognize items. For example, several studies have shown that increased study time (Roberts, 1972), increased familiarity, visualization (Bower, 1970), and the generation of the stimulus (Slamecka & Graf, 1978) can lead to improved memory retrieval.

Encoding quality also has been shown to affect several types of frequency and probability judgments. Greene (1988) examined the generation effect in a frequency estimation task and found that participants consistently underestimated the frequency of nongenerated words relative to generated words, reflecting the fact that the generated words had been encoded in memory with higher fidelity. Moreover, frequency estimates for the generated words were more accurate with respect to the objective frequencies. Williams and Durso (1986) found that frequency judgments were generally higher when participants were given instructions that facilitated encoding. Both of these results indicate that increasing how well information is encoded in memory will increase judgments of frequency.

Encoding quality also appears to affect the calibration of probability judgments. Juslin, Olson, and Winman (1996) manipulated whether the to-be-judged event was central or peripheral to the participants' focus of attention. Participants were underconfident when the stimulus event was central to the focus of attention but showed a modest amount of overconfidence when the stimulus event was peripheral to the focus of attention. Assuming that the amount of attentional resources devoted to the stimulus is directly related to quality of encoding (cf. Boronat & Logan, 1997; Logan, 1988), this suggests that the quality of encoding affects the calibration of probability judgments. Dougherty (2001) directly manipulated quality of encoding in a calibration task. Participants showed a modest amount of overconfidence when encoding quality was low but much less overconfidence when encoding was high. Taken together, these studies suggest that encoding quality is fundamental to the calibration of probability judgments: Overconfidence is greater when encoding quality is low.

The effect of encoding quality on frequency judgments and calibration can be accounted for by a multiple-trace memory model. Dougherty et al. (1999) simulated Greene's (1988) generation effect results using the MDM memory model. Consistent with Greene's results, MDM predicted that frequency judgments should increase as encoding quality (L) increases. MDM also produces decreasing overconfidence as encoding quality increases (Dougherty, 2001; Dougherty et al., 1999).

The preceding studies all indicate that improved encoding leads to improved judgment. However, this holds only for situations in which the to-be-judged stimuli have received unbiased encoding. Indeed, when the information in memory is itself biased by differential encoding, judgment is likely to be biased and distorted.

Effect of differential encoding on judgment. Increased encoding quality may actually lead to poorer judgment when the encoding process is biased. The natural environment is filled with both exciting and unexciting events that are either more or less important, and there is a natural tendency to allocate attentional resources to those events that are exciting and/or important (Durso & Gronlund, 1999). This differential allocation of attention is likely to lead to the differential encoding of information in memory: Events that receive a high amount of attention will be better encoded than events that receive only incidental attention (cf. Logan, 1988).

The differential encoding of information can have deleterious effects on judgment and decision making. For example, Lichtenstein, Slovic, Fischhoff, Layman, and Combs (1978) found that people's judgments of frequency for various causes of death were related to judgments of catastrophe. Participants tended to overestimate the frequency of those events that were perceived as more catastrophic. There are at least two interpretations of this effect. One interpretation is that perceptions of catastrophe are related to how often events are reported in the media. This interpretation places the locus of this overestimation in the environment, the result of biased reporting of events. A second interpretation is that people devote more attentional resources to catastrophic events and therefore encode them with a higher degree of fidelity than noncatastrophic events. This interpretation, in contrast, places the locus of overestimation within the decision maker, the result of differential encoding of stimuli (cf. Dougherty et al., 1999). Both differential reporting and differential encoding may contribute to the proclivity to overestimate rare and catastrophic events relative to more common but less catastrophic events.

Ogden, Dougherty, and Gettys (1999) directly investigated the effect of differential encoding on judgments of frequency. In their Experiment 2, Ogden et al. presented participants with a list of 31 adjectives. For 15 of the adjectives, participants were given instructions to self-reference the adjectives. For the remaining 16 adjectives, participants were required to respond whether the word contained the letter *i*. Ogden et al. hypothesized that the self-referenced words would be better encoded and that this would lead people to overestimate the frequency of the self-referenced words relative to the *i* words. Notice that the number of *i* words outnumbered the self-referenced words 16 to 15. Nevertheless, consistent with their hypothesis, the majority of their participants rated the self-referenced adjectives as more frequent, presumably because they had been encoded to a higher degree.

Begg, Armour, and Kerr (1985) investigated the effect of differential encoding on validity judgments. In their experiment, Begg et al. presented participants with a set of statements such as "Singapore has the 8th largest economy in the world." During the first stage of the experiment, participants studied a set of these statements. Differential encoding was induced by enticing participants to engage in more effortful processing of one set of statements relative to a second set of stimuli (Craik & Lockhart, 1972). In the second stage of the experiment, participants rated the validity of the statements studied in the first stage. Validity judgments were higher for the statements that received higher encoding. Assuming that validity judgments are based on the familiarity of the stimulus event (cf. Boehm, 1994), this result suggests that judged validity increases as encoding quality increases.

Both the Ogden et al. (1999) and the Begg et al. (1985) results can be accounted for by the MDM model. Dougherty et al. (1999) showed that introducing a biased-encoding mechanism into MDM was sufficient to predict an availability bias: MDM predicted that the better-encoded (but less frequent) events would be judged more frequent than the events that received low encoding (but were actually more frequent). The same mechanism can be used to account for the results of Begg et al. (1985). Better-encoded information is more easily accessible in memory, which in turn will lead participants to rate these items as more valid. In general, both of the preceding results can be viewed as special cases of availability biases in which biased encoding leads some instances to be more easily retrieved than others (Dougherty et al., 1999).

Thus far, we have discussed how encoding mechanisms can lead to both good and poor judgments in an instance-based representation. Good encoding generally leads to better judgment, unless the to-be-judged events have received differential encoding. Under conditions of differential encoding, judgment is bound to be poor simply because some stimuli are more accessible in memory than they "should" be. In any event, simple encoding processes are sufficient to account for a wide range of experimental results. In the next section, we examine how encoding processes in abstraction-based representations affect judgment.

Abstraction-Based Representations. Several decision models assume abstraction-based representations. For example, Pennington and Hastie's (1988, 1993) explanation-based decision model (the Story Model) assumes that memory consists of an "intermediate summary representation" of the decision situation. Rather than representing a veridical copy of the decision-relevant information in memory, people are assumed to construct an intermediate representation consisting of their *interpretation* of the information, much like the summary representation that would be constructed when reading a narrative (cf. Kintsch & van Dijk, 1978). For example, jurors are assumed to build a causal model – *a story* – that builds on the evidence presented in the trial. This causal model represents the juror's *interpretation* of the evidence. Accordingly, decisions, as well as the assessment of confidence in the decision, are assumed to be based on this intermediate summary representation (Pennington & Hastie, 1993).

A second abstraction-based model of decision making was proposed by Brainerd and Reyna (1990a) as part of their fuzzy-trace theory (FTT). Building on research in psycholinguistics (e.g., Bransford & Franks, 1971) and memory (e.g., Bartlett, 1932), Brainerd and Reyna (Brainerd & Reyna, 1990a; Reyna & Brainerd, 1990, 1995) assume that people encode information at several levels of abstractness (a fuzzy-to-verbatim continuum of possible memory traces). Traces can range from abstracted summaries and simplifications (the gist) to surface-level copies (verbatim details) of component events. For most applications, we need to consider only the endpoints of this continuum. A second assumption of FTT, germane to judgment and decision making, is a fuzzy-processing preference (Reyna & Brainerd, 1989); reasoning will tend to operate at the lowest level of specificity that can satisfactorily accomplish the task at hand (similar ideas were expressed by Moray, 1990, with regard to his lattice theory of mental models). A final assumption is that gist traces are retained longer than verbatim traces. How can the positing of a long-lasting gist-level representation, and a preference for using it, improve our understanding of judgment and decision making?

Effect of gist versus verbatim representation on judgment. Juslin, Winman, and Persson (1994, Experiment 1) investigated the effect of long versus short retention intervals and the meaningfulness of the stimuli on the calibration of probability judgments. Participants were presented with either nonmeaningful (nonsense syllables) or meaningful (text) stimuli. At test, participants were tested on their memory for the stimulus information and asked to rate their confidence in their memory for each retrieved item. Calibration was good for the meaningful material even after prolonged retention intervals (2 months) but deteriorated quickly for the more artificial nonsense syllables.

The preceding results can be interpreted using FTT. Juslin et al.'s (1994) participants could form a gist representation for meaningful text but not for nonsense syllables. Thus, participants could rely on their gist representation when judging the text information but had to rely on the verbatim representation when judging the nonsense syllables. Because gist information is retained longer (Brainerd & Reyna, 1990b), participants would be better calibrated for the textual information, especially after long intervals.

Effect of gist versus verbatim information on choice. Abstraction-based representations also have implications for choice behavior. For example, Reyna and Brainerd (1989, 1991) argued that framing effects are not due to the processing of numerical information (as traditional decision theories assumed; e.g., Lopes, 1987; Payne, Bettman, & Johnson, 1992) but are attributable to qualitative processing (i.e., reliance on gist). When faced with the choice of winning $100 for certain versus a 50% chance of winning $200 and a 50% chance of winning nothing, most people prefer the sure thing but reverse their choice when *winning* is replaced with *losing* (Reyna & Brainerd, 1989, 1991). This is difficult to explain from an expected-values perspective. Reyna and Brainerd (1991) showed that the inclusion of numerical information is not even necessary for observing framing effects. They replaced the numerical information with words like *some* and observed even larger framing effects, indicating that participants were not using the (verbatim) numerical information but some abstracted simplification (the gist) in making their choices. Reyna and Brainerd (1991) also showed that the occurrence of framing effects depended on the provision of the redundant zero-complement information (if there is a 10% chance of winning $200, the zero complement is the 90% chance of not winning $200). They argued that providing the zero complement instilled the pivotal qualitative contrast, triggering the encoding of the gist.

Wedell and Böckenholt (1990) provide a good example of how reasoners use the lowest level of representation that will accomplish a task. They examined how choices varied, depending on whether the participant anticipated one-time or repeated plays of a gamble. Anticipation of repeated plays produced a shift from gist to more verbatim processing. For example, if allowed to play the preceding gamble only once, most participants will be risk averse (take $100 for sure).

Categorical distinctions at the gist level are sufficient to make this decision. However, across repeated plays, the equivalent long-run pay-off between the two choices becomes clear, categorical distinctions no longer apply, and participants make finer distinctions, paying attention to the verbatim numerical information. These results might also be accounted for by assuming that some other aspect of the decision process changed with repeated plays. For example, the perception of the utilities may have changed with experience, as could subjects' risk preferences. Nevertheless, participants appear to operate at different levels of precision in different tasks and prefer to operate at the lowest possible level.

Summary of Representational Properties. MDM and FTT are two models that make extensive use of memory principles to explain a number of judgment and decision-making phenomena. However, it is useful to compare the two models because they complement one other. MDM can be characterized as possessing relatively complex processes that operate on a relatively simple representation (single level of traces), whereas FTT involves relatively simple processes that operate on a relatively complex representation (the fuzzy-to-verbatim continuum). In other words, some of the things that FTT tries to accomplish using its more complex representations, MDM tries to accomplish using its more complex processes (see the relevant discussion by Anderson, 1978). For example, MDM can accomplish gistlike abstraction (e.g., prototype effects) using its global matching process.

The models are also typically applied to different types of problems. MDM is a theoretical cousin of the exemplar-based categorization models (e.g., Medin & Schaffer, 1978) and was developed to account for data from frequentistic paradigms (repeated exposures of a single stimulus). In contrast, FTT is a theoretical cousin of text comprehension models (e.g., Kintsch & van Dijk, 1978) and is applied to more text-based reasoning paradigms (though FTT's verbatim level of traces enables it to account for frequentistic paradigms as well). Perhaps a model with the process complexity of MDM coupled with the representational complexity of FTT can integrate these disparate paradigms (see Estes, 1997, for such a model applied to memory phenomena).

Different types of decision problems rely on different types of memory representations. If the decision problem is specified verbally or is text-based, gistification processes may take precedence. However, if the decision problem relies on one's past frequentistic experience, verbatim, or exemplar, processing may take precedence. These two types of tasks correspond to two different experimental paradigms for studying judgment and decision making. Neither MDM nor FTT is sufficient to account for both paradigms. Future research should delineate the domains of these models more fully and specify the antecedent conditions that lead participants to rely on abstraction-based versus exemplar-based processing.

Retrieval from Memory

In the previous section, we illustrated how several decision-making phenomena arise from how information is stored or represented in memory. However, judgment and decision making can also be affected by how information is *retrieved* from memory. In this section, we discuss two characteristics of memory retrieval that affect judgment and decision making: (1) primacy and recency effects in judgment and (2) biased retrieval mechanisms.

Serial Position Effects in Judgment. Previous research on memory has revealed that people typically perform better at retrieving information from the beginning (primacy) and the end (recency) of a list of items relative to items that occur in the middle. These effects have been observed across a number of settings and occur for both long-term and short-term memory tasks (Baddeley, 1998). Given the ubiquity of order effects in recall, it should come as no surprise that primacy and recency effects occur in memory-based judgment and decision-making tasks as well (for a review of this literature and a model see Hogarth & Einhorn, 1992).

Weber, Goldstein, and Barlas (1995) found primacy and recency effects in a choice task using monetary gambles. Participants in their Experiment 2 were given a choice between two monetary gambles (G1 and G2), each of which had six different payoffs, depending on the role of a die (i.e., 1 = +$2.50, 2 = +$2.50, 3 = −$5, 4 = −$5, 5 = +$2.50, 6 = +$2.50). Participants were shown the six payoffs for one pair of gambles one at a time. Information displayed at the beginning and the end of this payoff presentation had the greatest impact on participants' preferences. This was particularly true when the positive outcomes occurred in runs at the beginning or the end of the presentation (i.e., −$5, −$5, +$2.50, +$2.50, +$2.50, +$2.50). Thus, participants were sensitive to the order in which the outcomes of the gambles appeared, showing a preference for gambles that had positive payoffs at either the beginning or end of the sequence.

Anderson and Hubert (1963) found a primacy effect in participants' impressions of a hypothetical person. In this experiment, participants were given a list of characteristics from which to form an impression about a hypothetical person. Participants were more likely to develop a positive impression if positive information was shown first, but tended to form a negative impression if negative information was shown first (cf. Srull, Lichtenstein, & Rothbart, 1985). Analysis of participants' memory for the characteristics revealed a higher rate of recall for items presented at the beginning of the list. Thus, the recall advantage for the characteristics presented first had a greater impact on participants' impressions.

Weber et al. (1991) argued that these same effects can be accounted for by assuming that a memory decay mechanism operates on a distributed-memory representation. In contrast to the instance-based representations discussed earlier, distributed-memory representations assume that informational items are stored in memory by superimposing all items into a single "composite" trace. Retrieval involves a recall of the composite memory trace rather than the specific instances stored in memory. Using the TODAM memory model, Weber et al. (1991) showed that a distributed representation was sufficient to account for primacy and recency effects in judgment, without assuming conscious recall of the individual items.

Weber et al. (1995) tested TODAM's account by examining set-size effects in an impression formation task. If a composite memory was stored, the set size of the attribute list should have no effect on the response times (RT) in the judgment task. As Weber et al. (1995) state, "the overall impression . . . requires only a 'read-out' from the common vector or matrix into which the individual items have been superimposed, an operation that is not a function of the number of items that went into the vector or matrix" (p. 41). In contrast, if judgment depends on the conscious recall of the individual items, there should be an effect of set size, with longer RTs associated with longer lists of attributes. Consistent with their prediction, Weber et al. found that RTs to make an attractiveness rating were unaffected by set size – suggesting that subjects based their judgments on a composite representation rather than on the recall of individual attributes.

Research by Hastie and Park (1986) suggested boundary conditions for judgmental primacy and recency effects. In a series of experiments,

Hastie and Park found that whether people show order effects in judgment depends on whether the judgments are being formed "on-line" as information is being received or whether the judgment is based on memory. On-line judgments involve a continuous updating of one's belief, judgment, or impression as each individual piece of information is encountered and does not involve the retrieval of information from memory. Memory-based judgments, in contrast, occur when one makes a judgment based on previously stored information. Hastie and Park found that participants tended to form judgments on-line if they were warned of the pending judgment task, but tended to base their judgments on their memory when not warned. Because on-line judgments do not require a memory retrieval operation, they were unaffected by the order in which information was presented; primacy and recency effects were found only when participants' judgments were based on memory.[1]

In sum, several studies have revealed primacy and recency effects in judgment and decision-making tasks. One account of these effects is suggested by Weber et al. (1991, 1995), who argued that primacy and recency effects in judgment can be accounted for by a composite memory model (i.e., TODAM), without assuming that participants consciously recall individual items from memory. One limiting condition is whether the judgment is on-line or memory based: Serial position effects in memory will affect judgment only when judgments are based on memory.

Biased Retrieval. In the section on memory representation, we showed that how information is initially represented in memory can bias judgment. For example, differential encoding can make some information more accessible than other information. This was assumed to be a fundamental property of how information is represented. However, memory also can be biased by the process of retrieval, even if information is represented in memory in a veridical and nonbiased fashion.

Biased retrieval can lead to various judgmental errors. For example, in conditional probability judgments, cuing the incorrect subset of instances in memory can lead to base-rate neglect (Gavanski & Hui, 1992; Sherman, McMullen, & Gavanski, 1992). Additionally, as Dougherty

---

[1] Hogarth and Einhorn's (1992) belief-adjustment model predicts primacy effects in judgment even for on-line judgments. This model assumes an anchoring-and-adjustment mechanism in which participants anchor on a prior belief and adjust in the face of new evidence. Consequently, information presented early in the decision task will have the greatest impact on the overall judgment because it serves to set the initial anchor.

et al. (1999) showed in their simulations of MDM, searching memory with a biased, or an underspecified, cue can affect the magnitude of people's probability judgment: The more details in the retrieval cue, the higher the predicted probability. In this section, we focus on the former source of bias.

A fundamental property of memory is that it is categorical (Rosch, Mervis, Gray, Johnson, & Boyes-Braem, 1976). Information encountered in the world is assumed to be organized into *natural categories*. For example, we may have *natural categories* for different types of animals (e.g., dogs, fowl, and tropical fish), different occupations (e.g., engineer, computer programmer, and psychologist), and different ethnicities (e.g., Hispanic, African American, and Caucasian).

Categories partition our knowledge of the world, and as such enable us to define subsets of information in memory along which judgments can be based (Gavanski & Hui, 1992; Sherman et al., 1992). For example, the judgment p(extrovert | male) requires participants first to delineate the subset (i.e., category) of instances stored in memory corresponding to males and then to assess the proportion who are extroverts (Gavanski & Hui, 1992). Crucial to making this judgment is the activation of the correct subset of instances in memory. As Dougherty et al. (1999) point out, the ability to activate the correct subset may be affected both by the representational structure of memory (e.g., natural categories) and by retrieval factors. They discussed three retrieval factors that may affect whether people activate the appropriate subset of instances: (1) category cueing, (2) individuating information, and (3) confusion of the inverse.

One factor that affects whether people activate the appropriate subset of instances in memory is category cueing or priming. Hanita, Gavanski, and Fazio (1997), for example, showed that priming a category leads people to base their judgment on the primed category, regardless of whether it is the appropriate category for the judgment. In their study, participants made conditional probability judgments such as p(likes tofu | likes to go to the movies). However, before making the judgment, participants were asked to recall either five people who like to go to the movies (instances from the appropriate subset) or five people who like tofu (instances from the inappropriate subset). This manipulation presumably primed one or another subset of instances. Participants deviated only slightly from the objective probabilities when the appropriate subset was primed (e.g., likes to go to the movies) but showed base-rate neglect when the inappropriate subset was primed (e.g., likes tofu). Similar results were obtained by Arkes and Rothbart (1985).

A second factor that may affect whether people activate the appropriate subset of instances is the amount of individuating information in the decision problem (Gavanski & Hui, 1992). For example, imagine that you are asked to judge the probability that Mary is an engineering major given that she carries a pocket calculator, enjoys building models, and enjoys mathematics (i.e., p (engineer | carries pocket calculator ∩ enjoys building models ∩ enjoys mathematics)). In this case, the appropriate subset of instances that are relevant to this judgment corresponds to the conjoint of the three characteristics.

Increasing the amount of individuating information can lead to two difficulties in memory retrieval. First, the task becomes more difficult as the amount of individuating information increases because the increase in information necessarily restricts the sample space (i.e., the number of instances that belong to the conjunctive category). Second, increasing the amount of individuating information may obscure which subset of instances should be searched. Both of these factors may lead people to use a simpler memory-search strategy – one in which they search whichever subset is most accessible in memory. In the engineering example, people are likely to search the subset corresponding to "engineers" because it would be more accessible than the conjoint category of "carries pocket calculator ∩ enjoys building models ∩ enjoys mathematics." Although this strategy is easier, it will result in base-rate neglect because the inappropriate subset of instances is searched.

A third factor that may affect whether the appropriate subset of instances is accessed is an explicit confusion of the inverse in which participants equate the likelihood (P(D | H)) with the posterior probability (P(H | D)). Several studies attest to people's tendency to equate these two probabilities. For example, Eddy (1982) showed that experienced physicians consistently confused the diagnosticity of a test with its posterior probability. Hamm (1993) presented participants with base-rate (P(H)) and likelihood (P(D | H)) information and asked them to assess the posterior probability (P(H | D)). Rather than computing and responding with the posterior probability, participants consistently responded with the likelihood (P(D | H)) information. The explicit confusion of the inverse may also extend to how people search memory. If participants do not distinguish between the two conditionals, then they may not search the appropriate subset of instances when making conditional likelihood judgments.

There are several factors that may affect participants' tendency to activate the inappropriate subset of instances in memory when making conditional likelihood judgments. We have discussed three such factors that operate at the retrieval stage: category cueing, individuating information, and confusion of the inverse. Although each of these factors has received some empirical support, there is no research to our knowledge that has investigated what happens when two or more of these factors operate simultaneously or are in competition. Future research should be aimed at delineating the conditions under which each mechanism operates.

Summary of Retrieval from Memory. In summary, judgment and decision making are affected by memory retrieval processes. We have discussed two of these factors. First, people show evidence of order effects. Information presented at the beginning and end of a list of decision-relevant information has the greatest impact on judgment. Second, judgment is affected by how information becomes active in memory. Although there has been some research on the process of memory retrieval in judgment and decision making, much more research is needed.

Experience and Domain Knowledge

An interesting characteristic of research on expert decision making is that experts do not always outperform novices – a stark contrast to the finding of studies in other cognitive domains (see Ericsson & Lehmann, 1996). The research on expertise in decision making is decidedly mixed, with experts in some domains exhibiting good decision quality and experts in other domains exhibiting poor decision quality (see Bolger & Wright, 1992; Shanteau, 1992; and Smith & Kida, 1991, for reviews). The contrast between (not so) expert decision making and superior expertise in other cognitive tasks has been referred to as the *process-performance paradox* (Camerer & Johnson, 1991). Presumably, expert decision makers have the same cognitive capabilities as experts in other domains, but nevertheless often fail to perform better than novices and typically do not do as well as a linear model (Goldberg, 1968).

Why is it that expert decision makers often do not perform exceptionally well? Two possible explanations for the variability in expert decision makers' performance have been proposed by Shanteau (1992) and Vicente (1998). Shanteau (1992) argued that expert performance is constrained by task characteristics: Experts tend to perform well in tasks that are static and have a high degree of predictability, and where feedback is readily available. Similarly, Vicente (1998) argued that expert performance is constrained by the inherent predictability of the environment: Experts working in environments that afford a high degree of predictability can exhibit a higher level of performance. For example, expert radiologists typically show exceptional performance in detecting abnormal x-rays (Myles-Worsley, Johnson, & Simons, 1988), a task that is static, has a high degree of predictability, and often provides the decision maker with confirmatory feedback. In contrast, expert clinicians typically show relatively poor accuracy in diagnosing mental disorders (Goldberg, 1959; Oskamp, 1965), a task that involves dynamic stimuli and lacks predictability, and where feedback is often missing or ambiguous. Although both task characteristics and the predictability of the environment are important components of judgment accuracy, these factors likely interact with basic-level memory processes. Little research has investigated the role of memory processes in expert decision making, although there are several relevant memory theories.

MINERVA-DM. A fundamental assumption of MDM is that each event encountered in the environment is encoded as a separate trace. This assumption has two important implications for the effect of experience on judgments of probability. First, as domain experience increases, the frequency of similar traces stored in memory will increase, thereby leading to the reduction of error variance in memory retrieval (due to the law of large numbers, increasing N leads to a decrease in variance). This type of error variance is analogous to Erev, Wallsten, and Budescu's (1994) response-error variance. Second, as domain experience increases, random variation associated with the sampling of environmental stimuli will decrease (Juslin, Olson, & Björkman 1997). In other words, memory will become a more or less veridical representation of the environmental cue structure – an extension of Gigerenzer et al.'s (1991) assumption of *cognitive adjustment*. Both sources of error variance are fundamental to the accuracy of people's probability judgments.

The roles of response-error variance and sampling-error variance in calibration have been investigated by several researchers. For example, Erev et al. (1994; Budescu, Wallsten, & Erev, 1997; see also Friedman & Massaro, 1998) revealed that the overconfidence phenomenon could be accounted for by a model that assumed that true judgments were perturbed by random error variance introduced into the response process. Increased response error led to increased overconfidence.

More recently, Juslin et al. (1997) used the binomial model to predict that overconfidence should decrease as the decision makers' experience in the judgment domain increases. This model assumes that one source of variation lies in the environment in the form of external sampling variation. When participants have limited experience in a judgment domain, the internal representation of the ecological structure contains error, such that the internal probabilities do not necessarily reflect the external ecological probabilities. However, as participants gain experience, the internal representation will approach the external structure and external sampling error will decrease (cf. Gigerenzer et al., 1991; Juslin et al., 1997).

MDM can be used to model both sources of random variation (Dougherty, 2001). Response variation is captured by MDM's computation on its memory vectors. However, in contrast to Erev et al. (1994), who assume that random variation arises from the *response* process, MDM assumes that random variation arises from the process of *memory retrieval*. Variation associated with the sampling of environmental stimuli can be accommodated by applying the assumption of cognitive adjustment to the way in which information is experienced in the external environment (Juslin et al., 1997). Because the internal representation (i.e., memory) is determined by one's experience, the amount of experience determines how closely the internal representation matches the external environment. As people gain experience, their internal representation will more closely approximate the cue structure of the external environment.

The distinction between response-error variance and retrieval-error variance is subtle but important, as measures taken to debias judgment will depend on where one places the locus of the random error. For example, if random error is assumed to arise from response processes, then efforts to debias judgment should be directed at how probabilities are elicited. However, if random error is the product of memory retrieval processes, then debiasing efforts should be directed at the processes of encoding and retrieval.

Simulation studies using MDM have revealed that both experience (an increase in the number of similar instances stored in memory) and encoding quality (increasing L) reduce error variance and improve calibration (Dougherty et al., 1999), suggesting that memory retrieval processes are fundamental to the overconfidence phenomenon (see Dougherty, 2001, for supporting data). Obviously, increased domain experience leads to an increase in the number of similar traces stored in memory. Similarly, encoding quality probably also improves with domain experience; Shanteau (1988) argued that domain experts are better at attending to relevant information than nonexperts. Again, if attention is necessary for encoding to take place (Boronat & Logan, 1997; Craik et al., 1996), experts may have enhanced encoding for domain-specific stimuli. Thus, increased experience may lead to better-calibrated probability judgments because experts have a more veridical memory base, a more extensive database of instances in memory, and enhanced encoding (Dougherty, 2001).

Logan's Theory of Automaticity. Logan (1988) proposed an exemplar model of automaticity to explain the speedup in problem-solving and memory tasks with training. The model assumes that there is a race between retrieving the solution to a problem from memory and computing the solution via an algorithm. If there are no prior experiences in memory, problem solving is assumed to be based on an algorithm. However, if there are relevant instances stored in memory, a race ensues between retrieving the solution directly and computing the solution via the algorithm. As task-relevant experience increases, the number of memory traces competing in the race increases, which increases the probability that the solution will be retrieved from memory rather than computed.

Logan's theory of automaticity may also describe what happens in rule-based decision making. Smith, Langston, and Nisbett (1992) make a cogent argument for the use of inferential rules (e.g., logical rules, statistical rules, rules for causal deduction, contractual rules, and cost-benefit rules) in guiding decision making. Presumably, in the absence of obvious choices, people engage in a form of deliberative decision making (Goldstein & Weber, 1995), whereby decision alternatives are enumerated, a decision strategy is chosen and implemented, and an explicit choice is made. This is to be expected when one has little experience with the judgment domain and the judgment task is novel. However, as one gains experience with a particular judgment task, processing might shift from rule-based to memory-based, as suggested by Logan's model of automaticity. In short, as experience increases, there is much less need to process inferential rules. Instead, situation-specific cues will trigger the retrieval of prestored solutions (Klein, 1997; see also case-based reasoning: Kolodner, 1993).

To date, decision researchers have studied only the endpoints of the expertise continuum. Traditional judgment and decision-making tasks using undergraduates as participants typically employ unfamiliar tasks, such as the choice between monetary gambles (Kahneman & Tversky,

1979). Other research has used domain experts working on highly familiar decision problems (e.g., Klein, 1997). Logan's (1988) theory predicts that participants would rely on algorithm-based processing in the former case and memory-based processing in the latter case (see Klein, 1997; Smith et al., 1992; Smith & Minda, 1998; but see Brainerd & Reyna, 1993, for a contrasting viewpoint).

Although previous research has shown that processing might switch from algorithm or rule-based to exemplar-based with experience, processing most likely is task dependent. Moray (1990) argued that the level of processing at which a person operates to complete a task depends on the task at hand. This type of task dependency was nicely illustrated by Gronlund, Ohrt, Dougherty, Perry, and Manning (1998) in a study investigating the role of memory in air traffic control. In this study, expert controllers were found to rely on a verbatim (i.e., exemplar) representation to remember altitude information but on a gist-type representation to remember speed information. Gronlund et al. argued that controllers relied on verbatim traces to remember altitude because that kind of information was needed to control traffic. In the air traffic control domain, it is important to know the *exact* altitude of most of the aircraft, whereas it is sufficient to know the *relative* speed (e.g., whether one aircraft is overtaking another).

One implication of Logan's (1988) theory is that participants should show relatively stable decisional behavior at the two endpoints of the expertise dimension. However, decision makers falling between these endpoints should show a high degree of variability in their decision modes, characterized by switching back and forth between rule-based and memory-based processing. One possible reason for the inconsistencies in expert decision making is that experts in some domains fall between the two expertise endpoints or are working on tasks that are atypical of their particular domains (see Shanteau, 1992; Smith & Kida, 1991, for reviews). For example, an expert who encounters a unique decision situation in a familiar context will not be able to base their judgment on their memory and instead will have to use a decision rule. Tasks that are complex and dynamic might have so many of these unique situations that the decision maker will never have an exemplar on which the judgment can be based and therefore will have to use rules or algorithms for decision making. Whether an expert will use memory-based processing will depend on how familiar they are with the particular judgment situation. If they are highly familiar, then processing will be memory-based, but if the situation is completely novel, they will use rule-based judgment. However, there may be a high degree of variability in expert judgment, characterized by a dynamic fluctuation between memory-based and rule-based decision making, when decision problems fall between highly familiar and completely novel.

Working Memory and Long-Term Working Memory. The idea that working memory has a limited capacity has had a lasting impact on judgment and decision researchers (Weber et al., 1995). As Weber et al. point out, decision researchers "have mostly made use of memory limitations to motivate a concern for issues of strategy selection" (p. 35). For example, Payne, Bettman, and Johnson's (1993) theory of adaptive decision making posits that people have a toolbox of heuristic-like decision strategies that reduce the computational load on the decision maker, and simulations of these strategies often assume a capacity within the normal range of 7 ± 2 chunks of information (e.g., attributes, alternatives). Likewise, fundamental to Simon's (1956) idea of bounded rationality is the idea that humans are finite information processors.

Research on expertise has challenged the traditional working memory model on grounds that it cannot account adequately for the performance of experts (Ericsson & Delaney, 1999). Experts have been shown to have superior memory performance in chess (Chase & Simon, 1973), bridge (Charness, 1979), and waitering (Ericsson & Polson, 1987), among many other domains. To account for this exceptional performance, Ericsson and Kintsch (1995) proposed long-term working-memory (LT-WM) theory. Traditional ideas of working memory (WM) can account for performance in unfamiliar activities but do not provide sufficient storage capacity for performing skilled activities. LT-WM is a retrieval structure in which pointers held in WM point to information stored in long-term memory (LTM). This allows experts to store information rapidly in, and to retrieve information efficiently from, LTM. Information stored in LT-WM can remain in LTM during an interruption (which clears WM), and access to this information can be reinstated by the reactivation of the relevant retrieval structure.

The majority of experts reviewed by Ericsson and Kintsch (1995) maintain a strong spatial character to their retrieval structures. For example, an expert waiter could remember the dinner orders of up to 20 patrons around a table by utilizing their location at the table. The retrieval structures of doctors making diagnoses is more hierarchical. In medical diagnosis, a large number of facts (more than 7 ± 2) must be stored in an accessible format prior to the recognition of the correct diagnosis. Medical experts create higher-level conceptual structures that they induce from patient data, which allow them to process information in a bottom-up mode using forward-reasoning strategies (Patel & Groen, 1991). Medical experts also can reorganize the data into these effective retrieval structures irrespective of their input order (Coughlin & Patel, 1987).

LT-WM theory has implications both for decision theories that posit that the capacity of WM moderates the choice of decision strategy (e.g., Payne et al., 1993) and for prescriptive measures designed to improve decision accuracy. LT-WM theory suggests that processing capacities for experts are less limited than was previously believed and that the selection of decision strategies by experts should not be contingent on a lack of processing capacity (at least to the same extent as for novice decision makers). In the absence of capacity limitations, expert decision makers should be able to use compensatory decision strategies that enable them to deal with more cues or more information simultaneously. One study that has shown evidence of experts ability to process more than 7 ± 2 chunks of information was done by Shanteau (1978), who found that expert livestock judges were able to use up to 11 pieces of information in judging the breeding quality of gilts. (Although Shanteau, 1978, showed that experts are *capable* of using up to 11 pieces of information, subsequent analyses demonstrated that experts often *do not* use significantly more cues or dimensions than non-experts due to the correlations among cues [Shanteau, 1988].)[2]

Prescriptively, LT-WM theory suggests that efforts taken to improve expert decision performance should attempt to capitalize on the experts' preexisting retrieval structures. One possible explanation of the process-performance paradox is that the decision tasks used to study expert decision making have not been amenable to the expert's preexisting LT-WM structures. For example, decision aids for doctors that tried to enforce a spatial rather than a hierarchical retrieval structure would be ineffective. Decision aids that are structured in a manner compatible with the experts' prior experience should enhance experts' decision quality.

---

[2] Although LT-WM extends the capacity of WM, it does not extend processing resources. However, to the extent that more information can be readily accessible with minimal draw on processing resources, experts should be able to use more information in making their decision. Thus, one would expect the use of compensatory strategies to be more common in experts.

Summary of Domain Expertise. Several cognitive models of memory can be applied to study expert decision making. All three models discussed in this section – MDM, Logan's theory of automaticity, and LT-WM theory – provide important insights into the memory processes that underlie and support expert decision making. Although these models are important in their own right, they are best appreciated when considered within the context of the decision task and by taking into account the predictability of the environment. For example, it is possible to model probabilistic environments with MDM by building these "environments" into MDM's instance-based memory representation. In fact, this is exactly what Dougherty et al. (1999) did in their simulations of the overconfidence and conservatism effects. By incorporating ecological assumptions into a memory processes model, it may be possible to determine the extent to which memory processes versus the environmental structure contribute to judgmental biases and decision making.

Summary

Our goal in this chapter has been to provide an organizing framework for research on memory and decision making, that is, to provide a guide for other researchers to pursue research on memory and decision making. In so doing, three characteristics of memory have been used to integrate a wide range of decision phenomena. In the first section, we described how different memory representations underlie different types of decisions. For example, instance-based theories (e.g., MDM) are more applicable when judgments are based on frequentistic information, whereas abstraction-based theories (e.g., the Story Model, FTT) are more useful for describing decisions that arise from narrative-type decision problems. We also showed that the factors that affect decision quality differ, depending on the type of decision model assumed. For example, instance-based representations are more sensitive to factors that affect how information is encoded in memory at the trace level (i.e., quality of encoding, differential encoding), whereas abstraction-based representations are more sensitive to contextual factors that determine the level of representation (e.g., gist versus verbatim) on which the decision is based.

In the second section, we showed how retrieval mechanisms can influence judgment and decision making. Several studies have revealed that the order in which information is presented influences participants' judgments: Information presented at the beginning and end of a list has the largest impact on judgment. Traditional theoretical interpretations of these effects posit that primacy and recency effects manifest themselves because of a retrieval advantage for information at the beginning and end of lists. However, Weber et al. (1991) showed that the same effects can be accounted for by a memory model with a composite (distributed) memory representation, without assuming that conscious recall takes place. A second aspect of retrieval that can bias judgment is whether the appropriate subset of instances in memory is activated by the retrieval cue. Activating the inappropriate subset of instances in memory can lead to base-rate neglect (Arkes & Rothbart, 1985; Hanita et al., 1997).

Research integrating memory and decision making is much less developed in the area of expertise. However, our analysis indicates several directions for future research. For example, the research by Dougherty (2001) on the calibration of probability judgments illustrates that a multiple-trace memory model can account for the improvement in calibration as a function of experience. Weber, Böckenholt, Hilton, and Wallace (1993) have similarly argued that a multiple-trace memory model can account for the generation of diagnostic hypotheses by experienced physicians. Logan's (1988) theory of automaticity can be used to describe how processing shifts from rule-based to memory-based. Finally, LT-WM theory suggests that expert decision makers can overcome the limitations of WM and use compensatory decision strategies – even in relatively complex decisions. These theories provide good starting points for researchers interested in studying the effects of experience on judgment and decision making.

Relationship Among Decision Models

The various models presented in this chapter all represent slightly different approaches to studying the relationship between memory and decision making. Indeed, all of the models discussed previously are quite distinct, as they describe fundamentally different memory processes and apply to fundamentally different types of decision situations. Figure 5.1 presents a two-dimensional space that is useful for comparing and contrasting several of the decision models presented in this chapter. The y-axis describes the familiarity of the decision situation; the two endpoints of this dimension represent the limiting cases: A decision situation can be completely novel or highly familiar. The x-axis describes the level of effortful processing required for the decision. For example,

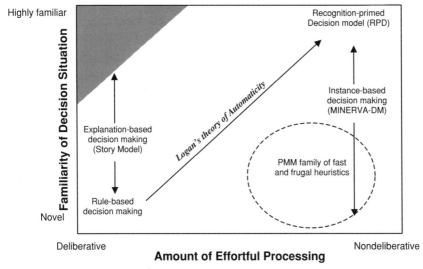

Figure 5.1 Diagram depicting relationships among several decision models.

it is possible for a decision to involve a highly deliberative process – the construction of a story or the use of a decision rule (e.g., conditional reasoning, cost-benefit analysis) or a highly automatic or nondeliberative process, such as the retrieval of instances for probability judgments or pattern recognition (see Goldstein & Weber, 1995, for a similar characterization of different decision modes). The two models absent from this space are FTT and LT-WM, which can be viewed as representational structures that underlie or support decision processes.

There are several interesting aspects of this space. First, and most obvious, the left and right sides of this space involve different types of processes. Decision processes that are deliberative involve explanation-based reasoning and rule use (left side), whereas decision processes that are nondeliberative involve instance-based memory processes (right side).

Second, the shaded area in the upper-left-hand corner of the space is empty. Although it is possible for a decision to be both deliberative and highly familiar, in practice this is unlikely to be the case. Considerable research has shown that as one gains experience in a domain, processing moves from deliberative to nondeliberative. For example, novice and low-ranked chess players tend to rely on deliberative search processes to select moves (Charness, 1991); however, as chess players gain experience, they increasingly rely on pattern-recognition (i.e., memory-based) processes (Gobet & Simon, 1996). Decision behavior can be characterized by this same shift.

The third interesting aspect of this space is the rather disjointed coverage of the various models: No single theory can be used to subsume the entire space. Gigerenzer et al.'s PMM family of fast and frugal heuristics is perhaps the only theoretical framework that captures both dimensions of this space – and even then, PMM covers only a small area, primarily because PMM was developed as a model of nondeliberative decision making. Klein (1997) presents one recent attempt to incorporate different areas of this space into a coherent theory. In his most recent version of the Recognition-Primed Decision (RPD) model, Klein includes both a pattern recognition process and a story-building/mental simulation process (cf. Pennington & Hastie, 1993). However, still lacking from his formulation is a process model for describing the antecedent conditions that lead people to use pattern-recognition processes versus story-building/mental simulation processes. Thus, Klein's revised RPD model is actually a combination of two disparate theories rather than a single unified process model.

The only theory that can be used to describe the relationship among different models is Logan's theory of automaticity. This theory describes how processing can move from rule-based to pattern-recognition processes as a result of increased domain experience or for decisions that are made repeatedly.

The disparate coverage of the models in Figure 5.1 indicates a need to build theories to describe when and how different models (and therefore different cognitive processes or decision modes) are implicated in different decision tasks. One promising approach might be to draw on dual-process theories of cognition. A nice illustration of this type of theory was proposed by Sloman (1996; see also Epstein, 1994; Evans, 1984, 1989; for a general characterization see Stanovich, 1999). In short, Sloman argues for two different reasoning systems: an associative system and a rule-based system. Table 5.1 summarizes the characteristics of these two systems (see also Stanovich, 1999). As can be seen, the associative system is assumed to be highly automatic and relatively fast, whereas the rule-based system is assumed to require deliberate processing and to be relatively slow. The associative system likely draws on evolutionary adapted mechanisms to make inferences and classification decisions, whereas the rule-based system uses decision rules (e.g., Bayes's theorem, SEU, cost-benefit analysis, conditional reasoning,

Table 5.1. *Properties of Associative and Rule-Based Systems*

Associative System	Rule-Based System
Associative	Rule-based
Holistic	Analytic
Automatic	Controlled
Evoked through similarity relations and pattern recognition	Evoked through analysis/ decomposition of decision problem
Relatively undemanding of cognitive capacity	Demanding of cognitive capacity
Relatively fast	Relatively slow
Acquisition by biology, exposure, and personal experience	Acquisition by cultural and formal training

Note: These characteristics were drawn from Stanovich (1999) and Sloman (1996).

syllogistic reasoning) learned through formal training or cultural norms. The associative system is assumed to be evoked by similarity relations, whereas the rule-based system is likely evoked after the decision problem is analyzed and decomposed. According to Sloman, the two systems are complementary but can arrive at different solutions simultaneously for the same reasoning problem. Although it is possible for the rule-based system to take precedence over the associative system, it cannot completely block it out (Epstein, Lipson, Holstein, & Huh, 1992; Sloman, 1996).

A second promising approach might be to combine two or more theories in this space. It might be possible to wed Kintsch's (1998) construction-integration model (see Rettinger & Hastie, this volume) to MDM (Dougherty et al., 1999) to model the constructive processes involved with text-based decision problems as well as the memory processes involved with instance-based judgments. This type of integrative model might provide a means of unifying the dimensions portrayed in Figure 5.1: MDM would naturally model decisions made via nondeliberative processes, whereas the construction-integration model would account for the more deliberative explanation-based and rule-based decisions. This approach is particularly appealing because both models are instantiated as simulation models, enabling quantitative predictions to be derived. Moreover, because the two models were developed to account for different types of reasoning processes, instance-based in the case of MDM and text-based in the case of construction-integration, a combination of the two models would provide a single model that could account for a wide range of experimental results. Such a model might assume that construction-integration and instance-based processing operate in parallel, with construction-integration processing dominating for novel decisions and instance processing dominating for routine decisions.

Of course, the preceding approaches are not exhaustive or mutually exclusive. Sloman's (1996) dual-process theory is only one type of dual-process model; similar frameworks have been proposed in cognitive and social psychology (see Stanovich, 1999). In addition to the class of dual-process models discussed previously, dual-process models of *memory* have enjoyed recent popularity in cognition (e.g., the conjoint-recognition model: Brainerd, Reyna, & Mojardin, 1999; the process-dissociation model: Jacoby, 1991). In contrast to most current global-matching models, dual-process models of memory assume separate processes for recognition and recall. As with most memory models, the implication of these models for judgment and decision making is still unknown. However, we believe they will bring novel insights to the cognitive processes that underlie and support decision making.

Conclusions

The behavioral decision-making literature is replete with interesting phenomena. Since its inception as a separate field of inquiry some 40 years ago, researchers have cataloged numerous empirical findings, a host of cognitive heuristics and their associated biases, and have investigated the boundary conditions of reasoning errors. However, missing from this stockpile of phenomena is an integrative theory to explain consistent findings. The accumulation of regularities is not a sufficient means of describing human judgment and decision making – unifying theories are necessary to summarize these regularities. Newell (1992) summarized this problem for workers in cognitive science:

> Elsewhere (e.g., Newell, 1990) I have estimated that there are of the order of three thousand good, quantitative regularities waiting to fuel the attempt to understand the nature of human cognition. This number is growing rapidly – about three or four hundred regularities a year, I reckon. Such an ample pool of regularities has consequences for us all, but especially to the experimentalists. It takes about ten good experiments to establish a regularity. Hence each good experiment an experimentalist performs provides about one tenth of the three thousandth and first addition to the body of knowledge now available. Remember

that, however out of fashion they may become, the old regularities do not wither in value – and that new regularities do not gain value by being this year's new crop. The point is not to discourage good experimentation – I would never do such a thing. The point is that we need to attend to how these regularities will be integrated into some sort of theory. Again, it is not that we are totally without theory. Cognitive science positively encourages theory, and many of the three thousand regularities are covered by good microtheories. But as the thirty years have shown us, these microtheories do not seem to accumulate into an integrated theory. . . .

If we go on as we have in the past – if we do not find some way of putting it all together – then we will soon face ten thousand regularities, then twenty thousand, then . . . Even the microtheories will then begin to approach a thousand. We face the prospect of being overwhelmed, of having such a huge data base of regularities that we can never work our way through it. It does not do to note that other sciences have hundreds of thousands or even millions of regularities. They have unified theories that provide the frameworks that keep these regularities tamed and useful. (pp 26–27)

We echo Newell's call for integrative theories. The decision-making literature is replete with phenomena, some old (e.g., hindsight bias, base-rate neglect, conjunction error) and some new (e.g., frequency effects). Rather than minimizing or dismissing the regularities born out of the heuristics and biases paradigm, our view is that all of these findings, both old and new, must be accounted for by any model that tries to integrate research on judgment and decision making. In this chapter, we have argued for a unifying framework for judgment and decision making based on memory theory. This framework can provide a process-oriented explanation for many of the regularities in the judgment and decision-making literature. Although we cannot yet point to a single model that provides the type of unifying theory that Newell (1992) alludes to, we have proposed several candidates (e.g., MDM, FTT, dual process models) that could profitably be explored.

Our review of the research on memory and decision making has revealed several directions for future research and theory development. Obviously, there is still a need to develop and explore more fully individual memory theories in the context of judgment and decision-making tasks. But we believe that a thorough investigation of the complex relationships between memory and decision making will ultimately benefit the field and lead to a better understanding of how memory processes and representations can both modify and support judgment and decision making.

Postscript

The first author is indebted to Charles (Chuck) F. Gettys, who passed away in May 1998, for his careful guidance throughout his graduate career. Chuck will be remembered for the many things he did, both at the professional and at the personal level. Professionally, Chuck will be remembered as an outstanding scientist, an excellent mentor, a gracious colleague, and a good friend. His mantra was "science must go on," a mantra he stuck to even after finding out that he had little time left to live, and one he insisted be followed after his death. On a personal level, Chuck will be remembered for his frank yet caring personality. He always found time to offer advice when he felt it would help.

References

Anderson, J. R. (1978). Arguments concerning representation for mental imagery. *Psychological Review, 85*, 249–277.

Anderson, J. R. (1989). A rational analysis of human memory. In H. L. Roediger III & F. I. M. Craik (Eds.), *Varieties of memory and consciousness: Essays in honour of Endel Tulving* (pp. 195–210), Hillsdale, NJ: Erlbaum.

Anderson, J. R. (1991). The adaptive nature of human categorization. *Psychological Review, 98*, 409–429.

Anderson, J. R. (1995). *Cognitive psychology and its implications* (4th ed.). New York: Freeman.

Anderson, N. H., & Hubert, S. (1963). Effects of concomitant verbal recall on order effects in personality impression formation. *Journal of Verbal Learning and Verbal Behavior, 2*, 379–391.

Arkes, H. R. (1991). Costs and benefits of judgment errors: Implications for debiasing. *Psychological Bulletin, 110*, 486–498.

Arkes, H. R., & Rothbart, M. (1985). Memory, retrieval, and contingency judgments. *Journal of Personality and Social Psychology, 49*, 598–606.

Baddeley, A. (1998). *Human memory: Theory and practice* (rev. ed.) Needham Heights, MA: Allyn & Bacon.

Bartlett, F. C. (1932). *Remembering.* Cambridge: Cambridge University Press.

Begg, I., Armour, V., & Kerr, T. (1985). On believing what we remember. *Canadian Journal of Behavioral Science, 17*, 199–214.

Boehm, L. E. (1994). The validity effect: A search for mediating variables. *Personality and Social Psychology Bulletin, 20*, 285–293.

Bolger, F., & Wright, G. (1992). Reliability and validity in expert judgment. In G. Wright & F. Bolger (Eds.), *Expertise and decision support* (pp. 47–76). New York: Plenum Press.

Boronat, C. B., & Logan, G. D. (1997). The role of attention in automatization: Does attention operate at encoding, or retrieval, or both? *Memory & Cognition, 25,* 36–46.

Bower, G. H. (1970). Analysis of a mnemonic device. *American Psychologist, 58,* 496–510.

Bower, G. H. (1961). Application of a model to paired-associate learning. *Psychometrika, 26,* 255–280.

Brainerd, C. J., & Reyna, V. F., (1990a). Can age × learnability interactions explain the development of forgetting? *Developmental Psychology, 26,* 194–204.

Brainerd, C. J., & Reyna, V. F. (1990b). Gist is the grist: Fuzzy-trace theory and perceptual salience effects in cognitive development. *Developmental Review, 10,* 3–47.

Brainerd, C. J., & Reyna, V. F. (1993). Memory independence and memory interference in cognitive development. *Psychological Review, 100,* 42–67.

Brainerd, C. J., Reyna, V. F. & Mojardin, A. H. (1999). Conjoint recognition. *Psychological Review, 106,* 160–179.

Bransford, J. D., & Franks, J. J. (1971). The abstraction of linguistic ideas. *Cognitive Psychology, 2,* 331–350.

Budescu, D. V., Wallsten, T. S., & Erev, I. (1997) On the importance of random error in the study of probability judgment. Part 1: New theoretical developments. *Journal of Behavioral Decision Making, 10,* 157–171.

Camerer, C. F., & Johnson, E. J. (1991). The process-performance paradox in expert judgment: How can experts know so much and predict so badly? In K. A. Ericsson & J. Smith's (Eds.), *Toward a general theory of expertise* (pp. 195–217). Cambridge: Cambridge University Press.

Charness, N. (1979). Components of skill in bridge. *Canadian Journal of Psychology, 33,* 1–16

Charness, N. (1991). Expertise in chess: The balance between knowledge and search. In K. A. Ericsson & J. Smith (Eds.) *Toward a General Theory of Expertise: Prospects and Limits* (pp. 39–63), New York, NY: Cambridge University Press.

Chase, W. G., & Simon, H. A. (1973). Perception in chess. *Cognitive Psychology, 4,* 55–81.

Clark, S. E., & Gronlund, S. D. (1996). Global matching models of recognition memory: How the models match the data. *Psychonomic Bulletin & Review, 3,* 37–60.

Coughlin, L. D., & Patel, V. L. (1987). Processing of critical information by physicians and medical students. *Journal of Medical Education, 62,* 818–828.

Craik, F. I. M., Govoni, R., Naveh-Benjamin, M., & Anderson, N. D. (1996). The effects of divided attention on encoding and retrieval processes in human memory. *Journal of Experimental Psychology: General, 125,* 159–180.

Craik, F. I. M., & Lockhart, R. S. (1972). Levels of processing: A framework for memory research. *Journal of Verbal Learning and Verbal Behavior, 11,* 671–684.

Dougherty, M. R. P. (2001). Integration of the ecological and error models of overconfidence using a multiple-trace memory model. *Journal of Experimental Psychology: General, 130,* 579–599.

Dougherty, M. R. P., Gettys, C. F., & Ogden, E. E. (1999). MINERVA-DM: A memory processes model for judgments of likelihood. *Psychological Review, 106,* 180–209.

Durso, F. T., & Gronlund, S. G. (1999). Situation awareness. In F. T. Durso, R. Nickerson, R. Schvaneveldt, S. Dumais, M. Chi, & S. Lindsay (Eds.), *The Handbook of Applied Cognition* (pp. 283–314). New York: Wiley.

Eddy, D. M. (1982). Probabilistic reasoning in clinical medicine: Problems and opportunities. In D. Kahneman, P, Slovic, & A Tversky's (Eds.), *Judgment under uncertainty: Heuristics and biases* (pp. 249–267). New York: Cambridge University Press.

Epstein, S. (1994). Integration of the cognitive and psychodynamic unconscious. *American Psychologist, 49,* 709–724.

Epstein, S., Lipson, A., Holstein, C., & Huh, E. (1992). Irrational reactions to negative outcomes: Evidence for two conceptual systems. *Journal of Personality and Social Psychology, 62,* 328–339.

Erev, I., Wallsten, T. S., & Budescu, D. V. (1994). Simultaneous over- and under-confidence: The role of error in judgment processes. *Psychological Review, 101,* 519–527.

Ericsson, K. A., & Delaney, P. F. (1999). Long-term working memory as an alternative to capacity models of working memory in everyday skilled performance. In A. Miyake & P. Shah (Eds.), *Models of working memory: Mechanisms of active maintenance and executive control* (pp. 257–297). New York: Cambridge University Press.

Ericsson, K. A., & Kintsch, W. (1995). Long-term working memory. *Psychological Review, 102,* 211–245.

Ericsson, K. A., & Lehmann, A. C. (1996). Expert and exceptional performance: Evidence of maximal adaptation to task constraints. *Annual Review of Psychology, 47,* 273–305.

Ericsson, K. A., & Polson, P. G. (1987). A cognitive analysis of exceptional memory for restaurant orders. In M. T. H. Chi, R. Glaser, & M. J. Farr (Eds.) *The nature of expertise* (pp. 23–70), Hillsdale, NJ: Erlbaum.

Estes, W. K. (1997). Process of memory loss, recovery, and distortion. *Psychological Review, 104,* 148–169.

Evans, J. St. B. T. (1984). Heuristic and analytic processes in reasoning. *British Journal of Psychology, 75,* 451–468.

Evans, J. St. B. T. (1989). *Bias in human reasoning: Causes and consequences.* London: Erlbaum.

Friedman, D., & Massaro, D. W. (1998). Understanding variability in binary and continuous choice. *Psychnomic Bulletin & Review, 5,* 370–389.

Gavanski, I., & Hui, C. (1992). Natural sample spaces and uncertain belief. *Journal of Personality and Social Psychology, 63,* 766–780.

Gigerenzer, G. (1991). How to make cognitive illusions disappear: Beyond "heuristics and biases." *European Review of Social Psychology, 2,* 83–114.

Gigerenzer, G. (1996). On narrow norms and vague heuristics: A reply to Kahneman and Tversky (1996). *Psychological Review, 103,* 592–596.

Gigerenzer, G., & Goldstein, D. G. (1996). Reasoning the fast and frugal way: Models of bounded rationality. *Psychological Review, 103,* 650–669.

Gigerenzer, G., Hoffrage, U., & Kleinbölting, H. (1991). Probabilistic mental models: A Brunswikian theory of confidence. *Psychological Review, 98,* 506–528.

Gobet, F., & Simon, H. A. (1996). The roles of recognition processes and look-ahead search in time-constrained expert problem solving: Evidence from grand-master-level chess. *Psychological Science, 7,* 52–55.

Goldberg, L. R. (1959). The effectiveness of clinicians' judgments: The diagnosis of organic brain damage from the Bender–Gestalt test. *Journal of Consulting Psychology, 23,* 25–32.

Goldberg, L. R. (1968). Simple models or simple processes? Some research on clinical judgments. *American Psychologist, 23,* 483–497.

Goldstein, W. M., & Hogarth, R. M. (1997). Judgment and decision research: Some historical context. In W. M. Goldstein & R. M. Hogarth (Eds.), *Research on judgment and decision making: Currents, connections, and controversies* (pp. 3–65). New York: Cambridge University Press.

Goldstein, W. M., & Weber, E. (1995). Content and discontent: Indication and implications of domain specificity in preferential decision making. In J. R. Busemeyer, R. Hastie, & D. L. Medin (Eds.), *The psychology of learning and motivation, Volume 32. Decision making from a cognitive perspective* (pp. 83–136). San Diego, CA: Academic Press.

Greene, R. L. (1988). Generation effects in frequency judgment. *Journal of Experimental Psychology: Learning, Memory and Cognition, 14,* 298–304.

Gronlund, S. D., Ohrt, D. D., Dougherty, M. R. P., Perry, J. L., & Manning, C. A. (1998). Role of memory in air traffic control. *Journal of Experimental Psychology: Applied, 4,* 263–280.

Hamm, R. M. (1993). Explanations for common responses to the blue/green cab probabilistic inference word problem. *Psychological Reports, 72,* 219–242.

Hanita, M., Gavanski, I., & Fazio, R. H. (1997). Influencing probability judgments by manipulating the accessibility of sample spaces. *Personality and Social Psychology Bulletin, 23,* 801–813.

Hastie, R., & Park, B. (1986). The relationship between memory and judgment depends on whether the judgment task is memory-based or on-line. *Psychological Review, 93,* 258–268.

Hintzman, D. L. (1988). Judgments of frequency and recognition memory in a multiple-trace memory model. *Psychological Review, 96,* 528–551.

Hintzman, D. L. (1991). Why are formal models useful in psychology? In W. E. Hockley & S. Lewandowsky (Eds.), *Relating theory to data: Essays on human memory in honor of Bennet B. Murdock* (pp. 39–56). Hillsdale, NJ: Erlbaum.

Hogarth, R. M., & Einhorn, H. J. (1992). Order effects in belief updating: The belief-adjustment model. *Cognitive Psychology, 24,* 1–55.

Jacoby, L. L. (1991). A process disassociation framework: Separating automatic from intentional uses of memory. *Journal of Memory and Language, 30,* 513–541.

Juslin, P., Olson, H., & Björkman, M. (1997). Brunswikian and Thurstonian origins of bias in probability assessment: On the interpretation of stochastic components of judgment. *Journal of Behavioral Decision Making, 10,* 189–209.

Juslin, P., Olson, N., & Winman, A. (1996). Calibration and diagnosticity of confidence in eyewitness identification: Comments on what can be inferred from the low confidence–accuracy correlation. *Journal of Experimental Psychology: Learning, Memory, and Cognition, 22,* 1304–1316.

Juslin, P., Winman, A., & Persson, T. (1994). Can overconfidence be used as an indicator of reconstructive rather than retrieval processes? *Cognition, 54,* 99–130.

Kahneman, D., Slovic, P., & Tversky, A. (1982). *Judgment under Uncertainty: Heuristics and Biases.* New York: Cambridge University Press.

Kahneman, D., & Tversky, A. (1973). On the psychology of prediction. *Psychological Review, 80,* 237–251.

Kahneman, D., & Tversky, A. (1979). Prospect theory: An analysis of decision under risk. *Econometrica, 47,* 263–291.

Kahneman, D., & Tversky, A. (1996). On the reality of cognitive illusions. *Psychological Review, 103,* 582–591.

Kintsch, W. (1998). *Comprehension: A paradigm for cognition.* Cambridge: Cambridge University Press.

Kintsch, W., & van Dijk, T. A. (1978). Towards a model of text comprehension and production. *Psychological Review, 85,* 363–394.

Klein, G. (1997). The recognition-primed decision (RPD) model: Looking back, looking forward. In C. E. Zsambok & G. Klein (Eds.), *Naturalistic decision making* (pp. 285–292). Mahwah, NJ: Erlbaum.

Kolodner, J. (1993). *Case-based reasoning.* San Mateo, CA: Morgan Kaufmann.

Lichtenstein, S., Slovic, P., Fischhoff, B., Layman, M., & Combs, B. (1978). Judged frequency of lethal events. *Journal of Experimental Psychology: Human Learning and Memory, 4,* 551–578.

Logan, G. D. (1988). Toward an instance theory of automatization. *Psychological Review, 95,* 492–527.

Lopes, L. L. (1987). Between hope and fear: The psychology of risk. *Advances in Experimental Social Psychology, 20,* 255–295.

Medin, D. L., & Schaffer, M. M. (1978). A context theory of classification learning. *Psychological Review, 85,* 207–238.

Mitchell, D. B., & Hunt, R. R. (1989). How much "effort" should be devoted to memory. *Memory & Cognition, 17,* 37–348.

Moray, N. (1990). A lattice theory approach to the structure of mental models. *Philosophical Transactions of the Royal Society of London, B327,* 577–583.

Myles-Worsley, M., Johnson, W. A., & Simons, M. A. (1988). The influence of expertise on x-ray processing. *Journal of Experimental Psychology: Learning, Memory, and Cognition, 14,* 553–557.

Newell, A. (1990). *Unified theories of cognition.* Cambridge, MA: Harvard University Press.

Newell, A. (1992). Unified theories of cognition and the role of SOAR. In J. A. Michon & A. Akyurek (Eds.), *Soar: A cognitive architecture in perspective* (pp. 25–79). Norwell, MA: Kluwer.

Ogden, E. E., Dougherty, M. R. P., & Gettys, C. F. (1999). *A test of two MINERVA-DM explanations of availability.* Unpublished manuscript, Department of Psychology. University of Oklahoma.

Oskamp, S. (1965). Overconfidence in case-study judgments. *Journal of Consulting Psychology, 29,* 261–265.

Patel, V. L., & Groen, G. J. (1991). The general and specific nature of medical expertise: A critical look. In K. A. Ericsson & J. Smith (Eds.), *Toward a general theory of expertise: Prospects and limits* (pp. 93–125). New York: Cambridge University Press.

Payne, J. W., Bettman, J. R., & Johnson, E. J. (1992). Behavioral decision research: A constructive processing perspective. *Annual Review of Psychology, 43,* 87–131.

Payne, J. W., Bettman, J. R., & Johnson, E. J. (1993). *The adaptive decision maker.* New York: Cambridge University Press.

Pennington, N., & Hastie, R. (1988). Explanation-based decision making: Effects of memory structure on judgment. *Journal of Experimental Psychology: Learning, Memory, & Cognition, 14,* 521–533.

Pennington, N., & Hastie, R. (1993). Reasoning in explanation-based decision making. *Cognition, 49,* 123–163.

Ratcliff, R. (1998). The role of mathematical psychology in experimental psychology. *Australian Journal of Psychology, 50,* 129–130.

Reyna, V. F., & Brainerd, C. F. (1989). *Fuzzy-trace theory of framing effects in choice.* Presented at the 30th annual meeting of the Psychonomics Society, Atlanta.

Reyna, V. F., & Brainerd, C. F. (1990). Fuzzy processing in transitivity development. *Annual of Operations Research, 23,* 37–63.

Reyna, V. F., & Brainerd, C. F. (1991). Fuzzy-trace theory and framing effects in choice: Gist extraction, truncation, and conversion. *Journal of Behavioral Decision Making, 4,* 249–262.

Reyna, V. F., & Brainerd, C. F. (1995). Fuzzy-trace theory: An interim synthesis. *Learning and Individual Differences, 7,* 1–75.

Roberts, W. A. (1972). Free recall of word lists varying in length and rate of presentation: A test of the total-time hypothesis. *Journal of Experimental Psychology, 92,* 365–372.

Rosch, E., Mervis, C. B., Gray, W. D., Johnson, D. M., & Boyes-Braem, P. (1976). Basic objects in natural categories. *Cognitive Psychology, 8,* 382–439.

Sachs, J. S. (1967). Recognition memory for syntactic and semantic aspects of connected discourse. *Perception & Psychophysics, 2,* 437–442.

Sedlmeier, P., Hertwig, R., & Gigerenzer, G. (1998). Are judgments of the positional frequencies of letters systematically biased due to availability. *Journal of Experimental Psychology: Learning, Memory, and Cognition, 24,* 754–770.

Shanteau, J. (1978). When does a response error become a judgmental bias? Commentary on "Judged frequency of lethal events." *Journal of Experimental Psychology: Human Learning and Memory, 4,* 579–581.

Shanteau, J. (1988). Psychological characteristics and strategies of expert decision makers. *Acta Psychologica, 68,* 203–215.

Shanteau, J. (1992). Competence in experts: The role of task characteristics. *Organizational Behavior and Human Decision Processes, 53,* 252–266.

Sherman, S. J., McMullen, M. N., & Gavanski, I. (1992). Natural sample spaces and the inversion of conditional probability judgments. *Journal of Experimental Social Psychology, 28,* 401–421.

Simon, H. (1956). Rational choice and the structure of the environment. *Psychological Review, 63*, 129–138.

Slamecka, N. J., & Graf, P. (1978). The generation effect: Delineation of a phenomenon. *Journal of Experimental Psychology: Human Learning and Memory, 4*, 592–604.

Sloman, S. A. (1996). The empirical case for two systems of reasoning. *Psychological Bulletin, 119*, 3–22.

Smith, E. E., Langston, C., & Nisbett, R. E. (1992). The case for rules in reasoning. *Cognitive Science, 16*, 1–40.

Smith, J. F., & Kida, T. (1991). Heuristics and biases: Expertise and task realism in auditing. *Psychological Bulletin, 109*, 472–489.

Smith, J. D., & Minda, J. P. (1998). Prototypes in the mist: The early epochs of category learning. *Journal of Experimental Psychology: Learning, Memory, and Cognition, 24*, 1411–1436.

Srull, T. K., Lichtenstein, M., & Rothbart, M. (1985). Associative storage and retrieval processes in person memory. *Journal of Experimental Psychology: Learning, Memory, and Cognition, 11*, 316–345.

Stanovich, K. E. (1999). *Who is rational?: Studies of individual differences in reasoning.* Mahwah, NJ: Erlbaum.

Tversky, A., & Kahneman, D. (1973). Availability: A heuristic for judging frequency and probability. *Cognitive Psychology, 5*, 207–232.

Vicente, K. J. (1998). *Building an ecological foundation for experimental psychology: Beyond the lens model and direct perception.* Paper presented at the Fourth Conference on Naturalistic Decision Making, Warrington, VA, May 15–17.

Weber, E. U., Böckenholt, U., Hilton, D. J., & Wallace, B. (1993). Determinants of diagnostic hypothesis generation: Effects of information, base rates, and experience. *Journal of Experimental Psychology: Learning, Memory, and Cognition, 19*, 1151–1164.

Weber, E. U., Goldstein, W. M., & Barlas, S. (1995). And let us not forget memory: The role of memory processes and techniques in the study of judgment and choice. In J. Busemeyer, R. Hastie, & D. L. Medin's (Eds.), *Decision making, The psychology of learning and motivation: Advances in research and theory* (Vol. 32, pp. 33–81). San Diego, CA: Academic Press.

Weber, E. U., Goldstein, W. M., & Busemeyer, J. R. (1991). Beyond strategies: Implications of memory representation and memory processes for models of judgments and decision making. In W. E. Hockley & S. Lewandowski (Eds.), *Relating theory to data: Essays on human memory in honor of Bennet B. Murdock* (pp. 75–100). Hillsdale, NJ: Erlbaum.

Wedell, D. H., & Böckenholt. U. (1990). Moderation of preference reversals in the long run. *Journal of Experimental Psychology: Human Perception and Performance, 16*, 429–438.

Williams, K. W., & Durso, F. T. (1986). Judging category frequency: Automaticity or availability? *Journal of Experimental Psychology: Learning, Memory, and Cognition, 12*, 387–396.

6   Comprehension and Decision Making

David A. Rettinger and Reid Hastie

ABSTRACT

How do the contents or subject matter of a decision problem affect the outcome of the decision? Are academic, legal, or gambling decisions with similar underlying *deep structures* made in the same fashion or does content have an effect on representations of the decision problems and on decision strategies? Formal decision theories focus on the invariant probabilities and values that define a decision problem and assume that surface content has little influence on the ultimate decision. However, psychological studies of decision processes find that content affects the framing and representation of decisions in ways that influence outcomes. Original empirical research is reported that demonstrates these effects. A recent model of text comprehension was applied to model the differences in problem representation that we hypothesized were the causes of the differences in behavioral outcomes. A computer simulation of the decision process illustrates the flexibility in representations and strategies that we hypothesize underlies these results. Some decisions are represented as narrative stories, and others are represented as decision trees. This research provides new insights into the mental representations used in decision making and how decision content influences people's choices by affecting those representations.

CONTENTS

Philosophers, behavioral scientists, and songwriters all report that life is a gamble. Given the vast literature examining human responses to simple gambles, we may be taking this precept a bit too literally. Lopes (1983), in fact, described the simple monetary gamble as playing the same central role for decision researchers that the fruit fly has played for geneticists. In the most common scientific method used to study human decision processes, research participants are asked to make ratings and choices among monetary gambles like those they would encounter in casinos. The prevailing view in the decision-making literature is that this is as it should be, because responses to simple gambles are generalizable to all of life's decisions. But perhaps we have accepted this cultural truism too quickly. We would like to challenge this assumption that all important decisions are like preferences among formal gambles. Instead, we advocate the view that the contents of a decision will dramatically affect not only choice outcomes, but the *way* the decision is made.

In order to explain these so-called content effects, we also advocate a cognitive approach to decision research and theorizing. Just as Dougherty and his colleagues (this volume) propose that many classic decision heuristics can be explained by understanding the nature of long-term memory, we propose that the role of content (among other effects) can be interpreted by understanding the way decisions are represented mentally. Expanding on a proposal by Kintsch (1998), we suggest that reading (or hearing about) a decision scenario is a special case of discourse comprehension and that common cognitive processes support both. Therefore, a major component in explaining and predicting what choice will be made is the understanding of how decision scenarios are comprehended, and the results of this comprehension process will vary with decision contents.

This chapter serves three purposes. First, it provides a brief review of the role of content in decision making (see Goldstein & Weber, 1995; Wagenaar, Keren, & Lichtenstein, 1988, for more complete coverage). Second, it reports empirical research demonstrating that when people are presented with formally identical decision scenarios in different content domains, their mental representations of the scenarios and their decision-making strategies differ. Third, it proposes a cognitive model (based on Kintsch's 1988, 1998, construction-integration theory) of decision making as primarily a comprehension process.

The Gamble Metaphor

Traditional theories (e.g., von Neumann & Morgenstern, 1953) hold that people make decisions based on the values and probabilities inherent in the outcomes, without respect to the domain of the problem or its representation. Therefore people make medical decisions the same way they make legal, financial, or academic decisions. This view is at odds with the claims of a number of psychologists (see Goldstein & Weber, 1995, for an excellent review), who believe that the contents of a problem will affect a person's reasoning about that problem. If the problem happens to be a decision, then people's decision strategies, and ultimately their preferences, will be determined by all of the elements of the problem, including probabilities and values, as well as the content domain and the form of the mental representation.

Acceptance of the *gamble metaphor* implies that a simple monetary gamble or lottery is an adequate description of all life decisions. This hypothesis first appeared in the writings of Bernoulli (1730–1733/1954), who assumed that simple gambles could stand in for more meaning-laden, familiar situations. This theme appears again in the work of von Neumann and Morgenstern (1953), who proposed that people's gambling behavior could be used to infer their *utility functions*, domain general descriptions of a hypothetical evaluation that would predict their behavior when making many individual and social decisions.

All decisions essentially require selecting options or courses of action that have outcomes marked by some degree of uncertainty. Given this assumption, the essence of all decision making is the process of estimating the likelihood of each outcome, determining the personal value of that outcome, and choosing the course of action that maximizes the subjective expected value. In the most extreme form of this argument, no factor outside of the personal probabilities and values has any effect on the decision. These prescriptions are expressed in several assertions about the invariance and regularity of decision-making processes across variations in problem contents that are implicit in conventional statements of decision theory (e.g., Dawes, 1988, pp. 158–159; 1998, pp. 504–505,

516–521; Tversky & Kahneman, 1986). Under these assumptions, it is appropriate to generalize from the decision processes observed in stylized gambles to other, more familiar situations.

Content Effects in Cognitive Tasks

A handful of researchers have reacted against the practice of utilizing "content-free" decision stimuli or ignoring whatever content might be present (see Goldstein & Weber, 1995; Wagenaar et al., 1988; Wang, 1996). If decision making is cognition, and it surely is, then research on the topic should take a cue from cognitive psychology and ask, "How do the contents of tasks affect their completion?" Such content effects have been identified in virtually every type of cognitive task that has been systematically studied. Two particularly good examples come from the early memory literature and from research on logical problem solving.

A particularly apt analogy is the one between Ebbinghaus's (1885) study of his memory for nonsense syllables and content-free judgments. Ebbinghaus believed that by studying nonsense syllables, he could examine memory that was free of contamination by meaning and pre-experimental associations. As a result, a number of issues quickly arose to which the nonsense syllable framework does not apply. For example, reconstructive memories for events in everyday life, like those induced by schemata (Bartlett, 1932; Bransford & Johnson, 1972; Brewer & Treyens, 1981), demand meaning-based encoding of memory. Just as Ebbinghaus advanced the study of memory by simplifying the materials, decision researchers have advanced our field by eliminating content from decisions.

The same problem that Ebbinghaus faced also needs to be addressed in the decision-making literature: Although eliminating (or controlling for) content improves experimental control, it precludes theoretical understanding of the potentially important effects of that content. The paradigm claiming that content-free stimuli represent all decisions is, by its very nature, unable to find the effects that demonstrate its inadequacy. Because simple gambles eliminate familiar, meaningful content, and because they represent the bulk of the decision literature, it is important to expand the preference judgment paradigm to include cases where the semantic content of decisions can play a role.

Perhaps the most widely studied content effects on cognition were first described by Wason (Wason & Johnson-Laird, 1972) in the domain of deductive reasoning. In Wason's classic four-card reasoning problem, people were given cards, each with a letter on one side and a number on the other. They were told to test the validity of a rule that applies to these cards: "If there is a consonant on one side of a card, then there is an even number on the reverse side." Cards showing a consonant, a vowel, an even number, and an odd number were then presented, with the question "Which cards must be turned over to check for rule violations?" Subjects were generally not able to solve the abstract form of the problem. However, when the same problem was described with contents referring to a scene in a tavern (where the rule requires one to be 18 years old in order to drink alcoholic beverages), subjects had no trouble pointing out that to test the rule completely, one must examine the cards that represent minors and the cards that depict beer drinkers.

This work led to the formation of two competing explanatory hypotheses: Either familiarity (Griggs & Cox, 1983) or concreteness (Manktelow & Evans, 1979) improves deduction. A more process-oriented explanation was proposed by Cheng and Holyoak (1985), who argued that people were using *pragmatic reasoning schemas* rather than abstract rules or concrete instances to perform these deductions. But Cheng and Holyoak also emphasized the critical importance of problem contents in activating relevant rules. This view is supported by their finding that when the same abstract problems just described were presented in terms of permission problems rather than as logical if-then rules, performance dramatically improved (see also Cosmides, 1989; Gigerenzer & Hug, 1992).

These results from the deduction literature are important because in the content-free condition the conclusion is that subjects are not very good at deduction. However, when given appropriate contents, with a rule that has causal or social significance, research participants are nearly perfect. Cheng and Holyoak's theory is now one of many explanations of these content effects (Cosmides, 1989, and Gigerenzer & Hug, 1992, are other examples). Although no definitive conclusion regarding content effects in deduction has been forthcoming, it is clear that these theoretical developments would have been impossible without an examination of the role of semantic content in the four-card problem. It is our position that a similar situation may apply in the decision-making literature; many of the anomalies of decision making observed for choices among gambles may not generalize to other content domains.

We hypothesize that changes in domain content (e.g., legal, financial, or human life) will influence decision making by affecting the cognition or information processing that underlies it, as well as the form of the mental representation of the decision situation. A simple model of the decision process, outlined in more detail subsequently, suggests that people take the decision as input, encode it into a mental representation, and then use that representation to make a decision. Changes in decision content can be expected to influence the mental representation by determining what type of representation is created; for example, will the relevant information be comprehended as a sequential story or as a multiple-branching decision tree structure? The content of a decision will affect the mental representation, and it will also influence what, if any, background knowledge will be imported into the situation representation. Furthermore, the content of a decision will influence the nature of the strategy that is used to decode the representation to make the decision. These two types of effects are the focus of this chapter.

Content and Decisions

The most familiar example of content effects on a decision process is the classic *reference point framing effect*. Framing effects occur when decision makers prefer different options due to manipulations of the options' surface descriptions, even when the basic options are identical (Levin, Schneider, & Gaeth, 1998). The classic example is Kahneman and Tversky's (1982) Asian disease problem, in which subjects are shown to be risk averse when options are framed as gains but risk-seeking for losses. The gain frame of the original problem reads as follows:

> Imagine that the U.S. is preparing for the outbreak of an unusual Asian disease, which is expected to kill 600 people. Two alternative programs to combat the disease have been proposed. Assume that the exact scientific estimate of the consequences of the programs are as follows:
> If program A is adopted, 200 people will be saved.
> If program B is adopted, there is 1/3 probability that 600 people will be saved and 2/3 probability that no people will be saved.
> Which of the two programs do you prefer?

A comprehensive meta-analysis by Kühberger (1998) has demonstrated that framing interacts with domain content, so that framing effects (differences in preferences between gain and loss descriptions) are twice as large for financial (Cohen's $d = .34$) and gambling ($d = .32$) domains as for social domains ($d = .16$) and substantially larger than for health decisions ($d = .26$). Similar results are reported by Schneider

(1992) in an empirical study in which she presented subjects with many decisions in a variety of domains. The most relevant result for present purposes is the finding that subjects showed larger framing effects for decisions involving human life than for other kinds of gains and losses (for decisions similar to the Asian disease problem), and were extremely risk averse for animal lives when species extinction was at stake. These sorts of results indicate the critical role of domain content and its interaction with decision frame.

Wagenaar et al. (1988) used the same principle of holding the underlying gamble structure constant while varying the domain content. They report studies in which they manipulated the content of a decision situation while holding the values and probabilities constant. Two stimulus problems with underlying structures based on the Asian disease problem involved human life and death. One asked research participants to decide which of two medical treatments to use in attempting to save the inhabitants of an island from a disease. The other was a decision about whether or not to use force to obtain the release of hostages. Wagenaar et al. also manipulated the perspective of the decision maker (medical officer/islander and parent/hostage negotiator), and the passive-active description (action or inaction) of the alternative courses of action. The content had complex effects on subjects' judgments. For example, subjects who took the islander perspective were more likely to choose an active solution regardless of its riskiness, whereas there were no differences in preferences for action or inaction in the other roles. The message from this study is that different *cover stories* attached to the same *underlying gamble* cause important differences in subjects' judgments.

The obvious interpretation of content effects is to suppose that these differences affect the mental representation of the decision situation. For example, the usual interpretation of framing effects is that certain values and probabilities are attended to and highlighted as inputs into a uniform decision process (usually a variant on the subjective expected utility theory). However, an additional route for content effects is via changes in the decision *strategy* followed by decision makers with different problem contents. Goldstein and Weber (1995) conducted a study of the differences in processing strategies in social decisions (choosing a spouse) versus consumer product decisions (buying a CD player). Processing strategy was manipulated by changing the type and order of evidence presented. Some items of evidence were presented in a format designed to promote the construction of an overarching schema like "childhood sweetheart" or "the Rolls Royce of CD players." This manipulation has been found to produce elaborate problem representations and narrative reasoning decision strategies. Other evidence was presented in a manner designed to create isolated feature list representations. This format for evidence promotes a traditional "tallying up pros and cons" decision strategy (see also Pennington & Hastie, 1988).

The hypothesis was that under normal circumstances, subjects would prefer to tally up pros and cons for CD players, but they would construct schematic stories when selecting a spouse. However, when the decision makers' preferred processing strategy was blocked by the evidence format manipulation, participants were expected to adopt the strategy that was favored by the presentation format. Goldstein and Weber found that decision makers distinguished more sharply between attractive and unattractive spouses when schema-based processing was facilitated. But for CD players the evidence format manipulation had little effect. (Presumably this was due to the fact that tallying pros and cons is easy to do even for schema-inducing formats.) Because the format manipulation interacts with domain content in influencing judgment, Goldstein and Weber concluded that content affected the decision *process*.

The Goldstein–Weber (1995) findings and all of the content effects described in this section represent a challenge to the expected utility family of decision models. At a minimum, such theories would need to be supplemented by auxiliary theoretical principles that could explain the differential weighting or combination rules that would be context dependent. Criticism of the heavy reliance on simple gambles is not the end of the story but rather the beginning. Now that we have determined that the gamble metaphor is incomplete, we must supplant it with both new theories and methods to examine them. These new theories must be able to account for the vast catalog of findings from minimal-content studies as well as the results of the content-enriched research mentioned here. They should also be comprehensive enough to provide alternative accounts of the variety of representations and strategies that are observed in any behavioral study of decision processes. Furthermore, they should allow for individual differences that include rational decision strategies, as well as the nonrational variations that have motivated the recent proliferation of nonexpected utility models (e.g., Luce, 2000).

Theoretical Framework and Predictions

We propose that the effects of decision content described previously are the result of fundamental changes in information processing strategies. This is in contrast to expected utility–based theories, which all assume that there is a single decision strategy that is invariant across decision domains. In these one-uniform-process models, content effects are ignored or are explained by hypotheses about encoding effects, like prospect theory's editing rules and psychophysical scaling functions. However, we advocate a shift to more comprehensive and more complex information processing models in order to explain these content effects.

Traditional information processing models require at least three cognitive components to provide a computational account of behavioral phenomena: encoding operations, an encoded cognitive representation, and decoding rules that operate on the representation to compute (the instructions for) a response. When all three components of a person's information processing sequence can be specified with a moderate degree of precision, we label the triplet an information processing strategy. The research outlined subsequently lends support to the construction-integration (Kintsch, 1998) architecture as a means of understanding the information processing that underlies these strategies. What do we already know about each of the three components of decision strategies?

Encoding Operations and Resulting Mental Representations

The first stage, comprising problem encoding or editing rules, has been a component of prospect theory, *reasons for* approaches, fuzzy-trace theory, and explanation-based decision-making accounts of framing and content effects. Although none of these accounts is sufficiently detailed to describe, for example, a working computer simulation of the encoding processes, there are several useful suggestions that inform our own efforts to develop descriptions of the comprehension process.

Kahneman and Tversky (1979) proposed a set of *editing rules* that decision makers are hypothesized to use when representing gambles. They include coding with respect to a reference point, segregating parts of gambles, cancellation of equivalent outcomes, and dominance detection. These rules are the mechanism by which complex gambles are converted from their presented format to the mental rubric of formal decision making. For example, separate outcomes with different probabilities and the same value will be aggregated to form a single prospect with a probability equal to the sum of the original separate outcomes.

Given appropriate editing rules, it is possible post hoc to account for almost any decision that we can observe. In order to make a priori predictions, the theory must be developed to determine how and when each editing rule is used. So far, no success on this front has been reported. In an important study, Fischhoff (1983) tested the editing rules of prospect theory by designing a set of decision problems that could be framed in three different ways. None of the studies using these problems found a relationship between the preferred frame and subjects' decisions. This suggests that decision making does not follow a single process rule in all content domains or that coding rules can explain decision differences across domains. We suggest that the editing phase is a complex process, interweaving domain-specific background knowledge with each novel decision as it is encountered, leading to one of several possible mental representations.

Reyna and Brainerd's (1995) fuzzy trace theory presents another, more sophisticated account of the encoding process. Their fundamental claim is that people use the simplest mental representation sufficient to perform any particular task. In decision-making tasks, people are predicted to recode the information known about the decision situation, extracting the gist of it to make their choice. The gist is considered to be a means of understanding a situation broadly, eliminating the details. For example, in the Asian disease problem, the gist is that there are two choices: a sure chance of saving some people and a risky plan that might save everyone, but might not save anybody. Decision makers evaluate these options by considering these *fuzzy amounts*, rather than particular numerical values, when choosing a course of action. Although we support the idea of simplification, we propose a more complete representation, at least at the outset, which may then be pruned and simplified based on assessments of relevance of individual details.

Beach (1990) has proposed image theory, in which the contents of the decision are accounted for by a framing process. The frame that a decision is given is influenced by the interaction between the content of the decision domain and the decision maker's images of the world. Decision makers have images that include information about mores and principles, about goals and how to achieve them, and about concrete strategies for solving specific problems. Beach and his colleagues predict that content will produce changes in decision strategies and ultimately in decisions by altering the image that summarizes the task. Different images bring different beliefs, rules, and principles into play for different decisions, depending on their content.

The *explanation-based decision making* approach proposes that a decision maker summarizes the current decision situation in terms of a plausible mental model of the important events and their causal relationships (Hastie & Pennington, 2000). This approach hypothesizes that causal situation models will play a central role in almost any complex everyday decision, although the specific form of the explanation is expected to vary from domain to domain (e.g., a legal decision is likely to depend on a narrative explanation, an engineering decision on a physical problem schema, and a medical decision on a physiological system model). Most of the research on explanations in decisions has involved legal decisions. For example, there is considerable empirical evidence that jurors construct a story or stories when judging a legal case, learn the appropriate verdict categories, compare the best story summary of what happened to each candidate verdict, and then decide which story–verdict fit is best (Pennington & Hastie, 1988, 1991, 1993). According to the theory, stories are created by an active process of comprehension in which information is integrated into a complex mental representation. That representation is composed of embedded *episodes*, sequences of events that are elaborated and explained by causal information (Kintsch, 1988; Trabasso & van den Broek, 1985). Subjects explain events using information from the trial (or specific instance), from their knowledge of similar events, and from knowledge about stories generally (e.g., effects follow causes). Pennington and Hastie (1991) describe stories as events linked by *causal chains*, which utilize necessity and sufficiency relationships among events.

The causal structure of stories plays an important role in explanation-based decision making because it provides a framework within which decision makers can evaluate individual pieces of evidence, draw on their experiences in the world to make inferences, and evaluate the evidence as a whole by comparing it to their broad understanding of the structure of stories. For certain decisions, particularly those in which domain content knowledge plays a major role, decision makers will be likely to rely on causal situation models as the central cognitive vehicle for their decisions. There is considerable empirical evidence from many diverse research programs that supports the generality of explanation-based strategies (see Hastie & Pennington, 2000, for a review).

A major tenet of our theory building has been to expand existing theories to account for content effects rather than to create a new explanation. The insight that mental representations in explanation-based decision making can potentially be simulated using the construction-integration framework (Kintsch, 1998) served as inspiration for our account of content effects. We assume that decisions are treated like other texts and that as in text comprehension, mental representations play a key role in decision making. Empirical methods used to inspect the encoding stage of processing directly require the use of extensive think-aloud verbal reports or other, labor-intensive information search measures (e.g. Pennington & Hastie, 1993). In the present research, we rely on behavioral measures of the resulting mental representation to infer what might have been happening earlier during the encoding phase.

Decoding Rules That Translate Mental Representations into Decisions

We also try to describe the mental operations that are performed on decision problem representations when selecting a choice or course of action. Of course, the structure and contents of the problem representation will exert constraints on the applicable operations. For example, if the representation does not include detailed numerical information (e.g., one of Reyna & Brainerd's 1995 *fuzzy representations*), arithmetical mental operations will not be applicable. At least three kinds of decoding operations need to be distinguished: arithmetic, narrative-scenario evaluation, and focus reaction.

As we shall discuss in greater detail, we propose that all of these operations can be described as different processes of decoding one's mental representation of a given decision. Each process uses similar elementary processes but in different combinations. Each operation relies on similar elementary processes but in different combinations, all embedded in the general *spreading activation* inference procedure that is part of the construction-integration architecture.

We can order these decoding processes along a continuum from most deliberate/analytic to most automatic/intuitive. The expected value calculation strategy would be located at the extreme analytic end of this continuum. The focus reaction strategies (e.g., "What's the worst outcome? How do I avoid it?") would be located at the other, intuitive end of the continuum. We hypothesize that the inferences and calculations prescribed by Kahneman and Tversky's prospect theory would lie in the middle of the continuum, an intuitive version of the arithmetic decoding strategies. Lopes's (1983) security-potential/aspiration theory would also lie toward the middle of the continuum as a relatively analytic form of focus reaction decoding processes. Fuzzy trace theory (Reyna & Brainerd, 1995) seems to allow all of these possible decoding rules but assumes that we have a bias for the simplest or most intuitive ones, a process that is a mixture of deliberate ("What are the elements of first-degree murder that the judge told me to consider?") and intuitive ("How *similar* is the defendant's conduct [in my story] to the conditions for premeditation?") elements.

To review, we have proposed that comprehension of the decision problem should be given a major, maybe a dominant, role in any theory of decision making in background knowledge–rich decision domains. The resulting model entails a three-stage process in which a decision situation is encoded and represented; the resulting representation is maintained, perhaps modified; and then that representation is decoded in order to make a choice among potential courses of action. The content of a decision scenario will dictate the encoding rules used and therefore the resulting mental representation. The content and the representation it engenders will operate together to determine the decoding rules one uses to make decisions.

Combining the Components into Strategies

We can combine the various representational hypotheses with the different decoding operations to yield a collection of possible decision strategies. The resulting collection can be simplified somewhat because some representation–decoding pairs are unlikely to occur. For example, expected value computations or prospect theory integrations are unlikely to be paired with a story representation. However, the analysis of possible strategies is also made more complicated by a fourth component of the general strategy that we will call *decision orientation*. Here we refer to the general orientation composed of the interactions between personal and situational variables that an individual has toward the options and outcomes. For example, some subjects will be security conscious and *maximin*-oriented, with an overriding motivation to avoid substantial losses, to protect themselves, and to guarantee the maximum (best) of all possible minimum outcomes under the worst-case scenario. In the same situation (and with the same problem representation), other subjects may be gain-oriented, aspiration-seeking, *maximax*-oriented, with a motivation to act so as to have the best chance of obtaining the most favorable outcome under a best-case scenario. Lopes and Oden (1999) have provided evidence that there are additional nuances to decision makers' orientations that involve even more subtle security level and level-of-aspiration combinations.

Table 6.1. *Factors Affecting Decision Strategy*

Factor	Increases Lead To:	Example
1. Personal importance	More narrative processing	Wagenaar et al. (1988): Are you affected by disease?
2. Familiarity	More narrative processing, then case-based reasoning for experts	Hastie and Pennington (unpublished data): Judges' expertise
3. Duration of outcomes	More narrative processing	Goldstein and Weber (1995): Rent or buy a home?
4. Moral relevance	More narrative processing	Schneider (1992): People or property at stake?

For our purposes, the important implication of decision orientation is that subjects with identical problem representations, following the same decoding process, may still make radically different choices because they differ in orientation. Again, we do not claim to have a complete theory of decision orientation, but the construction-integration theory approach we advocate is flexible enough to accommodate these sorts of individual differences.

Attributes of decision scenarios like the decision makers' personal involvement, familiarity with the content domain, and the presence of emotional or morally evocative events in scenarios will affect subjects' decision strategies. Goldstein and Weber (1995) have provided a clear formulation of this as an empirical question: How do problem contents influence the nature of the strategy employed by a decision maker? Table 6.1 provides a summary of the current wisdom, which can be summarized with reference to four general content factors.

Factor 1: Personal Importance

Wagenaar and his colleagues (1988) provide evidence that personal importance (i.e., whether the decision affects the decision maker or not) plays a role in decision making. Recall (from our earlier discussion) that in one condition subjects were presented a variant of the classic Asian disease problem (Tversky & Kahneman, 1981) and were told to take the point of view of either a potential victim of the disease or a public health official. Potential victims were more risk-seeking than nonvictims, and interestingly, when action was linked to risk, potential victims became more risk-seeking, whereas nonvictims became even less risk-seeking.

This interaction is difficult to explain with editing rules and suggests a difference at a deeper strategic level.

We expect that increased personal importance will lead to more thoughtful, cognitively demanding narrative processing. As the stakes increase, people may be less willing to be seen (even by themselves) as cold and therefore may be more likely to include information about their mores and values, as well as input in the form of societal pressure.

Factor 2: Familiarity

Decisions can be arranged along a continuum ranging from completely novel to those with which we have extensive experience (expertise). Most decisions, of course, lie somewhere in the middle: They are not absolutely novel, but we're far from expert. If decision makers are moderately familiar with a particular type of decision, it is predicted that they will elaborate the given information with their background knowledge. This will usually result in an explanation-driven style of decision making in which scenarios are entertained and evaluated, rather than a simple pro-and-con attribute weighting process. However, as decision makers become expert in a domain, case-based reasoning and reasoning by analogy will supersede an explanation-based strategy. Decisions are then based on the similarity of the current instance to previous ones or on rules generated as a result of experience. We know of little systematic research on the shift from inferences (rules) to cases (exemplars) in realistically complex domains, although there are many anecdotes that refer to the shift in legal and medical domains. In unpublished research, Hastie and Pennington asked a small ($n = 5$) sample of trial judges to decide the same realistically complex criminal cases that they had used in their jury research. They were surprised by the judges' quick, confident decisions, but then were less surprised when the judges reported that they were simply (simple for a domain expert) matching the current case to the most similar example from their rich memory of prior decided cases and "reading out" the right verdicts from the remembered cases.

Factor 3: Duration of Outcomes

Another possible difference among decisions concerns the subjective duration of the outcomes. For example, Goldstein and Weber (1995) contrasted the choice of an apartment to rent with the choice of a house to purchase with reference to the length of time that the outcome would be expected to last (e.g., 9 months versus 20 years). It is easy to imagine relying on a *satisficing*, pro-con attribute-counting strategy for choosing a rental house, especially when information about the long term is limited. However, as the duration of the outcome and the amount of longitudinal information increase, it is likelier that the decision maker will rely on temporally extended scenarios for each option. The implication is that a decision maker is more likely to create stories about a home purchase than about a rental. This will lead to a more narrative style of decision making as the duration of the outcome increases. Perhaps one value of the scenario is that it allows the decision maker to keep track of projected changes in his or her own values across time. For example, it is unlikely that when seeking a 9-month apartment rental, one would try to consider changes in family status or physical capabilities; however, these are natural considerations when choosing a house to purchase.

Factor 4: Moral Relevance

Another dimension along which decisions might vary is the number of morally relevant considerations they elicit. For example, a legal decision like whether or not to plead guilty to speeding has a moral element that is lacking from the consideration of purely financial consequences in a casino gamble or stock investment situation. A relevant finding in the framing effect literature is that framing effects are most robust when lives (human or otherwise) are at stake and less reliable and sizable when money or property is at risk (Kühberger, 1998; Schneider, 1992). This effect can be interpreted as at least partly the result of relying on moral factors or on a morality-centered decision strategy when life or health is at stake. In this case, subjects are likely to experience increased responsibility and invocation of moral reasoning, as well as simply working harder to elaborate the given information more fully. This will lead them toward narrative representations and the strategies associated with them. One might argue that the consideration of moral content simply activates the use of a different set of editing rules or a different value function than content that activates solely personal gains. However, it is also reasonable to propose that moral or emotional contents lead to nonmathematical reasoning. For example, some options may be so aversive that subjects choose to avoid them, even at a high cost. The moral or emotional content can lead to elaborated narrative processing as subjects try to create stories about each outcome and evaluate the stories. A related possibility is that in some contexts, noncompensatory habits will apply and people will simply not be willing to consider tradeoffs that involve *protected values* or *sacred attributes* (e.g., Baron & Spranca, 1997). A related possibility is that subjects faced with emotionally or morally evocative scenarios will seek the option that is least likely to engender strong regrets in the future.

Wang (1996) reminds us that decision strategies may be selected at the group or species level as well as in individual learning histories. Individual habits and strategies that maximize reproductive viability will be selected for any species over evolutionary time. Two attributes of decisions that are salient under this view are the social context of decisions (i.e., whether the decisions affect others and if those affected are kin) and the number of people affected. The data from Wang's studies were used as an argument for "[S]ignificant changes in choice preference" (p. 57) and for a change in judgment strategy. Decisions about family members reflect considerations of fairness that do not apply to other, nonfamily decisions. The social nature of the decision is also relevant to the selection of the decision strategy. Decisions about people, particularly family members, are affected by the number of people involved. Issues of fairness tend to predominate in decisions about small family groups yielding a preference for trying to save the entire group, whereas in larger groups a more detached strategy of saving the largest number of lives prevails. Subjects prefer to save as many people as possible, without regard to holding the group together. This can be viewed as a strategy shift away from utility maximization.

The effects of these four factors and their cognitive interpretations lend support to our claim that decision makers use a variety of strategies (and mental representations) rather than different policies within one general strategy when making decisions. One source of relevant information is subjects' self-reported strategies. Do those strategies vary systematically with domain content even when the actual decision remains the same? When subjects rely on narrative, regret-oriented, or aspiration-directed strategies, they should report and emphasize relevant aspects of the decision problem. When decision makers rely on simpler weight-and-add component utilities strategies, their reports and recall protocols will emphasize the probabilities and values explicitly mentioned in the problem statements, and their errors will be consistent with their edited and reweighted subjective values and probabilities. These two cases should be distinct in self-report data.

We created a taxonomy of seven decision strategies, informed by the four factors and by think-aloud reports collected from participants in a pilot study of risky decision making. Seven reliably identifiable strategies or heuristics for choosing between a risky option and a sure-thing option were discerned in the experimental participants' verbal reports. We have successfully used these categories both as checklists for experimental participants to complete (i.e., "Check each of the following descriptions that is a valid summary of the manner in which you made your decision") and as the basis for a content coding scheme applied to participants' open-ended think-aloud reports.

> *Numerical Calculations.* "I made a lot of arithmetic, numerical calculations to decide what to do."
>
> *Emotional Reactions.* "I focused on how I would feel if each outcome had happened."
>
> *Story Construction.* "I constructed a story in my head for each possibility and picked the best one."
>
> *Regret Focus.* "I asked myself: 'If I wind up with regrets, which choice will I regret least?' "
>
> *Morality Focus.* "I focused on the morality of the situation (right or wrong), including the best interests of society."
>
> *Choose-the-Favorite (high aspiration).* "I found the best outcome and picked the option that would give me the best chance to get it."
>
> *Avoid-the-Worst (security).* "I found the worst outcome and picked the option that would give me the best chance to avoid it."

Experimental Evidence

The goal of the current research program is to create a theory of decision making that uses multiple decision strategies (i.e., representations, decoding rules). Such a theory should be helpful in explaining why certain content domains lead to very different decisions. In order to test this general claim, we presented our subjects with a single decision in the form of a short scenario (from Rettinger, 1998; Rettinger & Hastie, 2001). The self-report, recall, and choice data from this study should demonstrate the effects of content on decision strategies and will serve as inputs for construction-integration simulations of the decision process.

The crucial manipulation was that although all participants received the same formal underlying decision problem, the domain content of the decision was varied. Participants received decisions in one of four domains: legal (what to do about a speeding ticket), grading (to write a final exam or a paper), stock (to keep or sell it), or a gamble (which option to wager on in a casino). They were asked to choose between a risky option, in which they could possibly gain $125 (or 12.5 grade points) but might also lose either $100 (10 points) or $300 (30 points), and a sure loss of $62.50 (6.25 points). Note that the expected value of the two options is identical. Points refer to the grading scenario, and the monetary options apply to the others.

The purpose of this methodology was to demonstrate that when the decision structure is identical, content variations still affect decisions. Data were also collected to test the hypotheses previously outlined: that these effects are the result of fundamental changes in the encoding, mental representations, and decoding of decision information. To this end, participants were asked not only to make a decision, but also to describe the strategy they used to make it. Having selected a course of action, subjects were asked to "Try to describe your thinking when you made your choice of what to do. Try to write down a list of 'rules' or procedures that you could tell to someone else so that they would think about the choice the same way you did and reach the same conclusion about what to do." Responses to this question were coded into the categories described previously.

Although self-reports of strategies have their limitations, including participants' lack of access to their own cognition (see Ericsson & Simon, 1984, for discussion of this issue), this question has been used successfully in the past to elicit strategies from subjects.

Participants' memory for the decision scenario (following a delay) was assessed to provide insight into the mental representations they relied on during decision making (Dellarosa & Bourne, 1985). They were given both free recall instructions ("Please summarize, in your own words, the decision scenario you just read. We want to know how complete and accurate your recall of the decision dilemma is, so try to include as much detail as you can and be as accurate as possible.") and a cued memory task, in which they were given an outline of the decision scenario and asked to fill in relevant details. This information about participants' memory for the decision and the strategies they used in making it is necessary to demonstrate that changes in decision content influence the cognitive processes underlying decision making.

In fact, subjects who saw the four different stories (but faced the same underlying decisions) exhibited different preferences for the risky

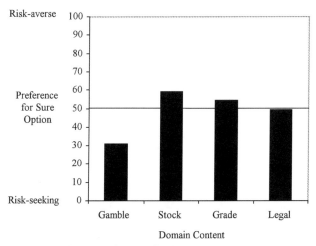

Figure 6.1 Subjects' preferences for the sure option in each content domain.

and sure options (see Figure 6.1). The dependent measure reflects the strength of subjects' preferences, with 0 reflecting 100% confidence in the risky option and 100 reflecting 100% confidence in the safe option. Analyses using dichotomous measures of preference yield the same pattern of results. When presented with the gamble scenario, subjects prefer the risky option ($m = 30.8$). By contrast, for the stock story, subjects are risk averse ($m = 59.2$), and ambivalent for the grade ($m = 54.3$) and legal stories ($m = 49.2$, $F(3, 99) = 3.69$, $p = .01$). It is particularly interesting to note that the gamble case is reliably different from the others ($F(1, 95) = 9.68$, $p = .002$), suggesting that the most popular laboratory problem content may elicit behavior that is different from behavior in other everyday contexts. These content effects are evidence for our claim that domain content plays an important role in decision making, but they do not tell us much about why these differences occur.

One possible explanation for the effects is simply that subjective values for the outcomes were different in the four contexts. To check for this possibility, participants rated their evaluations of all the outcomes in each problem on good–bad thermometer scales (see Rettinger & Hastie, 2001, for details of this methodology). This provided a measure of their subjective values for the risky and safe alternatives. Figure 6.2 shows that the average rated value for each option was invariant across content conditions. Furthermore, using these thermometer values and the probabilities stated in each problem for the risky and sure options provides

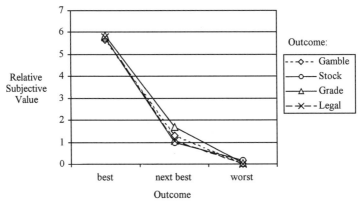

Figure 6.2 Subjects' valuation of options is invariant across conditions.

an estimate of each subject's utilities for the courses of action. This summary evaluation, according to traditional utility theories, should predict decisions. The thermometer values and probabilities are significant predictors of participants' decisions ($F(3, 84) = 3.04$, $p = .03$), but they account for only 10% of the variance in decisions. This can be interpreted to mean that although utility-based decision theories certainly play an important role in explaining decision behavior, there is much more going on in decision making. No single experimental condition is responsible for the entire effect, because the effectiveness of this model does not interact with the condition ($F(10, 71) = 1.39$, ns).

We propose that the domain content effects on the decision outcomes are best interpreted as evidence for changes in the choosers' information processing strategies. To explore this hypothesis, we looked for content effects on participants' self-reported decision strategies. We coded participants' open-ended verbal reports on their strategies into the seven strategy categories identified in prior research (see the preceding discussion) and checked to see if reported strategy differences were associated with different decisions. We found that reported strategies varied between the content domains (see Figure 6.3). The most popular strategy for the gamble scenario was choosing to avoid the worst possible outcome (41.7%). The calculation strategy was the most popular for the stock story (33.3%) and the grade story (50%), and legal subjects preferred a morality strategy (37.5%). Calculation was popular in all four conditions ($m = 37.5\%$), whereas regrets were mentioned by only two subjects (2.1%). In general, subjects used numerical (calculation, avoid worst, choose favorite) strategies most often in the grade

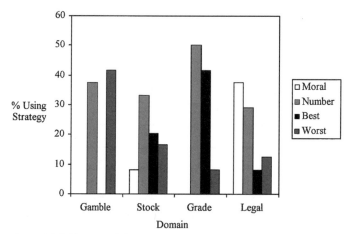

Figure 6.3 Self-reported decision strategies in each content domain.

case (100%), followed by the gamble (79.2%), stock (70.8%), and legal (50%, $\chi^2(3) = 16.44$) scenarios.

These differences in strategy are also associated with different choices. Participants using numerical strategies were more likely to choose the secure sure-thing option. This effect appears to be driven by the avoid-the-worst and numerical calculation strategies. The choose-the-favorite, regrets, story, and morality strategies were all associated with risky decisions ($\chi^2(6) = 33.94$, $p < .0001$). The different strategies were also placed on a continuum from most numerical to least numerical. The calculation strategy anchors the numerical end of the scale, and narrative strategies are at the nonnumerical end. This allows us to determine whether this attribute of the strategy was related to participants' decisions. Typically, participants who use less numerically oriented strategies tend to be risk-seeking, and those who are more numerical are risk averse ($F(1, 90) = 8.65$, $p = .004$).

Based on the finding that a manipulation of decision content led to differential strategy usage, and that different strategies led to different decisions, we tentatively conclude that one mechanism by which domain content influences outcome preferences is by changing the chooser's decision strategy. Of course, there are some notable qualifications on this inference. Foremost is its basis in correlations. A study in which subjects' decision strategies are manipulated orthogonally to decision content is necessary to infer causality. Such a follow-up study will address the heavy reliance on self-reports to determine strategy use. If we observe independent effects of manipulated decision strategy and contents, these will provide converging support for this claim.

A second anticipated effect of domain content is on the chooser's mental representation of the situation based on the (written) decision problem. We have suggested that different representations may arise as part of changes in decision strategy. Because changes in mental representation produce changes in the elements of the stimulus that are available and salient during the decision process and afterward, changes in domain content are predicted to result in differences in what information is recalled (Dellarosa & Bourne, 1985). This should be true even when the essential to-be-remembered information is identical across stories. Furthermore, one's decision also retroactively affects one's memory for the original scenario. Both of these processes are indicative of the complex cognitive processes that we propose underlie decision making (cf. Hawkins & Hastie, 1990).

Figure 6.4 shows the pattern of recall for the decision problem elements in each content condition. Both similarities and differences are clear. For example, subjects had the lowest recall for the 50% chance of a negative outcome element. Furthermore, recall was better for the worst outcome, particularly for its reported value ($300 or 30 points) than for the $100/10 point (25% chance) outcome. This was consistent with the

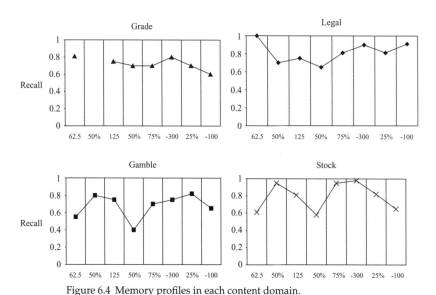

Figure 6.4 Memory profiles in each content domain.

frequent use of the avoid-the-worst strategy, which focuses attention on this piece of information.

An important difference among the representations is the perfect recall of the value of the sure loss ($62.50) in the legal condition, in contrast with the relatively poorer recall of that outcome in other conditions. This is indicative of the different representation used in this condition. We believe this occurred because participants in the legal condition were not relying merely on numerical considerations, but were deciding whether pleading not guilty was worthwhile relative to the sure loss. As a result, the sure loss would be salient and its recall is increased. Another notable difference is the improved recall of the likelihood and value of the gain in the stock scenario. This is consistent with the risk-seeking behavior in this condition, because participants who make the risky choice are likely to focus attention on the possible gain. The presence of these differences provides evidence to support our claim that surface changes in a decision scenario affect mental representation even of the decision's deep structure.

Computer Simulations

Although these results are informative, we are still left with fundamental questions about the mental representations underlying decision making. In particular, it is not at all clear how decisions are represented in the domains and whether domain content actually plays a role in determining the type of representation. In order to gain insight into these issues, computer simulations of subjects' mental representations were built. One important source of inspiration for these simulations was the relationship between explanation-based decision making (Pennington & Hastie, 1988) and construction-integration (Kintsch, 1998) accounts of mental representations.

Pennington and Hastie's notion of story structure has been influenced by research in the discourse processing domain, particularly Kintsch's construction-integration model of comprehension, which can be applied to preferential judgment. Kintsch (1988) proposed the construction-integration model with the goal of understanding discourse comprehension processes and their associated memory structures. The construction-integration model is implemented as a computer simulation that takes discourse in the form of propositions and "reads" it, creating a network of connections between concepts' in memory. The network can then be probed to answer questions about the text. For instance, its responses to words that are associated with main concepts in the text are facilitated (primed).

Construction-integration is a hybrid symbolic/connectionist model of how human readers comprehend text and other discourse. Texts are represented as a set of nodes that are connected by a network of links. Each node can be differentially active, and each link between nodes has a strength that specifies the relationship between nodes. Nodes represent propositions, which are units of meaning that include both arguments and predicate. For example, "the boy hit the girl" is represented as hit[boy, girl]. Propositions in a particular simulation are derived from the text itself and from the reader's long-term memory. Links are created between nodes when the propositions share an argument or are otherwise meaningfully related. Kintsch (1988, 1998) refers to the information that derives from the presented text as the *text base*, whereas the elaborated version that includes background knowledge is called a *situation model*.

Representations of a particular text are created by a two-stage process: first construction, then integration. During the construction stage, propositions are generated by importing them from the actual text and from one's long-term memory. All propositions from the text are initially included, as is all potentially relevant information from memory. Note that a great deal of information that is not ultimately relevant will be included by these procedures. Propositions that are related are linked together. Any two propositions that share an argument are connected. For example, hit[boy, girl] and run[girl, home] share *girl* and are thus linked. Information about girls from long-term memory is also imported and linked, so the proposition is a[girl, female] is added. It is possible to have negatively weighted links, whereby one node can inhibit another. Inhibition is useful for multiple interpretations of a text that are mutually exclusive and is used when implementing decision models. This process is predominantly bottom-up, using simple local rules to create a representation that sacrifices coherence for completeness.

Integration processes convert the constructed representation into a coherent one. Because link connections are promiscuous during construction, the goal of integration is to emphasize the important information in the story, thus developing a situation model. This is accomplished by spreading activation among nodes. Activation flows from node to node along links. Therefore, nodes that are connected by strong links will share more of their activation, and nodes with more activation spread more to their neighbors. An important point to note about integration is that, by convention, all nodes have activation levels between 0 and 1. This is enforced by normalizing the activations of all nodes, so that the one with the most activation is set to 1 and any nodes with negative activations are set to 0. Also by convention, all links and nodes are assumed to start out with equal activation, usually arbitrarily set to 1. Changes in these assumptions have been shown to have little or no effect on the final model output. The major result of the integration process is that nodes that are not well connected tend to have little or no activation, whereas better-connected ones gain the lion's share of the activation.

A critical aspect of the construction-integration model is the placement of information in long-term memory. Because the comprehension process is considered to be cyclical, information that is not currently being processed is sent to long-term storage. The strength of the long-term memory representation for each proposition is proportional to the activation it accrued during the previous processing cycles. Nodes that are kept active for more than one cycle have the opportunity to accrue even more activation in long-term memory. This process leads to the formation of a situation model in which the most important (as measured by connectedness) nodes gain the most activation. The model then predicts that subjects' memory will be best for the best-connected propositions, which form the situation model of the story.

Kintsch (1998) has proposed that comprehension can be construed as a broad framework for cognition. Among the tasks he has presented to the construction-integration model are nonpreferential judgments like the classic "Linda the feminist bank teller" (Kahneman & Tversky, 1982) and the Asian disease problems. Construction-integration networks, when probed, made the same conjunction errors as did Tversky and Kahneman's human subjects. This result suggests that it will be possible to use the same framework to model preferential choices like the ones discussed previously. Naturally, these preferences must be presented in discourse form both to human subjects and to the construction-integration model, but under these conditions, a model of comprehension can simulate the preferences of human subjects. This will be of particular interest, because this model is completely agnostic with regard to probability theory and, in fact, does not process numbers literally, only the valence of each proposition. If construction-integration is able to model subjects' decisions, and if its success depends on postulating different underlying text representations, this will be a strong argument for the role of content in preferential judgment.

Narrative Model

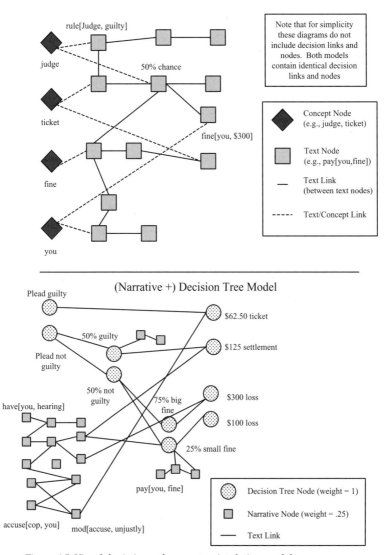

Figure 6.5 Visual depictions of computer simulation models.

Our research uses memory data to obtain clues about the nature of the decision problem representations. We use the construction-integration modeling notation and tools to frame specific hypotheses about mental models of decision problems (see later). We believe that a distinction between narrative and decision tree structures can explain some of the differences in choices that are caused by experimental decision framing and content manipulations. A third representational model, in terms of a list of problem elements, analogous to an accountant's spreadsheet is another plausible hypothesis about models of some decision situations. For present purposes, we will consider only these three representations: narrative-stories, decision trees, and lists of numbers (the first two of these are visually represented in Figure 6.5).

The narrative-story representation takes the form of a temporally ordered sequence of events linked together by antecedent–consequent or causal relationships. Complex events can include embedded events in a hierarchical structure, but the dominant ordering is temporal–causal. Pennington and Hastie (1988, 1991, 1993) have conducted extensive studies of these structures in the context of jurors' criminal trial decisions. They borrowed freely from the literature on text comprehension for hypotheses about the nature of these representations (e.g., Mandler & Johnson, 1977; Schank & Abelson, 1995). In the case where a decision problem includes several courses of action or options to choose, each option was represented as one main *story line*, with alternative contingent future paths subordinated to the main sequence within each option. The empirical signatures of reliance on a narrative-story decision problem model would be temporal ordering in recall, relatively high recall of nonnumerical material, and relatively high recall of information about causal relationships.

We hypothesize that a decision tree representation would preserve the format of a traditional decision problem, with several alternative courses of action, each conditioned on chance or cause nodes, leading to outcomes associated with consequences. We expect that a decision tree representation would be more balanced than a narrative representation and would not subordinate alternative future branches to a single dominant story line. We also expect that the decision tree representation would preserve and foreground numerical information more prominently than would a narrative model.

Finally, the tabular, numerical problem representation would be a bare-bones frame containing slots in which values would be assigned to variables according to the specifics of a decision problem. Attached procedures would execute the computations required by a rudimentary decision analysis expected-value formula. Nathan, Kintsch, and Young (1992) have proposed a graphic format for such *conceptual problem models*. We concur with their hypothesis that some explicit instruction or

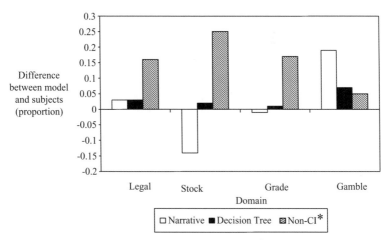

Figure 6.6 Decisions predicted by computer simulations compared to actual decisions. *Note:* Larger bars indicate bigger disparities between model and data.

training is necessary for the encoding, representation, and computational requirements of such a strategy.

The two former representations were implemented using the construction-integration rubric, and the latter was simulated using multiplication only. The decision process was simulated using a simplified decision rule in order to isolate the importance of mental representations. For all three simulations, the option that obtained the greatest activation from the representational network was chosen. The proportion of subjects choosing an option was operationalized as the proportion of activation accruing to each option. Although the number-list representation uses each subject's actual recall for the (sentence-level) elements of the decision scenario, the construction-integration models make predictions about what elements will be recalled. Correlations between these predictions and the subjects' actual recall are another criterion for judging the success of a model. A simulation is considered successful if it is able to predict both the proportion of subjects choosing each option and their memory for the decision scenario. If both criteria are met, then we conclude that the mental representation it simulates is similar to that used by the majority of subjects.

Turning now to the results of the simulations for subjects in each of the four domains, in Figure 6.6 we see the badness of fit for each model in each domain. Larger bars indicate greater deviance of each simulation model's predictions from the actual subjects as a group. In

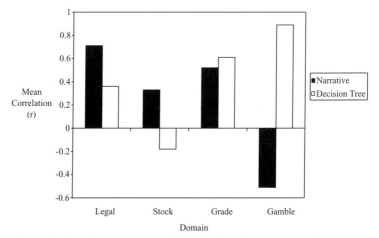

Figure 6.7 Correlations between subjects' recall and computer simulations' predictions of recall.

each condition, at least one simulation model can be ruled out. The non–construction-integration model fails utterly in all three content-rich domains, and the narrative model fails for gambles. Preferences are simulated well in the legal domain by the narrative and decision tree models, in the stock domain by the decision tree only, in the grade domain by the narrative and decision tree models, and in the gamble domain by the decision tree and subjects' memory models only.

The other criterion for a successful simulation is the correlation between the computer's predictions of memory for the text and subjects' actual memory. This test is critical, because it is difficult to argue that the simulation captures key elements of mental representations if our main measure of that representation is not well predicted. As Figure 6.7 shows, not all models fit this criterion equally well. In the legal domain, although both the decision tree and narrative representations fit the decisions equally well, the narrative simulation is notably better at predicting what parts of the story subjects remember, leading us to discard the decision tree model for this case. The reverse is true for the gamble domain. The narrative simulation is very poor at predicting what subjects remember, whereas the decision tree is excellent. The natural conclusion is that these subjects use decision trees and other, more formal representations. For the grade domain both models do fairly well, leading to the conclusion that subjects either use an intermediate representation or that there is no consensus representation within the group. For stocks, neither of the models does particularly well.

The most striking of these findings is that for legal stories the narrative representation seems most appropriate, and for the gamble, decision trees best simulate our subjects. These two domains, despite their identical underlying decision structure, produced quite different mental representations in our subjects. When combined with the strategy differences reported earlier, we find that manipulating domain content does change the information processing that underlies decision making, and that this leads to changes in subjects' preferences. Because of the relatively strong agreement between the human and simulated decision makers, we feel justified in concluding that construction-integration (Kintsch, 1998) can provide a rubric for understanding decision making. These simulations, when combined with Kintsch's (1998) model, provide evidence for the crucial role of mental representation in understanding the decision process and for construction-integration as a simulation of those representations.

Conclusions

The common theme running through the work described here is that decision making relies on a variety of cognitive processes and that domain content partly determines which strategies are followed. Whether it is reflected in the size of a framing effect (Schneider, 1992; Wagenaar et al., 1988), a change in decision strategy (Goldstein & Weber, 1995), or wholesale changes in the mental representation (Rettinger & Hastie, 2001), domain content has a pervasive influence on the decision-making process. We believe that the early findings on content effects summarized in this chapter point to a new and fruitful direction in decision-making research.

The notion that simple gambles are a metaphor for other life decisions is incomplete and sometimes misleading. We cannot generalize from decisions about monetary gambles to those regarding medical or legal decisions or even to other financial decisions. The context-specific information presented to decision makers plays a critical role in determining their decisions. The present research, in combination with the work of Goldstein and Weber (1995) and conceptual analyses by Tada and Weber (1998) and by Veinott and Yates (1998), supports the idea that decision content has profound effects on the decision process. People think about decisions differently as the contents change.

The content domain, personal relevance, moral content, and other aspects cause changes both in information processing strategy and in the way the informational inputs to decision processes are represented mentally.

We introduced an initial theory of decision representation based on Kintsch's (1988, 1998) construction-integration model of text comprehension. With the modest goal of taking an off-the-shelf representational scheme and applying it to the texts of decisions, we have illustrated a place for mental representation in the decision process. We were able to simulate changes in people's decisions that arise from changes in decision content, with reference to the way they comprehend the decision scenario. These simulations, which do not involve simply transforming the numerical outcomes, illustrate our assertion that mental representations are influenced by decision content. Future simulations will be necessary to understand just how content influences mental representations and how information is imported into them from one's background knowledge. Perhaps an integration of the construction-integration approach with Minerva-DM (Dougherty et al., this volume) or latent semantic analysis (Landauer and Dumais, 1997) would prove fruitful.

Two important follow-up lines of research will be crucial to the continuing advancement of our claims. First, because the current specification of content knowledge is arbitrary, a more systematic means of simulating this crucial aspect of the decision process is necessary. Both Dougherty et al. (this volume) and Landauer and Dumais (1997) have proposed models of long-term memory that could be combined with our construction-integration proposal. One way of considering our model is that it simulates on-line processing in great detail but is less concrete about the relationship with stored knowledge. By considering that relationship in a more principled manner, it should be possible to make stronger predictions of people's decisions while maintaining the basic framework we propose.

The second follow-up issue is that of individual versus aggregated simulations. Currently, our simulations explain the average memory and summarized decisions of groups of about 25 people. This is fine, but because every individual's knowledge base, decision preferences, and possibly even mental representations can (and likely do) differ, it will also be necessary to simulate individuals' decision making. This research will require a more discerning assessment of the knowledge used in making a decision, as well as a specification of each individual's mental representation in the construction-integration framework.

Decision making is a form of cognition, and cognitive explanations of the decision process can be fruitful and informative. Does the content domain of the cover story affect decision-making processes and outcomes? The present research provides a definite answer: "Yes." Cognitive models of comprehension provide mechanisms to explain content and other decision-making effects in the same terms that are applied to explain comprehension in other higher-order thought processes. Decision making relies on the same memory, reasoning, and perception processes that we use in other tasks. Of course, decisions contain unique features of their own, such as the application of subjective preferences and probabilities and the uncertainty inherent in predicting future events. In the future, this cognitive approach may not only help explain content effects, but may provide deeper understanding of other important phenomena in decision making. We therefore advocate information processing theories that integrate decision-making processes into the general context of computational models of cognition.

References

Baron, J., & Spranca, M. (1997). Protected values. *Organizational Behavior and Human Decision Processes, 70,* 1–16.

Bartlett, F. C. (1932). *Remembering: A study in experimental and social psychology.* New York and London: Cambridge University Press.

Beach, L. R. (1990). *Image theory: Decision making in personal and organizational contexts.* Chichester, U.K.: Wiley.

Bernoulli, D. (1954). Specimen theoriae novae de mensura sortis. *Commentarii Academiae Scientarum Imperialis Petropolitaneae, 5* (1730–1733), 175–192 (L. Sommer, Trans.). (Original work published 1738) [Exposition of a new theory on the measurement of risk] *Econometrica, 22,* 23–36.

Bransford, J. D., & Johnson, M. K. (1972). Contextual prerequisites for understanding: Some investigations of comprehension and recall. *Journal of Verbal Learning and Verbal Behavior, 11,* 717–726.

Brewer, W. F., & Treyens, J. C. (1981). Role of schemata in memory for places. *Cognitive Psychology, 13,* 207–230.

Cheng, P. W., & Holyoak, K. J. (1985). Pragmatic reasoning schemas. *Cognitive Psychology, 17,* 391–416.

Cosmides, L. (1989). The logic of social exchange: Has natural selection shaped how humans reason? Studies with the Wason selection task. *Cognition, 31,* 187–276.

Dawes, R. (1988). *Rational choice in an uncertain world.* San Diego, CA: Harcourt Brace Jovanovich.

Dawes, R. (1998). Behavioral decision making and judgment. In D. T. Gilbert, S. T. Fiske, & G. Lindzey (Eds.), *The handbook of social psychology* (Vol. 1, 4th ed., pp. 589–597). Boston: McGraw-Hill.

Dellarosa, D., & Bourne, L. E. (1985). Decisions and memory: Differential retrievability of consistent and contradictory evidence. *Journal of Verbal Learning and Verbal Behavior, 26*(6), 669–682.

Ebbinghaus, H. A. (1885). *Memory: A contribution to experimental psychology* (H. A. Ruger & C. E. Bussenues, 1913, Trans.). New York: Teachers College, Columbia University.

Ericsson, K. A., & Simon, H. A. (1984). *Protocol analysis: Verbal reports as behavior.* Cambridge, MA: MIT Press.

Fischhoff, B. (1983). Predicting frames. *Journal of Experimental Psychology: Learning Memory and Cognition, 9*, 103–116.

Gigerenzer, G., & Hug, K. (1992). Domain-specific reasoning: Social contracts, cheating, and perspective change. *Cognition, 43*, 127–171.

Goldstein, W. M., & Weber, E. U. (1995). Content and discontent: Indications and implications of domain specificity in preferential decision making. In J. Busmeyer, D. L. Medin, & R. Hastie (Eds.), *Decision making from a cognitive perspective* (Vol. 32, pp. 83–126). San Diego, CA: Academic Press.

Griggs, R. A., & Cox, J. R. (1983). The effects of problem content and negation on Wason's selection task. *Quarterly Journal of Experimental Psychology Section A: Human Experimental Psychology, 35A*(3), 519–533.

Hastie, R., & Pennington, N. (2000). Explanation-based decision making. In T. Connolly, H. R. Arkes, & K. R. Hammond (Eds.), *Judgment and decision making: An interdisciplinary reader* (2nd ed., pp. 212–228) New York: Cambridge University Press

Hawkins, S. A., & Hastie, R. (1990). Hindsight: Biased judgments of past events after the outcomes are known. *Psychological Bulletin, 107*, 311–327.

Kahneman, D., & Tversky, A. (1979). Prospect theory: An analysis of decision under risk. *Econometrica, 47*(2), 263–291.

Kahneman, D., & Tversky, A. (1982). The psychology of preferences. *Scientific American, 246*, 161–173.

Kintsch, W. (1988). The role of knowledge in discourse comprehension: A construction-integration model. *Psychological Review, 95*, 163–182.

Kintsch, W. (1998). *Comprehension: A paradigm for cognition.* Cambridge: Cambridge University Press.

Kühberger, A. (1998). The influence of framing on risky decisions. *Organizational Behavior and Human Decision Processes, 75*, 23–55.

Landauer, T. K., & Dumais, S. T. (1997). A solution to Plato's problem: The Latent Semantic Analysis theory of the acquisition, induction, and representation of knowledge. *Psychological Review, 104*, 211–240.

Levin, I. P., Schneider, S. L., & Gaeth, G. J. (1998). All frames are not created equal: A typology and critical analysis of framing effects. *Organizational Behavior and Human Decision Processes, 76*, 149–188.

Lopes, L. L. (1983). Some thoughts on the psychological concept of risk. *Journal of Experimental Psychology: Human Perception and Performance, 9*(1), 137–144.

Lopes, L. L., & Oden, G. C. (1999). The role of aspiration level in risky choice: A comparison of Cumulative Prospect Theory and SP/A Theory. *Journal of Mathematical Psychology, 43*, 286–313.

Luce, R. D. (2000). *The utility of gains and losses: Measurement-theoretical and experimental approaches.* Mahwah, NJ: Erlbaum.

Mandler, J. M., & Johnson, N. S. (1977). Remembrance of things parsed: Story structure and recall. *Cognitive Psychology, 9*, 111–151.

Manktelow, K. I., & Evans, J. S. (1979). Facilitation of reasoning by realism: Effect or noneffect? *British Journal of Psychology, 70*(4), 477–488.

Nathan, M. J., Kintsch, W., & Young, E. (1992). A theory of algebra-word-problem comprehension and its implications for the design of learning environments. *Cognition & Instruction, 9*(4), 329–389.

Pennington, N., & Hastie, R. (1988). Explanation-based decision making: Effects of memory structure on judgment. *Journal of Experimental Psychology: Learning, Memory, and Cognition, 14*(3), 521–533.

Pennington, N., & Hastie, R. (1991). A cognitive theory of juror decision making: The story model. *Cardozo Law Review, 13*, 519–557.

Pennington, N., & Hastie, R. (1993). A theory of explanation-based decision making. In G. Klein, J. Orasanu, R. Calderwood, & C. E. Zsambok (Eds.), *Decision making in action: Models and methods* (pp. 188–201). Norwood, NJ: Ablex.

Rettinger, D. A. (1998). *The role of comprehension in decisions: Framing and content effects.* Unpublished doctoral dissertation, University of Colorado at Boulder.

Rettinger, D. A., & Hastie, R. (2001). Content effects on decision making. *Organizational Behavior and Human Decision Processes, 85*(2), 336–359.

Reyna, V. F., & Brainerd, C. J. (1995). Fuzzy-trace theory: An interim synthesis. *Learning and Individual Differences, 7*, 1–75.

Schank, R. C., & Abelson, R. P. (1995). Knowledge and memory: The real story. In R. S. Wyer, Jr. (Ed.), *Knowledge and memory: The real story* (pp. 1–86). Hillsdale, NJ: Erlbaum.

Schneider, S. L. (1992). Framing and conflict: Aspiration level contingency, the status quo, and current theories of risky choice. *Journal of Experimental Psychology: Learning, Memory, and Cognition, 18*(5), 1040–1057.

Tada, Y., & Weber, E. U. (1998). *Psychological space of decision similarity and its influence on decision strategies.* Paper presented at the annual meeting of the Society for Judgment and Decision Making. November, Dallas, TX.

Trabasso, T., & van den Broek, P. (1985). Causal thinking and the representation of narrative events. *Journal of Memory and Language, 24*, 612–630.

Tversky, A., & Kahneman, D. (1981). The framing of decisions and the psychology of choice. *Science, 211*, 453–481.

Tversky, A., & Kahneman, D. (1986). Rational choice and the framing of decisions. *Journal of Business, 59*, s251–s278.

Veinott, E., & Yates, J. F. (1998). *A multi-dimensional scaling analysis of hard decisions.* Poster presented at the annual meeting of the Society for Judgment and Decision Making, November, Dallas, TX.

von Neumann, J., & Morgenstern, O. (1953). *Theory of games and economic behavior* (3rd ed.). Princeton, NJ: Princeton University Press.

Wagenaar, W. A., Keren, G., & Lichtenstein, S. (1988). Islanders and hostages: Deep and surface structures of decision problems. *Acta Psychologica, 67*, 175–189.

Wang, X. T. (1996). Domain-specific rationality in human choices: Violations of utility axioms and social contexts. *Cognition, 60*, 31–63.

Wason, P. C., & Johnson-Laird, P. N. (1972). *Psychology of reasoning: Structure and content*. Cambridge, MA: Harvard University Press.

7   Memory, Development, and Rationality:
      An Integrative Theory of Judgment and
      Decision Making

Valerie F. Reyna, Farrell J. Lloyd, and Charles J. Brainerd

ABSTRACT

In contrast to either heuristics-and-biases or adaptive-ecological approaches, fuzzy-trace theory embraces inconsistencies in human reasoning by assuming opposing dual processes. Recent advances in memory research are used to construct an integrative theory of judgment and decision making, with illustrations from real-world contexts such as medicine. Key principles include the following: (1) Reasoners encode multiple gist and verbatim representations, which confer cognitive flexibility. (2) However, reasoning operates at the least precise level of gist that the task allows, increasingly so with the development of expertise. (3) This simplified, qualitative processing is not a result of computational complexity but is the default mode of reasoning. Rather than classifying reasoning as rational or irrational, *degrees of rationality* are proposed based on the processing underlying different kinds of errors across many tasks, which we discuss (e.g., framing tasks, syllogistic reasoning, conjunctive and disjunctive probability judgment, base-rate neglect, and others). Therefore, rationality is not an immutable trait, but changes from task to task and from one stage of development to another.

CONTENTS

The study of judgment and decision making is at a crossroads. In the past, its success centered on demonstrating the foibles and fallacies of human reasoning (e.g., Kahneman, Slovic, & Tversky, 1982; Nisbett & Ross, 1980). Recent critics of this approach, however, have argued that human behavior is intelligent and well adapted to its naturalistic environment, which is poorly reflected in the problems posed in laboratories. Although there is widespread agreement that the field must progress beyond demonstrations of judgment-and-decision errors, there is sharp divergence of opinion about what direction to head in.

Confusion surrounds many foundational issues, such as whether well-known laboratory demonstrations are really errors. The choices boil down to two: We can reject the error data as irrelevant to human reasoning, or we can incorporate the standard demonstrations into an integrative theory that places them in a larger explanatory context. In this chapter, we pursue the second path, which brings us to a new conception of rationality that differs from both the standard irrationality view and recent adaptive/ecological approaches (e.g., Gigerenzer, 1994). This alternative conception of rationality characterizes judgment and decision making as neither irrational nor necessarily adaptive, but as exhibiting degrees of rationality, depending on the precise nature of reasoning processes (Reyna, 2000a; Reyna & Brainerd, 1995a).

In particular, we argue that a common core of processing principles explains such diverse effects as gain–loss framing, base-rate neglect, disjunctive probability judgment, and the conjunction fallacy, as well as their interaction with response types (e.g., choices, ratings, or point estimates), presentation formats (e.g., frequencies or probabilities), and motivational biases. These processing principles are drawn from an evidence-based theory of memory, reasoning, and development – fuzzy-trace theory – in which intuition is explicitly defined as an advanced mode of thought (e.g., Reyna & Ellis, 1994). Thus, we explain how the same intuitive processes that make reasoning more reliable, and that hold the key to rationality, also make systematic biases more reliable.

The Winter of Our Discontent

The discontent with standard demonstrations of judgment-and-decision errors is pervasive. Before we introduce an alternative view, we should describe the nature of this discontent. The putative violations of logic, probability theory, and basic axioms of decision making are dramatic and easy to replicate in classrooms and applied contexts (see Tables 7.1 and 7.2 for examples). Framing effects, the demonstration that the same options elicit risk aversion when they are described as gains but risk seeking when described as losses, have been replicated in medicine, accounting, labor bargaining, and many other real-life contexts. For

Table 7.1. *Decision Making: An Example of Framing Effects*

Decision Problem
  Imagine that the United States is preparing for the outbreak of an unusual
    Asian disease, which is expected to kill 600 people. Two alternative
    programs to combat the disease have been proposed. Assume that the
    exact scientific estimate of the consequences of the programs are as
    follows:
Options in Gain Frame
  Program A: 200 people saved.
  Program B: 1/3 probability that 600 people will be saved and 2/3 probability
    that no one will be saved.
Options in Loss Frame
  Program A: 400 people die.
  Program B: 2/3 probability that 600 people will die and 1/3 probability that
    no one will die.
Task
  Choose the preferred option.
Framing Effect
  Tversky and Kahneman (1981, p. 251) presented these gain and loss
    decisions to different groups of subjects. Most subjects chose Program A
    in the gain frame and Program B in the loss frame, although the two
    versions of the decision are identical.

Table 7.2. *Judgment: An Example of the Conjunction Fallacy*

Problem
   Linda is 31 years old, single, outspoken, and very bright. She majored in
   philosophy. As a student, she was deeply concerned with issues of
   discrimination and social justice, and also participated in antinuclear
   demonstrations.
Task
   Rank the following items in terms of probability:
   Linda is a teacher in an elementary school.
   Linda works in a bookstore and takes yoga classes.
   Linda is active in the feminist movement.
   Linda is a psychiatric social worker.
   Linda is a member of the League of Women Voters.
   Linda is a bank teller.
   Linda is an insurance salesperson.
   Linda is a bank teller and is active in the feminist movement.
Conjunction Fallacy Effect
   Tversky and Kahneman (1983, p. 297) gave subjects descriptions (e.g., of
   Linda) and asked them to rank the probability of several propositions that
   referred to individuals or classes in the descriptions. Subjects ranked
   conjunctions such as "bank teller and active in the feminist movement" as
   more probable than "bank teller" by itself, although the class of bank
   tellers includes feminist bank tellers (and therefore cannot be less
   probable).

---

example, patients and their physicians are more willing to undertake
risky therapies when outcomes are framed in terms of mortality (lives
lost), and negotiators are more willing to take risks (e.g., go out on
strike) when they perceive their options as losses (Kuhberger, 1998;
Levin, Schneider, & Gaeth, 1998). If we characterize these effects as spu-
rious, their importance and the importance of our field's contributions
over the last 30 years is diminished. Few researchers want to dismiss the
accomplishments of several decades, but they are ready for a change.

   A major source of dissatisfaction is that researchers see the standard
view as incomplete, not only because it emphasizes the shortcomings of
human reasoning but also because it fails to provide adequate processing explanations for effects. For example, the memory availability explanation for certain judgment biases – the availability heuristic – seems
underspecified, and studies have shown that memory and judgment are
not connected, as had been hypothesized (e.g., Shedler & Manis, 1986).
To many observers, however, the cure has been worse than the disease.
Some critiques of the standard view have been rhetorical (rather than
empirical), vague (although standard views of rationality are criticized,

no clear alternative definition is offered), and, worst of all, post hoc. Problems are said to be tricky or ambiguous, and interpretations of problems are offered to justify answers after results are known. Of course, it is a trivial matter to come up with post hoc speculations that account for findings. The problem has been that some critics have acted as though this speculation counts as evidence against the standard view, which it does not.

Similar confusion exists about the status of models or simulations as evidence bearing on human judgment and decision making. The initial belief that processing could be modeled has given way to skepticism about the ease of modeling processes that are not psychologically real. The standards for mathematical modeling and computer simulation are becoming more rigorous. Models that have large numbers of parameters are criticized increasingly for lack of parsimony (and lack of falsifiability), goodness-of-fit tests are demanded more often, and opaque mechanisms (e.g., neural nets) are being rejected because they are not testable. (For the latter models especially, it is crucial to distinguish between predictive validity, for which these models have achieved impressive results, and their validity as explanations of human behavior.) Once again, in the first wave of enthusiasm for change, rhetorical appeal and impressive simulations that lacked supporting human data were treated almost uncritically – as though they were evidence against the standard view; however, a new level of scrutiny is being applied to these approaches.

Perhaps the most insidious confusion that has characterized recent attacks on the standard view involves evolutionary arguments. The argument is of the general form that these biases or behaviors are the result of natural selection, and so would not exist if they were not adaptive. Although it is well within the bounds of scientific discourse to speculate about whether certain biases or behaviors might be adaptive, it is not correct to argue that the mere existence of a bias or behavior is evidence that it is adaptive. This argument is a classic misuse of evolutionary theory. As with the other non-evidence-based arguments discussed earlier, an equally plausible argument can often be constructed – after the fact – favoring the opposite bias or behavior. Therefore, despite a general uneasiness with the notion that nature could have left humanity so poorly equipped, evolutionary theory does not provide specific guidance as to the quality of any particular aspect of human reasoning.

One of the resolutions of this conflict between the standard view and ecological critiques has been to assert task specificity. That is, reasoning is flexible and depends on the specific features of the task. Thus, preferences cannot be inferred as global entities; instead, they are constructed anew, depending on the options that are presented (Payne, Bettman, & Johnson, 1992). Similar arguments have been made to explain judgments that seem to violate probability theory. Probability, it is argued, has multiple interpretations that shift from task to task, producing different results in different situations (Gigerenzer, 1994). Although these interpretations differ, supposedly they can all be considered logical, intelligent, and rational because tasks and situations differ. In the extreme, conflicting findings across tasks are handled by introducing different theories for different tasks. Researchers are again ambivalent about this resolution and would prefer global theories that *predict* behavior across paradigms. In fact, there is general agreement that integrative theorizing that spans domains is desirable, although its feasibility is questioned.

A Prolegomena to Integrative Theorizing: Why Memory Capacity Does Not Work

The seeds of the present debate about rationality were planted during the information processing revolution (e.g., Miller, 1956). Information processing theorists assumed that humans would process all relevant information precisely and coherently (if they were sufficiently motivated), but memory limitations lead to shortcuts or satisficing rather than optimizing (e.g., Hogarth, 1980; Nisbett & Ross, 1980; Simon, 1956). As in other research that relied on the computer metaphor, the idea that memory limitations constrain performance was rarely tested directly (e.g., see Reyna, 1992; Reyna & Brainerd, 1992). When those tests were performed, three conclusions emerged that we now discuss: (1) simplified processing does not reflect memory load, (2) tasks that produce errors make few memory demands, and (3) when tasks demand memory, reasoning performance is independent of those demands (for a review, see Reyna & Brainerd, 1995a).

Tables 7.1 and 7.2 describe two tasks that elicit errors, or at least biases, in judgment and decision making. In the conjunction fallacy task, for example, subjects rank the probability of a conjunction (e.g., feminist and bank teller) as greater than the probability of a more inclusive class (e.g., of bank tellers). Tversky and Kahneman (1983) ascribed this effect to the representativeness heuristic: that subjects make a similarity rather than a probability judgment (Table 7.2). Contrary to some characterizations of the standard view of heuristics and biases, Tversky and

Kahneman (e.g., Kahneman et al., 1982) consistently argued that human information processing is adaptive (heuristics being an example of such adaptation because they conserve information processing resources), and that heuristics ordinarily do not produce errors. Like Piaget or the psychophysicists, Tversky and Kahneman studied cognitive illusions such as the conjunction fallacy because such phenomena illuminate the nature of processing, not because they thought illusions are typical of ordinary cognition. Contemporary ecological theorists share Tversky and Kahneman's enthusiasm for human ingenuity and the need to conserve processing resources, but they disagree about whether certain behaviors are errors.

Indeed, there is long-standing evidence for cognitive economy, efficiency, or "fast and frugal" processing (e.g., Nisbett & Ross, 1980; Payne, et al., 1992). However, evidence for simplified processing is not the same as evidence pinpointing memory limitations as the cause of such simplified processing. For example, subjects often fail to process all of the quantitative information in complex multidimensional tasks and instead use noncompensatory qualitative reasoning (Fischer & Hawkins, 1993; Hogarth, 1980; Tversky, 1972). The frequent finding that subjects engage in simplified qualitative reasoning must be accommodated by any theory of judgment and decision making.

However, simplified qualitative processing occurs not only in complex tasks, but also under conditions in which memory capacity and other information processing limitations cannot be invoked to explain performance. Such processing occurs when a single problem or decision is presented, there are only two dimensions to process (e.g., outcomes and their probabilities), the information is written down, there is no time limit, and the relevant quantitative operations are easy to perform (e.g., weighing 600 lives saved by 1/3 to compare it to a sure outcome of 200 lives saved; see Table 7.1). Furthermore, memory limitations do not explain the fact that problems or decisions with identical memory constraints – for example, choosing between saving 200 lives and a 1/3 chance of saving 603 lives – produce evidence of quantitative processing. For this problem, as opposed to the standard Asian disease problem, subjects are sensitive to subtle quantitative differences in expected value that favor the gamble (Reyna & Brainerd, 1995a). Memory load, as traditionally defined, does not differ between the 600 and 603 versions of the Asian disease problem, and the quantitative burden is also comparable (dividing 600 or 603 by 3 is pretty simple). However, subjects apparently use a more exacting representation of quantities when they process the 603 version, but the shift seems to have little to do with conserving mental resources.

These shifting results illustrate the general problem of task variability, as defined by Reyna and Brainerd (1994), which must also be accommodated by any theory of judgment and decision making. In this usage, variability is real and does not reflect invalid assessment or shifts in the competencies required in different tasks. That is, substantial variability exists across tasks that cannot be explained away by superficial performance errors such as memory limitations. This task variability also cannot be explained away by general appeals to Type I or II error (i.e., by dismissing good performance as false-positive error or poor performance as false-negative error). Subjects exhibit different levels of reasoning involving the same formal principle (e.g., the appropriate use of base rates or sample size) when different tasks are used to assess the same reasoning competence (e.g., Jacobs & Potenza, 1991; Klaczynski & Fauth, 1997; Reyna & Brainerd, 1994).

Although variable, the logical or quantitative sophistication of judgment and decision-making performance appears to be orthogonal to memory constraints. Experiments that have directly assessed the stochastic dependency between memory and judgment in numerous tasks have found them to be routinely dissociated (e.g., Brainerd & Reyna, 1992a; Fisher & Chandler, 1991; Reyna, 1992, 1995; Reyna & Brainerd, 1995a, 1995b; Shedler & Manis, 1986; Woodard & Reyna, 1997). The role of memory limitations has been evaluated in diverse paradigms ranging from covariation estimation to probability judgment. Single and double dissociations between memory and judgment have been demonstrated. For example, conditions that impair memory for crucial task information do not necessarily affect judgment accuracy, and vice versa. Surprisingly, improving memory for details of task information has been shown to *decrease* reasoning accuracy under specific conditions (e.g., Brainerd & Gordon, 1994; Brainerd & Reyna, 1993). (See Brainerd and Reyna, 1992b, for a discussion of measurement issues, the denouement of which is that memory independence is confirmed.) These findings of memory independence and interference (and other problems; see Dempster, 1992) have contributed to growing dissatisfaction with the notion of working memory capacity or limitations as a viable construct in explaining reasoning and judgment (for alternatives to memory capacity, see, e.g., Chandler & Gargano, 1998; Hasher & Zacks, 1988; Pashler, 1997; Reyna, 1992; Reyna & Brainerd, 1989). Thus, the latest memory research undercuts the rationale behind both heuristics and fast-and-frugal processing, namely, the assumption that cognitive shortcuts occur because memory resources must be conserved.

Of course, it is crucial to distinguish concepts such as *mental effort* and *processing interference* from memory resources (e.g., Brainerd & Reyna, 1990a; Reyna, 1995). However, much of the evidence against relating memory resources to quality of reasoning also vitiates the role of mental effort. For instance, reasoners avoid quantitative processing when the mental effort that would be required is low (e.g., Fischer & Hawkins, 1993; Lovett & Singer, 1991; Reyna & Brainerd, 1994). In addition, increases in the mental effort required to make judgments or decisions can either increase or decrease accuracy. This is not to say that mental effort never affects the choice of strategies in reasoning. On the contrary, the study of tradeoffs involving mental effort and decision making has been a rich source of empirically sound research (e.g., Payne et al., 1992). Nevertheless, mental effort does not seem to be the driving force behind the use of heuristics in judgment or simple, qualitative processing in decision making.

Thus, the burgeoning memory literature provides two caveats for judgment-and-decision-making researchers. First, we can no longer refer casually to memory limitations as a cause of judgment-and-decision-making phenomena; we cannot claim that memory limitations cause behaviors when the dominant finding is that memory is independent of these behaviors. Second, at a minimum, it is incumbent on theorists to separate mental effort from discredited notions of capacity, and to distinguish between those phenomena that may be attributable to effort–accuracy tradeoffs and those that are not similarly attributable. Thus, although the computer metaphor has provided the explanatory framework for cognition for more than 30 years, major phenomena of judgment and decision making appear to be unrelated to computational capacity.

Alternatives to Generic Resources: Dual-Memory Models

To this point, we have discussed traditional memory models, which assume a generic processing resource in the sense that there is "one" memory that can be used to represent many types of information and can be tapped for a variety of purposes, including both representation and processing. In addition to the findings of memory–judgment independence, the generic capacity hypothesis has been assaulted by a number of other findings, chief among them being that capacity seems to be content-specific rather than generic (Brainerd & Reyna, 1990a; Hasher & Zacks, 1988) and that key empirical phenomena that were originally interpreted as capacity effects are most probably interference effects (Reyna & Brainerd, 1989). Further, qualitative data patterns that contradict one another have been produced that support the operation of different memory systems. (Distinctions between dual-memory systems have been used to explain traditional distinctions between short- and long-term memory, suggesting that the latter may be unnecessary. For instance, the time course of short-term memory can be captured by the evanescence of verbatim memory; see Reyna, 1992)

One example of qualitative data patterns that seem to contradict one another, but are explained by dual processes, is provided by Payne and Elie (1998) and Toglia, Neuschatz, and Goodwin (1999). (There are many other similar examples.) On the one hand, Payne and Elie (1998) reported that repeating presented words at study in a list of semantically related words increases later recognition of presented words and decreases acceptance of related words that were never presented. On the other hand, Toglia et al. (1999), using the same paradigm, showed that deep processing of the study list increased recognition of presented words, but it also increased acceptance of related words that were never presented. Improving "memory" seemed to have opposite effects in different studies, despite the fact that these studies used the same paradigm and the same types of materials (see also Table 7.3). Dual-memory processes (i.e., verbatim memory is primed in the first study and gist memory in the second) readily explain such contradictions (see Reyna, 2000b; Reyna & Lloyd, 1997).

In the study of dual-memory processes, there are three main approaches: (1) task-based (e.g., for a review, see Roediger, Weldon, & Challis, 1989), (2) process dissociation (e.g., Jacoby, 1991), and (3) conjoint recognition (Brainerd, Reyna, & Mojardin, 1999). In the task-based approach, one type of memory (usually called *controlled, conscious,* or *explicit*) is identified with performance on direct memory tasks (e.g., cued recall), and the other type (usually called *automatic, unconscious,* or *implicit*) is identified with performance on indirect tasks (e.g., fragment completion). For example, in fragment completion, the subject might study a list of words and then be given an ostensibly unrelated task and told to complete word fragments with words that come to mind. The number of words interpolated from the previously studied word list is taken as an indirect measure of implicit memory.

Table 7.3. *Findings from Dual-Memory Approaches That Challenge the One-Process Orientation*

Approach	Findings
Task-Based	Perceptual indirect performance (e.g., fragment completion) is improved by surface priming, but direct performance is unaffected. Direct performance (e.g., free recall) is improved by semantic priming, but perceptual indirect performance is unaffected.
Process Dissociation	The recollection parameter (an estimate of memory processes derived from the process-dissociation mathematical model) is affected by dividing attention and increasing list length, but the familiarity parameter is unaffected.
Conjoint Recognition	The identity parameter (an estimate of memory processes derived from the conjoint recognition model) for targets is affected by repetition priming, but the similarity parameter is not. The nonidentity parameter for distractors is increased by target priming, and the similarity parameter is decreased.

The second approach, process dissociation, is concerned with another dual-process distinction, namely, Mandler's (1980) recollection–familiarity distinction. Process dissociation uses a simple mathematical model, defined over a recognition memory design in which subjects make recognition decisions under two different instructions to estimate recollection and familiarity. The third approach, conjoint recognition, is concerned with another dual-process distinction, the identity–similarity distinction of fuzzy-trace theory. Conjoint recognition uses a mathematical model that is defined over recognition memory designs in which subjects respond under three different kinds of instructions to measure identity and similarity.

Although there is much discussion in the literature as to the relative merits of these approaches, together they have produced an impressive catalog of effects that are difficult to reconcile with contemporary one-process views of memory, such as SAM (Gillund & Shiffrin, 1984) and MINERVA (Hintzman, 1988). Some examples are shown in Table 7.3, most having to do with implicit or false memory effects (for a review, see Brainerd et al., 1999). However, it must be noted that global memory models were initially developed before the research literature on implicit memory emerged (but see Ratcliff, Van Zandt, & McKoon, 1995; Shiffrin & Steyvers, 1997).

In the next section, we show how one of the dual-memory models, fuzzy-trace theory, has been used to explain judgment and decision making (e.g., Brainerd & Reyna, 1990a; Reyna & Brainerd, 1991a, 1992, 1995a). Other researchers (e.g., Dougherty, Gettys, & Ogden, 1999) have also begun to apply existing memory models to judgment and decision making (although the shortcomings of the adopted one-process models have not been addressed; see Table 7.3). These efforts are promising for several reasons. First, they are empirically grounded rather than mainly rhetorical, having been derived from extensive research on human memory. In addition, the parent memory models are explicit; specific claims are made, rather than simply criticisms of the standard view. Although the one-process memory approaches to judgment and decision making are currently descriptive of known findings, their basis in theory suggests that they will ultimately inspire new predictions.

How Principles of Memory Explain Judgment and Decision Making: A Fuzzy-Trace Theory Analysis

We have reviewed a number of assumptions about the relation between memory and judgment that have been disconfirmed experimentally. Most important among these is the assumption, common to heuristics-and-biases as well as fast-and-frugal approaches, that capacity limitations explain judgment and decision-making shortcuts. In response to the mounting evidence for memory independence, we introduced fuzzy-trace theory in 1990 to explain this finding and to also accommodate the fact that information (held and operated on in memory) must somehow influence judgment and decision making (Reyna & Brainerd, 1990). A satisfactory resolution that incorporates the data is provided by assuming that reasoners extract independent verbatim and gist representations of information and rely primarily on the latter in judgment and decision making. This hypothesis explains the independence of reasoning and memory because, although reasoning relies on gist, memory tasks often require the finer precision to be found in independent verbatim representations. The *fuzzy-processing preference*, as it came to be known, also has advantages for reasoning, such as that gist representations are more stable over time and easier to manipulate than verbatim representations (e.g., Reyna & Brainerd, 1991a, 1992).

Developmentally, contrary to traditional theories, the reliance on simple qualitative gist representations appears to increase as reasoners gain expertise in a domain (e.g., Reyna & Brainerd, 1991a, 1995a). For example, young children do not show standard framing effects when there is no quantitative difference between gains and "losses." This failure to find framing differences cannot be attributed to developmental differences in risk attitudes for gains and losses. (Loss aversion is present in preschoolers; Reyna, 1996a.) The bias to respond to qualitative framing is cognitive and increases with age. According to fuzzy-trace theory, this trend of increasing reliance on gist as development advances applies to children acquiring basic knowledge (e.g., Moore, Dixon, & Haines, 1991; Reyna, 1996a; Reyna & Ellis, 1994; Spinillo & Bryant, 1991) and to adults acquiring expert knowledge (e.g., Reyna, Lloyd, & Whalen, 2001; Reyna, Lloyd, & Woodard, 1997; Shanteau, 1992).

Specifically, evidence from many tasks converged on the conclusion that reasoners encode multiple independent representations of the same information along a fuzzy-to-verbatim continuum, which ranges from verbatim surface details to vague gist that preserves the core meaning of inputs. These representations form a hierarchy of gist roughly analogous to scales of measurement (Reyna & Brainerd, 1995b). The fine-grained quantitative distinctions represented in verbatim memories are analogous to ratio-level information, and the categorical distinctions of lower-level gist are like crude nominal information. Reasoners operate at multiple levels between crude categories and precise quantities, however, including using ordinal-level distinctions in choosing between two gambles which are "more versus less" risky if they cannot be distinguished categorically (cf. Kuhberger, 1995; Reyna & Brainerd, 1995a). Technically, therefore, *dual* gist and verbatim memories refer to the two ends of a continuum of representations that varies in precision.

The availability of multiple representations at different levels of precision confers cognitive flexibility. Given the same information, reasoners can engage in qualitatively different kinds of processing, from fuzzy gist to verbatim-level processing. Whereas Piaget characterized reasoning as the application of logical rules, and information processing theorists characterized it as computation, we have identified reasoning with the fuzzy processes of intuition. Thus, although fuzzy-trace theory shares important features with other two-process theories, it differs in assuming that advanced reasoning is intuitive and parallel (cf. Sloman, 1996; for an overview of evidence, see Reyna & Brainerd, 1995a, 1998). Indeed, gist representations allow reasoners to treat superficially different problems similarly, supporting the consistency criterion of rationality (Tversky & Kahneman, 1986; see also Moray, 1990).

The fuzzy-processing principle governing judgment and decision making holds that reasoning tends to operate on the lowest (or least precise) level of gist that can be used to perform a task. For instance, the minimum distinction required to choose between $5,827 and $68 is that the first option involves more money; the exact difference is not necessary for establishing a preference. Research has produced many demonstrations that although fuzzy processing is the default, reasoners are cognitively flexible (e.g., Reyna & Brainerd, 1995a). They shift their level of representation, called *task calibration*, to adjust for such factors as response mode (more precise responses generally require more precise representations), tolerance for error in the particular situation, and the ambiguity of inputs (e.g., the usual variation of numerical scores along a dimension). In 1995, Reyna introduced a taxonomy of representations and tasks summarizing fuzzy-trace theory's claims about interference from memory representations that are inappropriate to certain tasks (e.g., verbatim interference in gist tasks). Thus, in contrast to most cognitive theories, especially computational ones, we characterized competent reasoning as parallel rather than serial, often operating on the barest senses of ideas prior to encoding all of the relevant details, and as fuzzy or qualitative rather than precise.

Reasoning principles or heuristics were also assumed to be represented vaguely in long-term memory as simple operations on qualitative gists as opposed to precisely articulated procedures (e.g., Reyna & Brainerd, 1991a, 1991b). For example, in framing problems for which subjects must choose between saving some lives for sure versus taking a chance and possibly saving no one, we have argued that decision makers respond on the basis of general principles such as "Saving some people is better than saving none" (see, e.g., Reyna & Brainerd, 1991b, 1995a for details). Evidence supporting these arguments includes nonnumerical framing effects, which are maintained when vague gist replaces all numerical information, and selective processing effects, in which focusing attention on relevant numbers wipes out framing effects but focusing on categorical contrasts such as saving some lives versus saving none (the latter contributes literally zero to predictions in prospect and other theories) enhances framing effects (e.g., Reyna & Brainerd, 1991b, 1995a). Other findings, such as that framing effects diminish if subjects are told that their choices will be executed repeatedly (which virtually eliminates categorical contrasts between some and none outcomes),

Table 7.4. *Examples of Principles Retrieved in Making Judgments and Decisions*

Equity Principle
    Everyone should have the same amount, everything else being equal (e.g.,
        salary, chance of survival).
Frequency Principle
    More numerous implies more probable, everything else being equal.
Cardinality Principle
    An ordering of classes with respect to inclusiveness is an ordering with
        respect to numerosity, everything else being equal.
Positive Preference Principle
    More is better than less (special case of general principle: some is better than
        none), everything else being equal (e.g., money gained, lives saved).
Negative Preference Principle
    Less is better than more (special case of general principle: none is better than
        some), everything else being equal (e.g., money lost, lives lost).

---

as opposed to once, are also consistent with fuzzy-trace theory's predictions (Gigerenzer, 1994; Keren, 1991; Wedell & Bockenholt, 1990, 1994).

Thus, fuzzy-trace theory does not imply that preferences are entirely constructed (cf. Payne et al., 1992) but are instead based on pre-existing values and principles that are not fully articulated in long-term memory (e.g., Rokeach & Ball-Rokeach, 1989). Qualitative memory representations address compatibility between the format of problems and values or principles. By representing problem information at a gist level, reasoners can map the problem onto comparably vague gist-level values and principles. Table 7.4 displays some of the values and principles that we have discussed over the years, ranging from morality to mathematics. These values or reasoning principles are not seen as universally valid in all problem situations, however.

The principle of equity, for instance, "Everyone should have the same chance of survival" (all things being equal) might compete against the principle that saving some lives is better than saving none (e.g., Reyna & Brainerd, 1991b; Tetlock, 1986). In the framing problems noted previously, many subjects would balk at the idea of saving 200 lives for sure if those 200 were selected because of race or income. This formulation of the problem would cue the equity principle, which is ordinarily not evoked in the standard formulation. Cuing the equity principle would likely shift preferences away from the sure option to the nondiscriminatory gamble (i.e., everyone has an equal chance to live or die). According to fuzzy-trace theory, the ability to recognize the relevance of general reasoning principles in specific and superficially disparate contexts is another feature of advanced reasoning.

An exciting development in recent research, one that portends well for the future, is the bringing together of concepts of values and emotion with those of cognitive representation and processing. Instead of arguing that cognition is not important and that emotion is, the most productive new approaches link what is already known about cognition with innovative ideas about emotion and motivation (e.g., Byrnes, 1998; Davidson, 1995; Isen, 1993; Klaczynski & Narasimham, 1998; Levin et al., 1998). For example, Klaczynski and Fauth (1997) have argued that emotion and cognition interact in specific ways in self-serving bias. When evidence supports their beliefs, subjects rely on a default mode of processing qualitative gist. When evidence contradicts cherished beliefs about the self, however, the same subjects engage in nonpreferred verbatim-level statistical reasoning, critiquing quantitative details.

Fuzzy-trace theory makes strong predictions about the form in which values, preferences, and emotion-laden attitudes are represented in long-term memory (namely, as fuzzy gists) and asserts that the valence of these dimensions determines behavior in judgment and decision tasks. In framing, for example, we have argued that some is preferred to none on positive dimensions such as "lives saved," whereas none is preferred to some on negative dimensions such as "lives lost" (e.g., Brainerd & Reyna, 1990a; Reyna & Brainerd, 1991a, 1991b, 1992, 1995a). We have also discussed similarities between moral values and decision principles, and how vaguely represented principles interact with task requirements, problem representations, retrieval of principles in context, and processing interference (e.g., Reyna & Brainerd, 1991a, 1992; see Table 7.5).

However, truly predictive theories of the effect of emotion on the quality of cognition are just beginning to be developed. Isen (e.g., 1993),

Table 7.5. *Degrees of Rationality: Analysis of Reasoning Errors*

Least Advanced
  1. Competence: Lack of knowledge of reasoning principle and how to apply it
  2. Representation: Interference from irrelevant verbatim details
  3. Representation: Failure to encode appropriate gist
  4. Representation: Interference from competing gists
  5. Retrieval: Failure to retrieve appropriate principle in context
  6. Processing: Errors in implementing reasoning principle
Most Advanced

for example, has shown that positive affect enhances human performance in a wide array of contexts. Some researchers have made the leap that emotion is a good guide for reasoning, perhaps an end in itself (i.e., rational behavior promotes happiness), with de rigueur evolutionary overtones. The tragedies that befall human beings when emotion clouds reason and judgment are ignored (Nisbett & Ross, 1980). Research that captures these subtleties, that explores the boundaries of emotion and cognition with a healthy respect for each of them, promises to be among the most practically important, bearing on such real-world issues as risk-taking in adolescence and the application of values in health care.

Degrees of Rationality: Judging Rationality Requires an Analysis of Reasoning Errors

Our analysis of rationality does not spring de novo from fuzzy-trace theory. Instead, we build on prior work concerning criteria for rationality, such as internal coherence and consistency with reality, but we suggest that some reasoning errors are "smarter" than others based on evidence of their order of emergence in cognitive development and on detailed process analyses of different types of errors (Reyna & Brainerd, 1994, 1995a). In order for judgment-and-decision-making research to be relevant to real-world issues, researchers must not shrink from clearly labeling some behaviors as irrational. Although prescriptive judgments about good and bad reasoning involve values and morality, and these must be separated from issues of fact, facts are germane to prescription. Rationality, in our view, goes beyond merely assisting people in achieving their own goals, no matter how misguided, inconsistent with reality, or self-destructive those goals might be. We count the selection of goals as fair game in judging the quality of cognition (see our subsequent comments about reconceptualizing the task). The title of a recent best-seller, *The Bed Was on Fire When I Lay Down on It*, provokes a chuckle about this obviously irrational behavior and, unfortunately, a twinge of recognition. Why does a teenager get into a car with a drunk driver? Why do people get married when they know they are making a mistake ("I knew it was a mistake, but the invitations had been sent out")? Why do they do it more than once? Is it enough to say that getting married and having fun are goals and that these behaviors satisfy those goals (e.g., Baron, 1988)? We contend that some goals should be questioned, and even rejected, although we realize that the value of others' goals may not be obvious. Research concerning the apparently rational tradeoffs favoring premature pregnancy among poor inner-city girls should give theorists pause in extrapolating their own limited experience to the goals of diverse groups (Loewenstein & Furstenberg, 1991). These subtleties do not imply that judging rationality is impossible, however, only that it is difficult without theoretical insight into the nature of thinking. What is needed, from our perspective, is an analysis that distinguishes different kinds of reasoning errors.

Knowledge of Reasoning Principles: Competence

Reasoning varies in quality, and this quality is judged when teachers assign grades, supervisors evaluate employees' problem-solving skills, and individuals characterize their own decisions as good or bad. According to fuzzy-trace theory, successful reasoning involves "selecting from among many relationships given as background facts, retrieving some among many principles that could be applied to such relationships, and, finally, applying the principles coherently" (Reyna & Brainerd, 1993, p. 105; see Table 7.5). Knowledge of the relevant reasoning principles (including how to apply them) is also necessary, but, empirically it has rarely been pinpointed as a major source of errors. Contrary to expectations of computational theories, reasoning errors typically occur despite excellent memory for relevant facts and the competence to solve problems correctly. Experiments that have teased apart sources of errors have shown that reasoners acted on the wrong representation for problems they were capable (in principle) of solving, or they failed to retrieve their knowledge, or they failed to implement knowledge that was retrieved.

These results support the intuitionist view of fuzzy-trace theory that reasoning is a dynamic, parallel, and uncertain process in which multiple representations of the same information are encoded, appropriate reasoning principles are cued with some probability, and the execution of processing is sometimes unreliable. This view contrasts with the usual definition of good reasoning as inherently serial (premise-like inputs are encoded, and then conclusions are drawn based on those inputs), logical, and precise. As we shall discuss, although there is growing acceptance of this alternative view of reasoning, theories differ in what to make of it. An easy, but unsatisfactory, explanation is to claim that dynamic variability is an issue of performance; in this way, the idea that reasoning competence is sound can be preserved. Instead, we decompose the concept of competence into particulars of rationality, that is, appropriate knowledge, representation, retrieval, and processing, given the task or question at hand (Table 7.5). This decomposition is predicated on detailed experimental evidence from many judgment and decision-making tasks (e.g., see Brainerd & Reyna, 1990b; Reyna, 1996a, 2000b; Reyna & Brainerd, 1991b, 1995a, 1998; Reyna & Ellis, 1994). We define rationality as the degree of adherence to appropriate processing in each particular. Each component of rationality for a given task is graded as shown in Table 7.5. Thus, ignorance of the reasoning principle – the nub of knowledge competence – is the worst error.

Verbatim Interference in Gist Tasks

The next, and slightly more intelligent, error is the representational mistake of operating on verbatim representations in a gist task. Literal thinking, whether it be lack of metaphorical understanding (A tie cannot be loud because loudness applies to sound; Reyna, 1996b; Reyna & Kiernan, 1995), lower levels of moral reasoning (Lying breaks the rules and should be punished regardless; Reyna & Brainerd, 1991a), or slavish adherence to the letter of what was said in an inference task (Brainerd & Reyna, 1993) fall into this category. Most judgment-and-decision-making tasks are gist tasks, such as transitive inference or discrimination among risk categories, that require the processing of meaning rather than rote retrieval of details (see Reyna, 1992, 1995). Because gist and verbatim representations of the same information can be distinguished a priori (i.e., imprecise semantic representations versus precise surface-level detail), it is possible to identify characteristic response patterns empirically. Clearly, a child who acknowledges that the experimenter said that the bird was in the cage and that the cage was under the table, but denies that the bird was under the table (because "you didn't say that"), is exhibiting verbatim interference in a gist task (especially given that the child can reason competently when asked to do so, as shown by Brainerd & Reyna, 1993). For such children, the better input sentences are remembered, the more likely it is that the true inference will be rejected (i.e., negative dependence). Verbatim interference in a gist task is demonstrated when reasoners substitute retrieval for thinking.

Failure to Encode Appropriate Gist

A somewhat more advanced error would be failure to encode the appropriate gist (perhaps encoding the correct facts but not their significance). This is the lack of recognition, conscious or unconscious, of abstract qualitative relations in the background information of a problem that are key to its solution. (Unlike the previous error, however, reasoners do not necessarily operate on verbatim representations.) In this case, reasoners "don't get it" in the sense that they do not understand what the judgment or decision is really about at a fundamental level (e.g., see Reyna & Brainerd, 1991a, 1995a, for reviews of relevant experimental evidence).

Von Winterfeldt and Edwards (1986) give some examples of this kind of error. They recount the true story of a 78-year-old academic facing progressive mental decline who had to decide whether to have a risky operation to restore blood flow to his brain. He decided to have the operation, but the actual sequence of events (he had a heart attack and was kept alive with "torturous life-sustaining procedures," p. 10) and the values that ultimately mattered were never considered in his decision about the surgery. The major omission in the decision process was the failure to consider that the alternative to successful surgery was not just death, but significant impairment of quality of life. Elaborate values matrices and decision trees were inadequate because the basic structure of the decision was flawed. At a verbatim level, innumerable possible outcomes are associated with surgery, but at a gist level, only major categories of outcomes matter. Unfortunately, the academic's decision analysis did not include a major outcome that ultimately occurred.

Similarly, in deciding whether to sue an uninsured motorist after a car accident, one of the authors failed to consider what "winning" a suit meant – that it did not necessarily mean obtaining a financial award and collecting it. Again, an elaborate decision analysis was not helpful because it failed to include an outcome that would have changed the decision maker's perspective on the problem. Both of these real-life examples concern unfamiliar decisions. The ability to recognize the basic structure of a decision can sometimes be learned through experience. Genetic counselors, for example, have greater experience than general medical practitioners in anticipating major outcomes of genetic testing for patients (e.g., Lloyd, Reyna, & Whalen, 2001), and in the case of the car accident, an experienced lawyer would presumably have realized that uncollected settlements are common.

The failure to encode appropriate gist often occurs in this early structuring phase of a decision or in predecision screening. Beach (e.g., 1990) and others have called for more attention to such predecision processes, and we agree, although we would place heavier emphasis on deeper processes of insight rather than peripheral processing

(Sternberg & Davidson, 1995). Evidence from verbal insight problems involving remote associates suggests that broad activation of gist meanings (coarse semantic coding) occurs in the right hemisphere, whereas narrow activation of precise meanings occurs in the left hemisphere (Bowden & Beeman, 1998; see also Schacter, Curran, Galluccio, Milberg, & Bates, 1996). Solutions to insight problems (e.g., What noun combines with each of three words to form a compound noun? FLY-WALL-NEWS; PAPER) can be activated in the right hemisphere, but they remain unconscious until interference subsides in the left hemisphere. As in our earlier discussion of knowledge competence, reasoners may have knowledge of the appropriate gist of decisions that is never consciously encoded into working memory. Remote associations about quality of life and uncollected monetary judgments may have been activated in the minds of our decision makers but were never brought into awareness.

Highly intelligent people can make this error of not encoding appropriate gist. Our grading of errors concerns the behavior (stupid) rather than the person (smart), although we acknowledge individual differences in reasoning (Stanovich & West, 1998, 2000). One of the most important questions for anyone interested in improving human judgment and decision making (educators, employers, psychotherapists) is why smart people, who often have the requisite competence, reason poorly or make stupid choices. In our view, lack of insight into the gist of a judgment or decision at this early structuring stage of processing is partly to blame. Although reasoners may overlook fundamental relationships in information at this stage when they make errors, when they are successful they may reconceptualize the judgment or decision task entirely (though appropriately). We have argued that this ability to ignore verbatim details and to perceive the underlying essence of a problem is a defining feature of rationality (e.g., Reyna, 1991; Reyna & Brainerd, 1993, 1994, 1995a).

Gist Interference

The next level of error involves active interference from competing gists. In this situation, the reasoner has encoded the appropriate gist representation of the problem but fails to use that representation. Reasoning is usurped by a competing (often accurate) conceptualization of the background information. Many theorists wish to stop here and claim that this reasoning is rational because it is internally accurate. The question is said to be tricky, but the reasoning is supposedly sound (see Reyna, 1991; Reyna & Brainerd, 1994, 1995a). The problem is that subjects fix on a salient gist representation that seems to answer the question or solve the problem, except that it does not.

For example, disputes in health care policy sometimes revolve around whether absolute or relative risk is at issue. Should health care resources be directed on the basis of rapid increases in relative risk (e.g., rate of women contracting acquired immune deficiency syndrome [AIDS] relative to men) or on absolute risk (e.g., the rate of AIDS among women)? Stone, Yates, and Parker (1994) investigated the gist representations involved in judgments of risk and showed how such representations become confused. Reyna and Brainerd (1993) presented a related example from a news report about dangerous playground equipment in which the probability of an accident given that a child was playing on a specific kind of equipment (e.g., slides) was confused with the probability that a child was playing on that equipment given that there was an accident. Decision makers confused these conditional probabilities and contemplated removing the most popular (played on the most often) rather than the most dangerous equipment from playgrounds.

In these examples, the wrong gist was an accurate representation of reality (e.g., a correct estimate of the wrong probability) but an inappropriate representation for the task at hand. Competing gists can produce powerful cognitive illusions because reasoners have an accurate representation of facts that seems to solve the problem. In the absence of processing interference (see later), interference from competing gists does not necessarily make reasoners feel confused; they have what they think is a perfectly adequate solution. If the question concerns which class has more (e.g., Are there more cows or more animals?), then salient information about relative numerosity (e.g., the number of cows) seems relevant, as opposed to the nonnumerical logic that animals include cows. If the question concerns dangerousness, then the frequency of accidents seems relevant. Thus, the illusion is particularly powerful if contextual cues seem to be compatible with the competing gist (Brainerd & Reyna, 1990b; Reyna, 1991).

Failure to Retrieve Relevant Reasoning Principles

If reasoning becomes derailed at the representational level, either because of failure to encode relevant relationships or because irrelevant relationships are more salient than relevant ones, the correct reasoning principle may not be retrieved (e.g., Reyna & Brainerd, 1991a). If the correct principle is not retrieved, manipulations that improve the mechanics of processing will not be effective (Brainerd & Reyna, 1990b; Reyna, 1991). Although we have discussed each kind of cognitive error separately, representation, retrieval, and processing are interconnected. Representational errors can lead reasoners down a garden path, so that the appropriate reasoning principles are not retrieved. However, relevant principles are also cued by the form of the question. A question of the form "Are there more *A*'s than *B*'s?" tends to elicit a relative magnitude principle (i.e., the set with the greater number of objects has more). The Piagetian class-inclusion question "Are there more animals or more cows?" is of this general form, and it (erroneously) elicits relative magnitude judgments in children. Children say that there are more cows than animals because they compare the relative magnitude of cows and horses (which are prominently displayed). The form of the Piagetian class-inclusion question is misleading (though this is not sufficient by itself to cause the class-inclusion error; Reyna, 1991). Although adults do not commit errors on the Piagetian task, they do show evidence of difficulty with such questions, including large increases in response time (e.g., Rabinowitz, Howe, & Lawrence, 1989), and they commit errors in opaque versions of class-inclusion tasks such as the conjunction fallacy (Reyna, 1991).

Retrieval failure – not noticing in a specific context that a known reasoning principle is relevant – is also a failure of insight, but it is less profound than misperceiving the problem information. This error tends to become apparent later in development, after representational errors decrease. Retrieval failures can sometimes be remedied easily, for example, by prefacing a subtle task with one in which the relevance of the reasoning principle is more obvious. Increasing nonspecific accessibility of the principle can be sufficient to ensure its application. Taking more time to respond can increase access to reasoning principles (as activation accumulates over time). For example, when children are told to wait at least 15 seconds before responding, class-inclusion errors are reduced. The Gestalt psychologists simply urged reasoners to "Think!" to decrease functional fixedness (e.g., Reyna 1991; Reyna & Brainerd, 1991a). Unlike errors involving competing gists, those that are due only to retrieval failure can typically be undone by drawing attention to the relevant principle. With practice in a task domain, reasoners become better able to recognize contextual cues to principles and call on them more reliably.

Processing Interference

Once retrieved, the reasoning principle must be applied coherently to the facts of the problem. Reasoners may have the knowledge to apply a principle and be aware of its relevance, but get bogged down in the mechanics of processing. Syllogistic reasoning, and other tasks involving overlapping classes, provide common examples of such processing interference (Johnson-Laird, 1983; Reyna, 1991, 1995). Given premises of the form All A are B and Some B are C, reasoners can lose track of the "marginal" members of the classes (e.g., the B's that are not A) and erroneously conclude that Some A are C. Conversion errors, assuming that All A are B means that All B are A, are another example of losing track of the marginals, the members that fall outside of a line of reasoning, say, from A to C (see also Wolfe, 1995). Such errors increase as processing interference increases but not as memory load increases. So, for example, as the overlap among classes increases, class-inclusion errors go up, but errors decrease as the number of nonoverlapping classes increases (Reyna & Brainerd, 1995a). Providing a notational system that allows reasoners to keep track of the entities being processed can eliminate processing errors. For example, using Venn diagrams or distinctive labels for superordinate classes significantly reduces errors in class-inclusion tasks (Agnoli, 1991; Reyna, 1991). We have argued that these kinds of processing errors do not reflect an absence of logical competence, but instead reflect sensitivity to interference from multiple sources in executing that competence. Because verbatim representations are especially susceptible to interference, reasoners who avoid processing details (and rely on more robust gist) can reduce these errors. However, processing interference is the least likely error to be overcome by advanced reasoners and continues to be a source of performance decrements into adulthood.

Summary of Errors

In summary, our conception of rationality is the degree to which reasoning fits a cognitive ideal whose components are knowledge, accurate representation of information, recognizing the gist of a problem, reliance on appropriate gist representations rather than surface details, resisting interference from inappropriate gist, retrieval of relevant reasoning principles in context, and implementing those principles coherently. Such practices provide global advantages to reasoning performance.

Accurate representation of information at multiple levels of precision confers cognitive flexibility in approaching different tasks. By *accurate*, we mean consistent (but not superficially identical) with reality (see Reyna & Brainerd, 1994, 1995a). Hence, ideal cognition satisfies both external correspondence with reality and internal coherence.

Coherence is achieved by perceiving the underlying essence, or gist, across superficially disparate problems. We agree with Tversky and Kahneman (e.g., 1986) that internal coherence or consistency is a minimal condition for rationality. In many well-known examples, coherence rests on semantic consistency, not on particular theories of probability. For example, in the conjunction fallacy, the meaning of the terms stipulates their class-inclusion relations. Once the classes are identified, whatever is true of the class must apply to an instance of that class. Numerical inferences, any inferences for that matter, must apply according to class-inclusion relations. In the same way, apples cannot be more numerous than fruits only because apples are defined as a type (subclass) of fruit. Differences among theories of numerosity, probability, and the like are superfluous as to whether an error has been committed.

Although knowledge, retrieval, and coherent implementation of abstract reasoning principles are required for ideal reasoning, the validity of principles is determined by their relevance in a context. Thus, if a Bayesian principle is relevant to solving a problem and a reasoner does not apply that principle, an error has been committed. (For example, if one is working with unknown or unreliable probabilities, Bayesian principles may not be relevant.) As we have seen, this error may be one of degree, depending on what other cognitive processes have occurred. Relevance, however, is determined by the requirements of the task itself a priori, not by what people do a posteriori.

Finally, we eschew the dominant information processing view of maximal rationality, or optimality, that "more is better" as far as processing relevant information goes. According to fuzzy-trace theory, processing more information more precisely, even if it were possible, is not the key to rationality. In practice, reasoners process verbatim details in parallel with gist and may spend more time processing the former than the latter. However, their judgments and decisions are ultimately determined by the least precise gist that they can use to perform the task (e.g., crude ordinal-level distinctions along quantitative dimensions in choice tasks, such as more versus less). Gist is not the result of a system overburdened by information that breaks down, but is the preferred mode of processing that must be disrupted in order for verbatim-level processing to occur.

A Comprehensive Theory of Inclusion Illusions: Conjunction, Disjunction, Conditional Probability, Base Rates, and Bayesian Updating

Inclusion illusions illustrate difficulties in representation (gist interference), retrieval, and processing. It has long been noted that children have difficulty processing relations among partially overlapping classes. Standard examples include the late acquisition of fractions (Spinillo & Bryant, 1991), physical properties involving proportionality (Moore, et al., 1991), and other ratio concepts, such as probability (Reyna & Brainerd, 1994). As we have noted, however, adults also have difficulty with class-inclusion tasks, as in the conjunction fallacy. Moreover, both children and adults can perform well at such tasks when the classes are labeled or some other mental bookkeeping system is used to keep the classes distinctive (e.g., Agnoli, 1991; Brainerd & Reyna, 1990b; Johnson-Laird, 1983). Research has established that the main difficulties in processing do not reflect a lack of understanding of ratio concepts or a failure of logical competence. For the most part, reasoners understand the semantic and logical relations among classes, but they lose track of classes during processing. In the ensuing confusion, competing gists usurp the role of relevant class relations, creating powerful cognitive illusions. So, for example, children compare a larger number of cows to a smaller number of horses and respond that there are more cows than animals. The cows-more-than-horses gist competes with the relevant relation between cows and animals. It must be emphasized that these effects cannot be attributed to trick questions or verbal ambiguity (e.g., Gricean conversational maxims that are used, post hoc, to justify alternative interpretations of the question). The ambiguity of questions allows the effect to occur but does not cause it. When the form of the question rules out misinterpretation, the effects are reduced slightly, but they remain significant (Brainerd & Reyna, 1990b; Reyna, 1991).

In 1991, Reyna used fuzzy-trace theory to explain these inclusion illusions, encompassing the conjunction fallacy, syllogistic reasoning, and other tasks (see also Davidson, 1995; Reyna & Brainerd, 1993, 1994, 1995a). Wolfe (1995) extended the analysis to additional aspects of conditional probability judgments, causal reasoning, and base-rate neglect. Table 7.6 summarizes our current claims about inclusion illusions. The table integrates the earlier analyses, but it also adds disjunctive probability judgments (i.e., the probability of A or B) to the account, providing a processing-level explanation for biases in judging explicit and implicit

Table 7.6. *An Integrative Theory of Inclusion Illusions*

Task	Superordinate	Gist	Nongist Class	Effect
Probability judgment	Total sample	Targets	Nontargets	Denominator neglect
Class inclusion	Animals	Cows	Horses	Cows > Animals
Conjunction fallacy	Bank tellers (BT)	Nonfeminist bank tellers	Feminist bank tellers	Feminist BT > BT
Disjunction bias	CAD; MI	Not MI CAD; MI CAD	MI CAD; MI Not CAD	CAD or MI = CAD
Conditional probability	P(A); P(B)	AB; BA	A Not B; B Not A	P(A/B) = P(B/A)
Syllogistic reasoning	B; C	AB; BC	B Not A; C Not B	Figural effects
Bayesian updating	Positive result	Disease, positive	No Disease, positive	Base-rate neglect

Note: CAD = coronary artery disease; MI = myocardial infarction.

disjunctions (Tversky & Koehler, 1994). This explanation draws on the data generated by support theory, as well as our own data, and shares the assumption that the effects have to do with the accessibility of concepts in memory.

Two specific claims are central to our argument. First, we assume that judgments about a class are made on the basis of the gist of that class. (This explanation is semantic in character and resembles our theory of metaphorical interpretation, that vague gists of word meanings are instantiated in context; see Reyna, 1996b; Reyna & Kiernan, 1995.) As the term implies, the *gist* of a class does not refer to its full extension (although the fuzziness of gist allows it to be applied more or less broadly, depending on the context). In Table 7.6, the gist of a class such as "bank tellers" (i.e., typical bank tellers) is distinguished from the nongist subclass of bank tellers, that is, atypical bank tellers. One might prefer to buy a Lincoln Continental rather than a Toyota Corolla but prefer new Corollas to old Lincolns. Initially, in the buying context, we tend to think of newer cars; the gist of a "Lincoln" is a shiny late-model luxury car. This gist assumption explains intransitivities in preferences and in similarity judgments because the gist of a class should change predictably in different contexts (e.g., Baron, 1988; Hogarth, 1980). Stone et al. (1994), for example, have shown how the gist interpretation of small quantities as essentially nil affects risk judgments. The meaning of *nil*, of course, depends on the nature of the dimensions involved in a judgment (i.e., a pinch of arsenic is not nil, but a pinch of flour is).

Specifically, the gist is the prototype of that class in that context: its larger, more frequent, stereotypical, causally salient, target (e.g., the winning color), or linked (e.g., in syllogistic reasoning) subclass (Table 7.6). For example, when we think of a bank teller, a conservative type springs to mind – nonfeminist bank tellers. Feminist bank tellers are not consciously rejected; they simply do not fit the gist of the class of bank tellers. In the conjunction fallacy task, therefore, subjects rank the probability that Linda fits the gist of a bank teller, a graded similarity judgment (Reyna & Brainerd, 1995a, 1998; see Tversky & Kahneman, 1983). Psychologically, it is not so much that subjects overestimate the probability that Linda is a feminist bank teller, but that they underestimate the probability that she is a bank teller.

Our second assumption is that reasoners usually avoid the complexities of overlapping classes by comparing nonoverlapping classes, specifically, the gist of one class to the gist of another distinct class or to a complementary nongist class. (A major difference between the explanation offered for the conjunction fallacy by the representativeness heuristic and by fuzzy-trace theory is the role of processing interference in reasoning with overlapping classes; see Reyna, 1991, and Brainerd & Reyna, 1990b, for empirical tests.) The more layers of overlapping classes (i.e., ratios of ratios), the more likely it is that reasoning errors will occur. Although reasoners focus on gist, they do not misunderstand what the classes refer to. Thus, in the class-inclusion task (Table 7.6), subjects think "cows" when they are asked about animals because that is the larger subclass of animals in that context. However, they also realize that the horses are animals and will answer questions about the horses correctly (class-inclusion errors are still common among 10-year-olds who are well aware that horses are animals). Moreover, when asked, children will explain that the cows and the horses are animals (and still claim that there are more cows than animals).

Emphasis on the gist of a class also helps explain *denominator neglect*, the tendency to focus on the positive instances of a class – the targets – rather than on nontargets (Reyna & Brainerd, 1993; Wolfe, 1995). The positive instances are the dieters who lost weight in a program, the "many ways to win" in the state lottery, the evidence that favors guilt, the number of times our opinions are confirmed, and so on. Denominator neglect is exemplified when subjects prefer drawing from a sample with four winning tokens out of eight to drawing from a sample with one winner out of two (Acredolo, O'Connor, Banks, & Horobin, 1989; Reyna & Brainerd, 1994; see Epstein, 1994, for similar findings with a different explanation). With one superordinate class and a simple probability judgment, focusing on gist merely introduces a bias in judgments that can be resisted if reasoners access information about the negative instances – the nongist class (e.g., dieters who did not lose weight, the many ways to lose the lottery, the nonwinning tokens).

The reference class (the denominator that contains nontargets) is not always so transparent, however. Consider the true story of two police officers found guilty of falsifying overtime forms. Their trial concentrated on the evidence for and against the truth of the overtime reports; records and witnesses were examined to prove that the officers could not have been on duty when they said that they were. Neither the defense nor the prosecution brought out the fact that a handful of questionable forms was culled from hundreds that these officers had filed over the years that showed no irregularities (the nontargets). Although it is impossible to estimate the exact probability of errors on such forms by chance alone, it is likely to be greater than zero.

The case of two samples of targets and nontargets is a simple generalization of the one-sample case. We expect specific manifestations of denominator neglect in the two-sample situation, however. As Reyna and Brainerd (1994) discussed, problems that involve comparing relative frequencies for two samples should be harder if the number of targets is fewer in the higher-probability sample (offset by fewer nontargets, hence a smaller denominator). Subjects compare gists for the two samples (the relative magnitude of targets) and pay less attention to the number of nontargets, which is why such examples have been called *interference* problems (Reyna & Brainerd, 1994).

As Table 7.6 shows, similar explanations apply to syllogistic reasoning, conditional probability, Bayesian updating, and disjunctive probability judgment. As we have mentioned with respect to syllogisms, given premises that link two classes such as A and B, subjects focus on the linked subclasses (e.g., the B's that are A's) rather than the parenthetical classes (e.g., B's that are not A's). Although this does not account for all syllogistic errors, it correctly predicts figural effects, such as the tendency to reach A–C conclusions given premises of the form A–B and B–C. In conditional probability judgments of the form $P(A/B)$, the conditional probability of A given B, subjects also focus on the B's that are A's and neglect the B's that are not A's. Because the joint probability of A and B is common to both conditional probabilities (only the denominator, or base rate of A or B, respectively, differs), subjects tend to confuse the two conditional probabilities. As fuzzy-trace theory predicts, the tendency to neglect the base rate (e.g., the probability of B that is composed of both the gist and nongist classes) was associated with the tendency to commit these conversion errors, that is confusing P(A/B) with P(B/A) (Wolfe, 1995). Bayesian updating is merely a special case of conditional probability judgment in which, for example, the sensitivity of a test (the probability of a positive result given disease) is confused with the positive predictive value (the probability of disease given a positive result; see Table 7.6). As in conditional probability judgment generally, base rates (i.e., pretest probabilities or prevalence rates) are inadequately considered when reasoners update their probabilities based on a test result (e.g., see Eddy, 1982, for numerous examples of this bias in medicine).

The final illustration of inclusion illusions concerns disjunctive probability judgment. Here we mainly discuss explicit disjunctions, although our analysis applies equally to implicit disjunctions. Implicit (e.g., the probability of death for a 20-year-old man) and explicit disjunctions (e.g., the probability of accidental death or death from all other causes for a 20-year-old man) ostensibly refer to the same overall class. As has been noted, explicit disjunctions provide retrieval cues that influence probability estimates (once again underlining the relevance of memory to judgment and decision making). In the aggregate, death seems a remote possibility for a young man until one is reminded, in the explicit disjunction, about the probability of car accidents and other sources of accidental injuries. Implicit and explicit disjunctions also differ in that varying the verbal description of classes is bound to introduce differences in sense, though not in reference (Johnson-Laird, 1983). Because the gist of a class is its sense or meaning, such different descriptions are likely to evoke different gists, leading to different probability judgments.

In other respects, we explain disjunction much the same way as our other examples of inclusion illusions. Consider judging the probability that a patient (e.g., one experiencing chest pain in an emergency room) either has clinically significant coronary artery disease (CAD) or is at imminent risk of a myocardial infarction (MI or heart attack). This disjunction is special because a national guideline on chest pain developed by the Agency for Health Care Policy and Research (now called the Agency for Health Care Research and Quality) has recommended that physicians make exactly this judgment. Over 6 million patients present to emergency rooms every year with chest pain, and many adverse outcomes (e.g., death) can be prevented by medication and other interventions if their risk is estimated accurately.

We presented 66 physicians with nine case descriptions, eliciting their probability judgments for CAD and MI separately, as well as the overall disjunction of CAD or MI (Reyna et al., 1997). Results showed that about one in five judgments violated logical constraints (e.g., the disjunctive probability was smaller than one or both of the separate probabilities). The most common result (55% of responses), however, was that the disjunctive probability exactly equaled the probability of CAD. Technically, this is not a logical violation if all patients at risk for MI also have significant CAD. Indeed, the gist for MI is the class of patients who are at risk for MI because of clinically significant CAD (the class of "MI and CAD"). Although MIs do occur without significant CAD (suggesting that physicians underestimated the disjunctive probabilities), this is not the typical etiology for MIs. Interestingly, the class of "MI and CAD" is the nongist class in judging the probability of CAD. Although most MIs are associated with CAD, CAD is usually present without a significant risk of MI. The risk of MI occurs later in the disease process. Thus, the class of "CAD and not MI" is the gist for coronary disease. As in two-sample probability judgment, physicians appear to combine the gists – CAD not MI and CAD MI – to estimate the disjunctive probability, which explains why most disjunctive judgments equal the probability of CAD (i.e., CAD not MI + CAD MI = CAD). The atypical class – MI not CAD – is neglected. Physicians are generally aware that MIs occur without CAD, but this nongist class falls outside of a salient causal chain from CAD to resulting MIs.

Thus, class-inclusion errors that were first studied in children can be found, in a somewhat more sophisticated form, among experts in cardiology. Like children, adults sometimes focus on salient relationships that are inappropriate to the question at hand. Adults, too, are subject to errors of representation, retrieval, and processing. Although such errors are less likely in adults than in children, they are not fundamentally different (Reyna & Brainerd, 1993). Regarding representations, adults are sometimes misled by salient patterns into responding to the wrong gist (Tversky & Kahneman, 1981, 1983). The same psychological processes that make representation and retrieval more reliable in adults make biases more reliable. With experience, adults come to recognize familiar patterns quickly and may leap to retrieval of well-known, but inappropriate, principles. Therefore, manipulating the cues in a problem produces systematic errors in reasoning (e.g., Kahneman et al., 1982; Reyna & Brainerd, 1991a). As inclusion illusions (e.g., denominator neglect), false recognition errors, and a host of other effects demonstrate, adults are less subject to interference, but they are not immune. Although development involves increasing resistance to interference and greater reliance on gist, mature processing has predictable pitfalls. However, reliance on gist allows mature reasoners to perceive the underlying patterns across superficially disparate problems, which is essential for achieving cognitive consistency – a fundamental criterion of rationality (Tversky & Kahneman, 1986). Thus, gist-based reasoning provides global advantages to performance, despite local pitfalls in solving particular problems.

The Role of Developmental Research in Judgment and Decision Making

As the analysis of class-inclusion errors illustrates, developmental research provides an important perspective on judgment and decision making in adults. The argument for the relevance of developmental research is analogous to the case for individual differences research, which has proven to be a rich source of evidence bearing on rationality (Stanovich & West, 2000). In particular, studying the origins of judgment and decision making deepens our understanding of adults in two ways: First, it supplies a separate body of evidence that can be used to select among competing theories. Because development is widely viewed as progress toward rationality, developmental trends bear directly on conceptions of rationality. There is no need to limit our discussion to speculation when abundant developmental evidence exists about how reasoning changes with experience and expertise. For example, as children get older, they become more likely to process qualitative gist; they also become more risk averse (Reyna, 1996a; Reyna & Ellis, 1994). These observations have implications for what we consider to be advanced reasoning.

Second, developmental research has provided sensible explanations of otherwise puzzling aspects of adult thinking. With respect to the classic cognitive developmental paradigms, errors decline with age. Computational skills clearly improve during childhood and, for some tasks, must be invoked (Moore et al., 1991). On the other hand, certain judgmental and decision-making biases increase with age. For example, Jacobs and Potenza (1991) found that young children's probability judgments were not biased by the *representativeness heuristic*, but use of the heuristic increased with age, and adults' judgments were inferior to those of children. Similarly, Davidson (1991) showed that older children were more likely to use noncompensatory reasoning in decision making compared to younger children. Reyna and Ellis (1994) found that the framing bias also increased with age, and, like probability judgment and decision making, risky decision making departed increasingly from the ideal quantitative model (see also Reyna & Brainerd, 1993).

These contradictions are puzzling because some of the same concepts are involved in developmental research and in the judgment and decision-making literature (see also Winer, Craig, & Weinbaum, 1992). Based on research in cognitive development, one would conclude that probability judgment improves as children grow older (Reyna & Brainerd, 1994). The implication would be that once those same children became adults, they would perform at least as well as, if not better than, young children. However, if we define *better* as processing ratios of frequencies, that implication is false. As we have seen, adults are likely to use relative magnitude of targets rather than ratios to judge probability (although they are capable of computing the correct ratios). Adults and older children are also more likely to reject appropriate quantitative information in a biasing context than younger children (Davidson, 1995; Jacobs & Potenza, 1991), and they are more likely to make intuitive rather than quantitative judgments when the latter are optional (Lovett & Singer, 1991). Finally, adults' errors in probability judgment have been demonstrated in numerous studies on heuristics and biases (Kahneman et al., 1982). It is not just that adult cognition is not quite as advanced as it should be. The biases research and the cognitive developmental research imply opposite views of adult competence in judgment and decision making.

The contradictions between the developmental and adult research point up the need to account for task variability. Fuzzy-trace theory accounts for this variability by distinguishing between knowledge competence and other sources of errors. We argue that adults generally have quantitative competence, but they tend not to engage in such processing unless compelled by the task. Young children's computational skills are more limited than those of adults. However, for many tasks, young children know the relevant concept and can sometimes demonstrate that competence. In probability judgment, sensitive techniques, such as functional measurement, reveal advanced competence even among first graders (Acredolo, et al., 1989; Jacobs & Potenza, 1991). Correct reasoning, however, involves more than competence. It also involves focusing on appropriate representations, as well as retrieval and implementation of appropriate principles (Tables 7.4 to 7.6). Each of these components has been shown to make independent contributions to successful reasoning (e.g., Reyna & Brainerd, 1995a). Thus, demonstrations of early competence in probability judgment place adult reasoning in perspective (Reyna & Brainerd, 1994). Developmental research, which assesses competence despite variations in performance, has provided a theoretical framework for evaluating adult reasoning errors.

Applications to a Naturalistic Context: A Fuzzy-Trace Theory of Medical Judgment and Decision Making

Using the elements of our arguments, it should be possible to explain the nature and development of decision making in naturalistic contexts. In particular, we shall draw together our discussions of the development of expertise, decision structuring (including hypothesis generation), and Bayesian updating to characterize natural reasoning in medicine. Our comments in this section are drawn from the clinical experience of physicians and the medical literature, as well as psychological research (Lloyd & Reyna, 2001; Lloyd et al., 2001; Reyna & Hamilton, 2001; Reyna et al., 1997, 2001).

The development of clinical expertise begins in medical schools, which traditionally emphasize verbatim memory for large amounts of information learned in very short time frames. This often takes the form of memorizing lists of information. It is a widely held belief that clinical decision making relies on a "fund of knowledge," and that much of this knowledge can be captured in lists. However, naturalistic clinical problem solving involves integration of facts and interpretation of data under conditions of uncertainty, a more gist-based process. Thus, although much of the inculcated knowledge is important, physicians typically experience discordance between the reasoning style of their academic training and the demands of clinical decision making.

Some clinicians respond to this discordance by redoubling their efforts to memorize all relevant information, a task that is becoming more difficult as the fund of knowledge expands. For example, only a decade ago, a handful of medications was available to treat most conditions. Today, there are often 10 or more, with highly similar names and features. The physician who attempts to recall and apply this verbatim information may be encouraged by the increased availability of protocols and guidelines, often also in the form of tables and lists. Clinical practice guidelines are available from government and private agencies, such as the U.S. Task Force for Preventive Health, American Heart Association,

National Cancer Institute, and others. In radiology alone, decision rules have recently been published for obtaining ankle films (i.e., rules for the appropriateness of ordering films), chest x-rays, and lumbosacral spine films (Heckerling et al., 1990; Jarvik, Deyo, & Koepsell, 1996; Stiell et al., 1994).

Technology has exacerbated the problem of information overload. A common reaction of experienced physicians to expert systems or computer decision support (e.g., Iliad, 1994; QMR, Gaspar & Ebell, 1995; or Dxplain, http://www.lcs.mgh.harvard.edu) is that they are useful for students but not practical for busy clinicians. They provide too much irrelevant detail and often compromise the basic structure of the decision by failing to include major diagnostic hypotheses. The development of Internet tools, the on-line accessibility of large warehouses of data and information, the electronic publication of Web-based textbooks such as *Harrison's Principles of Internal Medicine* (http:///www.harrisonsonlline.com), and services such as MDConsult (http:///www.mdconsult.com), with updates from major journals and medical organizations, have combined to provide a surfeit of verbatim information. However, the physician must be able to retrieve at least some information from memory and be able to apply it effectively in clinical decision making.

Few of these decision aids are designed to support the gist-based processing of medical experts (see Table 7.7 for an illustration of expert clinical reasoning). In contrast to the funds of knowledge and mnemonics of the verbatim approach, naturalistic medical decision making involves applying knowledge in ways that go beyond memorized examples (i.e., transfer), understanding the mechanisms of disease processes (e.g., understanding how pneumonia can be present and chest x-rays can be normal), generating relatively few highly probable diagnostic hypotheses, interpreting diagnostic tests, and converting the uncertain results of such tests into categorical decisions (e.g., admit or discharge). Probability judgments are inherent in these processes, though they are generally categorical (i.e., low, intermediate, or high). Much of the reasoning in diagnosis is qualitative and gist-based because of the need to integrate subjective and objective information in order to develop a working hypothesis.

The last several stages of decision making map onto elements of Bayesian updating that we have discussed: the determination of pretest probabilities and the interpretation of test results to take account of both pretest probabilities and test characteristics (e.g., sensitivity). This base

Table 7.7. *A Case History of Medical Judgment and Decision Making*

Presentation

A 67-year-old female seen in the emergency room complaining of left-sided
chest pain and shortness of breath is found to have a very low oxygen
saturation that requires over 40% oxygen to correct it to normal levels. She
was seen in the emergency room 2 days prior to this admission because of
complaints of a cough, fatigue, and malaise. At that time, she was given a
diagnosis of bronchitis and discharged on antibiotics.

History and Physical

Her past medical history is significant only for hypertension controlled by
medication. There is no significant family history of disease. She is retired
and lives in Arizona with her husband. She does not smoke tobacco or
drink alcohol. The physical exam revealed reduced breath sounds in the
right posterior lung fields and increased tactile fremitus consistent with
pneumonia. The rest of the exam was essentially normal. She had normal
vital signs except for a slightly increased respiratory rate. The chest x-ray
and blood tests were all reported as normal except for the blood gas
measurement, which revealed a low oxygen saturation of 84% (normal,
above 90%).

Differential Diagnoses

A working diagnosis includes pneumonia, pulmonary embolus, and
bronchitis. Although the chest x-ray does not reveal pneumonia, it may
be falsely negative because the clinical presentation of pneumonia may
precede radiographic evidence. Bronchitis does not usually cause reduced
oxygen saturation unless there is underlying lung disease or congestive
heart failure, and this clinical scenario suggests neither. By far the most
important diagnosis that must be considered is pulmonary embolism. It
typically occurs in patients who are bed bound or who have recently had
surgery. Patients with deep venous thrombosis of the lower extremities are
at especially high risk for a pulmonary embolism. The incidence in the
general population is about 1 in 1,000 persons. In this patient, the
unexplained hypoxia, which requires at least 40% oxygen, and the absence
of a viable alternative diagnosis suggest a high probability of pulmonary
embolism (85% or higher).

Diagnostic Tests

The test with the highest sensitivity and specificity for pulmonary embolism
is the pulmonary angiogram, but it is invasive. Alternative diagnostic tests
have been developed, including the ventilation-perfusion scan and the
spiral computed tomography (CT) scan. Other tests, including D-dimer and
ultrasonography of the lower extremities, are also sometimes used to aid in
the diagnosis of pulmonary embolism. The important clinical decision is

Table 7.7. *(continued)*

whether the patient requires anticoagulation with heparin and eventually with warfarin – a treatment that may require months to years in order to prevent the recurrence of the pulmonary embolism. Anticoagulation therapy is not without risk, as a small but significant number of patients on this therapy have life-threatening bleeding.

It is not appropriate to place the patient at an increased risk of bleeding unless a pulmonary embolism is confirmed by a reliable test. The spiral CT scan and the ventilation-perfusion scan are sufficiently specific to provide ample evidence of pulmonary embolism if positive, but they are not sufficient to exclude disease if negative and if the patient has a high probability of a pulmonary embolism.

Results and Decisions

A spiral CT scan was performed and was negative. To the verbatim decision maker, the negative CT scan may be interpreted as negative for pulmonary embolism. The patient may then be given an alternative diagnosis, such as bronchitis with unexplained hypoxia. However, the gist decision maker would likely order a pulmonary angiogram. If it is negative, the workup for the patient's hypoxia will be considered complete, although pneumonia remains a possibility. A pulmonary angiogram was ordered and a pulmonary embolism was diagnosed. The patient was placed on anticoagulation therapy, with a small risk of bleeding but a marked reduction in the risk of recurrence of a life-threatening pulmonary embolism.

rate or pretest probability is especially important in clinical medicine because of the imperfect predictive abilities of most diagnostic tests. Few gold-standard tests exist in medicine, and they are usually invasive, painful, or risky (e.g., exploratory surgery, tests requiring the insertion of catheters). The process that expert clinicians use to determine posttest predictive value is almost never verbatim calculation, but is a gist-based process (e.g., Lloyd & Reyna, 2001). The gist for interpretation of diagnostic tests may include qualitative principles such as the following: (1) When the pretest probability is high, the test's sensitivity must be very high in order to exclude the possibility of disease (usually one needs the gold standard). (2) When the pretest probability is low, the specificity of the test must be very high to exclude the possibility of disease. (3) Once results are obtained, positive and negative predictive values depend on the sensitivity and specificity of the diagnostic test and the pretest probability of disease (or base rate). Table 7.7 presents a case history of an actual patient that illustrates these aspects of medical judgment and decision making.

In summary, the development of medical expertise seems to involve processing fewer dimensions of information more simply, interpreting the gist of subjective symptoms, understanding how signs and symptoms reflect the underlying disease process, and acquiring qualitative principles to interpret probabilistic information. Often the available diagnostic tests are known to be insensitive or lack specificity for a particular clinical condition. However, they may be the best alternative to invasive, potentially harmful, and sometimes nonexistent gold standards. Such decision making determines patient outcomes and public health. Decision aids and technological tools that are compatible with naturalistic, gist-based decision processes are needed to bridge the gap between medical information and clinical implementation. Development of these aids must be accompanied by detailed task analyses so that biases are not inadvertently increased.

Overview

Rather than characterizing judgment and decision making as either correct or incorrect, or understanding as either present or absent, fuzzy-trace theory identifies different levels of reasoning. In order of sophistication, these range from failure to know a reasoning principle, to failure to appreciate the relevance of that principle in varied contexts, to failure to recognize and correct misdirections in reasoning that are due to interference (Reyna, 1995; Reyna & Brainerd, 1990, 1991a). Do the facts that these failures occur in mature reasoners, that some biases actually increase with age and expertise, and that reasoning is mostly intuitive (rather than logical or computational) indicate that human reasoning is irrational?

According to fuzzy-trace theory, although the competence necessary for rationality can often be demonstrated, acts of human reasoning are sometimes rational and sometimes irrational – and they vary by degrees. Fuzzy-trace theory provides a framework in which degrees of rationality can be specified. The empirical contradictions and variability that have been discussed exist within each mind, although they are exhibited across tasks. The same mind is both quantitative and qualitative, self-regulated and impulsive, fair-minded and self-serving, logical and emotional. Fuzzy-trace theorists differ from some recent theorists (e.g., Gigerenzer and colleagues) in that they acknowledge that many of these tendencies are not adaptive. There are stupid, self-defeating behaviors. The conjunction fallacy is one of them, and it is linked to interference errors, not to any particular theory of probability. The conjunction fallacy violates ordinal assumptions common to all of these theories and is not justified by verbal ambiguity, such as Gricean conversational maxims (which accounts for little variance in any case). Inclusion illusions, such as the conjunction fallacy, are attributable to interference from inappropriate gists, from irrelevant reasoning principles, and from processing of overlapping classes. Judgments focus on the gist of classes, producing neglect of nongist classes, and thus of superordinate classes and their base rates.

Therefore, although it could reasonably be argued that framing biases are not really errors (because the options are usually equivalent in expected value), reliance on gist in other contexts can lead to responses that are more difficult to defend (Reyna, 1991; Reyna & Brainerd, 1994). In those contexts, multiple sources of interference – from representation, retrieval, and processing – can compromise reasoning accuracy. However, across many types of tasks, reliance on gist minimizes these effects of interference, enhancing global reasoning accuracy.

More important, the developmental trend of increasing reliance on gist suggests that we are more rational than not. The most basic criterion of rationality is invariance: Responses to superficially different presentations of the same information should be consistent. The ineluctability of this position is brought home when a 5-year-old explains it: As one child said after completing gain (get two superballs) and loss versions (get four superballs and lose two) of the same framing task, "I get two superballs both ways, so there's no difference." This minimal condition of rationality has nothing to do with Bayesian versus frequentistic views of probability; it applies to both views. By operating on the underlying gist of information rather than on verbatim details, reasoning can be invariant across superficially different problems, which is key to rationality.

References

Acredolo, C., O'Connor, J., Banks, L., & Horobin, K. (1989). Children's ability to make probability estimates: Skills revealed through application of Anderson's functional measurement methodology. *Child Development, 60,* 933–945.

Agnoli, F. (1991). Development of judgmental heuristics and logical reasoning: Training counteracts the representativeness heuristic. *Cognitive Development, 6,* 195–217.

Baron, J. (1988). *Thinking and deciding.* Cambridge: Cambridge University Press.

Beach, L. R. (1990). *Image theory: Decision making in personal and organizational contexts.* New York: Wiley.

Bowden, E. M., & Beeman, M. J. (1998). Getting the right idea: Semantic activation in the right hemisphere may help solve insight problems. *Psychological Science, 9,* 435–440.

Brainerd, C. J., & Gordon, L. (1994). Development of verbatim and gist memory for numbers. *Developmental Psychology, 30,* 163–177.

Brainerd, C. J., & Reyna, V. F. (1990a). Gist is the grist: Fuzzy-trace theory and the new intuitionism. *Developmental Review, 10,* 3–47.

Brainerd, C. J., & Reyna, V. F. (1990b). Inclusion illusions: Fuzzy-trace theory and perceptual salience effects in cognitive development. *Developmental Review, 10,* 365–403.

Brainerd, C. J., & Reyna, V. F. (1992a). Explaining "memory free" reasoning. *Psychological Science, 3,* 332–339.

Brainerd, C. J., & Reyna, V. F. (1992b). The memory independence effect: What do the data show? What do the theories claim? *Developmental Review, 12,* 164–186.

Brainerd, C. J., & Reyna, V. F. (1993). Memory independence and memory interference in cognitive development. *Psychological Review, 100,* 42–67.

Brainerd, C. J., Reyna, V. F., & Mojardin, A. H. (1999). Conjoint recognition. *Psychological Review, 106,* 160–179.

Byrnes, J. P. (1998). *The nature and development of decision making: A self-regulation model.* Mahwah, NJ: Erlbaum.

Chandler, C. C., & Gargano, G. J. (1998). Retrieval processes that produce interference in modifed forced-choice recognition tests. *Memory and Cognition, 26,* 220–231.

Davidson, D. (1991). Developmental differences in children's search of predecisional information. *Journal of Experimental Child Psychology, 52,* 239–255.

Davidson, D. (1995). The representativeness heuristic and the conjunction fallacy effect in children's decision making. *Merrill-Palmer Quarterly, 41,* 328–346.

Dempster, F. N. (1992). The rise and fall of the inhibitory mechanism: Toward a unified theory of cognitive development and aging. *Developmental Review, 12,* 45–75.

Dougherty, M. R. P., Gettys, C. F., & Ogden, E. E. (1999). MINERVA-DM: A memory processes model for judgments of likelihood. *Psychological Review, 106,* 180–209.

Epstein, S. (1994). Integration of the cognitive and psychodynamic unconscious. *American Psychologist, 49,* 709–724.

Eddy, D. M. (1982). Probabilistic reasoning in clinical medicine: Problems and opportunities. In D. Kahneman, P. Slovic, & A. Tversky (Eds.), *Judgment under uncertainty: Heuristics and biases* (pp. 249–267). Cambridge: Cambridge University Press.

Fischer, G. W., & Hawkins, S. A. (1993). Strategy compatibility, scale compatibility, and the prominence effect. *Journal of Experimental Psychology: Human Perception and Performance, 19,* 580–597.

Fisher, R. P., & Chandler, C. C. (1991). Independence between recalling inter-event relations and specific events. *Journal of Experimental Psychology: Learning, Memory and Cognition, 17,* 722–733.

Gaspar, D. L., & Ebell, M. H. (1995). QMR: Quick Method Reference (Version 3.7) [Computer software]. San Bruno, CA: First Databank/Camdat Corp.

Gigerenzer, G. (1994). Why the distinction between single-event probabilities and frequencies is important for psychology (and vice versa). In G. Wright & P. Ayton (Eds.), *Subjective probability* (pp. 129–161). New York: Wiley.

Gillund, G., & Shiffrin, R. M. (1984). A retrieval model for both recognition and recall. *Psychological Review, 91,* 1–67.

Hasher, L., & Zacks, R. T. (1988). Working memory, comprehension, and aging: A review and a new view. In G. H. Bower (Ed.), *The psychology of learning and motivation* (Vol. 22, pp. 193–224). San Diego, CA: Academic Press.

Heckerling, P. S., Tape, T. G., Wigton, R. S. Hissong, K. K., Leikin, J. B., Ornato, J. P., Cameron, J. L., & Racht, E. M. (1990). Clinical prediction rule for pulmonary infiltrates. *Annals of Internal Medicine, 113*(9), 664–670.

Hintzman, D. L. (1988). Judgments of frequency and recognition memory in a multiple-trace memory model. *Psychological Review, 96,* 528–551.

Hogarth, R. M. (1980). *Judgment and choice: The psychology of decision.* Chichester, U.K.: Wiley.

Iliad [Computer software]. (1994). Salt Lake City, UT: Applied Medical Informatics.

Isen, A. M. (1993). Positive affect and decision making. In M. Lewis & J. Haviland (Eds.), *Handbook of emotion* (pp. 261–277). New York: Guilford Press.

Jacobs, J. E., & Potenza, M. (1991). The use of judgment heuristics to make social and object decisions: A developmental perspective. *Child Development, 62,* 166–178.

Jacoby, L. L. (1991). A process dissociation framework: Separating automatic from intentional uses of memory. *Journal of Memory and Language, 30,* 513–541.

Jarvik, J. G., Deyo, R. A., & Koepsell, T. D. (1996). Screening magnetic resonance images versus plain films for low back pain: A randomized trial of effects on patient outcomes. *Academic Radiology, 3 Suppl 1:S,* 28.31.

Johnson-Laird, P. N. (1983). *Mental models.* Cambridge, MA: Harvard University Press.

Kahneman, D., Slovic, P., & Tversky, A. (1982). *Judgment under uncertainty: Heuristics and biases.* New York: Cambridge University Press.

Keren, G. (1991). Additional tests of utility theory under unique and repeated conditions. *Journal of Behavioral Decision Making, 4,* 297–304.

Klaczynski, P. A., & Fauth, J. (1997). Developmental differences in memory-based intrusions and self-serving statistical reasoning biases. *Merrill-Palmer Quarterly, 43,* 539–566.

Klaczynski, P. A., & Narasimham, G. (1998). Representations as mediators of adolescent deductive reasoning. *Developmental Psychology, 34,* 865–881.

Kuhberger, A. (1995). The framing of decisions: A new look at old problems. *Organizational Behavior and Human Decision Processes, 62,* 230–240.

Kuhberger, A. (1998). The influence of framing on risky decisions. *Organizational Behavior and Human Decision Processes, 75*, 23–55.

Levin, I. P., Schneider, S. L., & Gaeth, G. J. (1998). All frames are not created equal: A typology and critical analysis of framing effects. *Organizational Behavior and Human Decision Processes, 76*, 149–188.

Lloyd, F. J., & Reyna, V. F. (2001). A Web exercise in evidence-based medicine using cognitive theory. *Journal of General Internal Medicine, 16*, 94–99.

Lloyd, F. J., Reyna, V. F., & Whalen, P. (2001). Accuracy and ambiguity in counseling patients about genetic risk. *Archives of Internal Medicine, 161*, 2411–2413.

Loewenstein, G., & Furstenberg, F. (1991). Is teenage sexual behavior rational? *Journal of Applied Social Psychology, 21*, 957–986.

Lovett, S. B., & Singer, J. A. (1991, April). *The development of children's understanding of probability: Perceptual and quantitative conceptions.* Paper presented at the biennial meeting of the Society of Research in Child Development, Seattle.

Mandler, G. (1980). Recognizing: The judgment of previous occurrence. *Psychological Review, 87*, 252–271.

Miller, G. A. (1956). The magical number seven plus or minus two: Some limits on our capacity for processing information. *Psychological Review, 63*, 81–97.

Moore, C. F., Dixon, J. A., & Haines, B. A. (1991). Components of understanding in proportional reasoning: A fuzzy set representation of developmental progressions. *Child Development, 62*, 441–459.

Moray, N. (1990). Designing for transportation safety in the light of perception, attention, and mental models. *Ergonomics, 33*, 1201–1213.

Nisbett, R. E., & Ross, L. (1980). *Human inference: Strategies and shortcomings of social judgment.* Englewood Cliffs, NJ: Prentice Hall.

Pashler, H. E. (1997). *The psychology of attention.* Cambridge, MA: MIT Press.

Payne, D. G., & Elie, C. J. (1998, November). *Repeated list presentation reduces false memories for pictures and words.* Paper presented at the annual meeting of the Psychonomic Society, Dallas, TX.

Payne, J. W., Bettman, J. R., & Johnson, E. J. (1992). Behavioral decision research: A constructive processing perspective. *Annual Review of Psychology, 43*, 87–131.

Rabinowitz, F. M., Howe, M. L., & Lawrence, J. A. (1989). Class inclusion and working memory. *Journal of Experimental Child Psychology, 48*, 379–409.

Ratcliff, R., Van Zandt, T., & McKoon, G. (1995). Process dissociation, single-process theories, and recognition memory. *Journal of Experimental Psychology: General, 124*, 352–374.

Reyna, V. F. (1991). Class inclusion, the conjunction fallacy, and other cognitive illusions. *Developmental Review, 11*, 317–336.

Reyna, V. F. (1992). Reasoning, remembering, and their relationship: Social, cognitive, and developmental issues. In M. L. Howe, C. J. Brainerd, & V. Reyna (Eds.), *Development of long-term retention* (pp. 103–127). New York: Springer-Verlag.

Reyna, V. F. (1995). Interference effects in memory and reasoning: A fuzzy-trace theory analysis. In F. N. Dempster & C. J. Brainerd (Eds.), *Interference and inhibition in cognition* (pp. 29–59). San Diego, CA: Academic Press.

Reyna, V. F. (1996a). Conceptions of memory development, with implications for reasoning and decision making. *Annals of Child Development, 12,* 87–118.

Reyna, V. F. (1996b). Meaning, memory and the interpretation of metaphors. In J. Mio & A. Katz (Eds.), *Metaphor: Implications and applications* (pp. 39–57), Hillsdale, NJ: Erlbaum.

Reyna, V. F. (2000a). Data, development, and dual processes in rationality. *Behavioral and Brain Sciences, 23,* 694.

Reyna, V. F. (2000b). Fuzzy-trace theory and source monitoring: A review of theory and false-memory data. *Learning and Individual Differences, 12,* 163–175.

Reyna, V. F., & Brainerd, C. J. (1989). Output interference, generic resources, and cognitive development. *Journal of Experimental Child Psychology, 47,* 42–46.

Reyna, V. F., & Brainerd, C. J. (1990). Fuzzy processing in transitivity development. *Annals of Operations Research, 23,* 37–63.

Reyna, V. F., & Brainerd, C. J. (1991a). Fuzzy-trace theory and children's acquisition of scientific and mathematical concepts. *Learning and Individual Differences, 3,* 27–60.

Reyna, V. F., & Brainerd, C. J. (1991b). Fuzzy-trace theory and framing effects in choice: Gist extraction, truncation, and conversion. *Journal of Behavioral Decision Making. 4,* 249–262.

Reyna, V. F., & Brainerd, C. J. (1992). A fuzzy-trace theory of reasoning and remembering: Paradoxes, patterns, and parallelism. In A. Healy, S. Kosslyn, & R. Shiffrin (Eds.), *From learning processes to cognitive processes: Essays in honor of William K. Estes* (Vol. 2, pp. 235–259), Hillsdale, NJ: Erlbaum.

Reyna, V. F., & Brainerd, C. J. (1993). Fuzzy memory and mathematics in the classroom. In R. Logie & G. Davies (Eds.), *Memory in everyday life* (pp. 91–119). Amsterdam: North-Holland.

Reyna, V. F., & Brainerd, C. J. (1994). The origins of probability judgment: A review of data and theories. In G. Wright & P. Ayton (Eds.), *Subjective probability* (pp. 239–272). New York: Wiley.

Reyna, V. F., & Brainerd, C. J. (1995a). Fuzzy-trace theory: An interim synthesis. *Learning and Individual Differences, 7,* 1–75.

Reyna, V. F., & Brainerd, C. J. (1995b). Fuzzy-trace theory: Some foundational issues. *Learning and Individual Differences, 7,* 145–162.

Reyna, V. F., & Brainerd, C. J. (1998). Fuzzy-trace theory and false memory: New frontiers. *Journal of Experimental Child Psychology, 71,* 194–209.

Reyna, V. F. & Ellis, S. C. (1994). Fuzzy-trace theory and framing effects in children's risky decision making. *Psychological Science, 5,* 275–279.

Reyna, V. F., & Hamilton, A. J. (2001). The importance of memory in informed consent for surgical risk. *Medical Decision Making, 21,* 152–155.

Reyna, V. F., & Kiernan, B. (1995). Children's memory and metaphorical interpretation. *Metaphor and Symbolic Activity, 10,* 309–331.

Reyna, V. F., & Lloyd, F. L. (1997). Theories of false memory in children and adults. *Learning and Individual Differences, 9,* 95–123.

Reyna, V. F., Lloyd, F. L., & Whalen, P. (2001). Genetic testing and medical decision making. *Archives of Internal Medicine, 161,* 2406–2408.

Reyna, V. F., Lloyd, F. L., & Woodard, R. (1997, October). *Deviations from practice guidelines for unstable angina.* Paper presented at the 19th annual meeting of the Society for Medical Decision Making, Houston, TX.

Roediger, H. L., Weldon, M. S., & Challis, B. H. (1989). Explaining dissociations between implicit and explicit measures of retention: A processing account. In H. L. Roediger & F. I. M. Craik (Eds.), *Varieties of memory and consciousness: Essays in honour of Endel Tulving* (pp. 3–41). Hillsdale, NJ: Erlbaum.

Rokeach, M., & Ball-Rokeach, S. J. (1989). Stability and changes in American value priorities, 1968–1981. *American Psychologist, 44,* 775–784.

Schacter, D. L., Curran, T., Galluccio, L., Milberg, W. B., & Bates. J. F. (1996). False recognition and the right frontal lobe: A case study. *Neuropsychologica, 34,* 793–808.

Shanteau, J. (1992). How much information does an expert use? Is it relevant? *Acta Psychologica, 81,* 75–86.

Shedler, J., & Manis, M. (1986). Can the availability heuristic explain vividness effects? *Journal of Personality and Social Psychology, 51,* 26–36.

Shiffrin, R. M., & Steyvers, M. (1997). Model for recognition memory: REM – retrieving effectively from memory. *Psychonomic Bulletin and Review, 4,* 145–166.

Simon, H. A. (1956). Rational choice and the structure of the environment. *Psychological Review, 63,* 129–138.

Sloman, S. (1996). The empirical case for two systems of reasoning. *Psychological Bulletin, 119,* 3–22.

Spinillo, A. G., & Bryant, P. (1991). Children's proportional judgments: The importance of half. *Child Development, 62,* 427–440.

Stanovich, K. E., & West, R. F. (1998). Individual differences in rational thought. *Journal of Experimental Psychology: General, 127,* 161–188.

Stanovich, K. E., & West, R. F. (2000). Individual differences in reasoning: Implications for the rationality debate? *Behavioral and Brain Sciences, 23,* 645–726.

Sternberg, R. J., & Davidson, J. E. (1995). *The nature of insight.* Cambridge, MA: MIT Press.

Stiell, I. G., McKnight, R. D., Greenberg, G. H., McDowell, I., Nair, R. C., Wells, G. A., Johns, C., & Worthington, J. R. (1994). Implementation of the Ottawa ankle rules. *Journal of the American Medical Association, 271*(11), 827–832.

Stone, E. R., Yates, J. F., & Parker, A. M. (1994). Risk communication: Absolute versus relative expressions of low-probability risks. *Organizational Behavior and Human Decision Processes, 60,* 387–408.

Tetlock, P. E. (1986). A value pluralism model of ideological reasoning. *Journal of Personality and Social Psychology, 50,* 819–827.

Toglia, M. P., Neuschatz, J. S., & Goodwin, K. A. (1999). Recall accuracy and illusory memories: When more is less. *Memory, 7,* 233–256.

Tversky, A. (1972). Elimination by aspects: A theory of choice. *Psychological Review, 79,* 281–299.

Tversky, A., & Kahneman, D. (1981). The framing of decisions and the psychology of choice. *Science, 211,* 453–458.

Tversky, A., & Kahneman, D. (1983). Extensional versus intuitive reasoning: The conjunction fallacy in probability judgment. *Psychological Review, 90,* 293–315.

Tversky, A., & Kahneman, D. (1986). Rational choice and the framing of decisions. *Journal of Business, 59,* 252–278.

Tversky, A., & Koehler, D. (1994). Support theory: A nonextensional representation of subjective probability. *Psychological Review, 101,* 547–567.

von Winterfeldt, D., & Edwards, W. (1986). *Decision analysis and behavioral research.* Cambridge: Cambridge University Press.

Wedell, D. H., & Bockenholt, U. (1990). Moderation of preference reversals in the long run. *Journal of Experimental Psychology: Human Perception and Performance, 16,* 429–438.

Wedell, D. H., & Bockenholt, U. (1994). Contemplating single versus multiple encounters of a risky prospect. *American Journal of Psychology, 107,* 499–518.

Winer, G. A., Craig, R. K., & Weinbaum, E., (1992). Adults' failure on misleading weight-conservation tests: A developmental analysis. *Developmental Psychology, 28,* 109–120.

Wolfe, C. (1995). Information seeking on Bayesian conditional probability problems: A fuzzy-trace theory account. *Journal of Behavioral Decision Making, 8,* 85–108.

Woodard, R. L. & Reyna, V. F. (1997, November). *Memory-reasoning independence in covariation judgment: A fuzzy-trace theory analysis.* Paper presented at the annual meeting of the Society for Judgment and Decision-Making, Philadelphia.

8   Integrating Themes from Cognitive and Social Cognitive Development into the Study of Judgment and Decision Making

Beth A. Haines and Colleen Moore

ABSTRACT

This chapter examines the development of judgment and decision-making skills. First, we discuss what studies of the development of problem solving and scientific reasoning show about the development of judgment and decision making. Second, we review some developmental research on the use of heuristics and biases from a social cognitive perspective. Third, we discuss evidence relevant to the development of the metacognition of judgment and decision making and the development of adaptive decision making. The research we review shows the importance of methodological, contextual, social, and motivational processes as influences on children's judgments and decision making. We suggest several directions for developmental work, as well as several ways developmental work may contribute to the understanding of adult judgment and decision making. Finally, we discuss implications of metacognitive training for improving strategy selection and execution and for reducing susceptibility to judgment and decision-making biases.

CONTENTS

What Developmental Work Contributes to the Study of Judgment and Decision Making

In this chapter we examine some recent literature relevant to the development of judgment and decision making in childhood and adolescence. Developmental research is similar to judgment and decision research in two ways: (a) in its emphasis on individual differences and (b) in its emphasis on improvement of performance toward an ideal state (rationality). But thinking developmentally also usually involves some features that are not as integral to mainstream judgment and decision research: (a) seeking an understanding of the origins of various judgment and decision strategies, biases, and heuristics; (b) concern with how the research participants perceive the structure of a judgment or decision task, and what goals and abilities they bring to the task; and (c) exploration of decision topics with the potential to impact daily functioning. We do not intend to imply that the field of judgment and decision making has not considered these last three features, but they are long-standing concerns that pervade developmental psychology. We will discuss these differences and similarities between a developmental perspective and mainstream judgment and decision research.

First, a developmental perspective emphasizes individual differences, mostly as a function of age and experience. Although developmental psychology, like most of the rest of psychology, is often a "psychology of the average" rather than a "differential" psychology (Cronbach, 1957), developmentalists consistently look for age group differences. An integral part of the study of age differences is the attempt to identify differences in cognitive and emotional states, strategies or response patterns across age groups, not just in summary measures, such as percentage correct. In the mainstream of judgment and decision making, several theoretical approaches have also emphasized at least some aspects of individual differences and the idea that there is a repertoire of strategies within individuals. For example, Social Judgment Theory using the Lens Model (Hammond, McClelland, & Mumpower, 1980) emphasizes individual differences in cue weights. Conjoint measurement and other approaches based on measurement axioms (Coombs, Raiffa, & Thrall, 1954; Luce, 1996) also examine individual data patterns and their correspondence to the models. Functional measurement (Anderson, 1974; Birnbaum, 1982; Mellers & Cooke, 1996; Shanteau & Skowronski, 1992) often tests only group average model fits, but sometimes it has been used to model individual differences in response patterns. The field also has a tradition of the study of expert judgment (Shanteau, 1992, and this volume), and recent work has begun to examine cultural effects on judgment and decision making (Weber, Hsee, & Sokolowska, 1998; Yates, Lee, Shinotsuka, Patalano, & Sieck, 1998). Also, Payne, Bettman, and Johnson (1993) have summarized evidence that people have a range of decision strategies from which they choose, depending on task demands, goals, and other situational constraints.

Second, both developmental and judgment and decision research emphasize the degree to which performance conforms to logic and rationality. More than 20 years ago, Harriet Shaklee (1979) pointed out that most theories of cognitive development (in particular, Piaget's theory) postulate that the child moves developmentally toward increasing use of formal logic or rationality. In contrast, judgment and decision-making researchers have expended great effort in cataloging the *failures* of adults to follow prescriptive models that provide the criterion of rationality. However, judgment and decision research has also expended great effort exploring ways of improving performance or *debiasing* (Yates, 1988). One developmental theory, fuzzy-trace theory, attempts to reconcile findings from developmental research and judgment and decision-making research by, in part, defining a new standard of rationality (Reyna & Brainerd, 1995). Fuzzy-trace theory asserts that people encode fuzzy or gist representations in parallel with more exact, verbatim representations. Although these multiple representations are available, people prefer to reason using the simplest representation that is effective. Consequently, according to fuzzy-trace theory, reasoners prefer to rely on gist, and with development, reasoning becomes increasingly gist-based. Reyna and Brainerd (1995) argue that although gist-based reasoning does not involve formal quantitative or logical manipulations, it shows *degrees of rationality.* That is, Reyna and Brainerd conclude that gist-based representations lead to reasoning that is consistent across isomorphic but superficially different tasks, consistent with reality, flexible, efficient, and minimizes reasoning errors overall.

In spite of these major similarities, a developmental approach differs from what is usually seen in the mainstream of judgment and decision research in that thinking developmentally implies thinking about the underpinnings and origins of judgment and decision-making strategies, heuristics, and biases. It is often the case that explanations of a phenomenon in the adult literature have unrecognized developmental implications. For example, if neglect of base-rate information and use of the representativeness heuristic is hypothesized to be due to limited information processing capacity, what developmental implications does this have? And how does the representativeness heuristic itself develop? If use of the representativeness heuristic is partly a function of a priori beliefs, category prototypes, or social stereotypes, then one would suppose that there would be developmental change as children acquire the system of beliefs, categories, and stereotypes of their culture. It is our view that an adequate theory of judgment and decision making should be able to accommodate observed developmental changes. Therefore, developmental data can be seen as providing some constraints on theories of judgment and decision making. Attention to the origins of strategies, heuristics, and biases could also be important in suggesting ways to improve decision making toward the ideal of rationality.

Another important aspect of most developmental research is a concern with the possibility that people of different ages perceive and subjectively structure the same judgment or decision problem in different ways or bring to the situation different goals and abilities. For example, because children of different ages differ in their verbal abilities, developmental researchers often attempt to simplify task instructions, materials, and response modes to suit the entire age range of interest. Developmentalists tend to be cautious about interpreting task performance as evidence of *lack* of an ability or lack of capacity to use a strategy, especially if such a conclusion is based on a single response criterion. Some of the research examples we will present show different results, depending on the response criterion – choice, rating scale judgments, or verbal explanations – and some of our research examples illustrate methods for assessing how people perceive and subjectively structure problems.

The important questions for a developmentalist to ask are "What develops?" and "How does development occur?" For judgment and decision making, the simple answer to the first question is that the judgment and decision heuristics, biases, and strategies seen in the adult must develop. Is there a developmental trend toward increasing rationality and less biased judgment and decision processes, or are rationality and the use of biases and heuristics developmentally separate? Although development must tend toward the judgment and decision phenomena observed in adults, the developmental trajectory is important too. With respect to the developmental trajectory, several other questions can be asked. Does the development of domain general cognitive skills constrain the types of judgment and decision processes seen? What is the developmental source of individual differences in judgment and decision making? How does the selection and monitoring of the effectiveness of judgment and decision strategies and heuristics for different tasks and settings develop (i.e., how does metacognition develop)? Does the developmental trajectory vary, depending on different task and context variables?

Although these questions cannot be thoroughly answered at present, toward answering these questions we summarize some selective aspects of two areas of developmental research: (a) cognitive development, with emphasis on our own work on proportional reasoning tasks, and (b) social cognition, including developmental judgment and decision research. We have chosen to present both cognitive and social cognitive development research because these two areas of developmental psychology also differ in their emphases in ways we see as relevant to the mainstream of judgment and decision-making research, and they differ to some extent in how they answer the question of what develops.

First, cognitive development research and theory has traditionally focused on questions of how age, cognitive stage, or cognitive level (i.e., capacity or competence) affects children's judgments, whereas social cognitive research (e.g., Crick & Dodge, 1994) has elaborated how a variety of other contextual and experiential factors affect children's judgments and decision making. Social cognitive and applied developmental judgment and decision research have challenged traditional models of cognitive development with findings that question the idea that development moves toward increasing logic and rationality in decision making. This obviously parallels the skepticism seen in the mainstream of judgment and decision research about whether people are rational. And although much social cognitive research shows developmental trends from simple to more complex judgment and decision strategies that use available information more fully, there is not a strict developmental progression in which immature strategies are discarded (cf. Moore, Hembree, & Enright, 1993). Rather, development is viewed as providing a repertoire of strategies and heuristics that increases with age.

Second, cognitive development research has presented children with reasoning tasks about science or school problems or about novel materials, whereas social cognitive and applied research typically uses problems based on interpersonal situations that are personally relevant or familiar to children. This tension between familiar and personally relevant versus novel judgment and decision settings is also seen in the mainstream judgment and decision literature. Novel materials are used when experimenters are trying to exclude people's preconceived ideas or knowledge and focus on their strategies. Familiar materials in a familiar context are used to examine the effects of factors such as knowledge, familiarity, emotions, and interpersonal influences on judgment and decision making. Different results are often obtained in developmental work using social and nonsocial contents.

Third, social cognitive and applied developmental research has begun to explore how children's emotional and social assessments and reactions affect their judgments and decisions. Cognitive development research has neglected the role of social and emotional factors largely due to an implicit attempt to exclude these factors by design. However, some cognitive researchers have recently questioned whether children are engaged by typical unfamiliar cognitive laboratory tasks, and they have been concerned about how low interest or low task engagement affects strategy selection and metacognitive monitoring of performance (Kuhn, 1993; Siegler, 1996). Further, emotional reactions might be elicited by the unfamiliarity of the task itself. Also, whether the goals that the child brings to the task or the goals that are conveyed by the investigator are to obtain a positive evaluation versus to acquire new skills can dramatically impact task performance (Dweck & Leggett, 1988; Henderson & Dweck, 1990). The mainstream of judgment and decision has recently begun to study the role of affect (Mellers, Schwartz, Ho, & Ritov, 1997; Schkade & Kahneman, 1998), but other judgment and decision research excludes affect by design, just as does cognitive development research.

Keeping these general issues in mind, we turn now to our review of developmental research.

Cognitive Development as the Development of Judgment and Decision Making

Piaget's theory of cognitive development is arguably the most important theory of cognitive development. Piaget's theory takes a structuralist approach that characterizes cognitive development in terms of developmental stages. The stages move from action-as-thought (sensorimotor) to intuitive, experience-based processing (concrete operations) toward increasingly rational, logic-based thought or *formal operations* (see Inhelder & Piaget, 1958, for a compendium on the development of formal operations). The basic idea of Piaget's theory is that children are not little adults, but that their thinking differs qualitatively from that of adults. Children's cognition was portrayed by most of Piaget's early interpreters for American psychology as relatively domain general; each stage was described as qualitatively distinct from the other stages and based on unifying structures of thought (Brainerd, 1978; Flavell, 1963). Cognitive stage as a theoretical construct can account for consistency in reasoning across domains. The problem, of course, is that empirical research shows little domain general consistency (Brainerd, 1978; Shatz, 1978).

Information processing theories of cognitive development (e.g., Case & Okamoto, 1996; Siegler, 1991, 1996) typically retain the assumption from Piaget's theory of increasingly sophisticated and ultimately rational reasoning with age, but they soften the assumption of domain generality through their focus on both situational and developmental differences in encoding, attention, memory retrieval, strategy choice, and strategy execution. In information processing approaches, improvement with age is viewed as due to developmental change in component processes, such as focusing on relevant information and ignoring irrelevant cues, memory retrieval, and choice of more logical and less biased strategies in their judgments. Both Piagetian and information processing approaches in contemporary interpretations (Chapman, 1988, pp. 340ff.; Siegler, 1996) disclaim broad domain-general structures, regarding development as occurring gradually and as consisting in part of an increase in the repertoire of strategies available.

A third approach, fuzzy-trace theory (Reyna & Brainerd, 1995), grew out of information processing approaches but challenged the information processing characterization of rational thinking that is based on formal computational logic. Reyna and Brainerd offer a dual-process account of rationality that suggests that people encode both verbatim representations (logical, quantitative) and gist (intuitive, qualitative, experiential) representations. People draw on the least detailed representation necessary to deal with the task at hand. Therefore, task parameters may require precise, logical approaches or may allow reliance on efficient and preferred gist representations. Developmental level is also expected to affect whether a child is able to select a verbatim representation because computational competence is expected to increase with age. Thus, fuzzy-trace theory, like information processing approaches, assumes that reasoning is domain specific but claims that gist-based representations, though sometimes logically flawed and prone to biases, show consistency across tasks – one possible criterion of rationality.

Many cognitive developmental studies of problem solving could be reinterpreted as studies of the development of judgment and decision making. The tasks used are usually multicue prediction tasks.

For example, a classic study by Siegler (1976) examined children's understanding of a simple two-arm balance scale. Weights were placed at different distances on either side of the fulcrum, and children aged 5 to 17 years were asked to choose which side of the balance would go down when the supports were removed. Siegler used a hierarchically structured set of decision trees to model four types of strategies. Based on the individual's pattern of choices, he classified each individual as using one of the four strategies. He found a developmental progression from a strategy that entailed use of only one cue (comparison of the number of weights on either side) to a strategy based on the normative model for the task (comparison of torque or weight × distance for each side of the balance scale). More sophisticated strategies were used with age, and training children to attend to a cue they ignored during a pretest (distance from the fulcrum) caused the children to use a more sophisticated strategy than they used initially.

Siegler's (1976, 1981) decision tree (or *rule assessment*) model is presented in virtually all introductory child development textbooks as a model *not* of how decision strategies develop, but of the development of children's *understanding* of proportional reasoning tasks. That is, the hierarchy of decision trees is used as a model of the mind (cf. Dawes, 1975).

Other researchers approached similar tasks using other methods. For example, Surber and Gzesh (1984) collected rating scale judgments and used functional measurement (Anderson, 1974) to model the judgments. Wilkening (1981) studied the development of judgments of time, distance, and velocity using rating scale responses and functional measurement. The results of Wilkening (1981) and Surber and Gzesh (1984) showed that there was not necessarily a developmental hierarchy ending in the normative multiplying model. In particular, whether the multiplying (or ratio) model provided an accurate description of the judgments depended on the variable being judged, as well as the age of the participants. In Wilkening's study, when velocity was judged (given time and distance), the ratings did not conform to the ratio model, and in Surber and Gzesh (1984), judgments of the weight needed to make the scale balance did not conform to the multiplying model (see Surber, 1987, for a more complete summary of this type of developmental research).

A controversy arose in the developmental literature over which method was superior for measuring cognitive developmental status on a task: functional measurement with rating scale responses or decision trees with choice responses (Gigerenzer & Richter, 1990; Kerkman &

Wright, 1988a, 1988b; Surber & Haines, 1987; Wilkening, 1988; Wilkening & Anderson, 1982). Notice that this controversy in developmental psychology was *not* over how the relevant judgment and decision strategies develop. Instead, the controversy was over what those judgment and decision strategies themselves reveal about the hypothetical underlying construct of *cognitive developmental status* or *task competence* and which method comes closer to representing the "true" developmental level of functioning of individuals on the task at hand. Such a controversy is almost unthinkable in the mainstream of judgment and decision research, where it is relatively common knowledge that choices and judgments can be based on different strategies.

Setting aside the controversy over whether choice or judgment methods are better, the last two decades of developmental research on problem solving show that children as young as 4 years of age can combine two quantitatively varied cues in an approximately linear model to make judgments or choices. As the number of cues in a task increases, the likelihood that younger children will ignore some of the cues increases (Anderson & Butzin, 1978; Singh & Singh, 1994). For choice tasks, younger children are more likely than older children to ignore one cue even when there are only two cues (Gigerenzer & Richter, 1990; Siegler, 1976, 1981). There are also clear developmental trends in most studies of this type that show that use of the normative model for a particular task increases with age.

When the relationship between one of the cues and the criterion in these multicue prediction tasks is inverse, larger developmental differences appear in both choice and judgment tasks than when cue and criterion are directly related. For example, in Wilkening's (1981) study, the 5-year-olds failed to use the time cue correctly in judging velocity, and in Surber and Gzesh's (1984) study, only 25% of the 5-year-olds and 65% of the second to eighth graders showed appropriate inverse relationships in judging variables in the balance scale task (for a more complete summary of developmental work on judgments of inverse relations between cues see Surber, 1984, 1985a).

Although our broad outline of these studies shows a developmental increase in appropriate cue use (which might be considered to be an increase in rationality), our characterization of the cognitive development research on multicue prediction tasks would be shown to have many contingencies attached to them if a more detailed examination of the original studies were presented (interested readers should see the review articles cited earlier). Some of those contingencies are whether the stimuli are social or nonsocial (Kuhn, Garcia-Mila, Zohar, & Anderson, 1995; Surber, 1985a, 1987; Surber & Haines, 1987), order of presentation of cues (Ahl, Moore, & Dixon, 1992), familiarity of the topic (Reed & Evans, 1987), and task engagement (Falk & Wilkening, 1998). These contextual and situational variables not only illustrate the fact that it is difficult to draw firm conclusions about the development of cognitive capacity, but also illustrate the importance of moving toward theories that explain why situational or contextual variables show developmental effects.

Subjective Problem Representation in the Development of Problem Solving

We summarize some of our own cognitive development research that illustrates the necessity of incorporating the influence of contextual variables into developmental theories of judgment and decision making. Our own approach emphasizes that a key factor in how a contextual variable influences performance is the way the variable alters (or fails to alter) the subjective representation of the problem constructed by a person.

In a series of studies using proportional reasoning problems, we manipulated whether the stimulus quantities were presented numerically versus perceptually with verbal labels (Ahl et al., 1992; Dixon & Moore, 1996, 1997; Haines, Moore, & Dixon, 1999; Moore, Dixon, & Haines, 1991). At the time we designed these experiments, we conceptualized them in terms of Hammond's (1996) concept of quasi-rationality along a *cognitive continuum*. Hammond, drawing on ideas from Brunswik (1956), proposed a distinction between judgment and decision strategies that are, on the one hand, *analytic* – based on explicit mathematical calculations or explicit steps of logic – versus, on the other hand, *intuitive* – based on implicit, automatic, and holistic processes and perceptual gratification. This distinction is also found in Piaget's developmental theory, with the hypothesized development being from qualitative and perceptual to formal operations (explicit, analytical reasoning). In Hammond's theory, numerical stimuli promote analytic processing, whereas perceptually quantified stimuli promote intuitive processing.

Our studies showed interesting developmental differences in the effects of numerically versus perceptually quantified/verbal stimuli. The largest differences occurred when a variable was inversely related to the criterion. For example, when judging the temperature that would result from combining two containers of water at different temperatures, the *larger* the quantity of the colder container, the *lower* the resultant temperature. In the presence of numerical stimuli, a substantial minority of children from second to eighth grade added the temperatures, yielding implausible judgments of the combined temperature (for example, two containers of water at 40°F yields 80°F water; Moore et al., 1991).

In another study, we also presented both the numerical and perceptually quantifiable versions of a temperature mixture task and manipulated the order in which the two versions were presented (Ahl et al., 1992). We hypothesized that presentation of the perceptual version before the numerical version would reduce the likelihood that the children would add the numerical temperatures. Based on Hammond's theory, the perceptual version of the task should push participants of all ages toward an intuitive approach to the task. We hypothesized that if people use their intuitive knowledge of the task structure to guide their formal or mathematical solutions, then solving the problem intuitively first ought to reduce the occurrence of blatantly incorrect mathematical solutions such as adding temperatures. The results were consistent with the hypothesis for the fifth and eighth graders.

The fact that order influenced the children's performance in the numerical version of the task suggests that an important developmental deficit for children compared to college students is in the spontaneous use of intuitive knowledge to select plausible mathematical strategies. Without experiencing the perceptual version of the task first, the fifth and eighth graders were less likely to form a representation of the problem that is coordinated with their knowledge of temperatures in the real world.

In two further studies, we examined in more detail how intuitive representation of the structure of a task is used in selecting math strategies (Dixon & Moore, 1996, 1997). The relevance of this topic to researchers in judgment and decision making is in the light it sheds on why people do not select the appropriate strategies (or normative models) to solve judgment and decision problems even when those strategies are in their repertoires. Our research shows that there are two separable causes for such failures on proportional reasoning tasks. First, a person may not represent the task subjectively in a way that leads to the appropriate normative model. Second, a person may not be able to construct the appropriate math strategy for the specific task even if the task is represented appropriately. Although appropriate task representation is a logical prerequisite to the use of a normative model, this idea that task representation is central to math strategy choice cannot be tested unless the subjective task representation can be measured or manipulated separately from the use of math strategies to solve the task. As in our previous studies, we accomplished this separation by presenting the same task without numerical values (perceptual/verbal version) and with numerical values.

In the first study (Dixon & Moore, 1996), participants judged the temperature of a mixture that resulted from combining two different quantities of water at different temperatures. All participants (2nd, 5th, 8th, and 11th graders and college students) completed the perceptual version of the task first, followed by the numerical version. Participants were asked to "think aloud" during the numerical task. We used the judgments of the perceptual version of the task to score each participant's understanding of several *principles* that correspond to aspects of the temperature mixture task. Creating principle scores from the judgments yielded a detailed profile of each person's intuitive task understanding. (Some researchers in problem solving might call this the *subjective problem space* [Hayes & Simon, 1976] or *problem representation* [Kuhn et al., 1995].) The results showed that the intuitive understanding constrained the math strategies such that intuitive understanding of a principle was necessary but not sufficient for use of a math strategy consistent with that task principle. That is, participants used math strategies that violated principles for which they showed good intuitive understanding, but they did not generate math strategies that instantiated principles they did not understand. This illustrates one source of suboptimal strategy use: A person may have appropriate intuitive knowledge or a subjective representation of the task but may not be able to invent the math to instantiate that knowledge.

Our second investigation (Dixon & Moore, 1997) used a reaction time task in two experiments to explore whether the task principles are subjectively represented and used in evaluating math strategies. In the first study, pairs of numerical temperature mixture problems with answers were presented to college students. Pairs of problems were used because some of the task principles require comparison across problems in order to judge whether the principle holds or is violated. The college students were asked to judge whether the *strategy* that produced the answers was correct or incorrect as quickly as possible. The problem pairs were designed such that they represented violations of different task principles. The degree of deviation from the correct values of the answers given with each problem pair varied independently of whether a principle was violated. Thus, if the subjective principles are actually used, violation of principle, but not deviation from correctness, should influence response time. The results were consistent with the idea that the task principles are subjectively represented and used.

In the second study (Dixon & Moore, 1997, Experiment 2), we used an acid mixture task (similar to that used by Reed & Evans, 1987) and manipulated understanding of one of the task principles. Although acid mixture is isomorphic to temperature mixture, it is not understood as well (Reed & Evans, 1987). College students and eighth graders were first given brief explanations of one of five task principles. Following this instructional manipulation, all participants completed a set of judgments with perceptual stimuli (with no numbers). These judgments were used to score intuitive understanding of the task principles. Finally, all participants evaluated the correctness of strategies for pairs of numerical problems, as in the previous experiment. We used multiple regression to test the hypothesis that the effect of the instructional manipulation on performance in the reaction time task would be mediated by intuitive understanding of the principles. The results supported this hypothesis. When instruction condition was partialed out, the principle scores were still significantly related to performance in the reaction time task. On the other hand, when the principle scores were partialed out, the relationship between instruction condition and performance in the reaction time task was reduced to nonsignificance.

Our research approach, and especially this last study, illustrates a *mentalistic* approach in which the key variable in determining performance is not an experimental manipulation or a contextual variable per se, but the mental states that are influenced by the manipulation (Dulany, 1991). In order to use a mentalistic approach, it is necessary to have measures of the cognitive states that are separate from the performances that they are intended to explain. This is especially true when a manipulation or a contextual variable is likely to have different effects on the problem representation of different individuals (or individuals of different ages). In theory, measures of relevant cognitive states (such as our measures of the intuitive task understanding) should relate more strongly to performance than do the contextual variables that influence those subjective states. This was shown in the last experiment previously described. Such mentalistic theories would differentiate implicit, intuitive understanding from explicit, conceptual understanding and would delineate how various contextual factors and task requirements trigger different representations and consequently different strategies.

In addition, mentalistic approaches invite explorations of the metacognitive control of problem solving and also of the roles of emotions and other motivational factors, such as goals (Dweck & Leggett, 1988). With their emphasis on individual differences, both developmental psychology and judgment and decision research are ripe to construct mentalistic theories that connect subjective psychological states to each other.

Social Cognitive Processing Approaches

Social cognitive developmental theories (e.g., Crick & Dodge, 1994; Dodge, 1986) have extended cognitive development theories by delineating social, interpersonal, emotional, and cultural variables that affect children's encoding and interpretation, response decisions, and behavioral enactment of decisions. We first summarize Crick and Dodge's (1994) social information processing framework and then describe some research findings relevant to the framework that have implications for judgment and decision research.

Crick and Dodge's (1994) "reformulated" model is nonlinear; it assumes that interpretation of stimuli and construction of responses may occur in parallel. The model contains six steps: "(1) encoding of external and internal cues, (2) interpretation and mental representation of those cues, (3) clarification or selection of a goal, (4) response access or construction, (5) response decision, and (6) behavioral enactment" (p. 76). The database in long-term memory is the hub of the model, as it is assumed to guide all processes. The database also changes in response to experience and feedback from each information processing step. Crick and Dodge hypothesize that children rely on simplifying cognitive structures (e.g., heuristics, schemas, working models) when processing internal and external cues. These simplifying structures are incorporated into the child's database and guide future on-line processing. For example, when presented with a problem, children may, in addition to creating a personalized representation of the external stimuli based on stored schemas or simplifying cognitive structures, consider the perspectives of others, make causal attributions, evaluate the personal significance of a problem, reflect on their past experiences in comparable situations, predict the likelihood that they will achieve their goals, and react emotionally to all of these inputs.

An interesting prediction made by Crick and Dodge (1994) is that rigidity in social information processing actually increases with age. They argue that based on early experiences, children construct their *working models* of the world – processing schemas, habits, and pathways that are used to interpret new experiences. These pathways or working models become increasingly efficient, complex, and automatic with experience, but they also become well established and resistant to change. Similarly Reyna and Brainerd (1995) argue that "the same psychological processes that make representation and retrieval more reliable in adults, make biases more reliable" (p. 44). That is, familiar cues and patterns may stimulate well-established, though biased, processing patterns. Thus, either an adaptive or a maladaptive processing pattern may come to function as a processing style, and may consequently interfere with processing of important situation-specific cues that are inconsistent with the working model. For example, a young child may acquire a pessimistic working model of the world through early experiences with parental neglect and abuse; this worldview is expected to affect processing patterns (e.g., leading to a pessimistic attributional style), and if these expectations are confirmed in later peer interactions and school experiences, it is plausible that particular processing patterns would become more stable and resistant to change (for a review of evidence regarding the origins of attributional style see Haines, Metalsky, Cardamone, & Joiner, 1999). This discussion of adaptive and maladaptive processing styles provides one developmental hypothesis about the origin of judgmental biases, especially the origin of individual differences in biases. In particular, it suggests that judgment biases should be more likely when children are making judgments that pertain to social situations familiar to them than when they are making judgments or decisions about novel materials or situations.

Crick and Dodge's approach also emphasizes the role of emotion in children's judgment, which has been neglected (mostly by design) in cognitive development research. For example, in their framework, emotional arousal is treated as an internal cue that may affect children's interpretation of situations and may motivate children to pursue particular goals. Factors seldom mentioned in cognitive problem-solving literature, such as social attributional processes, locus of control, and perceived vulnerability, also enter into social cognitive decision-making models. As Crick and Dodge (1994) suggest, emotionally arousing situations may trigger nonadaptive preemptive processing (i.e., simple, rapid, automatic processing), and differences in processing between children with behavior problems and other children are more likely to occur in situations that elicit highly automated processing than in situations that stimulate more reflective processing.

Evidence that children may selectively attend to or prioritize emotional cues is provided by Kindt, Brosschot, and Everaerd's (1997) finding (based on an emotional Stroop task) that children prioritized processing information related to physical harm. Similarly, MacLeod and Mathews (1991) claim that emotions affect the control of cognitive processes rather than the efficiency of basic processing mechanisms. On the other hand, children's cognitive assessments of a situation are also likely to affect their emotional interpretations of the situation. Crick and Ladd (1993) found that children's causal attributions affected whether or not they experienced feelings of distress in a situation. Thus, emotions are clearly implicated as affecting encoding and interpretation, and decision enactment, as well as being affected by cognitive interpretations.

A study illustrating that emotional factors influence decision making considered the role of identification in children's decisions about alcohol. The developmental concept of *identification* refers to the emotional ties that a child feels with a role model. The idea of identification comes originally from Freud but is given a central place in many theories of social development. Austin and Johnson (1997) examined whether media literacy training affected third graders' identification with people in advertisements, perceptions of alcohol advertisements themselves, and judgments of alcohol use norms, as well as their expectancies about alcohol use later in life. Therefore, their research considered not only cognitive factors such as perceived similarity, perceived realism, and understanding of persuasive intent, but also emotional processes, such as identification, desirability, and peer approval as fundamental aspects of children's judgments and hypothetical decisions about alcohol. The results showed that identification and the perceived desirability of alcohol had significant effects on children's alcohol use expectancies.

We turn now to a review of some empirical developmental studies of social cognition and judgment and decision making.

The Development of Biased Information Processing

Research done in the 1980s showed that aggressive children display certain processing biases, including the *hostile attributional bias* (they infer hostile intent in ambiguous provocation situations), as well as a tendency to evaluate aggressive responses to social conflict more positively than nonaggressive children (see Crick & Dodge, 1994, for a review). Crick and Werner (1998) studied social decision processes in school-age children classified as either relationally aggressive (i.e., aggression through teasing, excluding, and other manipulations of peer relationships) or overtly aggressive. Their results showed that situational factors affect whether biased processing is elicited from aggressive children. For example, overtly aggressive boys showed hostile response decision biases in instrumental contexts (e.g., being pushed from behind) but not in relational contexts (e.g., not being invited to a birthday party). In contrast, overtly aggressive girls evaluated overtly aggressive decisions positively in both instrumental and relational contexts. Furthermore, Crick and Werner found a developmental trend in which older boys evaluated overt aggression more positively and relational aggression more negatively than younger boys. This result is counter to a prediction of less decision bias and greater rationality with age, but it is consistent with gender stereotypes that characterize relational aggression as inappropriate for men.

Other research on judgment biases in children has mimicked adult studies of biases and heuristics (cf. Tversky & Kahneman, 1974) but has focused predominantly on determining whether children are prone to the same biases as adults. Most of the research has been conducted with school-age children and adolescents. Many types of heuristics and biases have been studied, including the representativeness heuristic and the conjunction fallacy, as well as self-serving biases. Most studies report that children are prone to many of the same biases as adults, though, as discussed subsequently, there is some evidence of interesting developmental trends in information use.

Work examining the representativeness heuristic and the conjunction fallacy in children as young as first graders (e.g., Davidson, 1995; Davidson, MacKay, & Jergovic, 1994; Jacobs & Potenza, 1991) provides some evidence regarding the hypothesis that biased judgments and decisions may increase with age (Reyna & Brainerd, 1995). Fuzzy-trace theory predicts that biased judgments increase with age because of increasing reliance on qualitative gist representations as children gain experience in a domain. Studies have found evidence that even first-grade children's *choices* reflect use of the representativeness heuristic, and that use of the heuristic by children is affected by domain (i.e., biases are more likely in social than in object domains), consistency between individuating and base-rate information, stereotypes, and general knowledge base.

Jacobs and Potenza (1991) examined children's choices, as well as their justifications for their choices about social and object domains. For example, in the object domain, children (in first, third, and sixth grades, as well as a comparison sample of college students) were asked to choose what color of socks would be drawn at random from a drawer, given base-rate information about the socks in the drawer, or what brand of bicycle should be purchased given information about the base rates of brand sales. For the social domain, children were asked to choose whether another child would take swimming or piano lessons, given base-rate information about the two types of lessons. For some problems, individuating information was added. For example, in the bicycle domain, information from a neighbor about the quality of the bicycle brands was added.

The results of Jacobs and Potenza's study showed some overall developmental trends; college students were more likely than children to make base-rate choices in object domains than in social domains when both individuating and base-rate information was presented. However, there were slight developmental *decreases* in base-rate choices when base-rate and individuating information was given in social domains. The *verbal justification* data suggested developmental increases in reliance on individuating rationales (i.e., information about the particular case in contrast to more objective base-rate information). That is, young children might be considered less biased than older children because they relied less on individuating information than older children did (i.e., younger children showed less use of the representativeness heuristic). This is a startling developmental result, but it agrees with the prediction from fuzzy-trace theory that judgmental biases based on social experiences should increase with age. However, is the result based on greater use of base-rate information by the younger children? Although the younger children did not mention the individuating information in justifying their choices, they also did *not* provide base-rate rationales for their choices. Instead, they frequently offered rationales based on idiosyncratic personal preferences or simple embellishments of the scenarios presented. This was the case even in object domains, in which both younger and older children were more likely than in social domains to make base-rate *choices*.

Another important result in the study by Jacobs and Potenza (1991) was that consistency between choices and rationales increased with age. This points to an important research question: What is the consistency between use of a judgment strategy or cue and verbal justification as well as verbal report of that judgment strategy or cue? This is a complex issue, aspects of which have been approached in a variety of ways by researchers of adult judgment and decision making (Ericcson & Simon,

1980; Goldstein & Beattie, 1991; Nisbett & Wilson, 1977; Lerner & Tetlock, this volume; Wills & Moore, 1996). For cue use and self-reports of cue weights, a review by Surber (1985b) showed moderate consistency. Developmental differences in consistency between verbal justification and strategy highlight the importance of studying individual variation and metacognition in judgment and decision making. Overall, the research of Jacobs and Potenza shows that children are more likely to rely on the representativeness heuristic in social than in object domains, and it highlights the importance of using multiple measures of the cognitive mechanisms underlying children's judgments. Obviously, articulating verbal rationales is a demanding task for young children that can itself induce age differences (see Brainerd, 1977, for a discussion of response criteria in developmental research). We turn to this issue again when we consider the development of metacognition.

Davidson and colleagues' work (Davidson, 1995; Davidson et al., 1994) provides further developmental evidence on the representativeness heuristic and the conjunction fallacy by showing that social stereotypes influence children's use of heuristics. Their work also illustrates that different conclusions may result from using different outcome measures – verbal justifications versus the choices themselves. In their study, second, fourth, and sixth graders were asked to choose whether a person would go for a walk or ride a bike (or choose a type of pie or a color of socks) given base-rate information and individuating information (age of the person – elderly or a child). Although age was the only individuating information, the task drew on age stereotypes such that the base-rate choice conflicted with a choice based on the stereotype. When presented with age information (i.e., the character was an elderly adult or a child), children made representativeness *choices* for social situations based on their stereotypes about the elderly rather than relying on base-rate information. Similar biases involving gender stereotypes have also been found in studies with children (e.g., Meehan & Janik, 1990). In Davidson et al.'s work, older children were more likely to articulate *rationales* consistent with their stereotypical choices than were younger children. However, one might question whether the lack of consistency between choice and rationale is based on a developmental difference in the use of social stereotypes as the basis for choice, a developmental difference in verbal expressive skill, or a difference in metacognitive awareness of what one is doing (or trying to do). Unfortunately, measuring metacognition usually requires collecting some kinds of verbal explanations.

Another interesting result in the work of Davidson et al. is that given information that was consistent with stereotypes about children (e.g., that children like to ride bikes), all children (second, fourth, and sixth grade) were more likely to base their rationales on scenario *embellishments* than on either base rates or stereotypes. This suggests that when they are given scenarios about a child, children make decisions based on their personal preferences and experiences, rather than using either base rates or stereotypes about their own group.

In summary, the research on the development of the representativeness heuristic suggests that children are more likely to use this heuristic in familiar social situations than in situations involving objects. Early in development or in domains that are highly personally relevant, children rely mainly on their idiosyncratic personal preferences and knowledge in making decisions, and it is not clear whether these types of scenario embellishments are connected to their processing of either the individuating or base-rate information or other situational cues. With increasing age, children are increasingly likely to draw on social stereotypes when making decisions about groups other than themselves, and they are increasingly likely to use objective base-rate information in object domains. Interestingly, children have been shown to be more likely to use base rates when larger numerical differences but identical ratios are used (4:8 vs. 2:4; cf. Reyna, 1995). This suggests that the way base-rate information is presented (Haines, Moore, & Dixon, 1999) could have a dramatic effect on how the problem is represented subjectively.

The differences found between children's choices and their verbal rationales in this line of research underscore the importance of considering differences among multiple dependent variables or methods in the assessment of the cognitive basis of children's judgments. The cleavage between the choice data and the verbal rationales at younger ages could suggest metacognitive differences, but this finding is hopelessly confounded with development of verbal expressive ability.

Confirmatory and Self-Serving Biases

Research on confirmatory and self-serving biases offers some interesting insights into the development of heuristic use. Much of the research on the self-serving bias has used a very limited age range (that is, children in fifth grade and older), and studies of confirmatory bias using nonsocial materials have also studied only children in late grade school and older (Kuhn et al., 1995; Shaklee & Mims, 1981). The self-serving and confirmatory bias is the tendency to treat evidence consistent with one's preexisting beliefs or personal goals more favorably than inconsistent evidence and to make judgments and decisions accordingly. The self-serving bias is a special case of confirmatory bias (Klayman & Ha, 1987). Existence of self-serving and confirmatory biases has been documented in research with children in social domains (e.g., Klaczynski, 2000; Klaczynski & Fauth, 1997; Klaczynski & Narasimham, 1998), environmental health (e.g., Holtgrave, Tinsley, & Kay, 1994), and everyday reasoning (Klaczynski, 1997), as well as in scientific domains (e.g., Kuhn, 1989, 1990, 1993). Typically these studies show few developmental differences, even with children as young as 7 years (Baron, Granato, Spranca, & Teubal, 1993; Byrnes, 1998).

The self-serving bias illustrates the importance of motivational and emotional factors in children's decision making. In this area of research, the use of everyday reasoning problems (e.g., justifying music preferences) and personally relevant social domains (e.g., religious beliefs) has brought to the foreground the significant impact of motivational factors on children's decision making. Motivation in such studies has usually been indexed by the relevance of the problem to children's lives or children's engagement with a problem. In such studies, motivation is hypothesized to increase the amount and type of cognitive resources allocated to a problem (this hypothesis also comes from Crick and Dodge's framework). In addition, evidence of a self-serving bias further suggests the importance of motivational goals in children's judgment and decision making.

In spite of the fact that in recent years theories of cognitive development have moved away from hypothesizing domain-general stages, some research has attempted to relate measures purported to assess domain-general cognitive abilities to self-serving bias in decision making (Klaczynski & Fauth, 1997). Klaczynski and Fauth used a test of logical thinking and Wason's (1966) well-known logical selection task to measure formal operational reasoning ability. Their intent was to test a prediction derived from Piaget's theory that formal operational thinkers should be less prone to self-serving biases. The idea behind this prediction is that once the ability to be rational is present, it should be used in all situations. (Of course, this prediction neglects important motivational and emotional factors.) The results showed that neither measure of general reasoning ability significantly predicted self-serving biases. Given the array of domain-specific factors that have been shown to affect decision making and judgment biases, this result is not surprising.

A key question arising from this research is whether the lack of support for domain-general stage theories reflects measurement issues (i.e., traditional means of assessing reasoning stage, like conservation or proportional reasoning tasks, have also been shown to be affected by a variety of task and contextual factors, and consequently may not be tapping a general underlying cognitive state accurately) or whether it is best to abandon the search for a single underlying cognitive state in children's cognition. Indeed, this is a fundamental issue in all of psychology: Are there general cognitive structures or competencies that underlie observed performance? We favor a multistate conception of cognitive development and cognition (as opposed to a domain-general stage concept) because the subjective problem representation of a task will depend on contextual factors, as shown in our own work on mixture problems, and on intraindividual variability (e.g., rooted in emotion and motivation), as shown in much of the social cognitive developmental work.

An important and interesting monograph on biased processing by Kuhn et al. (1995) studied evidence search, verbal explanations of inference processes, and belief revision as a function of a priori beliefs. The results showed that confirmatory bias depended on a priori belief, age, and task content (social or nonsocial). Both adults (community college students ranging in age from 22 to 47 years) and children (fourth graders, aged 8 to 10 years) participated in a multisession experiment. Participants worked on four different multicue causal inference problems. In the first session, each participant's a priori beliefs about the variables were assessed by asking whether or not each variable would make a difference in the outcome and why. Then in each session participants selected a limited set of trials (up to six) in which they manipulated combinations of variables and observed the results. Before each trial, the experimenter asked the participant, "Which features are you trying to find out about?" The participant was also asked to predict the outcome. After observing the outcome, the experimenter asked, "What do you think about how this one came out?" If the participant made an inference of causality for a feature, the experimenter asked for a justification, including what specific trial outcomes were relevant. Thus, detailed data were obtained on the reasoning used in drawing inferences.

The results showed that the confirmatory bias was stronger in the social tasks (inference of what causes good school performance given information about class size, gender of the principal, classroom noise level, presence of a teacher's assistant, and teacher's presence on the playground during recess, and inference of what causes children to like TV programs) than in the nonsocial tasks (inferences of distances traveled by toy boats and cars). The children's overall performance (percentage of prediction errors) was markedly better in the two nonsocial tasks than in the social tasks, whereas the adults did not show a large difference in prediction accuracy due to task content. For the adults, a priori belief that a variable was a cause of the outcome negatively influenced use of valid inferences in the social tasks but not in the nonsocial tasks. Hence, confirmatory bias was more apparent in the social tasks than in the nonsocial tasks. Children were particularly prone to confirmatory bias in their justifications, often ignoring the results of the experiments they constructed. Another interesting aspect of Kuhn et al.'s results is that some participants were clearly selective in applying their inference strategies in order to hold on to certain a priori beliefs. This selective strategy use was more likely in the social tasks than in the nonsocial tasks.

Klaczynski and Narasimham (1998) found evidence of self-serving biases and no developmental differences among 5th, 8th, and 11th graders in their *justifications* regarding religious beliefs. Klaczynski and Narasimham reported a "mere belonging" bias, such that children who personally identified with a religion were more critical of theory-inconsistent evidence than were children with negative views toward a religion, who, in turn, were consequently less biased by their personal theories. Developmental differences did emerge in Klaczynski and Narasimham's study in children's *ratings* that were not observed in their justifications. Fifth graders rated arguments (presented by the experimenter) that were supportive of their religious beliefs as stronger and more valid than did the two adolescent groups (8th and 11th graders). Thus, there was a developmental decrease in self-serving biases. Nevertheless, all groups showed the self-serving bias by rating supportive arguments as more valid and stronger than arguments that conflicted with their beliefs. Also, adolescents' ratings showed greater overall awareness of flaws in arguments (regardless of whether the argument conflicted with the participant's religious beliefs) than did the ratings of the fifth graders. Based on this latter result, the authors concluded that adolescents have the skills necessary for sophisticated analytical reasoning, but they use them selectively to preserve existing beliefs.

By coding the content of the rationales, Klaczynski and Narasimham examined whether self-serving biases arose out of cognitive mechanisms (i.e., protecting causal theories of how the world works) or ego-protective mechanisms (i.e., protecting self-concept and personal belief systems) and found that both kinds of rationales were comparably predictive of self-serving biases. Important questions are whether people are aware of their self-serving biases and whether there are developmental changes in such metacognitive awareness. The finding that reasoning skills increase with age, but that there is no corresponding decrease in self-serving biases with age, suggests that future research should also examine the role of metacognitive factors in regulating reasoning biases. When people have access to aspects of their own judgment and decision processes, there is at least the possibility of negotiation with others about the judgments and decisions that result (cf. Ebenbach & Moore, 2000). For topics such as religious beliefs with the potential to create intergroup conflict, such awareness of bias could be the key to avoiding open conflict.

In summary, Klaczynski and Narasimham (1998) and Kuhn et al. both found biased and selective strategy use. That is, rather than using their most sophisticated strategies on the most objectively challenging problems, children use their most sophisticated reasoning skills when their existing beliefs are challenged and rely on simpler schema-based processing when a situation or problem does not threaten their belief systems. These findings highlight the importance of including motivational factors in judgment and decision-making research. Research with preadolescent groups and younger children is particularly lacking in this area and is needed to trace the developmental trajectory more fully (see Baron & Brown, 1991, for an interesting collection of papers on teaching adolescents how to be more rational in their decision making). The findings presented here suggest improvement in reasoning skills and strategies with age but no corresponding decrease in biases with age. That is, some aspects of rationality (such as appropriate cue use) may increase with age but so may biased decision making. This pattern suggests a potential role for metacognition in regulating judgment and decision biases.

Development of Metacognition and Adaptive Judgment and Decision Making

An important issue both in developmental research and in the mainstream of judgment and decision-making research is how people decide what approach to use in a given setting. In some instances, strategies are chosen explicitly and deliberately, whereas in other instances strategy choice takes place automatically or implicitly. In developmental research there is a long history of concern with how children choose strategies, and with their awareness that they did use and can exert choice over strategies (Brown, Campione, & Barclay, 1979; Campione & Brown, 1977; Crowley, Shrager, & Siegler, 1997). A related and equally important issue is the extent to which children monitor the effectiveness of their strategies and adapt their behavior accordingly. This area is termed *metacognition* and was first explored for children's memory strategies (Flavell, 1970). The area is important in cognitive and social cognitive development because choice of appropriate strategies, monitoring, and regulation of those strategies are key to improving performance in most cognitive tasks (Crowley et al., 1997). Kuhn (1993), in her studies of the development of scientific reasoning, suggested that metacognitive skills are critical to the development of increasingly sophisticated reasoning skills and in the development of the avoidance of reasoning biases (such as the confirmatory bias). She says, ". . . the major challenge [children] face is not one of acquiring correct experimentation strategies, but of developing the ability to coordinate their existing theories with new evidence they generate, in an explicit, conscious, and controlled way; in other words, again, to think about their own thought" (p. 96). In judgment and decision making, Payne et al. (1993) emphasized the importance of adapting strategies to task demands and did discuss metacognition briefly. We discuss two lines of metacognitive research that are relevant to judgment and decision making. The first area focuses on strategy choice and offers a model of how explicit metacognitive processes interact with implicitly driven strategies. Second, we consider research on children's adaptive decision making and decision-making autonomy that highlights the roles of experience and personal responsibility in explaining children's decision-making processes.

Crowley et al. (1997) proposed a model describing the role of metacognitive mechanisms in strategy discovery using data on children's discovery of the *min* strategy for mental addition. The min strategy involves counting up from the larger addend in an addition problem and is an efficient improvement over young children's initial counting strategies when adding. The model is based on data from a *microgenetic* study over an 11-week period in which 4- and 5-year-old children were videotaped solving addition problems and interviewed afterward regarding their strategies. Children showed considerable variability in when and how the strategy was discovered and in the use of the min strategy following initial discovery. There was also variability in the extent to which children seemed aware of the discovery, and greater awareness was associated with faster generalization of the strategy.

Crowley et al. proposed a model of competitive negotiation between associative mechanisms and metacognitive mechanisms to account for these data on strategy discovery. Associative mechanisms are characterized as the implicit, fast, and experientially based strategies that evolve from trial-and-error practice in a particular domain, in this case, addition. In contrast, metacognitive mechanisms are explicit strategies that are consciously learned or invented, evaluated, and adapted through explicit reflection on their effectiveness. In comparison to associative mechanisms, metacognitive mechanisms are slow and demanding of mental effort, and are therefore likely to lose out in familiar domains where more efficient strategies are available. However, Crowley et al. hypothesize that the efficiency of associative strategies in familiar domains also frees the metacognitive system from strategy regulation, allowing it to monitor the associative system. Consequently, the metacognitive system has resources available to notice patterns, shortcuts, or alternative possibilities. Thus, Crowley et al. hypothesize that the monitoring process may suggest a new strategy to deal with familiar problems, and the metacognitive system will consequently compete for control of the problem-solving process. Furthermore, the bid for control may be weak, resulting in a subtle push toward a new path, but with little metacognitive awareness of what type of strategy change is evolving. Alternatively, the metacognitive system may make a strong bid to take over, explicitly directing strategy change and resulting in greater awareness of the parts of the new strategy.

Many factors are hypothesized to affect the speed and insight of metacognitive observations, including whether the child daydreams or concentrates on the task while the associative system functions and whether the child contemplates a strategy demonstrated by a peer or teacher. Crowley et al. also found that children did not try flawed strategies prior to discovering the min strategy and attribute this to children's goal sketch of addition. That is, they argue that a goal sketch (i.e., the basic principles of correct addition) results from repeated execution of a correct addition strategy. As the strategy becomes automatic with experience, only the essential subgoals are expected to remain in the representation (i.e., the goal sketch), allowing the cognitive system to try new strategies but constrained by these existing principles. Clearly, the extent to which a goal sketch can prevent adoption of flawed strategies depends on the extent to which the original strategy is grounded on formally correct principles.

The model of competitive negotiation between implicit experientially based processes and explicit metacognitive mechanisms provides a potential framework for addressing debates (cf. Reder, 1996) about the extent to which cognitive self-regulation is an explicitly conscious process. However, Crowley et al.'s model obviously contains hypotheses about the ontogenesis of the representation and the distribution of the resources of the metacognitive system that would be difficult to separate empirically.

The study by Kuhn et al. (1995) that compared causal inferences for social and nonsocial tasks is also pertinent to metacognition. A central conclusion drawn by Kuhn et al. is that "even when strategic competence is well in place, strategies are not consistently applied" (p. 109) because of failure in the general category of metacognition. The authors made a distinction between metastrategic and metacognitive competence. The term *metastrategic competence* is used to refer to the processes through which strategies are chosen, including understanding "how, when, and why the strategy should be used" (p. 109). One key aspect of metastrategic competence is the formation of an appropriate subjective task structure. Another aspect is adopting an appropriate task goal. Kuhn et al. also emphasized the important role of metastrategic knowledge in rejecting inadequate strategies, and interpreted the results from the adult sample as evidence that, over time, adults are likely to stop using ineffective strategies for both generating and interpreting evidence.

In contrast to metastrategic functions, the authors use the term *metacognitive competence* to refer to thinking about cognitive contents such as beliefs, theories, and their justifications. This competence is also important because good performance depends on separating observations, the implications of the observations, and the theories or beliefs. In the adults, the distinction between evidence and a priori belief was made more clearly for the nonsocial tasks, whereas for the children the distinction was equally fuzzy for both the social and nonsocial tasks. Thus, there is development in metacognition, but metacognitive failures occur even in adults, depending on the context.

Other studies relate to metacognition more indirectly but provide equally important insights into how children select strategies and adapt to their decision-making environment. Helwig and Kim (1999) studied children's perceptions of whether the decision-making context allows autonomous decision making or requires submission to authority.

This is obviously important in children's everyday lives. In their study, Helwig and Kim described decision situations to children (e.g., a family deciding what game to play, what educational content would be presented to third graders for a week, where a class should go on a field trip) and presented three decision procedure options (consensus, authority-based, and majority-rule vote). Children in first to sixth grade were interviewed about each option. The results showed that children chose consensus decision making as appropriate for peer contexts and certain situations within family contexts (e.g., choosing a game to play), whereas authority-based decision making was judged as appropriate in hierarchical situations within family and school contexts.

Children justified autonomous decision making on the basis of fairness, consensus, or democratic ideas. These justifications of autonomous decision making show a reliance on social norms as opposed to concepts such as personal rights or authority. Because the family is a major source of social norms, it would be expected that parental belief systems and socialization practices would have a significant impact on the extent to which children feel empowered to make autonomous decisions. Relevant to this interpretation, Helwig and Kim (1999) found that children's rationales for authority-based decisions often referred to the children's lack of competence to make a good decision. Children's assessments of inadequate competence to make autonomous decisions could reflect considerations of the complex goals operating in certain contexts (e.g., developing a good educational curriculum), which Helwig and Kim found among older children (fifth and sixth graders), or could reflect personal characteristics, such as learned helplessness or low self-esteem. In addition, young children were more likely than older children to endorse consensus-based decision making across contexts, even when cues for authority-based decisions were intended to be salient. Therefore, there does seem to be a developmental increase in choosing strategies that fit the social context – that is, adaptive decision making does show development. This study shows that children think decision methods should be adapted to the situation, but without studying what strategies are actually used. Hence, it can be regarded as a study of metacognition of decision strategies.

Another important implication of Helwig and Kim's study is that feeling competent and able to make independent decisions seems critical to cognitive engagement in the decision-making process. This result again points to the importance of emotional and motivational factors. For example, of particular interest are the types of strategies children generate when incentives to gain decision-making autonomy are high. Kelley, Mayall, and Hood (1997) reported that children desired control over their leisure time and that children were most critical of parental rules that they perceived as based only on their status as children. Using a qualitative method, they found that children reported a variety of strategies that they used to take control of their leisure time.

Perceived autonomy also plays an important role in much of children's real-life decision making. Perceived autonomy in legal situations is of practical importance to children who become involved in legal procedures. Peterson-Badali, Abramovitch, and Duda (1997) studied 7- to 12-year-old children and found that younger children frequently believed that lawyers could violate confidentiality in order to reveal what a minor client says to parents, judges, and police officers. Older children were more likely to understand confidentiality. Legal domains also require reasoning about correct or "right" and "wrong" decisions in a way that differs qualitatively from the moral conceptions of right and wrong that children are taught in home and school contexts. That is, a correct or right plea decision requires children to ignore actual guilt or innocence and consider the strength of the evidence. Making this distinction metacognitively is very important to using the distinction appropriately in everyday life. Peterson-Badali and colleagues (1997) studied this topic by presenting children 7 to 12 years old with scenarios about a protagonist who was arrested for committing an offense under various conditions of strength of evidence. Using qualitative interview methods, they found that a majority of children's hypothetical plea decisions were based on legal (strength of evidence) rather than moral criteria. However, these authors characterized children as relying primarily on an implicit understanding of the legal system and having serious misunderstandings of some legal concepts. The interaction between legal and moral domains represents an extremely complex, yet increasingly important, decision-making domain for children and an interesting arena for decision-making research.

Some research has examined the planfulness and exhaustiveness of children's information search strategies before making a decision, using information board methodology (Davidson, 1991, 1996; Gregan-Paxton & John, 1995, 1997). This research finds that young children frequently do less planful and more exhaustive searches than are beneficial. In contrast, older children use more focused and efficient noncompensatory search strategies (i.e., searching only certain dimensions designated as important and eliminating others). The exhaustive searches of the younger children are consistent with Reyna and Brainerd's (1995) fuzzy-trace theory in that the theory sees younger children as more enmeshed in details than older children. Young children do demonstrate some of the skills necessary for adaptive decision making, but only in decision-making environments that provide high support for their use (e.g., salient perceptual cues or clear cues about the costs of elaborate searching). Thus, research in this area suggests a developmental model in which children do use a variety of more sophisticated and less sophisticated strategies, depending on task parameters, rather than a simple developmental progression from less sophisticated to more sophisticated strategy usage. Furthermore, whether it is superior to eliminate by aspects (noncompensatory searching), as is evident in older children's and adults' information searches, depends on the task parameters and how the ideal decision is defined. In the adult decision-making literature, noncompensatory search strategies are not necessarily considered optimal because they fail to consider all dimensions or alternatives (see Byrnes, 1998, for a review). Consequently, it is important to separate selectivity (selecting the important dimension to search) and efficiency (avoiding search of the least important dimensions) in studying the development of adaptive decision making.

In summary, metacognitive research and theory highlight three processes that are key to children's judgment and decision making: selecting a strategy to approach a decision-making problem, monitoring the effectiveness of the strategy selected, and regulating the execution of the strategy according to both external feedback and metacognitive feedback (reassessing one's goals, reevaluating strategy options, assessing the efficiency of the strategy, etc.). For example, Helwig and Kim's research suggests that children's perceptions of their own autonomy in a decision-making situation will affect the strategy selection process. That is, they may choose to defer to an authority figure, or they may select strategies that will allow them to assume authority or attempt to obtain authority to make an independent decision. This type of metadecision will affect subsequent strategy selection for the task itself, as well as the amount of engagement in the task.

One issue in the metacognitive area is a need for research that separately measures metacognition and the performance metacognition supposedly regulates, as well as the accuracy of metacognitive monitoring (Nelson, 1996). Unfortunately, few studies have explicitly examined metacognitive development for judgment and decision making per se, and even recent cognitive and social cognitive development work emphasizing the importance of metacognition does not always measure the subjective states involved. For example, Kuhn et al.'s (1995) conclusion that metacognition is very important is based on relatively intrusive questioning of participants about many aspects of the inference task (for each trial, participants were probed to provide a prediction, conclusions, and justification of the conclusion). Although these questions are not quite *process tracing*, they do probe specific cognitive states involved in regulating task performance. A problem is that in order to study metacognition more effectively, the metacognitive measures must be separate from task performance itself.

A central issue for further research concerns the extent to which metacognition is explicit and deliberate (Metcalfe & Shimamura, 1994; Nelson, 1996). The model developed by Crowley et al. treats metacognition as primarily an explicit system that is independent of the more implicit associative cognitive system. Others have argued that certain strategy selection processes are implicit yet still metacognitive (Reder, 1996), as illustrated by the adaptive decision-making processes reviewed previously (e.g., Gregan-Paxton & John, 1997). That is, children adapt their decision-making processes with experience, but often with little apparent awareness or explicit regulation of the shifts in strategy they are making.

It is clear that the field of metacognition is in need of unifying constructs and terminology. For example, some, such as Crowley et al., seem to reserve the term *metacognition* for explicit and deliberately controllable processes. Others, such as Reder (1996), include in the metacognitive category most forms of self-regulation, including automatic and implicit processes. Research is also needed on how the metacognitive system interacts with other cognitive and affective systems. For example, how do motivational goals or personal beliefs interact with or direct the metacognitive system? Can we teach children (and adults) to monitor their cognitive processes more effectively and adapt them in the face of errors and biases?

Conclusions

Our selective review of developmental research shows that children's performance on judgment and decision tasks is influenced by a wide variety of contextual and internal variables. More sophisticated reasoning (and, ironically, perhaps more biased reasoning under conditions that threaten existing belief systems) is likely in social and interpersonal domains, in areas of high personal relevance, in situations in which task difficulty is low and strategy-supporting cues are salient, when familiarity is high, and when peer, parent, and cultural norms motivate task engagement. On the other hand, less complex, script-based processing and heuristic use is likely when external threats to belief systems are low, social norms are prescriptive and unchallenged, task difficulty is high, and familiarity and relevance are low. We have emphasized how internal variables (emotion, motivational goals, knowledge, etc.) interact with contextual variables to produce a subjective representation of the situation that may differ for different individuals.

Metacognitive regulation of judgment and decision strategies is hypothesized by several researchers to be the most efficient means of improving performance on judgment and decision tasks. Recent work in educational psychology on *self-regulated learning* shows promising results from attempting to connect cognitive and metacognitive strategies with motivational goals to enhance student achievement (Winne, 1996; Zimmerman & Risemberg, 1997). Both developmental psychology and the field of judgment and decision making focus on improving performance and reducing reasoning biases. Consequently, future research could profitably explore the metacognitive control of judgment and decision strategies. However, metacognitive control should not be studied just as an explicit and deliberate process; researchers should also be mindful of the possibility that strong influences on strategy regulation can derive from implicit cognitive processes as well. This implies that multiple methods should be used for studying metacognition, just as judgment and decision strategies are studied with multiple dependent variables (choice, ratings, justifications). Use of only verbal justifications as a measure of metacognition, for example, would tap only the easily verbalizable aspects of metacognition. Our review also shows that in studying metacognition, researchers should not neglect the ways in which an individual's goals, motivations, and the subjective representation of the problem affect strategy choice and regulation. These suggestions, though challenging, have potential to yield more comprehensive theories.

References

Ahl, V. A., Moore, C. F., & Dixon, J. A. (1992). Development of intuitive and numerical proportional reasoning. *Cognitive Development, 7*, 81–108.

Anderson, N. H. (1974). Cognitive algebra. In L. Berkowitz (Ed.), *Advances in experimental social psychology* (Vol. 7, pp. 1–101). New York: Academic Press.

Anderson, N. H., & Butzin, C. A. (1978). Integration theory applied to children's judgments of equity. *Developmental Psychology, 14,* 593–606.

Austin, E. W., & Johnson, K. K. (1997). Immediate and delayed effects of media literacy training on third graders' decision making for alcohol. *Health Communication, 9,* 323–349.

Baron, J., & Brown, R. (Eds.). (1991). *Teaching decision making to adolescents.* Hillsdale, NJ: Erlbaum.

Baron, J., Granato, L., Spranca, M., & Teubal, E. (1993). Decision-making biases in children and early adolescents: Exploratory studies. *Merrill-Palmer Quarterly, 39,* 22–46.

Birnbaum, M. H. (1982). Controversies in psychological measurement. In B. Wegener (Ed.), *Social attitudes and psychophysical measurement* (pp. 401–485). Hillsdale, NJ: Erlbaum.

Brainerd, C. J. (1977). Response criteria in concept development research. *Child Development, 48,* 360–366.

Brainerd, C. J. (1978). *Piaget's theory of intelligence.* Englewood Cliffs, NJ: Prentice Hall.

Brown, A. L., Campione, J. C., & Barclay, C. R. (1979). Training self-checking routines for estimating test readiness: Generalization from list learning to prose recall. *Child Development, 50,* 501–512.

Brunswik, E. (1956). *Perception and the representative design of experiments.* Berkeley, CA: University of California Press.

Byrnes, J. P. (1998). *The nature and development of decision making: A self-regulation model.* Mahwah, NJ: Erlbaum.

Campione, J. C., & Brown, A. L. (1977). Memory and metamemory development in educable retarded children. In R. V. Kail & J. W. Hagen (Eds.), *Perspectives on the development of memory and cognition* (pp. 367–406). Hillsdale, NJ: Erlbaum.

Case, R., & Okamoto, Y. (1996). The rule of central conceptual structures in the development of children's thought. *Monographs of the Society for Research in Child Development, 60,* Serial No. 246.

Chapman, M. (1988). *Constructive evolution: Origins and development of Piaget's thought.* New York: Cambridge University Press.

Coombs, C. H., Raiffa, H., & Thrall, R. M. (1954). Some views on mathematical models and measurement theory. *Psychological Review, 61,* 132–144.

Crick, N. R., & Dodge, K. A. (1994). A review and reformulation of social information-processing mechanisms in children's social adjustment. *Psychological Bulletin, 115,* 74–101.

Crick, N. R., & Ladd, G. W. (1993). Children's perceptions of their peer experiences: Attributions, loneliness, social anxiety, and social avoidance. *Developmental Psychology, 29,* 244–254.

Crick, N. R., & Werner, N. E. (1998). Response decision processes in relational and overt aggression. *Child Development, 69,* 1630–1639.

Cronbach, L. J. (1957). The two disciplines of scientific psychology. *American Psychologist, 12,* 671–684.

Crowley, K., Shrager, J., & Siegler, R. S. (1997) Strategy discovery as a competitive negotiation between metacognitive and associative mechanisms. *Developmental Review, 17,* 462–489.

Davidson, D. (1991). Developmental differences in children's search of predecisional information. *Journal of Experimental Child Psychology, 52,* 239–255.

Davidson, D. (1995). The representativeness heuristic and the conjunction fallacy effect in children's decision making. *Merrill-Palmer Quarterly, 41,* 328–346.

Davidson, D. (1996). The effects of decision characteristics on children's selective search of predecisional information. *Acta Psychologica, 92,* 263–281.

Davidson, D., MacKay, M., & Jergovic, D. (1994). The effects of stereotypes on children's use of decision heuristics. In L. Heath, R. S. Tindale, J. Edwards, E. J. Posavac, F. B. Bryant, E. Henderson-King, Y. Suarez-Balcazar, & J. Myers (Eds.), *Applications of heuristics and biases to social issues* (pp. 241–257). New York: Plenum Press.

Dawes, R. M. (1975). The mind, the model, and the task. In F. Restle, R. M. Shiffrin, N. J. Castellan, H. R. Lindman, & D. P. Pisoni (Eds.), *Cognitive theory* (Vol. 1, pp. 119–129). Hillsdale, NJ: Erlbaum.

Dixon, J. A., & Moore, C. F. (1996). The developmental role of intuitive principles in choosing mathematical strategies. *Developmental Psychology, 32,* 241–253.

Dixon, J. A., & Moore, C. F. (1997). Characterizing the intuitive representation in problem solving: Evidence from evaluating mathematical strategies. *Memory & Cognition, 25,* 395–412.

Dodge, K. A. (1986). A social information processing model of social competence in children. In M. Perlmutter (Ed.), *The Minnesota symposium on child psychology* (Vol. 18, pp. 77–125). Hillsdale, NJ: Erlbaum.

Dulany, D. E. (1991). Conscious representation and thought systems. In R. S. Wyer & T. K. Srull (Eds.), *Advances in social cognition* (Vol. 4, pp. 97–120). Hillsdale, NJ: Erlbaum.

Dweck, C. S., & Leggett, E. L. (1988). A social-cognitive approach to motivation and personality. *Psychological Review, 95,* 256–272.

Ebenbach, D. H., & Moore, C. F. (2000). Incomplete information, inferences, and individual differences. *Organizational Behavior and Human Decision Processes, 81,* 1–27.

Ericcson, K. A., & Simon, H. A. (1980). Verbal reports as data. *Psychological Review, 87,* 215–251.

Falk, R., & Wilkening, F. (1998). Children's construction of fair chances: Adjusting probabilities. *Developmental Psychology, 34,* 1340–1357.

Flavell, J. H. (1963). *The developmental psychology of Jean Piaget.* Princeton, NJ: Van Nostrand.

Flavell, J. H. (1970). Developmental studies of mediated memory. In H. W. Reese & L. P. Lipsitt (Eds.), *Advances in child development and behavior* (Vol. 5, pp. 181–211). New York: Academic Press.

Gigerenzer, G., & Richter, H. R. (1990). Context effects and their interaction with development: Area judgments. *Cognitive Development, 5,* 235–264.

Goldstein, W. M., & Beattie, J. (1991). Judgments of relative importance in decision making: The importance of interpretation and the interpretation of importance. In D. R. Brown & J. E. K. Smith (Eds.), *Frontiers of mathematical psychology: Essays in honor of Clyde Coombs* (pp. 109–137). New York: Springer-Verlag.

Gregan-Paxton, J., & John, D. R. (1995). Are young children adaptive decision makers? A study of age differences in information search behavior. *Journal of Consumer Research, 21,* 567–579.

Gregan-Paxton, J., & John, D. R. (1997). The emergence of adaptive decision making in children. *Journal of Consumer Research, 24,* 43–56.

Haines, B. A., Metalsky, G. I., Cardamone, A. L., & Joiner, T. (1999). Interpersonal and cognitive pathways into the origins of attributional style: A developmental perspective. In T. Joiner & J. C. Coyne (Eds.), *The interactional nature of depression* (pp. 65–92). Washington, DC: APA Press.

Haines, B. A., Moore, C. F., & Dixon, J. A. (1999). *Sources of asynchrony in the development of probability understanding.* Unpublished manuscript.

Hammond, K. R. (1996). *Human judgment and social policy: Irreducible uncertainty, inevitable error, unavoidable injustice.* New York: Oxford University Press.

Hammond, K. R., McClelland, G. H., & Mumpower, J. (1980). *Human judgment and decision making: Theories, methods and procedures.* New York: Praeger.

Hayes, J. R., & Simon, H. A. (1976). The understanding process: Problem isomorphs. *Cognitive Psychology, 8,* 165–190.

Helwig, C. C., & Kim, S. (1999). Children's evaluations of decision-making procedures in peer, family, and school contexts. *Child Development, 70,* 502–512.

Henderson, V. L., & Dweck, C. S. (1990). Motivation and achievement. In S. S. Feldman & G. R. Elliot (Eds.), *At the threshold: The developing adolescent* (pp. 308–329). Cambridge, MA: Harvard University Press.

Holtgrave, D. R., Tinsley, B. J., & Kay, L. S. (1994). Heuristics, biases, and environmental health risk analysis. In L. Heath, R. S. Tindale, J. Edwards, E. J. Posavac, F. B. Bryant, E. Henderson-King, Y. Suarez-Balcazar, & J. Myers (Eds.), *Applications of heuristics and biases to social issues* (pp. 259–285). New York: Plenum Press.

Inhelder, B., & Piaget, J. (1958). *The growth of logical thinking from childhood to adolescence.* New York: Basic Books.

Jacobs, J. E., & Potenza, M. (1991). The use of judgment heuristics to make social and object decisions: A developmental perspective. *Child Development, 62,* 166–178.

Kelley, P., Mayall, B., & Hood, S. (1997). Children's accounts of risk. *Childhood, 4,* 305–324.

Kerkman, D. D., & Wright, J. C. (1988a). An exegesis of two theories of compensation development: Sequential decision theory and information integration theory. *Developmental Review, 8,* 323–360.

Kerkman, D. D., & Wright, J. C. (1988b). A "misrepresentation" of method as theory. *Developmental Review, 8,* 368–375.

Kindt, M., Brosschot, J. F., & Everaerd, W. (1997). Cognitive processing bias of children in a real life stress situation, and a neutral situation. *Journal of Experimental Child Psychology, 64,* 79–97.

Klaczynski, P. A. (1997). Bias in adolescents' everyday reasoning and its relationship with intellectual ability, personal theories, and self-serving motivation. *Developmental Psychology, 33,* 273–283.

Klaczynski, P. A. (2000). Motivated scientific reasoning biases, epistemological beliefs, and theory polarization: A two-process approach to adolescent cognition. *Child Development, 71,* 1347–1366.

Klaczynski, P. A., & Fauth, J. (1997). Developmental differences in memory-based intrusions and self-serving statistical reasoning biases. *Merrill-Palmer Quarterly, 43,* 539–565.

Klaczynski, P. A., & Narasimham, G. (1998). Development of scientific reasoning biases: Cognitive versus ego-protective explanations. *Developmental Psychology, 34,* 175–187.

Klayman, J., & Ha, Y.-W. (1987). Confirmation, disconfirmation, and information in hypothesis testing. *Psychological Review, 94,* 211–228.

Kuhn, D. (1989). Children and adults as intuitive scientists. *Psychological Review, 96,* 674–689.

Kuhn, D. (1990). Developmental perspectives on teaching and learning thinking skills. *Contributions to human development* (Vol. 21). Basel: Karger.

Kuhn, D. (1993). Connecting scientific and informal reasoning. *Merrill-Palmer Quarterly, 39,* 74–103.

Kuhn, D., Garcia-Mila, M., Zohar, A., & Andersen, C. (1995). Strategies of knowledge acquisition. *Monographs of the Society for Research in Child Development, 60,* Serial No. 245.

Luce, R. D. (1996). The ongoing dialog between empirical science and measurement theory. *Journal of Mathematical Psychology, 40,* 78–98.

MacLeod, C., & Mathews, A. (1991). Biased cognitive operations in anxiety: Accessibility of information or assignment of processing priorities. *Behaviour Research and Therapy, 29,* 599–610.

Meehan, A. M., & Janik, L. M. (1990). Illusory correlation and the maintenance of sex role stereotypes in children. *Sex Roles, 22,* 83–95.

Mellers, B. A., & Cooke, A. D. J. (1996). The role of task and content in preference measurement. *Psychological Science, 7,* 76–82.

Mellers, B. A., Schwartz, A., Ho, K., & Ritov, I. (1997). Decision affect theory: Emotional reactions to the outcomes of risky options. *Psychological Science, 8,* 423–429.

Metcalfe, J., & Shimamura, A. P. (Eds.). (1994). *Metacognition: Knowing about knowing.* Cambridge, MA: MIT Press.

Moore, C. F., Dixon, J. A., & Haines, B. A. (1991). Components of understanding in proportional reasoning: A fuzzy set representation of developmental progressions. *Child Development, 62,* 441–459.

Moore, C. F., Hembree, S. E., & Enright, R. D. (1993). The unfolding of justice: A developmental perspective on reward allocation. In B. Mellers & J. Baron (Eds.), *Psychological perspectives on justice* (pp. 183–204). Cambridge: Cambridge University Press.

Nelson, T. O. (1996) Consciousness and metacognition. *American Psychologist, 51,* 102–116.

Nisbett, R. E., & Wilson, T. D. (1977). Telling more than we can know: Verbal reports on mental processes. *Psychological Review, 84,* 231–259.

Payne, J. W., Bettman, J. R., & Johnson, E. J. (1993). *The adaptive decision maker.* New York: Cambridge University Press.

Peterson-Badali, M., Abramovitch, R., & Duda, J. (1997). Young children's legal knowledge and reasoning ability. *Canadian Journal of Criminology, 39,* 145–170.

Reder, L. M. (1996). Different research programs on metacognition: Are the boundaries imaginary? *Learning and Individual Differences, 8,* 383–391.

Reed, S. K., & Evans, A. C. (1987). Learning functional relations: A theoretical and instructional analysis. *Journal of Experimental Psychology: General, 116,* 106–118.

Reyna, V. F. (1995). Interference effects in memory and reasoning. In F. N. Dempster & C. J. Brainerd (Eds.), *Interference and inhibition in cognition* (pp. 29–59). San Diego, CA: Academic Press.

Reyna, V. F., & Brainerd, C. J. (1995). Fuzzy-trace theory: An interim synthesis. *Learning and Individual Differences, 7,* 1–75.

Schkade, D. A., & Kahneman, D. (1998). Does living in California make people happy? A focusing illusion in judgments of life satisfaction. *Psychological Science, 9,* 340–346.

Shaklee, H. (1979). Bounded rationality and cognitive development: Upper limits on growth? *Cognitive Psychology, 11,* 327–345.

Shaklee, H., & Mims, M. (1981). Development of rule use in judgments of covariation between events. *Child Development, 52,* 317–325.

Shanteau, J. (1992). How much information does an expert use? Is it relevant? *Acta Psychologica, 81,* 75–86.

Shanteau, J., & Skowronski, J. J. (1992). The decision to donate organs. In J. Shanteau & R. J. Harris (Eds.), *Organ donation and transplantation: Psychological and behavioral factors* (pp. 59–67). Washington, DC: APA Press.

Shatz, M. (1978). The relationship between cognitive processes and the development of communication skills. In C. B. Keasey (Ed.), *Nebraska symposium on motivation 1977* (Vol. 25, pp. 1–42). Lincoln: University of Nebraska Press.

Siegler, R. S. (1976). Three aspects of cognitive development. *Cognitive Psychology, 8,* 481–520.

Siegler, R. S. (1981). Developmental sequences within and between concepts. *Monographs of the Society for Research in Child Development, 46* (2, Serial No. 189).

Siegler, R. S. (1991). *Children's thinking* (2nd ed.). Upper Saddle River, NJ: Prentice Hall.

Siegler, R. S. (1996). *Emerging minds: The process of change in children's thinking.* New York: Oxford University Press.

Singh, R., & Singh, P. (1994). Prediction of performance using motivation and ability information: New light on integrational capacity and weighting strategies. *Cognitive Development, 9,* 455–496.

Surber, C. F. (1984). The development of achievement related judgement processes. In J. Nicholls (Ed.), *The development of achievement motivation* (pp. 137–184). Greenwich, CT: JAI Press.

Surber, C. F. (1985a). Developmental changes in inverse compensation in social and nonsocial attributions. In S. Yussen (Ed.), *The development of reflection* (pp. 149–166). New York: Academic Press.

Surber, C. F. (1985b). Measuring the importance of information in judgment: Individual differences in weighting ability and effort. *Organizational Behavior and Human Decision Processes, 35,* 156–178.

Surber, C. F. (1987). The formal representation of qualitative and quantitative reversible operations. In J. Bisanz, C. Brainerd, & R. Kail (Eds.), *Formal methods in developmental psychology* (pp. 115–154). New York: Springer-Verlag.

Surber, C. F., & Gzesh, S. M. (1984). Reversible operations in the balance scale task. *Journal of Experimental Child Psychology, 38*, 254–274.

Surber, C. F., & Haines, B. A. (1987). The growth of proportional reasoning: Methodological issues. In R. Vasta & G. Whitehurst (Eds.), *Annals of child development* (Vol. 4, pp. 35–87). Greenwich, CT: JAI.

Tversky, A., & Kahneman, D. (1974). Judgment under uncertainty: Heuristics and biases. *Science, 185*, 1124–1131.

Wason, P. C. (1966). Reasoning. In B. Foss (Ed.), *New horizons in psychology* (pp. 135–151). Harmondsworth, UK: Penguin.

Weber, E., Hsee, C. K., & Sokolowska, J. (1998). What folklore tells us about risk taking: Cultural comparisons of American, German, and Chinese proverbs. *Organizational Behavior and Human Decision Processes, 75*, 170–186.

Wilkening, F. (1981). Integrating velocity, time and distance information: A developmental study. *Cognitive Psychology, 13*, 231–247.

Wilkening, F. (1988). A misrepresentation of knowledge representation. *Developmental Review, 8*, 361–367.

Wilkening, F., & Anderson, N. H. (1982). Comparison of two rule-assessment methodologies for studying cognitive development and knowledge. *Psychological Bulletin, 92*, 215–237.

Wills, C. E., & Moore, C. F. (1996). Perspective-taking judgments of medication acceptance: Inference from relative importance about the impact and combination of information. *Organizational Behavior and Human Decision Processes, 66*, 251–267.

Winne, P. H. (1996). A metacognitive view of individual differences in self-regulated learning. *Learning and Individual Differences, 8*, 327–353.

Yates, J. F. (1988). Analyzing the accuracy of probability judgments for multiple events: An extension of the covariance decomposition. *Organizational Behavior and Human Decision Processes, 41*, 281–299.

Yates, J. F., Lee, J. W., Shinotsuka, H., Patalano, A. L., & Sieck, W. R. (1998). Cross cultural variations in probability judgment accuracy: Beyond general knowledge and overconfidence? *Organizational Behavior and Human Decision Processes, 74*, 89–117.

Zimmerman, B. J., & Risemberg, R. (1997). Self-regulatory dimensions of academic learning and motivation. In G. D. Phy (Ed.), *Handbook of academic learning: Construction of knowledge* (pp. 105–125). San Diego, CA: Academic Press.

Part III

Incorporating Affect and Motivation in Decision Making

9 Values, Affect, and Processes in Human Decision Making: A Differentiation and Consolidation Theory Perspective

Ola Svenson

ABSTRACT

Differentiation and Consolidation (Diff Con) theory is a descriptive process theory that was created to provide a framework for empirical observations in behavioral decision research. Diff Con theory postulates not only that a decision process is a successful execution of one or several decision rules but also that a decision maker must find or create an alternative that is sufficiently superior in comparison with its competitor(s). This is accomplished in (1) holistic evaluation, (2) alternative and problem restructuring, and (3) applications of one or several decision rules. The stages of a decision process include identification of alternatives, attention to markers guiding the start of the decision process, elicitation of goals, screening and editing of alternatives, selection of reference and/or preliminary choice alternatives, and process and structural differentiation to reach a decision. Following the decision process, similar processes are activated in consolidating the chosen alternative. In the theory, attractiveness consists of affect/emotion and cognitive/value components. The chapter presents a detailed account of Diff Con theory including discussions of what drives differentiation and consolidation.

CONTENTS

The author wants to thank The Royal Netherlands Academy of Arts and Sciences for supporting a stay at the Netherlands Institute for Advanced Study in the Humanities and Social Sciences (NIAS) where the present chapter was written. The study was also supported by The Swedish Council for Research in the Humanities and Social Sciences. Carl-Martin Alwood, Robyn Dawes, Melissa Finucane, Maj-Lene Hedenborg, Richard Jennings, Ellen Peters, J. Edward Russo, Sanny Shamoun, and the reviewers are all thanked for their suggestions for improvements of earlier versions of the chapter.

The interest in human decision making may be as old as humanity it-self and in behavioral science as old as that science in itself. When Leon Festinger (1957, 1964) published his and his students' work on decision making, this was an important step in drawing attention to the psychological processes before and after a decision. Festinger was a social psychologist and did not identify himself as a decision researcher. He was more interested in the psychological processes after a decision than before. Before Festinger, Kurt Lewin also studied decision making (e.g., Lewin, 1951), and later Janis and Mann (1977) revived the interest in predecision processes, still with a social psychological but partly also with a dynamic psychology perspective.

With a few exceptions (see Svenson, 1979, for an overview), decision researchers had not been very interested in the psychological processes leading up to a decision before Janis and Mann published their book. Instead, most decision researchers used a structural approach, studying how decisions and judgments depend on variations of the parameters describing a decision problem. In the mid-1970s, a number of researchers including John Payne (1976) and the present author started process studies of decision making partly inspired by Herbert Simons's work in problem solving, but also partly in opposition to the very strong structural behaviorist tradition dominating decision research at the time. In the

1980s and 1990s, process studies were no longer strange anomalies in the decision research literature but already part of mainstream research. Differentiation and Consolidation theory should be seen as an attempt to create a frame of reference that can be used to create at least some order among contemporary process studies and other studies of human decision making.

Differentiation and Consolidation theory (Svenson, 1992) is primarily a descriptive theory having its roots both in decision theory (Abelson & Levi, 1985) and in the social psychological tradition of Festinger (1957, 1964). Early process studies of decision making were also important when the Differentiation and Consolidation (Diff Con) theory framework was created (Svenson, 1974, 1979). Earlier formulations of the theory (Svenson, 1992, 1996) did not explicitly acknowledge the effects of affect and emotion in human decision processes, a fact that was pointed out by Arkes (1996). It is evident from everyday life and other fields of psychology that affect and emotion play important roles in human behavior (Abelson, Kinder, Peters, & Fiske, 1982; Cacioppo & Gardner, 1999; Rosenberg, 1998). In addition, decision researchers are becoming increasingly interested in the effects of emotion and affect on human decision processes (Luce, Bettman, & Payne, 1997; Mellers, Schwartz, & Ritov, 1999). Toda (1980) suggested that most values could be derived from emotions. Sometimes the emotions have been rationalized into value systems, and sometimes they lead to biased information processing and reasoning about values when the decision maker tries to escape from the conscious influence of emotions (that are accepted or counteracted) in the decision process. Motivated reasoning illustrates this (Kunda, 1990). Recently, Mellers and her colleagues have treated anticipated emotions in a descriptive framework for decisions under risk (Mellers et al., 1999). Kahneman, Diener, and Schwarz (1999), Kahneman (1999), and Loewenstein and Schkade (1999) give important overviews of predicted cognitive/rational and affect/emotion attractiveness. During the past decade, Diff Con theory has also undergone significant changes in relation to its original version (Svenson, 1992), and these changes will be included in the revised version of Diff Con presented here.

The chapter will present Diff Con theory with a number of subheadings, some of which will be used as a brief overview of the areas of interest covered in the chapter: representation of decision alternatives, integrating affect and values in attractiveness representations, decision rules, levels of decision making, stages in the differentiation process, predecision differentiation, differentiation leading to a decision, post-decision consolidation, what drives differentiation and consolidation processes, and the role of uncertainty in Diff Con Theory.

Diff Con Theory: Cognitive, Evaluative, and Affective Emotional Processes

Diff Con theory provides a framework in which other theories can be located, but it deviates from other decision theoretic formulations in some important ways. One is that Diff Con theory implies that a decision process is not just a successful execution of one or several decision rules. Instead, Diff Con states that a decision maker must find or create an alternative that is *sufficiently* superior to its competitor(s). This is accomplished through (1) *holistic evaluation*, (2) *alternative and problem restructuring, and* (3) *application of one or several decision rules.* Diff Con theory also requires that the decision-making data are treated in ways other than those implied by most other theories. This and other ways in which Diff Con theory deviates from other contemporary approaches will be made clear later in the chapter. It is interesting to note that the idea of a sufficiently superior alternative is not new. To exemplify, Cartwright and Festinger (1943) wrote, "As it [the earlier theory] stands, any imbalance of forces, no matter how slight, is said to lead to a decision. Actually, a person usually will not announce his judgment before a given magnitude of difference between driving forces is reached" (p. 598). More recently, Decision Field theory (Busemeyer & Townsend, 1993) has been linked to Cartwright and Festinger in the treatment of the deliberation time before a decision can be made and the focus on latency before a decision is made (cf. Dror, Busemeyer, & Basola, 1999).

The process by which a sufficiently superior alternative is reached is named *differentiation*. Differentiation processes themselves cannot be observed, but they can be traced through measures of process and structural differentiation indicators. To illustrate, verbal reports can provide indicators of decision rules used in process differentiation. A decision maker may first say that he or she decides between jobs on the basis of only one attribute (e.g., salary). Then as the decision process proceeds, the decision maker may start talking about having to weigh salary against other attributes (e.g., distance to the job), indicating a second rule supporting the decision.

Changes over time of the rated attractiveness of aspects of decision alternatives is another indicator, this time of structural differentiation.

To exemplify attractiveness differentiation, the person making a decision about job offers A (nice job surroundings, low salary) and B (poor job surroundings, high salary) could find that although he or she initially was indifferent concerning the alternatives, the attractiveness of B's salary advantage gradually increases more and more over time, and B's disadvantage in job surroundings decreases. When the differentiation process goes on for some time, alternative B becomes sufficiently superior to A, and B is chosen.

Structural differentiation is always performed to reach a goal contingent on the situation. Differentiation means changes in the representation of the decision problem to increase the difference between alternatives according to one or several decision rules. In theoretical terms, a differentiation process is a hypothetical construct with aspects, images, and scenarios related to the decision alternatives. It is important to point out that indicators of, for example, structural differentiation manifest themselves in patterns of aspects, images, and scenarios.

When sufficient differentiation has been achieved, it is also important to maintain it. Therefore, postdecision processes work in support of the chosen alternative to maintain this alternative as the preferred gestalt separated from the nonchosen alternative, but also to protect the decision against poor outcomes, regrets, and so on. These processes are similar to predecision differentiation processes and are called *consolidation processes*.

Representation of Decision Alternatives

Decision processes, like other processes, are described in relation to a structure in which the processes take place. To illustrate, in order to describe how one job offer gradually improves over an alternative in a decision process (the process), it is necessary to postulate how the job offers should be described (structure) during this process. Otherwise, it would not be possible to describe the process.

Decision alternatives can be represented in a holistic way as entities in themselves in that structure. However, usually the structure is described in a more decomposed way using, for example, the alternative × attribute (or dimension) representation matrix. This is the most common structure onto which decision problems have been mapped in the past. Matrix representations of decision problems will be described in the first part of this section, along with holistic representations. Some other modes of representing decision alternatives will then be presented.

Finally, subjective representations of decision alternatives include cognitive value components and affective components; this topic will be elaborated in the last part of this section.

Holistic Representations

When decision alternatives are well known and/or easy to classify, each alternative can be represented as an entity in itself. The alternatives may be compared to templates or classified according to prototype alternatives. After this, the alternatives can be processed in accordance with already established routines or habits in the process of reaching and implementing a decision.

Matrix Representations

Complete Matrices. Matrix representations use alternative × attribute mappings of decision alternatives. As is well known, attributes are also called *dimensions* or *criteria* by some researchers and decision analysts. An aspect is the *primitive*, the smallest postulated unit in this representation, and it is associated with physical (e.g., a color), subjective (perceived color), and evaluative (e.g., attractiveness of the color) representations. The evaluative representations of aspects can be ordered along attractiveness scales on attributes.

Returning to the example of making a decision between two job offers, alternative A can be represented by 30 minutes of travel from home to the job. This is the *objective* physical representation of that aspect. When traveling or thinking of travel, the time may be perceived or *cognitively represented* as longer or shorter (depending on what activity is carried out while traveling, how monotonous the trip is, etc.). Finally, the *attractiveness* of the travel is determined by how the decision maker's value system maps onto the travel and his or her affective reaction to the travel. The values represent what the decision maker values in life (e.g., using public transportation is good) and the affective component represents reactions of an affective emotional kind (e.g., subway tunnels can be associated with claustrophobic reactions). Eagly and Chaiken (1993) make a corresponding distinction between evaluative and affective components in attitude formation. When a person makes a decision, values and affects are integrated into the attractiveness of the alternatives.

The properties of the attractiveness scales are important because they are intimately related to the kinds of rules that can be used when making a decision (Svenson, 1979). In general, applications of more complex rules require more complex and fine-grained representations. Attractiveness can be measured on rank-order scales, interval scales, or higher metric scales. In choosing between two jobs, the attractiveness of the salary attribute could be very precisely represented on an interval scale on which an increase in salary means an increase on an attractiveness interval scale. However, when judging the psychosocial climate of a workplace, a decision maker may rank order the jobs only on that attribute.

Even if aspects can be measured on one specific attractiveness scale, different attractiveness scales are not always commensurable (Svenson, 1979). So, for example, most people find it hard to apply commensurable attractiveness scales across lives saved and the costs of saving those lives. That is, people do not want to set a price on a life. Instead, they try to avoid making that tradeoff. To exemplify further, a job for the army could be so negative to a decision maker because it is for the army that this negative aspect cannot be traded off against any advantage on any other attribute. Then the military job attribute is not commensurable with other attributes. Baron and Spranca (1997) call attributes that are not commensurable *protected values* and elaborate on their characteristics.

The *importance* of different attributes for a decision can be represented on rank-order scales or on more advanced scales. To exemplify, the salary may be more important than the distance to a job (within a certain range) or it may be twice as important. In general, each alternative is represented by one aspect on each of the attributes in a matrix representation. However, sometimes different alternatives are represented at least partly by different attributes.

Incomplete Matrix Representations. Sometimes information is missing in a matrix representation. That is, one alternative lacks information on one of the attributes. To exemplify, in a decision about which house to buy, there may be no information about the energy needed for electric heating for one of the houses. There now exists a set of studies devoted to the problem of how incomplete matrix information affects decisions, starting with the seminal paper by Slovic and MacPhillamy (1974).

Nonmatrix Form Representations

Aspects. Perhaps the simplest way to represent a decision alternative is by sets of aspects. In the present context, an aspect corresponds to what can be called a *feature*, and it does not in the first place locate itself on an attribute. As mentioned previously, there are physical or objective aspects, such as "12 minutes," "34 meters long," or "37 degrees Celsius," that can be described independently of the decision maker. When a person perceives or experiences an aspect, this is a perceived or cognitive representation (short time, rather long distance, warm, red, etc.). When (cognitive) goals, value systems, and affects are activated, *attractiveness* becomes attached to the aspect.

Different decision alternatives can be represented by aspects on different attributes. Given the decision maker's past experiences, his or her goals, values, and affects in the situation, a degree of positive or negative attractiveness becomes associated to the aspect. An aspect may also be neutrally evaluated. To exemplify, the mention of a shop may elicit aspects that are mainly cognitively descriptive (5-minutes walk to it, visual image of shelves, a scenario in which a particular good is purchased, etc.). Note that this activates a set of specific aspects not associated with attractiveness evaluations. But the decision maker may also evaluate aspects and find that they are neutral (e.g., they neither contribute to nor hinder the achievement of a goal). However, quite often, spontaneous, automatic evaluations or more elaborate processes result in positive or negative attractiveness representations.

Aspects do not necessarily place themselves in an attribute space (in the preceding example, "distance" could be the first attribute, "size of shelves" the next, and so on). Aspects are postulated to be free-floating before the first attempt is made to order them for a certain purpose.

The aspects attracting focal attention at a certain moment depend on the situation (including goals, the decision problem, the decision problem context, etc.) and the person. This is a well-known fact from, for example, the psychology of attention. If, for example, the goal of a person is to find a shop in which he or she can buy a shirt, the aspects that become salient are likely to be different from those that become salient if he or she wants to buy a car. The salient aspects, when perceived, will also be associated with positive and negative attractiveness relating to either of the two goals. The sign "Auto Dealer" will have negative or neutral attractiveness for the person searching for a shirt but positive attractiveness for the person wanting to buy a car. However, there are also many aspects that are perceived but not salient at the moment and that may trigger values, affects, and new goals.

Images. Images are represented by, for example, physical objects and scenes. Images consist of cognitive representations, including sights, sounds, smells, touch, tastes, ideas, concepts, and words. Images can be decomposed into other images and aspects, but they can also be apprehended and processed as holistic units in themselves. A job offer may flash through a decision maker's mind as a scene in which he or she sits at a desk, and this elicits negative affect.

Images, as defined here, are primarily static in nature, although they may appear one after the other. Images are elicited when decision alternatives are encountered and processed. Images can be directly related to attractiveness or to attractiveness via their aspects.

Scenarios. When the time dimension is brought into an image and one or several chains of events are simulated in the decision maker's mind, this is called a *scenario*. Thus, when a job alternative is thought of as a series of conversations with customers asking difficult questions, this is a scenario representation of that job offer. Scenarios consist of other scenarios, images, and aspects. A scenario in itself, as a whole, may be associated with positive or negative attractiveness, or attractiveness of the scenario can be transmitted via images and/or aspects.

It may be difficult to determine to what extent the different cognitive and attractiveness components that represent a decision alternative are available to conscious observation by the decision maker. A scenario appearing in a person's mind may sometimes be quite easy to observe and report with its images and aspects. In other cases it can be harder, and in the extreme case, only unspecified evaluative and/or affective emotional experiences may form a memory trace after a scenario has flashed through a person's mind.

Alternatives in a Decision Need Not Be Represented in the Same Way

The alternatives in a decision problem can be represented in incomplete matrix representations if comparative information for one or more attributes is missing. But different alternatives can also be represented in fundamentally different ways in the same decision problem by the same decision maker. To illustrate, a decision problem can include one alternative represented as a scenario and another alternative represented as a set of aspects. This difference can depend on different degrees of familiarity with the alternatives or other factors. It is clear that decision makers' different representations of decision alternatives, such as those in the example, are not directly compatible with attributes × aspects representations. Another example is the decision on whether or not to stop smoking. The alternative of continuing to smoke has aspects that a smoker does not spontaneously order on the same set of attributes as the aspects of the alternative to stop smoking.

It should be stressed, however, that it is almost always possible for an analyst or a researcher to find a number of attributes to characterize the decision alternatives and to look at the situation in this perspective. But this perspective may not always be the most fruitful way of modeling the situation in order to find psychological regularities.

Integrating Affect and Values in Attractiveness Representations

The interest in affect and emotion is older than psychology itself (Solomon, 1993). But the very strong emphasis on cognitive functions in decision research during the past few decades has led to neglect of the roles of affect, emotional involvement, and affective components in decision processes. Most contemporary and earlier research on human decision making has focused mainly on cognitive aspects of the human decision process. The attractiveness of aspects has been treated as a relatively affect-free or emotion-free mapping of the decision maker's values and goals onto a decision problem. There are exceptions, however, in studies including emotion and affect in decision making in different ways (e.g., Isen, 1993; Janis & Mann, 1977; Johnson & Tversky, 1983; Kahneman & Snell, 1990; Lewicka, 1997; Zajonc, 1980). Assuming that most decision processes involve some interactions between affective and cognitive processes, it is postulated that each decision context, aspect, image, and scenario has links to affect and emotional reactions.

Affects and emotions have been approached and classified in different ways (LeDoux, 1995; Rosenberg, 1998). In the present context, affects are seen as including affective traits, moods, and emotions. Affective traits have the longest duration, are most pervasive, and broadest; moods are less pervasive but persist for some time. Finally, emotions are shortest in time, least pervasive, and most narrow (e.g., Rosenberg, 1998). Affect represents a mental and/or bodily feeling that is experienced by the decision maker. It has a positive or a negative character. Affective traits, moods, and emotions have several links to decision making. Affective traits could be related to decision styles. For example, one set of affective traits could be associated with slow differentiation processes or strong postdecision regrets impossible to counterbalance by consolidation processes. Emotions are transient but relatively stable over shorter periods of time. Emotions can be manipulated experimentally to a certain extent, and their effects on decision making can be investigated (Isen, 1993).

Affects can influence decision making in two ways. The influence can be on the *process* of decision making and/or on the representation of the decision problem, that is, its *structure*. In the former case, the way in which the information is processed is influenced (decision rules, completeness of the information search, order of the search, etc.); in the latter case, it is the attractiveness of that information that is influenced. To exemplify, a negative mood could correlate with processing of more negative information in a decision that also takes longer to make than when the decision maker is in a more positive mood.

Affect can also influence the structure of a decision problem, that is, the attractiveness of aspects, images, and scenarios. First, the overall evaluation may be affected. For example, an objectively identical salary in two job offers may be more positively evaluated when the decision maker is in a positive mood than when he or she is in a negative mood.

Affect also enters the decision problem structure through specific associations with holistic alternatives, aspects, images, or scenarios. When attractiveness is influenced by and partly composed of affect, this is the reflection of the decision maker's earlier experiences, with the same or similar alternatives now influencing the decision maker's present experience of a decision alternative.

Finally, decision problems can induce affect, closing the circle of causal relations. To be more specific, mood can be elicited by a decision problem. To illustrate, a set of awful job alternatives can induce a negative mood in the decision maker that differs from the mood induced by a corresponding set of wonderful job offers. Luce and her colleagues (Luce, 1998; Luce et al., 1997) have investigated mood (emotion) as a result of a decision problem and how emotions can affect choices.

When integrating affect into Diff Con theory, all these influences should be considered. The influence of affect on decision processes will be covered later when decision rules are treated. Next, we consider, in some detail, affect as one of the components shaping the structure of the decision problem, that is, the attractiveness of an aspect, image, or a scenario.

An affective reaction is often quick and can trigger responses (e.g., avoidance of different kinds) that are stimulus specific and controlled by their antecedents rather than by their consequences. The processes mediating these responses are largely automatic and require small amounts of energetic effort. (When the final decision is triggered by affective reactions, it will be described as an example of a level 2 decision later in this chapter.) To illustrate, a person's face can trigger positive affect, making the approach of that person the preferred alternative. Affective reactions can also trigger values activated when the attractiveness of an aspect, image, or scenario is shaped. For example, positive affect to the luxury of a house can function as a prime to comfort values when evaluating the following other house alternatives.

Affective reactions can be triggered by stimuli, such as individual aspects, images, or scenarios in a decision problem. The stimuli releasing the affective responses have earlier been associated with a somatic marker, according to Damasio (1994). Affective reactions (affecting the assessment of decision alternatives) and affective responses (directly affecting the response or choice alternative) can speed up decision processes. Decision processes can also be slowed down if the affective reactions are in conflict with each other or with cognitive attractiveness components.

Thus, somatic or affective markers can enable the decision maker to make decisions more quickly. Quicker decisions can have a survival value in some situations and are energy- saving in most situations. New stimuli can be linked to an affective response, but the response to the affect (select, approach or reject, avoid) will not change. When new aspects, images, or scenarios become associated with these responses they are called *secondary emotions* (Damasio, 1994). The secondary emotions tend to arise rapidly and are interesting because they can trigger not only responses but also affective reactions, which have great influence on the attractiveness of aspects, images, scenarios, and whole decision alternatives, as mentioned previously. Even though the Diff Con theory framework does not require all markers to be somatic, Damasio's model provides an interesting explanation of great value within the framework.

To summarize, an affective reaction may or may not have its roots in the context and/or the problem a decision maker is solving. Time pressure and stress can change the affective or emotional state of a decision maker and thereby the processes leading to a decision (Svenson & Maule, 1993). However, as illustrated earlier, affective reactions that interest us in this context are related to the alternatives in the decision problem. The affective reactions may be quick and appear at once, but they may also appear during an extended decision process when aspects, images, and scenarios are elicited and evaluated. But, as mentioned previously, a decision alternative as a whole can also elicit positive or negative affective reactions or responses. Svenson and Slovic (2002) found that a majority of the associations linked to decision alternatives were affectively loaded, but also that a significant number of associations were neutral.

Cognitively derived values represent relatively affect- and emotion-free cognitions about what is good and bad in different situations, including moral rules, ethics, and so on. As can be inferred from the preceding discussion, cognitively derived values constitute the other important component, along with the affective component, shaping the attractiveness of aspects, images, and scenarios.

Can these two components be disentangled in empirical investigations as well as in theory? If some necessary assumptions are fulfilled, this can be done. For example, some biological indicators can be assumed to be relatively more closely connected to affective components (Damasio, 1994), and verbal reports and ratings from decision makers can be assumed to reflect the relative strengths of the affective and cognitive components. The former assumption obviously invites neuropsychological measures in conjunction with decision making. The latter method can be used in, for example, studies asking subjects to indicate the relative strength of the cognitive (reason) component and the affect-emotion (emotion) component when the subjects evaluate the decision alternatives. Whereas the former method is widely accepted today, the latter method needs further research to explore its merits and limitations in separating the affect and value components.

Again, it is interesting to note that the two attractiveness components can be more or less antagonistic concerning the same aspect, image, or scenario. If the situation remains unclear, the ambiguity has to be resolved in some way during the differentiation process. If the reasons for the affective component are less well known to the decision maker than the reasons for the cognitive component, this might create a conflict that is more difficult to solve than a conflict between cognitive value-generated patterns of attractiveness. The attractiveness conflicts studied by Svenson and Hill (1997), in which, for example, interest was in conflict with job chances for the chosen alternative, presumably involved both kinds of conflict. However, at the time, there was no attempt to differentiate between the cognitive and affective components behind the conflicts.

Cognitive values can change under the influence of affect (Svenson & Maule, 1993). Correspondingly, there may be cases in which affect, emotions, and mood can change under the influence of cognitive processes driven by values. For instance, deliberate strategies for thinking about a problem may change or control the affects associated with a decision situation. This is exemplified by cognitive therapy, in which the patient learns how to control unwanted affective reactions. As mentioned earlier, Toda (1980) suggests that most values can be derived from emotions. Sometimes the emotions have been rationalized into value systems, and sometimes they lead to biased information processing and reasoning about values when the decision maker tries to escape from the conscious influence of emotions (that are accepted or counteracted) in the decision process. Recently, Mellers and her colleagues have treated anticipated emotions in a descriptive framework for decision making under risk (Mellers et al., 1999).

Alternatives in the same decision problem can be represented in different ways, as mentioned earlier. If, for example, one alternative is primarily associated with affect and the other with more cognitively derived values, they could be evaluated in different decision processes, one more suited for treating affect and the other for treating more cognitively represented values. Thus, alternatives in the same decision may vary both in the way they are represented (e.g., aspects, scenario) and in the cognitive-affective composition of attractiveness patterns.

To illustrate, in a decision between two vacation locations, the first alternative can trigger a scenario of pleasant events immediately, whereas the second alternative only invites a more deliberate evaluation of a written description of the travel. The choice of the first alternative can then be based on a different decision rule for evaluation than the choice of the second alternative. The first alternative may be chosen in, for example, a holistic evaluation. When the second alternative is preferred, this decision can be based on a compensatory decision rule weighing the pros and cons. For reasons of simplicity, when presenting Diff Con theory later, we initially assume that the integration of values and affect into an attractiveness pattern for each alternative has been reasonably successful.

Decision Rules

Decision rules describe principles for processing information in a decision problem. Earlier, I presented an overview of different decision rules (Svenson, 1979, 1992). The following discussion will only give a brief introduction.

There are decision rules that consider the aspects of one alternative at a time and decision rules that directly compare alternatives, sampling aspects across alternatives. In the former case, the result is an integrated attractiveness assessment (more or less conscious) of each alternative followed by a comparison. An example of this is a decision in which each of a set of job offers is evaluated first and then the best alternative is selected. In the other case, the decision is made in the process of evaluating the alternatives. Here the evaluation of job offers may start with salary across all alternatives, followed by job location, and so on. As mentioned earlier, there are also holistic rules. These rules use affective and / or cognitive processes leading to quick, integrated attractiveness assessments.

In *noncompensatory decision rules* the attractiveness of decision alternatives is compared across corresponding characteristics. To exemplify, in a conjunctive rule, all alternatives that fall short of meeting a criterion level on an attribute can be eliminated from the choice set processed later in the decision process. For example, all jobs that do not meet the decision maker's interest criterion level are rejected first. In another case, a decision maker can use the dominance rule and find that one alternative dominates another one (i.e., is better or equal on all compared attributes).

In *compensatory decision rules* the attractiveness of aspects of one attribute is traded off in comparisons across attributes and alternatives. Thus, positive aspects can compensate for negative aspects. The addition of the attractiveness rule belongs to this category of decision rules (Svenson, 1979). A compensatory decision compares advantages and disadvantages and integrates them so that one of the alternatives turns out to be superior to the other.

It is clear that decisions can also generate cognitions that are conflicting and not coherent, as well as affects from remaining conflicts, regret, frustration, or anger. Some of these cognitions and feelings are driving forces behind postdecision consolidation processes and decision outcome management.

Alternatives in the Same Decision Can Be Processed in Different Decision Rules

Different rules can be used in different stages of the differentiation process. For example, conjunctive rules can be used to eliminate alternatives in early phases of a process and compensatory rules to make the final choice.

In contrast to most contemporary decision researchers, I propose that different decision rules can apply to different alternatives in the same decision at the same time. This idea was introduced and exemplified in treating the different representations of different alternatives in the same decision situation. Alternatives represented in different ways invite the elicitation and application of different decision rules. The choice of a grocery that is part of one's habitual buying pattern invites a holistic classification, whereas the choice of a new product may elicit a more thorough decision process with pros and cons using a compensatory decision rule.

As another example, after some time it can be assumed that more cognitively driven habitual decisions have substituted for earlier, more affect-driven decisions in the same repeated decision situation. If a new affect-laden attractive alternative appears, the attractiveness of the habitually chosen alternative is predominantly cognitive in character, whereas the attractiveness of the new alternative can be predominantly affective. This may lead to different decision rules applied to the different alternatives if affective attractiveness representations tend to evoke other decision rules (e.g., noncompensatory rules) than cognitive representations do (e.g., compensatory rules).

Levels of Decisions

Earlier in this chapter, it was shown that decisions are made in different ways. Therefore, different scholars have classified decisions in different ways, with the underlying assumption that decisions in the same class have some common psychological characteristics. To fit Diff Con theory, decisions have been classified on four different levels. In general, the higher the level, the more energetic resources are used to make a decision. *Energetic resources* refer to both psychological and physiological energy resources. Because people want to minimize the use of energetic resources, they should want to make decisions on lower levels rather than on higher levels, given that the conditions while making the decisions remain the same.

In *level 1* decisions there is no assumption of any attractiveness representation at the moment the decision is made. Level 1 decisions can be made in quick habitual processes. The decision maker recognizes that a situation is similar to an earlier one and chooses the same alternative selected last time. This category includes many quick, largely automatic and unconscious decisions (Shiffrin & Schneider, 1977). Klein (1989) calls such decisions *recognition primed*, and Smith (1992) uses the exemplar model to describe them. Gärling (1992) calls these kinds of choices "decisions according to routines for performance of everyday activities."

Although level 1 decisions are related to cognitive value and affect-driven attractiveness in the past, they were disentangled from these before the decisions could be made. No attractiveness representation is therefore elicited when a decision is made on this level. Instead, other perceptual or cognitive principles (e.g., similarity by matching) guide level 1 decisions.

However, when the habits or categories were formed in the past, attractiveness based on values and affect were processed by decision rules at higher levels of decision making. Thus, level 1 decisions are seen as the result of an energetic effort-saving principle decreasing focal processing and energetic demands. In most daily life situations, level 1 decision are likely to govern most of our behavior. The everyday choice of milk is an example. Level 1 decisions may also represent predetermined strategies (e.g. always go by subway, always put on a seat belt, or always drive a little faster than the speed limit). Finally, level 1 decisions can function as subprocesses in higher-level decision processes and determine, for example, a preliminary or reference alternative.

In *level 2* decisions, the decision maker considers the attractiveness of one or a few aspects. The attractiveness of these aspects can be both value and affect driven. Level 2 decisions represent stereotypical and static mappings of the attractiveness of the alternatives (e.g., biggest is best). For example, no tradeoffs between conflicting attractiveness values are made. Decisions that are made in holistic processes relating to affect and/or cognitive attractiveness belong to this category as well.

In *level 3* decisions, the decision process is more complex. First, there can be within-alternative conflicts, with aspects, images, or scenarios having both positive and negative attractiveness. Second, there may be no or too few attractiveness values elicited by an alternative. Therefore, attractiveness has to be derived in primarily cognition-driven processes eliciting both affect and cognitive value components of attractiveness. Third, there can be attractiveness conflicts across alternatives. Decisions at this level can use tradeoffs between the attractiveness of aspects on different attributes, transform attributes into new ones, restructure the decision problem, and so on. For example, buying a digital TV may not be a very familiar decision for many people in 2003 and will therefore probably require careful processing as a level 3 decision. New alternatives can be elicited in this kind of decision if the existing options are inadequate.

As mentioned earlier, decisions on this level are fundamental precursors to many decisions at levels 1 and 2, which were once level 3 (or 4) decisions later transformed into simpler decisions.

In *level 4* decisions, the decision maker encounters or creates a new and unfamiliar problem in which new decision alternatives are elicited or created. Parts of the decision-making processes on this level include problem-solving processes. An example involves deciding how to travel from one location to another. The creation of decision alternatives includes making up composite alternatives. That is, an alternative is constructed that contains part of each of several different travel modes. This corresponds to a series of images or scenarios. For example, the constructive level 4 process may generate one (train + taxi) alternative competing with an (air + rental car) alternative. Langer (1994) calls level 4 decision making *active decision making* and argues that in comparison with the other levels of decision making, a greater proportion of this kind of active decision making should lead to greater self-esteem, enhanced perceived control, and less postdecision regret. Some of these postulates remain to be empirically demonstrated.

Earlier experience is a most important determiner of the level on which a decision will be made. Note, however, that decision processes on higher levels often contain subprocesses from lower levels. To illustrate, a careful creation of a transportation method to various job alternatives (level 4) also contains level 2 decisions eliminating some elements in the composition of alternatives. However, trait affect, mood, and emotions are just as important as the goals of the decision maker. For example, how important is the decision? Does the decision maker want to make a quick or a well-thought-through decision?

Stages in the Differentiation Process

When decision making is modeled as a process, the different stages and the simultaneous and/or sequential subprocesses become crucial for understanding the process. For example, the initiation phase of a decision process is very important for the rest of the decision process and the final choice. This phase, which is part of predecision differentiation, will be treated first in the next subsection, followed by other phases that can be engaged in the process of making a decision. The following discussion involves decisions at all levels.

Predecision Differentiation

Identification of Decision Alternatives, Markers, Goal Elicitation, Screening, and Editing. The initial processing of a decision problem is partly governed by *markers* that tell the decision maker where to start. Markers are salient aspects. To illustrate, a conspicuous, attractive color of a car can start a decision process between that car and other alternatives with comparisons on the color attribute. The salient color may also be so convincing that the car with that color is selected as the preliminary choice alternative, thereby influencing the decision process. Markers are related to the goal structure and the representation of a decision problem. Markers can also activate parts of a decision maker's goal structure, thereby partly determining the course of the decision process. As mentioned earlier, markers can be affective but can also be cognitive or perceptual associations to salient aspects.

It is asserted that markers are very important for decision processes and that they can be used in explaining important parts of otherwise unclear decisions and behavior. In particular, the effects of affective and unconscious markers can be hard to trace, as they may disappear beyond other processes. A marker in the form of a deviant aspect value does not have to be integrated in the process other than as an initiator of the process. To illustrate, a deviant typing format in a description of an alternative can serve as a marker for where to start a decision process, but otherwise may have no impact on the processing. Markers can also trigger level 1 and level 2 preliminary choice alternatives in processes embedded in level 3 and level 4 decisions; in this way, markers can influence final decisions.

In slower and more elaborate decision processes, *editing*, or early rearranging and grouping of the information, can take place during the initial phases of a decision process. Editing can also be initiated and partly governed by markers and is essential for minimizing the energetic resources spent in a decision (cf., Abelson & Levi, 1985; Coupey, 1994; Kahneman & Tversky, 1979; Ranyard, 1989; Tversky & Kahneman, 1992).

Identification of alternatives is very important in real-life decisions but often trivial in laboratory settings. Markers can sometimes be helpful in this process. *Screening* refers to a process in which some alternatives are eliminated early in the decision process (Beach, 1990) after not having reached a criterion level on one or several screening attributes. This process, mostly using a conjunctive decision rule, is seen as part of predecision differentiation. The selection of the screening attribute is determined by different factors, including the influence of markers.

Selection of Reference Alternative and Preliminary Choice Alternative. Diff Con theory includes processes for finding and explicitly or implicitly using *reference alternatives*. Reference alternatives serve as prototypes for what could be accepted as a worst case, what could be aspired for, what constitutes a really bad alternative, and so on. The aspects of a reference alternative provide guidance when evaluating the alternatives of a current decision problem. Thus, reference alternatives are used as benchmark alternatives, alternatives for which there exists an attractiveness mapping.

A reference alternative is not necessarily part of the decision set, but it can be an alternative that more or less consciously comes into the decision maker's mind. The reference alternative is similar to at least one of the alternatives available at the time or it is one of the alternatives in the decision set. A reference alternative can be selected in a level 1 quick process involving a classification without any evaluative component at the time; it can also be derived via quick, affective level 2 processes. Naturally, a reference alternative can also be found in more elaborate, conscious, and deliberate processes. A reference alternative can help to determine aspiration levels (Dembo, 1931), to define cutoff levels in a conjunctive decision rule, or to act as an anchor in other respects.

In many real-life situations, decision problems appear with only one alternative at a time. The problem is whether the alternative that appears should be accepted or rejected (cf. Fischhoff, 1996); then a reference alternative is useful. In formal terms, this kind of decision is often modeled as a choice between the status quo alternative and another alternative (cf. Kahneman, Knetsch, & Thaler, 1990; Samuelson & Zeckhauser 1988; Schweitzer, 1994; Svenson, 1990). Thus, the reference alternative becomes synonymous with the status quo alternative in these situations. To exemplify, Boles and Messick (1995) have illustrated the great importance of reference alternative as reflected in postdecision evaluations of a decision. In fact, depending on the reference alternative, winners were seen as less successful than losers having made the same decision (but with an unsuccessful outcome).

When there is more than one decision alternative to consider, Diff Con predicts that in most noninstantaneous decision processes, a *preliminary choice alternative* will be nominated. As mentioned earlier, the choice of a preliminary alternative can be the result of quick, holistic level 1 and level 2 decisions as well as of more elaborate processes.

The use of a preliminary preferred alternative means that the decision maker can save effort. This is because the load on working memory will be less if a preliminary choice exists. To illustrate, if all comparisons with other alternatives refer to only one alternative (the preliminary choice), this gives $N - 1$ comparisons (in a decision with N alternatives) instead of the greater number of all possible pairwise comparisons of the alternatives (if N is greater than 2). The preliminary choice alternative has also been called the *promising alternative* (Montgomery, 1983; Montgomery & Svenson, 1989). Because of the more than promising character of a real preliminary choice (also eliciting aspects, images, scenarios, and ideas about postdecision processes), the term *preliminary alternative* is used in Diff Con.

Differentiation Leading to a Decision

It is not always easy to determine when a decision process starts and when the individual more or less consciously realizes that there is a decision ahead. In the Diff Con framework, a pragmatic approach to this problem is chosen. Therefore, the differentiation process is assumed to start as soon as it is judged possible and meaningful to trace it. Following a decision, consolidation processes include not only the choice, but also implementation and monitoring of the decision.

The roles of markers, reference alternatives, and preliminary alternatives during the decision process were introduced in the preceding discussion. In the early stages of a decision process, a preliminary choice alternative may or may not exist. If a preliminary choice has been nominated, this makes the processing and structuring of information more focused, as it centers on the preliminary choice alternative, testing its possible future as the final choice. If there is no preliminary alternative, or if it has been rejected, early information processing often involves the screening process introduced previously or some other preliminary information processes such as information search. If and when a preliminary choice has been nominated, this alternative will have an advantage over its competitors. This will be elaborated in the following discussion.

Thus, Diff Con theory predicts that a preliminary choice alternative has a greater chance of becoming the final choice than other equally attractive alternatives just because it is the preliminary choice. This follows from the theory, which postulates that differentiation that takes place through testing the preliminary choice is biased toward that candidate. Evidence is now accumulating showing this in studies outside the Diff Con paradigm (cf. Frey, 1986; Russo, Medvec, & Meloy, 1996; Russo, Meloy, & Medvec, 1998; Shafir, 1993; Shafir & Tversky, 1992), in which more and neutral information is used to increase differentiation supporting the preliminary choice.

In Diff Con theory there are three differentiation processes: holistic, process, and structural. They can all be used with or without a preliminary choice alternative.

Holistic Differentiation. Holistic differentiation is quick and may be experienced by the decision maker as something like a classification process (not readily available for conscious control or awareness) leading to the selection of a preferred alternative (Estes, 1994; Klein, 1989). In this situation, there is a stimulus-reaction coupling that does not consider the consequences of the decision.

The driving force behind this process can be affective, with positive or negative reactions elicited instantaneously when a decision alternative appears. Then holistic differentiation takes place as a level 2 decision. Zajonc (1980) argues that such reactions are faster than cognitive processes. If this is true, it implies that largely affective reactions should be faster than cognitive value reactions.

Holistic decisions can be made without reference to attractiveness. In this case, pattern recognition takes place with reference to prototype decisions and/or decision alternatives. This occurs when a decision maker follows a habit. Another kind of holistic decision is to imitate the decisions of others. These two heuristics take place as level 1 decisions and predict most human real-life decision making.

Holistic differentiation often leads to a degree of differentiation that is sufficient for a final choice. As mentioned earlier, it is also an important subprocess in more complex differentiation processes, particularly the selection of a reference or preliminary alternative. Holistic processing may not apply to all alternatives in a decision. If it applies, let us say, to only one alternative, this could lead to the application of different decision rules to different alternatives concurrently in a decision process, as mentioned earlier.

Process Differentiation. Process differentiation includes the use of one or more decision rules (e.g., the conjunctive rule, the additive difference rule; cf. Beach, 1990; Svenson, 1979, 1992). The choices of rules applied to a decision problem depends on the individual, the context, the alternatives, and the structure of the decision problem. The frequently reported initial use of the conjunctive rule in the screening phase to reduce the number of options belongs to this category of differentiation. Changing the acceptance criteria on different attributes, in rules using such criteria, is a related kind of process differentiation. Traditional behavioral decision research has been focused on finding rules in which all alternatives are evaluated and processed the same way, and is therefore unprepared to cover the representation and processing asymmetries described earlier in this chapter.

Let us first exemplify process differentiation with a case involving which car to buy, in which all alternatives are processed by the same rules. Fuel consumption is an important attribute to which a conjunctive rule is applied. In the present case, the decision maker starts screening the available alternatives with the initial acceptance criterion level of 0.60 l per 10 km on the highway. Then the decision maker finds out that no available car meets this criterion level. He or she then revises the criterion level up to 0.65 l and resumes the screening. Next, the decision maker finds several possible alternatives.

According to Diff Con theory, the decision maker does more than use pass-fail classifications. It is also necessary to find a sufficiently superior alternative, which implies that the conjunctive rule has to be changed to fit Diff Con theory. So, in addition to making pass-fail decisions, the decision maker also has to assess by how much an alternative exceeds the criterion level. If only one alternative fulfills the differentiation criterion (implying a sufficiently large margin), that alternative can be selected to become the final choice. If this is not the case, other criterion levels or decision rules apply.

Thus, the conjunctive rule can be applied with successively stricter criteria of rejection in the early stages of a decision process to reduce the set of possible alternatives. In later stages of the differentiation process, the preliminary choice can be tested against other alternatives in other decision rules, including reference alternatives elicited in the situation.

When the affective and cognitive components forming the attractiveness pattern do not integrate naturally, ambivalence and conflict may be created in the decision maker. In some cases, affect-driven and cognitively value-driven evaluations may lead to disintegrated attractiveness assessments of aspects, images, and scenarios. As mentioned earlier, different rules may be applied to affect-driven and cognitively value-driven attractiveness representations.

Diff Con theory requires a sufficiently superior alternative to be chosen. Thus, as mentioned earlier, all decision rules used in this context have to be elaborated, as in the preceding case, with the conjunctive rule. Each rule must be able to determine which alternative is superior and how much better it is. If more than one decision rule is applied, with the same decision outcome, this can be considered as increasing the degree of differentiation (irrespective of the degree of logical redundancy). In this respect, differentiation may not correspond to rational decision making. For example, a differentiation process may include a first application of the additive difference rule followed by the use of the attractiveness rule applied to the two leading alternatives. In the differentiation process, both processes can support the leading alternative. Of course, in relation to normative theory, the two decision rules may be correlated and the decision process biased.

Structural Differentiation. Structural differentiation refers to changes in psychological representations of the decision alternatives. All such changes are made in relation to one or several decision rules. The rules, in turn, are governed by goals determined by values and affects induced by the problem and its context. Several different kinds of processes, including affective and cognitively driven components, are assumed to take place concurrently and are contingent on each other (cf. Svenson, 1992).

Structural differentiation processes are of different kinds, depending on which component of the structure is targeted. The target for restructuring can be (1) the attractiveness of aspects, images, and scenarios characterizing the decision alternatives, (2) the importance given to different characteristics or attributes, (3) the facts describing the decision problem, and (4) the way the alternatives are described (from minor changes in aspect, image, and scenario representations to complete redefinitions of decision problems).

Attractiveness restructuring concerns changes in the attractiveness of aspects, images, and scenarios. As mentioned earlier, attractiveness has both affective and cognitive value components, so a change in attractiveness can be rooted in both affects and values. As mentioned earlier, attractiveness restructuring is governed by decision rules setting the goals for the process. This means that the representation of a decision is restructured so that the support for one (or more) alternative(s), according to one or several decision rules, is increased. Restructuring is made possible through uncertainty in the mapping of goals on attractiveness representations, uncertainty about which goals to elicit in a situation and the relative importance of the different goals elicited in a particular situation.

To illustrate, a decision maker may be uncertain about how the alternatives in a decision relate to his or her goals of, say, being honest and being loved. The first of these goals is more cognitive and value driven, whereas the second goal is more emotional and affect driven. The decision maker may also feel uncertain about whether these values and affects are most relevant. The decision maker may also be uncertain about how the goals should be integrated in attractiveness representations. In this example, these uncertainties are genuine and the decision maker may want a clear solution. But in other cases, consciously or unconsciously, a decision maker may wish to keep these uncertainties unclear and use them as some kind of negotiation space, allowing a final structure that clearly differentiates one alternative from the others. When choosing a university program, a student may not wish to know about the employment chances (which may be poor) for those graduating from the program. Following a preliminary choice or the final decision, the employment attribute will be taken care of in structural differentiation and consolidation, now with the goal of supporting the preferred alternative (in a biased way, the normally inclined reader would say).

When affect is important, differentiation and consolidation can be performed in cognitive affect management (e.g., deliberate reasoning processes about affects). It is assumed that the affect component can be strong, changing more cognitively driven attractiveness representations in differentiation and consolidation and, in fact, transforming former largely cognitively driven attractiveness representations into more affect-driven ones – more affect-driven than the decision maker may be aware of.

Attribute importance restructuring refers to changes in the importance of a characteristic or an attribute. Note that an attribute is a principle for grouping aspects. For example, aspects with the same "label," such as color or price, can be grouped to form a color attribute and a price attribute, but less obvious groupings of aspects can also appear, such as a set of quite different aspects (e.g., visual, auditory) that may form an "esthetic" attribute.

In addition to label grouping, aspects can also be grouped together, depending on how they are assessed in the decision process. For example, the aspects on the most important attribute may be identified first, those second in importance next, and so on.

Another principle for the investigator in ordering aspects on attributes is the time order in which the aspects are attended to or appear in the decision makers' mind. In this way, the aspects are ordered according to their appearance in time. All aspects attended to first for each alternative are classified as one attribute, all aspects second in order forming another attribute, and so on. The different ways of grouping aspects are important because they relate to individual decision makers' decision processes and can therefore be used in data analyses when searching for regularities across individuals in human decision making (Svenson, 1996).

As, an example of importance restructuring using a label classification of attributes, a cost attribute may gradually be given more weight than a quality attribute in a differentiation process. To illustrate, in a choice between cars, one car is initially only marginally better than another one. In the ensuing differentiation process, the lower price of the preferred car is gradually given more weight in importance restructuring. In more formal terms, the differentiation may follow a weighted additive difference rule and may occur by gradually changing the relative importance of the weights among the two most important attributes.

Facts restructuring refers to changes in the representation of the facts describing a decision alternative. Again, such restructuring of aspects, images, and facts is performed in relation to a decision rule and in the process of supporting a preliminary choice.

A decision maker citing or searching for facts that are biased toward supporting the preliminary choice illustrates facts restructuring (Festinger, 1957; Frey, 1986). Facts restructuring parallels and interacts with attractiveness restructuring, and the two are sometimes substitutable for each other. This is also the case when memory retrieval of facts becomes gradually more supportive of an alternative. The price of a chosen commodity that is restructured after a decision (in a biased memory representation of the price) toward a lower price exemplifies postdecision facts restructuring (consolidation). If this takes place in postdecision processes, it can be called *hindsight* (Fischhoff, 1975) or *cognitive dissonance reduction* (Festinger, 1964).

Structural differentiation between two alternatives cannot be measured as, for example, a simple measure of the distance between two vectors of aspects characterizing the alternatives on different attributes; the greater the distance, the greater the differentiation. The picture is more complex than that. In some cases, differentiation may even imply that an alternative that is chosen becomes less valued on some attribute(s) in the differentiation process (although the attractiveness of the alternative as a whole stays the same or increases).

For example, some studies have shown that in order to differentiate-consolidate a value conflict (when the chosen alternative is worse on an important attribute), attributes that are already well above the sufficiently better criterion can be "sacrificed" and structured as less superior at the end of the process than at the beginning – but still sufficiently superior. To illustrate, when the preferred (job) alternative is worse on an important attribute (e.g., how interesting the job is) than its competitor, the focus is on reducing that conflict, turning it into an advantage, and letting the salary advantage decrease – as long as it is still sufficiently superior (Shamoun & Svenson, 2002; Svenson & Hill, 1997).

To exemplify further, a differentiation process with job alternatives A (nice surroundings, low salary) and B (poor job surroundings, high salary) could involve a process in which A becomes more similar to an earlier appreciated (reference) job C (very nice surroundings, very low salary) and B less similar to C. Note that A's salary disadvantage in relation to B could become even worse, and yet A is chosen because of its similarity to the earlier job C. In this case, differentiation was driven in relation to C as an alternative that one should choose. The poor salary is part of the C as well as of the A alternative, with an overall sufficient superiority leading to the choice of A over B.

Problem restructuring implies using available aspects, images, and scenarios in a search for new facts and/or alternative ways of representing the decision problem. This may involve new aspects, attributes, images, or scenarios supporting a preliminary choice and/or the creation of new alternatives. Markers are important in these creative processes. Perhaps the decision maker who is more attentive to potential markers and actively searches for different markers is more innovative in creating a new representation of a decision problem. New decision representations can, for example, involve completely new causal structures among available facts but can also incorporate new facts.

For a decision maker who has been trapped in a decision conflict, unable to make a reasonable choice, it is very important to be aware of the possibility of restructuring the decision problem. Such awareness and restructuring abilities can inoculate the decision maker from irrelevant affective reactions and stress (Svenson & Maule, 1993).

Reframing a decision problem (Kahneman & Tversky, 1979) during the decision process is one example of problem restructuring. In fact, the framing may be kept flexible to be settled first when a preliminary alternative has been selected. Problem restructuring can also involve changes of composite decision alternatives such as travels composed of different components (hotel, travel mode, time, etc.) or university studies (with different courses). But it may be even more important in situations where drastic restructuring is needed to solve a decision problem either to provide further support for a preliminary choice alternative or to generate a completely new alternative.

General Comments

The preliminary choice of an alternative means that the probability for this alternative to be finally chosen is greater than for other equally attractive alternatives. However, it does not mean that differentiation is always successful for the first preliminary choice. During the differentiation process, different facts and goals appear that influence the status of the preliminary choice. Thus, there are many factors that can lead to the rejection of a preliminary chosen alternative, such as new facts, partly different goals elicited during the process, and mappings of these goals changing during the decision process. If the preliminary choice alternative cannot remain the leading one, a new preliminary alternative or set of alternatives will be selected to move the decision process ahead.

From a theoretical perspective, differentiation and attractiveness are hypothetical constructs. Differentiation processes are reflected by indicators of differentiation, such as attractiveness ratings and descriptions of decision rules. However, it is hard to predict the exact pattern of indicator changes to which differentiation gives rise.

By analogy, it is possible to draw a tentative inference about a person's having access to more money (corresponding to the differentiation variable) from changes in his consumption pattern. So, if we know that the person buys more expensive things, we infer that he has more money. But with insufficient information, we do not know what particular consumption pattern he will develop when he gets more money. The situation is somewhat similar for Diff Con theory. It is possible to find that differentiation and/or consolidation seems to have occurred. But it is difficult to predict beforehand exactly how it will manifest itself at the present stage of development of the theory. Fortunately, there are some empirical results that can guide us along the road to more profound knowledge.

First, attractiveness restructuring seems to manifest itself for aspects ordered on attributes according to their importance. In general, the more important an attribute, the greater the chance of restructuring, provided that there is still room for differentiation. Ceiling effects sometimes preclude further restructuring on the most important attribute, leaving the strongest effects with the second most important attribute. Second, differentiation indicators depend on the pattern of attractiveness of the aspects in a decision problem. If, for example, the preliminary chosen alternative is initially far better on the most important attribute (e.g., costs), there seems to be less of a need to consolidate on that attribute than if it is just barely superior. When the attractiveness difference is already sufficient on the most important attribute (e.g., the chosen alternative is sufficiently cheaper), then there is room for attention to and consolidation of the second most important attribute (comfort). If the second most important attribute (e.g., comfort) also supports the chosen alternative, then there is less of a need to consolidate the decision than if it speaks against the preliminary chosen option (with an attractiveness conflict).

Decision makers can avoid the responsibility and pain of differentiating alternatives that are rather similar in attractiveness by just waiting. The world is dynamic, so in many cases there is a chance that, by just waiting, new facts will appear and attractiveness mappings and the situation will change, so that differentiation becomes easier. Of course, waiting gives opportunities for both externally (the external objective situation changes) and internally driven differentiation processes, but waiting may also lead in the end to the need to make decisions under adverse conditions and under time pressure and stress. It is assumed that different persons have different decision styles concerning when and how long they normally wait until making their final decisions. Finally, decision making is modeled in Diff Con as the result of a constructive process in which both values and decision rules are elicited in conjunction, and it is obvious that this approach has some elements in common with the constructive decision-making approach (e.g., Bettman, Luce, & Payne, 1998).

Postdecision Consolidation

After a decision is made, the decision maker's internal processes continue to work on the prior decision. Postdecision consolidation processes include the following phases: (1) postdecision consolidation, (2) implementation of the decision, (3) postimplementation consolidation and monitoring of the decision, (4) outcome of the decision, and (5) postoutcome consolidation and monitoring.

In the period immediately after a decision is made, the decision maker may feel that he or she has lost the opportunity to choose, has lost the unique good aspects of the rejected alternative(s), and is stuck with the bad aspects of the chosen alternative. This can create subjective tension or what can be called *cognitive* and/or *affective postdecision dissonance* (cf. Festinger, 1964) or *regret* (Loomes & Sugden, 1982), which has to be managed psychologically. The effects of these feelings also extend into the implementation period, when active exterior monitoring of the implementation of the decision may be possible.

The implementation of a decision can be associated with negative consequences, meaning that external factors can also lead to a feeling of regret or in other ways contribute to consolidation. Consolidation processes are active as responses to the previously discussed factors and are aimed at maintaining/creating cognitively and affectively superior representations of the chosen alternative after the decision as well. In some cases, in particular when decisions have been quick and perhaps immature, postdecision consolidation supporting the decision can be a late substitute for predecision processes (cf. Svenson, 1992).

Postdecision consolidation involves processes that are similar to those in the predecision differentiation phase (Svenson & Hill, 1997; Svenson & Shamoun, 1997). In addition, postdecision consolidation interacts with taking action or monitoring the decision when it is implemented so that the outcome of the decision comes as close as possible to the desired outcome. Thus, monitoring means that the decision maker acts to change the postdecision situation so that it turns out to be as favorable as possible and to restructure the mental representation to provide further support for the prior decision. In fact, this may imply a series of supporting decisions (Brehmer, 1992).

Postdecision affect and emotion monitoring is one way of structurally consolidating a prior decision. Affect and emotion monitoring is performed by processes that regulate which emotions a person has, when he or she experiences them, and how these affects and emotions are experienced and expressed. The selection of aspects supporting a prior decision is another (Festinger, 1957; Frey, 1986) example of postdecision structural consolidation.

Russo et al. (1998) state that postdecisional distortion, corresponding to consolidation, of aspects on attributes searched after a decision is about half as strong as the predecision distortion on the attributes searched before the decision. So far, consolidation has been modeled in Diff Con as mainly affecting information found and processed before the final decision. However, new information is also assumed to be sought and integrated before and after a decision has been made. Frey (1986) and Russo et al. (1998) demonstrate that additional information is also used to support an initial choice, thereby biasing the evaluation of the choice.

Postdecision consolidation is important in strengthening a decision, forming it into a habit, and developing a general strategy. Postdecision consolidation may be seen as one important factor in explaining how habits and conservatism in people's behavior are created and maintained.

What Drives Differentiation and Consolidation Processes?

The need to arrive at a choice can be defined as the chief overall driving force of all decision-making processes. Differentiation processes are applied to a decision problem to produce a final choice that is sufficiently superior to its competitors. Differentiation processes are driven by at least two partly independent sets of component forces.

Cognitive prototype "gestalt" factors influence the organization of psychological representations so that they conform to or approach earlier known or other simple cognitive structures or gestalts (Helson, 1933). In its pure form, this means that decision situations and problems are classified in certain ways and that incongruencies with these prototypical representations are treated in differentiation and consolidation processes. This set of driving factors can be related to predominantly cognitively driven explanations (Bem, 1965, 1967), to attribution theory (Kelley, 1967), and to self-serving biases (Greenwald, 1980). Holyoak and Simon (1999) elaborate the constraints that promote coherence in cognition and demonstrate how ambiguous inputs can be transformed into coherent decisions.

Another way of looking at differentiation and consolidation processes is to assume that an initial representation that does not fit with the desired one leads to arousal, which in turn drives *dissonance reduction*

(Festinger, 1957) in the form of differentiation and consolidation. Note that dissonance reduction has referred mainly to postdecision processes in the past (Festinger, 1964) but that dissonance reduction here applies also to the predecision phase. Empirical studies starting with that of Zanna and Cooper (1974) have shown that dissonant cognitions give rise to negative emotional arousal (cf. Eagly & Chaiken, 1993). One way of reducing this negative emotional arousal is to restructure a decision problem so that the cognitive dissonance is eliminated (by applying a decision rule or restructuring the problem). In Diff Con terms, cognitive dissonance would relate to both affect-driven and cognitively driven attractiveness. In the postdecision phase, it is natural to assume that dissonance reduction is driven also by negative consequences. Actually, Cooper and Fazio (1984) stated that dissonance reduction is driven only by negative consequences instead of inconsistency of cognitions. However, Harmon-Jones, Brehm, Greenberg, Simon, and Nelson (1996) showed that this is not necessarily the case. According to Diff Con theory, there is no need for negative consequences for differentiation and consolidation to take place.

The *stability and safety motive* constitutes a second set of component forces driving differentiation, is related to a safety or stability motive, and refers more clearly to a decision maker's predictions of aspects, images, or scenarios in the postdecision phase. This set of components drives predecision differentiation in a process that is explicitly related to the future much more than is the first set of factors. After a decision, the same set of components drives consolidation, so that in spite of adverse events and regret, the chosen alternative appears or becomes sufficiently better than its competitors. The purpose of safety and stability factors is to avoid spending unnecessary effort on decision reversals and changes of implementation plans following a decision.

As mentioned earlier, incentives to change a decision can originate in, for example, feelings of regret and unpredicted outcomes. Predecision differentiation positions the chosen alternative in as strong a position as needed or possible, and consolidation processes defend the achieved degree of superiority of the chosen alternative after the decision.

The Role of Uncertainty in Diff Con Theory

Because many contemporary decision research models treat decision making under uncertainty, it is appropriate to ask how Diff Con theory as a descriptive theory handles uncertainty. From empirical studies we know that decision makers attempt to eliminate uncertainty in their decisions (Huber, 1997). Diff Con–related research has treated uncertainty in different ways, and uncertainty can enter decisions in the following three different ways. First, uncertainty may concern what cognitively and affect-driven goals are relevant in a situation. What do I want to achieve and strive for? Second, uncertainty may exist concerning how the goals determined by affect and values should be mapped on the decision alternatives. How do I assign attractiveness to the alternatives given my goals? Third, uncertainty may concern outcome uncertainty. What is the likelihood for this or that event to follow a decision? Usually, the last of these uncertainties has been modeled in decision theories, exemplified by theories based on the expected utility concept.

Uncertainties concerning both future goals and attractiveness mappings are modeled in Diff Con theory as components in differentiation and consolidation. This kind of uncertainty can be utilized in restructuring the problem, providing greater support for a preliminary choice. The uncertainty can also affect the level of differentiation needed before a decision can be made. Huber (1997) demonstrated how decision makers restructured decision problems to avoid uncertainty before a decision could be made. Fischhoff, Slovic, and Lichtenstein (1980), Jungermann (1983), and Kahneman and Snell (1992) have treated the uncertainty of goals, and of present and future utilities in traditional decision theoretic frameworks, which is relevant for uncertainty concerning attractiveness in Diff Con theory as well.

Uncertainty concerning attractiveness representations, when the goals are clear, is also used in differentiation and consolidation processes without any specific uncertainty attribute. However, uncertainty concerning outcomes can be used in different ways. Sometimes such uncertainty can also be transformed into uncertainty about the attractiveness of the outcome. In other cases, uncertainty can be treated as a separate attribute, in particular when the decision problem is put in a probabilistic format. In the first presentation of Diff Con theory, uncertainty or subjective probability concerning events and outcomes was modeled in the former way (Svenson, 1992). However in some empirical work, uncertainty was such a conspicuous part of the decision problem (lottery) that it was modeled as an independent attribute (Svenson & Malmsten, 1996). Differentiation of uncertainty as an independent attribute in Diff Con theory can be related to wishful thinking (Cyert, Dill, & March, 1958; Slovic, 1966), and consolidation of the subjective probability attribute can be related to the hindsight phenomenon (Fischhoff, 1975).

Discussion

The Diff Con theory approach has recommendations for how human decision making can be studied empirically and how our understanding of human decision processes can be improved.

The representation of decision alternatives is different for different decision makers. The Diff Con approach recommends that the information for each subject be treated in accordance with that subject's representation before the data are aggregated across a group of subjects. This means that it is incorrect to compute means across attributes defined by their connotations (*labels*), except when all subjects share the same representation.

To illustrate this recommendation, assume a decision between two jobs characterized by salary (attribute 1) and how interesting the job is to the decision maker (attribute 2). Decision maker A thinks that salary is the more important attribute, whereas decision maker B considers interest more important. Aggregating data from the two decision makers within a label (salary and interest, respectively) would be suboptimal because the importance of the attributes is different for the decision makers. Instead, aggregation should be made within the most important and the second most important attributes, respectively. This is because it is assumed (and found empirically) that decision processes are regular across individuals, but only if an adequate representation can be found. In this case, the most important attribute is processed in the same way by both decision makers irrespective of the label. This means that A uses salary in the same way that B uses interest in reaching a decision. The less important attribute is processed in another way than the most important attribute but treated in the same manner by both decision makers.

The Diff Con approach also stresses the fact that decision alternatives in the same decision problem can be represented by aspects on completely different attributes. Then it becomes impossible to aggregate data within labels. However, aggregating data within attributes according to their importance is still possible.

Related to different representations of decision alternatives in the same decision problem, the Diff Con approach postulates that different decision rules can be applied to different alternatives in the same decision problem. To exemplify, one alternative may be processed in a holistic way under strong affective influence and another alternative by a more analytic and value-driven decision rule.

Affect and emotion are related to decision processes in different ways. First, affect in terms of the emotional state or mood of a decision maker can influence the process of making a decision (e.g., slowing it down). Second, it may affect all alternatives (e.g., making all of them look worse or better, depending on the mood). Third, an aspect of a decision alternative can trigger affects that, together with the value component, shape the attractiveness of that aspect. Fourth, a decision problem and its alternatives can themselves trigger affect (e.g., a set of very nice alternatives can create a positive mood).

Zajonc (1980) suggested that the experiences of feelings and affect are faster than cognitive processes related to the same stimulus. If that is so, then increased time pressure would, in general, lead to relatively greater influence from affective than from cognitive component forces. If affects, on the average, are faster than other cognitions, then earlier associations with a decision alternative should be relatively more affect related than later associations. Measures of affect can be achieved through ratings and measures of neuropsychological correlates of affect.

Introduction of affect as a component of attractiveness opens possibilities for a deeper understanding of decision processes. For example, conflicts between the affect and value components in a decision can now be modeled (e.g., Shiv & Fedorikhin, 1999; Slovic, Finucane, Peters, & MacGregor, 2002). Such conflicts can appear within one alternative and across alternatives. Within an alternative, the conflict creates affect–value ambivalence toward an alternative, and a conflict between alternatives introduces a decision under an affect–value goal conflict. If both are combined, a decision maker can choose an ambivalent alternative that was chosen under a goal conflict. In such a case, the need for consolidation can be strong to pacify the conflicts in the decision. Much work remains in both the theoretical and empirical domains of the Diff Con project, but hopefully, the present chapter has provided a framework for studies that can deepen our understanding of human decision processes.

References

Abelson, R. P., Kinder, D. R., & Peters, M. D. (1982). Affective and semantic components in political person perception. *Journal of Personality and Social Psychology, 42*, 619–630.

Abelson, R. P., & Levi, A. (1985). Decision making and decision theory. In G. Lindzey & E. Aronson (Eds.), *Handbook of social psychology* (3rd ed., pp. 231–309). New York: Random House.

Arkes, H. R. (1996). The temperature of Diff Con theory. *Organizational Behavior and Human Decision Processes, 65,* 268–271.

Baron, J., & Spranca, M. (1997). Protected values. *Organizational Behavior and Human Decision Processes, 70,* 1–16.

Beach, L. R. (1990). *Image theory: Decision making in personal and organizational contexts.* Chichester, UK: Wiley.

Bem, D. J. (1965). An experimental analysis of self-persuasion. *Journal of Experimental Social Psychology, 1,* 199–218.

Bem, D. J. (1967). Self-perception: An alternative interpretation of cognitive dissonance phenomena. *Psychological Review, 74,* 183–200.

Bettman, J. R., Luce, M. F., & Payne, J. W. (1998). Constructive consumer choice processes. *Journal of Consumer Research, 25,* 187–217.

Boles, T. L., & Messick, D. M. (1995). A reverse outcome bias: The influence of multiple reference points on the evaluation of outcomes and decisions. *Organizational Behavior and Human Decision Processes, 61,* 262–275.

Brehmer, B. (1992). Dynamic decision making: Human control of complex systems. *Acta Psychologica, 81,* 211–241.

Busemeyer, J. R., & Townsend, J. T. (1993). Decision field theory: A dynamic-cognitive approach to decision making in an uncertain environment. *Psychological Review, 100,* 432–459.

Cacioppo, J. T., & Gardner, W. L. (1999). Emotion. *Annual Review of Psychology, 50,* 191–214.

Cartwright, D., & Festinger, L. (1943). A quantitative theory of decision. *Psychological Review, 50,* 595–621.

Cooper, J., & Fazio, R. H. (1984). A new look at dissonance theory. In L. Berkowitz (Ed.), *Advances in experimental social psychology* (Vol. 17, pp. 229–264). New York: Academic Press.

Coupey, E. (1994). Restructuring: Constructive processing of information displays in consumer choice. *Journal of Consumer Research, 21,* 83–99.

Cyert, R. M., Dill, W. T., & March, J. G. (1958). The role of expectations in business decision making. *Administrative Science Quarterly, 3,* 307–340.

Damasio, A. R. (1994). *Descartes' error: Emotion, reason and the human brain.* London: Macmillan.

Dembo, T. (1931). Der Ärger als dynamisches Problem. *Psychologische Forschung, 15,* 1–144.

Dror, I. E., Busemeyer, J. R., & Basola, B. (1999). Decision making under time pressure: An independent test of sequential sampling models. *Memory and Cognition, 27,* 713–725.

Eagly, A. H., & Chaiken, S. (1993). *The psychology of attitudes.* New York: Harcourt Brace Jovanovich.

Estes, W. K. (1994). *Classification and cognition.* New York: Oxford University Press.

Festinger, L., (1957). *A theory of cognitive dissonance.* Stanford, CA: Stanford University Press.

Festinger, L. (1964). *Conflicts, decision and dissonance.* Stanford CA: Stanford University Press.

Fischhoff, B. (1975). Hindsight is not equal to foresight: The effect of outcome knowledge on judgment under uncertainty. *Journal of Experimental Psychology: Human Perception and Performance, 1*, 288–299.

Fischhoff, B. (1996). The real world; What good is it? *Organizational Behavior and Human Decision Processes, 65*, 232–248.

Fischhoff, B., Slovic, P., & Lichtenstein, S. (1980). Knowing what you want: Measuring labile values. In T. Wallsten (Ed.), *Cognitive processes in choice and decision behavior* (pp. 64–85). Hillsdale, NJ: Erlbaum.

Frey, D. (1986). Recent research on selective exposure to information. In L. Berkowitz (Ed.), *Advances in experimental social psychology* (Vol. 19, pp. 41–80). New York: Academic Press.

Gärling, T. (1992). The importance of routines for the performance of everyday activities. *Scandinavian Journal of Psychology, 33*, 170–177.

Greenwald, A. G. (1980). The totalitarian ego: Fabrication and revision of personal history. *American Psychologist, 35*, 603–618.

Harmon-Jones, E., Brehm, J. W., Greenberg, J., Simon, L., & Nelson, D. E. (1996). Evidence that the production of aversive consequences is not necessary to create cognitive dissonance. *Journal of Personality and Social Psychology, 70*, 5–16.

Helson, H. (1933). The fundamental propositions of gestalt psychology. *Psychological Review, 40*, 13–22.

Holyoak, K. J., & Simon, D. (1999). Bidirectional reasoning in decision making by constraint satisfaction. *Journal of Experimental Psychology, 128*, 3–31.

Huber, O. (1997). Beyond gambles and lotteries: Naturalistic risky decisions. In R. Ranyard, W. R. Crozier, & O. Svenson (Eds.), *Decision making: Cognitive models and explanations* (pp. 145–162). London: Routledge.

Isen, A. M. (1993). Positive affect and decision making. In M. Lewis & J. M. Haviland (Eds.), *Handbook of emotions* (pp. 261–277). New York: Guilford Press.

Janis, I. L., & Mann, L. (1977). *Decision making*. New York: Free Press.

Johnson, E. J., & Tversky, A. (1983). Affect, generalization, and the perception of risk. *Journal of Personality and Social Psychology, 45*, 20–31.

Jungermann, H. (1983). The two camps on rationality. In R. W. Scholz (Ed.), *Decision making under uncertainty* (pp. 63–86). Amsterdam: North Holland.

Kahneman, D. (1999). Objective happiness. In D. Kahneman, E. Diener, & N. Schwarz (Eds.), *Well-being: The foundations of hedonic psychology* (pp. 3–25). New York: Russell Sage.

Kahneman, D., Diener, E., & Schwarz, N. (1999). *Well-being: The foundations of hedonic psychology*. New York: Russel Sage Foundation.

Kahneman, D., Knetsch, J. L., & Thaler, R. H. (1990). Experimental tests of the endowment effect and the Coase theorem. *Journal of Political Economy, 98*, 1325–1348.

Kahneman, D., & Snell, J. (1990). Predicting utility. In R. M. Hogarth (Ed.), *Insights in decision making* (pp. 295–310). Chicago: University of Chicago Press.

Kahneman, D., & Snell, J. (1992). Predicting a changing taste: Do people know what they will like? *Journal of Behavioral Decision Making, 5*, 187–200.

Kahneman, D., & Tversky, A. (1979). Prospect theory: An analysis of decisions under risk. *Econometrica, 47*, 263–291.

Kelley, H. H. (1967). Attribution Theory in social psychology. In D. Levine (Ed.), *Nebraska symposium on motivation.* (Vol. 15, pp. 192–238). Lincoln: University of Nebraska Press.

Klein, G. A. (1989). Recognition – primed decisions. In W. B. Rouse (Ed.), *Advances in man–machine system research* (Vol. 5, pp. 47–92). Greenwich, CT: JAI Press.

Kunda, Z. (1990). The case of motivated reasoning. *Psychological Bulletin, 108,* 480–498.

Langer, E. (1994). The illusion of calculated decisions. In R. C. Schank & E. Langer (Eds.), *Beliefs, reasoning and decision making: Psycho-logic in honor of Bob Abelson* (pp. 33–53). Hillsdale, NJ: Erlbaum.

LeDoux, J. E. (1995). Emotion: Clues from the brain. *Annual Review of Psychology, 46,* 209–235.

Lewicka, M. (1997). Is hate wiser than love? Cognitive and emotional utilities in decision making. In R. Ranyard, W. R. Crozier, & O. Svenson (Eds.), *Decision making: Cognitive models and explanations* (pp. 90–106). London: Routledge.

Lewin, K. (1951). *Field theory in social science.* New York: Harper.

Loewenstein, G., & Schkade, D. (1999). Wouldn't it be nice? Predicting future feelings. In D. Kahneman, E. Diener, & N. Schwarz (Eds.), *Well-being: The foundations of hedonic psychology* (pp. 85–105). New York: Russel Sage Foundation.

Loomes, G., & Sugden, R. (1982). Regret theory: An alternative theory of rational choice under uncertainty. *The Economic Journal, 92,* 805–824.

Luce, M. F. (1998). Choosing to avoid: Coping with negatively emotion-laden consumer decisions. *Journal of Consumer Research, 24,* 409–433.

Luce, M. F. , Bettman, J. R., & Payne, J. W. (1997). Choice processing in emotionally difficult decisions. *Journal of Experimental Psychology: Learning, Memory and Cognition, 23,* 384–405.

Mellers, B., Schwarz, A., & Ritov, I. (1999). Emotion-based choice. *Journal of Experimental Psychology: General, 128,* 332–345.

Montgomery, H. (1983). Decision rules and the search for a dominance structure: Towards a process model of decision making. In P. C. Humphreys, O. Svenson, & A. Vari (Eds.), *Analyzing and aiding decision processes* (pp. 343–369). Amsterdam: North-Holland.

Montgomery, H., & Svenson, O. (1989). A think aloud study of dominance structuring in decision processes. In H. Montgomery & O. Svenson (Eds.), *Process and structure in human decision making* (pp. 135–150). Chichester, UK: Wiley.

Payne, J. W. (1976). Task complexity and contingent processing in decision making: An information search and protocol analysis. *Organizational Behavior and Human Performance, 16,* 366–387.

Ranyard, R. (1989). Structuring and evaluating simple monetary risks. In H. Montgomery & O. Svenson (Eds.), *Process and structure in human decision making* (pp. 195–207). Chichester, UK: Wiley.

Rosenberg, E. L. (1998). Levels of analysis and the organization of affect. *Review of General Psychology, 3,* 247–270.

Russo, J. E., Medvec, V. H., & Meloy, M. G. (1996). The distortion of information during decisions. *Organizational Behavior and Human Decision Processes. 66,* 102–110.

Russo, J. E., Meloy, M. G., & Medvec, V. H. (1998). Predecisional distortion of product information. *Journal of Market Research, 35*, 438–452.

Samuelson, W., & Zeckhauser, R. (1988). Status quo bias in decision making. *Journal of Risk and Uncertainty, 1*, 7–59.

Schweitzer, M. (1994). Disentangling status quo and omission effects: An experimental analysis. *Organizational Behavior and Human Decision Processes, 58*, 457–476.

Shafir, E. (1993). Choosing versus rejecting: Why some options are both better and worse than others. *Memory & Cognition, 21*, 546–556.

Shafir, E., & Tversky, A. (1992). Thinking through uncertainty: Nonconsequential reasoning and choice. *Cognitive Psychology, 24*, 449–474.

Shamoun, S., & Svenson, O. (2002). The effects of induced conflicts on decision and postdecision processes. *Scandinavian Journal of Psychology, 43*, 325–333.

Shiffrin, R. M., & Schneider, W. (1977). Controlled and automatic human information processing: II. Perceptual learning, automatic attending, and a general theory. *Psychological Review, 84*, 127–190.

Shiv, B., & Fedorikhin, A. (1999). Heart and mind in conflict: The interplay of affect and cognition in consumer decision making. *Journal of Consumer Research, 26*, 278–292.

Slovic, P. (1966). Value as a determiner of subjective probability. *IEEE Transactions on Human Factors in Electronics, HFE-7*, pp. 22–28.

Slovic, P., Finucane, M., Peters, E., & MacGregor, D. G. (2002). The affect heuristic. In T. Gilovich, D. Griffin, & D. Kahneman (Eds.), *Intuitive judgment: Heuristics and biases* (pp. 397–420). Cambridge: Cambridge University Press.

Slovic, P., & MacPhillamy, D. (1974). Dimensional commensurability and cue utilization in comparative judgment. *Organizational Behavior and Human Performance, 11*, 172–194.

Smith, E. R. (1992). The role of exemplars in social judgment. In L. L. Martin & A. Tesser (Eds.), *The construction of social judgments* (pp. 107–132). Hillsdale, NJ: Erlbaum.

Solomon, R. C. (1993). The philosophy of emotions. In M. Lewis & J. M. Haviland (Eds.), *Handbook of emotions* (pp. 3–15). London: Guilford Press.

Svenson, O. (1974). *A note on think aloud protocols obtained during the choice of a home*. Reports from the Psychological Laboratories. Stockholm: Stockholm University No. 421.

Svenson, O. (1979). Process descriptions of decision making. *Organizational Behavior and Human performance, 23*, 86–112.

Svenson, O. (1990). Some propositions for the classification of decision situations. In K. Borcherding, O. I. Larichev, & D. M. Messich (Eds.), *Contemporary issues in decision making* (pp.17–31). Amsterdam: Elsevier.

Svenson, O. (1992). Differentiation and consolidation theory of human decision making: A frame of reference for the study of pre- and postdecision processes. *Acta Psychologica, 80*, 143–168.

Svenson, O. (1996). Decision making and the search for psychological regularities: What can be learned from a process perspective? *Organizational Behavior and Human Decision Processes, 65*, 252–267.

Svenson, O., & Hill, T. (1997). Turning prior disadvantages into advantages: Differentiation and consolidation in real-life decision making. In R. Ranyard, W. R. Crozier, & O. Svenson (Eds.), *Decision making: Cognitive models and explanations* (pp. 218–232). London: Routledge.

Svenson, O., & Malmsten, N. (1996). Post-decision consolidation over time as a function of gain or loss of an alternative. *Scandinavian Journal of Psychology, 37*, 302–311.

Svenson, O., & Maule, A. J. (1993). *Time pressure and stress in human judgment and decision making.* New York: Plenum.

Svenson, O., & Shamoun, S. (1997). Predecision conflict and different patterns of postdecision attractiveness restructuring: Empirical illustrations from an important real-life decision. *Scandinavian Journal of Psychology, 38*, 243–251.

Svenson, O. & Slovic, P. (2002). *Word Associations, decision rules and choices.* Stockholm: Stockholm University, Department of Psychology, manuscript.

Toda, M. (1980). Emotion and decision making. *Acta Psychologica, 45*, 133–155.

Tversky, A., & Kahneman, D. (1992). Advances in prospect theory: Cumulative representation of uncertainty. *Journal of Risk and Uncertainty, 5*, 297–323.

Verplanken, B., & Svenson, O. (1997). Personal involvement in human decision making: Conceptualisations and effects on decision processes. In R. Ranyard, W. R. Crozier, & O. Svenson (Eds.), *Decision making: Cognitive models and explanations* (pp. 40–57). London: Routledge.

Zajonc, R. B. (1980). Feelings and thinking: Preferences need no inferences. *American Psychologist, 35*, 151–175.

Zanna, M. P., & Cooper, J. (1974). Dissonance and the pill: An attribution approach to studying the arousal properties of dissonance. *Journal of Personality and Social Psychology, 29*, 703–709.

10 Judgment and Decision Making: The Dance of Affect and Reason

Melissa L. Finucane, Ellen Peters, and Paul Slovic

"The heart has reasons that reason does not know at all."

Pascal

ABSTRACT

In this chapter, we propose a theoretical framework for understanding some of the ways that affect can influence judgment and decision making. Affect and emotion have been topics of study for centuries and, as a result, the literature is vast. One recent search found more than 5,000 citations to this topic over the previous 5 years (Cacioppo & Gardner, 1999). In this chapter we will obviously address only small portions of this literature. We hope, however, that the chapter will be viewed as an invitation for further exploration of the impact of affect on decisions. The theory we will introduce demonstrates the importance of affect in guiding evaluations and choices. We offer a parsimonious explanation for many patterns of results revealed in judgment and decision-making research and support the theory with some of our own data.

CONTENTS

Financial support for the writing of this chapter was provided by the National Science Foundation under Grants SES-9876587, SES-9975347, and SES-0112158. The authors gratefully acknowledge Leisha Wharfield for her help with manuscript preparation. This chapter was written through a thoroughly collaborative effort; an equal contribution was made by each author. Any opinions, findings, and conclusions or recommendations expressed in this chapter are those of the authors and do not necessarily reflect those of the National Science Foundation.

What Do We Mean by Affect?

Although researchers in the field of emotion have not yet agreed on a precise definition of *affect*, we use a specific definition throughout this chapter. We see affect as "goodness" or "badness" (1) experienced as a feeling state (with or without consciousness) and (2) demarcating a positive or negative quality of a specific stimulus. Stimulus representations associated with affect can include external events and objects as well as internal representations (e.g., memories). Individuals differ in the strength and speed of their positive and negative reactions, and stimuli themselves vary in the strength and speed with which they elicit positive and negative feelings. An affective reaction can be an enduring disposition strongly related to a stimulus (e.g., your child), but can also be a fleeting reaction or a weakly related response (e.g., to a chair). The affective quality of a stimulus may vary with the context: The strength of positive or negative feelings may depend on what aspects of a stimulus stand out as most salient at any particular time.

We distinguish affect from *emotion*, which generally refers to particular states (such as anger, fear, or happiness) that are "intense, short-lived, and usually have a definite cause and clear cognitive content" (Forgas, 1992, p. 230). We also distinguish affect from *mood*, which generally refers to a feeling (such as having the blues) that is low in intensity, can last for a few minutes or several weeks, has no object or has fleeting objects, and does not have to have a specific antecedent cause or cognitive content.

Distinguishing our conceptualization of affect from traditional characterizations of mood and emotion is critical. Unlike emotion, we view affect as having the capacity to be subtle and to be without elaborate appraisal properties; unlike mood, we view affect as having a direct (rather than an indirect) motivational effect. Similar to mood and emotion, however, affect can vary along both valence (positive, negative) and arousal (high, low) dimensions. In contrast to our definition of affect, Isen (1993) uses *affect* to refer to background mood, and other authors use it as a generic label or umbrella term that encompasses moods and emotions (e.g., Davidson, 1994; Forgas, 1995; Mayer, 1986; Petty, Gleicher, & Baker, 1991). The focus of this chapter is on potentially subtle feelings triggered by the object of judgment or choice and not on the influence of specific emotions or background mood state on the judgment or choice.

Our conceptualization of affect foreshadows how we think lability in judgments and decisions may arise. If affective feelings are as important as we assume, then differences in characteristics of the task and/or of the individual will impact the judgments and decisions that are made. For example, affective feelings toward a particularly salient aspect of a stimulus may strongly influence choices in one context, but in another context the same aspect may be less salient, produce less intense affective feelings, and exert only a weak influence on choice. On the other hand, individuals may differ from one another in the strength of their affective feelings such that, faced with the same context or task, Person X may have strong affective feelings that guide his or her decisions, whereas Person Y has weaker affective feelings that impact the decisions less forcefully. Judgments and choices may also result from an interaction between the characteristics of the person making the judgment or decision and the nature of the task.

In the following section, we draw together material to explain why we think affect plays a crucial role in evaluations and choices. Then we describe details of our theory of the role of affect in judgment and decision making, laying out some empirical predictions and offering some preliminary support for them. The final sections highlight the theoretical and applied implications of our model and suggest directions for future work.

Background and Review

Affect has played a key role in many theories about human behavior, but has rarely been recognized as an important component in research and theory in judgment and decision making (see Bentham, 1815/1969, for an important exception). Perhaps befitting the rationalistic origins of descriptive decision research, its main focus has been cognitive. Traditionally, researchers have concentrated on demonstrating whether or not individuals follow normative judgment and decision models, and reasoned deliberation has been implicitly assumed as the hallmark of good decision making. Studies over several decades, however, have given us ample descriptions of the diverse ways in which individuals deviate from the predictions of normative models and, in recent years, the importance of affect has been acknowledged increasingly by decision researchers. In this chapter, affect is being called upon as the basis for a coherent framework that explains rather than simply describes nonnormative judgments and decisions.

A strong early proponent of the importance of affect in decision making was Zajonc (1980), who argued that affective reactions to stimuli are often the very first reactions, occurring automatically and subsequently guiding information processing and judgment. According to Zajonc, all perceptions contain some affect. "We do not just see 'a house': We see a *handsome* house, an *ugly* house, or a *pretentious* house" (p. 154). He later adds, "We sometimes delude ourselves that we proceed in a rational manner and weigh all the pros and cons of the various alternatives. But this is probably seldom the actual case. Quite often 'I decided in favor of X' is no more than 'I liked X.' ... We buy the cars we 'like,' choose the jobs and houses we find 'attractive,' and then justify these choices by various reasons...." (p. 155). If Zajonc is correct, then affective reactions may serve as orienting mechanisms, helping us navigate quickly and efficiently through a complex, uncertain, and sometimes dangerous world.

Research by students of motivation, learning, memory, and social cognition is particularly relevant to the thesis of this chapter. This work includes studies by Mowrer (1960a, 1960b) on conditioned emotions, Epstein (1994) on rational and experiential modes of processing information, Fazio (1995) on the accessibility of affect associated with attitudes, and Gray (1990) on the learning of approach and avoidance behaviors. Theorists such as Mowrer and Epstein give affect a direct role in motivating behavior, implying that we integrate positive and negative feelings according to some sort of automatic, rapid *affective algebra*, whose operations and rules remain to be discovered. Epstein's (1994) view on this is concise:

> The experiential system is assumed to be intimately associated with the experience of affect, ... which refer[s] to subtle feelings of which people are often unaware. When a person responds to an emotionally significant event ... the experiential system automatically searches its memory banks for related events, including their emotional

accompaniments.... If the activated feelings are pleasant, they motivate actions and thoughts anticipated to reproduce the feelings. If the feelings are unpleasant, they motivate actions and thoughts anticipated to avoid the feelings. (p. 716)

Our theory is also based on important work done by Ariely (1998), Damasio (1994), Hsee (1995, 1998), Janis and Mann (1977), Johnson and Tversky (1983), Kahneman and Snell (1990), Mellers, Schwartz, Ho, and Ritov (1997), Loewenstein (1996), Loewenstein, Weber, Hsee, and Welch (2001), Rozin, Haidt, and McCauley (1993), Wilson et al. (1993), and others. Excellent work has also been done on the relation between mood states and decisions. Although beyond the scope of this chapter, interested readers should refer to the particularly extensive work on mood and positive affect by Isen (1993; Isen & Labroo, this volume) as well as research on the feelings-as-information hypothesis (Schwarz & Clore, 1983). More recently, Svenson (this volume) has begun to map the intricate interplay between affect and reason in his differentiation and consolidation theory of decision making.

Before describing our theoretical framework, we will present some core notions that have guided us, many of which have been derived from studies by other investigators. First, we highlight features of Damasio's somatic marker hypothesis that are relevant to our view of how affect impacts decisions. We link this work with research demonstrating that individual differences in affective information processing influence choice. Then we review findings in three types of studies that seem disparate but are closely linked theoretically: (1) the work by Mellers, Richards, and Birnbaum (1992) on what we shall call *affective mapping* in impression formation; (2) research by Hsee (1996, 1998) on evaluability; and (3) research by Slovic and colleagues on the dominance of probabilities and proportions in judgments and decisions about winning money and saving lives.

Damasio's Somatic Marker Hypothesis

One of the most comprehensive and dramatic theoretical accounts of the role of affect and emotion in decision making is presented by the neurologist Antonio Damasio and his colleagues (see Damasio, 1994; Damasio, Tranel, & Damasio, 1991). Damasio's theory is derived from observations of patients with damage to the ventromedial frontal cortices of the brain that has left their basic intelligence, memory, and capacity for logical thought intact but has impaired their ability to "feel" and to associate affective feelings with the anticipated consequences of their actions. Close observation of these patients combined with a number of experimental studies led Damasio to argue that this type of brain damage induces a form of sociopathy (Damasio, Tranel, & Damasio, 1990) that destroys the individual's ability to make rational decisions, that is, decisions that are in his or her best interests. Persons suffering this damage become socially dysfunctional even though they remain intellectually capable of analytical reasoning.

In seeking to determine "what in the brain allows humans to behave rationally," Damasio argues that thought is derived largely from images broadly construed to include a great variety of perceptual and symbolic representations. A lifetime of learning leads these images to become "marked" by positive and negative feelings linked directly or indirectly to somatic or bodily states (Mowrer, 1960a, 1960b, and other learning theorists would refer to this "marking" as *conditioning*).

Damasio and his colleagues tested the somatic marker hypothesis in a decision-making experiment in which subjects gambled by selecting cards from any of four decks. Turning each card resulted in the gain or loss of a sum of money. Whereas normal subjects and patients with brain lesions outside the prefrontal sectors quickly learned to avoid decks with attractive large payoffs but occasional catastrophic losses, patients with frontal lobe damage did not, thus losing a great deal of money. Although these patients responded normally to gains and losses when they occurred (as indicated by skin-conductance responses immediately after an outcome was experienced), they did not seem to learn to *anticipate* future outcomes (e.g., they did not produce normal skin-conductance responses when contemplating a future choice from a dangerous deck). In other words, they failed to show proper anticipatory responses, even after numerous opportunities to learn them. These anticipatory feelings (somatic markers or conditioned emotional responses) are an operational definition of affect as conceived in this chapter.

Individual Differences in Affective Reactivity

Damasio has shown that individuals with a certain kind of brain damage differ from the general population with respect to their inability to experience anticipatory affective reactions, and this inability degrades their decision-making capabilities. A growing body of research also has demonstrated that individual differences in affective processing in non-brain-damaged individuals similarly influence choices, judgments, and evaluations of affectively valenced stimuli (e.g., Larsen & Diener, 1987; Patrick, 1994).

Rusting and Larsen (1998), for example, demonstrated that higher extraversion scores (extraverts are thought to be very reactive to positive events) were associated with increased processing of, and better performance on tasks that involved, positive material (compared to negative and neutral material). Highly anxious individuals, on the other hand, are thought to be hyperreactive to negative cues, such that they will learn to make choices to avoid negative experiences more quickly than those who are not anxious (Zinbarg & Mohlman, 1998). Peters (1998; Peters & Mauro, 2000; Peters & Slovic, 2000) found that self-report measures of individual differences in affective reactivity were associated with choices made by college student participants in versions of the card-selection task originally designed by Damasio and his colleagues (Bechara, Damasio, Damasio, & Anderson, 1994). In multiple experiments using different versions of the task, greater self-reported reactivity to negative events was associated with fewer selections from decks with larger losing payoffs. Conversely, greater self-reported reactivity to positive events was associated with a greater number of selections from high-gain decks.

These results thus provide evidence that individuals rely in part on their feelings to recognize the best option in a decision or judgment situation. Those who are better able to process particular affective cues appear to arrive sooner at consistent and clear preferences for those cues.

The remaining core notions that form the background for our theory of affect in decision making come from research on images, affective mapping, evaluability, and proportion dominance, each of which will now be reviewed.

Imagery, Affect, and Decision Making

Many affective theories of behavior, such as Damasio's, revolve around the concept of *imagery*, broadly construed to include sounds, smells, real or imagined visual impressions, ideas, and words, to which positive and negative feelings have been attached through learning. Mowrer, for example, summarized a vast body of research on learning and motivation conducted during the first half of the 20th century by concluding that conditioned emotional responses to images "guide and control performance in a generally sensible, adaptive manner" (Mowrer, 1960a, p. 307).

Table 10.1. *Images, Ratings, and Summation Scores for Respondent 132*

Sample Subject	Image Number	Image	Image Rating
San Diego	1	Very nice	2
San Diego	2	Good beaches	2
San Diego	3	Zoo	2
San Diego	4	Busy freeway	1
San Diego	5	Easy to find way	1
San Diego	6	Pretty town	2
		Sum =	10
Denver	1	High	2
Denver	2	Crowded	0
Denver	3	Cool	2
Denver	4	Pretty	1
Denver	5	Busy airport	−2
Denver	6	Busy streets	−2
		Sum =	1

Note: Based on these summation scores, this person's predicted preference for a vacation site would be San Diego. Source: Slovic et al. (1991).

A number of empirical studies have demonstrated a strong relationship between imagery, affect, and decision making. Many of these studies have employed a technique based upon word associations. The approach involves presenting individuals with a target stimulus, usually a word or a very brief phrase, and asking them to provide the first thought or image that comes to mind. The process is then repeated a number of times, say three to six, or until no further associations are generated. Following the elicitation of images, subjects are asked to rate each image they give on a scale ranging from very positive (e.g., +2) to very negative (e.g., −2), with a neutral point in the center. Scoring is done by summing or averaging the ratings to obtain an overall index.

This method of images has been used successfully to measure the affective meanings that influence people's preferences for different cities and states (Slovic et al., 1991) as well as their support for or opposition to technologies such as nuclear power (Peters & Slovic, 1996).

Table 10.1 illustrates the method in a task where one respondent was asked to associate to each of two cities and, later, to rate each image affectively. The cities in this example show a clear affective preference for San Diego over Denver. Slovic et al. (1991) showed that summed image scores such as these were highly predictive of expressed preferences for living in or visiting cities. In one study they found that the image score predicted the choice of actual vacation sites during the *next* 18 months.

Subsequent studies have found affect-laden imagery elicited by word associations to be predictive of preferences for investing in new companies on the stock market (MacGregor, Slovic, Dreman, & Berry, 2000) and predictive of adolescents' decisions to take part in health-threatening and health-enhancing behaviors such as smoking and exercise (Benthin et al., 1995). Other studies have suggested that the images need not be conscious (e.g., Winkielman, Zajonc, & Schwarz, 1997) and have demonstrated alternative techniques for measuring affect (Peters, Flynn, & Slovic, in review).

Evaluability

The research with images points to the importance of affective impressions in judgments and decisions. However, the impressions themselves may vary not only in their valence but also in the precision with which they are held. It turns out that the precision of an affective impression substantially determines its impact on judgments.

We shall refer to the distributional qualities of affective impressions and responses as *affective mappings*. Consider, for example, some questions posed by Mellers et al. (1992): "How much would you like a potential roommate if all you knew about her was that she was said to be intelligent?" Or "Suppose, instead, all you knew about her was that she was said to be obnoxious?" Intelligence is a favorable trait, but it is not very diagnostic (e.g., meaningful) for likeableness; hence, its affective map is rather diffuse. In contrast, obnoxiousness will likely produce a more precise and more negative impression.

How much would you like a roommate said to be both intelligent *and* obnoxious? Anderson (1981) has shown that the integration of multiple pieces of information into an impression of this sort can be described well by a weighted average model in which separate weights are given to intelligence and obnoxiousness, respectively. Mellers et al. (1992) further showed that the weights in such integrative tasks are inversely proportional to the variance of the impressions. Thus we would expect the impression produced by the combination of these two traits to be closer to the impression formed by obnoxiousness alone, reflecting greater weight given to obnoxiousness due to its smaller variance (more precise affective mapping). The meaning of a stimulus image appears to be reflected in the precision of the affective feelings associated with

Table 10.2. *Attributes of Two Dictionaries in Hsee's Study*

	Year of Publication	Number of Entries	Any Defects?
Dictionary A	1993	10,000	No, it's like new
Dictionary B	1993	20,000	Yes, the cover is torn; otherwise, it's like new

that image. More precise affective impressions, that are subjectively experienced, reflect more precise meanings and carry more weight in impression formation, judgment, and decision making.

Hsee (1996, 1998) has developed the notion of *evaluability* to describe
the interplay between the precision of an affective impression and its
meaning or importance for judgment and decision making. Evaluability
is illustrated by an experiment in which Hsee asked people to assume
they were music majors looking for a used music dictionary. In a joint-
evaluation condition, participants were shown two dictionaries, A and
B (see Table 10.2), and asked how much they would be willing to pay
for each. Willingness to pay was far higher for Dictionary B, presumably because of its greater number of entries. However, when one group
of participants evaluated only A and another group evaluated only B,
the mean willingness to pay was much higher for Dictionary A. Hsee
explains this reversal by means of the *evaluability principle*. He argues
that, without a direct comparison, the number of entries is hard to evaluate, because the evaluator does not have a precise notion of *how good*
or *how bad* 10,000 (or 20,000) entries is. However, the defects attribute is
evaluable in the sense that it translates easily into a precise good/bad
response and thus it carries more weight in the independent evaluation.
Most people find a defective dictionary unattractive and a like-new one
attractive. Under joint evaluation, the buyer can see that B is far superior on the more important attribute, number of entries. Thus, number
of entries becomes *evaluable* through the comparison process.

The evaluability principle thus asserts that the weight of a stimulus
attribute in an evaluative judgment or choice is proportional to the ease
or precision with which the value of that attribute (or a comparison on
the attribute across alternatives) can be mapped into an affective impression. In other words, affect bestows meaning on information (recall the
work on semantic meaning by Osgood, Suci, & Tannenbaum, 1957), and
affective meaning influences our ability to use information in judgment
and decision making. Evaluability can thus be seen as an extension of

the general relationship between the variance of an impression and its weight in an impression-formation task (Mellers et al., 1992).

Hsee's work on evaluability is noteworthy because it shows that even very important attributes may not be used by a judge or decision maker unless they can be translated precisely into an affective frame of reference. As described in the next section, Hsee finds evaluability effects even with familiar attributes such as the amount of ice cream in a cup (Hsee, 1998). We will also demonstrate similar effects with other familiar concepts such as amounts of money or human lives.

Proportion Dominance

In situations that involve uncertainty about whether we will win or lose or that involve ambiguity about some quantity of something (i.e., how much is enough), there appears to be one information format that is highly evaluable, leading it to carry great weight in many judgment tasks. This is a representation characterizing an attribute as a proportion or percentage of something or as a probability. We shall refer to the strong effects of this type of representation as *proportion dominance*.[1]

Proportion or probability dominance was evident in the early study by Slovic and Lichtenstein (1968) that had people rate the attractiveness of various two-outcome gambles. Ratings of a gamble's attractiveness were determined much more strongly by the probabilities of winning and losing than by the monetary outcomes. This finding has been replicated many times (see, e.g., Goldstein & Einhorn, 1987, or Ordóñez & Benson, 1997).

Slovic (unpublished) tested the limits of probability dominance by asking one group of individuals to rate the attractiveness of playing a simple gamble (7/36, win $9) on a scale ranging between 0 (not at all attractive) and 20 (very attractive). A second group rated a similar gamble with a small loss (7/36, win $9; 29/36, lose 5¢) on the same scale of attractiveness. The data were anomalous. The mean response to the first gamble was 9.4. When a loss of 5¢ was added, the mean attractiveness jumped to 14.9, and there was almost no overlap between the distribution of responses around this mean and the responses for the group who judged the gamble that had no loss. A subsequent experiment found that the enhancement produced by adding a small loss held for choices as well as for rating responses.

---

[1] We thank Chris Hsee for suggesting this term.

A subsequent study employed a conjoint analysis in which each subject rated 1 of 16 gambles formed by crossing four levels of probability (7/36, 14/36, 21/36, 28/36) with four levels of payoff ($3, $6, $9, $12 in one study and $30, $60, $90, $120 in another). Although respondents said that they wanted to weight probability and payoff about equally in judging attractiveness (and thought they had done so), the actual weighting was more than five times greater for probability than for payoff.

These curious findings can be explained by reference to Hsee's evaluability concept and the notion of affective mapping. According to this view, a probability maps relatively precisely onto the attractiveness scale because probability has an upper and a lower bound (1 and 0) and people know where a given value, such as 7/36, falls within that range. They also know what 7/36 means – "I'm probably not going to win." In contrast, the mapping of a dollar outcome (e.g., $9) onto the attractiveness scale is diffuse, reflecting a failure to know how good or bad or how attractive or unattractive $9 is. Thus, the impression formed by the gamble offering $9 to win with no losing payoff is dominated by the relatively precise and unattractive impression produced by the 7/36 probability of winning. However, adding a very small loss to the payoff dimension brings the $9 payoff into focus and thus gives it meaning. The combination of a possible $9 gain and a 5¢ loss is a *very attractive* win/loss ratio, leading to a relatively precise mapping onto the upper end of the scale. Whereas the imprecise mapping of the $9 carries little weight in the averaging process, the more precise and now favorable impression of ($9; –5¢) carries more weight, thus leading to an increase in the overall favorability of the gamble.[2]

Another interpretation of the gamble study is that, despite a lifetime of experience with small amounts of money such as $9, we do not carry in our minds a fixed value or *utility* for $9 that is independent of context. The dependence upon context for understanding the "meaning" of $9 is evident by contemplating how you would feel about finding $9 lying on a sidewalk (probably quite happy) versus how you would feel about receiving $9 as your income tax refund (probably disappointed).

---

[2] We recognize that when subjects are asked to evaluate gambles by giving buying or selling prices, payoffs are weighted more heavily than probabilities because of anchoring and adjustment procedures induced through stimulus-response compatibility (Tversky, Slovic, & Kahneman, 1990). This shows the sensitivity of judgment processes to contextual factors and demonstrates that the applicability of the affect model will be context-dependent.

Proportion dominance surfaces in a powerful way in a very different context, the life-saving interventions studied by Baron (1997), Fetherstonhaugh, Slovic, Johnson, and Friedrich (1997), Jenni and Loewenstein (1997), and Friedrich et al. (1999). For example, Fetherstonhaugh et al. found that an intervention saving 4,500 lives out of 11,000 at risk was judged much more valuable than one saving 4,500 lives out of 250,000 at risk. However, when two or more interventions differing in lives saved were directly compared, number of lives saved became more important than proportion saved. Thus number of lives saved, standing alone, appears to be poorly evaluable, as was the case for number of entries in Hsee's music dictionaries. With a side-by-side comparison, the number of lives became clearly evaluable and important, as also happened with the number of dictionary entries.

Slovic (unpublished), drawing upon proportion dominance and the limited evaluability of numbers of lives, predicted (and found) that, in a between-groups study, people would more strongly support an airport-safety measure expected to save 98% of 150 lives at risk than to support a measure expected to save 150 lives. Saving 150 lives is diffusely good and hence only weakly evaluable, whereas saving 98% of something clearly is very good and hence highly evaluable and highly weighted in the support judgment.

Turning to a more mundane form of proportion dominance, Hsee (1998) found that an overfilled ice cream container with 7 oz of ice cream was valued more highly (measured by willingness to pay) than an underfilled container with 8 oz of ice cream (see Figure 10.1). This "less is better effect" reversed itself when the options were juxtaposed and evaluated together. Thus, the proportion of the serving cup that was filled appeared to be more evaluable (in separate judgments) than the absolute amount of ice cream.

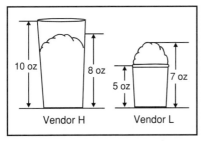

Figure 10.1 Stimuli in the ice cream study by Hsee (1998). Participants were given the sizes of the cups and the amounts of ice cream.

Summary

Briefly, we believe that the story emerging from the research just reviewed is as follows:

1. Affect, attached to images, influences judgments and decisions.
2. The evaluability of a stimulus image is reflected in the precision of the affective feelings associated with that image. More precise affective impressions reflect more precise meanings (i.e., greater evaluability) and carry more weight in impression formation, judgment, and decision making.[3]
3. Individuals differ in their reactivity to affective stimuli. As a result, reliable individual differences emerge regarding the influence of positive and negative affect on a person's decisions.
4. The anomalous findings from the experiments with gambles, ice cream preferences, and lifesaving interventions suggest that, without a context to give affective perspective to quantities of dollars, ice cream, and lives, these quantities may convey little meaning. Amounts of anything, no matter how common or familiar or intrinsically important, may in some circumstances not be evaluable. Probabilities or proportions, on the other hand, seem highly meaningful or evaluable, leading them to carry more weight in judgments and decisions than the quantities to which they apply.[4]

The Affect Heuristic

Description

In this section we propose a theory of how affect impacts judgment and decision making. The basic tenet is that positive and negative affective

---

[3] This does not mean that diffuse or vague affective experiences (e.g., good or bad moods) will fail to influence judgment and decision making. Their influence, however, tends to concern *how* we process information (e.g., systematically versus holistically) rather than *what* information we process and weight in decision making.

[4] We are not saying that people necessarily understand how to think probabilistically or produce judgments of probability. Rather, we are saying that people appear able to associate affective feeling states with probabilities and proportions. Thus, for example, they quickly see that a high probability of winning a prize is good and a low probability of winning is bad. Probabilities within a mid-range may, however, be poorly evaluable and carry little weight (see the discussion of the probability weighting function in Kahneman and Tversky, 1979).

feelings, attached to images, guide and direct judgments and decisions. We call this process the *affect heuristic*. In short, affect is a necessary bridge across the unexpected and the unknown. It facilitates information integration in judgments and decisions, guides reason, and gives priorities among multiple goals. We also consider it to be a powerful motivator of behavior (see Frank, 1988; LeDoux, 1996).

Despite what seem to be strong hints that many important findings in judgment and decision research may be understood by considering the role of affect, there are still rather few studies directly focusing on the influence of affective information processing upon performance in judgment and decision-making tasks.[5] One reason may be the lack of a sufficiently general but testable theoretical framework. The model we propose is intended as an initial attempt to fill this void.

To the extent that affect has captured the attention of researchers, two main perspectives seem to be emerging: One perspective emphasizes *expected affect*; the other emphasizes *experienced affect*. Some judgment and decision theorists include affect in their models as another attribute to be considered and deliberatively weighed in an evaluation or choice process. As such, individuals are thought to integrate the affect they *expect* they will feel in the future (e.g., disappointment or regret) as a consequence of their evaluations and choices (Bell, 1982; Mellers, 2000; Mellers et al., 1997). We postulate a different role for affect, however. Consistent with Damasio's views, our proposal is that mental representations of the decision stimuli evoke on-line affective *experiences* that influence people's perceptions and consequently their judgments and decisions. A similar view, labeled the *risk as feelings* hypothesis, has been proposed by Loewenstein et al. (2001). According to this view, all behavioral responses to risk are mediated by image-based emotional reactions or feelings that often diverge from cognitive evaluations of risk.

Our model has several parts to it (see Figure 10.2). To begin with, affective features that become salient in a judgment or decision-making process depend on characteristics of the individual and the task as well as the interaction between them. Differences among individuals in the way they react affectively, and differences across tasks regarding the evaluability (relative affective salience) of information, result in the affective

---

[5] The influence of mood on judgment has been extensively studied, (e.g., Bower, 1991; Isen, 1993; Schwarz & Clore, 1988) but has not directly addressed the question of how stimulus-specific affect is integrated in evaluations and choices.

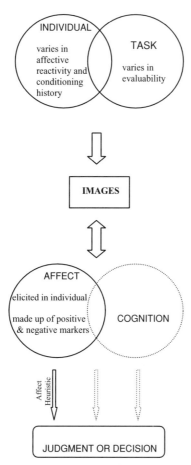

Figure 10.2 Theoretical framework of affective processes in judgment and decision making. (Dotted lines are used for cognitive elements because they are not the focus of this chapter.)

qualities of a stimulus image being *mapped* or interpreted in diverse ways. The salient qualities of real or imagined stimuli then evoke images (perceptual and symbolic interpretations) that may be made up of both affective and instrumental dimensions.

The mapping of affective information determines the contribution that stimulus images make to an individual's *affective pool* (lower left part of Figure 10.2). All of the images in people's minds are tagged or marked to varying degrees with affect. The affective pool contains all the positive and negative markers associated (consciously or unconsciously) with the images. The intensity of the markers varies with the images.

We propose that people consult or refer to the affective pool in the process of making judgments. Just as imaginability, memorability, and similarity serve as cues for probability judgments (e.g., the availability and representativeness heuristics), affect may serve as a cue for many important judgments. Using an overall, readily available affective impression can be easier and more efficient than weighing the pros and cons of various reasons or retrieving from memory many relevant examples, especially when the required judgment or decision is complex or mental resources are limited. This characterization of a mental shortcut leads us to label the use of affect a *heuristic*.

As indicated in Figure 10.2, characteristics of individuals and tasks also influence judgments and decisions. In addition, affective and cognitive features of judgment and decision processes are likely to interact with each other. However, the cognitive elements are not the focus of this chapter and are therefore depicted with dotted lines in the figure.

Empirical Predictions and Support

Earlier we traced the empirical origins of our theory in work on imagery, affective reactivity, evaluability, and proportion dominance. In this section we shall present some additional empirical predictions derived from the theory, along with findings from current research addressing those predictions. This research has tested the general hypothesis that affect serves to guide the formation of many types of judgments and decisions. It has also examined specific aspects of affective information processing. In particular, we have studied whether judgments about the risks and benefits of a technology may derive from a common source – affective reactions to the technology. In addition, we have studied the extent to which judgments of probability and risk are determined by affect-laden images.

Judgments of Risks and Benefits. In previous research, we have focused on the role of affect in explaining why risks and benefits tend to be negatively correlated in people's minds (and judgments) despite being positively correlated in the external environment. A study by Alhakami and Slovic (1994) found that the inverse relationship between the perceived risk and perceived benefit of an activity (e.g., using pesticides) was linked to the strength of the positive or negative affect associated with that activity. This result implies that people base their judgments of an activity or a technology not only on what they *think* about it but also on what they *feel* about it. If they like an activity, they are moved to judge the risks as low and the benefits as high; if they dislike it, they tend to judge the opposite – high risk and low benefit.

Alhakami and Slovic's (1994) findings suggested that use of the affect heuristic guides perceptions of risk and benefit. If so, providing information about risk should change the perception of benefit and vice versa. For example, information stating that the risk is low for some technology would lead to more positive overall affect that would, in turn, increase the perceived benefit. Indeed, we conducted this experiment (see Finucane, Alhakami, Slovic, & Johnson, 2000), providing four different kinds of information designed to manipulate affect by increasing or decreasing perceived risk and increasing or decreasing perceived benefit, as shown in Figure 10.3. In each case there was no

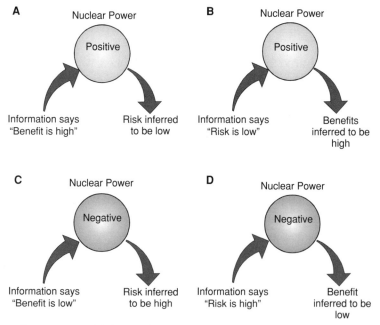

Figure 10.3 Model showing how information about benefit (A) or information about risk (B) could increase the overall affective evaluation of nuclear power and lead to inferences about risk and benefit that coincide affectively with the information given. Similarly, information could decrease the overall affective evaluation of nuclear power, as in C and D. *Source:* "The Affect Heuristic in Judgments of Risks and Benefits," by M. L. Finucane, A. Alhakami, P. Slovic, and S. M. Johnson. Copyright 2000 © John Wiley & Sons Limited. Reproduced with permission.

apparent logical relation between the information provided (e.g., risks) and the nonmanipulated variable (e.g., benefits). The predictions were confirmed. These data support the theory that risk and benefit judgments are influenced, at least in part, by the overall affective evaluation (which *was* influenced by the information provided).

The affect heuristic also predicts that using time pressure to reduce the opportunity for analytic deliberation (and thereby allowing affective considerations freer rein) should enhance the inverse relationship between perceived benefits and risks. In a second study, Finucane, Alhakami, Slovic, and Johnson (2000) showed that the inverse relationship between perceived risks and benefits increased greatly under time pressure, as predicted. These two experiments with judgments of benefits and risks are important because they support Zajonc's contention that affect influences judgment directly and is not simply a response to a prior analytic evaluation.

Slovic, MacGregor, Malmfors, and Purchase (1999) surveyed members of the British Toxicological Society and found that these experts, too, produced the same inverse relation between their risk and benefit judgments. As predicted, the strength of the inverse relation was found to be mediated by these experts' affective reactions toward the hazardous items being judged. In a second study, these same toxicologists were asked to provide a "quick intuitive rating" for each of 30 chemical items (e.g., benzene, aspirin, secondhand cigarette smoke, dioxin in food) on an affect scale (bad–good). Next, they were asked to judge the degree of risk associated with a *very small exposure to the chemical*, defined as an exposure that is less than 1/100th of the exposure level that would begin to cause concern for a regulatory agency. Rationally, because exposure was so low, one might expect these risk judgments to be uniformly low and unvarying, resulting in little or no correlation with the ratings of affect. Instead, there was a strong correlation between affect and judged risk of a very small exposure. When the affect rating was strongly negative, the judged risk of a very small exposure was high; when affect was positive, judged risk was small. Almost every respondent (95 out of 97) showed this negative correlation (the median correlation was −.50). Importantly, those toxicologists who demonstrated strong inverse relations between risk and benefit judgments in the first study also were more likely to exhibit a high correspondence between their judgments of affect and risk in the second study. In other words, across two different tasks, reliable individual differences emerged in toxicologists' reliance on affective processes in judgments of chemical risks.

Judgments of Probability, Relative Frequency, and Risk. Our model of affect and decision making has much in common with the model of *risk as feelings* proposed by Loewenstein et al. (2001) and with dual process theories put forth by Epstein (1994), Sloman (1996), and others. Epstein argues that individuals apprehend reality by two interactive, parallel processing systems. The *rational* system is a deliberative analytical system that functions by way of established rules of logic and evidence (e.g., probability theory). The *experiential* system encodes reality in images, metaphors, and narratives imbued with affective feelings.

To demonstrate the influence of the experiential system, Denes-Raj and Epstein (1994) showed that, when offered a chance to win a prize by drawing a red jelly bean from an urn, subjects often elected to draw from a bowl containing a greater absolute number but a smaller proportion of red beans (e.g., 7 in 100) than from a bowl with fewer red beans but a better probability of winning (e.g., 1 in 10). For these individuals, images of seven winning beans in the large bowl appeared to dominate the image of one winning bean in the small bowl.

We can characterize Epstein's subjects as following a mental strategy of *imaging the numerator* (i.e., the number of red beans) and neglecting the denominator (the number of beans in the bowl). Consistent with the affect heuristic, images of winning beans convey positive affect that motivates choice.

Although the jelly bean experiment may seem frivolous, imaging the numerator brings affect to bear on judgments in ways that can be both nonintuitive and consequential. Slovic, Monahan, and MacGregor (2000) demonstrated this in a series of studies in which experienced forensic psychologists and psychiatrists were asked to judge the likelihood that a mental patient would commit an act of violence within 6 months after being discharged from the hospital. An important finding was that clinicians who expressed their beliefs about a patient's violence risk in terms of a relative frequency judgment (e.g., of 100 patients like X, 10 could be expected to harm someone) subsequently labeled X as more dangerous than did clinicians who assigned an "equivalent" probability to X (e.g., X has a 10% chance of harming someone). Similar results have been found by Yamagishi (1997), whose judges rated a disease that kills 1,286 people out of every 10,000 as more dangerous than one that kills 24.14% of the population.

Not surprisingly, when clinicians were told that "20 out of every 100 patients similar to X are estimated to commit an act of violence during the first several months," 41% refused to discharge the patient.

But when another group of clinicians was told that "patients similar to X have a 20% chance of committing an act of violence," only 21% refused to discharge the patient (Slovic et al., 2000).

Follow-up studies showed that representations in the form of individual probabilities led to relatively benign images of one person who was unlikely to harm anyone, whereas the frequentistic representations created frightening images of violent patients.

Implications, Applications, and Future Directions

We believe that the affect model presents some exciting and profitable new research opportunities in the field of judgment and decision making. In this section we briefly highlight several promising areas of descriptive and prescriptive research.

Descriptive Research Opportunities

Affect and Attention. An important component of our model is that affect acts as an orienting disposition to facilitate efficient judgment and decision making. One specific way affect might orient an individual is by guiding his or her attention. Indeed, much research by social, clinical, and physiological psychologists demonstrates that mood and emotion can direct attention toward or away from particular features in the environment (e.g., Fazio, Roskos-Ewoldsen, & Powell, 1994; Mathews & MacLeod, 1994; Niedenthal, Setterlund, & Jones, 1994).

It may be that affect-driven attentional mechanisms underlie recent findings about which features of stimuli are given weight in retrospective evaluations. For instance, Kahneman, Fredrickson, Schreiber, and Redelmeier (1993) showed that memories of pain are based on evaluations of some features of the pain stimulus (peak and end magnitudes), but not on other features (duration) that are also important. Furthermore, research has demonstrated that the velocity with which an outcome changes over time affects satisfaction judgments (Hsee, Abelson, & Salovey, 1991). From this research, it seems that the beginning, end, and peak experiences should attract more attention than those at other time periods. Greater attention should also exist during periods with faster rates of change of affective intensity. To give a concrete example, perhaps people are more likely to attend to, feel positive toward, and invest money in the stock market if they have experienced a run of several increasingly large returns, compared to when they experienced a single constant return of equal or greater average magnitude.

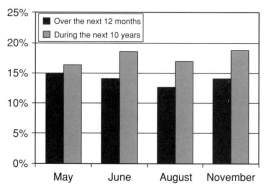

Figure 10.4 Annual return that investors said they expected on mutual funds.

Affect and Time Horizons. Anticipatory positive and negative affect appear to increase (probably at different rates) as one comes closer in time to experiencing an event (Miller, 1959). We hypothesize that heuristic reliance on affect, interacting with time horizons, could result in anomalous probability judgments. For example, one might expect that the anticipatory image of an Internal Revenue Service audit during the next 6 months would be more unsettling than the image of an audit during the next 5 years, leading the judged probability of the audit in the near term to be higher than that for the longer period.

Similarly, during 1997, a year in which the annual rate of return on mutual funds was near an all-time high, polls reported in the *New York Times* showed that fund investors expected even higher annual returns during the next 10 years. Almost identical results were found by Dreman, Johnson, MacGregor, & Slovic, 2001; see Figure 10.4. This odd result, which flies in the face of regression toward the mean, may have been due to images of current crises (e.g., the falling Asian market) and images of recent fluctuations in prices contributing negative affect and dampening the short-term expectation, whereas the long-term forecast may have been influenced by an image of a strong, healthy market, untarnished by imagery about current problems and short-term fluctuations. The generality of such forecasting anomalies and their link to time horizons, imagery, and affect warrant investigation, perhaps using the model of temporal construal proposed by Trope and Liberman (2000). According to this model, the nature and specificity of representational imagery change systematically with temporal distance.

Separate Consideration of Positive and Negative Affect. In this chapter, we have generally ignored possible distinctions between the influence of positive and negative affect. Research concerning affective motivation as well as the negativity bias, however, suggests that the distinction may be important (see reviews by Cacioppo, Gardner, & Berntson, 1997 and Baumeister, Bratslavsky, Finkenauer, and Vohs 2001). Univariate theorists hypothesize a single affective factor influencing behaviors (e.g., Epstein, Pacini, Denes-Raj, & Heier, 1996; Eysenck, 1967; Larsen & Diener, 1987), whereas bivariate theorists argue for separate positive and negative factors (Gray, 1970, 1982). Although researchers generally agree that the effects of positive and negative evaluative processes are antagonistic (a univariate view), Cacioppo and his colleagues proposed that there are two separate motivational substrates underlying positive and negative processes (Cacioppo et al., 1997). The net effect may be that as negative beliefs about an object increase, positive beliefs may decline in general. They argued that these effects are not always reciprocally controlled, however. For example, they found functional independence of positive and negative affect such that the level of positive affect, but not negative affect, toward a roommate predicted friendship and the amount of time spent with the roommate. As a result, it may be that changing the level of positive affect in a friendship may be more important to friendship-related thoughts and actions than changing the level of negative affect. Functional independence of positive and negative affect was also found by Abelson et al. (1982) and Peters et al. (in review). Evidence from classical conditioning, individual differences, and attitudes (e.g., Cacioppo & Berntson, 1994; Crites, Fabrigar, & Petty, 1994; Zinbarg & Mohlman, 1998; Zinbarg & Revelle, 1989) provides considerable support for the bivariate view. We expect that, in the future, researchers will find it important to examine separately the inputs of positive and negative affect on judgments and decisions.

Deliberative versus Nondeliberative Mechanisms. Although traditional decision research implicitly assumes deliberative processes in choice, it appears that affect can develop and influence decisions in nondeliberative ways as well (Chen & Bargh, 1999; Nisbett & Wilson, 1977; Zajonc, 2001). Take, for example, the mechanism of classical conditioning. In the studies by Damasio (1994) and Peters and Slovic (2000), reactions to the gains and losses experienced from drawing cards from each of the decks may have conditioned particular affective responses to the decks.

Attitude researchers have long recognized the relevance of classical conditioning principles to the attitude domain. Perhaps the best-known study of the effect of classical conditioning on the development of attitudes comes from Staats and Staats (1958, Experiment 1). They told subjects that their task was to learn two lists of words, one presented visually and one orally. The visually presented list consisted of the names of six nationalities (e.g., German, Italian), two of which served as the initially neutral stimuli (Dutch and Swedish). The orally presented list consisted of positive words (e.g., *gift, happy*), negative words (e.g., *bitter, failure*), and neutral words (e.g., *chair*). In the conditioning trials, each national name appeared visually on a screen, and then the experimenter pronounced a positive, negative, or neutral word from the second list. Subjects had to repeat this word aloud. After the conditioning procedure had ended, subjects were asked to rate each of the national names on a scale ranging from pleasant to unpleasant. Consistent with predictions, the national names were rated more positively if they had previously been paired with positive, rather than negative, words in the conditioning trials.

A particularly interesting test of the role of nondeliberative processes in the conditioning of attitudes was conducted by Krosnick, Betz, Jussim, and Lynn (1992). In two studies, they paired an initially neutral target with a series of photographs designed to elicit negative affect (e.g., a bloody shark) in half of their subjects and positive affect (e.g., a pair of kittens) in the other half of the subjects. Participants were exposed to the photographs, however, for a duration too brief (9–13 msec) for them to consciously recognize the photos. After the conditioning trials, participants indicated their attitudes toward the initially neutral target as well as other evaluative judgments. Krosnick et al. found that their conditioning procedures influenced attitudes even in the absence of conscious awareness of the existence or valence of the photographs.[6] Studies on the *mere exposure* effect have also demonstrated that affect is a strong conditioner of preference (Zajonc, 2001), whether or not the cause of that affect is consciously perceived (for a meta-analysis of over 200 experiments see Bornstein, 1989). The central finding is that, when objects (visual, auditory, gustatory, abstract, and social stimuli) are presented to an individual repeatedly, the mere exposure is capable of creating a positive attitude of preference for these objects.

---

[6] Krosnick et al. used a backward pairing procedure, however, so that their results do have alternative explanations, such as priming or mood effects.

Although many psychologists support the claim that classical conditioning comes about through automatic processes, other researchers (e.g., Insko & Oakes, 1966; Zinbarg & Mohlman, 1998) suggest that more deliberative mechanisms mediate the robust classical conditioning effect. Isolation of deliberative and nondeliberative elements is important in understanding attitudes as well as choice. The conditions under which affect operates as a deliberative or nondeliberative process in judgment and decision making raise questions for investigation.

Affect and Deliberative Capacity. The interplay between affect and reason also appears to be illuminated by conditions that reduce one's capacity for deliberation. One example of this is the study by Finucane, Alhakami, Slovic, and Johnson (2000), described previously, that found increased inverse relationships between perceived risks and perceived benefits under time pressure, supporting the hypothesized affect heuristic. Another example comes from Shiv and Fedorikhin (1999), who asked respondents to memorize either a two-digit number (low cognitive demand) or a seven-digit number (high cognitive demand). The respondents were then instructed to walk to another room to report this number. On the way, they were offered a choice between two snacks, chocolate cake (more favorable affect, less favorable cognitions) or fruit salad (less favorable affect, more favorable cognitions). The researchers predicted that the condition with high memory load (seven digits) would reduce the capacity for deliberation, thus increasing the likelihood that the more affectively favorable option (cake) would be selected. The prediction was confirmed. Chocolate cake was selected 63% of the time when the memory load was high and only 41% of the time when the memory load was low. Aging, which reduces attention and memory capacity, may act similarly to increase the reliance on affect relative to deliberation (see, e.g., Hess, 2000; Hess, Pullen, & McGee, 1996). Studies using time pressure, memory load, and distraction to manipulate cognitive load, as well as studies with elderly persons, could further illuminate the relative importance of affect and deliberation in decision making.

Measuring Affective Experiences. Naturally, given the early stage of development of our theory, it is critical to test the assumption that affective experiences play an influential role in directing evaluations and choices. Much of the research we have drawn on to illustrate the role of affect has not offered independent evidence that judgments and decisions are accompanied by physiological manifestations of the motivational properties of affect. Peters and Mauro (2000), however, recently demonstrated that physiological responses as well as self-reported affective reactivity were associated with choices. Future research would benefit from expanding measures of affect to other autonomic nervous system markers (e.g., skin conductance, facial myography) or activity in specific parts of the central nervous system (e.g., amygdala). Clarifying the relative contributions of analysis and affect across tasks and individuals is an important research direction.

Prescriptive Research Opportunities

Information Representation and Evaluability. Just as a golfer may be unable to execute repeatedly a proper drive off the tee, an individual may lack the skill to incorporate his or her desired "policy" into a judgment or decision, reliably and accurately, particularly when there are multiple conflicting attributes or objectives to integrate (Hammond, 1971). We propose that providers of information to decision makers consider using forms of graphic representation designed to make stimulus attributes more evaluable affectively. This may facilitate information integration and help individuals to better employ their knowledge and desired judgment policies.

Affective evaluability may underlie the findings of MacGregor and Slovic (1986), who studied the relative performance of four different graphic display types. The task involved predicting the completion times of runners in a marathon. Each runner was described by four cues: age, total miles run in training, fastest recent time for 10,000 meters (fastest 10K), and a self-rating of motivation. The information cues were presented in one of four graphic formats: a bar graph, a deviation display (i.e., deviation of a runner's score on a cue from the mean of the cue), a spoke display (see Figure 10.5a), and a face display (see Figure 10.5b). The face display was created by assigning each of the four cues to a particular feature of a schematic face. For this particular display format, the four facial features portrayed were eyebrow (age), eyes (total miles), nose (motivation), and mouth (fastest 10K). This assignment of cues to facial features was done to associate the most predictive cue (i.e., fastest 10K) with the more affectively salient facial feature (i.e., mouth) in the belief that this would give subjects the best chance to do well at the task. Subjects in the face-display condition were given additional instructions on how to interpret changes in facial features associated with changes in cue values. This was done by illustrating each facial feature

a

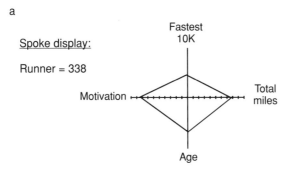

Spoke display:

Runner = 338

Fastest 10K

Motivation

Total miles

Age

b

Face display:

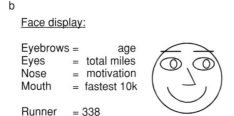

Eyebrows =   age
Eyes   = total miles
Nose   = motivation
Mouth   = fastest 10k

Runner   = 338

Figure 10.5 Formats for (a) the spoke display and (b) the face display. *Source:* "Graphic Representation of Judgmental Information," by D. MacGregor and P. Slovic, *Human-Computer Interaction*, 1986, Volume 2, pp. 179–200. Copyright 1986 by Lawrence Erlbaum Associates, Inc. Reprinted with permission.

separately, with other features removed, at the extremes of variation for each cue and at the cues' average value. A runner having the extremely low scores on all cues would be represented pictorially as a face with a frown, a short nose, eyes looking left, and low eyebrows. In contrast, extreme high scorers would be portrayed as a face with a smile, a long nose, eyes looking right, and high eyebrows.

When the most predictive cue (i.e., fastest 10K) was assigned to the mouth (and smile) of the face display, that display elicited judgments that were far superior to those of all other displays. When the cues were reassigned to other features, such that the smile or frown of the mouth was associated with a less important cue, performance on the facial display was reduced to the level of the other displays.

We hypothesize that the results obtained in this study are due in part to the evaluability principle. Information integration in judgment tasks is likely enhanced when the properties or features of an information display provide a convenient and salient mechanism by which affect can be used to integrate display components. In the case of MacGregor and

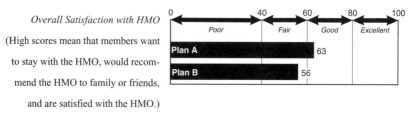

Overall Satisfaction with HMO
(High scores mean that members want
to stay with the HMO, would recommend the HMO to family or friends,
and are satisfied with the HMO.)

Figure 10.6 Bar display with affective categories.

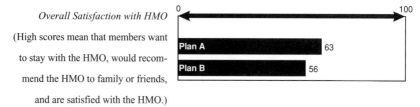

Overall Satisfaction with HMO
(High scores mean that members want
to stay with the HMO, would recommend the HMO to family or friends,
and are satisfied with the HMO.)

Figure 10.7 Bar display without affective categories.

Slovic (1986), facial features provide a powerful affective cue that can, under some circumstances, dramatically improve information integration in a relatively complex judgment task. Indeed, facial expressions in general are of significant importance in communicating emotional states between individuals (e.g., Eckman & Davidson, 1994; Eckman & Friesen, 1971).

Transforming graphical displays into faces may seem a rather extreme way to make information evaluable. It is likely, however, that equally strong effects can be obtained more subtly. Consider the ways that Peters, et al. (2000) displayed information to people asked to choose between two health maintenance organizations (HMOs). When numerical ratings of satisfaction with the HMO were superimposed against a template showing affective categories (poor, fine, good, excellent), as in Figure 10.6, this information was given more weight in the choice than it was when the categories were absent (Figure 10.7). Although these findings could be the result of providing additional meaning (other than affective meaning), subsequent tests of categorization alone (the category lines without the affective labels) suggest otherwise. Future research could further examine the role of affect by varying the affective content of the categories (Figure 10.6 could be presented with less affective labels such as low, medium, high) or by measuring the relative accessibility of affective and cognitive beliefs (see Verplanken, Hofstee, & Janssen, 1998).

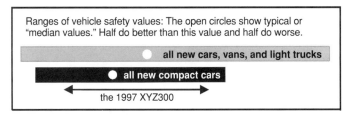

Figure 10.8 Proposed safety label for the 1997 XYZ300 automobile. *Source:* Adapted from NAS (1996).

Another example of how understanding the workings of affect and evaluability may help improve decision making comes from a study about providing consumers with information about the safety of new cars. The National Academy of Sciences (1996) analyzed the type of safety information that can be obtained from crash tests, accident data, and expert judgment and recommended that, to incorporate the inherent uncertainty of the estimates, this information be displayed on every new vehicle in the form of ranges (see Figure 10.8). Our understanding of evaluability suggests, however, that such range displays will make it hard for people to evaluate safety data when judging cars singly or even comparatively. Thus, safety will not be given the weight that consumers themselves would like it to receive and, instead, less intrinsically important but more affectively salient factors, such as color, style, and so on, will be overweighted relative to safety. Although safety measures may have little influence on buyers' choices when expressed as ranges, they may carry considerable weight when expressed in more precise and affectively meaningful formats, such as letter grades (A, B, C, D, etc.) or stars (much like ratings of hotels in Michelin guides).

Overcoming Psychophysical Numbing. Earlier, we described research by Fetherstonhaugh et al. (1997) indicating that numerical representations of losses of life were relatively nonevaluable. Very large numbers of lost lives were not valued differently than merely large numbers of lost lives. Someone once said "Statistics are human beings with the tears dried off." Another observed that "One person's death is a tragedy; 1,000 deaths is a statistic." Fetherstonhaugh et al. referred to these sorts of reactions as a form of *psychophysical numbing.*

Similar lack of emotion occurs when death takes place in a physically distant or culturally remote location (e.g., Africa or an urban ghetto). Can we devise ways to infuse affect into scenarios of catastrophe so as to reduce numbing and lead to preferences that do not devalue lives because of irrelevant contextual factors? In other words, how can we develop images and scenarios that bring life and meaning (affect) to statistics – that "put the tears back on," so to speak? One approach might be to utilize dramatic, personalizing visual images, the photo of one victim, for example, or a photo of the 38,000 pairs of shoes of victims placed around the United States Capitol to sensitize legislators to the 38,000 annual gunshot fatalities in the United States. Personalized vignettes or stories about victims could also be used. The potential power of personalization should not be underestimated, as demonstrated by society's willingness to expend extraordinary resources to save identified individuals (human or animal) who are endangered (Jenni & Loewenstein, 1997).

Risk, Affect, and Stigma. In ancient Greece, *stigma* referred to a mark placed on a person to signify infamy or disgrace. Someone thus marked was perceived to be unworthy or to pose a risk to society. Through its association with risk, the concept of stigma has recently been generalized to technologies, places, and products that are perceived to be unduly dangerous (Finucane, Slovic, & Mertz, 2000; Gregory, Flynn, & Slovic, 1995). A dramatic example of stigmatization is the near collapse of the British beef industry after it was learned that eating beef might be linked to a fatal brain disease (O'Brien, 1996).

As with the beef crisis in Britain, the impetus for stigmatization is typically some critical event, accident, or report that conditions negative affect to the mere thought of the product, place, or technology, motivating its avoidance. Returning to our model in Figure 10.2 and Table 10.1, above, we might ask whether stigmatizing characteristics are simply forms of negative somatic markers (like other negative images in the set) or whether they have special importance, perhaps as a form of *negative halo effect* that changes the integration model for all other positive and negative feelings.

Experiments could be designed to answer this question. One design might ask subjects to free-associate to a stimulus such as "eating beef." We would expect this to produce a variety of positive and negative associations, such as "tastes good" (+), "hamburgers" (+), "cholesterol" (−), "expensive" (−), and so on. Based upon previous imagery research, we would expect that subjects' attitudes toward consuming beef would be linearly related to the sum or average rated valence of the associations produced. Suppose that a percentage of subjects included a stigmatizing association, such as "mad cows" or "brain disease," as part of their set of positive and negative thoughts. Through parallelism tests of regression lines, it should be possible to determine whether the stigmatizing associations merely acted like other negative valences or whether they changed the integration rules governing the other affective information. At the extreme, we might find that presence of a stigmatizing negative rendered all positive associations impotent, similar to the extreme weights Baron and Spranca (1997) observed in their studies of protected values. Identification of negative thoughts as stigmatizing could be done by raters evaluating each negative on stigmatizing qualities such as (a) the risk or negative quality is abnormal or unnatural for the stimulus object; (b) the risk is new; (c) contact with the negative feature is involuntary or uncontrollable; and (d) the quality is immoral.

Stigma often remains even after the risk is removed. Risk communicators then face the difficult task of trying to calm unnecessary fears. Because stigma is based upon strong affective or emotional reactions, statistical or factual evidence is typically ineffective, as is the case with another strong affective phenomenon – *phobia*. With phobias, counterconditioning via exposure to desensitizing experiences works far better than rational appeals. For example, a subject who developed an inability to take pills following the Tylenol poisonings in 1981 was "cured" by starting with relaxation training and then being exposed very gradually to stimuli increasing in similarity to medicine pills (first, simply imagining pill taking, then taking a vitamin pill, etc.; see Pbert & Goetsch, 1988). Similar counterconditioning may be necessary to deal with the conditioned negative affect that drives stigmatization and avoidance behavior. Another form of desensitization may result from educating people about the benefits of the activity. Through the workings of the affect heuristic, this should reduce perceived risks, thus reducing stigma.

Conclusions

The important role of affect in guiding evaluations and choices is apparent. Drawing together patterns of results from judgment and decision-making research provides a testable model that we hope will encourage systematic investigation of the role of affect. Much is known after several decades of research on cognitive factors that influence judgment and decision processes, and it is now time to further our understanding of affective factors and their interaction with cognition.

Undoubtedly, the influence of affect will be context dependent: Characteristics of individuals, decision problems, and decision environments contribute both independent and interacting affective features to judgment and decision processes. Examining the elements of such a complex system is an exciting challenge. We have suggested several descriptive and prescriptive research directions to examine the extent of affective influence on judgment and decision-making processes. However, many other paths are likely to offer interesting and informative findings too, particularly if we capitalize on the wealth of information already available to us in the literature on emotion and cognition.

References

Abelson, R. P., Kinder, D. R., Peters, M. D., & Fiske, S. T. (1982). Affective and semantic components in political person perception. *Journal of Personality and Social Psychology, 42,* 619–630.

Alhakami, A. S., & Slovic, P. (1994). A psychological study of the inverse relationship between perceived risk and perceived benefit. *Risk Analysis, 14(6),* 1085–1096.

Anderson, N. H. (1981). *Foundations of information integration theory.* New York: Academic Press.

Ariely, D. (1998). Combining experiences over time: The effects of duration, intensity changes and on-line measurements on retrospective pain evaluations. *Journal of Behavioral Decision Making, 11,* 19–45.

Baron, J. (1997). Confusion of relative and absolute risk in valuation. *Journal of Risk and Uncertainty, 14(3),* 301–309.

Baron, J., & Spranca, M. (1997). Protected values. *Organizational Behavior and Human Decision Processes, 70,* 1–16.

Baumeister, R. F., Bratslavsky, E., Finkenauer, C., & Vohs, K. D. (2001). Bad is stronger than good. *Review of General Psychology, 5,* 323–370.

Bechara, A., Damasio, A. R., Damasio, H., & Anderson, S. W. (1994). Insensitivity to future consequences following damage to human prefrontal cortex. *Cognition, 50,* 7–15.

Bell, D. E. (1982). Regret in decision making under uncertainty. *Operations Research, 30,* 961–981.

Bentham, J. (1969). A table of the springs of action (1815). In P. McReynolds (Ed.), *Four early works on motivation* (pp. 477–512). Gainesville, FL: Scholars' Facsimiles & Reprints. (Original work published 1815).

Benthin, A., Slovic, P., Moran, P., Severson, H., Mertz, C. K., & Gerrard, M. (1995). Adolescent health-threatening and health-enhancing behaviors: A study of word association and imagery. *Journal of Adolescent Health, 17,* 143–152.

Bornstein, R. F. (1989). Exposure and affect: Overview and meta-analysis of research, 1968–1987. *Psychological Bulletin, 106,* 265–289.

Bower, G. H. (1991). Mood congruity of social judgments. In J. P. Forgas (Ed.), *Emotion and social judgments* (pp. 31–53). Oxford: Pergamon Press.

Cacioppo, J., & Berntson, G. (1994). Relationship between attitudes and evaluative space: A critical review, with emphasis on the separability of positive and negative substances. *Psychological Bulletin, 115*(3), 401–423.

Cacioppo, J. T., & Gardner, W. L. (1999). Emotion. *Annual Review of Psychology, 50*, 191–214.

Cacioppo, J. T., Gardner, W. L., & Berntson, G. G. (1997). Beyond bipolar conceptualizations and measures: The case of attitudes and evaluative space. *Personality and Social Psychology Review, 1*, 3–25.

Chen, M., & Bargh, J. A. (1999). Consequences of automatic evaluation: Immediate behavioral predispositions to approach or avoid the stimulus. *Personality & Social Psychology Bulletin, 25*, 215–224.

Crites, S., Fabrigar, L., & Petty, R. (1994). Measuring the affective and cognitive properties of attitudes: Conceptual and methodological issues. *Personality and Social Psychology Bulletin, 20*(6), 619–634.

Damasio, A. R. (1994). *Descartes' error: Emotion, reason, and the human brain.* New York: Avon.

Damasio, A. R., Tranel, D., & Damasio, H. (1990). Individuals with sociopathic behavior caused by frontal damage fail to respond autonomically to social stimuli. *Behavioural Brain Research, 41*, 81–94.

Damasio, A. R., Tranel, D., & Damasio, H. C. (1991). Somatic markers and the guidance of behavior: Theory and preliminary testing. In H. Levin, H. Eisenberg, & A. Benton (Eds.), *Frontal lobe function and dysfunction* (pp. 217–228). New York: Oxford University Press.

Davidson, R. J. (1994). On emotion, mood, and related affective constructs. In P. Ekman & R. J. Davidson (Eds.), *The nature of emotion: Fundamental questions* (pp. 51–96). New York: Oxford University Press.

Denes-Raj, V., & Epstein, S. (1994). Conflict between intuitive and rational processing: When people behave against their better judgment. *Journal of Personality and Social Psychology, 66*, 819–829.

Dreman, D., Johnson, S., MacGregor, D., & Slovic, P. (2001). A report on the March 2001 investor sentiment survey. *The Journal of Psychology and Financial Markets, 2*(3), 126–134.

Ekman, P., & Davidson, R. J. (1994). *The nature of emotion.* New York: Oxford University.

Ekman, P., & Friesen, W. (1971). Constants across cultures in the face and emotion. *Journal of Personality and Social Psychology, 17*, 124–129.

Epstein, S. (1994). Integration of the cognitive and the psychodynamic unconscious. *American Psychologist, 49*, 709–724.

Epstein, S., Pacini, R., Denes-Raj, V., & Heier, H. (1996). Individual differences in intuitive-experiential and analytical-rational thinking styles. *Journal of Personality and Social Psychology, 71*, 390–405.

Eysenck, H. J. (1967). *The biological basis of personality.* Springfield, IL: Thomas.

Fazio, R. H. (1995). Attitudes as object-evaluation associations: Determinants, consequences, and correlates of attitude accessibility. In R. E. Petty & J. A. Krosnick (Eds.), *Attitude strength: Antecedents and consequences* (pp. 247–282). Mahwah, NJ: Erlbaum.

Fazio, R. H., Roskos-Ewoldsen, D. R., & Powell, M. C. (1994). Attitudes, perception, and attention. In P. M. Niedenthal & S. Kitayama (Eds.), *The heart's eye: Emotional influences in perception and attention* (pp. 197–216). San Diego, CA: Academic Press.

Fetherstonhaugh, D., Slovic, P., Johnson, S. M., & Friedrich, J. (1997). Insensitivity to the value of human life: A study of psychophysical numbing. *Journal of Risk and Uncertainty, 14*(3), 282–300.

Finucane, M. L., Alhakami, A., Slovic, P., & Johnson, S. M. (2000). The affect heuristic in judgments of risks and benefits. *Journal of Behavioral Decision Making, 13*, 1–17.

Finucane, M. L., Slovic, P., & Mertz, C. K. (2000). Public perception of the risk of blood transfusion. *Transfusion, 40*, 1017–1022.

Forgas, J. P. (1992). Affect in social judgments and decisions: A multiprocess model. In M. Zanna (Ed.), *Advances in experimental social psychology* (Vol. 25, pp. 227–275). San Diego, CA: Academic Press.

Forgas, J. P. (1995). Mood and judgment: The Affect Infusion Model (AIM). *Psychological Bulletin, 117*(1), 39–66.

Frank, R. H. (1988). *Passions within reason: The strategic role of the emotions.* New York: Norton.

Friedrich, J., Barnes, P., Chapin, K., Dawson, I., Garst, V., & Kerr, D. (1999). Psychophysical numbing: When lives are valued less as the lives at risk increase. *Journal of Consumer Psychology, 8*, 277–299.

Goldstein, W. M., & Einhorn, H. J. (1987). Expression theory and the preference reversal phenomena. *Psychological Review, 94*, 236–254.

Gray, J. A. (1970). The psychophysiological basis of introversion–extraversion. *Behavior Research and Therapy, 8*, 249–266.

Gray, J. A. (1982). *The neuropsychology of anxiety: An enquiry into the functions of the septo-hippocampal system.* New York: Oxford University.

Gray, J. A. (1990). Brain systems that mediate both emotion and cognition. *Cognition and Emotion, 4*(3), 269–288.

Gregory, R., Flynn, J., & Slovic, P. (1995). Technological stigma. *American Scientist, 83*, 220–223.

Hammond, K. R. (1971). Computer graphics as an aid to learning. *Science, 172*, 903–908.

Hess, T. M. (2000). Aging-related constraints and adaptations in social information processing. In U. von Hecker, S. Dutke, & G. Sedek (Eds.), *Generative mental processes and cognitive resources: Integrative research on adaptation and control* (pp. 129–155). Dordrecht, the Netherlands: Kluwer Academic.

Hess, T. M., Pullen, S. M., & McGee, K. A. (1996). Acquisition of prototype-based information about social groups in adulthood. *Psychology and Aging, 11*, 179–190.

Hsee, C. K. (1995). Elastic justification: How tempting but task-irrelevant factors influence decisions. *Organizational Behavior and Human Decision Processes, 62*, 330–337.

Hsee, C. K. (1996). Elastic justification: How unjustifiable factors influence judgments. *Organizational Behavior and Human Decision Processes, 66*, 122–129.

Hsee, C. K. (1998). Less is better: When low-value options are valued more highly than high-value options. *Journal of Behavioral Decision Making, 11*, 107–121.

Hsee, C. K., Abelson, R. P., & Salovey, P. (1991). The relative weighting of position and velocity in satisfaction. *Psychological Science, 2*(4), 263–266.

Insko, C. A., & Oakes, W. F. (1966). Awareness and the "conditioning" of attitudes. *Journal of Personality and Social Psychology, 4*(5), 487–496.

Isen, A. M. (1993). Positive affect and decision making. In M. Lewis & J. M. Haviland (Eds.), *Handbook of emotions* (pp. 261–277). New York: Guilford Press.

Janis, I. L., & Mann, L. (1977). *Decision making.* New York: Free Press.

Jenni, K. E., & Loewenstein, G. (1997). Explaining the "identifiable victim effect." *Journal of Risk and Uncertainty, 14*(3), 235–258.

Johnson, E. J., & Tversky, A. (1983). Affect, generalization, and the perception of risk. *Journal of Personality and Social Psychology, 45*, 20–31.

Kahneman, D., Fredrickson, B. L., Schreiber, C. A., & Redelmeier, D. (1993). When more pain is preferred to less: Adding a better end. *Psychological Science, 4*, 401–405.

Kahneman, D., & Snell, J. (1990). Predicting utility. In R. M. Hogarth (Ed.), *Insights in decision making* (pp. 295–310). Chicago: University of Chicago Press.

Kahneman, D., & Tversky, A. (1979). Prospect theory: An analysis of decision under risk. *Econometrica, 47*, 263–291.

Krosnick, J. A., Betz, A. L., Jussim, L. J., & Lynn, A. R. (1992). Subliminal conditioning of attitudes. *Personality and Social Psychology Bulletin, 18*(2), 152–162.

Larsen, R. J., & Diener, E. (1987). Affect intensity as an individual difference characteristic: A review. *Journal of Research in Personality, 21*, 1–39.

LeDoux, J. (1996). *The emotional brain: The mysterious underpinnings of emotional life.* New York: Simon & Schuster.

Loewenstein, G. F. (1996). Out of control: Visceral influences on behavior. *Organizational Behavior and Human Decision Processes, 65*, 272–292.

Loewenstein, G. F., Weber, E. U., Hsee, C. K., & Welch, E. S. (2001). Risk as feelings. *Psychological Bulletin, 127*, 267–286.

MacGregor, D. G., & Slovic, P. (1986). Graphic representation of judgmental information. *Human-Computer Interaction, 2*, 179–200.

MacGregor, D. G., Slovic, P., Dreman, D., & Berry, M. (2000). Imagery, affect, and financial judgment. *Journal of Psychology and Financial Markets, 1*(2), 104–110.

Mathews, A., & MacLeod, C. (1994). Cognitive approaches to emotion and emotional disorders. *Annual Review of Psychology, 45*, 25–50.

Mayer, J. D. (1986). How mood influences cognition. In N. E. Sharkey (Ed.), *Advances in cognitive science* (Vol. 2, pp. 290–314). Chichester, UK: Ellis Horwood.

Mellers, B. A. (2000). Choice and the relative pleasure of consequences. *Psychological Bulletin, 126*(6), 910–924.

Mellers, B. A., Richards, V., & Birnbaum, M. H. (1992). Distributional theories of impression formation. *Organizational Behavior and Human Decision Processes, 51*, 313–343.

Mellers, B. A., Schwartz, A., Ho, K., & Ritov, I. (1997). Decision affect theory: Emotional reactions to the outcomes of risky options. *Psychological Science, 8,* 423–429.

Miller, N. (1959). Liberalization of basic S-R concepts: Extensions to conflict behavior, motivation and social learning. In S. Koch (Ed.), *Psychology: A study of a science* (Vol. 2, pp. 196–292). New York: McGraw-Hill.

Mowrer, O. H. (1960a). *Learning theory and behavior.* New York: Wiley.

Mowrer, O. H. (1960b). *Learning theory and the symbolic processes.* New York: Wiley.

National Academy of Sciences. (1996). *Shopping for safety: Providing consumer automotive safety information.* Washington, DC: National Academy Press.

Niedenthal, P. M., Setterlund, M. B., & Jones, D. E. (1994). Emotional organization of perceptual memory. In P. M. Niedenthal & S. Kitayama (Eds.), *The heart's eye: Emotional influences in perception and attention* (pp. 87–113). New York: Academic Press.

Nisbett, R. E., & Wilson, T. D. (1977). The halo effect: Evidence for unconscious alteration of judgments. *Journal of Personality and Social Psychology, 35,* 250–256.

O'Brien, C. (1996). Mad cow disease: Scant data cause widespread concern. *Science, 271,* 1798.

Ordóñez, L., & Benson, L., III. (1997). Decisions under time pressure: How time constraint affects risky decision making. *Organizational Behavior and Human Decision Processes, 71*(2), 121–140.

Osgood, C. E., Suci, G. J., & Tannenbaum, P. H. (1957). *The measurement of meaning.* Urbana: University of Illinois Press.

Patrick, C. J. (1994). Emotion and psychopathy: Startling new insights. *Psychophysiology, 31*(4), 319–330.

Pbert, L. A., & Goetsch, V. L. (1988). A multifaceted behavioral intervention for pill-taking avoidance associated with Tylenol poisoning. *Journal of Behavior Therapy and Experimental Psychiatry, 19*(4), 311–315.

Peters, E. (1998). *The springs of action: Affective and analytical information processing in choice.* Unpublished doctoral dissertation, University of Oregon, Eugene.

Peters, E., Flynn, J., & Slovic, P. (in review). Affective asynchrony and the measurement of the affective attitude component.

Peters, E., & Mauro, R. (2000, November). *Feeling our way through a complex world: Affective reactivity, physiology, and choice.* Paper presented at the Society for Judgment and Decision Making Conference, New Orleans.

Peters, E., & Slovic, P. (1996). The role of affect and worldviews as orienting dispositions in the perception and acceptance of nuclear power. *Journal of Applied Social Psychology, 26,* 1427–1453.

Peters, E., & Slovic, P. (2000). The springs of action: Affective and analytical information processing in choice. *Personality and Social Psychology Bulletin, 26,* 1465–1475.

Petty, R. E., Gleicher, F., & Baker, S. (1991). Multiple roles for affect in persuasion. In J. P. Forgas (Ed.), *Emotion and social judgments* (pp. 181–200). Elmsford, NY: Pergamon Press.

Rozin, P., Haidt, J., & McCauley, C. R. (1993). Disgust. In M. Lewis & J. M. Haviland (Eds.), *Handbook of emotions* (pp. 575–594). New York: Guilford Press.

Rusting, C. L., & Larsen, R. J. (1998). Personality and cognitive processing of affective information. *Personality and Social Psychology Bulletin, 24,* 200–213.

Schwarz, N., & Clore, G. L. (1983). Mood, misattribution, and judgments of well-being: Information and directive functions of affective states. *Journal of Personality and Social Psychology, 45,* 513–523.

Schwarz, N., & Clore, G. L. (1988). How do I feel about it? Informative functions of affective states. In K. Fiedler & J. Forgas (Eds.), *Affect, cognition, and social behavior* (pp. 44–62). Toronto: Hogrefe International.

Shiv, B., & Fedorikhin, A. (1999). Heart and mind in conflict: Interplay of affect and cognition in consumer decision making. *Journal of Consumer Research, 26,* 278–282.

Sloman, S. A. (1996). The empirical case for two systems of reasoning. *Psychological Bulletin, 119*(1), 3–22.

Slovic, P., Layman, M., Kraus, N., Flynn, J., Chalmers, J., & Gesell, G. (1991). Perceived risk, stigma, and potential economic impacts of a high-level nuclear waste repository in Nevada. *Risk Analysis, 11*(4), 683–696.

Slovic, P., & Lichtenstein, S. (1968). Relative importance of probabilities and payoffs in risk-taking. *Journal of Experimental Psychology Monograph, 78*(3), 1–18.

Slovic, P., MacGregor, D. G., Malmfors, T., & Purchase, I. F. H. (1999). *Influence of affective processes on toxicologists' judgments of risk* (Report No. 99-2). Eugene, OR: Decision Research.

Slovic, P., Monahan, J., & MacGregor, D. G. (2000). Violence risk assessment and risk communication: The effects of using actual cases, providing instructions, and employing probability vs. frequency formats. *Law and Human Behavior, 24*(3), 271–296.

Staats, A. W., & Staats, C. K. (1958). Attitudes established by classical conditioning. *Journal of Abnormal and Social Psychology, 57,* 37–40.

Trope, Y., & Liberman, N. (2000). Temporal construal and time-dependent changes in preference. *Journal of Personality and Social Psychology, 79,* 876–889.

Tversky, A., Slovic, P., & Kahneman, D. (1990). The causes of preference reversal. *American Economic Review, 80,* 204–217.

Verplanken, B., Hofstee, G., & Janssen, H. J. W. (1998). Accessibility of affective versus cognitive components of attitudes. *European Journal of Social Psychology, 28*(1), 23–36.

Wilson, T. D., Lisle, D. J., Schooler, J. W., Hodges, S. D., Klaaren, K. J., & LaFleur, S. J. (1993). Introspecting about reasons can reduce post-choice satisfaction. *Personality and Social Psychology Bulletin, 19*(3), 331–339.

Winkielman, P., Zajonc, R. B., & Schwarz, N. (1997). Subliminal affective priming resists attributional interventions. *Cognition and Emotion, 11*(4), 433–465.

Yamagishi, K. (1997). When a 12.86% mortality is more dangerous than 24.14%: Implications for risk communication. *Applied Cognitive Psychology, 11,* 495–506.

Zajonc, R. B. (1980). Feeling and thinking: Preferences need no inferences. *American Psychologist, 35,* 151–175.

Zajonc, R. B. (2001). Mere exposure: A gateway to the subliminal. *Current Directions in Psychological Science, 10*(6), 224–228.

Zinbarg, R. E., & Mohlman, J. (1998). Individual differences in the acquisition of affectively-valenced associations. *Journal of Personality and Social Psychology, 74*, 1024–1040.

Zinbarg, R. E., & Revelle, W. (1989). Personality and conditioning: A test of four models. *Journal of Personality and Social Psychology, 57*(2), 301–314.

11   Some Ways in Which Positive Affect
       Facilitates Decision Making and Judgment

Alice M. Isen and Aparna A. Labroo

ABSTRACT

This chapter suggests two perspectives that seem capable of contributing
to the development of decision-making research in the coming years: the
integration of positive affect into the decision-making literature, including
formal models of decision making, and the integration of understandings
from cognitive neuroscience into work on decision making. The chapter
summarizes recent work indicating that integration of each of these topics
is now possible and holds promise for advancing our understanding not
only of problem-solving and decision-making processes, but of affective
processes as well. In doing this, the chapter reviews some of the evidence
showing that positive affect promotes cognitive flexibility and thus facilitates problem solving and decision making in many situations. It calls
attention to the wide array of cognitive, motivational, and behavioral processes influenced by positive affect, and suggests ways that these effects
bear on decision making. The work also indicates that considering the
influence of positive affect in more detail, including its impact on cognitive organization and flexibility in problem solving, holds promise of
still greater advance in our understanding of decision processes. Finally, it
suggests ways that consideration of possible neuropsychological concomitants of positive affect, and neuropsychological processes more generally,
may provide additional tools for advancing understanding of affective,
cognitive, and decision processes.

CONTENTS

The authors thank Michael Doherty, Sandra Schneider, and James Shanteau for helpful
comments on the manuscript.

In recent years there has been increasing interest in affect as a topic of scientific investigation in psychology. This work has taken form in several ways: to some extent, as study of the experience of affect or emotions, through measures such as verbal self-reports; but more as study of the influence of affect on processes such as social interaction, motivation, cognition, and so on, using behavioral and cognitive measures; and, increasingly, as study of physiological and neuropsychological indicators or concomitants of emotions or feelings. As evidence of this, consider not only the large number of journal articles in the past few years involving affect, but also the several handbooks and journals devoted exclusively to the topic that have appeared recently. This includes the *Handbook of Emotions* (Lewis & Haviland-Jones, 2000), the *Handbook of Cognition and Emotion* (Dalgleish & Power, 1999), and others, the new APA journal *Emotion*, and the new Psychonomic Society journal *Cognitive, Affective, and Behavioral Neuroscience*, in addition to the already existing journals, *Motivation and Emotion* and *Cognition and Emotion*.

In many ways this represents a triumph of understanding. In earlier decades, affect was not a major focus of investigation, or was limited to verbal descriptions of emotional experience, and was certainly not considered as an integrated component of cognition. In fact, affect was typically omitted from cognitive theories and models. One exception to this generalization that, nonetheless, helps to illustrate the problem, was a computer model of thinking proposed by Simon (1967), in which affect was conceptualized as an "interrupt" or disruption in an otherwise goal-directed program. This exception, even though it allowed a place for affect in the system, was in keeping with earlier views of affect as nothing more than *arousal* (e.g., Duffy, 1934; Lindsley, 1951), and it helps to illustrate the marginal status and simplistic conceptualization that affect was afforded, when it was considered (see Isen, 2002b; Isen & Hastorf, 1982, for further discussion). In fairness to those earlier authors, however, it should be noted that there was not a lot of empirical evidence, especially regarding positive affect, on which they could base a more sophisticated consideration of affect.

In recent decades, however, the field has seen a steadily growing body of empirical research on the influence of positive affect on social interaction, cognitive processes, decision making, and risk taking (e.g., see Isen, 2000, for review), as well as work in applied contexts, extending and making use of these findings in domains such as organizational behavior, negotiation processes, coping processes and health psychology, consumer decision making and choice processes, and the like (e.g., Aspinwall, 1998; Barone, Miniard, & Romeo, 2000; Brief & Weiss, 2002; Carnevale & Isen, 1986; Isen, 2001; Kahn & Isen, 1993; Lee & Sternthal, 1999). Not only has our understanding of affect increased greatly, as a result of the newfound legitimacy of focusing on and studying affect, but this affective revolution has enriched our understanding of other subfields of psychology, such as cognition and decision making. We now know, for example, that positive affect (but not negative affect) is a category in memory used spontaneously by people to organize their thoughts, because studies have reported that positive affect as a state serves as a retrieval cue for positive material learned from a mixed list during the session (Isen, 1987; Isen, Shalker, Clark, & Karp, 1978; Lee & Sternthal, 1999; Teasdale & Fogarty, 1979; Teasdale & Russell, 1983). Even the emerging new cognitive neuroscience fields are being integrated with the study of affect, contributing to understanding of affect and benefiting from application of information learned from the affect literature (see, e.g., Ashby, Isen, & Turken, 1999; Depue & Collins, 1999; Heller, 1997; Isom & Heller, 1999). The realization that affect is a regular part of thought processes and motivation or processing goals has enriched conceptualizations in the fields of cognition and motivation, and those fields have grown more realistic and complex as a result. In addition, by identifying ways in which affect influences well-researched processes in, for example, cognitive psychology, we have learned a great deal about affect that would not have been possible by only focusing more obviously on affect, how it feels, and how people describe the experience of it.

Thus, the past three decades have seen a great enrichment in our understanding of affect, and some contribution to our understanding of cognitive processes as well, as a result of the field's recognition of affect as a regular influence on, or part of, cognitive processes. This integration has not been complete, however. In particular, the field of decision making has been somewhat slow to incorporate research on affect, especially positive affect, into its models and basic framework. This is true despite the fact that positive affect has been demonstrated to influence cognitive processes that are basic to decision making and has even been shown to influence actual decision processes themselves (e.g., Isen & Means, 1983; Isen, Rosenzweig, & Young, 1991; Kahn &

Isen, 1993). As noted, it is now becoming clear that positive affect plays an important, integral (not peripheral) role in shaping thinking and influencing plans, decisions, and behavior; thus, the time seems right for integrating affect into decision-making models and research as well.

The overarching goal of this volume is to consider new perspectives that may help shape and guide decision-making research in the coming years. The focus of this chapter, within that broader goal, is to call attention to two factors that are emerging as important considerations within cognitive and social psychology but that have not yet been represented extensively or regularly within decision research. These are (1) the influence of positive affect and (2) the contributions that may be obtained from considering the neuropsychological level of analysis.

To this end, this chapter will summarize some of the evidence showing that positive affect leads to cognitive flexibility and facilitates problem solving and decision making in many situations, and it will suggest that these kinds of findings have been observed so regularly that it would be appropriate for positive affect to be integrated in a regular way into decision-making models. We will then present some ideas about the kinds of processes that may underlie these effects, including a recent suggestion, on the neuropsychological level, that these effects may be mediated by the dopamine system in the brain (Ashby et al., 1999). And, finally, the chapter will suggest that our field may benefit from integrating current understandings of brain processes more regularly into our thinking about decision making and into the development of our decision-making models. This might lead to the development of new ways of conceptualizing the variables we study. Because of space limitations, our consideration of these issues must be brief, but we hope that this chapter will stimulate interest in these issues.

Background

We begin with a brief introduction to the nature of the affective states studied in this work. In accord with the methods and conventions of our field, we use operational definitions to define the affective states, and include converging operations to rule out alternative interpretations of the manipulations we use to induce affect (see, e.g., Isen, 1987, 1999, for more detail).

It is important to realize how small the interventions are that produce the effects to be described, how easily they are induced, how beneficial they usually are, and how persistent the effects are, because often when cognitive scientists or neuroscientists or, recently, economists do begin to think about affect, they think about intense, and usually negative, emotional events like rage, the death of a parent, dread, panic, and so on. From another perspective, it is fashionable now to speak about global *happiness* or well-being, usually assessed only by self-report in response to general questions, and to believe that affective state is stable (traitlike) and possibly even genetically determined, and that the only meaningful or impactful kind of affect results from stable affective dispositions or level of well-being. But what the body of work to be described here has shown is a stunningly large and impactful set of effects resulting from stunningly small – and positive – everyday occurrences. In addition, recent research is confirming that these effects can last and have impact for more than just a few minutes (e.g., Estrada, Isen, & Young, 1997) and that the impact of temporary affect is observable over and above that of any stable dispositions that may also contribute to determining behavior and/or performance outcomes (e.g., Weiss, Nicholas, & Daus, 1999).

The interventions that have produced cognitive and behavioral effects include things such as viewing a nonsexual, nonaggressive comedy film for 5 minutes (e.g., Isen, Daubman, & Nowicki, 1987); finding a coin in a public telephone (Isen & Levin, 1972); thinking positive thoughts or giving word associations to positive words (e.g., Isen, Johnson, Mertz, & Robinson, 1985); receiving a report of success on an unrelated task (e.g., Isen, 1970; Isen & Means, 1983; Isen et al., 1991); receiving a small free sample, gift, or coupon (e.g., Isen, Daubman, & Nowicki, 1987; Isen & Geva, 1987; Isen & Patrick, 1983; Kahn & Isen, 1993); or working in a room with pleasant ambiance (e.g., Bakamitsos, 2001; Baron, Rea, & Daniels, 1992). Note that although these are small incidental-seeming things, they are the kinds of things that are likely to occur frequently in everyday life and therefore may be of great practical significance.

Positive Affect Facilitates Problem Solving and Cognitive Flexibility

One of the most intriguing findings – and one of the most robust – in this affect literature is that positive affect, induced in simple ways such as these, promotes cognitive flexibility, innovation, problem solving, and creativity, including creative problem solving, in many different contexts. This has been found using several different measures or indicators of creativity and flexibility, including unusualness and diversity of word associations to neutral stimulus words (Isen et al., 1985); classification of atypical exemplars of neutral categories, both object categories and person categories (Isen & Daubman, 1984; Isen, Niedenthal, & Cantor, 1992); performance on a subset of the Remote Associates Test (Estrada, Isen, & Young, 1994; Isen, Daubman, & Nowicki, 1987), a test designed by the Mednicks (Mednick, Mednick, & Mednick, 1964) to be a measure of the trait of creativity; performance on Duncker's Candle problem, which is usually taken as requiring an innovative solution (Greene & Noice, 1988; Isen, Daubman, & Nowicki, 1987); unusualness of sensible responses in identifying similarities and differences between items (Hirt, Melton, McDonald, & Haraciewicz, 1996); and flexibility in considering alternatives among safe, enjoyable consumer-product choice options (Kahn & Isen, 1993). More recently, a study of physicians' diagnostic processes has also shown that positive affect promotes open-mindedness, flexibility, and willingness to accept disconfirming evidence in that kind of complex decision-making or problem-solving situation (Estrada et al., 1997).

Many of these effects have been found by researchers in many different laboratories, working in many different contexts, and involving many different populations, ranging from preschool children and young adolescents, through college student samples, and even including practicing physicians. This effect of happy feelings on flexible thinking has been observed in organizational settings (e.g., George & Brief, 1996; Isen & Baron, 1991; Staw & Barsade, 1993) and in the literature on consumer decision making, extending to the way consumers think about and decide to purchase and use products and services, the consideration sets they even consider when making choices, brand-related decisions such as brand loyalty and the acceptability of brand extensions, variety seeking, and many more (e.g., Barone et al., 2000; Kahn & Isen, 1993; Lee & Sternthal, 1999). One recent paper reported not only that positive affect improves people's memory for material learned at the session, but also that it accomplishes this by reducing the serial position effect, especially the impairment of memory for interior items caused by the primacy component of the serial position effect (Lee & Sternthal, 1999).

A growing body of research also indicates that positive affect can facilitate coping processes (e.g., Aspinwall & Taylor, 1997; Taylor and Aspinwall, 1996). Compatible effects have also been observed in applications such as solving interpersonal problems, as represented by negotiation and conflict-resolution situations (e.g., Carnevale & Isen, 1986). People in whom positive affect has been induced tend more than controls to take a problem-solving approach to these situations and come up with the kind of solution that involves thinking creatively about how to obtain the most for both sides. There is even an indication that they are better able to take the other party's perspective in the negotiation (Carnevale & Isen, 1986). Work in the coping literature indicates that under positive affect people also appear less "defensive" in stressful situations and tend to engage less in "defensive" interpersonal processes, such as downward comparison, competitive comparisons, making oneself feel better by focusing on the relatively worse outcome of another, or the flip side of that – feeling threatened by another person's success (e.g., Aspinwall, 1998; Aspinwall & Brunhart, 1996; Trope & Neter, 1994; Trope & Pomerantz, 1998).

It should be noted that these findings are in contrast with an earlier, widely held view that positive affect, by its nature, impairs systematic cognitive processing and leads to poor judgment and superficial thinking, either because it takes up cognitive capacity (e.g., Mackie & Worth, 1989) or because it signals that the environment is benign and does not require careful attention (e.g., Bless, Bohner, Schwartz, & Strack, 1990; Schwartz & Bless, 1991). (The latter view also assumes that if careful processing is not *required* in order for a person to *protect* himself or herself, it will not occur.) Another author adhering to a position essentially compatible with that is Forgas (1995, 2002), who has argued that affect may not always impact thought and behavior, but that when it does, it is disruptive of systematic processing and leads to superficial thinking. (These authors also assume that, just as positive affect leads to superficial processing, negative affect leads to careful thinking and problem solving; see, e.g., Forgas, 2002; Schwartz & Bless, 1991. The topic of the effects of negative affect on thought processes, itself controversial, is beyond the scope of this chapter.) The authors holding the view that positive affect is typically disruptive and leads to superficial cognitive processing have modified their position to some degree in recent years (e.g., Bless et al., 1996) as data have increasingly confirmed that the influence of positive affect is most frequently beneficial cognitively and leads to flexible consideration of tasks and material (e.g., Estrada et al., 1997; Fredrickson, 1998; Fredrickson, Mancuso, Branigan, & Tugade, 2000; Isen, 1993a; Isen, Daubman, & Nowicki, 1987; Isen et al., 1991; Staw & Barsade, 1993). However, for the most part, those authors have substituted a view that positive affect leads to "top-down" (influenced by existing cognitive structures and biases) processing rather than "bottom up" or data-driven processing and that therefore people in positive affect will be less responsive than controls to data and more responsive to their own biases (e.g., Bless et al., 1996; Forgas, 2002). Those authors propose that this view best fits with data showing that people in positive affect have better access to their existing cognitive structures (e.g., Bless et al., 1996).

Unfortunately, this view does not also fit with the growing body of data showing that positive affect facilitates flexibility – not rigidity – and openness to data, responsiveness to details of the materials and situation, and so forth (e.g., Aspinwall & Richter, 1999; Estrada et al., 1997; Isen et al., 1992; Urada & Miller, 2000; see Isen, 2000, for discussion). One possible resolution of this paradox that has been proposed is that positive affect may facilitate *both* use of internal structures *and* responsiveness to data from outside, as well as the ability to switch between these sources of information flexibly (Isen, 2000).

Thus, the view that positive affect leads to superficial, impaired processing has become untenable. In fact, recent work suggests that positive affect may actually free up capacity and in this way act as an additional resource or source of strength (e.g., Aspinwall 1998; Aspinwall & Brunhart, 1996; Isen, 1993; Isen, 2002a). This work suggests that positive affect leads to changes in cognitive organization, such as chunking, that then enable utilization of both existing cognitive structures *and* new information (e.g., Isen, 2000; Isen, Daubman, & Gorgoglione, 1987; Lee & Sternthal, 1999). This latter view is also supported by data showing that positive affect fosters integration of material (e.g., Isen, Daubman, & Gorgoglione, 1987; Isen, et al., 1991), a process that could facilitate chunking.

These facilitating effects of positive affect on cognitive elaboration and flexibility are relevant to decision making in several ways. Not only do they show that positive affect may influence the expected affective impact of the choice (which is especially relevant to a theory by Mellers, which will be discussed later in the chapter) and the decisions that are made in various circumstances, but they also indicate that this everyday affective state plays a role in many components of the decision process itself, from the range of options considered, to willingness to accept disconfirming evidence, and so forth.

Even more, however, the flexibility engendered by positive affect may play a role in reducing several biases that have been noted in the literature of cognitive and social psychology. We have already mentioned that one paper reported a reduction in the primacy component of the serial-position effect as a result of positive affect (Lee & Sternthal, 1999).

Another example may be found in the context of the work of Gilbert, Wilson, and their colleagues, who, in a series of studies investigating the accuracy of *affective forecasting*, or predictions of future affect, have identified what they call *durability bias*, or a tendency to predict that a future affective state will last longer than it actually does (e.g., Gilbert, Pinel, Wilson, Blumberg, & Wheatley, 1998). Interestingly, a recent study has shown that this bias can be reduced if people are led to think about other future activities besides the focal one about which they are being asked to predict the duration and intensity of their feelings in the future (Wilson, Wheatley, Meyers, Gilbert, & Axsom, 2000). That is, broadening attention beyond the one event – to think about other factors that will also be important or be present in the future situation – leads people to reduce their duration estimate of the impact of the focal event or emotion and thus alleviates this durability bias.

This is relevant in the present context, because positive affect is known to broaden attention (e.g., Fredrickson, 1998; Fredrickson et al., 2000; Isen, 1970, 1990; Isen et al., 1985) and stimulate cognitive elaboration, additional thoughts, and a diversity of thoughts (e.g., Greene & Noice, 1988; Isen et al., 1985; Kahn & Isen, 1993). That is, the flexibility that has been observed to result from positive affect involves cognitive elaboration, thinking of and about more different things, in response to a stimulus (e.g., Isen et al., 1985; Kahn & Isen, 1993). It has even been found that when people in positive affect focus on negative material such as potential loss or danger, they elaborate more and have more thoughts about the loss (e.g., Aspinwall, 1998; Isen & Geva, 1987). Thus, there is reason to believe that positive affect, because of increased flexibility and resultant cognitive elaboration, may alleviate focalism and the duration bias that has been observed, and thus may improve the accuracy of affective forecasts (or anticipated affect). This possibility is currently under investigation in our laboratory.

This prediction is similar to one that has been made (e.g., Isen & Stokker, 1996) regarding positive affect's influence on the *sunk-costs effect*. In the sunk-costs literature, it has been found that people tend to keep investing in a losing proposition in which they already have invested resources, to a greater extent than they would if they had not previously invested in the venture (e.g., Arkes & Blumer, 1985; Staw, 1976). However, here again, research suggests that prompting people to think of alternative ways to spend the money reduces the sunk-cost error (Northcraft & Neale, 1986). Thus, again, it seems plausible that, under some circumstances, positive affect may reduce this bias because of broadening attention and causing or allowing people to think spontaneously of alternative uses for the funds. In fact, preliminary findings support this suggestion (Isen & Stokker, 1996), and work on this topic is continuing.

At the same time, the data indicate that decisions made under conditions of positive affect are not necessarily automatic, nor are the effects of affect irresistible. This is illustrated in several studies that showed significant interactions between affect and the nature of the materials or other conditions of the experiment (see Isen, 2000, 2002b, for review and further discussion). Affect does not operate like the application of a lens or the donning of rose-colored glasses. A person's plans, goals, and consideration of the relevant materials play their appropriate roles in the presence of affect.

Flexibility in Negotiation. As noted, one study, looking at the impact of positive affect on the process and outcome of negotiation in an integrative-bargaining situation, found that among negotiators bargaining face-to-face, those in whom positive affect had been induced achieved better outcomes, and had a more pleasant session, than those in whom no affect had been induced (Carnevale & Isen, 1986). In fact, both parties achieved the best outcome possible from the negotiation, whereas in the control condition, participants typically broke off the negotiation without reaching any agreement. It was apparent that people in the positive affect condition took a problem-solving approach (rather than contending, withdrawing, or yielding), aimed at obtaining the most for both parties, and that it was the flexibility that is represented by a problem-solving approach that enabled the good outcome achieved. This seems likely because people in the positive affect condition were better able to report, at the end of the session, what the other person's payoff schedule was – a fact not divulged during the negotiation – and this, in turn, suggests that they were taking the other person's perspective during the session.

One may wonder what the impact of positive affect would be in a zero-sum type of negotiation, where it is not possible for the parties to make tradeoffs among elements in the negotiation because there is only one item and one response opportunity per round. Recently, a series of studies was conducted investigating this question, using two forms of the Prisoner's Dilemma situation. The two forms used were the standard one, in which the payoffs were structured so that it was to the player's advantage to choose the "defect" response, and the second form was what we called a *trust* situation, in which the payoffs were structured so that it was to the player's advantage to choose the "cooperate" response as long as he or she could trust the other party to cooperate as well. In these studies there were repeated rounds with ostensibly the same coplayer (actually a nonexistent coplayer), and after each round dummy feedback was provided about which response the coplayer had chosen on the previous round. On each round, the participant chose to cooperate or defect (compete) and then received feedback about what the coplayer supposedly had done on that round.

Results showed that the positive-affect and control subjects did not differ on the first round of negotiation, or on Round 2 or 3, on which they received feedback that the coplayer had competed; but on Round 4, which was the first round after the participant received feedback saying that the coplayer had chosen the cooperate response, people in the positive-affect condition chose the cooperate response significantly more often than the controls (Labroo, Isen, & Shanteau, 2000). Such a tit-for-tat strategy has been shown by Axelrod (1984, pp. 27–54) to be the optimal strategy in negotiation situations. Controls switched to the cooperate response on Round 5 and thereafter; but the important point in the present context is that the positive-affect group showed more flexibility and responded immediately to the coplayer's response. It should also be noted that in a real negotiation situation, the one-round lag between the affect and control groups' responsiveness could make a huge difference, as a real coplayer might not continue to choose the cooperate response when the participant was unresponsive to his or her cooperative overture on Round 4 (as control participants were). Therefore, the positive-affect group's flexibility and immediate responsiveness could make even more difference than it did here, where dummy feedback ensured that the coplayer kept cooperating despite the control participant's lack of responsiveness. In terms of the actual outcome in the negotiation, those in the positive-affect condition outperformed the controls in the trust game and did not differ from controls in final score in the standard situation (Labroo et al., 2000).

Variety-Seeking Among Safe, Enjoyable Products. For another example of the impact of the flexibility engendered by positive affect, several studies have found that people in whom positive affect was induced made more switches and entertained a larger and more diverse consideration set, compared with controls, when considering choices among safe, enjoyable products such as snack foods (Kahn & Isen, 1993). Significant interactions supported the point that this held true only as long as the items were not of questionable taste/quality. If there was doubt about the products, people in positive affect did not differ from controls. This is an example, then, of a case in which positive affect influenced the actual choices, increasing switching and preference for variety; and it is an example of a study that reported a significant interaction between affect and the nature of the materials, showing that people in positive affect are not prisoners of their affect but have, and exercise, the ability to choose based on the meaning of the situation to them. At the same time, it is important to note that variety-seeking is not the same as risk-seeking or sensation-seeking. It refers only to variety or exploration among safe, enjoyable products.

Risk-Taking. In contrast with variety-seeking, risk-seeking typically refers, at least in common parlance, to dangerous behavior (although, technically, it refers to variance; see Isen, Nygren, & Ashby, 1988, for further discussion of this point). Studies on the impact of affect on risk-taking show results that differ from those related to variety-seeking. In contrast with the increased switching and variety-seeking observed to result from positive affect in safe situations, results of several studies indicate that positive affect does not generally lead to increased risk-taking (even defined as a preference for variance) if the risk is real and meaningful (e.g., Isen & Geva, 1987; Isen & Patrick, 1983). The common misconception of most people is that positive affect will lead to increased risk-taking, or throwing caution to the wind; but actually, the research has shown that this happens only where the risk is small or hypothetical (not real). In contrast, in situations where the risk is real and sizable or meaningful, positive affect leads to *reduced* risk-taking in comparison with controls (Isen & Geva, 1987; Isen & Patrick, 1983).

The reason for this may be that when people are feeling happy, they have more to lose if they lose a gamble (they stand to lose their affective state as well as their stake), and possibly for this reason they avoid the chance of a meaningful loss. Follow-up studies, in fact, have found that the negative utility of a given loss is greater for people in positive-affect conditions, and that under conditions of positive affect, people who are in a situation of possible loss show more thoughts about losing than do control subjects (Isen & Geva, 1987; Isen et al., 1988). Thus, possible loss seems to loom even larger for people who are feeling happy than for people in whom positive affect has not been induced. Another follow-up study reported that positive affect seems to lead people to give more weight to the hedonic impact of the outcome than to the probability of that outcome (Nygren, Isen, Taylor, & Dulin, 1996).

Again, however, it should be noted that these studies show significant interactions between affect and level of risk, or reality of risk, indicating that positive affect does not lead people to lose sight of the details of the situation or to lose the ability to differentiate between real threat or danger and hypothetical or mild negative consequence. Moreover, the finding that positive affect increases the perceived negative utility of a loss, and the resultant hypothesis that this may be the reason that people in positive affect resolve the situation by avoiding the risky alternative, should not cause us to lose sight of all of the other effects induced by positive affect simultaneously. That is, we should not assume that affect maintenance is the *only* motive induced by positive affect. Studies show that people in positive affect readily focus on negative material if it is to their long-term benefit or if the situation calls for it (e.g., Aspinwall, 1998; Isen & Geva, 1987; Trope & Pomerantz, 1998). Thus, it is important to keep in mind that (1) affect maintenance and, in general, the estimate of affective outcome are not the only influences that positive affect may have on decision making; and (2) people in positive affect are able to make choices, and in fact are more flexible and more able to respond to various aspects of the situation appropriately.

Decision Making

Several studies have demonstrated that, beyond influencing the component processes that could be involved in decisions, in actual decision contexts positive affect influences the decision-making process. These studies, taken together, indicate that under conditions of positive affect, the decision process is both more efficient and more thorough, as long as the task is one that is meaningful, interesting, or important to the decision maker. For example, in a study involving a choice among hypothetical cars for purchase, subjects were given folders of information pertaining to nine dimensions for each of six cars. They reasoned aloud as they went about the task, and the session was taped and later transcribed for analysis. Results indicated that people in whom positive affect had been induced were more efficient in the way they went about the task (Isen & Means, 1983). Although their ultimate choices did not differ from those of control subjects, they reached a decision sooner, showed less redundancy in the search process, and eliminated two dimensions from consideration, but only dimensions that were of low importance (as judged by controls following the task).

When this same paradigm was used to study the decision-making processes of young medical care providers in training (fourth-year medical students who had completed 1 full year of clinical experience, including a rotation in internal medicine or pediatrics), it was found, again, that those in whom positive affect had been induced were more efficient and showed less confusion, although the particular measures that reflected these characteristics were a bit different from those in the car-choice study (Isen et al., 1991).

In this study, subjects were asked to identify which of six patients, each of whom had been found to have a solitary pulmonary nodule on x-ray, was most likely to have lung cancer, based on data on nine different dimensions (e.g., previous chest x-ray, cough, smoking history, weight loss, etc.), using the same format as for the car-choice problem. All participants found the correct answer to the problem.

Protocol analyses, which were done by two independent raters who were not aware of a respondent's condition while reading his or her protocol, showed that people in the positive-affect condition completed the assigned task (to decide which stimulus person was most likely to have cancer) significantly earlier in their protocols. Thus, as in the earlier car-choice study, the positive-affect subjects were more efficient, in that they solved the assigned problem sooner. But the measure that showed this was not total time on task, as it had been in the earlier study, because in this study, subjects in the positive-affect condition did not stop working when they solved the problem posed by the experimenter, as participants in the earlier (car-choice) study had done. Instead, interestingly, the positive-affect subjects were significantly more likely than controls to do more than was asked – to go beyond the assigned task. Primarily what they did, to a significantly greater extent than control subjects, was to attempt to diagnose the remaining cases, and in some instances they suggested treatments. Thus, they were more thorough in their consideration of the materials. In addition, protocol analyses indicated that clinicians in whom positive affect had been induced tended significantly more than controls to integrate dimensions and to think configurally, and they showed significantly less evidence of confusion.

The findings of these car-choice and medical-decision studies suggest that, under conditions of positive affect, people tend to integrate material for decision making and to be less confused by a large set of propositions. This allows them to work faster and either finish earlier (as in the car-choice task) or to turn attention to other important tasks within the materials (as in the medical-diagnosis task).

A follow-up study examined medical doctors' diagnostic process in a more realistic task and setting (Estrada et al., 1997). In this study, which was conducted in a busy hospital during a busy day, participants were practicing physicians specializing in internal medicine. The study asked them to reason aloud as they solved a diagnostic task that they were given; again, sessions were tape-recorded and the transcripts were analyzed later. Affect was induced by means of a small bag of candy, modified just slightly from the standard candy-bag gift used in previous research.

Three sets of results were collected: scores on the subset of items from the Remote Associates Test, used previously to show the influence of positive affect on creative problem solving (e.g., Isen, Daubman, & Nowicki, 1987); protocols of the doctors' decision processes while solving the diagnostic problem; and responses to a questionnaire given at the end of the session assessing two sources of the doctors' motivation for the practice of medicine (humanistic vs. extrinsic).

These results show that physicians in whom positive affect had been induced scored significantly higher on the creativity measure, as had been found previously for other populations. They also reported relatively more humanistic than extrinsic motivation for practicing medicine compared with controls (Estrada et al., 1994). On the diagnostic task itself, results indicated that the doctors in the positive-affect condition were significantly earlier in their protocols to recognize and integrate the symptoms and signs with the correct domain of the illness and to begin considering the correct type of disease (Estrada et al., 1997). This is not where they concluded what the disease was, but where they first seriously began considering the correct disease domain. It is taken as an indication of integration of information or correct-hypotheses generation. This is where they first "put things together" and realized the correct domain of the problem/illness, and on this measure, doctors in the positive-affect condition were significantly earlier than controls.

These analyses showed no difference between the groups in their confirmation process, and no evidence that the doctors in the positive-affect condition jumped to conclusions or were superficial in their decision process in any way. In fact, analysis of the protocols revealed that physicians in the positive-affect condition showed significantly *less* distortion or ignoring of information that did not fit with a hypothesis they were already considering (Estrada et. al., 1997).

Supplementary post hoc analyses, designed to investigate whether there was any evidence that people in the positive-affect condition achieved these seemingly better results by jumping to the diagnosis prematurely, or were superficial in their consideration of the evidence, showed no evidence of superficial, faulty, or flawed processing. In fact, there was some tendency for the doctors in the positive-affect condition to show greater care and thoroughness, and less superficiality in their decision process, as all differences were in the direction consistent with that conclusion and reached customarily accepted levels of significance. Because of the large number of comparisons in this post hoc analysis of the protocols, however, one may want to be conservative in analyzing these differences. Using a Bonferroni procedure and setting the alpha for these comparisons at .003, these differences are not significant. Thus, although it appeared that the positive-affect doctors were even *better* than the controls in these dimensions also (careful, less superficial, considered more possibilities, etc.), from these supplementary analyses one can at least feel confident in saying simply that those in positive affect are *not worse* than controls.

Decision-Making Models. Recently, one group of decision theorists has proposed a model that considers one aspect of affect as a fundamental component of the decision-making model (Mellers, 2000; Mellers, Schwartz, Ho, & Ritov, 1997). Mellers and her colleagues focus on people's expectation of the emotional experience that will be associated with the outcomes of decisions, and they suggest that choices between risky options may depend on maximizing the expected emotional experience, rather than only on maximizing the expected utility of the chosen outcome. Although at first it may seem that these two (expected utility and expected emotional experience) would be the same, Mellers and colleagues point out that factors such as degree of expectedness or surprise may play a role in resultant feelings, as may comparison with alternative options possible in the situation (whereas presumably such factors would not influence expected utility). Thus, the model they propose as a result adds consideration of factors such as counterfactuals to the more traditional elements of probability and utility of the alternative outcomes. In this way, the Mellers model builds on traditional decision approaches and adds consideration of one aspect of affect in a systematic way.

Another recent paper attempts to broaden this effort by distinguishing between the effect of anticipated and anticipatory emotions

(Loewenstein, Weber, Hsee, & Welch, 2001). *Anticipated emotion* refers to the aspect of feelings relating to how one expects to feel as a result of the choice, which is similar to the focus that Mellers and colleagues adopted. Loewenstein et al. (2001) contrast that with *anticipatory emotion*, by which they appear to mean emotions or feelings that the decision maker is experiencing while making the decision; and they call for a focus on anticipatory emotion, referring to anticipated emotion as nothing more than cognition. However, in presenting the distinction, they explain anticipatory emotions as "immediate, visceral reactions (e.g., fear, anxiety, dread) to risks and uncertainties" (p. 267), so that it is difficult to tell whether the authors intend this category (and, indeed, their paper in general) to be about feelings broadly or only about a subset of feelings – intense, negative, danger-related, focused emotion.

Even if intended to apply only to intense, negative affect, the effort by Loewenstein et al. (2001) to distinguish between anticipated and anticipatory emotion actually breaks down, even in their paper, when the authors attempt to operationalize the distinction. Beyond that, in practice it is difficult to keep anticipated emotion from actually becoming anticipatory emotion, for example, because excitement at a prospect may make one feel elated, or consideration of a feared outcome may induce fear or dread. And it is difficult to determine when that has happened. In addition, factors such as unexpectedness, and aspects of the context, and the degree of experience one has with the emotion-generating object could influence the nature and degree of anticipatory affect toward any given stimulus. For example, a dog's owner usually does not experience as much dread, if any, upon seeing her dog as does a stranger to the dog who has recently been bitten by another dog. In fact, many instances of anticipatory affect may arise actually from anticipated affect, based on one's assessment of one's strengths versus one's vulnerabilities. Therefore, empirical work establishing Loewenstein et al.'s proposed distinction, its parameters, and its implications would be needed if the distinction is to be sustainable and understood in a more useful way.

Judging from many of the examples and arguments used in the paper by Loewenstein and colleagues, it is possible that the model proposed by those authors applies only to intense, negative emotion. In that case, the applicability of the approach in the paper by Loewenstein et al. may be restricted to those relatively few instances in which, by definition, people's reasoning about a decision is overwhelmed or short-circuited by some intense emotion or by a set of circumstances that limits their ability to cope with the problem. Although, at one point, Loewenstein and colleagues claim that their view is consistent with a view of emotion as beneficial to the person and adaptive, for the most part their argument seems more compatible with a view that that emotion derails or overrides thinking and good judgment, and causes people to make errors, take inappropriate actions, or fail to speak and think clearly (e.g., Loewenstein et al., 2001, p. 269). As such, it is similar to earlier models and conceptualizations, such as Simon's (1967), described in the introductory section of this chapter, in that it views affect narrowly and limits affect's influence on cognitive processes or decision making to peripheral effects such as disruption or impulsive responding.

As we have seen thus far in this chapter, however, the work on positive affect's influence on decision making does not focus solely on positive affect's influence on estimation of anticipated feelings as the only, or even the primary, impact of positive affect on decision making. And it does not indicate that affect's only influence is to disrupt logical, effective thinking. To the contrary, the work reviewed in this chapter calls attention to many effects of positive affect – effects on anticipated feelings and the motivations and behaviors to which they give rise, but also effects on cognitive organization, options considered, flexibility in considerations, and perspectives taken, to name just a few – and it has shown that positive affect can be an important facilitator of logical, effective, flexible thinking and problem solving. That is, the research has shown that working or deciding *happily* can have important facilitating effects compared to just working.

The Influence of Positive Affect on Cognitive Processes: Integrating a Neuropsychological Perspective

Although the finding that positive affect leads to creativity and flexibility in thinking is robust and has been obtained many times and in many different contexts, it is not well understood. One possible mechanism that has been suggested is that because positive affect cues positive material, and because positive material is extensive and diverse, a complex, rich cognitive context is created by positive affect, as it cues its diverse sets of ideas (e.g., Isen, 1984). Work by precognitive psychologists of the 1950s and 1960s established that complex context fosters creative or unusual responding (e.g., Cramer, 1968), and thus the suggestion has been made that positive affect fosters innovativeness and creative responding because it alters the cognitive milieu in this way and makes it rich and diverse, providing many additional cues.

Yet it is still not clear why a complex context itself leads to innovation, nor are many of the other effects of positive affect on cognition and social behavior addressed by that explanation. For example, as noted earlier, after a period of debate in the affect literature, there is now growing evidence that positive affect promotes both efficient and thorough problem solving and generally enhances cognitive ability and processes (e.g., Bless et al., 1996; Estrada et al., 1997; Isen, 1993a, 2000; Isen et al., 1991; Lee & Sternthal, 1999). But what enables thinking processes to be enhanced by simple happy feelings? If they foster chunking and improve the ability to organize and integrate cognitive material, as has been proposed, what processes enable or underlie this ability?

Today, in view of the tremendous advances in understanding of brain processes and their relationship to thought and behavior that have resulted from the nation's "Decade of the Brain" in health research and cognitive research, it is inviting to consider what role brain processes may play in these effects. That is, it is reasonable to inquire whether we can advance our understanding of how positive affect comes to have many of these effects on cognitive processing, social behavior, and other products of decision making by understanding the brain processes underlying or associated with positive affect, or with the processes and abilities that positive affect fosters (such as a complex context and flexible thinking). Such brain processes that are identified as relevant to positive affect and its effects, then, may offer still more clues about what else to expect of positive affect.

Recently, in fact, a neuropsychological theory of the relationship between positive affect and enhanced cognitive processes has been offered (Ashby et al., 1999). This proposal suggests that the neurotransmitter dopamine and the brain dopamine system may play an important role in the effects that positive feelings have on thought processes and social behavior, and may therefore help us to understand these effects – and may even shape our view of them. That is, many of the behavioral and cognitive effects of positive affect may be mediated by the dopamine system in the brain and the activation of certain brain regions that are rich in dopamine receptors.

Reasoning from the fact that dopamine is associated with reward and learning from reward, it was proposed that dopamine may also be present at increased levels at times of positive affect. Although other neurotransmitters, such as serotonin, may play a role as well, and may even act in concert with dopamine to determine specific nuances of behavior or subtleties of different emotions or affective states, the dopamine system may be particularly important, because excitatory dopamine receptors are abundant in regions of the brain that have been found to underlie effective thinking (e.g., frontal areas), and in particular to underlie flexible attention deployment and set-switching (the anterior cingulate region; see Ashby et al., 1999, for discussion).

Research has shown that dopamine in the anterior cingulate region of the brain is associated with flexible attention deployment and set-switching, and enables switching attention and taking different perspectives in the context of a task. Thus, this neuropsychological theory of the influence of positive affect on cognitive processes proposes that dopamine release into the anterior cingulate may underlie the relationship between positive affect and cognitive flexibility or creativity, as the ability to shift attention and take different perspectives enables the person to see things in different ways, seemingly simultaneously, and be flexible. This, then, would implicate dopamine in many of the effects of positive feelings that have been observed: creativity, openness to information, exploration, integration of ideas, effective problem solving, focus on important negative information when that is needed, ability to keep others' perspectives as well as one's own in mind seemingly simultaneously, and responsiveness to others' behavior, including moves in a negotiation situation, just to name a few.

Positive affect has also been found to increase helping and generosity in many circumstances (see Isen, 1987, for review), findings that themselves have been conceptualized as the products of decision-making processes (e.g., Isen & Levin, 1972). The dopamine hypothesis also may help to explain these findings, as the ability to switch perspectives may facilitate kindness and generosity to others. As people can shift attention and perspective, they are better able to see things from other people's perspectives, and may therefore be more generous and understanding. Compatibly with this suggestion, one of the remarkable things that was first noted in the helping literature was that when people in positive affect help others, that does not mean that they deprive themselves; rather, the evidence shows that they are simultaneously kind to both others and themselves. This finding is completely compatible with the dopamine hypothesis regarding the mediation of positive affect's influence on thinking and behavior, because that view suggests that positive affect enables people to take both their own and another's perspective, in effect, simultaneously or in quick succession. So, they are likely to be equally concerned with their own and the other's outcomes, or can see how the other's outcome is important or at least what is likely to happen to the other person.

The proposal that some of the important influences of positive affect on cognition and social behavior are mediated by release of dopamine suggests some effects that positive affect should have and some that it should not (see Ashby et al., 1999, for further discussion). For example, as we have already seen, dopamine in the anterior cingulate fosters flexible set-switching and alternative perspective taking. Other regions rich in dopamine receptors are other frontal regions, the olfactory bulb, and the olfactory cortex. This would lead us to predict salutory effects of positive affect on thinking, memory consolidation, deciding, and olfactory processing. Because there are not dopamine receptors in visual and auditory areas, we would not expect positive affect to influence vision and hearing. Clearly, much remains to be explored relating to the dopamine hypothesis, but these kinds of predictions provide more specific targets than we have had in the past, and hopefully it will contribute to our understanding and suggest additional hypotheses and research directions.

One of the most exciting things about integrating cognitive neuroscience with work on social, affective, and decision-making phenomena is that it provides the possibility of establishing a dialogue between decision psychologists and neuroscientists. For decision psychology, one advantage of such a dialogue may be that of defining our concepts more precisely or in a more useful way, a way that maps onto processes that are better understood – as, for example, realizing the possible importance of cognitive set-switching in determining choices and judgments, rather than relying on more static determinants or on the simple "on" or "off" status of particular strategies (e.g., asking whether the decision maker is employing so-called systematic reasoning). Rather than conceptualizing processes arbitrarily, piecemeal, as they are discovered, or in terms only of apparent function, it may be possible to conceptualize them in terms of brain processes and functions about which something else is known – as, for example, in the case of cognitive set-switching. Thus, this neurological theory can add to our tools for studying the impact of affect on thinking and decision making; and integrating recent advances in neuroscience into our understanding of decision making and judgment more generally can lead to exciting new developments in the field.

However, it should be emphasized that we are not endorsing reductionism, as if the neuropsychological level of analysis were the only important level on which to obtain information. This level of analysis cannot replace studies conducted on the cognitive and behavioral levels. Rather than viewing these levels of analysis (e.g., neurological vs. behavioral or cognitive) as opposing one another as ways to advance understanding, it is possible, instead, to attempt to bring them together and integrate work from these multiple levels. That is, understandings from the neurological level can help to inform and guide our search for behavioral and cognitive, as well as other neurological, effects and determinants of feelings, judgments, and decisions. Similarly, research on the behavioral and cognitive levels can point to neurological processes that may be critical. Indeed, it was studies on the behavioral and cognitive levels of analysis that led to our understanding that positive affect promotes flexibility and creativity, and thus to the realization that the ability to switch perspectives is an important process facilitated by positive affect, and thence to the hypothesis that dopamine may mediate at least some of the cognitive and behavioral effects of positive affect.

Before concluding, it is important to note that discovery of the role of neurological processes in any of these relationships should not cause us to assume that the effects are genetic, immutable, automatic, or irresistible, or to lose sight of the fact of continual learning and plasticity in human behavior and cognitive processes (e.g., Cabib & Puglisi-Allegra, 1999; Heller, 1997; Isom & Heller, 1999). When neurological mechanisms mediating behavior are identified, it is sometimes tempting to attribute them, and the behavior or cognitive processes they mediate, to genetic or innate factors, or to see them as the product of very early learning, or as somehow immutable or very difficult to change. Yet, there is no need to assume that all neurological structures and processes are innate or unchangeable. In fact, there is growing evidence that neurological changes also result from learning and experience throughout the life span (Cabib & Puglisi-Allegra, 1999; Heller, 1997; Isom & Heller, 1999).

Likewise, one need not assume that these effects and processes are automatic, even if a neurological process is identified. In fact, the evidence underscores the role of people's plans, goals, understandings, and expectations in determining their reactions to the situations in which they find themselves – which suggests that the effects are not automatic and irresistible (Isen & Diamond, 1989; Posner, 1978; Posner & Snyder, 1975). Evidence showing significant interactions between affect and the nature of the materials or situations suggests that people's interpretations and goals play a role in the impact of affect on thinking and behavior. For example, although people in positive affect were more likely than controls to categorize marginal examples of neutral person types as more fitting into an overarching positive category (e.g., bartenders as members of the category "nurturant people"), they were not more likely to do the same with a negative category (e.g., placing geniuses in the category "mentally unstable people"; Isen et al., 1992). For another example, people in positive affect, compared with controls, showed improved satisfaction and job perceptions for enriched job tasks but not for unenriched ones (Kraiger, Billings, & Isen, 1989). If dopamine in the anterior cingulate associated with positive affect or complexity helps to increase flexibility and alternative perspective-taking, for example, nonetheless the particular way in which this added potential for flexibility is implemented, or not implemented, still depends on people's resolution of the possibilities, constraints, contingencies, and so forth that they understand. This we know from the many studies now showing interactions between affect and situational aspects of the task (e.g., Bodenhausen, Kramer, & Susser, 1994; Isen, Christianson, & Labroo, 2001; Isen & Geva, 1987; Isen et al., 1985, 1992; Isen & Patrick, 1983; Kahn & Isen, 1993; Kraiger et al., 1989; Martin, Ward, Achee, & Wyer, 1993, Urada & Miller, 2000, just to note a few). How people implement their added flexibility depends upon other factors in the situation, as well as on the affect and the dopamine themselves. Thus, the ultimate cognitive and behavioral effects of dopamine release in the anterior cingulate are nonetheless mediated by factors in the situation influencing people's plans, goals, and purposes. Dozens of studies point to the importance of these purposive factors.

In conclusion, this review has demonstrated that positive affect has a substantial facilitating impact on organization of thought, cognitive flexibility and elaboration, evaluation of evidence, negotiation tactics and responsiveness, variety-seeking and risk-taking propensities, and the efficiency and thoroughness of decision strategies. Further, we have seen that integrating a neuropsychological perspective with the behavioral and cognitive work on the influence of affect can aid our understanding markedly. We hope that this review of some of the work on positive affect and cognition, including decision making, will call attention to the potential contributions to be had from expanding our decision-making models in these ways. In particular, we suggest that the time may be right to include consideration of the impact of positive affect on decision making, and to integrate understandings from neuropsychology into our understanding of decision making.

References

Arkes, H. R., & Blumer, C. (1985). The psychology of sunk cost. *Organizational Behavior and Human Decision Processes, 35*(1), 124–140.

Ashby, F. G., Isen, A. M., & Turken, A. U. (1999). A neuropsychological theory of positive affect and its influence on cognition. *Psychological Review, 106*, 529–550.

Aspinwall, L. G. (1998). Rethinking the role of positive affect and self-regulation. *Motivation and Emotion, 22*, 1–32.

Aspinwall, L. G., & Brunhart, S. M. (1996). Distinguishing optimism from denial: Optimistic beliefs predict attention to health threats. *Personality and Social Psychology Bulletin, 22*, 99–103.

Aspinwall, L. G., & Richter, L. (1999). Optimism and self-mastery predict more rapid disengagement from unsolvable tasks in the presence of alternatives. *Motivation and Emotion, 23*(3), 221–245.

Aspinwall, L. G., & Taylor, S. E. (1997). A stitch in time: Self-regulation and proactive coping. *Psychological Bulletin, 121*, 417–436.

Axelrod, R. (1984). *The evolution of cooperation.* New York: Basic Books.

Bakamitsos, Y. (2001). *When and how does mood make a difference?* Paper presented at the annual meeting of the Society for Consumer Psychology, Scottsdale, AZ.

Baron, R. A., Rea, M. S., & Daniels, S. G. (1992). Effects of indoor lighting (illuminance and spectral distribution) on the performance of cognitive tasks and interpersonal behaviors: The potential mediating role of positive affect. *Motivation and Emotion, 16*, 1–33.

Barone, M. J., Miniard, P. W., & Romeo, J. B. (2000). The influence of positive mood on brand extension evaluations. *Journal of Consumer Research, 26*, 386–400.

Bless, H., Bohner, G., Schwartz, N., & Strack, F. (1990). Mood and persuasion: A cognitive response analysis. *Personality and Social Psychology Bulletin, 16*, 331–345.

Bless, H., Clore, G. L., Schwarz, N., Golisano, V., Rabe, C., & Wolk, M. (1996). Mood and the use of scripts: Does a happy mood really lead to mindlessness? *Journal of Personality and Social Psychology, 71*, 665–679.

Bodenhausen, G. V., Kramer, G. P., & Susser, K. (1994). Happiness and stereotypic thinking on social judgment. *Journal of Personality and Social Psychology, 66*, 621–632.

Brief, A. P. & Weiss, H. M. (2002). Organizational behavior: Affect in the workplace. *Annual Review of Psychology, 53*, 279–307.

Cabib, S., & Puglisi-Allegra, S. (1999). Of genes, environment, and destiny. *Behavioral and Brain Sciences, 22*, 519.

Carnevale, P. J. D., & Isen, A. M. (1986). The influence of positive affect and visual access on the discovery of integrative solutions in bilateral negotiation. *Organizational Behavior and Human Decision Processes, 37*, 1–13.

Cramer, P. (1968). *Word association.* New York: Academic Press.

Dalgleish, T., & Power, M. (1999). *The handbook of cognition and emotion.* Sussex, UK: Wiley, 521–539.

Depue, R. A., & Collins, P. F. (1999). Neurobiology of the structure of personality: Dopamine, facilitation of incentive motivation, and extraversion. *Behavioral and Brain Sciences, 22,* 491–569.

Depue, R. A., Luciana, M., Arbisi, P., Collins, P., & Leon, A. (1994). Dopamine and the structure of personality: Relation of agonist-induced dopamine activity to positive emotionality. *Journal of Personality and Social Psychology, 67,* 485–498.

Duffy, E. (1934). Emotion: An example of the need for reorientation in psychology. *Psychological Review, 41,* 184–198.

Estrada, C. A., Isen, A. M., & Young, M. J. (1994). Positive affect influences creative problem solving and reported source of practice satisfaction in physicians. *Motivation and Emotion, 18,* 285–299.

Estrada, C. A., Isen, A. M., & Young, M. J. (1997). Positive affect facilitates integration of information and decreases anchoring in reasoning among physicians. *Organizational Behavior and Human Decision Processes, 72,* 117–135.

Forgas, J. P. (1995). Mood and judgment: The affect infusion model (AIM). *Psychological Bulletin, 117:* 39–66.

Forgas, J. P. (2002). Feeling and doing: Affective influences on interpersonal behavior. *Psychological Inquiry, 13,* 1–28.

Fredrickson, B. L. (1998). What good are positive emotions? *Review of General Psychology, 2,* 300–319.

Fredrickson, B. L., Mancuso, R. A., Branigan, C., & Tugade, M. M. (2000). The undoing effect of positive emotions. *Motivation and Emotion, 24*(4), 237–258.

George, J. M., & Brief, A. P. (1996). Motivational agendas in the workplace: The effects of feelings on focus of attention and work motivation. In L. L. Cummings & B. M. Staw (Eds.), *Research in organizational behavior* (Vol. 18, pp. 75–109). Greenwich, CT: JAI Press.

Gilbert, D. T., Pinel, E. C., Wilson, T. D., Blumberg, S. J., & Wheatley, T. P. (1998). Immune neglect: A source of durability bias in affective forecasting. *Journal of Personality and Social Psychology, 75*(3), 617–638.

Greene, T. R., & Noice, H. (1988). Influence of positive affect upon creative thinking and problem solving in children. *Psychological Reports, 63,* 895–898.

Heller, W. (1997). Emotion. In M. Banich (Ed.), *Neuropsychology: The neural bases of mental function.* New York: Houghton Mifflin.

Hirt, E. R., Melton, R. J., McDonald, H. E., & Harackiewicz, J. M. (1996). Processing goals, task interest, and the mood–performance relationship: A mediational analysis. *Journal of Personality and Social Psychology, 71,* 245–261.

Isen, A. M. (1970). Success, failure attention and reactions to others: The warm glow of success. *Journal of Personality and Social Psychology, 17,* 107–112.

Isen, A. M. (1984). Toward understanding the role of affect in cognition. In R. Wyer & T. Srull (Eds.), *Handbook of social cognition* (pp. 179–236). Hillsdale, NJ: Erlbaum.

Isen, A. M. (1987). Positive affect, cognitive processes and social behavior. In L. Berkowitz (Ed.), *Advances in experimental social psychology* (pp. 203–253). New York: Academic Press.

Isen, A. M. (1990). The influence of positive and negative affect on cognitive organization: Implications for development. In N. Stein, B. Leventhal, & T. Trabasso (Eds.), *Psychological and biological processes in the development of emotion* (pp. 75–94). Hillsdale, NJ: Erlbaum.

Isen, A. M. (1993a). Positive affect and decision making. In M. Lewis & J. Haviland (Eds.) *Handbook of emotions* (pp. 261–277). New York: Guilford Press.

Isen, A. M. (1993b). The influence of positive affect on cognitive organization: Some implications for consumer decision making in response to advertising. In A. Mitchell (Ed.), *Advertising exposure, memory, and choice* (pp. 239–258). Hillsdale, NJ: Erlbaum.

Isen, A. M. (1999). Positive affect. In T. Dagleish & M. Power (Eds.), *Handbook of cognition and Emotion* (pp. 521–539). Sussex, UK: Wiley.

Isen, A. M. (2000). Positive affect and decision making. In M. Lewis & J. Haviland-Jones (Eds.). *Handbook of emotions* (2nd ed., pp. 417–435). New York: Guilford Press.

Isen, A. M. (2001). An influence of positive affect on decision making in complex situations: Theoretical issues with practical implications. *Journal of Consumer Psychology, 11*, 75–85.

Isen, A. M. (2002a). A role for neuropsychology in understanding the facilitating influence of positive affect on social behavior and cognitive processes. C. R. In Snyder & S. J. Lopez, (Eds.), *Handbook of positive psychology*. New York: Oxford University Press.

Isen, A. M. (2002b). Missing in action in the AIM: Positive affect's facilitation of cognitive flexibility, innovation, and problem solving. *Psychological Inquiry, 13*, 57–65.

Isen, A. M., & Baron, R. A. (1991). Positive affect in organizations. In L. Cummings & B. Staw (Eds.), *Research in organizational behavior* (pp. 1–52). Greenwich, CT: JAI Press.

Isen, A. M., Christianson, M., & Labroo, A. A. (2001). *The nature of the task influences whether positive affect facilitates task performance.* Manuscript, Cornell University.

Isen, A. M., & Daubman, K. A. (1984). The influence of affect on categorization. *Journal of Personality and Social Psychology, 47*, 1206–1217.

Isen, A. M., Daubman, K. A., & Gorgoglione, J. M. (1987). The influence of positive affect on cognitive organization: Implications for education. In R. E. Snow & M. J. Farr (Eds.), *Aptitude, learning, and instruction* (pp. 143–164). Hillsdale, NJ: Erlbaum.

Isen, A. M., Daubman, K. A., & Nowicki, G. P. (1987). Positive affect facilitates creative problem solving. *Journal of Personality and Social Psychology, 52*, 1122–1131.

Isen A. M., & Diamond, G. A. (1989). Affect and automaticity. In J. Uleman & J. A. Bargh (Eds.), *Unintended thought* (pp. 124–152). New York: Guilford Press.

Isen, A. M., & Geva, N. (1987). The influence of positive affect on acceptable level of risk: The person with a large canoe has a large worry. *Organizational Behavior and Human Decision Processes, 39*, 145–154.

Isen, A. M., & Hastorf, A. H. (1982). Some perspectives on cognitive social psychology. In A. H. Hastorf & A. M. Isen (Eds.), *Cognitive social psychology* (pp. 1–31). New York: Elsevier North-Holland.

Isen, A. M., Johnson, M. M. S., Mertz, E., & Robinson, F. G. (1985). The influence of positive affect on the unusualness of word association. *Journal of Personality and Social Psychology, 48*, 1413–1426.

Isen, A. M., & Levin, P. F. (1972). The effects of "feeling good" on helping: Cookies and kindness. *Journal of Personality and Social Psychology, 21*, 384–388.

Isen, A. M., & Means, B. (1983). The influence of positive affect on decision-making strategy. *Social Cognition, 2*, 18–31.

Isen, A. M., Niedenthal, P., & Cantor, N. (1992). The influence of positive affect on social categorization. *Motivation and Emotion, 16*, 65–78.

Isen, A. M., Nygren, T. E., & Ashby, F. G. (1988). The influence of positive affect on the perceived utility of gains and losses. *Journal of Personality and Social Psychology, 55*, 710–717.

Isen, A. M., & Patrick, R. (1983). The influence of positive feelings on risk taking: When the chips are down. *Organizational Behavior and Human Performance, 31*, 194–202.

Isen, A. M, Rosenzweig, A. S., & Young, M. J. (1991). The influence of positive affect on clinical problem solving. *Medical Decision Making, 11*, 221–227.

Isen, A. M., Shalker, T., Clark, M., & Karp, L. (1978). Affect, accessibility of material in memory, and behavior: A cognitive loop? *Journal of Personality and Social Psychology, 36*, 1–12.

Isen, A. M., & Stokker, L. G. (1996). *Positive affect reduces the "sunk-cost" effect.* Unpublished manuscript, Cornell University.

Isom, J., & Heller, W. (1999). Neurobiology of extraversion: Pieces of the puzzle still missing. *Behavioral and Brain Sciences, 22*, 524.

Kahn, B., & Isen, A. M. (1993). The influence of positive affect on variety-seeking among safe, enjoyable products. *Journal of Consumer Research, 20*, 257–270.

Kraiger, K., Billings, R. S., & Isen, A. M. (1989). The influence of positive affective states on task perceptions and satisfaction. *Organizational Behavior and Human Decision Processes, 44*, 12–25.

Labroo, A. A., Isen, A. M., & Shanteau, J. (2000). *The influence of positive affect on strategic decision making in "Prisoner's dilemma" situations.* Paper presented at the annual meeting of the Society for Judgment/Decision Making, New Orleans.

Lee, A., & Sternthal, B. (1999). The effects of positive mood on memory. *Journal of Consumer Research, 26*, 115–127.

Lewis, M., & Haviland-Jones, J. M. (2000). *Handbook of emotions* (2nd ed., pp. 417–435). New York: Guilford Press.

Lieberman, M. D., & Rosenthal, R. (2001). Why introverts can't always tell who likes them: Multiasking and nonverbal decoding. *Journal of Personality and Social Psychology, 80*(2), 294–310.

Lindsley, D. B. (1951). Emotion. In S. S. Stevens (Ed.), *Handbook of experimental psychology* (pp. 473–516). New York: Wiley.

Loewenstein, G. F., Weber, E. U., Hsee, C. K., & Welch, N. (2001). Risk as feelings. *Psychological Bulletin, 127*, 267–286.

Mackie, D. M., & Worth, L. T. (1989). Cognitive deficits and the mediation of positive affect in persuasion. *Journal of Personality and Social Psychology, 57*, 27–40.

Martin, L. L., Ward, D. W., Achee, J. W., & Wyer, R. S., Jr. (1993). Mood as input: People have to interpret the motivational implications of their moods. *Journal of Personality and Social Psychology, 64*, 317–326.

Mednick, M. T., Mednick, S. A., & Mednick, E. V. (1964). Incubation of creative performance and specific associative priming. *Journal of Abnormal and Social Psychology, 69*, 84–88.

Mellers, B. A. (2000). Choice and the relative pleasure of consequences. *Psychological Bulletin, 126*(6), 910–924.

Mellers, B. A., Schwartz, A., Ho, K., & Ritov, I. (1997). Decision affect theory: Emotional reactions to the outcomes of risky options. *Psychological Science, 8*(6), 423–429.

Northcraft, G. B., & Neale, M. A. (1986). Opportunity costs and the framing of resource allocation decisions. *Organizational Behavior and Human Decision Processes, 37*(3), 348–356.

Nygren, T. E., Isen, A. M., Taylor, P. J., & Dulin, J. (1996). The influence of positive affect on the decision rule in risk situations: Focus on outcome (and especially avoidance of loss) rather than probability. *Organizational Behavior and Human Decision Processes, 66*, 59–72.

Posner, M. I. (1978). *Chronometric explorations of mind*. Hillsdale, NJ: Erlbaum.

Posner, M. I., & Snyder, C. R. R. (1975). Attention and cognitive control. In R. L. Solso (Ed.), *Information processing and cognition: The Loyola Symposium* (pp. 55–85). Hillsdale, NJ: Erlbaum.

Schwartz, N., & Bless, H. (1991). Happy and mindless, but sad and smart? The impact of affective states on analytic reasoning. In J. P. Forgas (Ed.), *Emotion and social judgment* (pp. 55–71). Oxford: Pergamon Press.

Simon, H. A. (1967). Motivational and emotional controls of cognition. *Psychological Review, 74*, 29–39.

Staw, B. M. (1976). Knee-deep in the Big Muddy: A study of escalating commitment to a chosen course of action. *Organizational Behavior and Human Decision Processes, 16*, 27–44.

Staw, B. M., & Barsade, S. G. (1993). Affect and managerial performance: A test of the sadder-but-wiser vs. happier-and-smarter hypotheses. *Administrative Science Quarterly, 38*, 304–331.

Taylor, S. E., & Aspinwall, L. G. (1996). Mediating and moderating processes in psychosocial stress: Appraisal, coping, resistance and vulnerability. In H. B. Kaplan (Ed.), *Psychosocial stress: Perspectives on structure, theory, life-course, and methods* (pp. 71–110). San Diego, CA: Academic Press.

Teasdale, J. D., & Fogarty, S. J. (1979). Differential effects of induced mood on retrieval of pleasant and unpleasant events from episodic memory. *Journal of Abnormal Psychology, 88*, 248–257.

Teasdale, J. D., & Russell, M. L. (1983). Differential aspects of induced mood on the recall of positive, negative and neutral words. *British Journal of Clinical Psychology, 22,* 163–171.

Trope, Y., & Neter, E. (1994). Reconciling competing motives in self-evaluation: The role of self-control in feedback seeking. *Journal of Personality and Social Psychology, 66,* 646–657.

Trope, Y., & Pomerantz, E. M. (1998). Resolving conflicts among self-evaluative motives: Positive experiences as a resource for overcoming defensiveness. *Motivation and Emotion, 22,* 53–72.

Urada, D. I., & Miller, N. (2000). The impact of positive mood and category importance on crossed categorization effects. *Journal of Personality and Social Psychology, 78*(3), 417–433.

Weiss, H. M., Nicholas, J. P., & Daus, C. S. (1999). An examination of the joint effects of affective experiences and job beliefs on job satisfaction and variations in affective experiences over time. *Organizational Behavior and Human Decision Processes, 78*(1): 1–24.

Wilson, T. D., Wheatley, T. P., Meyers, J. M., Gilbert, D. T., & Axsom, D. (2000). Focalism: A source of durability bias in affective forecasting. *Journal of Personality and Social Psychology, 78*(5), 821–836.

12 What Do People Really Want?
Goals and Context in Decision Making

Sandra L. Schneider and Monica D. Barnes

ABSTRACT

In standard economic and decision theory, it has been assumed that all decision makers have the same goal: to maximize expected utility. This chapter
presents evidence of alternative goals of decision makers and alternative
frameworks for understanding how these goals motivate decision making.
Decisions that are likely to influence an individual's policies are also likely
to be driven by specific goals. The results of an exploratory study show that
people believe their decisions are motivated by approximately eight distinct factors that cut across gender, age, and time horizon. These include relationship, financial, personal satisfaction, career, education, leisure, health,
and instrumental goals. These goals are further elaborated with respect to
motives identified as essential within evolutionary and motivational theories. The importance of incorporating these goals into theories of decision
making is discussed. In addition, the value of temporal and situational
contexts in decision making is explored, as well as the need to address
issues such as goal conflict, goal compatibility, and priorities.

CONTENTS

Replete with terms such as *probability, utility, rationality, optimizing, maximizing, attributes, alternatives, decision weights, heuristics, biases,* and *errors,* the classic vocabulary of decision-making research says a great deal about common assumptions of the critical variables of investigation. Much less common in the vocabulary are concepts such as *goals, priorities, balance, conflict, involvement, time, happiness, hope, fear, control, self-regard, fairness,* or *meaning.* Although there are exceptions (e.g., Isen, 1993; Lopes, 1987; Schneider, 2001; Weber, Baron, & Loomes, 2001), approaches to decision making often seem to focus on the process of decision making, without much attention to the goals and motives of the decision maker. Indeed, goals are often presumed in the form of utility maximization, and decision makers are sometimes deemed irrational for apparently not adhering to this as their primary goal (e.g., Dawes, 1988; Luce & Raiffa, 1957; Schoemaker, 1982; von Neumann & Morgenstern, 1944).

One of the concerns with the latter approach is that goals are likely to be far richer than what can be captured in utility-maximizing models. At the very least, empirical and theoretical attention to goals seems prerequisite to any meaningful understanding of decision-making processes or outcomes. The study of goals can elucidate why people make decisions, what kinds of decision strategies they adopt, and what constraints are experienced throughout the decision-making process.

The Decision Context

Most theories of decision making are concerned with *how* people make decisions (e.g., Baron, 1988; Dawes, 1988; Yates, 1990). Although this is indeed an important area of study, there is often little attempt to evaluate scientifically what may be the more fundamental question: *Why* do people make decisions? Until we understand how external circumstances, inherited predispositions, and psychological processes combine to evoke decision processes, we are unlikely to develop a deep understanding of how these processes operate in practice.

Perhaps the simplest answer to the "why" question is that people make decisions in order to guide behavior. This answer may seem less than satisfying because it is too open-ended. At any given moment, there may be infinitely many behaviors that one could consider. The simple answer does not provide any insight into how people define decision situations so that they can identify which sorts of things might be considered among the possible options. But that may also be what makes this kind of answer valuable. It does not allow us to bypass fundamental issues concerning how we come to define decision situations (Day, 1988; Newell & Simon, 1988; Svenson, 1999) and what it is that people feel they need to make decisions about. Much of the essence of decision making may be lost in theoretical frameworks, implying that choices and option sets present themselves or can be treated as given (see also Goldstein & Weber, 1995).

Policy Decisions: Guides for Day-to-Day Behavior

So where do we begin in thinking about decisions as guides to behavior? Is it reasonable to assume that the bulk of our behavior results from decision making? There has been a relatively long-standing controversy about the extent to which our behaviors are consequences of conscious decision making (e.g., Bargh & Chartrand, 1999; Cialdini, 1993; Langer, 1978, 1997). People are often described as operating on "automatic pilot" or as being "lazy thinkers." There seem to be many instances in which we are engaged in complex goal-directed behavior, but we are not engaged in much thought or conscious decision making.

Obviously, reflexes and autonomic responses are among those behaviors that do not require decisions. But there are many more complex behaviors that we perform in a more or less automatic fashion. Highly practiced behaviors, for instance, become routinized until they can be carried out without conscious attention. (Consider the classic demonstrations by Newell & Rosenbloom, 1981, and by Shiffrin & Schneider, 1977.) Several researchers have distinguished between decisions that require little thought and those that are more complex. Svenson's (1999) *level 1 decisions* and Klein's (1997) *recognition-primed decisions* are described as relatively routine decisions that are made without much thought. They simply require a recognition process to initiate the decision to enact a familiar behavior pattern (e.g., deciding to enter an intersection when the traffic signal turns green).

Others have described these types of decisions (or at least a subset of them) as *policies* (e.g., Chapman, 1997; Redelmeier & Tversky, 1992). Policies are decision routines that originally occurred through conscious attention and evaluation, but that over time have become part of a routine (e.g., brushing one's teeth or taking vitamins). This perspective serves to remind us that routine sequences of behavior are typically dependent on thoughtful decision making in their origins. Decisions are likely to be essential in determining most of the routines that will be developed to ease our day-to-day decision-making burden. Where will a person choose to work? How will the person choose to get there? These types of decisions, once made, can be the basis for developing routines. However, without these decisions, it is unlikely that people could develop meaningful action plans.

Decisions that contribute to the establishment of behavioral routines can be thought of as personal *policy decisions*. Once a person makes a decision with policy implications for routine behaviors, the routine can be established and then carried out repeatedly without much additional decision making, unless something interferes with the routine or there is a change in the person's goals. Policy decisions are likely to be considered important in that they imply a commitment to a continuing course of action, and they also imply a person's priorities. By establishing these things in advance, policy decisions reduce the risk that resulting automatic or routine behavior will be inconsistent with desired goals.

The decision to buy a home, for instance, is a policy decision in that it establishes a routine concerning where a person will reside for an extended period. Buying a home suggests a commitment to continuing to return to that place on a daily basis. It also implicitly suggests priorities in the form of tradeoffs between conflicting goals and values. Goals concerning cost, type of dwelling, dwelling attributes, neighborhood, proximity to work or school, and so on will each be given more or less weight in determining the choice. If more than one person (e.g., a couple or family) is involved in the purchase, negotiating goal priorities is also likely to be involved. Having a home also reduces the need to decide on a continuing basis where one will go to seek food and shelter. Without a home, one can imagine that these needs would consume much conscious thought and prevent attention to higher-order goals and decisions.

It is our contention that personal policy decisions are of fundamental significance in people's lives but that research on decision making has paid very little attention to these types of choices as a class. Nor has there been any focus on the impact that these types of decisions are likely to have on life satisfaction and quality of life. Instead, the typical approach has intentionally decontextualized the decision-making process in order to identify quantifiable and generalizable variables that might be combined to develop general (descriptive, normative, and prescriptive) rules of decision making. Although it sounds like a reasonable strategy, removing the context in decision making may be equivalent to throwing out the baby with the bath.

Goals and the Decision Context

Decision context is likely to provide structure to a decision situation and provide constraints on subjective values. For instance, the choice between a new stereo system and a gallon of water may seem obvious, unless of course the context involves being stranded in a desert. Context is also important in evaluating the meaning of outcomes. Decision consequences have typically been evaluated in terms of the rationality of the process generating the outcome, and not in terms of how the consequences are experienced by the decision maker (see also Peterson, Miranda, Smith, & Haskell, this volume). The strict decision-making criteria for rationality in the form of consistency and coherence (for a review see Hammond, 2000) may not in practice be nearly as important as criteria such as personal satisfaction and fulfillment. This is especially so when circumstances are changing. When contexts change, preferences are also likely to change as priorities shift.

Though decontextualizing decision situations has been a popular strategy in the interest of deriving basic principles, the study of decision making has not been completely devoid of context. Decision research has typically focused on decision contexts involving monetary or material goals, usually expressed as gambles (see Goldstein & Weber, 1995). Research paradigms adopting this focus have the advantage of working with goals that are easy to operationalize and manipulate. Furthermore, monetary units seem to provide a medium for capturing subjective value or subjective utility across a large set of decision domains (e.g., Garrod & Willis, 1999; Hausman, 1993). However, monetary units may not be an acceptable currency for representing subjective values, just as financial goals may not adequately substitute for the wide range of goals that we aspire to in our lives. In many cases, financial goals may be in conflict with other types of goals.

Consider, for instance, a couple's decision about whether to have children. This is clearly a policy decision in that the couple will establish a multitude of long-standing routines as a function of the choice made. However, the decision does not seem to be reducible in any satisfying way to monetary equivalents. Financial concerns may well be an element in the couple's decision, but many might reasonably feel that the couple is missing the point should they attempt to reduce the decision to one involving monetary equivalents for the value of expected experiences. Even if one argues that value can be measured with a more generic utility unit that is not monetary in essence, there is still the question of whether or how the value of various aspects of the decision options can be made comparable. And even this ignores the need for the couple to communicate and negotiate with one another to arrive at a mutually agreeable decision.

The tendency to rely on monetary decision goals is problematic not only because it trivializes the difficulties in integrating values across disparate dimensions, but also because it obscures the need to understand the goals that motivate decisions. Increasing material wealth is likely to be an important goal for many people in many situations, but comparisons between the importance of financial goals and other types of goals have not been seriously considered. Within the domain of decisions that are likely to have policy implications for daily living, financial considerations are likely to play a key role. However, to understand how the need to decide emerges and how contextual variables may impact the decision process, we must also be aware of other critical goals that may support or conflict with financial interests.

In the remainder of this chapter, we first describe an exploratory study examining the goals that people spontaneously report as driving their decisions. We then compare these results to expectations derived from theoretical perspectives on motivation and evolutionary processes in order to develop a more holistic sense of critical decision variables. The contrast between this holistic perspective and traditional utility theories of decision making is then used to suggest that substantial advances in the field are likely to require attention to situational and temporal contexts, as well as the interplay between goals and priorities.

Goals That Drive Decisions: An Exploratory Study

Because decisions guide behavior, the goals that motivate the decision process become of fundamental interest in understanding why decisions are made and in providing benchmarks for measuring the qualitative success of decisions. One way to discover goals that are influential

Table 12.1. *Breakdown of the Number of Participants According to Age and Gender*

Group	Age in Years	No. of Females	No. of Males
Young adults	18–29	85	34
Midcareer adults	30–44	81	63
Late-career adults	45–59	79	57
Senior adults	60–95	<u>15</u>	<u>16</u>
TOTALS:		260	170

in decision making is to simply ask people about the goals that their decisions are intended to support. In our exploratory study, we did just that. We collected descriptive data from a large group to explore the types and frequency of commonly sought-after goals, both in the short run and in the long run. We examined the goals of males and females in four groups ranging from young adults to senior citizens, and we inquired about three different time horizons. In this way, we hoped to cover a wide spectrum of people, situations, and temporal considerations so that we would obtain at least a taste of the diversity that may exist in the goals that drive personal policy and day-to-day decisions.

Method

Participants. The sample consisted of 260 females and 170 males ranging in age from 18 to 95 years. Students in an undergraduate psychology class were invited to participate in the study and were also given the opportunity to recruit up to four of their acquaintances who were over the age of 29. The breakdown of participants into age groups is presented in Table 12.1. Participants in the young adult group consisted entirely of students from the class, and the remaining groups consisted primarily of their family members, relatives, and neighbors. Because this is a sample of convenience, results must be interpreted cautiously. Nevertheless, the general pattern of results may be instructive.

Measures and Procedure. Participants were asked to complete three tasks, all prefaced by the following statement: "We make lots of decisions in our lives aimed at accomplishing a variety of different goals. I am interested in what some of these goals are." Each of the tasks was then listed, with the admonishment to please complete the given task before proceeding to the next. The first task read: "Think about your entire life. List 3 of your

Lifetime Goals." The second task read: "Think about the next 3–5 years of your life. List 3 of your *Goals for the Next 3–5 Years."* The third and final task read: "Think about the next week of your life. List 3 of your *Goals for the Next Week."* Participants were given as much time as necessary (typically about 5 to 10 minutes) to complete the task, inserting their goals in an open-ended format.

Response Coding. The nine responses (three goals × three time horizons) of each participant were transcribed into cells in a spreadsheet. In order to evaluate the responses, phrases were coded to develop categories of goals. The preliminary coding scheme was developed by a single coder who attempted to arrange goals into fewer than a dozen categories. To our surprise, this task was much simpler than we expected. Ten categories emerged, and after review, two of the categories were subsumed under other existing categories, leaving a final set of eight categories.

Two independent coders were then trained in the coding system and asked to categorize each of the goals in the spreadsheet. Agreement among coders was nearly perfect, with occasional exceptions, typically when items seemed to represent more than one category. These statements were discussed and then categorized by reaching a consensus among all coders. In some cases, it was obvious that a goal involved more than one category. These cases were double-coded to designate the desire to reach more than one goal simultaneously. (For example, the goal of "having a satisfying and high-paying career" was coded both as a career goal and as a financial goal.)

Results

The overriding purpose of the analysis was to determine the most common types of goals people report as motivating their decision making. A secondary goal was to gain a preliminary sense of how these goals may vary as a function of gender, age, and the time horizon for planning. The first part of the analysis focused on the eight goals that emerged repeatedly in participants' responses, with a discussion of differences in the goals' prevalence for males and females and across the four age groups identified in the previous section. The second part of the analysis focused on the time horizon of the goals, looking at variations in the types of goals that operate within windows of weeks or years or a lifetime.

Table 12.2. *Sample Goals*

Relationship	Financial
To be happily married	To own my own home
To have/enjoy a family	To get/stay out of debt
Close relationships with friends and family	To make a good living
Career	Instrumental
To have a rewarding career	To clean the house
To start my own business	To keep up with the yard
To have a career in _____	To be more organized
Personal	Health
To be respected	To stay healthy
To be happy	To maintain a healthy diet
To be a good person	To exercise regularly
Leisure	Education
To travel (to _____)	To graduate from college
To have more free time	To earn a Ph.D.
To learn or engage in a hobby	To get a degree in _____

Eight Recurring Goals in Decision Making. Although our survey covered a wide range of age groups and three distinct time horizons, there emerged a small and cohesive set of goals that people reported as motivations for most of their decisions. These goal categories are listed in Table 12.2 along with representative sample items.

On average, the most frequently mentioned type of goal concerned *relationships* with others. Ninety percent of the 430 participants included at least one relationship goal in their set of reported goals. Most often, these relationship goals referred to family members, especially partners and children. The popularity of relationship goals was similar across all groups of participants. The percent of participants reporting at least one relationship goal ranged from a low of 82% for males aged 45–59 to a high of 100% for females aged 60–95. Overall, there was no significant difference in the percentage of males and females reporting relationship goals. The vast majority of people routinely reported decision-making goals aimed at establishing and maintaining high-quality relationships with others.

As might be expected based on the emphasis in the literature, *financial goals* were also routinely reported. Over three-quarters of the participants felt that financial concerns served an important motivational function in their decision making. Although the proportions for males and females were comparable, there was a marked difference in prevalence across age groups. Neither the younger (18–29) nor the older (60–95) groups of participants were as concerned about financial goals as the middle-aged groups (30–59). Over 80% of the middle-aged groups focused on financial goals, compared to about 60% in the younger and older groups.

Career goals were the next most likely type of goal, with 67% of participants mentioning them. Although career goals tended to be slightly less common among women (64%) than men (72%), this trend was not reliable taken as a whole ($\chi^2[1] = 3.38$, $p < .07$). However, within the age range of 30–59 years, career goals among men (78%) were much more prevalent than among women (62%), $\chi^2[1] = 8.67$, $p < .01$. For both women and men, about three-fourths of the youngest groups (18–29) reported goals related to their career, whereas the oldest groups were far less likely to be interested in career goals (only 15%).

Perhaps the most unexpected category of goals is what we refer to as *instrumental goals*. These goals include a wide variety of tasks focused on maintaining the quality of life at home or at work. These tasks often involve establishing or restoring order or cleanliness, but they may also involve repairs, home improvements, and increased efficiency through better organization. Males and females shared a concern for these instrumental goals, with approximately 65% of both groups listing at least one such goal. Across age groups, the pattern was similar to that found for financial goals. Whereas 74% of the middle-aged groups (30–59) included instrumental goals among their priorities, only about half of the people in the youngest (18–29) or oldest (60–95) groups reported goals concerning these types of issues.

For the first four categories just described, males and females shared the same ranking of relative goal popularity. For the fifth category, however, males and females began to deviate from one another slightly. For females the next most commonly cited goal involved *personal or spiritual well-being*, whereas for males the next most popular goal involved engaging in *leisure activities*. The difference in the popularity of personal goals between females (61%) and males (55%) was small and potentially unreliable ($p = .23$). The rates of personal goal setting among the youngest group (18–29) of males compared to females were indistinguishable (65%), with the suggestion that if there are potential gender-based discrepancies, they may be confined to the older groups (though post hoc tests only approached significance).

In contrast, there was a marked difference in the endorsement rates of leisure goals by males (57%) and females (43%), $\chi^2[1] = 8.50$, $p < .01$.

The patterns across age groups was also quite different for males and females. For males, leisure goals followed the same pattern as described previously in the case of financial and instrumental goals. The 30–59 age groups (60%) were more likely to list leisure goals than either the younger or older group (44%). For females, leisure goals were least likely to appear for those in the 30–45 age bracket (33%), intermediate for the 18–29 and 45–59 age groups (45%), and by far the most likely to be included for those in the 60–95 age group (67%).

For both males and females, *health goals* were sixth in the rankings of relative likelihood. About 55% of persons of both genders felt that health-related goals motivated some of their decision making. The trend across age groups was similar for males and females. As one might predict, health goals became increasingly popular as the age bracket increased, from an endorsement rate of about 40% in the youngest group (18–29) to about 80% in the oldest group (60–95).

The final goal category that was prevalent in the responses of participants involved *education*. Interestingly, females (52%) were much more likely than males (35%) to list educational goals, $\chi^2[1] = 11.77$, $p < .001$. Although over 90% of both male and female participants were concerned about education in the youngest age bracket, education was a much more common goal among females aged 30–59 years (33%) than among similarly aged males (21%). This pattern among the middle-aged groups is just the opposite of what was found for career goals, potentially suggesting that more of the men in the sample fulfilled their educational goals in earlier years compared to the women.

About 10% of the goals listed for both males and females fell into a miscellaneous category. In most cases, it was not possible to categorize these responses because the ultimate purpose of the stated goal could not be discerned. For example, a relatively common response within this category was "move to _____." However, nothing in the response indicated why the person wanted to move to the designated location. With further prodding, it seems likely that the response would fall into one or more of the eight categories just described.

Decision Goals and Time Horizons. Participants volunteered goals for three different time horizons: the next week, the next 3–5 years, and their lifetime. The three different time horizons were examined to begin to get a sense of how goals are likely to vary as a function of the amount of time one has to make decisions aimed at fulfilling the goal. Figure 12.1

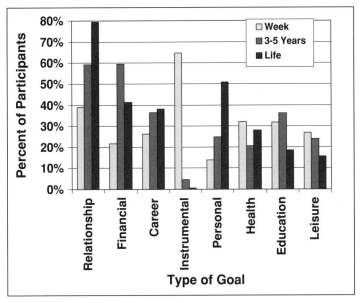

Figure 12.1 Percentage of participants who reported goals in each of the eight categories compared across three different time horizons.

presents a graph of the percentage of participants reporting goals within each of the eight previously identified categories, separated according to the time horizon in which the goal was reported.

Although Figure 12.1 shows the eight goal categories listed roughly from most to least frequently endorsed overall, it is obvious that time horizon has a strong influence on the likelihood that particular types of goals will be identified as priorities. The only goals that remain prominent across all three time horizons are the relationship goals, with over one-third of the participants endorsing a relationship goal in the next week, in the next 3–5 years, and in their lives.

In the short term, the instrumental goals stand out above all others. Almost two-thirds of the participants listed these kinds of maintenance or organizational goals as one of their top three goals for the upcoming week. The prevalence of instrumental goals is mediated almost entirely by time horizon, with 5% or fewer endorsing these types of goals within longer time periods. Although speculative, it seems that preoccupation with these types of goals in the short term is likely to make it more difficult to focus on other potentially more fulfilling goals.

Over 80% of the youngest participants were motivated by education goals in the short term, and over one-third of the older groups reported short-term health goals. As mentioned previously, almost 40% of participants also included relationship goals in their next week's priorities. Financial, career, and leisure goals were somewhat less common in the short term, and personal satisfaction goals were among the least likely when considering decision needs for the next week.

When the horizon shifted to 3–5 years, relationship and financial goals were among most participants' priorities, especially among the middle-aged groups. Career and education goals were among the most common in 3- to 5-year planning for those in the younger age brackets. Health goals were again typical among members of older groups, and leisure goals were especially frequent among middle-aged males. Personal satisfaction goals were included by about 20% of participants across most age brackets.

Relationship goals clearly predominated when goals for life were considered. Personal satisfaction goals were also quite likely to be among people's goal priorities for their lives. For other goals, the patterns were quite similar to those for the 3- to 5-year horizon. Career and education goals were common in younger groups, financial goals were especially likely in middle-aged groups, and health goals were typical among older groups. Instrumental goals were essentially nonexistent within a lifetime horizon.

One might have expected greater similarity across age groups when reflecting on lifetime priorities, given that participants were instructed to consider goals for their entire lives. The differences across age groups could be cohort effects given that the different age groups have lived through different historical time periods (though the pattern of results seems rather predictable independent of group historical differences). Alternatively, it may be that participants interpreted the survey question to refer to the remainder of their lives rather than their lives from the beginning. Yet another possibility is that people's mental time horizons are not flexible enough to encompass an entire lifetime, with a bias toward goals that currently seem of long-term importance. Regardless, people in all age brackets tended to agree that relationship, personal satisfaction, and financial goals were priorities within the scope of their lives.

Summary and Study Conclusions

There were highly consistent themes in the goals that this sample of people reported as influences on their decision making. Using only eight categories of goals, it was possible to identify the themes of 90% of the stated goals in this study (and possibly more if additional clarifying information had been available). For both genders, all age groups, and all time horizons, relationship goals were among the most common goals. Moreover, the likelihood of reporting relationship goals increased as the time horizon grew.

Goals in the service of short-term decision making were dominated by an instrumental focus on maintaining order, good repair, and cleanliness in the home and workplace. These instrumental goals essentially introduced a lack of correspondence between short- and long-term goals. It may be that the immediacy of these instrumental goals routinely diminishes the capacity of decision makers to focus on more fulfilling longer-term goals.

As might be expected based on the monetary focus of so much of the decision literature, financial goals were frequent, especially within longer time frames and among those who were in the 30–59 age bracket. Personal satisfaction goals were also typical priorities for all groups of participants in longer time frames. Education and career goals were reported to motivate much of the decision making of younger groups, whereas health concerns were prominent among older participants. Leisure goals received moderate support across all three time horizons and were especially pronounced for middle-aged males.

To the extent that these findings seem predictable or mundane, one might anticipate that these goals are typically incorporated in the study of decision making. However, the tools of decision science currently seem ill-equipped to provide useful insights into how decisions are shaped by these goals. Consider the idiosyncrasies inherent in decisions driven by relationship goals. Negotiation, decision analysis, and game theory literatures (e.g., Bazerman & Neale, 1993; Keeney & Raiffa, 1993; Luce & Raiffa, 1957; Shubik, 1982; Thompson, Levine, & Messick, 1999) provide relevant and helpful perspectives with respect to the allocation of certain types of resources. However, concepts such as *payoff structures, probability estimates,* and *certainty equivalents* may not provide convincing analogies to the issues that seem tractable or essential in real-world relationship contexts. Similar concerns seem warranted with regard to the other goal categories. The structure of these types of decisions may not be discernible without sensitivity to the human context that is responsible for these goals.

Evolutionary and Motivational Perspectives on the Human Context

To understand what drives decision making and the behavior that results, more is required than a simple exploratory study. There is a long
history of research and theory focusing on the fundamental processes
that motivate behavior (if not decision making per se). Although a complete review is beyond the scope of this chapter, it may be instructive
to summarize some of the more common themes, with a focus on how
these fundamental goals and motives are likely to impact decision making. A review of both evolutionary and motivation literatures reveals
survival, relationship, and mastery motives as essential.

Survival Motives and Basic Needs

From an evolutionary perspective, the primary goal of any organism
is survival. Darwin's (1859, 1871) notion of *survival of the fittest* is by
now cliché. Survival, of course, requires fulfillment of basic needs
through acts such as eating and drinking. Not surprisingly, survival
needs figure prominently in most major theories of human motivation.
They are represented in the primary drives identified by behaviorists
such as Hull (1943, 1952) and encompass the lowest level of Maslow's
(1962, 1970) hierarchy of needs. Other needs relating to survival are
found in the second level of Maslow's hierarchy: ensuring safety through
adequate shelter and ample resources. Although we may rarely think
about it, these needs are undoubtedly powerful motivating forces when
unmet, and are prerequisites to even considering the pursuit of higher-
order goals. For those who face threats to survival like starvation and
exposure to the elements, decisions are likely to focus exclusively on
these goals until basic needs are met.

Although basic survival needs were not among the eight goals identified in our exploratory study, there are at least three obvious links.
First, health concerns were among the eight commonly reported goals
of participants. Although they were prevalent primarily among older
adults, this is probably because the health of younger adults was not
perceived to be threatened.

The basic needs were more broadly reflected in a second type of goal,
namely, the instrumental goals. Considering Maslow's hierarchy and
the primacy of basic needs, it becomes increasingly obvious why instrumental goals are so prevalent in day-to-day plans. These goals, which

appeared almost exclusively in the short term, included items reflecting basic needs such as going grocery shopping, getting the heating system repaired, and cleaning the house. Instrumental goals may serve the function of preventing basic needs from evolving into threats that would require long-term attention or concern. For this reason, instrumental goals are likely to be salient, immediate, and recurring, with clear-cut criteria for acceptable outcomes. Under normal conditions, the recurring nature of most basic needs may supply the necessary conditions for effective routines to develop. Once policy decisions are in place, many basic needs may be met with little conscious decision-making effort. In contrast, higher-order goals are likely to require more conscious thought and long-term behavioral commitments to reach meaningful levels of achievement.

The third type of goal related to basic needs is the financial category of goals. For basic needs, monetary goals may have substantial value as a surrogate, provided that the decision context is one in which there is a functioning market economy. With enough money, problems of adequate food and shelter can be addressed. Financial success can also contribute to the likelihood of achieving other higher-order goals such as reaching educational and career aspirations. Both aspects of the role of finances were evident in our data, with some financial goals focused on being able to buy or rent a home or obtain money to pay household bills and others focused on obtaining high-paying jobs. Nevertheless, financial goals may be particularly powerful with respect to basic needs. Indeed, the role of money in perceived happiness and satisfaction in life has been shown to be quite strong in situations of relative poverty, where challenges to basic needs are more likely, but insignificant in cases where basic needs have been adequately met (for a review see Argyle, 1999).

Relationships and Sexual Motives

Our relationships with others are fundamental parts of our lives and one of the major predictors of life satisfaction (Myers, 1999). Based on evolutionary and motivational theories as well as common sense, it is no surprise that relationship issues figure prominently among people's goals.

Some form of attachment to others is common to all mammals, especially infant–parent bonds. Parental and romantic attachments are also typical. These attachments involve the desire to be near particular individuals, the experience of distress when separated from these individuals, and reduced stress levels when in the presence of one another (Mason & Mendoza, 1998). Basic brain mechanisms have been found to promote these types of attachments in mammals (for reviews see Carter, 1998; Insel & Young, 2000). These mechanisms encourage us to seek approval from others, and they enhance the desire to be involved in meaningful relationships.

Not surprisingly, the primacy of our relationships with other humans is reflected in most major theories of human motivation. Hull (1943, 1952) recognized the need for sex as among the primary biological drives of organisms. Within Maslow's (1962, 1970) hierarchy, relationship goals comprise the third and fourth levels, although the goals are characterized more in interpersonal rather than biological terms. Maslow described the need for love or belongingness and the need for esteem from others as the primary interpersonal concerns that we strive to meet once the more basic survival needs have been satisfied. Murray (1938) described the need for affiliation as 1 of 20 important human needs. Early research (e.g., Atkinson, Heyns, & Veroff, 1954; Heckhausen, 1980) operationalized the need for affiliation as being concerned with interpersonal security, desire to feel accepted by others, and fear of rejection from others. This approach was criticized for focusing too heavily on avoiding social rejection and was later expanded to include the need for intimacy, which focuses on engaging in close, positive interpersonal relations (Boyatzis, 1973; McAdams, 1982). Relationship goals are also seen as primary in recent motivational theories focused more narrowly on the organization of controlled (or conscious) human behavior. For instance, in their self-determination theory, Deci and Ryan (1985, 1991; Ryan, 1993) identify relatedness as one of three essential psychological needs.

Empirical evidence has also suggested the importance of relationship goals in subjective well-being. For instance, Kasser and Ryan (1993, 1996; Ryan, Sheldon, Kasser, & Deci, 1996) found that those who placed more emphasis on fulfilling relationships over other, more extrinsic goals such as financial success tended to report greater self-actualization, vitality, and psychological well-being, and exhibited lower incidences of depression and anxiety. Also, success with close relationships (i.e., a successful marriage) has been linked to greater subjective well-being or life satisfaction, as well as better health and a longer life span (for a review see Myers, 1999). It has also been shown that those who value relationships as a means to other ends rather than as something of intrinsic worth tend to be psychologically less well off (Blais, Sabourin,

Boucher, & Vallerand, 1990; Rempel, Holmes, & Zanna, 1985; Seligman, Fazio, & Zanna, 1980).

Evolutionary theory also emphasizes relationships to the extent that they are necessary for procreation. Darwin (1859, 1871) argued that two major forces drive the evolution of living beings: competition for survival (natural selection) and competition for reproduction (sexual selection). Although natural selection has been a fundamental guiding principle of evolutionary biology since Darwin's time, sexual selection has only recently been reconsidered as a potentially powerful driving force behind the evolution of sexually reproducing species (for a review see Miller, 2000).

Competition for survival is a process wherein those who are best suited for their environment live longer into adulthood and thus have more opportunity to pass their genes on to future generations. As we have discussed, the basic motives of hunger, thirst, pain avoidance, and so on contribute to the success of this competition. Relationship motives may also be important to survival, particularly with respect to the formation of social groups and societies. The formation of social groups has enhanced survival chances through a number of advantages, such as the distribution of labor (and the resulting developments in domain expertise), the reduction of redundancies (e.g., by housing more than one individual in a given dwelling), and improved protection in the form of strength in numbers.

Nevertheless, surviving to a ripe old age is almost trivial from an evolutionary perspective unless survival increases the odds of passing along one's genes. This aspect of evolutionary selection is referred to as the *competition for reproduction*. Organisms must find mates, preferably mates who will provide healthy genes to offspring and, in the case of humans at least, who will provide support in raising those offspring to adulthood. This increases the chances that children survive into adulthood and produce grandchildren, thus continuing the life span of genes.

One might expect that the only implication of sexual selection is that we would have evolved with a strong desire to mate and that we would regularly seek out potential mates. However, the ramifications may be much more powerful and extend to a much larger domain of behaviors than was previously recognized. In the competition for reproduction, an organism is at an advantage if it can influence the choices of other members of its own species. In other words, success in the competition for reproduction is likely to depend on the ability to attract partners and to persuade them to agree to mate. The pressure to reproduce successfully is distinct from the pressure to survive in that it is directly linked to the preferences of same-species organisms and is not so dependent on the idiosyncrasies of the environment. According to Miller (2000), this fact may help us understand long-standing goals that promote the development of language, social skills, physical attractiveness, and other attributes that are helpful in securing mating prospects.

Miller (2000) argues that sexual selection may have played a key role in the evolutionary development of our higher-order thought processes. Sexual selection involves choosing to mate with those who show evidence of having the best possible genes to pass on to our offspring (increasing the survival prospects of our children) and, in turn, making ourselves attractive enough to convince these high-quality individuals to mate. In order to encourage those with the best genes to mate with us and give us support in making sure that our children survive into adulthood, many of our mental abilities may have evolved to elicit liking, status, and support from others.

Our physical attractiveness, ability to entertain others, athletic ability, respectable careers, good educations, and caring and generous demeanors are all ways in which we can elicit admiration and respect from others. These abilities may provide benefits from an evolutionary perspective not only when dealing directly with potential mates, but also when dealing with relatives, potential friends, and others who have the ability to increase our social status (increasing our mating prospects) or provide social support in times of need (increasing the survival potential of ourselves and our offspring). If Miller (2000) is correct about the evolutionary implications of relationship goals, then most decision contexts may ultimately have relationship goals at their essence. Certainly, the preponderance of relationship goals that were manifest in reports of people throughout various stages of their lives and across several time horizons confirms that decisions with consequences for relationships are worthy of particular attention in research and theory.

Mastering the Environment

Another set of primary motivators focuses on the need to acquire knowledge, skills, and other positive attributes in order to make sense of and exert some control over the world. Several theories of motivation have pointed to these goals as being of primary importance in human motivation. White (1959) proposed that competence should be included among the basic drives outlined by Hull and others. He argued that competence is essential in that it involves being able to deal with the environment in an efficacious manner. This obviously has survival implications, but it also serves as a catalyst for curious, explorative, and creative behaviors. White described the striving for competence as a major motivator, with success producing feelings of effectance.

This need to feel that one can deal with the challenges of life in an effective manner is the essence of several other motivational theories. Murray (1938) developed the concept of *need for achievement*, which involves striving to overcome obstacles in an efficient and competent manner as well as being able to exercise power. This need is seen as arising from positive previous experiences of achievement. The concept of need for achievement was later elaborated by Atkinson (1964), who stressed that need for achievement interacts with another motivation, that of avoiding failure. The theory of achievement motivation asserts that striving to meet the challenges of life in a successful manner is important for people, and can have implications for the types of endeavors people choose to take on as well as the outcomes of those endeavors.

Maslow's (1962, 1970) hierarchy also reflects recognition of the importance of mastery experiences, though perhaps at a loftier scale. The need for self-actualization, which is the highest goal of humans in his hierarchy, taps into humans' need to grow and expand their skills and attributes, thereby increasing their ability to live with continued successes.

Attribution theory (Heider, 1958; Jones & Davis, 1965; Kelley, 1967, 1972; Weiner, 1985), which has had a huge impact in social psychology, is founded on assumptions about the importance of mastery. The link between experience of control and psychological well-being has become fundamental to the theory. There is an abundance of evidence documenting that lack of a sense of control can lead to learned helplessness and depression (Abramson, Seligman, & Teasdale, 1978; Seligman, 1975). Weiner (1985) introduced the popular expression *locus of control*, and provided evidence of the importance of perceptions of control and need for achievement in relation to attribution theory.

In his highly influential theory, Bandura (1977, 1982) also addressed mastery motives through the introduction of the concept of *self-efficacy*, the expectation that one can perform desired actions successfully. As with need for achievement, the level of self-efficacy that a person experiences is modulated by the outcomes of previous attempts to meet challenges, and high levels of self-efficacy are related to success in tasks.

Deci and Ryan's (Deci & Ryan, 1985, 1991; Ryan, 1993) needs for competence and autonomy also reflect an organism's need for mastery over its environment. As with relationships goals, these researchers (Kasser & Ryan 1993, 1996, Ryan et al., 1996) found that people who place more emphasis on personal growth over other, more extrinsic goals report greater self-actualization, vitality, and psychological well-being and exhibit lower incidences of depression and anxiety.

These needs have been central in psychological theorizing on motivation and can also be examined in light of evolutionary pressure. Mastery contributes to the competition for survival by increasing the ability to make predictions about and control one's environment. Mastery may also contribute to the competition for reproduction in that demonstrating competence can help to win the esteem of others, including potential mates.

Mastery goals of at least three different types were evident in the results of our study. The goals associated with education, career, and personal satisfaction were typically aimed at improving the ability to control various aspects of the environment. Even leisure goals were often associated with mastery. Many of these goals involved activities that require or contribute to mastery, such as participating in sports, working with volunteer groups, and exploring new places.

Among the most popular personal satisfaction goals were items that seem to reflect the perceived importance of social responsibility and of obtaining pleasure from life. These themes appeared in goals such as "I want to be a good person" and "I want to find happiness." Although these goals may not seem to be focused exclusively on mastery, they are goals that depend critically on gaining competence in social and personal realms. There has recently been an increasing focus in the literature on socioemotional skills and their benefits for successfully negotiating social environments.

Damasio (e.g., 1994), for instance, has suggested that reasoning behavior is fundamentally tied to the functioning of emotion centers in the brain. Damage to these centers has routinely been associated with profound losses in the ability to behave in a socially acceptable fashion, with severely debilitating consequences. Similarly, Goleman (1995) has presented evidence in support of his contention that *emotional intelligence* is a more reliable predictor of most measures of success than the kinds of academic intelligence captured by constructs such as IQ. In addition, socioemotional selectivity theory (Carstensen, Isaacowitz, & Charles, 1999) suggests that social goals serve at least two critical functions: knowledge acquisition and emotion regulation. The knowledge acquisition function involves gaining useful information for future behavior from observation of and interaction with others. Emotion regulation, a goal that is hypothesized to take on increasing importance as life progresses, involves efforts to surround oneself with people who can help to promote one's positive affect and to avoid negative affect. A sense of social competence and prevalence of positive affect or outlook have been linked with any number of benefits with respect to quality of life (e.g., Peterson, 2000; Scheier & Carver, 1993).

More commonly cited mastery-related goals have also been associated with benefits, many of which may be socially based as well. Argyle (1999) summarized findings from several large surveys examining the relationship between a large variety of demographic variables and measures of subjective well-being. He concluded that both nonwork (i.e., leisure) and work feelings of satisfaction are positively associated with life satisfaction, even when factors such as income and education are controlled for (see also Warr, 1999). Research has also revealed a small correlation between education and positive affect, but this relationship seems to result from the differential opportunities for employment afforded to educated persons.

Summary

Within motivational and evolutionary theory, at least three categories of goals repeatedly stand out as vital to survival and quality of life. These include basic physiological and safety needs, relationship goals, and mastery goals. Evidence of the importance of each of these types of goals continues to mount. Moreover, the goals that people believe motivate their decision making are largely consistent with these emphases. Instrumental, health, and financial goals are likely to support basic needs, though the routine success of most people in satisfying these needs may obscure the link between decision making and fulfillment of these goals. Consistent with expectations from both motivation and evolution literatures, relationship goals are among the most commonly reported motivators of decision making. The importance of relationship goals is likely to be pervasive, potentially contributing to several of the other commonly reported goals. Finally, the importance of mastering the environment in social as well as physical and intellectual spheres was evident in the desire to achieve education, career, personal satisfaction, and leisure goals.

Goals and Decision Making

The results of our exploratory study and emphases within motivational and evolutionary literatures suggest that a small but varied set of goals is likely to figure prominently in decision making. The fact that these goals resurface repeatedly suggests that they have fundamental importance worth capturing in decision theories. The parameters of interest in theorizing are likely to be expanded, if not restructured, by thinking about decision making as a motivated process. As such, decision-making processes can be evaluated in terms of their effectiveness in achieving a specific and limited set of goals that have different meanings and impacts across the life span, and across shorter and longer time horizons. In concluding this chapter, we briefly discuss two issues that will undoubtedly loom large in this perspective. These issues are concerned with the essential value of temporal and situational contexts and the need to address goal compatibility and conflict.

Temporal and Situational Contexts

The old adage that time is money suggests an interplay and interchangeability between these two fundamental resources. Yet traditional decision theory has been much more concerned with money than with time. It is not simply that economic aspects of decision making have been seen as more important than temporal aspects, but that temporal variables (with the notable exception of temporal discounting) have in many cases been explicitly excluded or deemed irrelevant.

Ignoring temporal context, or the differences in one's situation that occur as a function of time, creates a distorted view in which the importance of goals is easily lost. Without time considerations, decision making is stripped of its fundamentally dynamic character.

Context and the Utility of Experience. The most obvious and critical case of downplaying the importance of time involves the von Neumann and Morgenstern (1944; see also Luce & Raiffa, 1957) axioms on which the normative status of expected utility theory rests. In particular, the principle of *reduction of compound prospects* requires that a person be indifferent between a gamble that occurs in stages and a single gamble that represents the same final outcomes. Many have argued that it is irrational to care about intermediate outcomes and that final outcomes are all that matters. This is equivalent to saying that decision makers should not be affected by changes in the time frame for experiencing outcomes (nor should they be influenced by changes in the number of events that need to occur before some arbitrarily designated final outcome is experienced).

On the other hand, many counter that there is a *utility of gambling* that may lead to preferences for a staged lottery over one that involves a single set of equivalent consequences. People might reasonably value (either positively or negatively) the process of gambling or they might value extending the gambling game across time. If they do, however, then they do not ascribe to the principle of reduction of compound prospects, and there is therefore no reason to believe that utility measures can or should be able to represent their preferences.

Soon after the introduction of the von Neumann–Morgenstern axioms, Daniel Ellsberg (1954) pointed out the implausibility of the assumption of no utility of gambling:

> [A] sensible person might easily prefer a lottery which held several intermediate drawings to determine who was still "in" for the final drawing. . . . The crucial factor is "pleasure of winning," which may be aroused by intermediate wins even if one subsequently fails to receive the prize. Many, perhaps most, slot-machine players know the odds are very unfavorable, and are not really motivated by hopes of winning the jackpot. They feel that they have had their money's worth if it takes them a long time to lose a modest sum, meanwhile enjoying a number of intermediate wins. . . . Von Neumann and Morgenstern single out axiom 3:C:b, which excludes this type of behavior, as the "really critical" axiom – that one which gets closest to excluding a 'utility of gambling.'" (pp. 281–282)

In any generalization of expected utility theory to real-world scenarios beyond contrived monetary gambles, the axiom of reduction of compound prospects essentially asserts that there is no *utility of experience*. Given that all of life involves risky decision making, this axiom might lead to the obviously ridiculous position that one should be indifferent to living life versus simply finding out the final state at the end of life. Finagling the issue by asserting that there is some arbitrary period of time that can be considered a unitary decision event seems unsatisfactory. Inasmuch as goal striving and progress toward goals are integral to the essence of life, the desire to experience intermediate successes and failures is at the crux of what rationality may entail in any meaningful application.

The importance of experience itself needs to become a part of theories of judgment and decision making. Moreover, the importance of different kinds of experiences at different developmental stages of life is

Table 12.3. *A Pair of "Identical" Prospects Used to Illustrate Framing Effects*

You are given $200 and offered one of the following options:	
Option 1	You will receive an additional $100.
Option 2	A fair coin is tossed.
	Heads you receive an additional $200.
	Tails you receive no additional money.
You are given $400 and must choose one of the following penalties:	
Penalty Option 1	You must return $100.
Penalty Option 2	A fair coin is tossed.
	Heads you must return $200.
	Tails you may keep all money received.

Source: Adapted from Dawes (1988, p. 34).

also critical (see, e.g., Ryff, 1995). Even in our exploratory study, we saw clear links between certain types of goals and age. These undoubtedly influence decision making in meaningful ways. Time horizons are also critical, not just for computing discount functions, but also for recognizing the need to negotiate between conflicting goals. In particular, the need to satisfy more basic goals may prevent movement toward higher-order goals. In a decision situation, this could produce what appears to be a suboptimal choice if viewed relative only to the longer-term goal. Including the temporal context of decisions allows the injection of greater meaning into our understanding of decision processes.

Context and the Value of Reference Dependence. Reference dependence is another form of context that provides meaning. However, the decision literature presents a conflicted view of the importance of reference dependence. For instance, Dawes (1988, p. 8) argues that rationality requires that one make decisions based on current assets. This sounds as though context is a critical consideration and that the current state of affairs should be adopted as the relevant reference point. On other occasions, however, many decision researchers have argued that changing a reference point should not influence the decision (e.g., Tversky & Kahneman, 1981). Consider Table 12.3, which consists of the problem used by Dawes (1988) to illustrate the irrationality of framing effects. Dawes and others (e.g., Kahneman, Knetsch, & Thaler, 1991) suggest that it is irrational to prefer Option 1 in the first case and Option 2 in the second, as the two problems are identical; hence, a person should prefer the same option under both descriptions. The two versions, however, are identical only if one forbids decision makers to consider the original monetary gifts (either $200 or $400) as part of their current assets. With the original gift (a *sunk gain*, in effect) thus removed from consideration, there is no longer any argument that a particular relationship should exist between preferences for the two different lotteries (unless one wishes to argue that it is irrational to treat losses differently than gains).

Framing effects, more generally, may not be irrational to the extent that a different frame may communicate or imply a different context for the decision, particularly with respect to implied goals. Consider the Asian Disease problem, wherein people's preferences often differ, depending on whether options to fight the hypothetical deadly disease are framed in terms of the lives that may be saved or the lives that may be lost. Schneider (1992) points out that the two situations imply different assumptions about the status of the 600 individuals inflicted with the disease:

> If people need to be saved, it must be that the perceived given state of affairs presupposes their death. It is only for a status quo that accepts the deaths as imminent that the construct of *saving* has meaning. In much the same way, the construct of *losing* only has meaning when associated with a status quo that implies their unthreatened existence. The framing of a decision problem is tantamount to a manipulation of the perceived status quo. (p. 1055)

If assumptions about the most appropriate status quo are shared by others, then it makes especially good sense to choose differently as a function of what is accepted as the current state of affairs and thus as the most appropriate goal. Decision outcomes include social outcomes, such that a shared sense of a goal is likely to determine how people react to particular outcomes and to the people who made the decisions. In fact, Schneider and Jackson (in preparation) have recently shown that the framing of a decision situation influences both of these things. Thus, having a sense of the most appropriate frame or goal for a decision, given the temporal and situational constraints, allows an individual to predict more accurately the reactions of others to his or her decisions.

The role of frames in communicating temporal and situational contexts has recently been demonstrated empirically. McKenzie and Nelson (2001) have recently shown that frames allow the speaker to effectively communicate information about the state of affairs at the time when a change takes place (for example, as a consequence of a decision). They demonstrated that both speakers and listeners are more likely to use the phrase "glass half full" to refer to a glass that was previously empty, and to use the phrase "glass half empty" to refer to one that was previously full. Hence, the frame is used to communicate the most appropriate reference point.

Even Tversky and Kahneman, who coined the term *framing effect* and provided the first demonstration (i.e., the Asian Disease problem, 1981), have more recently come to the conclusion that the implications of reference dependence for the rationality of decision making cannot be determined a priori or across the board:

> The effects of reference levels on decisions can only be justified by corresponding effects of these reference levels on the experience of consequences. For example, a bias in favor of the status quo can be justified if the disadvantages of any change will be experienced more keenly than its advantages.... We conclude that there is no general answer to the question about the normative status of loss aversion or other reference effects.... (Tversky & Kahneman, 1991, pp. 1057–1058)

Reference points provide information about the current situation including goals, commitments, and priorities. For this reason, reference points are likely to help guide individuals in defining the decisions they need to make, in identifying choice options, in determining relevant attributes, and in developing subjective values. Without reference points, a choice situation loses a fundamental source of meaning (see also Finucane, Peters, & Slovic, this volume).

Choice situations will also be seen very differently at different times throughout the life cycle and when different goals are perceived as the priority (see, e.g., Markman & Brendl, 2000). Similarly, choices will seem quite different for those in different circumstances. Indeed, constructs such as *marginal utility* cannot be defined in the absence of a reference point (i.e., we need to establish the current quantity to identify the margin).

Nevertheless, dependence on reference points may also leave us susceptible to accepting arbitrary or misleading assumptions when the state implied by the reference point draws our attention away from other critical facets of the situation. The inconsistent behavior seen in studies of framing effects, for example, could signal important contextual shifts in goals or it could signal an unintended and undesirable attentional phenomenon. For instance, the preference reversals that occur when a decision format changes from a choice context to a selling price context (e.g., Slovic, Fischhoff, & Lichtenstein, 1982) may or may not be irrational, depending on whether and how the goals in the two contexts differ. In some cases, differences in preference may be caused by inadvertent and potentially harmful biases introduced by a simple change in perspective that has no implication with respect to goals or the value of outcomes. By focusing on the importance of behavioral goals, research efforts may be more likely to distinguish the variables that predict or comprise the advantages and disadvantages of reliance on reference points (see also Baron, 1988).

Goal Compatibility, Goal Conflict, and Priorities

Attention to changing goals across contexts is also likely to encourage an appreciation of the need to better understand the impact of goal compatibility and goal conflict. Although typical goals for behavior may consist of a relatively small set, these goals are nevertheless qualitatively different from one another, yet in many respects they are dependent on one another. The notion of *utility* begins to become problematic when one asks, "Utility with respect to which goal(s)?" An option may have considerable apparent positive utility with respect to education and career, but at the same time may have negative utility with respect to key relationships or leisure. Deriving a single value to represent an option's utility may force an unnatural combination rule for dealing with incompatible goals.

Averaging leads to the frequently erroneous conclusion that goals are independent of one another and can readily compensate for one another. For instance, by averaging, career aspirations should be able to trade off with education goals, such that one might give up important education goals to pursue career aspirations. Although this may occasionally be possible, more often educational goals are prerequisite to career goals. Several other kinds of interdependencies are likely to exist between goals, and these different interdependencies will require different types of mathematical combination rules to describe adequately how the value or utility of outcomes changes with interactions among goals. At the very least, awareness of multiple interdependent goals makes apparent the need to gain a better qualitative understanding of how goals tend to relate to one another, how these goal relationships influence satisfaction with decisions, and how goal interactions may have implications for measuring decision quality.

There has been some research attention to the difficulties in making tradeoffs among potential outcomes (e.g., Keeney & Raiffa, 1993; Weber et al., 2001). Frequently, the tradeoff between money and risk is emphasized, with policy implications in mind. At other times, the focus is on conflicts between multiple parties who are each stakeholders in a decision, or conflicts between the well-being of an individual versus the collective good. Perhaps, in the near future, we will see a growing emphasis on the conflict among the kinds of goals identified here.

That is not to say that conflict is the only possible relationship among goals. Some goals are compatible with one another, or choices can be made in such a way as to satisfy more than one goal. It turns out that this kind of multiple goal satisfaction may be critical to the quality of decisions and to psychological well-being. Evidence is now emerging to show that those who adopt strategies that are likely to help satisfy multiple goals tend to be happier and healthier (Sheldon & Emmons, 1995; Sheldon & Kasser, 1995; Vaillant, 2000). The challenge of satisfying multiple goals also opens the door for direct associations between creative and decision processes. Better decisions may be those wherein the decision situation and the possible options are defined in a way that facilitates several goals or that minimizes conflicts among goals (similar to good problem solving, e.g., as defined by Newell & Simon, 1988). Indeed, creativity has been linked to higher levels of perceived comfort in handling and resolving goal conflicts (Sheldon, 1995; see also Isen & Labroo, this volume).

Finally, although goal compatibility and goal conflict offer tremendous potential as critical variables in decision research, the set is not complete without consideration of priorities. One might easily imagine that goal priorities can be represented as values corresponding to the importance of goals such as relationship, career, and so on. However, this kind of representation is not likely to capture the interaction among different goals and how the priorities of goals are dependent on one another. Financial or health concerns may be more potent when raising a family, for instance. Beyond this interdependence, however, is the larger issue of how to set priorities to maximize effective behavior and both long- and short-term satisfaction. These types of issues are likely to generate some of the toughest challenges to making high-quality decisions.

We started this chapter with the question: What do decision makers really want? Based on our study and a review of the related literature, we have identified several things that they want. Decision makers want to be safe and healthy, they want to have fulfilling relationships, and they want to experience some successes in the domains of education, career pursuits, personal development, and leisurely activities. Decision makers may have other types of goals as well, but the critical point is that people make decisions because they want to move toward satisfying their goals. To move successfully toward goals, it is essential that decision makers pay close attention to both temporal and situational contexts so that they can monitor their direction of movement with respect to any given goal across any given period of time. Decision makers may also want to change goals or goal priorities as temporal and situational contexts change.

Because there are many possible goals and because these goals are likely to change over time, decisions may be more realistically construed as constraint satisfaction problems rather than utility maximization problems. How can people make decisions in a way that can address all (or even most) of the goals they might like to achieve in life's finite amount of time, especially when goal achievement is not entirely under their own control? A decision science focused on answering this question may be more likely than traditional approaches to be able to help people make satisfying and meaningful decisions.

References

Abramson, L. Y., Seligman, M. E. P., & Teasdale, J. (1978). Learned helplessness in humans: Critique and reformulation. *Journal of Abnormal Psychology, 87,* 49–74.

Argyle, M. (1999). Causes and correlates of happiness. In D. Kahneman, E. Diener, & N. Schwarz (Eds.), *Well-being: The foundations of hedonic psychology* (pp. 353–373). New York: Russell Sage Foundation.

Atkinson, J. W. (1964). *An introduction to motivation.* New York: D. Van Nostrand.

Atkinson, J. W., Heyns, R. W., & Veroff, J. (1954). The effect of experimental arousal of the affiliation motive on thematic apperception. *Journal of Abnormal and Social Psychology, 49,* 405–410.

Bandura, A. (1977). Self-efficacy: Toward a unifying theory of behavior change. *Psychological Review, 84,* 191–215.

Bandura, A. (1982). Self-efficacy mechanism in human agency. *American Psychologist, 37,* 122–147.

Bargh, J. A., & Chartrand, T. L. (1999). The unbearable automaticity of being. *American Psychologist, 54*(7), 462–479.

Baron, J. (1988). *Thinking and deciding.* New York: Cambridge University Press.

Bazerman, M. H., & Neale, M. A. (1993). *Negotiating rationally.* New York: Free Press.

Blais, M. R., Sabourin, S., Boucher, C., & Vallerand, R. J. (1990). Toward a motivational model of couple happiness. *Journal of Personality and Social Psychology, 59,* 1021–1031.

Boyatzis, R. E. (1973). Affiliation motivation. In D. C. McClelland & R. S. Steele (Eds.), *Human motivation : A book of readings*. (pp. 252–276). Morristown, NJ: General Learning Press.

Carstensen, L. L., Isaacowitz, D. M., & Charles, S. T. (1999). Taking time seriously: A theory of socioemotional selectivity. *American Psychologist, 54*(3), 165–181.

Carter, C. S. (1998). Neuroendocrine perspectives on social attachment and love. *Psychoneuroendocrinology, 23*(8), 779–818.

Chapman, G. B. (1997, November). *Explicit decisions, personal policies, and self-control.* Paper presented at the annual meeting of the Psychonomic Society, Philadelphia.

Cialdini, R. B. (1993). *Influence: Science and practice* (3rd ed.). New York: William Morrow.

Damasio, A. R. (1994). *Descartes' error: Emotion, reason, and the human brain.* New York: Grosset/Putnam.

Darwin, C. (1859). *On the origin of species by means of natural selection.* London: John Murray. (Reprinted in 1964 by Harvard University Press.)

Darwin, C. (1871). *The descent of man, and selection in relation to sex* (2 vols.). London: John Murray. (Reprinted in 1981 by Princeton University Press.)

Dawes, R. M. (1988). *Rational choice in an uncertain world.* New York: Harcourt Brace Jovanovich.

Day, R. S. (1988). Alternative representations. In G. H. Bower (Ed.), *The psychology of learning and motivation: Advances in research and theory* (Vol. 22, pp. 261–305). San Diego, CA: Academic Press.

Deci, E. L., & Ryan, R. M. (1985). *Intrinsic motivation and self-determination in human behavior.* New York: Plenum.

Deci, E. L., & Ryan, R. M. (1991). A motivational approach to self: Integration in personality. In R. Dienstbier (Ed.), *Nebraska Symposium on Motivation Vol. 38: Perspectives on motivation* (pp. 237–288). Lincoln: University of Nebraska Press.

Ellsberg, D. (1954). Classic and current notions of "measurable utility." *Economics Journal, 64*, 528–566.

Garrod, G., & Willis, K. G. (1999). *Economic valuation of the environment: Methods and case studies.* Northampton, MA: Edward Elgar.

Goldstein, W. M., & Weber, E. U. (1995). Content and discontent: Indications and implications of domain specificity in preferential decision making. In J. R. Busemeyer, R. Hastie, & D. L. Medin (Eds.), *The psychology of learning and motivation, Vol. 32: Decision making from a cognitive perspective* (pp. 83–136). San Diego, CA: Academic Press.

Goleman, D. (1995). *Emotional intelligence.* New York: Bantam Books.

Hammond, K. R. (2000). Coherence and correspondence theories in judgment and decision making. In T. Connolly & H. R. Arkes (Eds.), *Judgment and decision making: An interdisciplinary reader* (2nd ed., pp. 53–65). New York: Cambridge University Press.

Hausman, J. A. (Ed.). (1993). *Contingent valuation: A critical assessment.* New York: North-Holland.

Heckhausen, H. (1980). *Motivation und handeln.* New York: Springer-Verlag.

Heider, F. (1958). *The psychology of interpersonal relations.* New York: Wiley.

Hull, C. L. (1943). *Principles of behavior.* New York: Appleton-Century-Crofts.

Hull, C. L. (1952). *A behavior system.* New Haven, CT: Yale University Press.

Insel, T. R., & Young, L. J. (2000). Neuropeptides and the evolution of social behavior. *Current Opinion in Neurobiology, 10,* 784–789.

Isen, A. M. (1993). Positive affect and decision making. In M. Lewis & M. Haviland (Eds.), *Handbook of emotion* (pp. 261–267). New York: Guilford Press.

Jones, E. E., & Davis, K. E. (1965). From acts to dispositions: The attribution process in person perception. In L. Berkowitz (Ed.), *Advances in experimental social psychology* (Vol. 2, pp. 219–266). New York: Academic Press.

Kahneman, D., Knetsch, J. L., & Thaler, R. H. (1991). Anomalies – the endowment effect, loss aversion, and status-quo bias. *Journal of Economic Perspectives, 5*(1), 193–206.

Kasser, T., & Ryan, R. M. (1993). A dark side of the American dream: Correlates of financial success as a central life aspiration. *Journal of Personality and Social Psychology, 65,* 410–422.

Kasser, T., & Ryan, R. M. (1996). Further examining the American dream: Differential correlates of intrinsic and extrinsic goals. *Personality & Social Psychology Bulletin, 22*(3), 280–287.

Keeney, R. L., & Raiffa, H. (1993). *Decisions with multiple objectives: Preferences and value tradeoffs.* New York: Cambridge University Press.

Kelley, H. H. (1967). Attribution theory in social psychology. In D. Levine (Ed.), *Nebraska symposium on motivation* (Vol. 15, pp. 192–238). Lincoln: University of Nebraska Press.

Kelley, H. H. (1972). The process of causal attribution. *American Psychologist, 28,* 107–128.

Klein, G. (1997). The recognition-primed decision (RPD) model: Looking back, looking forward. In C. E. Zsambok & G. Klein (Eds.), *Naturalistic decision making. Expertise: Research and applications* (pp. 285–292). Hillsdale, NJ: Erlbaum.

Langer, E. J. (1978). Rethinking the role of thought in social interaction. In J. H. Harvey, W. Ickes, & R. F. Kidd (Eds.), *New directions in attribution research* (Vol. 2, pp. 35–58). Hillsdale, NJ: Erlbaum.

Langer, E. J. (1997). *The power of mindful learning.* Reading, MA: Addison-Wesley.

Lopes, L. L. (1987). Between hope and fear: The psychology of risk. In L. Berkowitz (Ed.), *Advances in experimental social psychology* (Vol. 20, pp. 255–295). San Diego, CA: Academic Press.

Luce, R. D., & Raiffa, H. (1957). *Games and decisions: Introduction and critical survey.* New York: Wiley.

Markman, A. B., & Brendl, C. M. (2000). The influence of goals on value and choice. *The Psychology of Learning and Motivation, 39,* 97–128.

Maslow, A. H. (1962). *Toward a psychology of being.* Princeton, NJ: Van Nostrand.

Maslow, A. H. (1970). *Motivation and personality* (2nd ed.). New York: Harper & Row.

Mason, W. A., & Mendoza, S. P. (1998). Generic aspects of primate attachments: Parents, offspring, and mates. *Psychoneuroendocrinology, 23*(8), 779–818.

McAdams, D. P. (1982). Intimacy motivation. In A. J. Steward (Ed.), *Motivation and society* (pp. 133–171). San Francisco: Jossey-Bass.

McKenzie, C. R. M., & Nelson, J. D. (2001, November). *What a speaker's choice of frame reveals: Reference points, frame selection, and framing effects.* Paper presented at the annual meeting of the Psychonomic Society, Orlando, FL.

Miller, G. (2000). *The mating mind: How sexual choice shaped the evolution of human nature.* New York: Doubleday.

Murray, H. A. (1938). *Explorations in personality.* New York: Oxford University Press.

Myers, D. G. (1999). Close relationships and quality of life. In D. Kahneman, E. Diener, & N. Schwarz (Eds.), *Well-being: The foundations of hedonic psychology* (pp. 353–373). New York: Russell Sage Foundation.

Newell, A., & Rosenbloom, P. S. (1981). Mechanisms of skill acquisition and the law of practice. In J. R. Anderson (Ed.), *Cognitive skills and their acquisition* (pp. 1–56). Hillsdale, NJ: Erlbaum.

Newell, A., & Simon, H. A. (1988). The theory of human problem solving. In A. M. Collins & E. E. Smith (Eds.), *Readings in cognitive science: A perspective from psychology and artificial intelligence* (pp. 33–51). San Mateo, CA: Morgan Kaufmann.

Peterson, C. (2000). The future of optimism. *American Psychologist, 55,* 44–55.

Redelmeier, D. A., & Tversky, A. (1992). On the framing of multiple prospects. *Psychological Science, 3*(3), 191–193.

Rempel, J. K., Holmes, J. G., & Zanna, M. P. (1985). Trust in close relationships. *Journal of Personality & Social Psychology, 49*(1), 95–112.

Ryan, R. M. (1993). Agency and organization: Intrinsic motivation, autonomy, and the self in psychological development. In J. Jacobs (Ed.), *Nebraska Symposium on Motivation: Vol. 40. Developmental perspectives on motivation* (pp. 1–56). Lincoln: University of Nebraska Press.

Ryan, R. M., Sheldon, K. M., Kasser, T., & Deci, E. L. (1996). All goals are not created equal: An organismic perspective on the nature of goals and their regulation. In P. Gollwitzer & J. A. Bargh (Eds.), *The psychology of action: Linking cognition and motivation to behavior* (pp. 7–26). New York: Guilford Press.

Ryff, C. D. (1995). Psychological well-being in adult life. *Current Directions in Psychological Science, 4*(4), 99–104.

Scheier, M. F., & Carver, C. S. (1993). On the power of positive thinking: The benefits of being optimistic. *Current Directions in Psychological Science, 2,* 26–30.

Schneider, S. L. (1992). Framing and conflict: Aspiration level contingency, the status quo, and current theories of risky choice. *Journal of Experimental Psychology: Learning, Memory, and Cognition, 18,* 1040–1057.

Schneider, S. L. (2001). In search of realistic optimism: Meaning, knowledge, and warm fuzziness. *American Psychologist, 56*(3), 250–263.

Schoemaker, P. J. H. (1982). The expected utility model: Its variants, purposes, evidence and limitations. *Journal of Economic Literature, 20,* 529–563.

Seligman, M. E. P. (1975). *Helplessness: On depression, development, and death.* San Francisco: W. H. Freeman.

Seligman, M., Fazio, R. H., & Zanna, M. P. (1980). Effects of salience of extrinsic rewards on liking and loving. *Journal of Personality & Social Psychology, 38*(3), 453–460.

Sheldon, K. M. (1995). Creativity and goal conflict. *Creativity Research Journal, 8,* 299–306.

Sheldon, K. M., & Emmons, R. A. (1995). Comparing differentiation and integration within personal goal systems. *Personality & Individual Differences, 18,* 39–46.

Sheldon, K. M., & Kasser, T. (1995). Coherence and congruence: Two aspects of personality integration. *Journal of Personality & Social Psychology, 68,* 531–543.

Shiffrin, R. M., & Schneider, W. (1977). Controlled and automatic human information processing: II. Perceptual learning, automatic attending and a general theory. *Psychological Review, 84*(2), 127–190.

Shubik, M. (1982). *Game theory and the social sciences: Concepts and solutions.* Cambridge, MA: MIT Press.

Slovic, P., Fischhoff, B., & Lichtenstein, S. (1982). Responsibility, framing, and information-processing effects in risk assessment. In R. Hogarth (Ed.), *New directions for methodology of social and behavioral science: Question framing and response consistency* (No. 11). San Francisco: Jossey-Bass.

Svenson, O. (1999). Differentiation and consolidation theory: Decision making processes before and after a choice. In P. Juslin & H. Montgomery (Eds.), *Judgment and decision making: Neo-Brunswikian and process-tracing approaches* (pp. 175–197). Mahwah, NJ: Erlbaum.

Thompson, L. L., Levine, J. M., & Messick, D. M. (Eds.). (1999). *Shared cognition in organizations: The management of knowledge.* Mahwah, N.J.: Erlbaum.

Tversky, A., & Kahneman, D. (1981). The framing of decisions and the psychology of choice. *Science, 211,* 453–458.

Tversky, A., & Kahneman, D. (1991). Loss aversion in riskless choice: A reference-dependent model. *Quarterly Journal of Economics, 106,* 1039–1061.

Vaillant, G. E. (2000). Adaptive mental mechanisms: Their role in a positive psychology. *American Psychologist, 55,* 89–98.

Von Neumann, J., & Morgenstern, O. (1944). *Theory of games and economic behavior.* Princeton, NJ: Princeton University Press.

Warr, P. (1999). Well-being and the workplace. In D. Kahneman, E. Diener, & N. Schwarz (Eds.), *Well-being: The foundations of hedonic psychology* (pp. 392–412). New York: Russell Sage Foundation.

Weber, E. U., Baron, J., & Loomes, G. (2001). *Conflict and tradeoffs in decision making.* New York: Cambridge University Press.

Weiner, B. (1985). An attributional theory of achievement motivation and emotion. *Psychological Review, 92,* 548–573.

White, R. W. (1959). Motivation reconsidered: The concept of competence. *Psychological Review, 66,* 297–333.

Yates, J. F. (1990). *Judgment and decision making.* Englewood Cliffs, NJ: Prentice Hall.

Part IV

Understanding Social and Cultural Influences on Decisions

13 Bridging Individual, Interpersonal, and Institutional Approaches to Judgment and Decision Making: The Impact of Accountability on Cognitive Bias

Jennifer S. Lerner and Philip E. Tetlock

ABSTRACT

Research on accountability takes an unusual approach to the study of judgment and decision making. By situating decision makers within particular accountability conditions, it has begun to bridge individual, interpersonal, and institutional levels of analysis. We propose that this multilevel approach can enhance both the study of judgment and choice and the application of such research to real-world settings. To illustrate the multilevel approach, we present a review of accountability research, organized around an enduring question in the literature: Under what conditions will accountability improve judgment and decision making? After considering the shortcomings of two seemingly straightforward answers to this question, we propose a multifactor framework for predicting when accountability attenuates bias, when it has no effect, and when it makes matters even worse. Key factors in this framework draw from multiple levels of analysis.

CONTENTS

Psychological theories of judgment and choice have tended to view decision makers as isolated individuals. While elucidating cognitive processes that occur within the individual, they have tended to overlook the impact of interpersonal and institutional settings on thought and action. By contrast, organizational and political theories have tended to view decision makers as the instruments of institutional norms, rules, and constraints. While elucidating social and political processes that occur outside of the individual, they have tended to overlook the impact of intrapsychic processes. We argue that the study of accountability – pressure to justify one's views to another – can bridge these historically distinct approaches. It can do so by providing a natural link between individual decision makers and the relationships within which decision makers work and live. Bridging these approaches not only has the potential to improve the applicability of decision-making research to real-world settings, it also has the potential to improve basic theories of judgment and decision making.

In the first section of this chapter, we introduce accountability as a universal feature of social life and discuss the social foundations of accountability. In the second section, we review the effects of accountability on putative *biases* identified in the judgment and decision-making literature. In particular, we consider two overarching hypotheses about the effects of accountability. According to the first hypothesis, accountability will attenuate judgment and decision-making biases to the extent that accountability increases cognitive effort. According to the second hypothesis, accountability will amplify the dominant responses to judgment and decision-making problems – thereby attenuating bias on easy problems and amplifying bias on difficult problems. Finding that neither hypothesis receives substantial empirical support, we identify two factors that play an especially important role in determining when accountability will attenuate bias, when it will have no effect, and when it will make matters even worse. We then review evidence for these factors and propose incorporating them into a multifactor framework of accountability effects. Finally, in the concluding section, we identify specific ways in which accountability research can enhance both the study of judgment and choice and the application of judgment and choice research to real-world settings.

Accountability as a Universal Feature of Social Life

Social Functions of Accountability

Many theorists – from political philosophers (Hobbes, 1660/1968) to organizational behaviorists (Katz & Kahn, 1978; March & Olsen, 1995), to social psychologists (Schlenker, 1980; Scott & Lyman, 1968; Semin & Manstead, 1983; Tetlock, 1992) – have viewed accountability as a prerequisite for social order. Although accountability ground rules obviously vary dramatically across cultures and history (Bersoff & Miller, 1993; Hong & Chiu, 1992), the underlying functions of accountability are strikingly similar. Accountability systems represent sociocultural adaptations to the perennial problem of how to coordinate relationships among individuals. Whatever the ideological or cultural value system underlying the social system – be it a decentralized market or a command economy – accountability guidelines prescribe the norms and guidelines in a collectivity (Lerner & Tetlock, 1994; Tetlock, 1998) and how to deal with those who deviate from them (Stenning, 1995). "Accountability serves as a critical rule and norm enforcement mechanism – the social psychological link between individual decision-makers on the one hand and social systems on the other" (Tetlock, 1992, p. 337). Because the transaction costs of relying on purely external forms of accountability would be prohibitive, most social control takes the form of internalized accountability. People monitor their own judgments and decisions by considering the justifiability of alternative courses of action. Indeed, this idea is a cornerstone of the symbolic interactionist approach to thought. George Herbert Mead maintained that "the very process of thinking is, of course, simply an inner conversation that goes on. . . . He thinks it out, and perhaps writes it in the form of a book; but it is still part of social intercourse in which one is addressing other persons and at the same time addressing one's self, and in which one controls the address to other persons by the response made to one's own gesture" (1934, p. 141).

Modeling Thought as Internalized Dialogue

As long as people are concerned about maintaining their identities as moral, competent beings, a central function of thought is making sure that one acts in ways that can be persuasively justified or excused to observers. Indeed, the process of considering the justifiability of one's choices may be so prevalent that decision makers not only search for convincing reasons to make a choice when they must explain that choice to others, they search for reasons to convince themselves that they have made the "right" choice (cf. Shafir, Simonson, & Tversky, 1993). As Kuhn (1992) argues, the ability to generate persuasive justifications for beliefs may be "the most significant way in which higher-order thinking and reasoning figure in the lives of most people" (p. 155).

A number of researchers have made the case that concerns about the justifiability of action loom large in all judgments and choices (Gonzales, Kovera, Sullivan, & Chanley, 1995; Hsee, 1995; McGraw, Best, & Timpone, 1995; Schlenker, 1980, 1985; Scott & Lyman, 1968). For example, Shafir and colleagues (1993) demonstrated in a series of studies that the justifiability of reasons figured into participants' choices even when participants neither expected to explain their judgments nor even to interact with anyone. When participants were presented with only two options, it should not have mattered whether the experimenter asked them to select the option "they preferred" or the option "they would reject." Nevertheless, participants' selections varied as a function of elicitation procedures; they relied on positive features of each option when they were told to *choose* an option and negative features when they were told to *reject* an option (Shafir et al., 1993). The researchers explained that although this phenomenon defies a value maximization perspective, it readily fits a reason-based choice perspective: "reasons for choosing are more compelling when we choose than when we reject, and reasons for rejecting matter more when we reject than when we choose" (Shafir et al., 1993, p. 18). To recap, both theoretical and empirical arguments suggest that thought may be usefully modeled as dialogue – even when decision makers are not explicitly held accountable.

Defining Accountability in the Judgment and Choice Literature

Although implicit accountability may be an inevitable feature of real-world decision environments, accountability here refers to an explicit expectation that one will be called upon to justify one's beliefs, feelings, or actions to others (Scott & Lyman, 1968; Semin & Manstead, 1983; Tetlock, 1992). Additionally, accountability implies that positive or negative consequences hinge on the acceptability of one's justification. In a few field studies, the acceptability of one's justification carries such concrete consequences as performance-contingent career advances or setbacks. More typically, however, the acceptability of one's justification carries only intangible consequences (e.g., approval or disapproval from the audience). Specifically, most laboratory studies create a situation in which people expect to explain their actions to someone they have never met before and never expect to meet again. What is remarkable about this literature is that – despite the prevalence of these minimalist manipulations – participants still reliably respond as if audience approval matters. And they do so even when the decisions at hand require them to express deeply held moral/ethical beliefs (see Brief, Dukerich, & Doran, 1991; Pennington & Schlenker, 1999). Two implications follow from the fact that researchers achieve these effects with such weak manipulations. First, it implies support for the social interactionist view that concerns about how the self relates to others – even temporarily significant others – drive cognition. Second, it implies that much more substantial effects may result from accountability in everyday life – where the acceptability of one's justification carries significant consequences.

Accountability Is Not a Unitary Phenomenon. Just as many distinct subtypes of accountability appear in real-world settings, distinct subtypes also appear in judgment and decision-making research. For example, one may be accountable to an audience (a) whose views are known or unknown (Tetlock, 1983a, 1985); (b) who is interested in accuracy or in expediency (Mero & Motowidlo, 1995); (c) who is interested in the quality of one's judgment processes in specific judgment outcomes (Siegel-Jacobs & Yates, 1996; Simonson & Staw, 1992); (d) who is reasonably well informed or who is naive (Fitzpatrick & Eagly, 1981); and (e) who has a legitimate reason for inquiring into the reasons behind a decision maker's judgments or who has no legitimate reason (Cvetkovich, 1978; Gordon & Stuecher, 1992). In addition, the conditions under which one is accountable can vary dramatically. For example, one may learn of being accountable prior to encoding judgment-relevant evidence or only afterward (e.g., Tetlock, 1983b, 1985; Tetlock & Kim, 1987; Thompson et al., 1994). Similarly, one may learn of being accountable prior to irrevocably committing oneself to a course of action or only afterward (e.g., Ross & Staw, 1986, 1993; Staw, 1980; Staw & Fox, 1977; Staw & Ross, 1989).

These qualitative differences – in the nature of the audience and in the context of accountability – are by no means trivial. Both laboratory and field studies reveal that distinct kinds of accountability activate distinct social and cognitive coping strategies (for reviews, see Lerner & Tetlock, 1994, 1999; Tetlock, 1992). Importantly, only certain types of accountability elicit the kind of open-minded and critical thinking that may improve judgments and choices – a point to which we return in the third section.

The Effects of Accountability on Putative Biases: Examining Support for Two Hypotheses

Multiple studies find that predecisional accountability to an audience with unknown views is especially likely to stimulate effortful, self-critical thought (for review, see Lerner & Tetlock, 1999). As such, it has received more attention in the judgment and decision-making literature than any other kind of accountability. But employing this specific kind of accountability by no means ensures improved judgment. Rather, the effects observed in studies employing this kind of accountability are highly variable.

To organize our review of these studies, we attempt to fit two different hypotheses to the literature. Each provides a relatively straightforward, face-valid scheme for predicting when predecisional accountability to an audience with unknown views will attenuate, have no effect on, or amplify bias. According to the first hypothesis, accountability will amplify the dominant responses to judgment and decision-making problems – thereby attenuating bias on *easy* problems and amplifying bias on *difficult* problems. According to the second hypothesis, accountability will attenuate biases to the extent that it increases cognitive effort.

Hypothesis One: Does Accountability Facilitate Accuracy on Easy Judgments and Inhibit Accuracy on Difficult Judgments?

The idea that accountability's effect depends on the difficulty of the judgment or decision task arises from classic drive (Hull, 1943; Spence, 1956) and social-facilitation (Zajonc, 1965) theories. According to this view, dominant responses are amplified by motivation; and the dominant response to easy problems is, by definition, the "right" answer, whereas the dominant response to difficult problems is wrong (see Pelham & Neter, 1995). For example, researchers invoking this hypothesis posit that "easy judgments about persuasion arguments almost always benefit from motivational manipulations, more demanding person-perception judgments sometimes benefit from motivational manipulations, and highly demanding judgments under uncertainty almost never benefit from motivational manipulations" (Pelham & Neter, 1995, p. 581). For simplicity, we refer to this account as the *Motivation-Difficulty hypothesis.*

Several major problems, which we have described in detail elsewhere (see Lerner & Tetlock, 1999), arise when applying the Motivation-Difficulty hypothesis to the accountability literature. In this chapter, we focus on the most important problems: determining (a) what constitutes a difficult task and (b) if accountability inhibits performance on such tasks. Some advocates of the Motivation-Difficulty hypothesis classify judgments under uncertainty (i.e., judgments in which probability values are unknown) as difficult tasks based on the idea that no amount of motivation improves accuracy when assessing the precise probability of unusual events (Pelham & Neter, 1995, p. 582). If their classification of difficult judgments as those that are made under uncertainty is right, then several lines of accountability research fail to support the Motivation-Difficulty hypothesis. Each finds that accountability improves judgments under uncertainty.

Specifically, the record shows that overconfidence in judgment accuracy (see Lichtenstein, Fischhoff, & Phillips, 1982) decreases with accountability (Kassin, Castillo, & Rigby, 1991; Siegel-Jacobs & Yates, 1996; Tetlock & Kim, 1987). Accuracy in assessing covariation improves with accountability (Murphy, 1994); as does awareness of one's judgment process – indicated by greater correspondence between (a) the cues that participants say they are using to make choices and (b) the cues that regression models from participants' data reveal they are using (Cvetkovich, 1978; Hagafors & Brehmer, 1983; Weldon & Gargano, 1988). Conjunction errors (i.e., when the likelihood of two events is judged greater than the probability that one of the events will occur alone, e.g., Tversky & Kahneman, 1982) are also reduced by accountability (Simonson & Nye, 1992). Moreover, two especially pervasive tendencies – (1) anchoring on an initial value and insufficiently adjusting a numerical estimate up or down from that anchor (Tversky & Kahneman, 1974) and (2) weighting sunk costs when considering future investments (Arkes & Blumer, 1985) – are also reduced by accountability (Brockner, Shaw, & Rubin, 1979; Kruglanski & Freund, 1983; Simonson & Nye, 1992; Simonson & Staw, 1992). If we accept the idea (suggested by Motivation-Difficulty researchers) that judgments under uncertainty constitute difficult judgments, then these well-replicated results contradict the Motivation-Difficulty hypothesis's prediction that accountability will fail to improve judgment in difficult tasks. Theoretically, this hypothesis could be supported if we were able to redefine what constitutes a difficult task, but that would require so many post hoc judgment calls that the original advantage of parsimony would be lost.

Hypothesis Two: Does Increased Cognitive Effort Attenuate Bias?

The idea that thinking harder equates to thinking better has intuitive appeal. Considering the tendency for decision makers to use low-effort heuristics and *satisficing* techniques (for reviews, see Dawes, 1998; Kahneman, Slovic, & Tversky, 1982), any factor that encourages systematic forms of thought could be beneficial.

To be sure, some research documents that accountability leads research participants to think harder and better. For example, accountability prompted participants in an attribution study to focus on the facts presented in fictional tort cases rather than to simply infer a judgment based on their present feelings (Lerner, Goldberg, & Tetlock, 1998). Increased cognitive effort among accountable participants has also been shown to decrease susceptibility to a host of common biases such as the *fundamental attribution error* (Tetlock, 1985), oversensitivity to the order in which information appears (Kennedy, 1993; Kruglanski & Freund, 1983; Schadewald & Limberg, 1992; Tetlock, 1983b; Webster, Richter, & Kruglanski, 1996), and overconfidence (Kassin et al., 1991; Siegel-Jacobs & Yates, 1996; Tetlock & Kim, 1987).

Quite often, however, thinking harder (as a result of accountability) does not equate to thinking better. At least two factors moderate the relationship between effortful thought and bias attenuation. The first factor involves characteristics of the judgment and decision-making process; the second involves characteristics of the judgment and decision-making task.

A Process Moderator. Although both confirmatory thought and exploratory thought can be high-cognitive-effort responses to accountability, they differ in important ways. Whereas confirmatory thought involves a one-sided attempt to rationalize a particular point of view, exploratory thought involves evenhanded consideration of alternative points of view. In short, although both exploratory and confirmatory thought can be effortful, one takes place in the service of self-justification, whereas the other takes place in the service of optimizing a judgment/decision.

Generally speaking, the timing of accountability determines which process will occur. Whereas predecisional accountability prompts exploratory thought and the goal of making an optimal judgment/ decision, postdecisional accountability prompts confirmatory and self-justifying thoughts (for review, see Lerner & Tetlock, 1999). A useful example appears in research on the sunk cost effect (i.e., escalating resource commitments to prior courses of action even when future costs from the course of action will exceed future benefits; see Arkes & Blumer, 1985). Whereas postdecisional accountability amplifies the commitment to prior courses of action (Conlon & Wolf, 1980; Fox & Staw, 1979), predecisional accountability attenuates commitment (Brockner et al., 1979; Simonson & Staw, 1992). In the former situation, learning of the need to justify their actions only after committing themselves to a decision led participants to think of as many reasons as they could to bolster their decision. By contrast, in the latter situation, learning of the need to justify their actions prior to forming an opinion allowed participants to consider impartially whether or not to continue their commitment. In sum, increased cognitive effort can take the form of confirmatory or exploratory thought.

A Task Moderator. Depending on the type of the task, biases can arise from different sources. Sometimes judgment bias arises from insufficient attention to relevant cues in a task – what Arkes (1991) calls *strategy-based errors*. According to Arkes, people engage in a cursory review of available information when the effort or cost associated with a thorough review of cues in a particular task is greater than the benefit. At other times, bias arises from overuse of available cues – what Kerr, MacCoun, and Kramer (1996) call *sins of commission* or what Hastie and Rasinski (1988) call *using a bad cue*. According to Kerr and colleagues, people make sins of commission when a task contains a proscribed cue that is normatively irrelevant but not obviously so. Importantly, the effects of accountability and increased cognitive effort hinge on whether a bias arises from underuse or overuse of cues. Whereas accountability will attenuate the first kind of bias, it will amplify the second.

To illustrate this moderator, first consider a prototypical strategy-based error: the tendency of perceivers to rely on category rather than attribute information. Kruglanski and Freund (1983) showed that accountability attenuates this bias. When Israeli participants graded a paper by an Ashkenazi (high status group) writer under no accountability, the scores were higher than when they graded a paper known to be from a Sepharadic (low status group) writer. In effect, the stereotyped-category label shaped grade assignments among unaccountable participants. This reliance on category labels disappeared, however, when participants believed that they had to explain their grade assignments to other members of the group. When accountable, participants paid greater attention to the actual attributes of the paper (for similar results, see Boudreau, Baron, & Oliver, 1992; Pendry & Macrae, 1996).

Now consider a prototypical sin of commission (i.e., bias arising from use of a normatively proscribed cue): the dilution effect. This effect occurs when nondiagnostic evidence dilutes the predictive power of diagnostic evidence (Nisbett, Zukier, & Lemley, 1981; Zukier, 1982) and is amplified by predecisional accountability to an unknown audience (Tetlock & Boettger, 1989). When attempting to predict a student's grade point average, accountable and unaccountable participants gave weight to irrelevant information contained in a thumbnail sketch of the student (e.g., the number of plants a student keeps) but accountable participants were even more likely to do so. Compared to accountable participants, unaccountable participants relied more on the sole valid predictor – namely, the number of hours the student studied per week. In short, accountability amplified bias by increasing indiscriminate use of information (for similar results, see Gordon, Rozelle, & Baxter, 1988; Hattrup & Ford, 1995; Siegel-Jacobs & Yates, 1996; Tetlock, Lerner, & Boettger, 1996).

To recap, increased cognitive effort sometimes attenuates biases in judgment and decision making; at many other times it does not – it even amplifies some biases. Rather than exerting a main effect on outcomes, both judgment *process* factors (e.g., exploratory versus confirmatory efforts) and judgment *task* factors (e.g., the initial source of bias) moderate the effect of cognitive effort on bias.

Toward a Multifactor Framework for the Effects of Accountability

Having failed to find support for two face-valid hypotheses – one positing a main effect, the other a first-order interaction – we now elaborate on an alternative scheme for predicting the effects of accountability on bias. Building on the process and task moderators identified in the previous section, this framework posits that the effects on bias depend on interactions among multiple factors, including *the type and timing of accountability*; the *original source of the judgment/choice bias*; *individual differences among decision makers* (e.g., in knowledge of decision rules and in sensitivity to social pressures); *social constraints on the decision process* (e.g., time pressure); and *the degree to which accountability systems are perceived as legitimate.* Elsewhere, we have reviewed these and other moderators (see Lerner & Tetlock, 1999). Due to limitations of space, we focus here on two especially important factors that provide the basis for a new framework: the type and timing of accountability and the original source of the judgment/choice bias.

Key Factors

Type and Timing of Accountability. As discussed in the previous sections, accountability is not a unitary phenomenon. Different kinds of accountability activate qualitatively and quantitatively distinct forms of thought. Here we briefly sketch predictions for the relation between type of accountability and resulting thought processes (for elaboration, see Lerner & Tetlock, 1999).

When decision makers learn of accountability only after encoding judgment/choice cues, they are likely to anchor on initial values and adjust their estimates insufficiently (Tetlock & Kim, 1987). Similarly, learning of accountability only after committing themselves to a particular judgment/choice will trigger confirmatory thoughts and bolstering of their initial selections (Conlon & Wolf, 1980; Fox & Staw, 1979). Predecisional and preencoding accountability are, therefore, necessary preconditions for integratively complex thought. They are not, however, sufficient. If the decision makers know the views of the prospective audience, conformity is the most likely reaction (Tetlock, Skitka, & Boettger, 1989). Moreover, even if decision makers are unaware of the audience's views, they may believe that an audience favors expedient decisions rather than accurate decisions and respond accordingly (Mero & Motowidlo, 1995; Siegel-Jacobs & Yates, 1996). Finally, whether the decision maker perceives accountability as legitimate and unobtrusive or not should moderate the kind of thought accountability triggers. Decision makers who sense that an illegitimate audience wants to influence their beliefs may react in a variety of counterproductive ways. They may respond by asserting their own views even more vigorously (Baer, Hinkle, Smith, & Fenton, 1980; Brehm, 1966, 1972; Heilman & Toffler, 1976) or by disengaging from the task (Cvetkovich, 1978; Enzle & Anderson, 1993). Figure 13.1 provides a schematic representation of these predictions. We hasten to note that these predictions necessarily

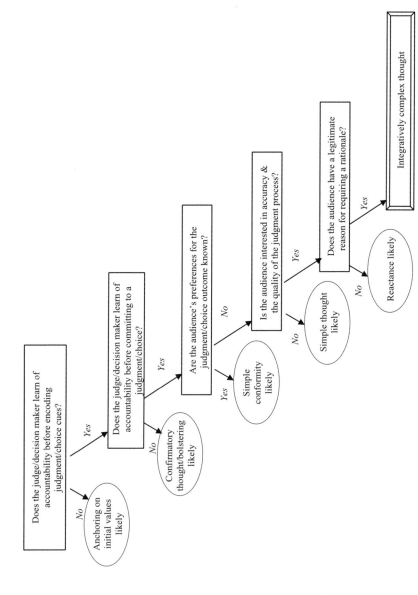

Figure 13.1 Effects of the type and timing of accountability on complexity of thought.

simplify the possible range of responses. Depending on the situational context, other nonintegratively complex responses (e.g., buck passing and procrastination) may also occur (see Tetlock & Boettger, 1994).

To recap, the framework predicts that integratively complex and open-minded thought is most likely to be activated when decision makers learn prior to forming any opinions that they will be accountable to an audience (a) whose views are unknown, (b) who is interested in accuracy, (c) who is reasonably well informed, and (d) who has a legitimate reason for inquiring into the reasons behind participants' judgments/ choices.

Importantly, the framework assumes that even among studies that trigger integratively complex thought, accountability effects will be highly variable across judgment and choice tasks, sometimes improving, sometimes having no effect on, and sometimes degrading judgment and choice. To specify the determinants of these respective outcomes, we introduce the second factor in our framework.

Source of Bias. The framework predicts that predecisional accountability to an unknown audience will *attenuate bias* on tasks to the extent that (a) a given bias results from lack of self-critical attention to the judgment process and (b) improvement requires no special training in formal decision rules, only greater attention to the information provided. This prediction is consistent with Arkes's (1991) view that increases in cognitive effort attenuate strategy-based errors. The rationale is as follows. When participants expect to justify their judgments, they want to avoid appearing foolish in front of the audience. They prepare themselves by engaging in an effortful and self-critical search for reasons to justify their action. This leads participants to (a) survey a wider range of conceivably relevant cues; (b) pay greater attention to the cues they use; (c) anticipate counterarguments, weigh their merits impartially, and factor those that pass some threshold of plausibility into their overall opinion or assessment of the situation; and (d) gain greater awareness of their cognitive processes by regularly monitoring the cues that they allowed to influence judgment and choice.

Predecisional accountability to an unknown audience will, however, *have no effect on bias* to the extent that (a) a given bias results from lack of special training in formal decision rules (e.g., Bayes's theorem, expected utility theory) that are unfamiliar to the decision maker (see Simonson & Nye, 1992) and (b) no amount of increased effort illuminates these rules. This prediction is consistent with several recent theories positing that bias correction hinges not only on the motivation to correct but also on the ability to correct one's mental processes (Kerr et al., 1996; Wegener & Petty, 1995; Wilson & Brekke, 1996).

Finally, it is useful to distinguish between judgment and choice tasks when predicting the conditions under which predecisional accountability to an unknown audience will *amplify bias*. To be sure, the same overarching motive underlies bias amplification in both judgment tasks and choice tasks: a desire to avoid appearing foolish in front of the audience. This motivation plays out differently, however, in judgment and choice tasks. In *choice tasks*, accountability to an unknown audience will amplify bias to the extent that a given bias arises because the choice option that appears easiest to justify also happens to be the biased option (Simonson, 1989; Simonson & Nye, 1992). That is, a desire to avoid appearing foolish in front of the audience heightens (a) the need to ensure that one's choice is securely based on reasons and thus (b) the preference for options that are easy to justify (Shafir et al., 1993).

In *judgment tasks*, predecisional accountability to an unknown audience will amplify bias to the extent that a given bias results from naive use of normatively (but not obviously) irrelevant cues. That is, when a bias results from a lack of awareness that certain cues are proscribed, the desire to avoid appearing foolish in front of an audience only makes matters worse: It heightens use of all cues, even irrelevant ones.

Evidence for Hypotheses

In support of our predictions concerning the type of accountability and the integrative complexity of thought, several studies find that timing plays a pivotal role in moderating thought. If decision makers learn of accountability before exposure to judgment/choice cues, accountability can activate integratively complex thought and reduce biases (e.g., over-attribution, overconfidence in the accuracy of one's predictions, and the primacy effect; see Tetlock, 1983b, 1985; Tetlock & Kim, 1987). By contrast, if decision makers learn of being accountable only after encoding the information, they do not retroactively compensate for a faulty encoding process.[1] Another key timing issue concerns whether decision

---

[1] In one rare circumstance, postexposure accountability and an explicit emphasis on the value of forming accurate judgments reduced bias. Specifically, participants who initially encoded evidence in heuristic fashion returned to the evidence and reprocessed it in a more systematic fashion (Thompson et al., 1994).

makers learn of accountability before committing themselves to a particular judgment/choice. For example, accountable decision makers who reported their thoughts *after* making attitudinal commitments bolstered their initial attitude and formed less integratively complex and more rigidly defensive views (Lambert, Cronen, Chasteen, & Lickel, 1996; Morris, Moore, Tamuz, & Tarrell, 1998; Tetlock et al., 1989).[2]

In support of predictions concerning the views of the audience, several studies have found that when audience views are known prior to forming one's own opinion, conformity becomes the likely coping strategy (see Cialdini, Levy, Herman, Kozlowski, & Petty, 1976; Jones & Wortman, 1973; Klimoski & Inks, 1990; Tetlock, 1983a; Tetlock et al., 1989). Similarly, if decision makers are unaware of specific views but sense that the audience wants a particular decision outcome, they will focus on achieving that outcome to the detriment of an open-minded, careful decision process (c.f. Mero & Motowidlo, 1995; Siegel-Jacobs & Yates, 1996).

Finally, several studies find that perceived legitimacy plays an important role. In cases where accountability was perceived as overly intrusive or illegitimate, predecisional accountability to an unknown-view audience failed to play its typical role in activating integratively complex thought. Rather, overly intrusive accountability led participants to disengage from the tasks (Enzle & Anderson, 1993) and to assert their own initial views more vigorously (Baer et al., 1980; Brehm, 1966, 1972; Heilman & Toffler, 1976).

To recap, when decision makers do not feel locked into any prior commitment, when they learn of accountability prior to encoding cues, and when their audience is legitimately interested in the reasons behind a careful decision process, decision makers are likely to engage in *preemptive self-criticism* (Tetlock, 1983a; Tetlock et al., 1989). That is, they think in more self-critical, integratively complex ways in which they consider multiple perspectives on the issue and try to anticipate the objections that "reasonable others" might raise to positions that they might take.

Turning to our *bias attenuation* prediction, predecisional accountability to an unknown audience has repeatedly been shown to improve

---

[2] The dominant tendency to bolster initial thoughts does interact with situational and individual factors. Specifically, the timing of an anticipated discussion and the relative importance of the issue moderate complexity (Cialdini et al., 1976), as do the relative expertise of the audience (Fitzpatrick & Eagly, 1981) and individual differences in dogmatism (Tetlock et al., 1989).

judgments and decisions via increases in the integrative complexity of thought. As examples, predecisional accountability to an unknown audience has increased consideration of often overlooked situational attributions for a target's behavior (Lerner et al., 1998; Tetlock, 1985; Wells, Petty, Harkins, Kagehiro, & Harvey, 1977); use of effortful, systematic judgment strategies (Ashton, 1992; Cvetkovich, 1978; Doney & Armstrong, 1996; Ford & Weldon, 1981; McAllister, Mitchell, & Beach, 1979; Murphy, 1994; Weldon & Gargano, 1988); attention to effort-demanding cues in persuasive messages (Chaiken, 1980); awareness of judgmental processes, and as a result, improved consistency of cue utilization, consensus within auditing groups, and consistency of judgment strategy use across a rater's judgments (Hagafors & Brehmer, 1983; Johnson & Kaplan, 1991; Siegel-Jacobs & Yates, 1996). (For similar effects, see Boudreau et al., 1992; Kassin et al., 1991; Kennedy, 1993; Kruglanski & Freund, 1983; Mero & Motowidlo, 1995; Pendry & Macrae, 1996; Schadewald & Limberg, 1992; Simonson & Nye, 1992; Tetlock, 1983a; Tetlock & Kim, 1987; Webster et al., 1996).

In sum, accountability attenuates bias on tasks to the extent that (a) suboptimal performance resulted from lack of self-critical attention to the judgment process and (b) improvement required no special training in formal decision rules, only greater attention to the information provided. For example, heightened awareness of judgment processes led accountable participants to disregard their own previously aroused affect (Bodenhausen, Kramer, & Süsser, 1994; Lerner et al., 1998) because it takes no special training in formal decision rules to realize that one's mood should not influence unrelated judgments.

In support of our *no effect on bias prediction*, several studies have found that accountability failed to modify biases that were exclusively attributable to lack of knowledge regarding formal decision rules. For example, accountability has no effect on insensitivity to sample size and insensitivity to base-rate information (Simonson & Nye, 1992). Presumably most participants lack the knowledge that one should reduce estimates of sampling variance in proportion to sample size (Kahneman & Tversky, 1982) or that one should adjust probability estimates for the frequency of a specific event in some relevant population (Kahneman et al., 1982). (For similar examples, see Selart, 1996; Simonson & Nye, 1992.) Moreover, the only examples of accountability improving judgments requiring formal rules are those in which participants had previously received training in the relevant rules (cf. Wilson & Brekke, 1996). For example, when MBA students (trained in subjective expected utility theory and its application to investment decisions) were made accountable for their future investments, they became willing to write off sunk costs (Simonson & Nye, 1992; Simonson & Staw, 1992). Confirming that these participants knew formal decision rules, 84% of them later stated an awareness of the principle that sunk costs should be written off.

In support of our *bias amplification* prediction for *choices*, accountability has amplified bias in several tasks where the option perceived as easiest to justify also happened to be the biased option. The compromise effect – the tendency for a product to gain attractiveness simply because it becomes a middle option in a choice set (Simonson, 1989; Simonson & Nowlis, 2000) – nicely illustrates this phenomenon. Accountable participants were especially likely to select the product that represented the compromise option because they thought that products with middle-of-the-road features were more easily defensible than options that were superior on one dimension but inferior on another (Simonson & Nowlis, 2000). Similar findings were obtained for the attraction effect (Simonson, 1989) and ambiguity aversion (Curley, Yates, & Abrams, 1986) – two effects in which the option perceived as easiest to justify also happens to be the biased option.

In support of our *bias amplification* prediction for *judgments*, accountability to an unknown audience has repeatedly been shown to amplify indiscriminate use of information in prediction tasks (Gordon et al., 1988; Hattrup & Ford, 1995; Siegel-Jacobs & Yates, 1996; Tetlock & Boettger, 1989). Research on the dilution effect, described earlier, serves as a useful example. Because the dilution effect stems from use of normatively irrelevant evidence, motivating accountable participants to become more vigilant thinkers sent accountable participants off on inferential wild-goose chases in which they attempted to weave together into a coherent story the disparate pieces of normatively – but not obviously – irrelevant information contained in diluted conditions (Tetlock & Boettger, 1989; Tetlock et al., 1996). In short, when bias arises from the use of normatively (but not obviously) irrelevant information, accountability amplifies bias by increasing indiscriminate use of that information.

At this point, readers may wonder how the conclusion that accountability amplifies use of normatively irrelevant cues can be reconciled with the fact that irrelevant cues are present in virtually all real-life problems. Why doesn't accountability always amplify judgment bias? The answer is straightforward: Amplification hinges on the context in which cues are presented, such as whether the cues have been presented to the judge by someone presumed to have knowledge about the task. When the judge receives information from someone presumed to be knowledgeable (e.g., the experimenter), the judge will follow the reasonable assumption that all information provided is relevant to the task at hand (see Grice, 1975; Schwarz, Strack, Hilton, & Naderer, 1991; Sperber & Wilson, 1986). From this vantage point, the presentation of information in experiments can be likened to a conversation between the researcher and the participant – an interaction in which participants assume that the experimenter (their conversational partner) is following a widely accepted norm of stating only relevant information in social discourse (see Grice, 1975; Sperber & Wilson, 1986).

If the preceding predictions hold, it should be possible to reduce this indiscriminate use of normatively irrelevant information by leading participants to question the otherwise reasonable assumption (when participating in experiments) that all information provided by the experimenter is somehow relevant to the task at hand. Tetlock et al. (1996) tested this hypothesis on the dilution effect. Some participants were explicitly told that the axioms of conversation (assume the relevance of all information) did indeed apply and that the experimenter had carefully screened the information provided participants to ensure its relevance for the prediction task. Other participants were explicitly told that the information might or might not be relevant to the prediction task. Still other participants were not given any explicit guidance one way or the other concerning the relevance of the information. Accountable participants demonstrated a robust dilution effect when conversational norms were explicitly primed, as well as in the no-priming control condition, but no dilution at all when conversational norms were explicitly deactivated. Nonaccountable participants demonstrated the dilution effect across norm activation (information relevant) conditions, with the strongest effect under the activation of conversational norms. In other words, accountable participants were fully capable of disregarding irrelevant information, but only when they believed that conversational norms no longer required them to search for relevance in communications from others. So long as they believed conversational norms applied, their judgments were at least as biased as those of nonaccountable participants.

Synthesis. Among the various kinds of accountability, predecisional accountability to an unknown-view audience is most likely to trigger integratively complex thought. This form of accountability is likely to attenuate biases that arise from lack of critical attention to one's decision processes and failure to use all relevant cues. By contrast, this same form of accountability is likely to amplify bias to the extent that (a) a given judgment bias results from using normatively (but not obviously) proscribed information or (b) a given choice bias results from the fact that the option that appears easiest to justify also happens to be the biased option. Finally, this form of accountability is likely to have no effect on biases that result exclusively from lack of special training in formal decision rules (for additional evidence supporting these predictions, see Lerner & Tetlock, 1999). The previously described moderators are not an exhaustive list, but they provide a solid basis for building a broader multifactor framework.

Conclusions: Benefits of Accountability Research for the Study of Judgment and Choice

Although accountability is an inevitable feature of decision environments, it has been overlooked by psychological theories of judgment and choice. In the past two decades, however, an exciting field has begun to document the ways in which accountability systematically shapes judgment process and content. A driving question in this emerging field has been: Can accountability inoculate decision makers from commonly observed cognitive biases? As the previous section documented, we can now answer this question. We can now predict how specific forms of accountability interact with characteristics of decision makers and properties of the task environment to shape judgment and choice.

In this final section, we move from organizing the empirical effects of accountability to considering the broader benefits accountability research brings to the study of judgment and choice. We focus on two kinds of benefits: enhancing theoretical development and improving applications of research to real-world settings.

Enhancing Theoretical Development

In the judgment and decision-making literature, a bedrock assumption has been that individuals are motivated to form accurate judgments (see Kelley, 1967). Based on this assumption, researchers label departures from accuracy (e.g., departures from Bayes's Theorem and Subjective Expected Utility) as errors or biases. It is worth noting, however, that social and institutional contexts can alter the goals held by decision makers. For example, accountability can lead decision makers to place greater value on getting along with their conversation partner by respecting norms than on judgment accuracy (Dulany & Hilton, 1991; Grice, 1975; Hilton, 1990; Krosnick, Li, & Lehman, 1990; Lerner & Tetlock, 1999; Schwarz et al., 1991; Tetlock, 1992). As a result, the dilution effect may appear to be evidence of irrationality in one social or institutional context, but may be judged quite rational within another (what Tetlock, 1998 calls a *normative boundary condition* on classification of effects as errors or biases).

Numerous other studies support the notion that decision-making goals shift as a function of social and institutional contexts (e.g., Chen, Shecter, & Chaiken, 1996; Cialdini, Kallgren, & Reno, 1991; Goldberg, Lerner, & Tetlock, 1999; Kunda, 1990). For example, Thompson (1995) found that negotiators flexibly shifted their goals according to their constituency's views. When negotiators believed they would be rewarded for their objectivity, accountable bargainers were better able to perceive interests compatible with the other party than were unaccountable bargainers. By contrast, when they believed they would be rewarded for their partisanship, accountable bargainers were less able to see compatible interests than were unaccountable bargainers. In short, accountability research implies that before labeling a response tendency a cognitive error or bias, we should consider the interpersonal, institutional, or political goals of the decision maker.

Improving the Application of Judgment and Decision-Making Research to Real-World Settings

In an age where everyone from physicians to politicians faces demands for greater accountability, the judgment and decision-making literature can make a timely contribution. Specifically, incorporating the real-world pressures of accountability into judgment and decision-making research sheds light on how best to structure reporting relationships in organizations. Already we know that accountability is not a cognitive cure-all for lazy or unresponsive workers, as conventional wisdom suggests. Rather, only highly specialized subtypes of accountability lead to increased effort, and more cognitive effort is not inherently beneficial; it sometimes makes matters even worse. Moreover, there is ambiguity and room for reasonable disagreement over what should be considered worse or better judgment when we place cognition in its social or institutional context.

At this stage, our grasp of how accountability effects observed in the laboratory will translate to real-world settings is still highly tentative.

Moreover, the details of how one integrates theoretical and empirical work across levels of analysis remain to be ironed out. Nevertheless, this review suggests that placing judgment and decision making in its accountability context helps to put in perspective (a) how the political, institutional, and social settings may require us to rethink what counts as judgmental bias or error and (b) how accountability ground rules can be engineered to encourage desired, and discourage undesired, forms of human information processing.

References

Arkes, H. R. (1991). Costs and benefits of judgment errors: Implications for debiasing. *Psychological Bulletin, 110*(3), 486–498.

Arkes, H. R., & Blumer, C. (1985). The psychology of sunk cost. *Organizational Behavior and Human Decision Processes, 35*, 125–140.

Ashton, R. H. (1992). Effects of justification and a mechanical aid on judgment performance. *Organizational Behavior and Human Decision Processes, 52*(2), 292–306.

Baer, R., Hinkle, S., Smith, K., & Fenton, M. (1980). Reactance as a function of actual versus projected autonomy. *Journal of Personality and Social Psychology, 38*, 416–422.

Bersoff, D. M., & Miller, J. G. (1993). Culture, context, and the development of moral accountability judgments. *Developmental Psychology, 29*, 664–676.

Bodenhausen, G. V., Kramer, G. P., & Süsser, K. (1994). Happiness and stereotypic thinking in social judgment. *Journal of Personality and Social Psychology, 66*, 621–632.

Boudreau, L. A., Baron, R. M., & Oliver, P. V. (1992). Effects of expected communication target expertise and timing of set on trait use in person description. *Personality and Social Psychology Bulletin, 18*, 447–451.

Brehm, J. W. (1966). *A theory of psychological reactance*. New York: Academic Press.

Brehm, J. W. (1972). *Responses to loss of freedom: A theory of psychological reactance*. Morristown, NJ: General Learning Press.

Brief, A. P., Dukerich, J. M., & Doran, L. I. (1991). Resolving ethical dilemmas in management: Experimental investigations of values, accountability, and choice. *Journal of Applied Social Psychology, 21*, 380–396.

Brockner, J., Shaw, M. C., & Rubin, J. Z. (1979). Factors affecting withdrawal from an escalating conflict: Quitting before it's too late. *Journal of Experimental Social Psychology, 15*, 492–503.

Chaiken, S. (1980). Heuristic versus systematic information processing and the use of source versus message cues in persuasion. *Journal of Personality and Social Psychology, 39*, 752–766.

Chen, S., Shecter, D., & Chaiken, S. (1996). Getting at the truth or getting along: Accuracy-versus impression-motivated heuristic and systematic processing. *Journal of Personality and Social Psychology, 71*, 262–275.

Cialdini, R. B., Kallgren, C. A., & Reno, R. R. (1991). A focus theory of normative conduct: A theoretical refinement and reevaluation of the role of norms in human behavior. *Advances in Experimental Social Psychology, 24,* 201–234.

Cialdini, R. B., Levy, A., Herman, C. P., Kozlowski, I. T., & Petty, R. E. (1976). Elastic shifts of opinion: Determinants of direction and durability. *Journal of Personality and Social Psychology, 34,* 663–672.

Conlon, E. J., & Wolf, G. (1980). The moderating effects of strategy, visibility, and involvement on allocation behavior: An extension of Staw's escalation paradigm. *Organizational Behavior and Human Performance, 26,* 172–192.

Curley, S. P., Yates, J. F., & Abrams, R. A. (1986). Psychological sources of ambiguity avoidance. *Organizational Behavior and Human Decision Processes, 38,* 230–256.

Cvetkovich, G. (1978). Cognitive accommodation, language, and social responsibility. *Social Psychology, 2,* 149–155.

Dawes, R. (1998). Behavioral decision making and judgment. In D. T. Gilbert, S. T. Fiske, & G. Lindzey (Eds.), *The handbook of social psychology* (Vol. 1, pp. 497–548). New York: Oxford University Press.

Doney, P. M., & Armstrong, G. M. (1996). Effects of accountability on symbolic information search and information analysis by organizational buyers. *Journal of the Academy of Marketing Science, 24,* 57–65.

Dulany, D. E., & Hilton, D. J. (1991). Conversational implicature, conscious representation, and the conjunction fallacy. *Social Cognition, 9,* 85–110.

Enzle, M. E., & Anderson, S. C. (1993). Surveillant intentions and intrinsic motivation. *Journal of Personality and Social Psychology, 64*(2), 257–266.

Fitzpatrick, A. R., & Eagly, A. H. (1981). Anticipatory belief polarization as a function of the expertise of a discussion partner. *Personality and Social Psychology Bulletin, 7,* 636–642.

Ford, J. K., & Weldon, E. (1981). Forewarning and accountability: Effects on memory-based interpersonal judgments. *Personality and Social Psychology Bulletin, 2,* 264–268.

Fox, F. V., & Staw, B. M. (1979). The trapped administrator: The effects of job insecurity and policy resistance upon commitment to a course of action. *Administrative Science Quarterly, 24,* 449–471.

Goldberg, J. H., Lerner, J. S., & Tetlock, P. E. (1999). Rage and reason: The psychology of the intuitive prosecutor. *European Journal of Social Psychology, 29,* 781–795.

Gonzales, M. H., Kovera, M. B., Sullivan, J. L., & Chanley, V. (1995). Private reactions to public transgressions: Predictors of evaluative responses to allegations of political misconduct. *Personality and Social Psychology Bulletin, 21,* 136–148.

Gordon, R. A., Rozelle, R. M., & Baxter, J. C. (1988). The effect of applicant age, job level, and accountability on the evaluation of job applicants. *Organizational Behavior and Human Decision Processes, 41,* 20–33.

Gordon, R. A., & Stuecher, U. (1992). The effect of anonymity and increased accountability on the linguistic complexity of teaching evaluations. *Journal of Psychology, 126,* 639–649.

Grice, H. P. (1975). Logic and conversation. In P. Cole & J. L. Morgan (Eds.), *Syntax and Semantics, 3: Speech Acts* (pp. 41–58). New York: Academic Press.

Hagafors, R., & Brehmer, B. (1983). Does having to justify one's judgments change the nature of the judgment process? *Organizational Behavior and Human Performance, 31,* 223–232.

Hastie, R., & Rasinski, K. A. (1988). The concept of accuracy in social judgment. In D. Bar-Tal & A. W. Kruglanski (Eds.), *The social psychology of knowledge* (pp. 193–208). Cambridge: Cambridge University Press.

Hattrup, K., & Ford, J. K. (1995). The role of information characteristics and accountability in moderating stereotype-driven processes during social decision making. *Organizational Behavior and Human Decision Processes, 63,* 73–86.

Heilman, M. E., & Toffler, B. L. (1976). Reacting to reactance: An interpersonal interpretation of the need for freedom. *Journal of Experimental Social Psychology, 12,* 519–529.

Hilton, D. J. (1990). Conversational processes and causal explanation. *Psychological Bulletin, 107,* 65–81.

Hobbes, T. (1660/1968). *Leviathan.* Baltimore: Penguin Books.

Hong, Y., & Chiu, C. (1992). A study of the comparative structure of guilt and shame in a Chinese society. *Journal of Psychology, 126,* 171–179.

Hsee, C. (1995). Elastic justification: How tempting but task-irrelevant factors influence decisions. *Organizational Behavior and Human Decision Processes, 62*(3), 330–337.

Hull, C. L. (1943). *Principles of behavior: An introduction to behavior theory.* New York: Appleton-Century-Crofts.

Johnson, V. E., & Kaplan, S. E. (1991). Experimental evidence on the effects of accountability on auditor judgments. *Auditing: A Journal of Practice and Theory, 10,* 96–107.

Jones, E. E., & Wortman, C. (1973). *Ingratiation: An attributional approach.* Morristown, NJ: General Learning Press.

Kahneman, D., Slovic, P., & Tversky, A. (Eds.). (1982). *Judgment under uncertainty: Heuristics and biases.* New York: Cambridge University Press.

Kahneman, D., & Tversky, A. (1982). On the psychology of prediction. *Psychological Review, 80,* 237–251.

Kassin, S. M., Castillo, S. R., & Rigby, S. (1991). The accuracy–confidence correlation in eyewitness testimony: Limits and extensions of the retrospective self-awareness effect. *Journal of Personality and Social Psychology, 5,* 698–707.

Katz, D., & Kahn, R. L. (1978). *The social psychology of organizations.* New York: Wiley.

Kelley, H. H. (1967). Attribution theory in social psychology. *Nebraska Symposium on Motivation, 15,* 192–238.

Kennedy, J. (1993). Debiasing audit judgment with accountability: A framework and experimental results. *Journal of Accounting Research, 31,* 231–245.

Kerr, N. L., MacCoun, R. J., & Kramer, G. P. (1996). Bias in judgment: Comparing individuals and groups. *Psychological Review, 103,* 687–719.

Klimoski, R., & Inks, L. (1990). Accountability forces in performance appraisal. *Organizational Behavior and Human Decision Processes, 45,* 194–208.

Krosnick, J. A., Li, F., & Lehman, D. R. (1990). Conversational conventions, order of information acquisition, and the effect of base rates and individuating information on social judgments. *Journal of Personality and Social Psychology, 59,* 1140–1152.

Kruglanski, A. W., & Freund, T. (1983). The freezing and unfreezing of lay-inferences: Effects on impressional primacy, ethnic stereotyping and numerical anchoring. *Journal of Experimental Social Psychology, 19,* 448–468.

Kuhn, D. (1992). Thinking as argument. *Harvard Educational Review, 62*(2), 155–178.

Kunda, Z. (1990). The case for motivated reasoning. *Psychological Bulletin, 108,* 480–498.

Lambert, A. J., Cronen, S., Chasteen, A. L., & Lickel, B. (1996). Private versus public expressions of racial prejudice. *Journal of Experimental Social Psychology, 32,* 437–459.

Lerner, J. S., Goldberg, J. H., & Tetlock, P. E. (1998). Sober second thought: The effects of accountability, anger and authoritarianism on attributions of responsibility. *Personality and Social Psychology Bulletin, 24,* 563–574.

Lerner, J. S., & Tetlock, P. E. (1994). Accountability and social cognition. In V. S. Ramachandran (Ed.), *Encyclopedia of human behavior* (Vol. 1, pp. 3098–3121). San Diego, CA: Academic Press.

Lerner, J. S., & Tetlock, P. E. (1999). Accounting for the effects of accountability. *Psychological Bulletin, 125*(2), 255–275.

Lichtenstein, S., Fischhoff, B., & Phillips, L. D. (1982). Calibration of probabilities: The state of the art to 1980. In D. Kahneman, P. Slovic, & A. Tversky (Eds.), *Judgment under uncertainty: Heuristics and biases* (pp. 306–354). Cambridge: Cambridge University Press.

March, J. G., & Olsen, J. P. (1995). *Democratic governance.* New York: Free Press.

McAllister, D. W., Mitchell, T. R., & Beach, L. R. (1979). The contingency model for the selection of decision strategies: An empirical test of the effects of significance, accountability, and reversibility. *Organizational Behavior and Human Performance, 24,* 228–244.

McGraw, K. M., Best, S., & Timpone, R. (1995). "What they say or what they do?" The impact of elite explanation and policy outcomes on public opinion. *American Journal of Political Science, 39,* 53–74.

Mead, G. H. (1934). *Mind, self, and society from the standpoint of a social behaviorist* (Vol. 1). Chicago: University of Chicago Press.

Mero, N., & Motowidlo, S. (1995). Effects of rater accountability on the accuracy and favorability of performance ratings. *Journal of Applied Psychology, 80*(4), 517–524.

Morris, M., Moore, P. C., Tamuz, M., & Tarrell, R. (1998, August). *Learning from a brush with danger.* Paper presented at the annual meeting of the Academy of Management, San Diego, CA.

Murphy, R. (1994). The effects of task characteristics on covariation assessment: The impact of accountability and judgment frame. *Organizational Behavior and Human Decision Processes, 60,* 139–155.

Nisbett, R. E., Zukier, H., & Lemley, R. (1981). The dilution effect: Nondiagnostic information weakens the implications of diagnostic information. *Cognitive Psychology, 13*, 248–277.

Pelham, B. W., & Neter, E. (1995). The effect of motivation of judgment depends on the difficulty of the judgment. *Journal of Personality and Social Psychology, 68*(4), 581–594.

Pendry, L. F., & Macrae, C. N. (1996). What the disinterested perceiver overlooks: Goal-directed social categorization. *Personality and Social Psychology Bulletin, 22*, 249–256.

Pennington, J., & Schlenker, B. R. (1999). Accountability for consequential decisions: Justifying ethical judgments to audiences. *Personality and Social Psychology Bulletin, 25*, 1067–1081.

Ross, J., & Staw, B. M. (1986). Expo 86: An escalation prototype. *Administrative Science Quarterly, 31*, 274–297.

Ross, J., & Staw, B. M. (1993). Organizational escalation and exit: Lessons from the Shorehem nuclear power plant. *Academy of Management Journal, 36*, 701–732.

Schadewald, M. S., & Limberg, S. T. (1992). Effect of information order and accountability on causal judgments in a legal context. *Psychological Reports, 71*, 619–625.

Schlenker, B. R. (1980). *Impression management: The self-concept, social identity, and interpersonal relations.* Monterey, CA: Brooks/Cole.

Schlenker, B. R. (Ed.). (1985). *The self and social life.* New York: McGraw-Hill.

Schwarz, N., Strack, F., Hilton, D., & Naderer, G. (1991). Base rates, representativeness, and the logic of conversation: The contextual relevance of irrelevant information. *Social Cognition, 9*, 67–84.

Scott, M. B., & Lyman, S. (1968). Accounts. *American Sociological Review, 33*(1), 46–62.

Selart, M. (1996). Structure compatibility and restructuring in judgment and choice. *Organizational Behavior and Human Decision Processes, 65*, 106–116.

Semin, G. R., & Manstead, A. S. R. (1983). *The accountability of conduct: A social psychological analysis.* New York: Academic Press.

Shafir, E., Simonson, I., & Tversky, A. (1993). Reason-based choice. *Cognition, 49*, 11–36.

Siegel-Jacobs, K., & Yates, J. F. (1996). Effects of procedural and outcome accountability on judgment quality. *Organizational Behavior and Human Decision Processes, 66*, 1–17.

Simonson, I. (1989). Choice based on reasons: The case of attraction and compromise effects. *Journal of Consumer Research, 16*, 158–174.

Simonson, I., & Nowlis, S. (2000). The role of explanations and need for uniqueness in consumer decision making: Unconditional choices based on reasons. *Journal of Consumer Research, 27*, 49–68.

Simonson, I., & Nye, P. (1992). The effect of accountability on susceptibility to decision errors. *Organizational Behavior and Human Decision Processes, 51*, 416–446.

Simonson, I., & Staw, B. M. (1992). Deescalation strategies: A comparison of techniques for reducing commitment to losing courses of action. *Journal of Applied Psychology, 77*(4), 419–426.

Spence, K. W. (1956). *Behavior theory and conditioning*. New Haven, CT: Yale University Press.

Sperber, D., & Wilson, D. (1986). *Relevance: Communication and cognition*. Cambridge, MA: Harvard University Press.

Staw, B. M. (Ed.). (1980). *Rationality and justification in organizational life* (Vol. 2). Greenwich, CT: JAI Press.

Staw, B. M., & Fox, F. V. (1977). Escalation: The determinants of commitment to a chosen course of action. *Human Relations, 30*, 431–450.

Staw, B. M., & Ross, J. (1989). Understanding behavior in escalation situations. *Science, 246*, 216–220.

Stenning, P. C. (Ed.). (1995). *Accountability for criminal justice*. Toronto: University of Toronto Press.

Tetlock, P. E. (1983a). Accountability and complexity of thought. *Journal of Personality and Social Psychology, 45*(1), 74–83.

Tetlock, P. E. (1983b). Accountability and the perseverance of first impressions. *Social Psychology Quarterly, 46*, 285–292.

Tetlock, P. E. (1985). Accountability: A social check on the fundamental attribution error. *Social Psychology Quarterly, 48*(3), 227–236.

Tetlock, P. E. (1992). The impact of accountability on judgment and choice: Toward a social contingency model. *Advances in Experimental Social Psychology, 25*, 331–376.

Tetlock, P. E. (1998). Losing our religion: On the collapse of precise normative standards in complex accountability systems. In R. Kramer & M. Neale (Eds.), *Influence processes in organizations: Emerging themes in theory and research* (pp. 121–144). Thousand Oaks, CA: Sage.

Tetlock, P. E., & Boettger, R. (1989). Accountability: A social magnifier of the dilution effect. *Journal of Personality and Social Psychology, 57*, 388–398.

Tetlock, P. E., & Boettger, R. (1994). Accountability amplifies the status quo effect when change creates victims. *Journal of Behavioral Decision Making, 7*, 1–23.

Tetlock, P. E., & Kim, J. I. (1987). Accountability and judgment processes in a personality prediction task. *Journal of Personality and Social Psychology, 52*, 700–709.

Tetlock, P. E., Lerner, J. S., & Boettger, R. (1996). The dilution effect: Judgmental bias, conversational convention, or a bit of both? *European Journal of Social Psychology, 26*, 915–934.

Tetlock, P. E., Skitka, L., & Boettger, R. (1989). Social and cognitive strategies for coping with accountability: Conformity, complexity, and bolstering. *Journal of Personality and Social Psychology, 57*, 632–640.

Thompson, E. P., Roman, R. J., Moskowitz, G. B., & Chaiken, S. (1994). Accuracy motivation attenuates covert priming: The systematic reprocessing of social information. *Journal of Personality & Social Psychology, 66*(3), 474–489.

Thompson, L. (1995). They saw a negotiation: Partisanship and involvement. *Journal of Personality and Social Psychology, 68*, 839–853.

Tversky, A., & Kahneman, D. (1974). Judgment under uncertainty: Heuristics and biases. *Science, 185*, 1124–1131.

Tversky, A., & Kahneman, D. (1982). Extension versus intuitive reasoning: The conjunction fallacy in probability judgments. *Psychological Review, 90*, 293–315.

Webster, D. M., Richter, L., & Kruglanski, A. W. (1996). On leaping to conclusions when feeling tired: Mental fatigue effects on impressional primacy. *Journal of Experimental Social Psychology, 32,* 181–195.

Wegener, D. T., & Petty, R. E. (1995). Flexible correction processes in social judgment: The role of naive theories in corrections for perceived bias. *Journal of Personality and Social Psychology, 68*(1), 36–51.

Weldon, E., & Gargano, G. M. (1988). Cognitive loafing: The effects of accountability and shared responsibility on cognitive effort. *Personality and Social Psychology Bulletin, 14,* 159–171.

Wells, G. L., Petty, R. E., Harkins, S. G., Kagehiro, D., & Harvey, J. (1977). Anticipated discussion of interpretation eliminates actor–observer differences in the attribution of causality. *Sociometry, 40,* 247–253.

Wilson, T. D., & Brekke, N. (1996). Mental contamination and mental correction: Unwanted influences on judgments and evaluations. *Psychological Bulletin, 116*(1), 117–142.

Zajonc, R. B. (1965). Social facilitation. *Science, 149,* 269–149.

Zukier, H. (1982). The dilution effect: The role of the correlation and the dispersion of predictor variables in the use of nondiagnostic information. *Journal of Personality and Social Psychology, 43*(6), 1163–1174.

14 Cognitions, Preferences, and Social Sharedness: Past, Present, and Future Directions in Group Decision Making

Tatsuya Kameda, R. Scott Tindale, and James H. Davis

ABSTRACT

Research on group decision making has focused on how group-member preference distributions map into group-level preferences. One of the key findings from this research is that majority/plurality factions tend to control the group's final decision. Thus, preferences shared by most of the group members tend to become the group's preference. Findings at the cognitive level have also shown that the degree to which cognitions are shared among members affects group decisions. These sociocognitive processes tend to work in concert with the social processes concerning preferences, but they can either enhance or counter preference-level faction size effects. Additionally, socially shared cognitions can both improve and impede group decision performance. This chapter attempts to review key aspects of the group decision-making literature, focusing both at the preference level and at the cognitive level. Similarities between the findings at both levels are explored in relation to the importance of social sharedness for group performance.

CONTENTS

Preparation of this chapter was supported by the Japanese Ministry of Education, Science, Sports, and Culture Grant 11610096 (Tatsuya Kameda, Principal Investigator), National Science Foundation Grant SBR 9730822 (R. Scott Tindale, Principal Investigator), and National Science Foundation Grant SBR 9507955 (James H. Davis, Co-Principal Investigator).

Research on group decision making has several distinctive roots in the social sciences. Besides psychological and sociological approaches to how people make decisions as a collective (e.g., Coleman, 1990; Witte & Davis, 1996), group decision making has been a major research topic in the interdisciplinary area of *social choice theory*, in which economics and political science intersect (Arrow, 1963; Black, 1958; Fishburn, 1973; Ordeshook, 1986). Although these disciplines differ in many ways in terms of how and on what to focus (e.g., empirical versus analytical emphasis, consensus versus choice), perhaps one of the most profound differences is how they characterize *legitimate* inputs for collective choices – what elements are regarded as acceptable inputs to render group decisions (e.g., preference orders, intensity of preferences, justifications).

In this chapter, we start with a discussion of this legitimate input issue. We then demonstrate that distinguishing two levels of inputs, namely, preference and cognition, provides a useful overarching conceptual picture for synthesizing our empirical knowledge about decision making in consensus groups. In so doing, we also show that, at both levels, social sharedness plays a vital, perhaps the most critical, role in determining actual consensus processes and outcomes. *Social sharedness* here refers to the degree to which preferences and cognitions are shared among members at the outset of group interaction (cf. Tindale & Kameda, 2000). We argue that this notion serves as a common thread for understanding various features of group decision making and also as a useful heuristic guide for future research endeavors.

Two Natural Levels in Social Aggregation

Social Choice versus Consensus

To discuss the legitimate input issue in group decision making, let us first think about aggregation processes in a *public choice* such as an election.

As exemplified by a single-ballot system, almost all aggregation methods in public choice situations regard any background information other than preferences to be irrelevant. The only legitimate input for collective choice is individual *preference* (most typically a preference order), formally represented by a vote. More specifically, as far as it is expressed, any vote (whether it is a well-thought-out choice or a capricious one, whether it represents a strong preference or a weak preference, etc.) counts exactly the same in the social aggregation operation. Such a treatment of preference as the supreme (or untouchable) unit in social decision making dates back to the ideas of 18th-century theorists, including Condorcet, Borda, and others, and has been accepted as the standard view in the modern social choice literature (see Mueller, 1989, for a recent review). Furthermore, as Sen (1977) suggests, it is generally unrealistic in a large-scale election to consider a social aggregation mechanism that incorporates inputs other than expressed preferences (i.e., votes).

However, despite its theoretical clarity and practical usefulness in many public choice situations, the notion of supremacy of preferences is not so well established in an everyday group decision-making context featuring a face-to-face interaction (e.g., the committee). In consensual decision making, people tend to presume some background information to play special functions beyond mere preferences. Indeed, people's trust in and justification for the use of consensual decision making seem to rest on this presumption in an essential way – an intuitive but strong belief that cognitive/affective components underlying preferences can be or should be shared among group members through face-to-face dialogue.

Verdict-Driven versus Evidence-Driven Process

Hastie, Penrod, and Pennington's (1983) observation about jury decision making illustrates this legitimate input issue well. These researchers identified two contrasting aggregation styles, verdict-driven versus evidence-driven, in mock jury deliberation. The *verdict-driven* style refers to a consensus process in which a jury is divided into factions based on verdict preferences from the outset of deliberation. Typically, these juries open deliberations with a public ballot; jurors then act as advocates for their positions, aligned in opposing factions by expressed preferences. The *verdict-driven* juries conduct polling frequently until they reach a final verdict.

In contrast, the *evidence-driven* style refers to a deliberation process in which jurors collaborate to review evidence closely and try to reach a common understanding of what actually happened in the focal case. Instead of aligning themselves into opposing factions by verdict preferences, these jurors focus on constructing the single most credible story that summarizes the events at the time of the alleged crime; verdict statements and polling typically do not occur until later in deliberation.

From our perspective, the preceding Hastie et al. observation illustrates *dual meanings of "consensus."* Just as individual preferences serve as natural inputs for consensus (e.g., the verdict-driven process), individual cognitions or knowledge representations serve as meaningful inputs as well (e.g., the evidence-driven process). Preferences and cognitions are both treated as legitimate inputs (notably, sometimes the latter being even more legitimate) in consensual decision making.

A question arises about what this duality implies for group decision making. Although cognitions or knowledge representations are often related to preferences, their mapping is usually imperfect. Then how is group decision making characterized when we regard *preference* as a unit of social aggregation and when we regard *cognition* or *knowledge* as a unit of aggregation? Are different mechanisms in operation at each level of the social aggregations or does the same type of social mechanism govern the aggregations in general? In the following, we examine representative theories and empirical research in the small group decision-making literature from this dual perspective.

Aggregation at the Preference Level

Social Decision Scheme Model

Just as preference structures over alternatives dominated the early individual decision-making literature, the process of aggregating the preferences of group members in order to achieve consensus has played a major role in theory and research on group decision making. Probably the most comprehensive conceptual system for describing such aggregation processes is Davis's (1973, 1996; Stasser, Kerr, & Davis, 1989) Social Decision Scheme (SDS) theory. SDS theory starts with the assumption that small group interaction can be seen as a *combinatorial process* wherein preferences for decision alternatives across group members must be combined in such a way as to allow the group to reach consensus on a single group choice. This combinatorial process can vary as a function of the group task, the environment, and other factors and is described in terms of an SDS matrix.

In the general case, the theory assumes that an individual decision maker must select one of n mutually exclusive and exhaustive response alternatives, A_j, $j = 1, 2, 3, \ldots, n$. It also assumes that individual decisions are characterized by a discrete probability distribution, $p = (p_1, p_2, \ldots, p_n)$, over n alternatives, and similarly for groups, $P = (P_1, P_2, \ldots, P_{n'})$. However, situations are possible (e.g., jury decisions) where $n \neq n'$, in that the number of response outcomes for groups, $n' = 3$ (i.e., guilty, not guilty, hung), may differ from the number, $n = 2$ (i.e., guilty, not guilty), defined for individuals. Prior to discussion, the r individual group members may array themselves over the n response alternatives in

$$C(n + r - 1; r) = \frac{(n + r - 1)!}{r!(n - 1)!}$$

different ways. For example, the members of a six-person group can array themselves over two choice alternatives in seven different ways, that is, (6, 0), (5, 1), ..., (0, 6). Such an array is referred to as a *distinguishable distribution*, in which response alternatives but not individual group members are distinguishable, just as in voting. The probability, π_i of the ith distribution, $i = 1, 2, \ldots, m$, of member preferences occurring may be estimated in two different ways. Some applications allow for a direct estimate by counting the relative frequency with which the ith distribution is observed to occur (e.g., inspecting prediscussion preferences within the group). In other cases, π_i must be estimated indirectly using the multinomial distribution

$$\pi_i = \begin{pmatrix} r \\ r_1, r_2, \ldots, r_n \end{pmatrix} p_1^{r_1} p_2^{r_2} \cdots p_n^{r_n}$$

using observed estimates for the individual choice probability distribution, $\hat{p}_i$.

Given a particular distribution of opinions in a group, the relevant problem is to ascertain the probability that the group will choose a given alternative. This process is obviously a function of the social interaction, as well as of various prescribed rules or laws governing the particular group. Although the process may be rather complex, it can be given an explicit summary form by defining the conditional probability, d_{ij}, of the group choosing the jth choice alternative given the ith distinguishable distribution. The general statement of the theoretical relation between the initial preference distribution and the final group outcome may be cast as an $m \times n'$ stochastic matrix, D, called a *social decision scheme matrix*.

Table 14.1. *Social Decision Scheme Matrices for Two Models:*
Proportionality and Majority-Equiprobability Otherwise

Individual Distribution		Proportionality		Majority-Equiprobability Otherwise	
		Group Distributions			
A	B	A	B	A	B
6	0	1.00	0.00	1.00	0.00
5	1	0.83	0.17	1.00	0.00
4	2	0.67	0.33	1.00	0.00
3	3	0.50	0.50	0.50	0.50
2	4	0.33	0.67	0.00	1.00
1	5	0.17	0.83	0.00	1.00
0	6	0.00	1.00	0.00	1.00

Table 14.1 shows two examples of SDS matrices for six-person groups with two choice alternatives.

The *D* matrices in Table 14.1 represent two different processes. The majority-equiprobability otherwise SDS presupposes that whenever a majority of the members favor a particular decision alternative, that alternative will be chosen by the group. In cases where no majority exists (a 3–3 split), each alternative is equally likely to be the group's choice. The proportionality SDS assumes that the probability that a group will choose a particular alternative is the proportion of members favoring that alternative. Thus, the proportionality SDS assumes that factions within the group are only as powerful as the relative size of that faction, whereas the majority-equiprobability otherwise model assumes that majority factions are quite powerful and typically define the group's choice. (Of course, when $d_{ij} = .00$ or 1.00, it should be understood that such values represent entries that are actually very near .00 or 1.00.)

Given a particular SDS matrix, the group probability distribution, $P = (P_1, P_2, \ldots, P_{n'})$, is obtained from

$$P = \pi D,$$

where $\pi = (\pi_1, \pi_2, \ldots, \pi_m)$. This general model can be used in two different ways in relation to research on small groups. First, group outcome distributions predicted by any given SDS model can be tested against observed distributions of group decisions. Thus, for example, the predictions from the two models presented in Table 14.1 could be compared against observed data to assess which model better accounts for the data.

This allows for a priori tests of various assumptions underlying how decision-making groups reach consensus. However, the general model can also be used in a model-fitting capacity. Given a particular π vector, an estimated SDS model can be obtained for a specific set of group decision data. Estimated SDS models can be seen as a description of the consensus processes for the particular task/situation in which the data were collected. (For a more detailed and comprehensive discussion of the model-testing vs. model-fitting applications of SDS theory, see Kerr, Stasser, & Davis, 1979.)

The SDS approach has generated a large body of research addressing how groups reach consensus in a variety of decision situations (e.g., Davis, 1980, 1982; Davis, Kameda, Parks, Stasson, & Zimmerman, 1989; Kameda, 1991; Kameda & Sugimori, 1993, 1995; Tindale & Davis, 1983, 1985). Although a number of factors have been found to influence group decision processes (Davis, 1982; Laughlin, 1980), one of the more consistent and robust findings from this research has been that majorities/pluralities win most of the time. This is particularly true when no demonstrably correct alternative exists (Laughlin & Ellis, 1986). When groups cannot demonstrate that a particular alternative is empirically or axiomatically correct (or optimal) during discussion, "correctness" tends to be defined by the group consensus, and larger factions tend to define the group consensus. Majority/plurality-type processes have been observed to describe the consensus process of groups working on a variety of decision tasks/situations, including mock juries (Kameda, 1991; Tindale & Davis, 1983), risk-taking (Davis, Kameda, & Stasson, 1992; Kameda & Davis, 1990), duplex bets (Davis, Kerr, Sussman, & Rissman, 1974), choosing political candidates (Stasser & Titus, 1985), reward allocation decisions (Tindale & Davis, 1985), and hiring job candidates (Tindale, 1989).

Continuous Judgment

One of the limitations of the SDS modeling approach is that it is restricted to decisions defined by discrete decision alternatives. The model does not apply to continuous response formats because the number of distinguishable distributions becomes infinite. Recently, Davis (1996) formulated a continuous judgment model analogous to the SDS model that has many of the same properties discussed previously for majority/plurality models (see also Gigone & Hastie, 1996, for a social judgment theory model for continuous responses). The model, referred to as the

Social Judgment Scheme (SJS) model, is based on position discrepancies (distance among preferences) along the response continuum among the members of a group. The model assumes that the group's decision, G, is a weighted sum of the r members, preferences, x_j, $j = 1, 2, \ldots, r$, where c_j is the weight of the jth member. That is,

$$G = c_1 x_1 + c_2 x_2 + \cdots + c_r x_r.$$

Given that the members' preferences can be observed a priori, only the weights must be defined further. The consensus weight of the jth member depends on the *centrality* of the member's position relative to other members of the group. The closer that member's position is to other members' positions, the more weight that member is given in defining the group consensus. Thus, the weight of the jth member is defined by

$$c_j = \frac{\sum_{j'=1}^{r} f(|x_j - x_{j'}|)}{\sum_{j=1}^{r} \sum_{j'=1}^{r} f(|x_j - x_{j'}|)}$$

In the preceding equation, the social influence function is defined as

$$f(|x_j - x_{j'}|) = \exp[-\theta(|x_j - x_{j'}|)], \quad j \neq j'$$

where θ is a positive constant. In practical applications of the model to date, $\theta = 1.00$.

This model tends to give little if any weight to the most discrepant member of the group and fairly heavy weight to the most central member(s). Even though factions per se cannot be defined, the group decision tends to be defined mainly by members who are similar (in proximity along the response dimension) to each other, at the expense of members whose positions are fairly discrepant. Thus, the SJS model essentially assumes a dominant role of central members in guiding the consensus, much like the majority/plurality models discussed previously. Although formulated relatively recently, the model has fared well in empirical tests thus far (Davis, Au, Hulbert, Chen, & Zarnoth, 1997).

Macro Consequences of Consensus Processes Guided by Socially Shared Preferences

As we have seen, group aggregation processes tend to be guided by initial majorities or pluralities in a discrete choice situation, or by members whose opinions are mutually close (i.e., central in the group) in a continuous judgment case, when the demonstrability of a preferred solution is low. In other words, the degree of *social-sharedness* in members' preferences at the onset of the interaction plays a critical role in determining the final consensus outcomes. This is an important observation, because most social decision-making situations that require discussion among people generally fall into this category of ambiguous cases in terms of the demonstrability of solutions. Then, what macro-level consequences are theoretically implied by such processes guided by shared preferences? We think that two macro consequences are particularly important, *group polarization* and *manipulability of group decisions*.

Group Polarization. In the June 1994 election for the European Parliament conducted in Britain, the Labour Party, and the Conservative Party, and the Liberal Democratic Party obtained 44%, 28%, and 17% of the *votes*, and acquired 70%, 20%, and 2% of the *seats*, respectively, in the parliament. The Labour Party, which was relatively advantageous in terms of the number of votes obtained, won the landslide victory in terms of the final seats in the parliament. The electoral system used in this election was a single-seat constituency system coupled with a *plurality* rule.

As readers correctly guess, consensual decision making guided by initial majorities/pluralities produces exactly the same accentuation effect at the group level. To illustrate, let us imagine a hypothetical investment decision-making situation. There are three choice alternatives, which can be ordered in terms of their risk levels – low risk, moderate risk, and high risk. Suppose that an n-member representative committee, randomly chosen from some population, is to discuss this investment issue and to make a final decision. We assume that consensual decision making in this committee is essentially governed by a *majority/plurality process*, as mentioned earlier. Figure 14.1 displays distributions of individual preferences in the population and theoretical distributions of group decisions assuming a simple majority/plurality process.

As Figure 14.1 demonstrates, it is clear that the risky alternative, which is most dominant at the individual level (i.e., the population level), becomes more dominant at the group level, whereas the other weaker alternatives become even weaker at the group level. For example, the most popular, high-risk alternative is supported by 60% of the individuals in the population. The theoretical probability that this alternative will be adopted as a group choice is amplified to 68% in a five-member committee and to 73% in a nine-member committee. On

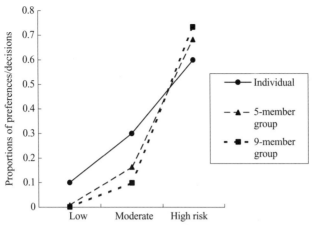

Figure 14.1 Majority/plurality processes and group polarization.

the other hand, the least popular, low-risk alternative (supported by only 10% of the individuals) is adopted as a group choice only .8% of the times by the five-member committee and .08% by the nine-member committee. The change in choice probabilities from the individual level is more evident with the increase in group size, as can be seen from the comparison between the five- and nine-member groups.

Notice that such an accentuation or *group polarization effect* in the micro → macro transformation *never* occurs if group aggregation is summarizable as a *proportionality process* (cf. the left panel of Table 14.1). If proportionality governs the consensus process in the representative committee, the distribution of group choices should be *identical* to the distribution of individual preferences. Furthermore, although the preceding illustration used a discrete choice case, the same argument applies to a continuous judgment case as well. If the aforementioned SJS-like process characterizes group aggregation in the committee, any skewness in the population distribution (i.e., the individual preference distribution) toward a particular end of a response continuum would be exacerbated in the group response distribution due to the higher likelihood of committee members having preferences in the smaller tail. In contrast, a simple *averaging process* in the committee should yield exactly the opposite effect, viz., a *less skewed* distribution at the group level than at the individual level. The group polarization phenomenon, which is observed widely in social decision making beyond risky situations, was a vigorous research topic in social psychology in the 1970s. Although several "individually oriented" explanations have been proposed

(Sanders & Baron, 1977; Vinokur & Burnstein, 1974), notice that our view of this phenomenon focuses directly on the social aggregation process. A consensus process affected by social sharedness (e.g., a majority/plurality or an SJS-like aggregation) can theoretically produce polarization at the group level even when there is no attitude preference change in individuals due to social interaction. Thus, individual attitude change is not a necessary condition for group polarization (see Davis 1973, and Lamm & Myers, 1978, for a further discussion on this point).

Besides their obvious political implications, these group polarization phenomena are important in relation to decision accuracy. Suppose that a focal group decision task may potentially trigger some *cognitive bias* (cf. Kahneman, Slovic, & Tversky, 1982). If there is no external evidence proving why biased preferences are wrong, and/or if members lack logical or statistical backgrounds to understand those corrective arguments, then consensual processes would essentially be determined by shared preferences at the outset of the interaction. Then the quality of group decisions should depend on what kinds of preferences are shared at the outset in a given group stochastically. In this sense, the probability of an individual member's *biased* preference is a key. If this individual probability is larger than a critical social threshold (e.g., 50% in the case of a simple majority process), then consensual decision making leads groups astray. Improvement by grouping is expected only when the individual bias-proneness is smaller than the social threshold (cf. Kerr, MacCoun, & Kramer, 1996). Furthermore, as can be seen in the comparison of the five- and nine-member groups in Figure 14.1, increasing the group size accentuates such a group polarization tendency even further. Using a larger group means that the variance of group-decision qualities is also enlarged statistically – either a great success or a fiasco, depending on the size of individual bias-proneness relative to the critical social threshold in a focal context.

Manipulability of Group Decisions. Another important implication of a consensus process guided by shared preferences is procedural manipulability of group outcomes. The most famous example of this sort, focusing particularly on majority/plurality aggregation, is Condorcet's voting paradox. When a group decides among three or more alternatives (say x, y, and z), cyclical majorities can exist. For example, if members' preference orders are $x > y > z$, $y > z > x$, and $z > x > y$, respectively, in a three-person group, the majority in the group (two of three members) prefer x over y, y over z, and z over x. Thus, cyclicity (intransitivity) exists in the preferences of majority members. In such a situation, the group choice outcome via *majority rule* depends on a particular path by which pairwise votings are conducted – a phenomenon called *path dependency* of voting. Obviously, a chairperson who can choose which voting order to take can potentially manipulate the group's decision outcome to personal advantage (see Black, 1958, for further discussion of paradoxes of voting).

Although the preceding example is taken from a voting situation, manipulability accruing from a majority/plurality process may also play a substantive role in consensual decision making. For instance, Kameda (1991) demonstrated such a procedural manipulation in a situation where a group needs to consider several key conditions to render a final decision. An example might be investment decision making, in which several key criteria must be satisfied to make a final investment decision. Now, two contrasting discussion procedures are conceivable in these situations. In one procedure (*compound* procedure), the chairperson solicits members' overall conclusions from the outset. Analogous to the verdict-driven juries (Hastie et al., 1983), the chairperson encourages members to express their overall preferences – to invest or not. In contrast, the other procedure (*elemental* procedure) takes the opposite approach, focusing on collaborative evaluations of the key criteria. Somewhat analogous to the evidence-driven juries observed by Hastie and others, the chairperson asks for members' judgments of each of the conditions respectively (e.g., whether condition 1 is satisfied). Although these two procedures are both plausible and seemingly neutral, the choice of a procedure substantially impacts on the final group outcome, as illustrated in Table 14.2.

Table 14.2 displays a hypothetical opinion configuration of three members working on the investment decision task. Suppose that there are two key conditions to be satisfied to make the investment and that person A serves as the chairperson of this committee. As shown in Table 14.2, whereas member A prefers to invest, the other two members

Table 14.2. *An Illustrative Example of Group Decision Making Involving Several Conditional Judgments*

Member	Condition 1	Condition 2	Preference
A	Yes	Yes	Invest
B	Yes	No	Not invest
C	No	Yes	Not invest

do not. Therefore, provided that the consensual process is guided by a majority process, member A has little chance to prevail if the discussion centers on exchanging members' *preferences* (*compound procedure*). However, what if member A adopts the elemental procedure instead, stating, "To avoid a rough decision, why don't we examine each of the conditions carefully? Let's start with condition 1 . . . , etc." Assuming that each member is faithful to his or her original judgments, the same majority process should yield a positive collective judgment for each of the two criteria. Therefore, as the chairperson, member A can conclude the group discussion as follows: "We seem to have reached a conclusion after a careful deliberation. Both conditions for investment are satisfied" – the conclusion the chairperson prefers.

More formally, if the individual members' decision probabilities combine conjunctively, as in the preceding example, the binomial theorem (cf. Davis, 1973) yields the result that the probability of investment will *always* be higher with the elemental procedure than with the compound procedure. Specifically, in this example, the elemental procedure can theoretically increase the probability of the "investment" decision by the maximum margin of .13 for a 3-person group, .23 for a 6-person group, and .37 for a 12-person group compared to the compound procedure. Thus, the elemental procedure is more advantageous to the chairperson if this person desires to invest; if he or she prefers not to invest, the compound procedure should serve the chair's interest. Using four- and six-person groups, Kameda (1991) confirmed that consensus outcomes can be manipulated procedurally, as just discussed. Even when a group was instructed explicitly to discuss the issue until they reached a *unanimous* agreement (i.e., majority voting was thus discouraged), the two procedures affected consensus outcomes, as implied by the binomial model. Furthermore, no members were aware of the manipulation; group outcomes were essentially accepted as fair and satisfactory (cf. Lind & Tyler, 1988).

As illustrated in this example, the functioning of a majority/plurality process makes the *paradox of voting* a central issue to consensual decision making that lacks an explicit formal voting procedure. In a similar vein, continuous group decisions can also be guided toward a particular individual's personal advantage through procedural manipulation utilizing social sharedness tactically. Although space does not allow us to discuss them here, various forms of such procedural influences have been studied in the small group decision-making literature, including effects of sequential straw polling (Davis, Stasson, Ono, & Zimmerman,

1988), local majorities (Davis et al., 1989; Kameda & Sugimori, 1995), consensus rules (Davis, Kerr, Atkin, Holt, & Meek, 1975; Miller, 1989), agenda setting (Stasson, Kameda, & Davis, 1997), and so on. (See Davis, Hulbert, & Au, 1996, and Kameda, 1996, for further discussion on procedural influence on consensual decision making.)

Aggregation at the Cognitive Level

One of the main reasons groups are often perceived to be superior to individuals in terms of decision quality or accuracy is that groups bring more cognitive resources to the particular decision task (Tindale & Davis, 1983). Each member's knowledge, expertise, past experiences, and so on can be added to the whole and applied to the evaluation of the problem or decision at hand. Indeed, such a view provides a major justification for *consensual* decision making, expecting that important cognitive components can be brought in or newly shared among group members through face-to-face dialogue. However, like earlier research on problem solving (cf. Davis, 1969), more recent research specifically looking at information processing in groups has shown that groups do *not* necessarily harness these cognitive resources in an optimal way (Stasser & Titus, 1985). As we will see in this section, such suboptimal information processing in groups is often brought by *social sharedness* at the cognitive level. In a recent review article, Hinsz, Tindale, and Vollrath (1997) view information processing in groups as "the degree to which information, ideas, or cognitive processes are *shared*, and are *being shared*, among the group members . . ." (p. 43; italics added). In line with this view, we argue that the degree of social sharedness at the cognitive level is another central factor for understanding consensual decision making and is both consistent with, but different from, the aggregation processes at the preference level.

The Hidden Profile Approach

Although much of the early work on group decision making focused mainly on preferences, there were some exceptions (Graesser, 1982; Vinokur & Burnstein, 1974). Vinokur and Burnstein's work on Persuasive Arguments Theory was an attempt to explain group polarization at the information level. They argued that group members shifted their opinions in the direction of the majority (or, more accurately, in the direction of the dominant pole of the dimension) because group discussion generated novel and more persuasive arguments favoring the dominant pole (typically risk or caution on the items used). Thus, according to their theory, unique or unshared information was of central importance. Information that was shared by all group members would have little if any impact when brought up during discussion because everyone already knew it. Novel information, because it was unshared, would influence the preferences of the group members and subsequently, the final group choice.

However, more recent research has demonstrated exactly the opposite. Stasser and Titus (1985) designed a paradigm for studying the effects of shared and unshared information on group decision making that had a major impact on the field of small group research. The paradigm is referred to as the *hidden profile* approach, and the basic finding has been called the *common knowledge effect* (Gigone & Hastie, 1996). Stasser and Titus had four-person groups choose one of three political candidates based on information profiles about the candidates. However, in some of the conditions, different group members got different information. For one of the candidates (e.g., Candidate B), all four group members received all of the positive information about that candidate but only part of the negative information. For a different candidate (e.g., Candidate A), they received all of the negative information but only part of the positive information. Given the total pool of information, most people would have perceived Candidate A as best among the three. However, the superiority of Candidate A was *hidden* from particular group members because of the way in which the information was distributed. If group members shared all of the information available to them, they should have been able to see that Candidate A was superior. However, in the condition just described, most of the groups chose Candidate B. Given the way the information was distributed among the group members, most of the members' individual preferences were for B. Therefore, at the preference level, most groups had a majority for B and subsequently chose B.

Even though, at the time, this was a rather surprising finding, Stasser (1988) argued that two rather simple processes can account for this effect. First, research has shown that the likelihood of a piece of information being recalled by a group is a function of the number of members presented with that information (Hinsz, 1990; Tindale & Sheffey, 1992). Thus, shared information is more likely to be recalled than unshared information at the group level. In addition, even with perfect recall, the probability that a piece of information gets brought up is also a function of the number of members who have it. Based on these assumptions,

Stasser and Titus (1987) formulated their Information Sampling Model to explain the common knowledge effect found in their hidden profile studies. The model (similar in structure to Lorge and Solomon's 1955 Model A for predicting correct problem solutions by groups) basically assumes that the probability, $p(D)$, that a given piece of information will be discussed is 1 minus the probability that no one mentions the item during discussion. Making simplified assumptions about independence, and so on, this notion may be written as

$$p(D) = 1 - [1 - p(M)]^n$$

where $p(M)$ is the probability of any given individual's mentioning a given item and n is the number of members having that item. When only one member knows a given piece of information, $p(D) = p(M)$. However, as n increases, so does $p(D)$, so that shared information is always more likely to be brought up during group discussion than unshared information. Larson, Foster-Fishman, and Keys (1994) showed that as discussion time increases, the likelihood of unshared information being brought up relative to shared information also increases. However, groups may easily reach a consensus (due to majority processes) before all the available information can be mentioned.

Although the common knowledge effect is fairly robust and has been replicated a number of times, there are some procedural mechanisms, common to consensus-seeking discussions, that can attenuate the effect. For example, both Sawyer (1997) and Sheffey, Tindale, and Scott (1989) have shown that allowing group members to keep a record of the information presented to them reduces, but does not eliminate, the effect. Sawyer also found that instructing group members not to form a priori judgments helps to reduce the effect, although this has not always been found to be effective (Sheffey et al., 1989). Also, Stasser and Stewart (1992) found that framing the task as a problem to be solved (implying a correct answer) led to greater sharing of unshared information during discussion. Finally, Stewart and Stasser (1995) demonstrated that assigning roles associated with the information distribution (e.g., "you are the expert on candidate X") led to more discussion of unshared information, but only when the roles were known by all of the group members.

Decomposing the Common Knowledge Effect

Much of the work just described used decision tasks with discrete decision alternatives and assessed the effects of shared and unshared information by looking at the group's response distributions and how much shared and unshared information was brought up during discussion. Although informative, such measures do not explicitly assess how the information was used, nor do they measure the potential importance of each type of information for both individual and group decisions. Using a different type of decision task, Gigone and Hastie (1993, 1996) attempted to address both of these issues and to explicate further the processes underlying the common knowledge effect. Their work is based on the Brunswik (1956) *lens model* approach to judgment, as developed within the context of Social Judgment Theory (SJT; Brehmer & Joyce, 1988; Hammond, Stewart, Brehmer, & Steinmann, 1986). The lens model describes the judgment process as a mapping of cues to a criterion using a weighted linear function, where the actual cue weights in the environment can be used to assess the viability of the mental model that a particular judge uses to predict the criterion. Gigone and Hastie generalized these ideas to a group judgment situation where different group members may have access to different cues. The full model defines the group judgments as a linear function of (a) a weighted average of members' preferences (where members' preferences are seen as a representation of a linear combination of the cues using weights specific to a particular member), (b) a weighted linear combination of the cues at the group level, (c) a weighted linear combination of whether each cue was pooled (discussed), and (d) an interaction term involving each cue and whether it was pooled, which represents the extent to which the weight for a particular cue depends on whether the cue is pooled (see Gigone & Hastie, 1996, for a more detailed description of the model).

Gigone and Hastie (1993) had groups of three students make 32 judgments about students' grades in an introductory psychology class based on six cues. Each cue was provided to either one, two, or all three group members. As predicted from the common knowledge effect, cues were more important (received greater weight) for the group judgments when they were presented to more group members. Although there were some inconsistencies, the relationship between cue weight and number of group members having access to the cue tended to be linear, particularly for cues that were considered important. Also, the probability that a cue was pooled increased as a function of the number of members having access to the cue. However, two rather interesting findings also emerged. First, the interaction term (cue by pooling) did not add significantly to the model. Second, when the full model was tested, the only term that added significantly to predicting the group judgments was the members' preferences. Thus, their results seem to indicate that the distribution of information in the group impacts the group judgment only indirectly through its effects on the members' preferences. Although more recent research has shown that the pooling of unshared information potentially may add to group judgment accuracy over and above members' preferences in some circumstances (Winquist & Larson, 1998), the Gigone–Hastie findings are quite consistent with the majority/plurality models discussed in the previous section. The degree to which information is shared impacts on information pooling during discussion, but it also impacts the member preference distribution. If the information is distributed in such a way as to produce a majority/plurality favoring a less than optimal decision alternative (as the hidden profile procedure does), then it is highly likely that groups will fail to reach a consensus on the optimal alternative. Thus, social sharedness at the cognitive level leads to a shared preference structure that ultimately drives the consensus process.

Shared Task Representations and Cognitive Centrality

The research on the common knowledge effect tends to show that shared cognitions play a central role in group decision making. In addition, it shows that shared cognitions and shared preferences tend to correspond with one another. However, two recent lines of research have shown that this correspondence is not necessary for shared cognitions to impact on group decisions. The first of these is based on the notion of a *shared task representation* (Tindale, Smith, Thomas, Filkins, & Sheffey, 1996) and stems conceptually from earlier work by Laughlin (1980; Laughlin & Ellis, 1986) on group problem solving. In contrast to judgmental tasks where no demonstrably correct solution exists, Laughlin has shown that, for tasks where the correctness of an alternative can be demonstrated, a minority faction favoring a demonstrably correct solution will tend to win out over an incorrect majority. In defining *demonstrability*, Laughlin and Ellis (1986) argued that a key feature is a system of axioms or beliefs that are shared among the group members. This shared belief system serves as a background for the members understanding the logic behind the correctness of a given alternative. Thus, using the shared belief system, minority factions arguing for a correct alternative can win out over majorities favoring an incorrect alternative.

Tindale et al. (1996) generalized this notion and argued that whenever a shared task representation exists, alternatives consistent with the representation will be easier to defend, and thus will be more likely to end up as the group's collective choice. Accordingly, the task representation that is shared does not have to support axiomatic "correctness" and may even be inconsistent with normatively correct positions. For example, mock juries given the "reasonable doubt" instruction tend to show asymmetries in the SDS models that best describe preference aggregation (MacCoun & Kerr, 1988; Tindale, Davis, Vollrath, Nagao, & Hinsz, 1990). Research has consistently demonstrated that both majorities and minorities favoring a "not guilty" verdict (which is consistent with the reasonable doubt processing objective given to the jury) are more powerful than majorities and minorities favoring a "guilty" verdict. In addition, incorrect representations, such as faulty decision strategies that most people use (Kahneman et al., 1982), can lead minorities favoring normatively incorrect alternatives to win out over majorities favoring normatively correct positions (Tindale, 1993; Tindale et al., 1996).

Recent research has shown that shared representations potentially operate in two different ways to affect group decisions. First, Smith, Tindale, and Steiner (1998), using a sunk cost problem, found that sunk cost arguments were persuasive, even if brought up by only a minority of members. Thus, arguments that are consistent with the shared representation can be especially influential in a group decision context. Second, a recent study by Tindale, Anderson, Smith, Steiner, and Filkins (1998), continuing a program of research looking at the estimation of conjunctive probabilities by individuals and groups (Tindale, Sheffey, & Filkins, 1990; Tindale, Filkins, Thomas, & Smith, 1993), videotaped the group discussions for conjunctive probability problems. Earlier research had shown that minorities making nonnormative estimates were more powerful than majorities making normative estimates. The videotaped group discussions showed that groups rarely discussed strategies concerning how to make the estimates, but rather simply exchanged information concerning their individual judgments. Quite often (more than 60% of the time), groups went with a single member's judgment. In those conditions where individuals were likely to make nonnormative estimates, groups were even more likely to do so, regardless of the preference distribution in the group. Thus, it seems that shared task representations can impact group decisions even when only preference information is exchanged. As long as a given individual preference is plausible within the shared representation, the group members will find it acceptable without thorough debate.

Virtually all of the aforementioned research has focused on the impacts of shared *cognitions* or *knowledge* per se on consensus. Little emphasis has been placed on group *members' status* or *power* as a function of degree of knowledge sharing with other members. For example, one member may share a substantial amount of information with other members, whereas another member may share only a portion of it. Because shared information has a greater impact on final group decisions, it seems likely that members having more shared information may acquire pivotal power in the group. This idea was tested in a recent set of studies by Kameda, Ohtsubo, and Takezawa (1997). Using a social network framework, Kameda et al. formulated a model to represent the degree to which any given member was "cognitively central" in the group. Much like Davis's (1996) SJS model, which locates members' preference centrality, Kameda et al.'s measure of *cognitive centrality* defines members in terms of their degree of centrality in the *sociocognitive network*. The greater the degree of overlap between the information held by a given member and the information held by other members on average, the greater the degree of centrality for that member.

Kameda et al. (1997) ran two studies to assess whether cognitively more central members would be more influential in their groups, regardless of their preference status (i.e., whether they were in minority or majority factions). In Study 1, they had three-person groups discuss whether a defendant in a highly publicized trial deserved the death penalty. By coding the contents of knowledge each member held prior to the group interaction, they calculated a cognitive centrality score for each member in each group. They then used the members' cognitive centrality scores to predict participation rates and opinion change after group discussion. Members' rankings in terms of centrality were positively related to their rankings in terms of participation. For members in minority factions, their degree of centrality also predicted (inversely) their amount of opinion change, though centrality was unrelated to opinion change for majority members.

In Study 2, Kameda et al. manipulated the information given to each group member to create two different situations. In one condition, the most cognitively central member of the group was a lone minority (in terms of preference) against a two-person majority. In the other condition, the most cognitively central person was part of the two-person majority, with the minority member being the least cognitively central. When the minority person was most cognitively central, the group went with the minority position (over the majority position) 67% of the time. When the minority person was least cognitively central, the minority won only 42% of the time. In addition, groups were considerably more confident in the conditions in which the central minority person's preference was chosen by the group. Thus, being the most cognitively central person in the group allows that person a greater degree of influence, even when holding a minority position in terms of preference. Kameda et al. (1997) argue that such enhanced social power accrues from perceptions of expertise for the cognitively central member in the focal knowledge domain.

Robust Influence of Social Sharedness: Some Suggestions for Future Research

In this chapter, we have examined representative theories and empirical findings about group decision making by focusing on the dual meanings of consensus – aggregation at the preference level and aggregation at the cognitive level. It seems clear that there is a marked similarity between the two levels of social aggregation. On both levels, social sharedness, the degree to which preferences and cognitions are shared among members prior to group interaction (cf. Tindale & Kameda, 2000), plays a vital function in determining consensus processes and outcomes. To recapitulate, a majority/plurality process (or an SJS-like process in a continuous judgment) essentially underlies the *preference*-level aggregation, especially when axiomatic (logical) or empirical correctness is difficult to establish. As side effects, these social processes make group decisions more polarized than individual decisions statistically and also make them vulnerable to arbitrary procedural manipulation. On the *cognitive* level, shared information or knowledge plays critical roles in guiding consensus. Shared information tends to be attended to more thoroughly than unshared information during group discussion, and indirectly impacts the final consensus via members' initial preferences. Persuasiveness of arguments or credibility of a member in a given task domain is also critically affected by shared knowledge.

Research on each level of aggregation, taken together, points to the general group phenomenon that *initial sharedness* of knowledge prepares the ground for consensus while severely constraining *shareability of knowledge* among members, viz., what type of knowledge can be newly shared by whom through communication. Somewhat analogous to Thomas Kuhn's notion of *paradigm* (Kuhn, 1962), such a cyclical process in group communication constitutes a *closed loop*.

Given the fundamental influence of social sharedness in consensual decision making, several directions for future research may be suggested along this line. One important direction, both theoretically and practically, may be to specify the ways for consensus groups to exit from the aforementioned closed loop. Recent work by Stasser and his colleagues (e.g., Wittenbaum, Vaughan, & Stasser, 1998) aims to address this issue by focusing on tacit task coordination among members. For example, if members are mutually aware of respective expertise in a group, exchange of unshared information (e.g., unique knowledge relevant to each member's expertise) should be facilitated, which may provide one way out of the closed loop (Stewart & Stasser, 1995). In fact, Kameda et al.'s (1997) notion of cognitive centrality may explain one way that such *meta-knowledge* (knowledge about the locus of knowledge – who knows what, whose knowledge is most reliable, etc.) emerges in a group *voluntarily*. Needless to say, disentangling the closed loop theoretically and finding various ways out constitutes an important research agenda toward effective group performance – a shared concern across various social science disciplines. Such a perspective also seems to provide a useful guideline for engineering research that aims to develop various *groupwares* implemented on computer systems (e.g., Smith, 1994).

Another important research direction may be to clarify how social sharedness at the preference and cognitive levels interplays in consensus processes. For example, when do they differ, and if they do, which level takes precedence and why? Factors associated with a context/situation in which a group decision is sought may be critical in answering such questions. Time pressure, for example, would probably lead to focusing on social sharedness at the preference level at the expense of the cognitive level (cf. Hinsz et al., 1997). The SJT paradigm developed by Gigone and Hastie (1993, 1996) also seems to be useful in exploring these issues. However, at this point, many related interesting questions are still open, awaiting future empirical investigations.

Potentially the most important line of research relating to social sharedness concerns *why* it is such a powerful force in group decision making. For example, majorities may contain only one more member than a competing minority, yet they define the group consensus nearly 100% of the time. Thus, their power is often far greater than their relative numbers. In addition, shared information not only gets brought up more often, but also is weighted more heavily in the final group judgment (Gigone & Hastie, 1996). Thus, the power of social sharedness at the cognitive level is not just a function of the greater probability of shared information being brought up. Although this topic has received little attention to date, recent theory and research on the *social nature of reality* (cf. Hardin & Higgins, 1996) may provide a useful framework for understanding the power of social sharedness. Knowing that one shares preferences with the largest faction within a group may instill greater confidence in the correctness of one's position, and hearing that others share information you already have may help to establish socially the validity of the information.

With a similar goal, it seems worthwhile to examine the degree of *net efficiencies* that various types of social influences, as discussed in this chapter, may achieve in group decision making. For example, intrigued by the recent adaptive decision-making arguments (e.g., Fiedler, 1996; Gigerenzer & Goldstein, 1996; Payne, Bettman, & Johnson, 1993), Kameda and Hastie (1999) explored the accuracy of various *group decision heuristics* (i.e., commonly used aggregation methods) under uncertainty by a series of Monte Carlo computer simulations. These researchers found that a simple majority/plurality aggregation, albeit being fairly cheap in terms of necessary social/cognitive calculation costs, achieves an accuracy level essentially comparable to that of much more effortful aggregation algorithms (see also Sorkin, Hays, & West, 2001; Sorkin, West, & Robinson, 1998). Such a finding may explain why majority/plurality aggregation is so robust in group decision making, as reviewed in this chapter. Given the increased focus on adaptive aspects of human decision making, examining various functions of social sharedness in guiding consensus from an adaptive perspective seems theoretically quite promising (cf. Kameda & Nakanishi, 2002).

As we have discussed in this chapter, social sharedness plays a fundamental role in consensual decision making that features face-to-face interaction (e.g., the committee). We believe that this notion serves as a useful common thread for understanding various features of group decision making and also generates many intriguing questions for future research endeavors.

References

Arrow, K. J. (1963). *Social choice and individual values* (2nd ed.). New Haven, CT: Yale University Press.

Black, D. (1958). *The theory of committees and elections.* Cambridge: Cambridge University Press.

Brehmer, B., & Joyce, C. R. B. (Eds.). (1988). *Advances in psychology: Vol. 4. Human judgment: The SJT view.* North Holland: Elsevier.

Brunswik, E. (1956). *Perception and the representative design of psychological experiments.* Berkeley: University of California Press.

Coleman, J. S. (1990). *Foundations of social theory.* Cambridge, MA: Harvard University Press.

Davis, J. H. (1969). *Group performance.* Reading, MA: Addison-Wesley.

Davis, J. H. (1973). A theory of social decision schemes. *Psychological Review, 80,* 97–125.

Davis, J. H. (1980). Group decision and procedural justice. In M. Fishbein (Ed.), *Progress in social psychology* (Vol. 1, pp. 157–229). Hillsdale, NJ: Erlbaum.

Davis, J. H. (1982). Social interaction as a combinatorial process in group decision. In H. Brandstatter, J. H. Davis, & G. Stocker-Kreichgauer (Eds.), *Group decision making* (pp. 27–58). London: Academic Press.

Davis, J. H. (1996). Group decision making and quantitative judgments: A consensus model. In E. Witte & J. H. Davis (Eds.), *Understanding group behavior: Consensual action by small groups* (Vol. 1, pp. 35–59). Mahwah, NJ: Erlbaum.

Davis, J. H., Au, W., Hulbert, L., Chen, X., & Zarnoth, P. (1997). Effect of group size and procedural influence on consensual judgment of quantity: The example of damage awards on mock civil juries. *Journal of Personality and Social Psychology, 73,* 703–718.

Davis, J. H., Hulbert, L., & Au, W. (1996). Procedural influence on group decision making: The case of straw polls – observation and simulation. In R. Y. Hirokawa & M. S. Poole (Eds.), *Communication and group decision making* (2nd ed., pp. 384–425). Beverly Hills, CA: Sage.

Davis, J. H., Kameda, T., Parks, C., Stasson, M., & Zimmerman, S. (1989). Some social mechanics of group decision making: The distribution of opinion, polling sequence, and implications for consensus. *Journal of Personality and Social Psychology, 57,* 1000–1014.

Davis, J. H., Kameda, T., & Stasson, M. (1992). Group risk taking: Selected topics. In F. Yates (Ed.), *Risk-taking behavior* (pp. 163–199). Chichester, U.K.: Wiley.

Davis, J. H., Kerr, N. L., Atkin, R. S., Holt, R., & Meek, D. (1975). The decision processes of 6- and 12-person mock juries assigned unanimous and two-thirds majority rules. *Journal of Personality and Social Psychology, 32,* 1–14.

Davis, J. H., Kerr, N. L., Sussman, M., & Rissman, A. K. (1974). Social decision schemes under risk. *Journal of Personality and Social Psychology, 30,* 248–271.

Davis, J. H., Stasson, M., Ono, K., & Zimmerman, S. K. (1988). The effects of straw polls on group decision making: Sequential voting pattern, timing, and local majorities. *Journal of Personality and Social Psychology, 55,* 918–926.

Fiedler, K. (1996). Explaining and simulating judgment biases as an aggregation phenomenon in probabilistic, multiple-cue environments. *Psychological Review, 103,* 193–214.

Fishburn, P. (1973). *The theory of social choice.* Princeton, NJ: Princeton University Press.

Gigerenzer, G., & Goldstein, D. G. (1996). Reasoning the fast and frugal way: Models of bounded rationality. *Psychological Review, 103,* 650–669.

Gigone, D., & Hastie, R. (1993). The common knowledge effect: Information sharing and group judgment. *Journal of Personality and Social Psychology, 65,* 959–974.

Gigone, D., & Hastie, R. (1996). The impact of information on group judgment: A model and computer simulation. In E. Witte & J. H. Davis (Eds.), *Understanding group behavior: Consensual action by small groups* (Vol. 1, pp. 221–251). Mahwah, NJ: Erlbaum.

Graesser, C. C. (1982). A social averaging theorem for group decision making. In N. H. Anderson (Ed.), *Contributions of information integration theory* (Vol. 2, pp. 1–40). New York: Academic Press.

Hammond, K. R., Stewart, T. R., Brehmer, B, & Steinmann, D. (1986). Social judgment theory. In H. R. Arkes & K. R. Hammond (Eds.), *Judgment and decision making: An interdisciplinary reader* (pp. 56–76). New York: Cambridge University Press.

Hardin, C. D., & Higgins, E. T. (1996). Shared reality: How social verification makes the subjective objective. In R. M. Sorrentino & E. T. Higgins (Eds.), *Handbook of motivation and cognition: The interpersonal context* (Vol. 3, pp. 28–84). New York: Guilford Press.

Hastie, R., Penrod, S., & Pennington, N. (1983). *Inside the jury*. Cambridge, MA: Harvard University Press.

Hinsz, V. B. (1990). Cognitive and consensus processes in group recognition memory performance. *Journal of Personality and Social Psychology, 59*, 705–718.

Hinsz, V. B., Tindale, R. S., & Vollrath, D. A. (1997). The emerging conception of groups as information processors. *Psychological Bulletin, 121*, 43–64.

Kahneman, D., Slovic, P., & Tversky, A. (Eds.). (1982). *Judgment under uncertainty: Heuristics and biases*. Cambridge: Cambridge University Press.

Kameda, T. (1991). Procedural influence in small-group decision making: Deliberation style and assigned decision rule. *Journal of Personality and Social Psychology, 61*, 245–256.

Kameda, T. (1996). Procedural influence in consensus formation: Evaluating group decision making from a social choice perspective. In E. Witte & J. H. Davis (Eds.), *Understanding group behavior: Consensual action by small groups* (Vol. 1, pp. 137–161), Mahwah, NJ: Erlbaum.

Kameda, T., & Davis, J. H. (1990). The function of the reference point in individual and group risk decision making. *Organizational Behavior and Human Decision Processes, 46*, 55–76.

Kameda, T., & Hastie, R. (1999). *Social sharedness and adaptation: Adaptive group decision heuristics*. Paper presented at the 17th Subjective Probability, Utility, and Decision Making Conference, Mannheim, Germany.

Kameda, T., & Nakanishi, D. (2002). Cost-benefit analysis of social/cultural learning in a non-stationary uncertain environment: An evolutionary simulation and an experiment with human subjects. *Evolution and Human Behavior, 23*, 373–393.

Kameda, T., Ohtsubo, Y., & Takezawa, M. (1997). Centrality in socio-cognitive network and social influence: An illustration in a group decision making context. *Journal of Personality and Social Psychology, 73*, 296–309.

Kameda, T., & Sugimori, S. (1993). Psychological entrapment in group decision-making: An assigned decision rule and a groupthink phenomenon. *Journal of Personality and Social Psychology, 65*, 282–292.

Kameda, T., & Sugimori, S. (1995). Procedural influence in two-step group decision making: Power of local majorities in consensus formation. *Journal of Personality and Social Psychology, 69*, 865–876.

Kerr, N. L., MacCoun, R. J., & Kramer, G. P. (1996). Bias in judgment: Comparing individuals and groups. *Psychological Review, 103*, 687–719.

Kerr, N. L., Stasser, G., & Davis, J. H. (1979). Model testing, model fitting, and social decision schemes. *Organizational Behavior and Human Performance, 23*, 399–410.

Kuhn, T. (1962). *The structure of scientific revolutions.* Chicago: University of Chicago Press.

Lamm, H., & Myers, D. G. (1978). Group induced polarization of attitudes and behavior. In L. Berkowitz (Ed.), *Advances in experimental social psychology* (Vol. 11, pp. 145–195). New York: Academic Press.

Larson, J. R., Jr., Foster-Fishman, P. G., & Keys, C. B. (1994). Discussion of shared and unshared information in decision-making groups. *Journal of Personality and Social Psychology, 67*, 446–461.

Laughlin, P. R. (1980). Social combination processes of cooperative, problem-solving groups on verbal intellective tasks. In M. Fishbein (Ed.), *Progress in social psychology* (Vol. 1, pp. 127–155). Hillsdale, NJ: Erlbaum.

Laughlin, P. R., & Ellis, A. L. (1986). Demonstrability and social combination processes on mathematical intellective tasks. *Journal of Experimental Social Psychology, 22*, 177–189.

Lind, A. E., & Tyler, T. R. (1988). *The social psychology of procedural justice.* New York: Plenum Press.

Lorge, I., & Solomon, H. (1955). Two models of group behavior in the solution of eureka-type problems. *Psychometrica, 20*, 139–148.

MacCoun, R., & Kerr, N. L. (1988). Asymmetric influence in mock jury deliberations: Juror's bias for leniency. *Journal of Personality and Social Psychology, 54*, 21–33.

Miller, C. E. (1989). The social psychological effects of group decision rules. In P. Paulus (Ed.), *Psychology of group influence* (2nd ed., pp. 327–355). Hillsdale, NJ: Erlbaum.

Mueller, D. C. (1989). *Public choice II.* New York: Cambridge University Press.

Ordeshook, P. C. (1986). *Game theory and political theory.* New York: Cambridge University Press.

Payne, J. W., Bettman, J. R., & Johnson, E. J. (1993). *The adaptive decision maker.* Cambridge: Cambridge University Press.

Sanders, G. S., & Baron, R. S. (1977). Is social comparison irrelevant for producing choice shift? *Journal of Experimental Social Psychology, 13*, 303–314.

Sawyer, J. E. (1997). *Information sharing and integration in multifunctional decision-making groups.* Paper presented at the annual meeting of the Society of Judgment and Decision Making, Philadelphia.

Sen, A. (1977). Social choice theory: A re-examination. *Econometrica, 45*, 53–89.

Sheffey, S., Tindale, R. S., & Scott, L. A. (1989). *Information sharing and group decision-making.* Paper presented at the annual convention of the Midwestern Psychological Association, Chicago.

Smith, C. M., Tindale, R. S., & Steiner, L. (1998). Investment decisions by individual and groups in "sunk cost" situations: The potential impact of shared representations. *Group Processes and Intergroup Relations, 2*, 175–189.

Smith, J. B. (1994). *Collective intelligence in computer-based collaboration.* Hillsdale, NJ: Erlbaum.

Sorkin, R. D., Hays, C., & West, R. (2001). Signal-detection analysis of group decision making. *Psychological Review, 108*, 183–203.

Sorkin, R. D., West, R., & Robinson, D. E. (1998). Group performance depends on the majority rule. *Psychological Science, 9*, 456–463.

Stasser, G. (1988). Computer simulation as a research tool: The DISCUSS model of group decision making. *Journal of Experimental Social Psychology, 24*, 393–422.

Stasser, G., Kerr, N. L., & Davis, J. H. (1989). Influence processes and consensus models in decision-making groups. In P. Paulus (Ed.), *Psychology of group influence* (2nd ed., pp. 279–326). Hillsdale, NJ: Erlbaum.

Stasser, G., & Stewart, D. D. (1992). Discovery of hidden profiles by decision-making groups: Solving a problem vs. making a judgment. *Journal of Personality and Social Psychology, 63*, 426–434.

Stasser, G., & Titus, W. (1985). Pooling of unshared information in group decision making: Biased information sampling during discussion. *Journal of Personality and Social Psychology, 48*, 1467–1478.

Stasser, G., & Titus, W. (1987). Effects of information load and percentage of shared information on the dissemination of unshared information during group discussion. *Journal of Personality and Social Psychology, 53*, 81–93.

Stasson, M., Kameda, T., & Davis, J. H. (1997). A model of agenda influences on group decisions. *Group Dynamics, 1*, 316–323.

Stewart, D. D., & Stasser, G. (1995). Expert role assignment and information sampling during collective recall and decision making. *Journal of Personality and Social Psychology, 69*, 619–628.

Tindale, R. S. (1989). Group vs. individual information processing: The effects of outcome feedback on decision-making. *Organizational Behavior and Human Decision Processes, 44*, 454–473.

Tindale, R. S. (1993). Decision errors made by individuals and groups. In N. Castellan, Jr. (Ed.), *Individual and group decision making: Current issues* (pp. 109–124). Hillsdale, NJ: Erlbaum.

Tindale, R. S., Anderson, E. M., Smith, C. M., Steiner, L., & Filkins, J. (1998). *Further explorations of conjunction errors by individuals and groups.* Paper presented at the British Psychological Society Social Psychology Section Conference, Canterbury, UK.

Tindale, R. S., & Davis, J. H. (1983). Group decision making and jury verdicts. In H. H. Blumberg, A. P. Hare, V. Kent, & M. F. Davies (Eds.), *Small groups and social interaction* (Vol. 2, pp. 9–38). Chichester, U.K.: Wiley.

Tindale, R. S., & Davis, J. H. (1985). Individual and group reward allocation decisions in two situational contexts: The effects of relative need and performance. *Journal of Personality and Social Psychology, 48*, 1148–1161.

Tindale, R. S., Davis, J. H., Vollrath, D. A., Nagao, D. H., & Hinsz, V. B. (1990). Asymmetrical social influence in freely interacting groups: A test of three models. *Journal of Personality and Social Psychology, 58*, 438–449.

Tindale, R. S., Filkins, J., Thomas, L. S., & Smith, C. M. (1993). *An attempt to reduce conjunction errors in decision-making groups.* Poster presented at the meeting of the Society for Judgment and Decision Making Meeting, Washington, D.C.

Tindale, R. S., & Kameda, T. (2000). "Social sharedness" as a unifying theme for information processing in groups. *Group Processes and Intergroup Relations, 3,* 123–140.

Tindale, R. S., & Sheffey, S. (1992). *Optimal task assignment and group memory.* Paper presented at the Nags Head Conference on Groups, Networks, and Organizations, Highland Beach, FL.

Tindale, R. S., Sheffey, S., & Filkins, J. (1990). *Conjunction errors by individuals and groups.* Paper presented at the annual meeting of the Society for Judgment and Decision Making, New Orleans.

Tindale, R. S., Smith, C. M., Thomas, L. S., Filkins, J., & Sheffey, S. (1996). Shared representations and asymmetric social influence processes in small groups. In E. Witte & J. H. Davis (Eds.), *Understanding group behavior: Consensual action by small groups* (Vol. 1, pp. 81–103). Mahwah, NJ: Erlbaum.

Vinokur, A., & Burnstein, E. (1974). The effects of partially shared persuasive arguments on group induced shifts: A group problem solving approach. *Journal of Personality and Social Psychology, 29,* 305–315.

Winquist, J. R., & Larson, J. R. (1998). Information pooling: When it impacts group decision making. *Journal of Personality and Social Psychology, 74,* 371–377.

Witte, E., & Davis, J. H. (Eds.). (1996). *Understanding group behavior: Consensual action by small groups* (Vol. 1). Mahwah, NJ: Erlbaum.

Wittenbaum, G. M., Vaughan, S. I., & Stasser, G. (1998). Coordination in task-performing groups. In R. S. Tindale, J. Edwards, F. B. Bryant, & E. J. Posavac (Eds.), *Social psychological applications to social issues: Vol. 4. Applications of theory and research on groups* (pp. 177–204). New York: Plenum Press.

15 The Accentuation Principle in Social Judgment: A Connectionist Reappraisal

J. Richard Eiser

ABSTRACT

What kinds of processes allow us to represent complex information about our world so that we can arrive at a judgment or decision? Theories of social categorization commonly assume that individuals tend to accentuate the differences between objects (or target persons) identified as belonging to distinct classes. Such interclass accentuation has traditionally been interpreted as reflecting motivations for simplicity, consistency, or (in an intergroup context) self-distinctiveness, in ways that imply that participants engage in symbolic reasoning about the class membership of objects. It is argued that such findings are better interpreted as reflecting processes of associative learning and parallel constraint satisfaction. Two simulations are reported, in which feed-forward connectionist neural networks easily reproduce patterns of data reported by Tajfel and Wilkes (1963) and Eiser and Mower White (1975). These findings suggest that accentuation effects can be explained as the consequence of learned associations between multiple inputs processed in parallel, without the need to postulate explicit reasoning concerning class membership or the neglect of information concerning individual objects.

CONTENTS

Judgments and Decisions: What Kinds of Processes?

In psychology, we build our theories with words. Even if we insist that we are using words only in a technical sense, even if we follow up verbal statements with mathematical formulae, it is difficult to discard the baggage of associations that such words bring with them from their use in everyday language. And everyday language is, of course, replete with *folk psychology* assumptions about how people think and feel and why they act in the ways they do. *Judgment* and *decision* are two such words. Both in ordinary usage and in much psychological research, they seem to refer to capacities in which human beings can take special pride. To call someone a *decision maker* (let alone a *judge*) implies high status or responsibility. People are praised for *sound judgment* and censured for *poor judgment*. Company executives are trained in *decision skills*. And so on. Wherever we find these words, the implication is that we are observing something that marks people out as rather clever, either individually by comparison with other human beings or, at very least, by comparison with other species.

The debate is not over whether judgment and decision making are indeed clever activities, but in what such cleverness or intelligence consists. A common assumption seems to be that these activities *necessarily* involve highly rationalistic processes including, for example, the deliberate and explicit use of logical and/or symbolic reasoning, calculation of likely consequences of planned behaviors, consideration of the statistical nature of evidence, and so on. In short, people use *rules*. Of course, it is recognized that people make mistakes, but even such lapses are frequently attributed to the fact that they use imperfectly valid rules or *heuristics* (Nisbett & Ross, 1980; Tversky & Kahneman, 1974) rather than no rules at all.

One difficulty with all of this is that we rarely have any direct evidence of what rules people may or may not be using other than from the *outcome* of their judgment and decision processes. We tend to assume that, if people achieve a desired outcome or provide the correct answer to some problem set by an experimenter, it is because they have engaged in appropriate reasoning procedures. However, the use of explicit rules is not a necessary condition for solving any decision problem. Even if a problem is defined so that anyone following a specific procedure will find the solution, someone else might still find the solution through the use of some other (albeit less efficient or general) rule or reasoning procedure, or even no explicit rule at all. Moreover, the use of explicit rules or reasoning procedures is often not even a sufficient condition for finding the correct solution, particularly when critical parameters of the problem are unknown or imprecisely defined.

Uncertainty is part of the natural order of things, at any rate outside the laboratory. Whereas participants in decision experiments may be told in advance exact numerical probabilities of particular actions producing a given outcome, or of a given object having a particular attribute, most real-life decisions are made without the benefit of such prior calculations. We inhabit, and somehow cope with, a hugely complex physical and social environment in which many of the events of most significance to us are intrinsically uncertain. Our success at navigating such complexity is the main justification for claiming a capacity for *intelligent* judgment and decision making, and the main task of research in judgment and decision making is to describe and explain this capacity. What kinds of processes allow us to represent complex information about our world so that we can arrive at a judgment or decision?

In this chapter, I shall explore the relationship between two approaches to this broad question that have traditionally been considered somewhat separately from each other. The first approach proposes that we handle complexity in our environment through a process of categorization. In other words, we represent our world in terms of classes of objects and events. Traditionally, categorization has been regarded as reliant on the use of symbolic concepts and associations, but I shall argue that this assumption is unnecessary. The second approach applies notions of connectionist learning to the general question of how we represent patterns of attributes and events in our environment. The assumption is that we have the capacity for processing multiple sources of information about our environment *in parallel*, that is, simultaneously. Crucially, such processing involves encoding associations between attributes and between events and their consequences. Whereas judgments and decisions, according to the *symbolic* view, rely on the cognitive *manipulation* of meaningful concepts, according to the connectionist view they are typically a kind of compromise between diverse influences and tendencies.

Categorization and Accentuation

Much research in both cognitive (Harnad, 1987; Smith & Medin, 1981) and social psychology (Eiser & Stroebe, 1972; Fiske, 1993; Smith & Zárate, 1992) has been concerned with how individuals sort objects or events into categories and use information about category membership when judging individual class members. A long-held assumption is that individuals tend to *accentuate* (relative to some comparison standard) the differences between stimuli (objects or persons) defined as belonging to distinct groups or categories (Bruner, Goodnow, & Austin, 1956; Campbell, 1956). Tajfel (1959) used this principle as the basis for one of the most influential cognitive accounts of prejudice and social stereotyping (Tajfel, 1969). This principle was extended to the field of attitudinal judgment (Eiser, 1971, 1990) and to processes of social identity formation, self-categorization, and intergroup relations (Tajfel, 1982; Turner, 1991).

The starting point for such work was the classical psychophysical question of how people report their *psychological* sensations of stimuli of varying *physical* magnitude or intensity. Context effects on judgment had already been extensively studied (e.g. Helson, 1964) but, almost always, stringent controls were put in place to ensure that the stimuli presented differed from each other only in terms of a *single* dimension or attribute (e.g., size). The critical question posed by Tajfel was: What happens when stimuli vary simultaneously in terms of more than one dimension? In terms of any relevance to *social* perception and judgment, the answer to this question is absolutely crucial, because people are manifestly complex and multidimensional. So too, albeit to a lesser extent, are many familiar physical objects, such as coins, which vary in both size and value (Tajfel, 1957). As a simple case, then, what happens when stimuli that vary along some continuum such as size *also* can be classified into distinct groups on the basis of some additional arbitrary cue, so that the larger stimuli fall into one class and the smaller stimuli into another? Tajfel (1959) proposed that stimuli belonging to different classes should be judged as more different from each other when information about class membership is available than when it is not.

Tajfel and Wilkes (1963) confirmed this prediction of an *accentuation of interclass differences* in a study in which participants estimated the lengths of lines presented with or without a category label (A or B) that differentiated the shorter lines from the longer ones. They also hypothesized that the presence of a superimposed classification should lead to a reduction of intraclass differences, that is, a tendency for members of the *same* class to be judged as more similar to each other. However, the evidence for this latter effect is somewhat more mixed in their own and subsequent studies. Importantly, such effects were discussed not in terms of how multiattribute stimuli were represented *as such*, but in terms of how one attribute (class membership) affected judgment of another (length). In the terms introduced by Eiser and Stroebe (1972), the question was how judgments along the *focal* dimension of length were influenced by a *peripheral* cue (A vs. B) that was not explicitly judged but was potentially informative if correlated with the focal dimension. As Tajfel and Wilkes (1963) put it:

> The class identification of a stimulus provides a *supplementary source of information* about the relationship of its magnitude to the magnitude of the other stimuli, whether identified as belonging to the same class or a different class. (p.103)

Simplicity and Order

In the context of social identity and prejudice, the "supplementary information" in question would be social group membership (e.g., ethnicity, gender). Tajfel (1969, p. 82) specifically claimed that stereotypes "introduce simplicity and order" and allow us to "achieve as much stereotyped simplification as we can without doing unnecessary violence to the facts." But exactly how does attention to the peripheral attribute of class membership introduce simplicity and order? The answer implied by the *cognitive miser* metaphor (Fiske & Taylor, 1991) is that this involves a neglect of differentiating information relating to individual members or exemplars of a given class. If we have too much information to deal with, so the story goes, we merely pick on some easily recognized attribute while ignoring the rest.

However, this is only one way of thinking about simplicity. From the point of view of decision making and judgment, what we need is not a predilection to *neglect* information, but a capacity to *recognize* patterning and covariation within the *data structure* offered by our environment. Hence, when we attend to categorical cues and class membership, this is not necessarily because this saves us the effort of processing information about the individual class members, but rather because we have learned (or been told) that relevant characteristics of the individuals are predictable from their class membership. In a similar vein, Chater (1996, 1999) has argued that simple representations are those that describe predictable *patterns* of information most efficiently. Categorization thus reflects what the individual has *learned* about the relevant objects of judgment and the covariation between their attributes.

Connectionism and Learning

It is fair to say that early research on accentuation mostly took such learning for granted, rather than treating it as integral to the categorization process. An exception is a study by Campbell (1956), in which a form of interclass accentuation was described as a *composite habit* acquired through learned associations between stimulus attributes and responses. By contrast, research on *connectionism* gives learning a central place in cognitive processes. The growing interest in the potential application of connectionism to social psychology and related areas is exemplified in a number of recent publications (Eiser, 1994; Read & Miller, 1998; Smith, 1996; Smith & DeCoster, 2000).

For readers less familiar with the principles of connectionism, the following is a simple summary. The basic building blocks of a connectionist system are, firstly, *units* and, secondly, *connections*. Because these were originally conceived of as analogous, respectively, to neurons and synaptic connections, connectionist systems are commonly called *neural networks*. Some units may be designed (or defined) as input receptors, others as outputs, and others (in many applications, termed *hidden units*) fulfill an intermediate role between input and output. At any given moment, each unit has a specific level of energy or *activation*, and each connection between any two units has a specific strength or *weight*. The connection weights control the extent to which activation spreads from one unit to another. In computer simulations, the activation of a given unit at a given time is calculated from the activations of all other units connected to it multiplied by the relevant connection weights. Cognitive and behavioral states (discriminations, preferences, response choices, etc.) are represented in a connectionist system by the pattern of activation across a set of units. Memory is represented by the pattern of connection weights. The levels of the unit activations and the connection weights are not (typically) fixed, but are continually being updated through interaction with a given data structure. This updating is analogous to *learning* in a person or an animal. A number of *learning algorithms* have been devised to modify the connection weights so that state of a system achieves a better representation of the data structure with which it presented. The algorithms most commonly used involve either the minimization of the difference between the output of the system and some specified *target* or the strengthening of connections between any pair of units that are simultaneously active. The former is termed *supervised learning*, and can be considered as analogous to instrumental conditioning, whereas the latter, termed *unsupervised learning*, is more analogous to Pavlovian conditioning.

Much connectionist research is concerned with the relative merits of different learning algorithms and network *architectures* (configurations of units) for the modeling of cognitive processes, including categorization. I shall not address such technical issues directly. Rather, I shall explore a more conceptual implication of a connectionist approach. Research on social judgment and categorization has commonly assumed (explicitly or implicitly) that individuals engage in a form of symbolic reasoning, particularly regarding the consistency of information that defines a given object of judgment (or a target person) as a member or a particular group or class. It has been further assumed that the categorical distinctions yielded by such reasoning do not merely reflect the *data structure* of the individual's social environment, but are guided by some kind of motivational principle – be it a need for simplicity and order, self-distinctiveness, or whatever. Neural networks have no in-built motivation, but are designed to identify any patterning or covariation that exists in any data structure with which they are presented. They are not (except by deliberate manipulation) preset to treat any specific cue or input as more informative than any other. Rather, they identify, during the process of learning itself, which cue combinations are the most informative and what reliance should be placed on particular cues. This can be expressed by saying that neural networks operate by attempting to satisfy *parallel constraints* rather than being governed by specific logical rules.

Simulating Accentuation Effects

In order to provide a simple illustration of the relevance of connectionist principles to such phenomena, I shall now describe two computer simulations. The strategy to be adopted is first to choose a data structure in which interclass accentuation has been observed and then to present it to a neural network (using a standard learning algorithm and architecture). If the network can "learn" to represent the data structure by finding an appropriate pattern of connections, then this establishes that accentuation effects could, in principle, be regarded as the product of a form of parallel constraint satisfaction. The pattern of connection weights can then be inspected to identify the nature of these constraints. Presentation of novel input patterns without further modification of the connection weights then provides a test of the generalizability of any accentuation tendency to new stimulus configurations.

I must stress that this is merely an attempt to illustrate, in connectionist terms, the *consequences* of category learning within the accentuation theory paradigm, as observed in previous empirical studies. What follows does not amount to a simulation of how any individual participant might learn the relationships between, say, focal and peripheral attributes without explicit feedback. The purpose here is rather to identify a pattern of connection weights consistent with observed group data and then to examine the outputs generated by this pattern to new inputs.

Study 1: Simulating Accentuation with a Single Classification

Tajfel and Wilkes (1963) conducted a widely cited experiment to test Tajfel's (1959) hypothesis that a superimposed classification would lead to an accentuation of interclass differences. Participants were required to estimate the length of eight lines, ranging from 16.2 to 22.8 inches, projected individually onto a screen. In the critical experimental conditions, the four shortest lines were distinguished from the four longest by alphabetic labels. (In the following, I shall refer to the label attached to the shorter lines as A, and to the label attached to the longer lines as B, although the direction of the relationship was balanced in the actual experiment.) In the control conditions, the stimuli were presented either without any labels or with the labels attached at random to the lines of different lengths. Tajfel and Wilkes (1963) report the mean estimates for the experimental and combined control conditions separately over two sessions. The most striking effect relates to the estimated interval between the fourth and fifth longest stimuli. Over the two sessions, this averages 1.9 inches in the experimental condition, compared with a control estimate of 1.1 inches and an actual interval of 0.9 inch.

Method

A computer simulation was conducted using a standard three-layer feed-forward network and employing the back-propagation of error learning rule. In simple terms, this means that the network was connected so that activations are fed forward from a layer of input units (representing stimulus attributes) to a layer of hidden units, and thence to the output layer (in this case, consisting of just one output unit). The activation of the output unit is then compared with the correct target value (the mean estimate observed in the original experiment), and an error term is derived. Finally, the connection weights (first from the hidden to the ouput layer and then from the input to the hidden layer) are modified so as to reduce this error. This procedure is then repeated over a number of presentations of the stimulus series (*epochs*) until a criterion of low error is reached over the set of input patterns (stimulus series) as a whole. The software employed was PlaNet version 5.6 (Miyata, 1990). Parameter settings were a learning rate of 0.2, a momentum of 0.9, and a randomization of initial weights within the range ±0.1.

Sixteen input patterns were presented to the network, with the targets corresponding to the means for the eight stimuli in the experimental and control conditions, averaged over the two sessions. The targets were recoded (linearly) as continuous values within a range from 0 (= 15.5 inches) to 1 (= 25.5 inches). The network architecture involved 1 output unit, 2 hidden units, and 11 input units, all taking binary values of 0 or 1. The first two input units were coded as 0,0 for all stimuli in control conditions, 1,0 for the four shortest lines, and 0,1 for the four longest lines in the experimental conditions (i.e., the first unit, if positive, coded the presence of the label A and the second B). The remaining nine units coded the relative lengths of the stimuli, according to the scheme shown in Table 15.1. The coding of each stimulus thus depends on positive activations from two input units, one of which is shared with the adjacent stimulus to the "shorter" side and the other with the adjacent stimulus to the "longer" side (except for the two end stimuli, which share only one unit). This enables the network to represent the relative positions of the stimuli.

Results

The network easily learned to reproduce the set of 16 target outputs, reaching the default error limit of 0.0001 in 562 epochs. The first column of Table 15.2 shows the contributions of each input unit to the output

Table 15.1. *Coding of Patterns in the Simulation of Tajfel and Wilkes (1963)*

Actual Length in Inches	Input Coding	Target Coding Control	Experimental
16.2	i j 1 1 0 0 0 0 0 0 0	0.10	0.06
17.0	i j 0 1 1 0 0 0 0 0 0	0.18	0.14
17.9	i j 0 0 1 1 0 0 0 0 0	0.26	0.21
18.8	i j 0 0 0 1 1 0 0 0 0	0.37	0.32
19.7	i j 0 0 0 0 1 1 0 0 0	0.48	0.52
20.7	i j 0 0 0 0 0 1 1 0 0	0.59	0.64
21.7	i j 0 0 0 0 0 0 1 1 0	0.72	0.75
22.8	i j 0 0 0 0 0 0 0 1 1	0.89	0.94

Note: i, j refer to inputs 1 and 2. These take values 0,0 in the Control condition; in the Experimental condition, they take the values 1,0 for the four shortest stimuli and 0,1 for the four longest.

activations (i.e., the sum of the products of the relevant input–hidden and hidden–output connections). These can be interpreted as similar to regression coefficients, in that a positive score means that the relevant input would predict a higher output (response) and a negative score a lower output. As can be seen, the contributions of the units representing the two labels were in the direction predicted. The label A made a negative contribution, thus leading to a lower value for the output (a shorter estimate), and the label B made a positive contribution. The contributions of the remaining input units are also consistent with a picture of a separation of the two stimulus classes. Those units exclusively used to encode shorter lines (3–6) all made negative contributions (and increasingly so toward the extreme of the distribution), whereas those used to encode longer lines (8–11) all made positive contributions.

Having established a set of connection weights that allowed the network to reproduce the observed means from the inputs with minimal error, the network was then tested on a set of novel input patterns. Specifically, five patterns with 1s on input units 3–7 (in turn) were presented with and without a 1 on input unit 1 (i.e., the A label), and five patterns with 1s on input units 7–11 were presented with and without a 1 on input unit 2 (i.e., B), all other inputs being 0. This amounts simply to a test of the generalization of the superimposed classification to hypothetical stimuli half a *step* shorter or longer than those actually used in the experiment, with input unit 7 representing the midpoint of the distribution. In addition, the network was tested on two patterns (input

Table 15.2. *Results of the Simulation of Tajfel and Wilkes (1963)*

Inputs	Contributions to Output	Outputs to Test Patterns		
		Without A/B	With A	With B
Input 1 (A)	−0.23	0.39[a]		
Input 2 (B)	0.31		0.50[b]	
Input 3	−1.67	0.11	0.09	
Input 4	−0.97	0.26	0.22	
Input 5	−1.11	0.29	0.24	
Input 6	−0.57	0.41	0.35	
Input 7	−0.58	0.42	0.36	0.46
Input 8	−0.10	0.51		0.57
Input 9	0.06	0.53		0.58
Input 10	0.99	0.65		0.69
Input 11	2.51	0.86		0.88
Bias: hidden units	−0.11			
Bias: output unit	1.39			

[a] Output when input 1 is set to 1, all other inputs to 0.
[b] Output when input 2 is set to 1, all other inputs to 0.

unit 1 or 2 only) representing the class labels by themselves, without any other stimulus information.

The remaining columns of Table 15.2 show the outputs generated by the network to these novel inputs. As can be seen, these were all more extreme or polarized in the presence of a relevant classification label than without it, supporting the hypothesis of an accentuation of interclass differences. The size of these displacements is somewhat reduced toward the extremes of the distribution but is still in the direction of increased polarization. This suggests that any reduction of intraclass differences in these data need not be attributable to assimilation to some class prototype. Instead, it may be a by-product of the fact that the interclass accentuation effects are stronger closer to the class boundary, because it is here that the class membership cue is least redundantly informative.

It is also worth noting that testing the network on the class membership cues alone (with all the inputs corresponding to the separate stimuli "switched off") shows only modest polarization. That is, it produces outputs that are less polarized, on average, than those yielded by combinations of the inputs corresponding to stimulus values (line lengths) and class membership. The implication is that accentuation occurs not because individuating stimulus information is ignored in favor of class membership, but as a consequence of individuating stimulus and class membership information being learned in association with each other.

Study 2: Simulating Accentuation with Multiple Cues

Tajfel (1959) formulated his theory to account for judgment in the presence of a single superimposed classification or peripheral cues. However, in real life we can categorize objects and persons in a number of different ways. This is illustrated by the application of accentuation theory to the field of attitudinal judgment. Here the main phenomenon to be explained is the influence of people's own attitudes on their judgments of statements expressing different opinions on some issue.

According to Sherif and Hovland (1961), judgments of attitude statements are governed by a principle termed *assimilation-contrast*. This assumes that people will use their own position on an issue as a comparison standard or "anchor" when interpreting statements made by other people. Statements that fall within a person's *latitude of acceptance* will be assimilated (i.e., judged as closer) to his or her own position, whereas those falling within the *latitude of rejection* will be contrasted (i.e., judged as further away).

Dissatisfied with the explanation offered by Sherif and Hovland (1961), I argued (Eiser, 1971) that assimilation-contrast might reflect the effect of participants using their own agreement and disagreement with the statements as a subjective *superimposed classification*, hence accentuating the differences (in positions along the pro–anti continuum) between statements they accepted and rejected. In support of this, I found accentuation effects similar to those of Tajfel and Wilkes (1963) when student subjects rated 64 statements concerning the nonmedical use of drugs along a scale from "extremely permissive" to "extremely restrictive." In the experimental condition, the 32 more prodrug (permissive) items were presented as coming from one newspaper and the 32 more anti-drug items from another newspaper. An anomaly in the relationship of participants' own attitudes to their judgments was then addressed. According to both the assimilation-contrast model and the basic version of accentuation theory, people with extreme own positions, either pro *or* anti, should give more polarized ratings than neutral participants. However, in previous studies (mainly using the issue of racial attitudes), only the pro participants showed the predicted polarization compared with neutrals, with antis showing the least polarization of all.

In an attempt to explain this, a new principle was added to accentuation theory. Superimposed classifications should lead to polarization (interclass accentuation) only on response continua that are congruent with the classification. This is an acute issue in which the continua are labeled by terms carrying *value connotations*. For instance, describing a statement as *unfavorable* toward African Americans could imply an attribution of prejudice, hence a negative evaluation. This would be congruent with the attitudes of more liberal respondents, who would anyway reject such statements. However, less liberal respondents might personally agree with such statements but be reluctant to accept that they expressed a negative prejudice. (It was suggested that antidrug participants in the Eiser, 1971, study would have been similarly reluctant to describe their own position by the negative label *restrictive*.) In simple terms, participants should show more polarization if their "own end" of the scale was evaluatively positive, so that they could use an evaluatively positive label to describe those statements with which they agreed and a negative term to describe those statements with which they disagreed. Expressed more technically, both participants' own agreement-disagreement and (their perceptions of) the value connotations of the response scale could be considered as superimposed cues, which could "reinforce" each other if they were congruent but "inhibit or cancel each other out" (Eiser, 1971, p. 3) if they were incongruent. This argument begs to be recast in terms of parallel constraint satisfaction.

A direct test of this principle is achieved by having participants rate the same set of statements on a series of response scales, some of which are labeled so that the pro end is more evaluatively positive than the anti end (henceforth P+ scales), and others (A+) scales where the anti end is the more positively labeled. In a study using the issue of teenagers' attitudes toward adult authority (Eiser & Mower White, 1974), participants whose own attitudes were more proauthority gave more polarized ratings on P+ scales (e.g., disobedient–obedient), whereas those with more antiauthority attitudes polarized more on A+ scales (e.g. adventurous–unadventurous).

The simulation to be described uses data obtained from a sequel to this study (Eiser & Mower White, 1975). As before, teenage students had to rate 10 short statements supposedly made by other young people. Five of these expressed clearly proauthority opinions and five expressed antiauthority positions. The students' task was to rate their impressions of the person who had made each statement on a series of eight scales, four of which were P+ and four A+. Ratings were made on continuous

100-mm lines, scored from 0 at the antiauthority extreme to 100 at the proauthority extreme. A check on the effectiveness of this manipulation of value connotations was incorporated by asking participants to rate the concepts "The kind of person I most like" and "The kind of person I most dislike" on each scale. Participants rated their own agreement with each statement. These further ratings also were made on 100-mm scales.

The interactive effect (on polarization of judgment) of participants' attitudes and the scale value connotations found by Eiser and Mower White (1974) was successfully replicated. However, the design was elaborated by experimentally superimposing an additional classification. For one-third of the sample (Direct condition), the five anti statements were presented as made by (different) boys and the five pro statements as made by girls. For another third (Reverse condition), the boys made the pro statements and the girls the anti ones, and for the remaining third (Control condition), the statements were presented without names of either gender. The prediction was that, overall, ratings should show more polarization (interclass accentuation) when the pro and anti item groups could be differentiated by the gender of the source than when they could not. This was confirmed, but the effect was moderated (albeit more weakly) by yet another predicted interaction. Suppose (went the argument) some of the scale labels were seen as more applicable to boys and others to girls. If this happened, the gender classification should lead to interclass accentuation on scales that allowed a "masculine" term to be used to describe a boy and a "feminine" term to describe a girl, but not if such gender connotations of the scale terms were incongruent with the supposed gender of the person who had made the statement being judged. To test this idea, half of the scales (Marked scales) were preselected so that the more anti term was also seen as more applicable to boys and the more pro term as more applicable to girls (e.g., bold–timid). The other four (Unmarked) scales were chosen so that neither term was seen as more applicable to boys or to girls.

With the sample split into three attitude groups (pro, neutral, and anti) on the basis of their own agreement-disagreement with the statements, the basic design is a $3 \times 3 \times 2 \times 2 \times 2$ factorial (Superimposed Classification $\times$ Attitude Group $\times$ Gender $\times$ A+ vs. P+ $\times$ Marked vs. Unmarked $\times$ Item Group), with the last three factors being within subjects. This is clearly an elaborate study, but it has been chosen for simulation precisely for this reason. Participants rated the statements in the context of multiple cues. If the rather intricate logic of the experimental hypotheses can be a bit taxing to revisit, it is hardly credible that the young participants obligingly provided confirmatory data by explicitly working out this logic for themselves. It is far more plausible to suggest that they responded to such multiple cues *in parallel* on the basis of associations acquired before and during the experiment. This suggestion would be supported by evidence that a device designed for parallel processing, a neural network, could satisfactorily identify the data structure produced by these multiple cues.

Method

As in the previous simulation, the neural network employed was a standard three-layer feed-forward network trained by back-propagation of error. The same software and parameter settings were employed as before. The network architecture comprised 1 output unit, 2 hidden units and 9 input units. Instead of combining the data from different conditions into a single training procedure, eight separate simulations were conducted. Each of these involved presenting to the network mean data from a separate cell of the (between-subjects) design, excluding the control conditions (those without a superimposed classification) and those with neutral attitudes. Thus, the simulations distinguished males and females, the direct and reverse classification conditions, and two attitude groups (pro and anti). The (target) data for each simulation consisted of the mean ratings for the relevant cell of each of the two groups of statements (averaged over the five statements within each statement group) on each of the four types of scale resulting from the 2×2 design of value and gender connotations. Thus 8 target outputs were employed in each training procedure. All target scores were re-coded from 0 to 1 (corresponding to 0 to 100 in the original data), with higher scores representing more pro ratings.

The input units were coded according to the following scheme. First, as an estimate of the position of each item group without the influence of attitude, scale type, or superimposed classification, the mean rating for the item group provided by same-gender participants in the control condition was calculated, averaged over all scales, and entered on *input unit 1* as a continuous variable with the range 0–1. *Input units 2 and 3* (binary values) coded the gender connotations of the scale: 1,0 for unmarked and 0,1 for marked. *Input units 4 and 5* (binary values) coded the superimposed classification: 1,0 for an anti source (male source in the direct condition, female in the reverse) and 0,1 for a pro source (female source in the direct condition, male in the reverse). *Input units 5 and 6* coded the value connotations of the scale based on the mean ratings by the relevant subgroup of the concepts "The kind of person I most like" and "The kind of person I most dislike." Preference for the more anti term (i.e., A+) was coded by a positive score (dislike–like difference) on *input unit 5*, 0 on input unit 6. Preference for the more pro term (i.e., P+) was coded by 0 on input unit 5 and a positive score (like–dislike difference) on *input unit 6*. *Input units 7 and 8* coded agreement and disagreement as separate unipolar scores. *Input unit 7* took a continuous value between 0 (undecided/disagree) and 1 (maximum agreement). *Input unit 8* took a continuous value between 0 (undecided/agree) and 1 (maximum disagreement).

Results

The neural network easily learned the patterns presented within each of the eight cells. The numbers of epochs required to reach the default error limit of 0.0001 were, for males, direct-pro, 718, direct-anti, 525, reverse-pro, 836, and reverse-anti, 99; and, for females, direct-pro, 654, direct-anti, 1,536, reverse-pro, 263, and reverse-anti, 127. The independent contributions of each input unit were calculated as in Study 1. These are shown in the first two columns of Table 15.3, averaged separately over the results of the simulations on the four pro and four anti subgroups. Several features are noteworthy. First, the control group rating (input unit 1) makes a rather small contribution to prediction of the target: Although it discriminates the pro and anti item groups, it makes no distinction between types of scales. The contributions of input units 2 and 3 are also small. More importantly, within the same column, that is, for the same attitude group, they have the same sign. This means that no simple differentiation between scales marked or unmarked for gender connotations was achieved by the network. However, input units 4 and 5 combine to show a generally strong effect of the superimposed classification, consistent with an accentuation of interclass differences between statements attributed to sources of different gender. Strong positivity effects are observed for value connotations. For A+ scales (input unit 6), the negative sign means that lower (i.e., more anti) ratings are predicted by the network for both item groups. For P+ scales (input unit 7), the positive sign means that higher (more pro) ratings are predicted. The contributions of input units 8 and 9 confirm the division of

Table 15.3. *Results of the Simulation of Eiser and Mower White (1975)*

Inputs	Contributions to Output		Outputs to Test Patterns[a]	
	M for Pros	M for Antis	M for Pros	M for Antis
Input 1 (control rating)	0.25	1.02	0.52	0.58
Input 2 (unmarked)	−1.71	0.41	0.46	0.60
Input 3 (marked)	−1.04	0.12	0.47	0.59
Input 4 (anti source)	−5.11	−1.98	0.34	0.47
Input 5 (pro source)	2.35	2.66	0.65	0.71
Input 6 (A+)	−5.73	−6.77	0.32	0.27
Input 7 (P+)	6.24	3.30	0.82	0.73
Input 8 (agreement)	1.16	−0.82	0.58	0.54
Input 9 (disagreement)	−0.76	−0.14	0.49	0.58
Bias: hidden units	−2.68	0.70		
Bias: output unit	2.10	−0.85		
Inputs 6 and 8			0.34	0.25
Inputs 6 and 9			0.31	0.26
Inputs 7 and 8			0.85	0.70
Inputs 7 and 9			0.79	0.73
			M for direct	M for reverse
Inputs 2 and 4			0.44	0.39
Inputs 2 and 5			0.66	0.62
Inputs 3 and 4			0.36	0.39
Inputs 3 and 5			0.69	0.62

[a] Input 1 is set to 0.5 (i.e., the scale midpoint) throughout. Test patterns consist of the other listed inputs set to 1 and all other inputs set to 0.

the sample into attitude groups, showing that pro participants tend to rate as more pro the items with which they agree and as more anti those with which they disagree. For anti participants, the network identified a tendency for agreement to predict more anti ratings but not a tendency for disagreement to predict more pro ratings.

The ability of the network to generalize to new patterns was then tested. The test patterns involved setting input unit 1 to 0.5 in all instances (equivalent to a control rating at the scale midpoint) and then setting specific other input units (singly or in pairs) to 1 or 0. The outputs produced to these test patterns, shown in the third and fourth columns of Table 15.3, signify the extent to which the specific inputs "pulled" the output above or below the scale midpoint. In addition to test patterns involving single inputs, more complex patterns were presented to test specific hypotheses of Eiser and Mower White (1975).

Those involving combinations of inputs 6, 7, 8, and 9 relate to the hypothesis that polarization should be more marked on scales where the value connotations are congruent with participants' own attitudes. In the original study, this was tested by looking at the mean item group differences for A+ and P+ scales for different attitude groups. In the simulations, account is taken of the (A+ and P+) value connotations of the different scales, as *judged* by the participants within each group (on average). Also, the extents of agreement and disagreement are treated as inputs, even though (as for the single input test patterns) the results are presented as averages of the simulations for the pro and anti groups separately.

These data show, first of all, the very strong positivity effect also apparent when inputs 6 and 7 are presented singly. In other words, outputs are much higher (more pro) when scales are judged as P+ rather than as A+. In addition, lower (more anti) outputs are predicted by the network for antis than for pros when scales are more A+, and higher (more pro) outputs are predicted for pros than for antis when scales are more P+. However, the simulation demonstrates that the extent of agreement/disagreement still has an effect that is not wholly one of maximizing evaluative congruity: Considering both A+ and P+ scales together, antis still give more anti ratings to statements with which they agree than to those with which they disagree, whereas the relationship for pros is in the reverse direction. (Note that in the original study, the attitude groups were defined on the basis of the same agree–disagree ratings that were used here to generate inputs 8 and 9. However, the criteria for defining an individual as pro, neutral, or anti varied within the different experimental conditions so as to secure equal cell sizes. Thus, some of the group differences in ratings could still be attributable to differences in agreement or disagreement in ways that were not identified in the original analysis.)

Social Categorization and Symbolic Reasoning

The principle of interclass accentuation has been a recurrent theme in social psychological theories. In the four decades since Tajfel's (1959) original statement, the empirical generality of the basic effect has been demonstrated in several areas, but explicit analysis of the underlying process has advanced more slowly. Many of the category distinctions with which social psychologists are most concerned (e.g., social identities and group memberships) are highly valued and symbolic. Perhaps for this reason, there may have been a presumption that social categorization must be essentially a higher-order symbolic process.

I am not arguing against the proposition that much social life is highly symbolic, both in terms of its products and in terms of the significance of the communicative acts through which it is constituted and organized. This can all be true, but still the question remains of how we process complex combinations of stimulus information of any kind. To adopt a connectionist approach is not to deny our capacity for higher-order symbolic reasoning, but rather to be agnostic (and somewhat skeptical) concerning the need to invoke such a capacity as an explanation when the critical phenomena can be accounted for by simpler associative processes. In short, the appeal of this approach is its conceptual parsimony. The key is the assumption that the brain (or any analogous device) can process several stimulus events at the same time, and detect the relationships between them, without the need for explicit reasoning. A connectionist neural network is not a brain, but it is a device capable of detecting patterns in stimulus events, self-evidently without any conscious thought.

The simulations reported in this chapter demonstrate the capacity of a connectionist neural network to reproduce both simple and complex examples of social categorization. The specific networks employed here achieve this through adjusting the weights of the connections between the units until the output to each vector of input values sufficiently matches the desired target (derived from the observed empirical data from the studies in question). The fact that the process can be so described carries important implications. Firstly, the process is iterative and automatic. Secondly, the input to this process is a *vector*, or list, of numerical values, and this vector is responded to as a whole. From the point of view of the network, there is no distinction between focal and peripheral attributes. What is important is their configuration with each other. It is not a matter of one cue by itself coming to be used to the exclusion of other attributes because it requires too much effort to respond to complex stimulus combinations. For a parallel processing system (of which these networks are extremely simple examples), it is really no effort at all. Nor, indeed, would it be any effort for such networks to produce several different outputs (in parallel) to the same input patterns. Although only a single output unit was employed here, networks with vectors of multiple outputs are extremely common in connectionist research, and would offer an alternative approach to the simulation of judgments on multiple response scales (as in Study 2).

Limitations of the Current Simulations

It is important to stress that the simulations reported have a very limited objective: to demonstrate that certain patterns of data in social judgment can be identified and reproduced by a parallel processing system. No claim is made that the kind of network used is the only, or even the best, that could be devised for performing such tasks, still less that it is a direct analogue of what went on in the brains of participants in the original experiments. The focus here has been on the end product of the categorization process rather than the specific form of learning by which such categorization is produced.

In considering how one might extend the present approach to study the process of category learning in such experiments, the first point to remember is that the participants themselves performed their task without explicit feedback. That is to say, participants were not given any information about the discrepancy between their actual judgments and any "correct" target value, whereas the back-propagation-of-error algorithm used in the simulations specifically calculates such a discrepancy. An attempt to model how an individual might learn the associations between different stimulus attributes over time, prior to formulating a response on a given rating scale, would therefore require unsupervised rather than supervised learning (for an example of unsupervised learning of social information, see Eiser, Claessen, & Loose, 1998). It would also demand, at least for Study 2, a more detailed coding of the attributes of the individual statements than was attempted here. More generally, the inputs would need to represent specific individual stimulus events, in the order in which they occurred for individual judges, whereas the present simulations were designed only to reproduce average data patterns over sets of stimulus items, response scales (in Study 2), and groups of participants.

Complexity and Social Judgment: A Paradox

Despite all of this, the success of these simple simulations underlines a paradox within most theories of social judgment. Evidently, social objects and events are highly complex, multidimensional stimuli. If we had to describe fully all the detectable and potentially relevant attributes of another person, or even an attitude statement, we would have neither the time nor the words to do so. Yet we seem to be able to make judgments about such social stimuli relatively easily and speedily. Such ease and speed are important to remember in the context of current discussions of dual process models of cognition. For instance, Smith and DeCoster (2000) include categorization as an example of a process dependent on *associative learning* rather than the use of symbolic *rules* but still characterize it as a form of slow learning. I find the term *slow* rather unconvincing in this context, because participants in accentuation experiments typically appear to learn category distinctions (i.e., show polarization of judgment in comparison to control groups) within remarkably few trials (i.e., after just the first few items are presented). Their more general argument could also be taken to imply some backtracking from Smith's (1996) earlier advocacy of connectionist ideas. Despite evidence from neuroscience that symbolic rule use may occur mainly in different parts of the brain from those involved in slow associative learning, there remains a need to explain how rules differ from associations in principle and how, wherever in the brain they might be found, they could be physically instantiated other than in terms of coordination between the activations of different complexes of neurons. Clearly, there are implications here for the kinds of network models that could be proposed as "neurally plausible," but it seems far too early to set limits on the range of phenomena potentially interpretable in accordance with connectionist principles.

Our reactions to social stimuli are complex and multidimensional, including affective, cognitive, and behavioral responses. From a connectionist or parallel processing perspective, such complexity is unexceptional and unproblematic. However, the associative processes that transform complex inputs into complex outputs need not (and typically cannot) be accessible to awareness or introspection. By contrast, much social psychological theory typically treats social judgment as the product of a form of *reasoning* involving symbolic representations expressed through language. Early extensions of accentuation theory to attitudinal judgment (e.g., Eiser, 1971; Eiser & Stroebe, 1972) are also open to this criticism, because consistency was regarded initially as a motivational principle operating at a symbolic level rather than the product of associative learning (but see Eiser, 1987). Likewise, despite the introduction of the notion of *value connotations* into debates concerning attitudinal judgment, these connotations, albeit socially conditioned, were treated as part of the intrinsic meaning of words or speech acts (cf. Nowell-Smith, 1956). The paradox, though, is that although we can use language to express the forms of reasoning that *might* underlie some very simple forms of categorization, linguistic reasoning does not seem able to capture at all easily what happens when we deal with more complex and interactive patterns of information.

It is plausible (though unnecessary) to surmise that a participant in the Tajfel and Wilkes (1963) study might have reasoned that "This line labeled with an 'A' is probably shorter because other 'A' lines are short." It could just about be plausible that a student with antidrug attitudes in the Eiser (1971) study could have reasoned that "This statement opposes drugs, and so I agree with it. On the other hand, I don't want to rate it as 'extremely restrictive' because *restrictive* seems to me to be a negative word, and so would imply that I disagreed with the statement." However, it already stretches the bounds of credibility to suggest that such explicit reasoning accompanied the rating of every single statement in the set of 64 (while participants were also attending to the supposed source of the statements as emanating from one of two newspapers).

Move on to the Eiser and Mower White (1975) experiment simulated in Study 2, and the proposition that categorization was based on explicit reasoning is completely implausible. A participant would have had to interpret complex linguistic content from the statement itself, notice the gender of the name of the person who supposedly made the statement, notice both the gender and value connotations of each of the rating scales, formulate a view of the personal acceptability of the statement, and, in the light of this, make a rating on the relevant judgment scale. To spell out all these separate and interacting influences in terms of explicit symbolic reasoning would also create a misleading impression that the whole operation was performed serially, that is, in an arbitrary sequential order. The alternative perspective is that the processing of multiattribute social stimuli is performed in parallel and, for this very reason, typically cannot be succinctly or accurately expressed in ordinary language.

Complex Systems

This chapter has attempted to illustrate the applicability of a connectionist approach to the field of social judgment. As such, it addresses two potential groups of readers. For cognitive scientists, there is, of course, nothing new in the message that neural networks can make categorical discriminations. However, cognitive science has sometimes appeared reluctant to consider more complex examples from the fields

of social cognition and social interaction, many of which pose exciting conceptual and technical challenges. For social psychologists and
other researchers in judgment and decision making, this is an invitation
to reconsider the level at which we attempt to describe the cognitive
processes that underlie social judgment and behavior. By formulating
our theories at too high (i.e., symbolic or intentional) a level, we may
have succeeded only in producing a plethora of constructs that offer
little more than a redescription of the phenomena they purport to explain. Worse, as our discipline expands its scope, we seem to need yet
more such constructs to describe the phenomena we find. *Accentuation*
is just one such construct. Although it at least derives from a tradition in
which researchers were looking for continuities across subdisciplinary
boundaries, it is, nonetheless, still a description of an effect rather than a
process. If, instead, we ask how this, and other such effects, could be produced through the processing of information within a complex system,
we may move toward a theory with greater parsimony and generality
than has been typical within our discipline for quite some time.

The phrase *complex system* is crucial to this claim of generality. For
as long as I can remember, there have been ideological debates over
whether social psychology is truly social or too individualistic, and
which traditions within social psychology can claim to be more social than others. Most of these debates have generated more heat than
light, primarily because both sides seem to have implicitly assumed that
groups and individuals must be inherently different, but nobody can really agree how they are. The field of judgment and decision making has
not been helped by this quarreling going on in the background. Easily
characterized as concerned with the products of *individual* rationality,
research in this area has tended to be neglected by many social psychologists, even sometimes when it deals specifically with issues of social
relevance.

If, instead of fixating on the content of issues, we attempt to ask questions about processes, many of these difficulties potentially disappear.
What is a process? In the simplest terms, it is how something affects
something else. What is a system? It is a set of things that affect each
other, and a complex system is (simply!) a system with lots and lots of
things that affect each other. Applied to individual cognition, connectionism argues that the mind/brain is a complex system. We can begin
to model this system as a set or sets of interconnected units, with varying levels of activation and connections of different strengths (weights),
modified by experience.

A central insight of this approach is that the system as a whole has properties (e.g., attitudes, capacity for rational thought, a sense of self) that are *not* attributable to its individual component parts, but emerge from the interaction of such parts with each other (Eiser et al., 1998; Nowak, Vallacher, Tesser & Borkowski, 2000). Neurons don't have attitudes, for instance, but people – because they have brains composed of interconnected neurons – do. But this insight applies not just when one is comparing people with neurons, but also when one is comparing groups or societies with their constituent members. Norms, constitutions, consensus, and dissent are group properties that depend upon, and emerge from, how individuals relate to each other. In other words, *both* individuals *and* groups are examples of complex systems, and studying how such systems operate may lead us to conclusions that apply at both levels. Social and individual psychology are therefore of a piece with one another, and the intellectual traffic, the adoption of concepts, need not simply be one way, from the individual to the social, but can go in both directions. As the philosopher David Hume (1740) once put it:

> we may observe that the true idea of the human mind, is to consider it as a system of different perceptions or different existences, which are link'd together by the relation of cause and effect, and mutually produce, destroy, influence, and modify each other.... In this respect, I cannot compare the soul more properly to anything than to a republic or commonwealth, in which the several members are united by the reciprocal ties of government and subordination, and give rise to other persons, who propagate the same republic in the incessant changes of its parts. (p. 307)

References

Bruner, J. S., Goodnow, J. J., & Austin, G. A. (1956). *A study of thinking.* New York: Wiley.

Campbell, D. T. (1956). Enhancement of contrast as composite habit. *Journal of Abnormal and Social Psychology, 53,* 350–355.

Chater, N. (1996). Reconciling simplicity and likelihood principles in perceptual organisation. *Psychological Review, 103,* 566–581.

Chater, N. (1999). The search for simplicity: A fundamental cognitive principle? *Quarterly Journal of Experimental Psychology, 52A,* 273–302.

Eiser, J. R. (1971). Enhancement of contrast in the absolute judgment of attitude statements. *Journal of Personality and Social Psychology, 17,* 1–10.

Eiser, J. R. (1987). *The expression of attitude.* New York: Springer-Verlag.

Eiser, J. R. (1990). *Social judgment.* Buckingham: Open University Press.

Euser, J. R. (1994). *Attitudes, chaos and the connectionist mind.* Oxford: Blackwell.

Eiser, J. R., Claessen, M. J. A., & Loose, J. J. (1998). Attitudes, beliefs and other minds: Shared representations in self-organizing systems. In S. J. Read & L. C. Miller (Eds.), *Connectionist models of social reasoning and social behavior* (pp. 313–354). Mahwah, NJ: Erlbaum.

Eiser, J. R., & Mower White, C. J. (1974). Evaluative consistency and social judgment. *Journal of Personality and Social Psychology, 30,* 349–359.

Eiser, J. R., & Mower White, C. J. (1975). Categorization and congruity in attitudinal judgment. *Journal of Personality and Social Psychology, 31,* 769–775.

Eiser, J. R., & Stroebe, W. (1972). *Categorization and social judgement.* London: Academic Press.

Fiske, S. T. (1993). Social cognition and social perception. *Annual Review of Psychology, 44,* 155–194.

Fiske, S. T., & Taylor, S. E. (1991). *Social cognition* (2nd ed.). New York: McGraw-Hill.

Harnad, S. (1987). (Ed.). *Categorical perception: The groundwork of cognition.* Cambridge: Cambridge University Press.

Helson, H. (1964). *Adaptation-level theory.* New York: Harper & Row.

Hume, D. (1740). *A treatise of human nature.* Extracted in D. Robinson (1998) (Ed.), *The mind* (p. 307). Oxford, Oxford University Press.

Miyata, Y. (1990). *A user's guide to PlaNet version 5.6: A tool for constructing, running and looking into a PDP network.* Boulder, CO: Computer Science Department, University of Colorado.

Nisbett, R. E., & Ross, L. (1980). *Human inference: Strategies and shortcomings of social judgment.* Englewood Cliffs, NJ: Prentice-Hall.

Nowak, A., Vallacher, R. R., Tesser, A., & Borkowski, W. (2000). Society of self: The emergence of collective properties in self-structure. *Psychological Review, 107,* 39–61.

Nowell-Smith, P. H. (1956). *Ethics.* Harmondsworth, U.K.: Penguin Books.

Read, S. J., & Miller, L. C. (Eds.). (1998). *Connectionist models of social reasoning and social behavior.* Mahwah, NJ: Erlbaum.

Sherif, M., & Hovland, C. I. (1961). *Social judgment: Assimilation and contrast effects in communication and attitude change.* New Haven, CT: Yale University Press.

Smith, E. E., & Medin, D. L. (1981). *Categories and concepts.* Cambridge, MA: Harvard University Press.

Smith, E. R. (1996). What do connectionism and social psychology offer each other? *Journal of Personality and Social Psychology, 70,* 893–912.

Smith, E. R., & DeCoster, J. (2000). Dual-process models in social and cognitive psychology: Conceptual integration and links to underlying memory systems. *Personality and Social Psychology Review, 4,* 108–131.

Smith, E. R., & Zárate, M. A. (1992). Exemplar-based model of social judgment. *Psychological Review, 99,* 3–21.

Tajfel, H. (1957). Value and the perceptual judgment of magnitude. *Psychological Review, 64,* 192–204.

Tajfel, H. (1959). Quantitative judgement in social perception. *British Journal of Psychology, 50,* 16–29.

Tajfel, H. (1969). Cognitive aspects of prejudice. *Journal of Social Issues, 25,* 75–97.

Tajfel, H. (1982). (Ed.). *Social identity and intergroup relations.* Cambridge: Cambridge University Press.

Tajfel, H., & Wilkes, A. L. (1963). Classification and quantitative judgement. *British Journal of Psychology, 54*, 101–114.

Turner, J. C. (1991). *Social influence.* Buckingham: Open University Press.

Tversky, A., & Kahneman, D. (1974). Judgment under uncertainty: Heuristics and biases. *Science, 185*, 1124–1131.

16 The Sociocultural Contexts of Decision Making in Organizations

Mark F. Peterson, Shaila M. Miranda, Peter B. Smith, and Valerie M. Haskell

ABSTRACT

Culture conditions the context within which a decision-making group engages in decision-making processes. Culture concepts come from multiple-nation studies and from focused studies of culture and decision making. In this chapter, we review how culture may affect decision context characteristics such as whether decision makers are selected to legitimize the choice process or to contribute information needed to make choices (logic of participation), whether decisions are made sequentially or simultaneously (rationale of time), and whether the purpose of decision making is simply to formulate a choice or to fulfill social functions such as socializing members or legitimating premade choices. By influencing the social context of decision making, culture affects information acquisition issues such as how much explicit or tacit information is used. Culture also influences how situations are framed and which situations are identified as requiring an explicit decision, how conflicting views are handled while developing alternatives, and the strength of propensities to select alternatives based on culturally sensitive value priorities. These considerations are applied to how cultural differences and communication technology combine in international virtual teams.

CONTENTS

The need to incorporate culture into decision theory has become increasingly pressing. The history of decision theory is a case study in scientific progress from modeling a limited, manageable portion of a phenomenon toward incorporating ever more ambiguity and complexity. At each step, the simplifying assumptions that had previously helped to make analysis practicable have been discarded. At the present stage of decision theory, remaining assumptions about the universality of social psychological processes continue to eclipse cultural aspects of the social nature of decision making, and limit our ability to anticipate and comprehend the implications of decision making in many contexts.

Much of the decision-making literature has made the simplifying assumption that individual decision makers do a considerable amount of cognizing on their own, without drawing from other parties. Some group and organizational analyses of decision making, however, do recognize aspects of its social quality (e.g., Thompson, Levine, & Messick, 1999; see also the chapters in this volume by Kameda, Tindale, & Davis, and Lerner & Tetlock). As examples, other parties can contribute factual information to a focal decision maker or they can offer ways of structuring decision making and understanding (e.g., Saunders & Miranda, 1998). Although social considerations always condition decision making, cultural considerations make it particularly imperative that we examine the social situation. Further, the literature on culture suggests that social aspects of decision making are even more central in many societies than they are in those societies in which decision making has been most often studied (Miller, Hickson & Wilson, 1996).

Our discussion of culture and decision making is based on the premise that decision making, particularly in organizations, is a culturally embedded social activity. We develop several aspects of this premise and provide an example of their application to an increasingly significant phenomenon – electronically mediated decision making by geographically dispersed, culturally diverse, virtual teams.

A Model of Culture, Context, and Decision Making

Our discussion of the implications that culture has for decision making in organizations will be structured around the three elements portrayed in the model shown in Figure 16.1: culture, the context of decision making, and the explicit decision-making process. This model suggests that culture affects the immediate context within which a relatively bounded set of people accept responsibility to make some sort of choice. The context of decision making comprises relatively stable characteristics of the situation, beginning when a set of decision makers enter into the process of decision making and continuing throughout the decision process. Characteristics of this context affect the explicit process of decision making. The cultural and contextual components of our model will be briefly outlined to set the

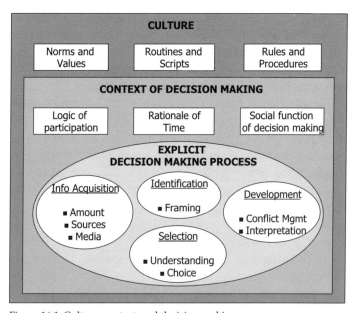

Figure 16.1 Culture, context, and decision-making process.

stage for a more elaborate treatment of their influences on the decision process.

Approaches to the Study of Culture

In our model, the term *culture* is used to designate the norms and values, routines and scripts, and rules and procedures that shape the ways of thinking, behaving, and interacting that are especially evident in a particular society. Although some qualities of societal culture also have meaning for collectivities of limited scope such as work organizations, our principal concern here will be with societies that encompass all aspects of daily life. The social-psychological and organizational literatures about culture that are most useful for understanding its implications for decision making tend to emphasize national culture delimiters while usually recognizing, although less often empirically representing, others (e.g., region, ethnicity).

There is an extensive culture literature in social psychology (e.g., Smith & Bond, 1999) and organizational studies (e.g., Ashkanasy, Wilderom, & Peterson, 2000) that is potentially relevant to decision making. At the present point in the field's development, major perspectives on societal culture have been developed around social science perspectives on values. One marker in this historical development is Inkeles and Levinson's (1969) integrative review of the psychological and sociological literature about culture. Hofstede (1980a, 2001; Hofstede & Peterson, 2000) developed this framework into the now ubiquitous culture dimensions of individualism versus collectivism, large versus small power distance, high versus low uncertainty avoidance, and masculinity versus femininity. Perhaps the most significant psychological taxonomy of values has been Rokeach's (1973). Schwartz (1994) has built from this base to develop a framework that reduces the U.S. ethnocentrism reflected in the specific values represented in Rokeach's model. Schwartz has developed it to identify individual-level value dimensions applicable throughout the world (e.g., self-direction, security, achievement). From these he has derived in turn seven societal-level culture dimensions (e.g., conservatism, intellectual autonomy, affective autonomy). Trompenaars (1993) has developed a taxonomy of culture dimensions (e.g., universalism versus particularism) from the values elements of Parsons's structural-functional theory of action, perhaps the most influential grand theory in sociology through the middle years of the 20th century (Parsons & Shils, 1951).

The next generation of culture dimensions is now emerging that represents attempts to improve on the earlier projects of Hofstede and others. Inglehart (1990) and his colleagues represent culture by drawing from a variety of sociological analyses of values. A major theme in this research is the view that culture is enduring but not absolutely unchanging. Inglehart argues that cultures have tended to move from traditionalism to modernism to postmaterialism. An ongoing project, Project GLOBE, being organized by Robert House, is well along the road to providing an update and a refinement of the Hofstede scheme (Dickson, Aditya, & Chhokar, 2000).

Although each of these frameworks maintains an internal consistency that helps to organize culture theory and answers a number of the theoretical challenges noted by critics (Child, 1981; Roberts, 1970), constructing a single framework that includes all of them is premature. For example, each framework has something to say about the relationship of a person to society, but the links across projects in how this theme is treated are uncertain. For example, trying to equate Hofstede's conception of individualism-collectivism with Schwartz's individual-level distinction between self-direction and security creates a level of analysis problem, and trying to equate Hofstede's conception with Schwartz's societal contrast of conservatism with both intellectual autonomy and affective autonomy is conceptually awkward.

The majority of scholars (e.g., Erez & Earley, 1993; Triandis, 1995) have identified individualism-collectivism as the most important aspect of culture and have worked through many of its nuances and implications. Apart from individualism versus collectivism, some conceptual analyses rooted in anthropological theory also continue. In particular, Maznevski and colleagues (1997) seek to operationalize Kluckhohn and Strodtbeck's (1961) constructs for characterizing societies. Numerous studies based on single constructs with speculative relationships to the more comprehensive frameworks are also being conducted. A book-length review of cross-cultural psychology by Smith and Bond (1999) provides a comprehensive overview of the field. Given the complex literature base available for the present analysis of culture and decision making, we have chosen to focus on implications of the relatively comprehensive culture frameworks. We have also selectively chosen examples from more narrowly focused projects that are either receiving particular attention in cross-cultural research or show particular relevance to decision making.

The Cultural Context of Decision Making

Many applications of culture research to social phenomena treat culture as part of the larger context within which social phenomena occur (e.g., Erez & Earley, 1993). Saunders and Jones (1990) have proposed that culture shapes many aspects of the context of decision making, including *temporal factors* such as when the decision maker becomes aware of the need to make a decision, the number of simultaneous decisions, and time pressures; *social factors* such as established values and patterns of interaction; and *problem-specific factors* such as perceived importance and problem characteristics.

In highlighting context as the intersection of culture with the decision-making process, we focus on three aspects: the logic of participation (substantive or symbolic), the impact of time, and the social function of decision making. These are not necessarily exhaustive elements of context, but rather represent elements that earlier research has found important and through which culture becomes salient in the decision-making process.

Logic of Participation. A decision can be important because of the substance of the choice being made or because of the symbolism of the decision-making process itself. Societal tendencies to emphasize either substance or symbolism are linked to cultural values and institutions. A society's emphasis on substance implies that individuals' status as decision participants is tied to their ability to provide information needed to solve problems or to their experience in structuring the decision process. An emphasis on symbolism means that status is tied to a person's political role in providing the decision-making process with influence or legitimacy in the view of external parties.

Much research on decision making has focused on the substantive nature of participation: Individuals are seen as holding information and opinions that are necessary for a rich, informed solution (e.g., Stasser, Taylor, & Hanna, 1989). However, an increasing body of knowledge points to the impact of symbolic variables on the decision-making process. For example, user participation in information system development leads to successful implementation of the system largely because personal involvement by the user facilitates user "buy-in" (e.g., Robey & Rodriguez-Diaz, 1989). Another example, presented by Turner, Pratkanis, Probasco, and Leve (1992), suggests that symbolic factors such as image are important. In particular, they demonstrated that groups with an "alibi" for a potentially poor decision circumvented the groupthink that can occur when a group feels the need to exercise excessive caution to protect its image. As a result, such groups tended to make better decisions. In both studies, the selection of who will be involved and their willingness to contribute substantively in decision making are affected by the symbolism of who they are and whether their image to parties outside the decision-making group is protected.

The utility of substance relative to symbolism is increased in societies that have developed institutions that provide a basis for enforcing agreements (Doney, Cannon, & Mullen, 1998; Hagen & Choe, 1998). Such institutions can be relatively explicit, as in the typical European and European-heritage legal systems that enforce contracts. They can also be strong, yet less explicit, as in the case of Japanese institutions that tend to identify and informally isolate parties considered to be deviant. In some societies, personal ties provide alternatives to either explicit or strong implicit institutions supporting trustworthiness. Societal values supporting individualism (rather than collectivism) and universalism (rather than particularism) have been argued to correlate positively with societal institutions that create trust through written agreements (Hofstede, 1980a; Trompenaars & Hampden-Turner, 1998). These cultural characteristics are likely to promote selection of decision-making participants on the basis of information and experience rather than on the basis of holding politically influential positions.

In contrast to issues of substance, culture can also affect the symbolic or ceremonial status of participants, and hence of the decision process. Aspects of culture related to the salience of status differentials, and what determines the status of particular social actors, have implications for the parties who participate in decision making and the influence they have in the process. Rather than explicitly study how people relate to each other in the decision-making process, much of the decision-making literature assumes that all parties in a decision process have equal status and contribute information equally to the content of the decision (Miller et al., 1996). Moving this expectation to other cultural contexts requires us to question this belief.

Some research questions whether a nonpolitical, equal contribution can be assumed by pointing to the considerable effort that is sometimes needed in order to promote equal contributions. For example, studies within the United States have frequently heralded electronic group support systems for facilitating equal influence by group members, irrespective of disparities in members' status (e.g. Zigurs, Poole, & DeSanctis, 1988). However, the cultural dependence of even this technique for promoting equal influence is evident in other research. In an experimental study contrasting the Singaporean and U.S. cultures, status differentials were manipulated via the use of a confederate who was working toward a higher educational degree (a graduate degree) than were the study participants (an undergraduate degree) (Tan, Wei, Watson, & Walczuch, 1998). The confederate was instructed to take a position that varied considerably from that of the rest of the group. Findings of this study indicate that disparities in influence persisted for a longer period in the Singapore groups than in the U.S. groups. Using computer-mediated communication significantly reduced the effect of status differentials in the Singaporean groups (Tan et al., 1998). In another study, utilizing a design similar to Asch's (1956) work on influence, researchers found that although computer-mediated communication forestalled the influence of a group majority (composed of three experimental confederates) on participating subjects (one subject per group) in an individualist culture (the United States), this technology did not have a similar effect on influence in a collectivist culture (Singapore) (Tan, Wei, Watson, Clapper, & McLean, 1998). They attribute this difference to the lesser likelihood that minorities in collectivist cultures would take advantage of the ability of this technology to promote equal influence. In general, research to date suggests that the logic for choosing participants, whether based strictly on task-related knowledge to make substantive contributions or on status, has culturally contingent implications. However, these implications are only beginning to be specified.

Impact of Time. A second influence that culture may have on the decision context is through its implications for time use. Various aspects of time are the focus of an extensive body of research on decision making. For example, Gersick (1988, 1989) found that the anticipation of a midpoint or endpoint in the decision-making process prompted a marked change in behavior in decision-making groups. McGrath's Time, Interaction, Performance (1991) model has prompted considerable empirical attention to the issue of time in decision making. In this model, McGrath proposed that decision-making groups demonstrate complex temporal patterning in their sequencing of activities. For example, the temporal patterning of activities by an organization's strategy planning group tends to correspond to or be "entrained" with external events such as changes in market or economic cycles, or to changing trends in expectations of analysts or regulators who actively monitor the organization. Brown and Eisenhardt (1997) found that the activities of successful project teams were paced by strategies or events in the organizational context (see also Wally & Baum, 1994).

Cultural differences in typical time use are likely to influence the decision-making context with respect to the value placed on time efficiency and pace. For example, dependence on trust in relationships rather than on enforcing institutions has implications for time use in decision making (e.g., Inglehart, 1990). Developing trust in a particular person can take time. A culture's emphasis on collectivist values can have a substantial impact on the amount of time taken to make decisions. Indonesian village councils (i.e., local governments in Java; Bailey, 1965), as well as organizations in Japan (Maguire & Pascale, 1978), for example, have been reported to reach their decisions by seeking consensus even if the process necessitates protracted deliberations. Perhaps time considerations are one reason why the consultative Japanese *ringi* system is much less widely used than in the past (Misumi, 1984). Some cultures are accustomed to handling multiple decisions simultaneously (polychronic) rather than handling one decision at a time (Bluedorn, 2000; Hall, 1983). So the time taken to handle a set of x_n decisions could be equal in polychronic and monochronic cultures, but the former would handle them simultaneously, whereas the latter would sequence them. This difference means that the time needed to handle a given decision is less in monochronic cultures, but viewed more broadly, the time needed to handle any given set of decisions could be equal. The cultural predisposition toward trust and decision sequencing, then, shapes the temporal context of decision making.

Social Function of Decision Making. Culture plays a strong role in the varying emphases on the social function relative to the task function of decision-making groups. Research on decision making has long acknowledged socioemotional maintenance and development as important functions of decision-making groups (Bales, 1970; Kelly & McGrath, 1985). Indeed, Smith and colleagues (1989) draw from Misumi (Misumi & Peterson, 1985) to show that whereas task and socioemotional behaviors were seen as orthogonal to one another by U.S. respondents, in the United Kingdom, Hong Kong, and Japan the two aspects of behavior were interrelated. Task functions were seen as having interpersonal consequences and vice versa. Thus, in most cultures, social aspects of participants such as their interaction patterns derive from culture and impinge upon the decision-making process.

Decision making is usually assumed to be purposive in an economically rational fashion. Although organizational researchers no longer assume that individuals involved in the process are motivated solely by economic rationality, they do assume that the overriding objective of decision making is to arrive at an economically viable or profitable solution for the organization. However, the latent functions of organizational decision making can have substantial elements of socialization and legitimation (Weick, 1995). That is, the decision-making process can be intended to bring newcomers into an understanding of the actions that more powerful parties will take, or to announce predetermined choices in a way that gains ceremonial acceptance.

The global dissemination of U.S. participative decision-making schemes can create situations in which existing power differentials cause participation to be radically reinterpreted. For instance, Juralewicz (1974) reports a case from Puerto Rico, where invitations to participate led employees to infer that management was incompetent. Hofstede's (1980a) *power distance* construct has a strong element of fear of openly objecting to the preferences of more powerful parties. Smith and Peterson (1988) suggest that decision making in a Japanese context can at times take the form of less powerful parties seeking to infer what more powerful parties want. Hofstede (1980b) cautions managers to avoid taking participative decision-making procedures designed for rational decision making into situations in which, implicitly, the decision-making context tends to be to legitimize premade choices.

A consideration of the participants' perspective on decision making suggests cultural differences in whether participants are likely to view the decision-making context as one principally for (a) making rational choices; (b) socializing newcomers or particular others; (c) discovering and establishing the legitimacy of premade choices; or (d) jointly making sense of events, with little emphasis placed on the impact of the explicitly announced choices.

Implications of Culture and Context for Decision-Making Processes

An organizational decision is commonly represented as explicit commitment to devote a set of resources under the control of a powerful party or parties to a course of action or a goal over a period of time.

For example, the construction of an organization's product strategy expresses a commitment to devote a large portion of corporate resources to reaching certain product development and sales targets over a relatively long time frame. The process of decision making is that which leads up to the announcement of this commitment. Given such a formulation, relatively little of what occurs in organizations, let alone in life more generally, is well represented as a sequence of decisions.

Weick (1995) follows a well-established tradition in organizational studies by describing much of what happens in organizations as based on relatively nondeliberative "enactment" rather than explicit decision making. Decisions are not viewed as being made and followed. Instead, memories of a decision announced in the past are viewed as being combined with other, more immediate cues to influence behavior at any given moment. Much of cognitive social psychology similarly indicates that most of what people do is not rationalized to the point of even consciously reaching an explicit determination that "I will now do the following" (see, e.g., Bargh & Chartrand, 1999; Wegner & Bargh, 1998). Rather, behavior is the reproduction of unconsciously internalized routines or behavior patterns that initially may have been the culmination of conscious cognition but that have become habitual through repetition (Berger & Luckmann, 1966/1990). Although a complete understanding of organizational action and human behavior must include these more implicit processes, our focus here is on the implications that culture and context have for those instances in organizations that can best be described as controlled or explicit decision making.

The process of explicit decision making is one in which social parties draw information from sources through various media to define and deliberate about the goals or course of action to which they will express a commitment. Researchers have begun to identify cultural preferences in the use of information sources, the use of particular media, and the nature and meaning of choices. Consistent with Mintzberg, Raisinghani, and Theoret (1976), we model the decision-making process as involving three phases: identification, development, and selection. Consistent with later work by Mintzberg and colleagues (Langley, Mintzberg, Pitcher, Posada, & Saint-Macary, 1995), however, we do not view these phases as necessarily sequential, but simply as activities that a decision-making group undertakes. Borrowing from Saunders and Jones (1990), we add the activity of information acquisition to these phases.

Information Acquisition

The parties who directly participate in decision making do so by drawing from a variety of *sources* through a variety of *media* to both obtain information and communicate to other decision participants. Culture scholars have argued that preferences for particular sources and media, in turn, are associated with preferences for particular kinds of information. Information that enters into decision making varies from relatively discrete bits of information that decision makers incorporate into their deliberations to information that contributes to structuring the decision process itself (Saunders & Jones, 1990). For example, decision making about annual budgets in local governments uses discrete bits of information that permit revenue projections. These budgeting deliberations also make use of information about an influential party's belief about the sequence of steps that should be followed or the priorities that should be given most weight when doing budgeting (Peterson, Elliott, Bliese, & Radford, 1996).

Cultural Preferences for Sources of Meaning and Information. One series of studies indicates that the sources that organization members draw from to make sense of work situations and produce decisions about how to handle them are linked to characteristics of a nation's culture (Peterson, 1998; Peterson & Smith, 2000). These studies examine the extent to which managers report using different sources of information to handle various specified work events.

Smith, Peterson, and Gilani (1995) showed that managers report different use of each of eight sources in six developing countries: Brazil, India, Iran, South Korea, Nigeria, and Uganda. These sources are formal rules and procedures, unwritten rules, subordinates, staff specialists, colleagues, superiors, personal experience and training, and widely accepted beliefs. Even among this small number of nations, reliance on personal experience and training is positively associated with Hofstede's (1980a) scores for individualism and negatively associated with his scores for power distance (i.e., acceptance that power differences are a normal part of life). They also reported national differences in the relationship between managers' evaluations of how well selection situations are handled and the sources the managers report being most heavily used. For example, use of personal experience and training is positively associated with handling selection well in five of the six nations (all except Nigeria), whereas reliance on formal rules and procedures is positively associated with effectiveness in India, South Korea, Nigeria, and Uganda.

In an expanded set of nations based on the same survey instrument, Smith, Dugan, Peterson, and Leung (1998) reported the average responses of managers in 23 nations in handling differing opinions within one's own department. Referencing their data against Hofstede's (1980a) dimensions, they report more reliance on subordinates and colleagues in low power distance nations and more reliance on personal experience and training in relatively individualistic nations.

Peterson et al. (1996) presented results from a study of U.S. and Japanese local governments. Respondents were asked about the extent to which they use 10 sources to handle nine sorts of work events. The sources represented explicit, implicit, and ad hoc reliance on rules, leaders, peers, subordinates, and self. The events were selected to represent differences in uncertainty, importance, and use of various resources (human, financial, material, multiple). The results show relatively little overall difference in the use of these sources between the two nations, although there was greater reliance on external boards in Japan. The results show consistency between the two nations in using superiors' and staffs' opinions to handle important events. However, the profiles reflecting interactions between nation and type of event showed differences at some points. For instance, superiors were used to handle events that involved personnel resources more in Japan than in the United States.

This line of research provides an empirical base supporting what has previously been largely speculation about the implications culture has for information use. Individualistic cultures are often argued to give decision makers considerable autonomy to structure problems for themselves, whereas collectivist cultures are said to encourage decision makers to refer to the interests of a larger in-group even though they may not be physically present as part of the decision making. The individualistic preference would support drawing discrete bits of information from any party who can provide it, regardless of his or her status. Although each link in this line of argument is yet to be fully tested, comparative research about cultural preferences for sources and media suggests that the more speculative analyses derived from the large-scale studies of national values reviewed previously are on the right track.

Cultural Preferences for and Implications of Media. Intercultural interactions occur through an ever broader variety of media as telecommunication technology improves and diffuses. Initially, media research attempted to characterize media based on their properties and to "fit" media to different types of tasks. Two theories have driven this perspective: media richness theory (Daft & Lengel, 1986) and social presence theory (Short, Williams, & Christie, 1976). More recently, some scholars have proposed that cultural and practical considerations (e.g., the written language script) make some media more appropriate to and more frequently used in some cultures than in others (Straub, 1994).

One proposal has been that cultural individualism entails a preference for *low-context* information, requiring a great deal of explication, as compared to *high-context* information that relies on extensive background knowledge and nonverbal cues (Hall, 1976). Hence, individualism is associated with making heavy use of lean, less personal media that efficiently transmit explicit factual information, whereas collectivism is associated with the use of richer, more personal media, such as is provided by face-to-face interaction. The preceding is the most direct inference and suggests that communication in high-context cultures requires nonverbal cues not available from thin media such as e-mail. However, members of high-context cultures may well find significance in simple cues to provide the hints they need to give communication a context. Simple cues that can be communicated even in lean media such as a sender's title, organization, manner of greeting (e.g., Dear. . ., Hello. . ., Bob:) or other indications of status in high-context cultures may be sufficient to evoke background knowledge of the sender and the institution the sender represents. In the latter case, Peterson and Smith's (2000) discussion of the implicit and explicit uses of the sources of meaning reviewed previously indicates that cues to meaning may in effect be intuitions of probable intentions of the communication partner based on internal representations of social roles rooted in past interactions.

For high-context cultures, we would anticipate greater stresses in using thin media for decision making during the early phases of a relationship than we would expect for low-context cultures. Once relationships are developed, we would anticipate that lean media could be used to make decisions at least as effectively as in high-context cultures. Although ordinarily used nonverbal cues might be missing, relationship-based cues would be available to supplement them. For low-context cultures, we would anticipate less variability in the use of lean versus rich media throughout the relationship. This expectation is based on another line of research.

Other scholars suggest that whether some set of media is experienced as being rich or high in social presence may be culturally variable even where the extensiveness of their use is equivalent. Straub (1994) found that Japanese workers viewed e-mail and fax messages as lower in social presence than did U.S. workers. He predicted that the cultural dimension of uncertainty avoidance, an element of which is a preference for explication (Hofstede, 1980a), and the pictorial rather than phonetic nature of the written word in Japan would result in e-mail's being perceived as less useful, and consequently used less often, among Japanese than among, U.S. workers. This prediction was confirmed. Straub, Keil, and Brenner (1997) found that whereas adoption of e-mail was strongly influenced by its usefulness and ease of use in the United States and in Switzerland, these variables failed to explain e-mail's adoption in Japan. They attributed this finding to the fact that rich media reduce uncertainty, support status differentials, provide social cues, and support assertiveness. Therefore, in the case of the Japanese, who are high in uncertainty avoidance, power-distance, and collectivism, the cultural need for rich media of communication overrides rational criteria for media usage.

On balance, the literature about cultural factors influencing media preference to the present point has begun to structure the theoretical considerations in analyzing this issue and has provided some evidence for culture effects, but the research continues to lag changes in communication technology.

Identification

The identification phase of decision making consists of recognizing and diagnosing the problem or decision situation (Langley et al., 1995). As described in Figure 16.1, identifying the decision is highly constrained by one's view of the related context, which, as we suggested, is influenced by one's culture. The identification process in many ways amounts to how one frames the decision problem (Kahneman, Slovic, & Tversky, 1982; Whyte, 1991; see Levin, Schneider, & Gaeth, 1998, for a review).

One of the pivotal cultural aspects of decision making is determining when something will be identified as requiring a decision. Maznevski and Peterson (1997) argue that the kinds of events noticed and attended to, and hence the issues that provoke decision making, are culturally dependent. Working from Kluckhohn and Strodtbeck's (1961) culture constructs, they suggest that the events a person notices will be affected by the culture into which the person has been socialized. For example, an individual's tendency to notice and think carefully about a slow-down in sales will be culturally dependent. An individual socialized into a *mastery*-oriented culture, in which it is considered normal and desirable for people to exert control over nature, will be scanning for events providing just such cues to potential environmental problems affecting sales that can be controlled and solved. An individual socialized into a *harmony*-oriented culture, in which adapting oneself to external conditions is typical, may be oblivious to such events, unless the events also produce disharmony in social relationships (Maznevski & Peterson, 1997, p. 72).

Insofar as high-context cultures prefer explication, a larger number of situations in such cultures will call for choices to be made consciously and announced publicly. For example, engaging in a collective process to formulate mission statements and corporate strategies is one way in which executives in individualistic U.S. and northern European cultures draw attention to situations requiring choices. In this way, cultures oriented toward exerting control over nature rather than living in harmony with it (Kluckhohn & Strodtbeck, 1961; Schwartz, 1994) may emphasize explication of decisions as a way of marshaling social support for collective projects.

Even in situations that are perceived as requiring a decision, cultural predispositions, and the social contexts they support, can have profound influences on how the decision situation is initially perceived. For example, Schlegelmilch and Robertson (1995) found that U.S. managers were more likely to classify issues of employee drug and alcohol abuse, theft, and discrimination as ethical issues that should trigger decision making about corporate policies in these areas than were managers from the United Kingdom, Germany, and Austria.

The identification of a decision situation as one that involves risk, and the assessment of the acceptability of that risk, are also affected by culture and context. McDaniels and Gregory (1991) reviewed studies from Hungary, Norway, Sweden, and Japan and reported numerous cultural differences in risk perceptions. For instance, Hungarian samples perceived lower levels of risk for most hazards, maintained more of a focus on everyday risks, and were less concerned about low-probability/high-consequence events than was an American sample (see Englander, Farago, Slovic, & Fischhoff, 1986).

Douglas and Wildavsky (1982) argue that the perception of risk is a collective phenomenon socially constructed in order to maintain a particular way of life. The social contexts generated by these constructions influence the way people sort out which risks are worthy of attention. Douglas (1985), for example, found that industrial and technological risks were more likely to be interpreted as opportunities in social contexts emphasizing hierarchical rather than egalitarian norms. Moreover, Weber and Hsee (1998) have pointed to social context as a central factor in explaining why the Chinese tend to be more risk-seeking in situations that involve financial risk and less risk-seeking in situations that involve social risk. A focus on one's network of relationships, and reliance on these relationships both as a cushion for loss and as an essential component of future happiness, may cause financial risks to seem less dire and social risks to seem crucial.

Although the relevant context may provide guidelines for identifying or framing the decision-making situation, the way that one views a decision is likely to differ from individual to individual even within the same culture. Decisions in organizational, and especially multicultural, contexts may become particularly complicated, as individual perspectives need to be communicated, integrated, and perhaps negotiated. These processes are typically construed as part of the development phase.

Development

The development phase of decision making involves designing alternate courses of action. This necessitates processing various types of information and identifying criteria for success. Such information processing occurs cognitively as well as politically, particularly in organizations and other group contexts. Thus, in this phase of decision making, we find processes of conflict management and interpretation functioning to develop more completely the implications of the decision situation and the ramifications that various possible actions have both for the decision-making group and for others whom they represent.

Dealing with conflict is a frequently studied example of the development phase in cross-cultural research. There are often said to be two aspects to conflict – *issue-based conflict* that is directed at the task and *interpersonal conflict* that is directed at persons (Deutsch, 1969). U.S. researchers have demonstrated that issue-based conflict, including that in demographically diverse groups, leads to favorable task-related outcomes, whereas interpersonal conflict has a negative effect on task outcomes (Johnson & Tjosvold, 1983; Pelled, Eisenhardt, & Xin, 1999).

A few comparative studies of culture and conflict management have been reported. Van Oudenhoven, Mechelse, and De Dreu (1998) compared approaches to conflict management among managers from five European nations, all of whom worked for the same multinational corporation. They contrasted problem-solving, assertive, and empathic approaches. In decisions involving one's superior, a problem-solving approach was used significantly more frequently by Danish, British, and Dutch managers than by Belgians and Spaniards. These results are consistent with the power-distance scores for these five nations. Kirkbride, Tang, and Westwood (1991) found that compromising and avoiding were favored styles among a large sample of Hong Kong managers. However, these studies reported no evaluations of the effectiveness of the different approaches.

A few other studies have considered cultural contingencies in the relative effectiveness of conflict management strategies. Graham and his colleagues have reported an extensive series of studies of buyer–seller negotiations in 17 different nations (Esteban, Graham, Ockova, & Tang, 1993; Graham, Mintu, & Rodgers, 1994). Their overall hypothesis has been that those who adopt a problem-solving approach will be less successful unless their opponent does likewise. Most studies in this series have used small samples, and it is not clear whether differing results are attributable to sample variance or to cultural difference. Samples include those from the United States and Russia (Graham, Evenko, & Rajan, 1992), Taiwan (Graham, Kim, Lin, & Robinson, 1988), Germany, Great Britain (Campbell, Bommer, & Yeo, 1993), Mexico, and French Canada (Adler, Graham, & Schwartz, 1987). This promising series of studies opens up as many questions as it answers. If a mutual problem-solving approach is the most effective one in all the contexts sampled, then what are the contextual cues that decision makers will attend to in each context that lead them to interpret the need for problem solving rather than competition?

Apart from conflict, another aspect of the identification phase is interpretation. Interpretation is a sociocognitive process that involves mapping or modeling the information obtained and relating different pieces of information to one another (Miranda, 2000). In interpreting information, our cultural frames inevitably come into play (e.g., Weick, 1995). Morris and Peng (1994), for example, observed a tendency toward situation-centered explanations of behavior among the Chinese, whereas Americans were more likely to adopt person-centered explanations of behavior. The Chinese also pay more attention to their environment, a practice that serves to enhance the accuracy of their memory (Ji, Schwarz, & Nisbett, 2000). This suggests that in individualist contexts, the choice of approach will be more strongly driven by personality, whereas in collectivist contexts it will depend more on selection of behaviors appropriate to the context.

Selection and Changed Understandings

Selection is the choice among alternatives. It entails the screening and evaluation of proposed alternatives and the authorization or sanctioning of a specific course of action. In the Mintzberg et al. (1976) model, this represents the final stage of the decision-making process, analogous to the choice phase in Simon's (1965) model. Mintzberg and colleagues' recent reconceptualization of the decision-making process as *issue networks* emphasizes the interlinked and interpretive aspects of decision making. That is, although there may be some practical and analytic convenience in identifying an endpoint in a decision-making process, the delimitation of a set of activities as "decision making" is somewhat arbitrary. From this perspective, the selection phase, as the culmination of the decision-making process, may serve to identify, constrain, or enable subsequent discussion of issues or decisions (Langley et al., 1995).

Because each of the major comparative studies of culture noted at the outset is built on societal preferences for some values over others, each one has obvious implications for preferences for decision criteria that favor corresponding values. For example, individualist cultures are argued to be relatively more biased toward alternatives favoring the well-being of the individuals making the decision and to their contractually identifiable principals (such as whoever they are working for at the moment), whereas collectivist cultures are argued to be biased toward alternatives favoring a less explicitly defined and longer-lasting in-group (Peterson, Rodriguez, & Smith, 2000). Hofstede (1998) would argue that societies that tend to value material acquisition and personal achievement (*masculine* or *ego-oriented* societies, in his terms) favor corresponding decision criteria. Decision criteria preferences in societies that value supporting weaker parties and nonmaterialistic aspects of quality of life (*feminine* or *socially oriented* societies, in his terms) are likely to reflect these alternative values.

Beyond preferences for particular criteria and corresponding to the preceding discussion of cultural differences in noticing when an explicit choice is needed, culture may affect the significance of making an explicit choice. Conformity pressures are greater in collectivist contexts (Bond & Smith, 1996), so the taking of an explicit position may be avoided if it is likely to be challenged. Explicit verbal statements are more likely to influence subsequent thought and action in low-context (often individualist) than in high-context (often collectivist) cultures (Hall, 1976). Explication is likely to be preferred in what Kluckhohn and Strodtbeck (1961) refer to as *mastery* cultures as distinct from *harmony* or *subjugation* cultures (Maznevski & Peterson, 1997).

Differences in cultural context may also affect how the likelihood versus the magnitude of projected losses is weighted when decisions are made about the acceptability of risk. When examining judgments about the riskiness of monetary lotteries by business students and security analysts, Bontempo, Bottom, and Weber (1997) found that samples from the United States and the Netherlands weighted the probability of loss more heavily, whereas samples from Hong Kong and Taiwan focused on the magnitude of those losses. In another study, Weber and Hsee (1998) examined how differences in risk perception were related to differences in the willingness to pay for financial investment options. Among participants from the United States, Germany, Poland, and China, the Chinese judged the risks to be lowest and were willing to pay the most, whereas the opposite was true for the Americans.

Culture has also been shown to shape confidence in one's choice. One trend that has been identified is a greater overconfidence in the accuracy of probability judgments by Asians (except the Japanese) than by Americans and Europeans (Yates et al., 1989; Yates, Lee, & Bush, 1997). This tendency toward overconfidence has been associated with a focus on gathering confirming rather than disconfirming evidence (Yates, Lee, & Shinotsuka, 1996; Yates, Lee, Shinotsuka, Patalano, & Sieck, 1998). Overconfidence has also been linked to fatalistic attitudes and less differentiated cognitive functioning (Wright & Phillips, 1980), which in turn have been shown to be related to a focus on family (Yang, 1981) and authoritarian socialization (Hossain, 1988).

Cultural influences on choice and the evaluation of previously made choices are also found in the priority placed on justice. The Japanese, for instance, are more strongly oriented toward maintaining relationships than on ensuring just outcomes (Ohbuchi, Fukushima, & Tedeschi, 1999). Furthermore, in the group-centered decision making of the

Navajo, compensation is made to those who do not benefit from the group's choice (Maruyama, 1982), demonstrating the value of connectedness as central to the legitimacy of an outcome.

Even the basis of fairness evaluations varies culturally. For instance, Tyler and Bies (1990) suggest that cultures that accept the authority of powerful decision makers tend to value procedural justice over justice based on outcome fairness. However, there is little support for this proposal. Pearce, Bigley, and Branyiczcki (1998) found procedural justice equally predictive in the United States and in the presumably more hierarchical Lithuania. Farh, Earley, and Lin (1997) found procedural justice to be less predictive than distributive justice of organizational citizenship behavior in Taiwan, another hierarchical culture. In a reformulation based on the now extensive literature on justice, Leung (1997) contends that key variables include whether the allocator and recipient are in-group or out-group members and whether the allocator benefits from allocations. Both of these factors will influence the effect of culture on the allocation of reward and the perceived justice of allocations.

Yates and Lee (1996) describe the folk-precedent matching method in Chinese decision making. Here the collectivist cultural norm creates a social context in which precedents based on the actions of respected others are presumed to be more important than analytic processes in resolving choices. Thus, the Chinese decision maker tends to define a decision situation not as a comparison of option attributes or utilities, but as a search for the most fitting precedent (such as may be found in cultural stories and legends) in order to determine an appropriate course of action. Hsu (1970) as well as Markus and Kitayama (1991) suggest that networks of relationships form a fundamental basis upon which Chinese perceptions of the world are constructed. This collectivist focus at such a fundamental level dictates a social context emphasizing role-based rather than cost-benefit-based decisions (Weber, Tada, & Blais, 1999, as cited in Weber & Hsee, 2000). It may also place limits on competition and create long-term moral obligations, as well as promote ethical over utilitarian concerns (Tse, Lee, Vertinsky, & Wehrung, 1988). Hence, in the identification phase, decision goals in collectivist cultures are likely to emphasize connectedness over individual profit.

Cultural Differences in Decision Making

Our review of culture and decision-making research shows intersections of the literature identifying the problems of decision theory, as reflected in the main categories noted in Figure 16.1, with large-scale comparative studies and a variety of studies of specific decision-related topics. Although many gaps remain and a considerable amount of empirical work is needed to replace theoretical speculation, movement has been evident in recent years. Progress in understanding particular aspects of culture in relation to the decision process is reflected in focused research programs such as those about media preferences and risk orientation. The speculative links between large-scale values-based research and aspects of social process are beginning to be filled in by comparative studies of their implications for typically used or preferred sources of meaning. The literature on culture and decision making is also beginning to set the stage for analyses of decision making in new kinds of situations not anticipated to be important even 20 years ago.

Decision Making by International Virtual Teams

The previous sections highlight the many ways in which sociocultural factors can influence decision making. As we have suggested, the various components of Figure 16.1 apply to any number of situations in which organizations encounter cultural differences. Practical applications include (a) determining which policies and practices to follow uniformly throughout an organization's global operations and which ones to adapt to local cultures (Bartlett & Ghoshal, 1992); (b) developing mechanisms for transferring management practices, including decision-making practices, across national boundaries (e.g., Peterson, Peng, & Smith, 1999); and (c) addressing problems of intercultural interaction, such as those that occur in multicultural management teams within a single organization (e.g., Earley & Mosakowski, 2000) or in multicultural groups managing relations between joint venture or strategic alliance partners (e.g., Salk & Brannen, 2000). We turn now to a special type of this last sort of application to provide an example of some of the considerations about culture and context in decision making that we have already discussed. The rapid development of computer-mediated interaction over the past decade or so has increased intercultural interaction in business decision making. The intercultural element of these interactions adds a complexity that is not present in single cultures. *Virtualness* can be a consequence of *geographical* and/or *temporal separation* (e.g., DeSanctis & Monge, 1999). Although our emphasis will be on teams of people separated by distance and culture, some of the literature that can be applied to this problem comes from studies of electronically mediated communication by people contributing to decision-making discussions at different times but at a single locale.

The rapid increase in intercultural virtual teams has caught analysts sleeping. There is very little empirical research directly addressing cross-cultural virtual teams, so developing theory in this area requires us to integrate literatures about virtual domestic teams and culture differences with the limited literature about intercultural interactions. Because most research on culture has compared cultures rather than studied intercultural interactions, most of our examples thus far have assumed situations in which decision-making participants all share a common culture. Although a few studies about international, multicultural teams that meet face-to-face have appeared very recently (e.g., Gibson, 1999; Salk & Brannen, 2000), the literature on the topic is typically conceptual rather than empirical (DiStefano & Maznevski, 2000; Granrose & Oskamp, 1997; Maznevski & Peterson, 1997). Multicultural groups within a single nation have been studied more often.

The domestic diversity literature suggests that international virtual teams are likely to face unique stresses and to have some unique advantages when making decisions, and the small amount of research on international organizational settings suggests the same. Research about the effectiveness and social processes that occur in demographically diverse groups within a single nation have produced inconsistent results (Williams & O'Reilly, 1998). Attempts to reconcile the inconsistencies have looked for aspects of diversity (e.g., ethnic versus task-related skill diversity) that operate differently and for the sorts of tasks for which diversity has different implications. More recent research confirms that different types of diversity are likely to have different effects. Value diversity tends to create emotional stresses and constrains performance, whereas task-related informational diversity can promote performance and purely demographic diversity (separated from value and informational diversity) can promote positive attitudes (Jehn, Northcraft, & Neale, 1999; Pelled et al., 1999).

Domestic diversity tends to differ from international diversity in two respects. Despite some particular sort of diversity reflected in these domestic studies, members of diverse groups within a single nation typically share substantial similarities, often more than they realize, in their sociocultural situation. These members can also draw from shared institutional experiences that may be typical of their nation (e.g., the particular sort of voting method used in national political decisions) and organization to establish fairly rapidly a shared social context for decision making (cf. Thompson et al., 1999). Even when systematically selected on the basis of demographic characteristics, so that they share different subcultural identities, members of demographically diverse groups in a single nation also are typically more aware of one another's subcultural backgrounds and their implications than is typical in international interactions.

To analyze international virtual teams, we need to replace the assumption of a relatively shared cultural situation with that of a largely unshared cultural situation. Studies of international top management teams (Elron, 1997) and multicultural teams within a single organization (Earley & Mosakowski, 2000) provide some encouragement that international teams can overcome their stresses and take advantage of their potential when making decisions.

The Sociocultural Context

Following Figure 16.1, our analysis of international virtual teams will first consider culture and its implications for the context within which such teams function. Then we will consider each of the four elements of the explicit decision-making process – information acquisition, identification, development, and selection. The literature about culture differences in decision making that was reviewed earlier suggests that team members from different national cultures will have different assumptions about the decision-making process. For example, Maznevski and Chudoba (2000) found cultural differences to impact assumptions about responsibility and task performance in global virtual teams. Such differences in assumptions generate different interaction preferences across team members.

Despite their differences, members of internationally dispersed virtual teams will share a few cultural and technological commonalities. For example, the fact that they use sophisticated electronic information technology and operate out of work organizations reflects acceptance of a significant level of modern values (Inglehart, 1990). Virtual teams are not likely to be composed of people from premodern groups who favor traditional agrarian and craft-based work and economic arrangements. They are made up of people who implicitly accept the utility of working for or with organizations. Within the context of an organizational hierarchy, these people are likely to include in their values the accomplishment of some sort of work for which their team has responsibility.

The decision to use electronic media rather than wait for ordinary mail or opportunities for face-to-face interaction reflects a value placed on efficient time use. Inglehart (1990) identifies global forces reflecting the influence of technological and economic modernity on the diffusion of these sorts of societal values.

Despite these few commonalities, however, the cultural variability among members of geographically dispersed cross-cultural virtual teams provides a substantially weaker base for establishing a shared context for decision making than is available for domestic virtual teams. The understandings that form the social context for decision making are likely to be very limited at the outset of the decision process. For example, who defines the parameters of the decision task and the criteria for determining decision effectiveness? Is it the member with the greatest technical competence, the oldest member, the member from the same nation as the corporation's headquarters, the highest-ranking member in the organization hierarchy, or some coalition of these individuals? As a consequence, the energy that the team devotes to constructing and carrying out a decision-making process and the potential for misunderstandings based on varying assumptions about the process will be high. The potential for an international virtual team to create a unique set of understandings, not typical of any one of the cultures from which the members come, about the way decision making will be carried out will also be high. Attention to the immediate content of the decision task will tend to be interrupted more frequently by issues associated with the understandings that form the social context for decision making than will be the case in domestic virtual teams.

How then are we to anticipate the social context of decision making as it develops and the way in which the decision-making process will operate? The literature about the structure of relationships, transactions, or exchanges that occur in the absence of a common institutional framework suggests that the development of social ties, characterized by cohesiveness and trust, is pivotal to more specific aspects of the social process. Some insights about how cohesion and trust develop are provided by research on culturally homogeneous computer-mediated group work (DeSanctis & Monge, 1999). Even within virtual teams in a single locale, technology use can retard the development of cohesive social ties (e.g., Chidambaram, 1996; Walther, 1995). In a multicultural setting, Jarvenpaa, Knoll, and Leidner (1998) note that "swift" trust emerged in about half of the international virtual teams that they studied. *Swift trust*, as the term implies, arises quickly and promotes effective interaction in virtual teams (Meyerson, Weick, & Kramer, 1996). Jarvenpaa et al. (1998) find that swift trust is a function of three things – the culturally influenced individual difference of a "propensity to trust," as well as ability (skills) and integrity (disciplined work habits). However, swift trust is relatively fragile and needs to be guarded (Jarvenpaa et al., 1998). Thus, early in an international virtual team's development, the social ties necessary for a shared social context that facilitates effective decision making are, at best, weak and tenuous and, at worst, may not exist. In time, a more robust shared social context may develop in international virtual teams, particularly as the team occasionally supplements its ordinary electronic communication with richer media for interaction, that is face-to-face or phone (Maznevski & Chudoba, 2000).

Information Acquisition in the Decision-Making Process

Characteristics of electronic media combine with the sociocultural context of decision making to shape the amount of information an international virtual team obtains and the sources it relies on to obtain and interpret information.

Medium. The functioning of geographically dispersed virtual teams hinges on common characteristics of electronic communication. The electronic medium is one of the only options available to long-distance teams that have time efficiency as a priority. Although this constrains the transmission of rich cues common in face-to-face interaction, it has some positive consequences for the amount of information brought to bear in the decision-making process and for the diversity of information sources utilized (Huber, 1990; Saunders & Miranda, 1998). Nevertheless, there is a concern that it is liable to impact subsequent stages of the decision-making process negatively.

Although the need for virtualness constrains media choices, some choice does still exist. Virtual teams can and do convene occasionally for face-to-face meetings and interact via phone. Maznevski and Chudoba (2000) found that, when possible, effective international virtual teams attempted to engage media appropriate to the changing requirements of the particular tasks at hand at any given point in the decision process. By contrast, ineffective teams did not, utilizing e-mail to discuss complex strategic issues and face-to-face meetings for collecting simple information.

Amount of Information. Research on computer-mediated teams shows that the introduction of the electronic medium resulted in increased communication (Hiltz, Johnson, Turoff, 1986; Whittaker & Sidner, 1997) and more information use (Saunders & Miranda, 1998). This leads us to anticipate more comprehensive information acquisition in international virtual teams than in teams that do not rely predominantly on the electronic medium. However, we need to examine the nature of the information acquired more closely. Not all information is explicit or discursive. In fact, the most meaningful information may be tacit (Pfeffer & Sutton, 2000). Although the electronic medium encourages the acquisition of explicit information, the acquisition of tacit information may require a richer medium. As discussed earlier in relation to cultural preferences for media, there are reasons to anticipate that members of international virtual teams who are from cultures that rely heavily on high social presence and rich media may not show the increase in communication that has been found in largely U.S. virtual team research.

Information Sources. Although little empirical work exists on the effect of computer-mediated communication on the number of sources sought by decision makers, this medium is believed to make potential information sources considerably more accessible (e.g., Bostrom & Anson, 1992; Huber, 1990). Technology facilitates easy retrieval of electronic information (Huber, 1990). Such information retrieval is not constrained by factors such as status or affect that may otherwise constrain information access (Bostrom & Anson, 1992). Further, cultural differences are likely to encourage individual team members to consult and draw the team's attention to different sources, thereby increasing the variety of sources consulted by the team as a whole (Maznevski & Peterson, 1997). For example, one person, who for reasons of cultural background is particularly attentive to hierarchy, may enter into the electronic record what he or she sees as the views of organizational superiors on the decision problem at hand and ask other participants what their superiors think. Another person, who for cultural reasons identifies particularly strongly with a work group, may encourage attention to the views of colleagues, and yet another from a society in which religious or political ideology is highly salient may raise issues of national norms.

Hence, even compared to situations of domestic diversity or domestic virtual teams, international virtual teams have an unshared cultural context that could potentially produce a more comprehensive analysis. On the other hand, it could also contribute to information overload, or deadlock due to reference to the interests and views of too many parties. However, researchers find that the electronic medium itself can help preempt such overload: The permanence of information available via the electronic medium enables individuals to process the information at their own pace (Schultze & Vandenbosch, 1998). Yet, the tradeoffs between potentials and stresses remain a highly speculative question for empirical research. The increased use of these teams means that the need for just this sort of empirical research is becoming quite pressing.

The Identification Phase of Decision Making

The identification process is one of decision framing. Research on decision framing in diverse domestic groups suggests that the inclusion of participants with diverse perspectives will cause the group to frame the decision in multiple fashions (Whyte, 1991). The even more unshared sociocultural context of international virtual teams is likely to yield individuals with diverse perspectives, thereby introducing more complex framing and a larger variety of perspectives on the decision. Although multiple perspectives may facilitate the decision-making process, it also complicates it in ways that may be difficult to resolve. Developing a shared framing of a decision problem is likely to be particularly challenging (Thompson et al., 1999).

In domestic groups, the electronic medium has been demonstrated to help groups overcome some of the process losses typical of conventional face-to-face interaction (e.g., Gallupe, DeSanctis, & Dickson, 1988; Vogel & Nunamaker, 1988). Features such as anonymity, simultaneous input, process structuring, extended information processing, and electronic recording and display alleviate typical group problems such as monopolization of the discussion or domination by a single member or minority, information loss due to time constraints or member shyness, or groups wandering off task (Bostrom & Anson, 1992). In this way, the electronic medium may therefore contribute to the development of effective and shared frames (Miranda, 1994). To the extent that similar problems, notably those of status differences among members, are particularly characteristic of international face-to-face groups, the electronic medium may be expected to help even more than in the domestic context. Moreover, the electronic medium can keep people focused on the task and issues currently at hand, given that the written word provides a focal point for the group's interaction (Bostrom & Anson, 1992) and that the group's interaction can be more effectively structured within electronic media (DeSanctis & Gallupe, 1987). We lack evidence as to how often these potential benefits for decision framing are actually achieved by cross-national virtual teams.

The Development Phase of Decision Making

The development process builds from the framing of a decision to the more complete analysis and interpretation of what led up to the situation prompting a need for a decision and what the implications of the decision situation might be for various involved parties. Successful development depends not only on the availability of information, but also on communication patterns and mechanisms for resolving conflict. Again, international virtual teams experience both the benefits and limits of cultural difference and the electronic medium.

Conflict Management. Domestic research on electronic communication indicates that although the medium suppresses dysfunctional interpersonal conflict, it also tends to dampen the issue-based conflict that is essential to productive exploration of options (Miranda & Bostrom, 1993–1994). Nevertheless, the electronic medium has been found to facilitate more productive integrative conflict management strategies to incorporate creatively the interests of multiple parties (Sambamurthy & Poole, 1992), while suppressing distributive strategies requiring tradeoffs between interests (Miranda & Bostrom, 1993–1994).

Interpretation. Miranda (2000) discusses two reasons why the electronic medium may impede interpretation. First, because the electronic medium improves access to information, and the amount of information that is brought to bear on a specific decision, it may cause information overload, albeit temporarily. This corresponds to Thorngate's (1997) notion of *attention economics*: The more information we possess at a given time, the less we are able to attend to all of it adequately. Second, the electronic medium suppresses the communication of socioemotional cues (e.g., Sproull & Kiesler, 1986). These cues assist in interpretation by providing an emphasis on certain information that imbues it with meaning. Further, the suppression of socioemotional cues makes it difficult to communicate affect (e.g., Galegher & Kraut, 1994). The communication of positive affect, or emotional contagion, has been found to favorably impact information processing and creative problem solving (e.g., Estrada, Isen, & Young, 1997; Staw & Barsade, 1993). Because interpretation is fundamentally a creative process, the suppression of emotional communication via the electronic medium can be expected to stymie interpretation.

Some researchers have proposed that the electronic medium need not block social cues (e.g., Lee, 1994). The reader of a message or piece of information may infer such cues based on his or her knowledge of the organizational context and of the author of the message or information (Carlson & Zmud, 1999). However, in the case of intercultural virtual teams, such knowledge is likely to be quite limited. These teams are embedded in disparate national cultural systems and probably in organizational subcultural systems that tend to color their members' contexts. Disparate cultural values make it more difficult for individual teammates to anticipate each other's behaviors (e.g., Zucker, 1986). Hence, an unshared culture is likely to compound the negative effects of the electronic medium and virtualness on the decontextualization of virtual teams.

This raises a concern about whether cross-cultural virtual teams are likely to be successful in developing a viable social context of understandings without the supplement of face-to-face meetings. However, Miranda (2000) proposes that although the electronic medium may have certain inherent limitations, it also possesses the advantages of allowing dynamic reorganization of time, associations, and concepts. These characteristics may encourage efficient communication, relationship building, and information processing as well as creative interpretation and problem solving. Exploring the impact of these tradeoffs on the costs and benefits of relying on the electronic medium becomes particularly pressing in the multicultural context.

The Selection Phase of Decision Making

Although we have distinguished the decision-making process from other interpretation processes as one in which an explicit choice is required, the selection phase of decision making includes not only choice, but also changed understandings that result from decision-making activities. In the case of international virtual teams, these understandings will be about the way electronic media can be used, as well as about the roles of team members and the understandings formed about the decision task.

Choice. The domestic literature on computer-mediated group work demonstrates better choices by distributed teams compared to face-to-face teams for certain types of activities. Notably, computer-mediated teams outperform face-to-face teams on generative, brainstorming types of activities (e.g. Jessup & Tansik, 1991). However, the technology appears unable to support convergent types of tasks with strong organization and evaluation components (Chin, Hayne, & Licker, 1992). Logically, incorporating decision-aiding technologies that facilitate the analysis of proposed alternatives against multiple criteria should assist in choosing effectively among alternatives. The preceding discussion of cultural preferences for particular decision criteria suggests that members of virtual teams from different cultures are likely to be particularly attuned to different criteria (e.g., task versus social, individual versus collective). We would anticipate that the sorts of technical or task-related criteria that can be legitimately discussed openly and explicitly would be handled well in virtual teams, and that members of cultures placing emphasis on such criteria would be particularly influential and satisfied with the outcomes. A decision's utility for personal, family, or other social criteria may well be downplayed. Societies accustomed to taking such criteria heavily into account may require periodic face-to-face interaction to supplement the virtual side of the team's work. Some research suggests interactions between culture and task in predicting the quality of choices. Culturally rooted differences reflected in team members' field independence and collective orientation interact with task characteristics and expressed efficacy to predict group effectiveness (Gibson, 1999).

Understanding. The effective implementation of a team's choice requires that the surrounding social system be understood in a manner consistent with the choice made. In other words, successful implementation necessitates a change in understandings. Here again, the electronic medium may prove useful in codifying and disseminating revised organizational definitions necessary for successful implementation. However, team diversity may require the revised understandings to be presented differently to the different constituencies to facilitate assimilation and buy-in of the new definitions. Participation in and implementation of decisions by team members from collectivist cultures will be critically dependent on the degree to which they perceive themselves to hold in-group status. Members of collectivist work teams work harder and show more commitment than when working individually, but only when they have in-group status (Earley, 1993). If they perceive themselves to have a peripheral or nominal membership in a virtual team, low activity and minimal implementation are more probable.

A shared culture facilitates a shared social context; similarly, physical proximity facilitates the embedding of decision-making activities in a similar context for all members of a team, thereby permitting them to index a shared situation. This is critical for shared meaning, which, in turn, is essential to collective action. Thus, the key need in building effective use of cross-cultural virtual teams is that they find ways to build a team culture that is their own. This may well require occasional face-to-face contact in order to enable team members to acquire "rich" data about one another.

Conclusion

The cultural biases of scholars have long affected social science. Roberts (1970) and Hofstede (1980b) pointed out ways in which the cultural biases of U.S. scholars have affected what is studied and what is concluded in organizational research. Erez (1990) documents preferences in the organizational behavior topics studied by researchers who are located in various parts of the world. Miller et al. (1996) note similar cultural biases in studies of organizational decision making. They point out that assumptions emphasizing the value of rational decision making reflect the cultural view of the West rather than a fundamental truth. Miller et al. then characterize decision making in parts of the world that are likely to place comparatively more emphasis on loyalty to individuals and the personal touch, hierarchy based on status, centralization, and politicized decision processes. If we are to overcome the ethnocentrism of our research endeavors, we must find optimal ways of incorporating the concept of culture into our studies.

Future Challenges

Although the analysis of culture has become increasingly sophisticated, considerable controversy remains. The limitations of using studies comparing Country A and Country B to understand how individual members of both countries will work together in teams are generally recognized (e.g., Boyacigiller & Adler, 1991; Peterson, Brannen, & Smith, 1994). Current debates focus on which culture dimensions are most useful or parsimonious, whether generalizations about whole nations are valid, and the significance of national rather than demographic or cultural boundaries (e.g., Hofstede & Peterson, 2000; Smith & Bond, 1999). Van de Vijver and Leung (1997) call attention to both the usefulness and the inherent limitations in establishing linguistic and conceptual equivalence in measures.

It is evident from the studies reviewed in this chapter that the only contrast identified by cross-cultural researchers that has been widely drawn on by researchers in decision making is that between individualism and collectivism. Although there is certainly value in noting the contrasts between Western and Asian styles of decision making, further progress requires more fine-grained analyses. Some researchers have recommended that we look to the work of other disciplines, including ethnographic methodology, in order to develop indigenous psychologies (Kagitcibasi & Berry, 1989; Smith & Bond, 1999). Similarly, Betancourt and Lopez (1993) endorse bottom-up research, in which researchers build theories only after careful examination of aspects of cultural variation. Cooper and Denner (1998) appeal for "explicit interdisciplinary, international and intergenerational discussions of culture and psychological processes" (p. 562).

An alternative way forward is to build much stronger bridges between measures of cultural variance and the actual decision makers involved in a given study. Rather than assert that a given culture is collectivist, on the basis that Hofstede's (1980a) data showed it to be so, the cultural values of those sampled can be surveyed. This makes it possible to test the extent to which particular cultural values mediate variance in the actions of decision makers. Weber and Hsee (2000) provide a detailed exposition of this strategy, as applied to the field of decision making. Morris et al. (1998) show how Schwartz's (1994) measure of values mediates differences in approaches to conflict management. Although they used a standard measure, their procedures enabled them to detect different effects within India, the Philippines, Hong Kong, and the United States rather than a simple East–West contrast. Continuing efforts on this frontier offer the promise of a richer understanding of how decision making among identifiable societies is likely to vary. This, in turn, will open the doors to developing a global perspective on decision making.

The Place for Culture in Models of Decision Making

A tempting way to make the culture concept easier to handle is to try to treat it as an individual difference characteristic. This approach to culture reflects an individualistic orientation. Trying to represent culture in terms of its manifestation by individuals is awkward for two reasons. First, psychological discussions of individual characteristics rely on the existence of a shared context that gives meaning to individual actions. Although analyses of differences among cultures sometimes can make comparisons based on reasonably equivalent meanings, at other times cultural differences shape the basic meaning of concepts. For example, we have noted that even the meaning of "making a decision" in the sense of committing resources to a course of action may be culturally variable enough that comparing average levels of decision making across different societies would miss the point.

The second reason is that although individual differences are principally conceived as just that – individual differences – cultural characteristics include a person's embeddedness in a network of interpersonal relationships. More pointedly in some parts of the world than in others, individuals are not best viewed as the focal points of choices. They can equally be implements of a family (variously conceptualized), a community, or an organization. Culture needs to become an integral part of decision theory in its own right, rather than being thought of simply as a predictor of more established factors that influence thought, choice, action, and interaction.

In this chapter, we have discussed the importance of considering the cultural contexts of decision making. We have also explored the modern phenomenon of virtual teams, arguing that cultural contexts play a critical role in shaping the integrative processes involved in decision making. In doing so, the purpose of this chapter has been to emphasize that cultural contexts can no longer be assumed away when studying decision making. To do so in today's complex decision-making environments would yield ethnocentric results of rather limited application.

References

Adler, N. J., Graham, J. L., & Schwartz, T. (1987). Business negotiations in Canada, Mexico, and the U.S. *Journal of Business Research, 15,* 411–429.

Asch, S. E. (1956). Studies of independence and conformity 1. A minority of one against a unanimous majority. *Psychological Monographs, 70,* 1–70.

Ashkanasy, N. M., Wilderom, C. P. M., & Peterson, M. F. (Eds.). (2000). *Handbook of organizational culture and climate*. Thousand Oaks, CA: Sage.

Bailey, F. G. (1965). Decisions by consensus in councils and committees. In M. Banton (Ed.), *Political systems and the distribution of power* (pp. 1–20). New York: Praeger.

Bales, R. F. (1970). *Personality and interpersonal behavior*. New York: Holt, Rinehart, & Winston.

Bargh, J. A., & Chartrand, T. L. (1999). The unbearable automaticity of being. *American Psychologist, 54*, 462–479.

Bartlett, C. A., & Ghoshal, S. (1992). *Transnational management*. Boston: Irwin.

Berger, P. L., & Luckmann, T. (1990 [1966]). *The social construction of reality: A treatise in the sociology of knowledge*. New York: Anchor Books.

Betancourt, H., & Lopez, S. R. (1993). The study of culture, ethnicity, and race in American psychology. *American Psychologist, 48*, 629–637.

Bluedorn, A. C. (2000). Time and organizational culture. In N. Ashkanasy, C. Wilderom, & M. F. Peterson (Eds.), *Handbook of organizational culture and climate* (pp. 117–128). Thousand Oaks, CA: Sage.

Bond, R. A., & Smith, P. B. (1996). Culture and conformity: A meta-analysis of studies using Asch's (1952b, 1956) line judgment task. *Psychological Bulletin, 119*, 111–137.

Bontempo, R. N., Bottom, W. P., & Weber, E. U. (1997). Cross-cultural differences in risk perception: A model based approach. *Risk Analysis, 17*, 479–488.

Bostrom, R. P., & Anson, R. G. (1992). The face-to-face electronic meeting: A tutorial. In R. P. Bostrom, R. T. Watson, & S. T. Kinney (Eds.), *Computer augmented teamwork: A guided tour* (pp. 16–33). New York: Van Nostrand Reinhold.

Boyacigiller, N. A., & Adler, N. J. (1991). The parochial dinosaur: Organization science in a global context. *Academy of Management Review, 16*, 262–390.

Brown, S., & Eisenhardt, K. M. (1997). The art of continuous change: Linking complexity theory and time-paced evolution in relentlessly shifting organizations. *Administrative Science Quarterly, 42*, 1–34.

Campbell, D., Bommer, W., & Yeo, E. (1993). Perceptions of appropriate leadership style: Participation versus consultation across two cultures. *Asia Pacific Journal of Management, 10*, 1–19.

Carlson, J. R., & Zmud, R. (1999). Channel expansion theory and the experiential nature of media richness perceptions. *Academy of Management Journal, 42*, 153–170.

Chidambaram, L. (1996). A study of relational development in computer supported groups. *MIS Quarterly, 29*, 143–165.

Child, J. (1981). Culture, contingency, and capitalism in the cross-national study of organizations. *Research in Organizational Behavior, 3*, 303–356.

Chin, W., Hayne, S., & Licker, P. (1992). The group consolidation problem during GSS usage: A new approach and initial empirical evidence. *Journal of Information Technology Management, 3*, 15–27.

Cooper, C. R., & Denner, J. (1998). Theories linking culture and psychology: Universal and community-specific processes. *Annual Review of Psychology, 49,* 559–584.

Daft, R. L., & Lengel, R. H. (1986). Organizational information requirements, media richness and structural design. *Management Science, 32,* 554–571.

DeSanctis, G., & Gallupe, R. B. (1987). A foundation for the study of group decision support systems. *Management Science, 35,* 589–609.

DeSanctis, G., & Monge, P. (1999). Communication processes for virtual organizations. *Organization Science, 10,* 693–703.

Deutsch, M. (1969). Conflicts: Productive and destructive. *Journal of Social Issues, 25,* 7–41.

Dickson, M. W., Aditya, R. N., & Chhokar, J. S. (2000). Definition and interpretation in cross-cultural organizational culture research: Some pointers from the GLOBE research program. In N. M. Ashkanasy, C. P. M. Wilderom, & M. F. Peterson (Eds.), *Handbook of organizational culture and climate* (pp. 447–464). Thousand Oaks, CA: Sage.

DiStefano, J. J., & Maznevski, M. L. (2000). Creating value with diverse teams in global management. *Organization Dynamics, 29,* 45–63.

Doney, P. M., Cannon, J. P., & Mullen, M. R. (1998). Understanding the influence of national culture on the development of trust. *Academy of Management Review, 23,* 601–620.

Douglas, M. (1985). *Risk acceptability according to the social sciences.* New York: Russell Sage Foundation.

Douglas, M., & Wildavsky, A. (1982). *Risk and culture: An essay on the selection of technological and environmental dangers.* Berkeley: University of California Press.

Earley, P. C. (1993). East meets west meets mideast: Further explorations of collectivistic versus individualistic work groups. *Academy of Management Journal, 36,* 319–348.

Earley, P. C., & Mosakowski, E. (2000). Creating hybrid team cultures: An empirical test of transnational team functioning. *Academy of Management Journal, 43,* 26–49.

Elron, E. (1997). Top management teams within multinational corporations: Effects of cultural heterogeneity. *Leadership Quarterly, 8,* 393–412.

Englander, T., Farago, K., Slovic, P., & Fischhoff, B. (1986). A comparative analysis of risk perception in Hungary and the United States. *Social Behavior: An International Journal of Applied Social Psychology, 1,* 55–66.

Erez, M. (1990). Toward a model of cross-cultural industrial and organizational psychology. In H. C. Triandis, M. D. Dunnette, & L. M. Hough (Eds.), *Handbook of industrial and organizational psychology* (2nd ed., Vol. 4, pp. 559–608). Palo Alto, CA: Consulting Psychologists Press.

Erez, M., & Earley, P. C. (1993). *Culture, self-identity, and work.* New York: Oxford University Press.

Esteban, G., Graham, J. L., Ockova, A., & Tang, S. (1993). *Hofstede, Rokeach and culture's influence on marketing negotiations.* Unpublished paper, University of California, Irvine.

Estrada, C. A., Isen, A. M., & Young, M. J. (1997). Positive affect facilitates integration of information and decreases anchoring in reasoning among physicians. *Organizational Behavior and Human Decision Processes, 72,* 117–135.

Farh, J. L., Earley, P. C., & Lin, S. C. (1997). Impetus for action: A cultural analysis of justice and organizational citizenship in Chinese society. *Administrative Science Quarterly, 42,* 421–444.

Galegher, J., & Kraut, R. E. (1994). Computer-mediated communication for intellectual teamwork: An experiment in group writing. *Information Systems Research, 5,* 110–139.

Gallupe, R. B., DeSanctis, G., & Dickson, G. W. (1988). Computer-based support for group problem finding: An experimental investigation. *MIS Quarterly, 12,* 277–298.

Gersick, C. J. G. (1988). Time and transition in work teams: Toward a new model of group development. *Academy of Management Journal, 31,* 9–41.

Gersick, C. J. G. (1989). Marking time: predictable transitions in task groups. *Academy of Management Journal, 32,* 274–309.

Gibson, C. (1999). Do they do what they believe they can? Group efficacy and group effectiveness across tasks and cultures. *Academy of Management Journal, 42,* 138–152.

Graham, J. L., Evenko, L. I., & Rajan, M. N. (1992). An empirical comparison of Soviet and American business negotiations. *Journal of International Business Studies, 23,* 387–418.

Graham, J. L., Kim, D. K., Lin, C. Y., & Robinson, R. (1988). Buyer–seller negotiations around the Pacific Rim: Differences in fundamental exchange processes. *Journal of Consumer Research, 15,* 48–54.

Graham, J. L., Mintu, A. T., & Rodgers, W. (1994). Explorations of negotiation behaviors in ten foreign cultures, using a model developed in the United States. *Management Science, 40,* 72–95.

Granrose, C. S., & Oskamp, S. (Eds.). (1997). *Cross-cultural work groups.* Thousand Oaks, CA: Sage.

Hagen, J. M., & Choe, S. (1998). Trust in Japanese interfirm relations: Institutional sanctions matter. *Academy of Management Review, 23,* 589–600.

Hall, E. T. (1976). *The hidden dimension.* New York: Doubleday.

Hall, E. T. (1983). *The dance of life: The other dimension of time.* New York: Doubleday.

Hiltz, S. R., Johnson, K., & Turoff, M. (1986). Experiments in group decision-making: Communication process and outcome in face-to-face versus computerized conferences. *Human Communication Research, 13,* 225–252.

Hofstede, G. (1980a). *Culture's consequences: International differences in work-related values.* Beverly Hills, CA: Sage.

Hofstede, G. (1980b). Motivation, leadership, and organizations: Do American theories apply abroad? *Organizational Dynamics, 8,* 42–63.

Hofstede, G. (1998). *Masculinity and femininity.* Thousand Oaks, CA: Sage.

Hofstede, G. (2001). *Culture's consequences* (2nd ed.). Thousand Oaks, CA: Sage.

Hofstede, G., & Peterson, M. F. (2000). Culture: National values and organizational practices. In N. M. Ashkanasy, C. P. M. Wilderom, & M. F. Peterson (Eds.), *Handbook of organizational culture and climate* (pp. 401–416). Thousand Oaks, CA: Sage.

Hossain, R. (1988). Perceptual processes in the Chinese. In M. H. Bond (Ed.), *The psychology of the Chinese people* (pp. 67–83). Oxford: Oxford University Press.

Hsu, F. L. K. (1970). *Americans and Chinese: Purpose and fulfillment in great civilization*. Garden City, NY: Natural History Press.

Huber, G. P. (1990). A theory of the effects of advanced information technologies on organizational design, intelligence, and decision making. *Academy of Management Review, 15*, 47–71.

Inglehart, R. (1990). *Culture shift in advanced industrial society*. Princeton, NJ: Princeton University Press.

Inkeles, A., & Levinson, D. J. (1969). National character: The study of modal personality and sociocultural systems. In G. Lindzey & E. Aronson (Eds.), *Handbook of social psychology* (2nd ed., pp. 418–506). Reading, MA: Addison-Wesley.

Jarvenpaa, S., Knoll, & Leidner, D. (1998). Is anybody out there? Antecedents of trust in global virtual teams. *Journal of Management Information Systems, 14*, 29–64.

Jehn, K. A., Northcraft, G. B., & Neale, M. A. (1999). Why differences make a difference: A field study of diversity, conflict, and performance in workgroups. *Administrative Science Quarterly, 44*, 741–763.

Jessup, L. M., & Tansik, D. A. (1991). Decision making in an automated environment. *Decision Sciences, 22*, 266–280.

Ji, L., Schwarz, N., & Nisbett, R. E. (2000). Culture, autobiographical memory, and social comparison: Measurement issues in cross-cultural studies. *Personality and Social Psychology Bulletin, 26*, 585–593.

Johnson, D. W., & Tjosvold, D. (1983). Constructive controversy: The key to effective decision making. In D. Tjosvold & D. W. Johnson (Eds.), *Productive conflict management: Perspectives for organizations* (pp. 41–61). New York: Irvington.

Juralewicz, R. S. (1974). An experiment in participation in a Latin American factory. *Human Relations, 27*, 627–637.

Kagitcibasi, C., & Berry, J. W. (1989). Cross-cultural psychology: Current research and trends. *Annual Review of Psychology, 40*, 493–531.

Kahneman, D., Slovic, P., & Tversky, A. (1982). *Judgment under uncertainty: Heuristics and biases*. Cambridge: Cambridge University Press.

Kelly, J. R., & McGrath, J. E. (1985). Effects of time limits and task types on task performance and interaction of four-person groups. *Journal of Personality and Social Psychology, 49*, 395–407.

Kirkbride, P. S., Tang, S. F. Y., & Westwood, R. I. (1991). Chinese conflict preferences and negotiating behaviour: Cultural and psychological influences. *Organization Studies, 12*, 365–386.

Kluckhohn, C., & Strodtbeck, F. L. (1961). *Variations in value orientations*. Evanston, IL: Row, Peterson.

Langley, A., Mintzberg, H., Pitcher, P., Posada, E., & Saint-Macary, J. (1995). Opening up decision making: The view from the black stool. *Organization Science*, *6*, 260–279.

Lee, A. S. (1994). Electronic mail as a medium for rich communication: An empirical investigation using hermeneutic interpretation. *MIS Quarterly*, *18*, 143–157.

Leung, K. (1997). Negotiation and reward allocations across cultures. In P. C. Earley & M. Erez (Eds.), *New perspectives on international industrial/ organizational psychology* (pp. 640–675). San Francisco: New Lexington.

Levin, I. P., Schneider, S. L., & Gaeth, G. J. (1998). All frames are not created equal: A typology and critical analysis of framing effects. *Organizational Behavior and Human Decision Processes*, *76*, 149–188.

Maguire, M. A., & Pascale, R. T. (1978). Communication, decision-making and implementation among managers in Japanese and American companies. *Sociology and Social Research*, *63*, 1–22.

Markus, H. R., & Kitayama, S. K. (1991). Culture and the self: Implications for cognition, emotion, and motivation. *Psychological Review*, *98*, 224–253.

Maruyama, M. (1982). Mindscapes, workers, and management: Japan and the U.S.A. In S. Lee & G. Schwendiman (Eds.), *Japanese management* (pp. 53–71). New York: Praeger.

Maznevski, M. L., & Chudoba, K. M. (2000). Bridging space over time: Global virtual team dynamics and effectiveness. *Organization Science*, *11*, 473–492.

Maznevski, M. L., DiStefano, J. J., Gomez, C., Noorderhaven, N. G., & Wu, P. C. (1997). *The cultural orientations framework and international management research*. Presented at the annual meeting of the Academy of Management, Boston.

Maznevski, M. L., & Peterson, M. F. (1997). Societal values, social interpretation, and multinational teams. In C. S. Granrose & S. Oskamp (Eds.), *Cross-cultural work groups* (pp. 61–89). Thousand Oaks, CA: Sage.

McDaniels, T. L., & Gregory, R. S. (1991). A framework for structuring cross-cultural research in risk and decision making. *Journal of Cross-Cultural Psychology*, *22*, 103–128.

McGrath, J. E. (1991). Time, interaction, and performance (TIP): A theory of groups. *Small Group Research*, *22*, 147–174.

Meyerson, D., Weick, K. E., & Kramer, R. M. (1996). Swift trust and temporary groups. In R. M. Kramer & T. R. Tyler (Eds.), *Trust in organizations: Frontiers of theory and research* (pp. 166–195). Thousand Oaks, CA: Sage.

Miller, S. J., Hickson, D. J., & Wilson, D. C. (1996). Decision making in organizations. In S. R. Clegg, C. Hardy, & W. R. Nord (Eds.), *Handbook of organization studies* (pp. 293–312). Thousand Oaks, CA: Sage,

Mintzberg, H., Raisinghani, D., & Theoret, A. (1976). The structure of "unstructured" decision processes. *Administrative Science Quarterly*, *12*, 246–275.

Miranda, S. M. (1994). Avoidance of groupthink: Meeting management using group support systems. *Small Group Research*, *25*, 105–136.

Miranda, S. M. (2000, August). *A theory of technology and depth of meaning: Focusing on dynamic reorganization of time, associations, and concepts*. Presented at the annual meeting of the Academy of Management, Toronto.

Miranda, S. M., & Bostrom, R. P. (1993–1994). The impact of group support systems on group conflict and conflict management. *Journal of Management Information Systems, 10*, 63–96.

Misumi, J. (1984). Decision-making in Japanese groups and organizations. In B. Wilpert & A. Sorge (Eds.), *International perspectives on organizational democracy* (pp. 525–539). Chichester, U.K.: Wiley.

Misumi, J., & Peterson, M. F. (1985). The Performance-Maintenance Theory of Leadership: Review of a Japanese research program. *Administrative Science Quarterly, 30*, 198–223.

Morris, M. W., & Peng, K. (1994). Culture and cause: American and Chinese attributions for social and physical events. *Journal of Personality and Social Psychology, 67*, 949–971.

Morris, M. W., Williams, K. Y., Leung, K., Larrick, R., Mendoza, M. T., Bhatnagar, D., Li, J., Kondo, M., Luo, J. L., & Hu, J. C. (1998). Conflict management style: Accounting for cross-national differences. *Journal of International Business Studies, 29*, 729–748.

Ohbuchi, K. I., Fukushima, O., & Tedeschi, J. T. (1999). Cultural values in conflict management: Goal orientation, goal attainment, and tactical decision. *Journal of Cross-Cultural Psychology, 30*, 51–71.

Parsons, T., & Shils, E. A. (Eds.). (1951). *Towards a general theory of action.* Cambridge, MA: Harvard University Press.

Pearce, J. L., Bigley, G. A., & Branyiczki, I. (1998). Procedural justice as modernism: Placing industrial/organizational psychology in context. *Applied Psychology: An International Review, 47*, 371–396.

Pelled, L. H., Eisenhardt, K. M., & Xin, K. R. (1999). Exploring the black box: An analysis of work group diversity, conflict and performance. *Administrative Science Quarterly, 44*, 1–28.

Peterson, M. F. (1998). Embedded organizational events: Units of process in organization science. *Organization Science, 9*, 16–33.

Peterson, M. F., Brannen, M. Y., & Smith, P. B. (1994). Japanese and U.S. leadership: Issues in current research. In S. B. Prasad (Ed.), *Advances in international comparative management* (Vol. 9, pp. 57–82). Greenwich, CT: JAI Press.

Peterson, M. F., Elliott, J. R., Bliese, P. D., & Radford, M. H. B. (1996). Profile analysis of the sources of meaning reported by U.S. and Japanese local government managers. In P. Bamberger, M. Erez, & S. B. Bacharach (Eds.), *Research in the sociology of organizations* (pp. 91–147). Greenwich, CT: JAI Press.

Peterson, M. F., Peng, T. K., & Smith, P. B. (1999). Using expatriate supervisors to promote cross-border management practice transfer: The experience of a Japanese electronics company. In J. K. Liker, W. M. Fruin, & P. S. Adler (Eds.), *Remade in America: Transplanting and transforming Japanese productions systems* (pp. 294–327). New York: Oxford University Press.

Peterson, M. F., Rodriguez, C. L., & Smith, P. B. (2000). Agency theory and event management. In P. C. Earley & H. Singh (Eds.), *Innovations in international and cross-cultural management* (pp. 131–182). Thousand Oaks, CA: Sage Press.

Peterson, M. F., & Smith, P. B. (2000). Sources of meaning, organizations, and culture: Making sense of organizational events. In N. M. Ashkanasy, C. P. M. Wilderom, & M. F. Peterson (Eds.), *Handbook of organizational culture and climate* (pp. 101–116). Thousand Oaks, CA: Sage.

Pfeffer, J., & Sutton, R. I. (2000). *The knowing–doing gap: How smart companies turn knowledge into action.* Boston: Harvard Business School Press.

Roberts, K. H. (1970). On looking at an elephant: An evaluation of cross-cultural research related to organizations. *Psychological Bulletin, 74*, 327–350.

Robey, D., & Rodriguez-Diaz, A. (1989). The organizational and cultural context of systems implementation: Case experience from Latin America. *Information and Management, 17*, 229–240.

Rokeach, M. (1973). *The nature of human values.* New York: Free Press.

Salk, J. E., & Brannen, M. Y. (2000). National culture, networks, and individual influence in a multicultural management team. *Academy of Management Journal, 43*, 191–202.

Sambamurthy, V., & Poole, M. S. (1992). The effects of variations in capabilities of GDSS designs on management of cognitive conflict in groups. *Information Systems Research, 3*, 224–251.

Saunders, C., & Jones, J. W. (1990). Temporal sequences in information acquisition for decision making: A focus on source and medium. *Academy of Management Review, 15*, 29–46.

Saunders, C., & Miranda, S. (1998). Information acquisition in group decision making. *Information and Management, 34*, 55–74.

Schlegelmilch, B. B., & Robertson, D. C. (1995). The influence of country and industry on ethical perceptions of senior executives in the U.S. and Europe. *Journal of International Business Studies, 26*, 859–882.

Schultze, U., & Vandenbosch, B. (1998). Information overload in a groupware environment: Now you see it, now you don't. *Journal of Organizational Computing and Electronic Commerce, 8*, 127–148.

Schwartz, S. H. (1994). Cultural dimensions of values: Towards an understanding of national differences. In U. Kim, H. C. Triandis, C. Kagitçibasi, S. C. Choi, & G. Yoon (Eds.), *Individualism and collectivism: Theory, method and applications* (pp. 85–119). Newbury Park, CA: Sage.

Short, J., Williams, E., & Christie, B. (1976). *The social psychology of telecommunications.* New York: Wiley.

Simon, H. (1965). *The shape of automation.* New York: Harper & Row.

Smith, P. B., & Bond, M. H. (1999). *Social psychology across cultures* (2nd ed.). Needham Heights, MA: Allyn & Bacon.

Smith, P. B., Dugan, S., Peterson, M. F., & Leung, K. (1998). Individualism-collectivism and the handling of disagreement: A 23 country study. *International Journal of Intercultural Relations, 22*, 351–367.

Smith, P. B., & Peterson, M. F. (1988). *Leadership, organizations and culture.* London: Sage.

Smith, P. B., Peterson, M. F., & Gilani, Z. (1995). Cultural diversity in managing the employee selection event. In R. N. Kanungo & D. Saunders (Eds.), *New approaches to employee management* (Vol. 3, pp. 143–153). Greenwich, CT: JAI Press.

Smith, P. B., Peterson, M. F., Misumi, J., Bond, M. H., & Tayeb, M. H. (1989). On the generality of leadership styles across cultures. *Journal of Occupational Psychology, 62*, 97–110.

Sproull, L., & Kiesler, S. (1986). Reducing social context cues: Electronic mail in organizational communication. *Management Science, 32*, 1492–1512.

Stasser, G., Taylor, L. A., & Hanna, C. (1989). Information sampling in structured and unstructured discussions of three- and six-person groups. *Journal of Personality and Social Psychology, 57*, 67–78.

Staw, B. M., & Barsade, S. G. (1993). Affect and managerial performance: A test of the sadder-but-wiser vs. happier-and-smarter hypotheses. *Administrative Science Quarterly, 38*, 304–332.

Straub, D. W. (1994). The effect of culture on IT diffusion: E-mail and FAX in Japan and the U.S. *Information Systems Research, 5*, 23–47.

Straub, D. W., Keil, M., & Brenner, W. (1997). Testing the technology acceptance model across cultures: A three country study. *Information and Management, 33*, 1–11.

Tan, B. C. Y., Wei, K. K., Watson, R. T., Clapper, D. L., & McLean, E. (1998). Computer-mediated communication and majority influence: Assessing the impact in an individualistic and a collectivist culture. *Management Science, 44*, 1263–1278.

Tan, B. C. Y, Wei, K. K., Watson, R. T., & Walczuch, R. M. (1998). Reducing status effects with computer-mediated communication: Evidence from two distinct national cultures. *Journal of Management Information Systems, 15*, 119–141.

Thompson, L. L., Levine, J. M., & Messick, D. M. (Eds.). (1999). *Shared cognition in organizations: The management of knowledge.* Mahwah, N.J.: Erlbaum.

Thorngate, W. (1997). More than we can know: The attentional economics of internet use. In S. Kiesler (Ed.), *Culture of the internet* (pp. 296–297). Mahwah, NJ: Erlbaum.

Triandis, H. C. (1995). *Individualism and collectivism.* Boulder, CO: Westview.

Trompenaars, F. (1993). *Riding the waves of culture.* London: Brealey.

Trompenaars, F., & Hampden-Turner, C. (1998). *Riding the waves of culture* (2nd ed.). New York: McGraw-Hill.

Tse, D. K., Lee, K.-H., Vertinsky, I., & Wehrung, D. A. (1988). Does culture matter? A cross-cultural study of executives' choice, decisiveness, and risk adjustment in international marketing. *Journal of Marketing, 52*, 81–95.

Turner, M. E., Pratkanis, A. K., Probasco, P., & Leve, C. (1992). Threat, cohesion, and group effectiveness: Testing a social identity maintenance perspective on groupthink. *Journal of Personality and Social Psychology, 63*, 781–796.

Tyler, T. R., & Bies, R. J. (1990). Beyond formal procedures: The interpersonal context of procedural justice. In J. S. Caroll (Ed.), *Applied social psychology and organizational settings* (pp. 77–98). Hillsdale, NJ: Erlbaum.

Van de Vijver, F., & Leung, K. (1997). *Methods and data analysis for cross-cultural research.* Thousand Oaks, CA: Sage.

Van Oudenhoven, J. P. L., Mechelse, L., & de Dreu, C. K. W. (1998). Managerial conflict management in five European countries: The importance of power distance, uncertainty avoidance and masculinity. *Applied Psychology: An International Review, 47*, 439–455.

Vogel, D. R., & Nunamaker, J. F. (1988). Group decision support system impact: Multi-methodological exploration. *Information & Management, 18*, 15–28.

Wally, S., & Baum, J. R. (1994). Personal and structural determinants of the pace of strategic decision making. *Academy of Management Journal, 37*, 932–956.

Walther, J. (1995). Relational aspects of computer-mediated communication: Experimental observations over time. *Organization Science, 6*, 186–203.

Weber, E. U., & Hsee, C. K. (1998). Cross-cultural differences in risk perception, but cross-cultural similarities in attitude towards perceived risk. *Management Science, 44*, 1205–1217.

Weber, E. U., & Hsee, C. K. (2000). Culture and individual judgment and decision making. *Applied Psychology: An International Review, 49*, 32–61.

Weber, E. U., Tada, Y., & Blais, A. R. (1999). *From Shakespeare to Spielberg: Predicting modes of decision-making*. Working paper, Ohio State University.

Wegner, D. M., & Bargh, J. A. (1998). Control and automaticity in social life. In D. Gilbert, S. Fiske, & G. Lindzey (Eds.), *Handbook of social psychology* (4th ed., pp. 446–496). New York: McGraw-Hill.

Weick, K. E. (1995). *The social psychology of organizing*. Reading, MA: Addison-Wesley.

Whittaker, S., & Sidner, C. (1997). Email overload: Exploring personal information management of email. In S. Kiesler (Ed.), *Culture of the Internet* (pp. 277–295). Mahwah, NJ: Erlbaum.

Whyte, G. (1991). Decision failures: Why they occur and how to prevent them. *Academy of Management Executive, 5*, 23–31.

Williams, K. Y., & O'Reilly, C. A. (1998). Demography and diversity in organizations. In B. M. Staw & R. M. Sutton (Eds.), *Research in organizational behavior* (Vol. 20, pp. 77–140). Stamford, CT: JAI Press.

Wright, G., & Phillips, L. D. (1980). Cultural variation in probabilistic thinking: Alternate ways of dealing with uncertainty. *International Journal of Psychology, 15*, 239–257.

Yang, K. S. (1981). Social orientation and individual modernity among Chinese students in Taiwan. *Journal of Social Psychology, 113*, 159–170.

Yates, J. F., & Lee, J. W. (1996). Chinese decision making. In M. H. Bond (Ed.), *Handbook of Chinese psychology* (pp. 338–351). Hong Kong: Oxford University Press.

Yates, J. F., Lee, J. W., & Bush, J. G. (1997). General knowledge overconfidence: Cross-national variations, response style, and "reality." *Organizational Behavior and Human Decision Processes, 70*, 87–94.

Yates, J. F., Lee, J. W., & Shinotsuka, H. (1996). Beliefs about overconfidence, including its cross-national variation. *Organizational Behavior and Human Decision Processes, 65*, 138–147.

Yates, J. F., Lee, J. W., Shinotsuka, H., Patalano, A. L., & Sieck, W. R. (1998). Cross-cultural variations in probability judgment accuracy: Beyond general knowledge overconfidence? *Organizational Behavior and Human Decision Processes, 74*, 89–117.

Yates, J. F., Zhu, Y., Ronis, D. L., Wang, D. F., Shinotsuka, H., & Toda, W. (1989). Probability judgment accuracy: China, Japan and the United States. *Organizational Behavior and Human Decision Processes, 43,* 147–171.

Zigurs, I., Poole, M. S., & DeSanctis, G. L. (1988). A study of influence in computer-mediated group decision making. *MIS Quarterly, 12,* 625–644.

Zucker, L. G. (1986). Production of trust: Institutional sources of economic structure, 1840 to 1920. In B. M. Staw (Ed.), *Research in organizational behavior* (Vol. 8, pp. 53–111). Stamford, CT: JAI Press.

Part V

Facing the Challenge of Real-World Complexity in Decisions

17 The Naturalistic Decision-Making Perspective

Rebecca Pliske and Gary Klein

ABSTRACT

Researchers affiliated with the Naturalistic Decision-Making (NDM) perspective study how people use their experience to make decisions in field settings. In this chapter we present an overview of the NDM perspective by providing a brief history of its development, a description of the types of models and methods used by NDM researchers, and examples of the types of research currently included in this approach. We also summarize several studies conducted with weather forecasters that have used both the traditional and naturalistic perspectives in order to illustrate the relationship between the approaches. We conclude with a discussion of the strengths and weaknesses of the NDM perspective.

CONTENTS

We would like to thank Beth Crandall for reviewing this manuscript.

Case 1. A fireground commander was called to a simple house fire in a one-story house in a residential neighborhood. The fire was in the back, in the kitchen area. The lieutenant led his hose crew into the building, to the back, to spray water on the fire, but the fire just roared back at them. He thought this was odd because the water should have had more of an impact. They tried dousing it again and got the same results. They retreated a few steps to regroup. Then the lieutenant started to feel that something was not right. He didn't have any clues; he just didn't feel right about being in that house, so he ordered his men out of the building – a perfectly standard building with nothing out of the ordinary. As soon as his men left the building, the floor where they had been standing collapsed. Had they still been inside, they would have plunged into the fire below.

Case 2. A neonatal intensive care nurse was working with a tiny infant born at 25–26 weeks whom nobody really expected to live. When the baby was about 2–3 days old, she noted that he was having real fine tremors in his extremities on one side. She told the charge nurse that she thought the baby was having seizures (a far more serious condition). The next night he was still having fine tremors, and they seemed to be increasing in frequency and strength. With each tremor, his oxygen saturation dropped. He also was doing some tongue thrusting, but it was so mild that it looked like a sucking reflex (although 25-week-old infants normally do not have this reflex). The nurse assumed that it was seizure activity. By the third night, she was able to convince one of the physicians that the baby might be having seizures. Diagnostic tests were ordered, and he was found to have a grade 4 bleed. He was put on phenobarbital, the seizures were resolved, and he eventually went home with no damage.

Researchers using the Naturalistic Decision-Making (NDM) perspective have studied these decision makers (and many others) to obtain a better understanding of how experienced people make high-stakes decisions. This chapter provides an introduction to the NDM perspective by providing a brief history of its development, a description of the types of models and methods used by NDM researchers, and an overview of the types of research currently included in this approach. We also illustrate the relationship between the NDM perspective and more traditional decision research by describing research with weather forecasters that has been conducted using both perspectives. We conclude with a discussion of the strengths and weaknesses of the NDM perspective.

Overview of the NDM Perspective

What Is the NDM Perspective?

NDM has been defined as the study of how people use their experience to make decisions in field settings (Zsambok & Klein, 1997). A key element in this definition is the emphasis on experience. In laboratory-based research, experience is often viewed as a confounding factor because if the experimental and control groups differ with regard to task experience, the results of the study may be difficult to interpret. Therefore, studies are often conducted with novel tasks to ensure that subjects have little or no prior experience. However, NDM researchers believe that many important decisions are made by people with domain experience and, therefore, that it is important to learn how people use their experience to make these decisions.

Several different researchers have attempted to describe the NDM perspective by enumerating the characteristics of the decisions NDM researchers study in field settings. Orasanu and Connolly (1993) described a variety of task conditions including time pressure, uncertainty, dynamic conditions, ill-defined goals, feedback loops, multiple players, high stakes, and organizational constraints that are studied by NDM researchers. Cannon-Bowers, Salas, and Pruitt (1996) added several other considerations – multiple goals, decision complexity, quantity of information, and level of expertise – and linked these to the decision task, the decision maker, or the environment.

Zsambok (1997) took a different approach to defining the NDM perspective. She identified the following four criteria to contrast research conducted from the NDM perspective with more traditional types of research:

1. the features of the task and setting (NDM researchers study tasks and settings that are context rich rather than impoverished)
2. the nature of the research participants (NDM researchers tend to study experienced performers rather than novices)
3. the purpose of the research (NDM researchers focus on describing the strategies people use rather than detecting deviations from a normative standard of performance)
4. the locus of interest with the decision episode (NDM researchers study prechoice processes such as the development of situation awareness rather than focusing primarily on the moment of choice)

Brief History of the NDM Perspective

The beginning of the NDM perspective is typically traced to the first NDM conference held in 1989 in Dayton, Ohio. (Although there are many different lines of decision-making research consistent with the NDM framework that were conducted prior to this conference, this brief history focuses only on the research most closely affiliated with the NDM perspective.) Thirty researchers attended the first meeting in Dayton to try to find some common themes for research programs that up to that point had been conducted in parallel. Papers based on discussions of the working groups conducted as part of the first NDM conference were subsequently published in *Decision Making in Action: Models and Methods* (Klein, Orasanu, Calderwood, & Zsambok, 1993). A second NDM conference was held in 1994 and was attended by over 100 researchers; this conference resulted in another book (*Naturalistic Decision Making* by Zsambok & Klein, 1997). In 1995, a new technical group on Cognitive Engineering and Decision Making was formed as part of the Human Factors and Ergonomics Society to provide additional opportunities for researchers using the NDM perspective to communicate their research results. NDM conferences are now being held on a regular basis (see *Decision Making Under Stress: Emerging Themes and Applications* by Flin, Salas, Strub, & Martin, 1997, for the papers presented at the third NDM conference held in Aberdeen, Scotland, in 1996; and *Linking Expertise and Naturalistic Decision Making* by Salas & Klein, 2001, for the papers presented at the fourth NDM conference held in Virginia in 1998).

The NDM perspective was developed by researchers who were motivated by curiosity about how people are able to make decisions in field settings characterized by stress, time pressure, and uncertainty. For example, Klein, Calderwood, and Clinton-Cirocco (1986) studied fireground commanders who supervise teams of fire fighters; Wohl (1981) studied Navy command and control; and Rasmussen (1983) studied the nature of errors in nuclear power plants. It became clear to researchers who were studying decision making in field settings that even though decision makers were required to work under time pressure, they were still able to do a good job. It also became clear that these decision makers did not have sufficient time to deliberate between a variety of options; instead, they were able to use their experience to act quickly under time pressure even when there was a good deal of uncertainty about the outcomes of their actions. These observations motivated field researchers to learn more about the cognitive processes involved in these decision-making situations.

The relatively rapid growth of the NDM community was facilitated by support from several of the funding agencies that sponsor behavioral science research. The types of settings studied by NDM researchers were of great interest to the military and aviation communities. Research on training and equipment design issues had reached a point where the behavioral problems had become fairly well understood (e.g., how to train persons in a set of procedures, how to design a set of cockpit controls emphasizing the human factor). However, the cognitive demands faced by the decision maker within these settings were not well understood. What decisions are involved in this task? What cues and strategies do experienced decision makers use? What types of errors are likely to be made? Thus, the NDM perspective grew to meet the demands of research sponsors who wanted to have a better understanding of how people in the military, aviation, and other applied settings perform their jobs.

The NDM perspective has attracted applied researchers seeking opportunities to improve job performance. These researchers conduct studies to describe how skilled performers make decisions in order to identify ways to improve the quality of decision processes and outcomes. NDM researchers attempt to learn how experience is being used in a domain and where the barriers are to developing and applying that experience. These research efforts have been guided, in part, by the models described in the next section.

NDM Models

Lipshitz (1993) described nine different models related to the NDM perspective, including Pennington and Hastie's theory of explanation-based decision making (Pennington & Hastie, 1988), Montgomery's work on dominance structures (Montgomery, 1993), Beach's Image Theory (Beach, 1990), Hammond's work on Social Judgment Theory (Hammond, Stewart, Brehmer, & Steinmann, 1975), and Rasmussen's decision ladder (Rasmussen, 1983). Additional models have been developed since Lipshitz completed his review (e.g., Cohen, Freeman, & Thompson, 1998; Endsley, 1995).

The model most closely associated with the NDM perspective is the Recognition-Primed Decision (RPD) model first proposed by Klein and his colleagues (Klein et al., 1986). This model was originally developed to explain how fireground commanders used their experience to select a course of action without having to compare different options. The findings of Klein et al. raised two key questions: First, how could the commanders be sure of carrying out effective courses of action without generating a set of options from which to choose? Second, how could the commanders evaluate a course of action without comparing it to others? Klein et al. examined their interview data, which included 156 decision points, and developed the RPD model to answer these questions.

The answer to the first question (how the commanders did not have to generate a set of options) was that the commanders could use their experience to size up a situation and thereby recognize the typical action to take. They could generate a reasonable option as the first one considered. They were not trying to find the optimal solution, but rather to arrive quickly at a workable solution that could be enacted in time to arrest the spread of a fire that might be growing exponentially.

The answer to the second question (how the commanders could evaluate an option without comparing it to others) was that once the commanders identified a typical course of action, they would evaluate it by imagining it, mentally simulating it to see if it would work in the situation they were facing. If the course of action was found satisfactory, it would be initiated without any further delay. If they found any flaws, they would switch to a problem-solving mode to repair the flaws. If they could not repair the flaws, they would reject the course of action and consider the next most typical reaction, repeating the process until they found a workable option.

In short, the commanders were able to use their experience to identify a workable course of action as the first one they considered. If they needed to evaluate a course of action, they conducted a mental simulation to see if it would work.

The RPD model shown in Figure 17.1 (Klein, 1998) is an extension of the model originally proposed by Klein et al. (1986). The revised model includes three different types of cases faced by decision makers. The revised model describes many different components of the decision-making process; however, these processes can be accomplished very rapidly – almost instantaneously. The simplest type of case is one in which a decision maker sizes up a situation, forms expectancies about what is going to happen next, determines the cues that are most relevant, recognizes the reasonable goals to pursue in the situation, recognizes a typical reaction, and carries it out. This type of case is considered to be a decision because reasonable alternative courses of action could have

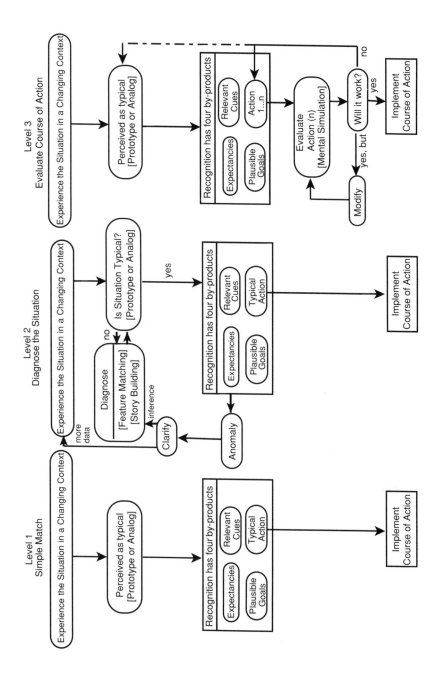

565

been taken. Other decision makers, perhaps with less experience, might have selected these alternatives. Therefore, a decision point hypothetically existed even though the decision maker did not treat it as such.

The second panel of Figure 17.1 shows a more difficult type of case in which the decision maker is not entirely certain about the nature of the situation. Perhaps some anomaly arises that violates his or her expectancies and forces the decision maker to question whether the situation is perhaps different than it seems. The decision maker must deliberate about what is happening. A key aspect in this type of case is the use of diagnosis to link the observed events to causal factors; by establishing such a linkage, the decision maker obtains an explanation for the events.

Diagnosis is important for the RPD model because the nature of the situation can largely determine the course of action adopted. Often decision makers will spend more time and energy trying to determine what is happening, and distinguishing between different explanations, than comparing different courses of actions. Diagnostic activity is initiated in response to uncertainty about the nature of the situation. The purpose of the diagnosis is either to evaluate an uncertain assessment of the situation or to compare alternative explanations of events. Two common diagnostic strategies are *feature matching* and *story building*. Story building often involves a type of mental simulation in which a person attempts to synthesize the features of a situation into a causal explanation that can be evaluated and used in a number of ways. The decision maker tries to find the most plausible story, or sequence of events, in order to understand what is going on.

The third panel of Figure 17.1 shows that once decision makers arrive at an understanding of a situation, they will recognize a typical course of action for that situation and then evaluate it by mentally simulating what will happen when they carry out the action. In this way, if they spot weaknesses in their plan, they can repair the weaknesses and improve the plan.

One of the important characteristics of the RPD model is its account of how mental simulation is useful in evaluating options without requiring comparisons to other options. If the mental simulation process is not considered, the RPD model is sometimes characterized as a simplistic pattern-matching process in which people apply standard rules or operating procedures. At its most basic level, the RPD model is about condition–action sequences. These may appear to be standard operating procedures, except that close inspection often shows that a great deal of experience is needed to reliably make the judgment about when the antecedent condition has been achieved. For example, a pilot may know the rule that if the weather looks threatening, it is best to find an alternative route. But what constitutes threatening weather?

It is important to note that as a descriptive account, the RPD model does not offer direct prescriptive guidance. However, the model offers suggestions about which cognitive processes (e.g., judging typicality, prioritizing cues, generating expectancies, conducting mental simulations) need strengthening through either training or system design in order to improve performance in situations characterized by time pressure, risk, and uncertainty. The RPD model does not help researchers to distinguish between good and poor decisions or to identify errors. Instead, the RPD model describes how people make decisions without analyzing the strengths and weaknesses of alternative courses of action under high stress; it illustrates how experts use their experience to adopt the first course of action they generate.

Methods

NDM researchers study decision makers in field settings using a variety of methods. In this section, we briefly summarize two of these methods, *cognitive task analysis* (CTA) and *simulations*.

NDM researchers use CTA methods to describe the cognitive skills needed to perform a task proficiently. These methods extend traditional behavioral task analysis methods because they explore the cognitive processes underlying the behavioral components of a job. A detailed description of CTA is beyond the scope of this chapter. For more details about these methods, see Cooke (1994) and Jonassen, Tessmer, and Hannum (1999).

CTA methods include both knowledge elicitation techniques and knowledge representation techniques, and they typically involve interviews about retrospective accounts of incidents or observed samples of performance. Some of these methods have been adapted from laboratory techniques, others from techniques used to perform knowledge engineering for knowledge-based systems (e.g., Gordon & Gill, 1997; Hoffman, Crandall, & Shadbolt, 1998; Militello & Hutton, 1998; Woods, 1993).

Hoffman et al. (1998) describe one of the CTA methods specifically developed by NDM researchers to study experienced decision makers in their natural setting. This method, called the *Critical Decision Method*, involves a knowledge elicitation technique in which in-depth interviews are conducted with subject matter experts who are asked to recount a challenging or critical incident in which their skills affected the outcome. The incident is then probed for decision points, shifts in situation assessment, critical cues leading to a specific assessment, cognitive strategies, and potential errors. The knowledge elicited from these in-depth interviews can be represented in a variety of ways. These include narrative accounts of the critical incident and Cognitive Requirements Tables that list the specific cognitive demands for the task in question, as well as contextual information needed to develop training requirements or system design recommendations.

NDM researchers also use simulations to learn more about how people make decisions in work settings. Woods (1993) contends that the most powerful approach to NDM research is to conduct studies in simulated environments. By conducting such studies, researchers can achieve control over cues and can collect a wide variety of both quantitative and qualitative measures. For example, Kanki, Lozito, and Foushee (1989) scored both verbal and physical behaviors of actual commercial airline pilots who were videotaped while performing complex tasks in a high-fidelity flight simulator. The criterion for including a study involving a simulated task within the NDM perspective is that the simulation needs to be of sufficient functional quality to be relevant to proficient decision makers in the domain of interest. If the task engages experienced decision makers and requires them to use their expertise, then it is likely that the results of the study will be applicable to the field setting.

Scope of the NDM Perspective

The NDM perspective has attracted researchers from a variety of backgrounds, and this is reflected in the wide range of topics currently included in this perspective. Current research within the NDM perspective is related to research in cognitive science (Beach, Chi, Klein, Smith, & Vicente, 1997), expertise (Ericsson & Charness, 1994; Shanteau, 1992), situation awareness (Endsley, 1990; Sarter & Woods, 1991), ecological psychology (Hancock, Flach, Caird, & Vicente, 1995), and situated cognition (Suchman, 1987).

Not all of the NDM research is descriptive. Hypothesis testing, although infrequent, has occurred. Thus, some of the research conducted within the NDM perspective has tested the assertions of the RPD model.

For example, Klein, Wolf, Militello, and Zsambok (1995) investigated whether people can use their previous experience with a situation to subsequently generate a reasonable course of action as the first one they consider by studying 16 skilled chess players. With the assistance of a chess master, they selected four reasonably challenging chess positions and presented each of these to players whose official ratings were at a C level (mediocre) or an A level (very strong). Each player was tested individually and was asked to think aloud while trying to generate a move to play. The data consisted of the first option articulated by the player. When the players had repeated this process for all four boards, they were asked to rate the quality of all the legal moves on each of the boards.

Figure 17.2 shows the percentage of first moves and all possible moves receiving each of five move quality ratings. The figure shows that across the full set of legal moves, most were rated as poor ones. However, the very first move that the chess players considered was rated very highly using the players' own assessments. This means that, according to their own standards, the first moves were good ones. Still, one might wonder how good these first moves were by objective standards. To investigate this issue, Klein et al. (1995) used judgments of quality made by grandmasters. These ratings also indicated that the very first moves

Figure 17.2 Percentage of first moves and all possible moves receiving each of five move quality ratings. *Source:* Klein et al. (1995).

generated by the players were good ones. Only one-sixth of the legal moves merited grandmaster points, but four-sixths of the first moves selected were of high quality according to the grandmasters' ratings. Therefore, the first moves generated by the players were significantly better than chance.

The RPD model also claims that experienced decision makers can adopt a course of action without comparing and contrasting possible courses of action. Kaempf, Klein, Thordsen, and Wolf (1996) found support for this claim. They studied 78 instances of decision making in operational Navy anti–air warfare incidents involving AEGIS cruisers. These were, for the most part, actual encounters with potentially hostile forces in which several courses of action theoretically existed. The 78 instances were probed retrospectively, during interviews, to determine the rationale for the decision. Kaempf et al. estimated that in 78% of the cases, the decision maker adopted the course of action without any deliberate evaluation, and in 18% of the cases the evaluation was accomplished using mental simulation. In only 4% of the cases was there any introspective evidence for comparisons of the strengths and weaknesses of different options.

In addition to the research conducted by Klein and his colleagues, other researchers have also demonstrated support for the RPD model in a variety of settings. For example, Randel, Pugh, Reed, Schuler, and Wyman (1994) probed electronic warfare technicians while they were performing a simulated task and found that 93% of the decisions involved serial (i.e., noncomparative) deliberations, in accord with the RPD model. Only 2 of the 38 decisions studied were classified as showing comparisons between options. Mosier (1991) obtained similar findings in a study of pilots who were videotaped during a simulated mission. Pascual and Henderson (1997) also obtained data supporting the prevalence of recognitional decision making in a study of Army command-and-control personnel. Driskell, Salas, and Hall (1994) found that training Navy officers to follow vigilant procedures (e.g., systematically scanning all relevant items of evidence and reviewing the information prior to making a decision) resulted in worse performance than if the Navy officers were allowed to use "hypervigilant" procedures that were compatible with recognitional decision making (e.g., scanning only the information items needed to make a decision, in any sequence, and reviewing items only if necessary).

Much of the research in the NDM prospective has been funded by the Department of Defense and, therefore, has focused on the application areas of interest to these sponsors. However, other (nonmilitary) domains also have been studied. In particular, there has been continued interest in studying expert decision makers in a variety of medical settings (e.g., Cook, 1998; Crandall & Getchell-Reiter, 1993; Dominguez, Flach, Lake, McKellar, & Dunn, in press; Militello & Lim, 1994; Miller, Kyne, & Lim, 1994). For example, Dominguez et al. interviewed 10 highly experienced and 10 less-experienced surgeons as they watched videotapes of challenging gallbladder removal cases. The surgeons talked aloud about the videotaped surgeon's decision to convert from the laparoscopic method for removing the gallbladder to the traditional open-incision method. When using the laparoscopic method, the surgeon is handicapped by degraded perceptual information that can increase the probability of certain types of errors. Dominguez et al. conducted extensive protocol analyses of the verbal transcripts from the interviews. These analyses indicated that the more experienced surgeons made significantly more inferences and predictions from perceptual information than the less experienced surgeons. The more experienced surgeons also expressed more awareness of the boundary conditions for safe operations.

A relatively recent focus of NDM research has been on training the decision-making skills of military personnel. Fallesen and his colleagues at the U.S. Army Research Institute for the Behavioral and Social Sciences (Fallesen, 1995; Fallesen, Michel, Lussier, & Pounds, 1996) have developed a comprehensive cognitive skills training program. They call their program Practical Thinking to contrast it with theoretical or formal methods. Fallesen and his colleagues were asked to develop a Practical Thinking course to be implemented as part of the U.S. Army's Command and General Staff Officers Course. The goal of this course was to increase officers' skills for reasoning and deciding in battle command situations. Fallesen et al. reviewed existing cognitive instruction programs to identify training approaches applicable to their goal. Based on this review, they developed course materials that included lessons on multiple perspectives (i.e., thinking outside the box), metacognitive skills that allow the individual to guide his or her thinking deliberately, techniques for identifying hidden assumptions, practical reasoning techniques (e.g., demonstrations of reasoning fallacies), and integrative thinking techniques to increase students' understanding of the relationships among events and concepts.

Cohen and his colleagues (Cohen et al., 1998; Cohen, Freeman, & Wolf, 1996) have also developed an approach to training decision-making skills, which they call Critical Thinking Training. Cohen et al. (1998) describe the results of two studies they conducted with a total of 95 military officers (drawn from the Navy, Marines, Army, and Air Force) to evaluate the effectiveness of this training. In both studies the officers were asked to play the role of the Tactical Action Officer in a Combat Information Center in a battleship. The training included several sessions on a low-fidelity computer-based simulator of the Combat Information Center. During these sessions, the participants learned how to use tools such as a *hostile intent story template* to facilitate the development of alternative explanations for potential threats (e.g., an enemy airplane or ship) that appeared on their computer screens. Cohen et al. assessed the effectiveness of their training by having their participants complete questionnaires assessing the intent of a particular threat (e.g., an enemy airplane) and justifying their assessments. Participants were also required to generate alternative possible assessments, identify conflicting evidence, and describe actions they would take at a specified point in the scenario. In general, the results of the Cohen et al. study support the effectiveness of the Critical Thinking Training they have developed.

Some of our own research efforts have also focused on the development of an approach for training decision skills (Klein, 1997; Pliske, McCloskey, & Klein, 2001). The rationale for our approach is based on our belief that good decision-making performance depends on decision makers' expertise in the domain in which they work. Therefore, in order to improve decision-making performance, we have developed an instructional program for helping the decision maker develop domain expertise. This program was based on a survey of the literature on expertise (e.g., Chi, Glaser & Farr, 1988; Ericsson, 1996), which identifies strategies experts use in order to learn more rapidly and effectively. These strategies include engaging in deliberate practice, so that each opportunity for practice has a goal and evaluation criteria; compiling an extensive experience bank; obtaining feedback that is accurate and diagnostic; building mental models; developing metacognitive skills; and becoming more mindful of opportunities for learning. Based on this review and our own experience working with experts in a variety of domains, we developed a set of training tools to be used in conjunction with low-fidelity paper-and-pencil simulations. We have used these tools to train U.S. Marine Corps squad leaders and junior officers as well as fire fighters. Based on evaluations made by the participants in our training workshops and their supervisors, it appears that this may be an effective way to improve decision-making skills.

Comparison of the NDM Perspective to Traditional Decision Research

Decision-making research conducted from the NDM perspective can be compared to research conducted from the more traditional perspectives on a variety of characteristics. In this section, we use these characteristics to contrast the different perspectives. Then we illustrate the relationship between the two perspectives by briefly describing some research that has been conducted on weather forecasting.

Characteristics of the Two Perspectives

Traditional decision research has been guided by normative decision models such as Expected Utility Theory, whereas research within the NDM perspective has not. The work of Tversky and Kahneman (1973) and others (cf. Kahneman, Slovic, & Tversky, 1982) has shown that decision makers tend to apply a variety of heuristics even when these heuristics result in suboptimal performance. One interpretation of this work is that these heuristics bias the judgment of subjects and need to be counteracted through either training or system design (Hammond, Keeney, & Raiffa, 1998). Another interpretation is that these heuristics are strengths based on the use of experience. The NDM research that has been based on the RPD model's claims that decision makers can use their experience to size up a situation as typical, can identify a typical reaction to the situation, and can evaluate that reaction by using mental simulation. The RPD model incorporates several of the heuristics described by Tversky and Kahneman. The recognition of a situation as typical makes use of both the availability (Tversky & Kahneman, 1973) and representativeness heuristics (Kahneman & Tversky, 1972), and the mental simulation described in the RPD model makes use of the simulation heuristic (Kahneman et al., 1982). When used by skilled personnel, these heuristics can be very effective, particularly in time-pressured and uncertain settings for which analytical strategies cannot be used.

Traditional research has focused primarily on the moment of choice, whereas the NDM perspective has focused more on situational assessment. Beach (1996) has argued that decision making must involve the comparison of different options. We disagree and argue that limiting the term *decision making* to situations that involve a clear choice between options is too restrictive. NDM researchers have repeatedly documented that experienced decision makers can (and do) implement courses of action without deliberating over their various options (Driskell et al., 1994; Kaempf et al., 1996; Randel et al., 1994). It is also important to note that some traditional research studies were conducted on predecision processes such as hypothesis and option generation before the NDM perspective was formally recognized (e.g., Gettys & Fisher, 1979; Gettys, Pliske, Manning, & Casey, 1986; Pitz, Sachs, & Heerboth, 1980).

Traditional research has been primarily theory-driven, whereas NDM research is primarily problem-driven. Most of the research conducted by NDM researchers has been conducted by applied researchers who have been funded to provide their sponsors with recommendations as to how training can be improved or how a system can be better designed to support the decision maker. There has been very little research based on the NDM perspective conducted in academic settings. In contrast, practitioners have been applying traditional decision approaches such as multiattribute utility theory and Brunswik's lens model to real-world problems (e.g., Hammond, Hamm, Grassia, & Pearson, 1987; Russo & Schoemaker, 1989), whereas their academic colleagues generate the theoretically based research on these approaches. One explanation for the fact that little NDM research is conducted in academic settings is that the qualitative methods used to study decision makers in field settings are not typically taught to graduates students, nor are they widely accepted within traditional graduate programs in psychology.

Traditional researchers have been more concerned with internal validity issues, whereas NDM researchers have been more concerned with external validity issues. By definition, NDM research is focused on decision makers in their natural settings, so it is not surprising that NDM researchers stress the importance of ecological validity over the need for methodological rigor. Likewise, because many of the researchers who conduct traditional research on decision making were trained to be experimental psychologists, it is not surprising that their research is done in controlled settings that lend themselves to the use of traditional laboratory methods. The common ground for the two perspectives may be the use of simulations. As discussed previously in this chapter, NDM researchers use simulation studies to study decision makers completing realistic tasks in controlled settings.

Although there are definite differences between the types of research typically conducted within the traditional and naturalistic perspectives, there are also some gray areas where the two perspectives overlap. In the next section, we briefly describe one domain, weather forecasting, which has been the focus of study for researchers from several different perspectives.

Multiple Approaches to Studying Weather Forecasters

Weather forecasters have been studied for many years by decision researchers. Although a comprehensive review of this research is well beyond the scope of this chapter, we have selected three examples of research conducted with weather forecasters to illustrate the overlap between the different decision-making perspectives.

Some of the earliest work was done by Murphy and his colleagues (Murphy & Brown, 1984; Murphy & Winkler, 1974, 1977). Prior to 1965, National Weather Service forecasters did not add probabilistic judgments to their forecasts. That is, they predicted that it would either rain or not rain, but they did not add the now familiar statements like "There is a 30% chance of showers tomorrow." Murphy and his colleagues investigated forecasters' use of these subjective probability statements. Although many lay people may disagree, according to Murphy and Winkler (1977) weather forecasters are well calibrated. *Calibration* has traditionally been defined as the extent to which decision makers' confidence matches their accuracy when making a set of judgments. When Murphy and Winkler studied precipitation forecasts made by individual weather forecasters in Chicago, they found that these forecasters' accuracy judgments generally matched their confidence judgments. For example, they examined 2,916 judgments made by one particular forecaster, and when he predicted that there was a 60% chance of rain, it actually rained on approximately 60% of those occasions. In this example of research on weather forecasting, expert decision makers were studied in their natural environment using methods of mathematical modeling that are typically applied in much more controlled environments.

Stewart and his colleagues have used the Lens Model as a framework for studying the judgments made by weather forecasters (Stewart, Heideman, Moninger, & Reagan-Cirincione, 1992; Stewart & Lusk, 1994). For example, Stewart et al. (1992) conducted three studies using different types of simulated weather scenarios to examine how increases in the amount and quality of information affect the quality of expert judgments. The participants in their studies were meteorologists from several different locations within the continental United States. None of them were operational meteorologists at the time of the study, although over half of them had operational experience; some of the meteorologists were atmospheric science students, and others were researchers interested in forecasting. Across the three studies, Stewart et al. manipulated the amount and quality of the information given to the meteorologists. For example, in the most limited information condition, the meteorologists were required to make predictions of severe weather from maps showing radar reflectivities, without any additional information about the storms represented on the maps. In contrast, in the full information condition, the meteorologists worked on advanced weather forecasting workstations that included radar and satellite images, surface maps, and output from different computer-generated forecasting models. Overall, Stewart et al. found that forecast accuracy in predicting the severe storms was low, and increased only modestly as the amount and quality of information increased substantially. They also found that the reliability of forecasts (as measured by consensus among the forecasters) actually decreased as the amount of information increased. In this example, decision makers with varying levels of expertise were studied using simulations of varying levels of fidelity.

Pliske, Crandall, and Klein (in press) describe a cognitive task analysis of weather forecasters that was conducted to provide recommendations on how to improve forecasting performance for U.S. Air Force weather forecasters. Interviews and observations were conducted with 42 forecasters at 12 different locations in the continental United States. Small-group interviews were conducted with some of the National Weather Service forecasters who predicted the weather for the 1996 Olympic games in Atlanta. In-depth interviews were conducted with 29 U.S. Air Force forecasters using knowledge elicitation tools such as the Critical Decision Method. The experience level of these forecasters varied from 4 months to 21 years, with an average of approximately 10 years of experience. Qualitative analyses of the data obtained in these interviews identified a set of critical cognitive elements involved in the weather forecasting process. The results indicated that there were no standard information-seeking strategies used by the forecasters, but skilled forecasters flexibly adapted their information-seeking strategies based on their interpretation of the "weather problem of the day." One of the key findings of this study was that U.S. Air Force weather forecasters were operating with virtually no feedback on the accuracy of their performance. Although in most situations this information could be made available to the forecasters, it was not. Without the opportunity to learn from their experience, many of these forecasters had failed to develop into highly skilled performers. In this example, decision makers with widely different experience levels were studied in their natural setting using a qualitative approach.

These studies on weather forecasters illustrate that research from a variety of perspectives can be used to increase our understanding of the cognitive processes underlying the judgments and decisions made by experienced decision makers. These examples also point out that there are similarities, as well as differences, between these different research perspectives. The work of Murphy examines the accuracy of predictions but not the process by which accurate predictions are obtained. The work of Stewart et al. (1992, 1994) addresses the value of data for forecasters at different skill levels, thereby looking at a variable that may contribute to accuracy. In contrast, Pliske et al. (in press) studied the process rather than accuracy. These examples also illustrate that the distinction between the traditional and naturalistic approaches is not always clear. In this case, the examples from the more traditional approaches (the work by Murphy and Stewart and their colleagues) included experienced participants, which is more typical of research conducted from the naturalistic perspective. In the next section, we discuss several issues that currently divide the NDM perspective from the more traditional approaches to the study of decision making.

Criticisms of the NDM Perspective

In an invited address at the fourth NDM conference, Yates (1998) offered a summary of some of the criticisms made by traditional researchers regarding the NDM perspective. We will now discuss several of these points.

NDM theories have been called deficient because they are imprecise and untestable. To some extent, this criticism is valid. The RPD model, for example, is imprecise in that it does not specifically explain how the pattern matching or judgment of typicality occurs, nor does it explain how decision makers generate new actions. In its defense, however, the RPD model was not developed to address these questions.

NDM researchers have also been criticized for using flawed research methods. For example, they typically use small sample sizes and rely on subject matter experts' verbal reports for much of their data. As we have discussed, NDM researchers emphasize external validity over internal validity issues. Because NDM research is focused on experienced decision makers, NDM researchers use subject matter experts as their primary data source.

Although some NDM research involves observational/behavioral data, most of these researchers rely heavily on verbal report data. They are willing to accept the inaccuracies inherent in this type of data in order to study decision makers in their natural settings. The time-intensive, qualitative data analysis methods typically used by NDM researchers limit the number of participants that can reasonably be included in a study. Given the small sample sizes typically used, it is often impossible for NDM researchers to use traditional parametric statistics to establish the reliability of their findings.

NDM researchers frequently rely on subject matter experts' performance as the criterion for good decision making. Traditional decision researchers object to this approach because they have repeatedly documented situations in which experts fail to adhere to normative models. For example, researchers have demonstrated that physicians, as well as lay persons, are subject to framing effects using Tversky and Kahneman's (1981) Asian Disease problem (McNeil, Pauker, Sox, & Tversky, 1982). After describing the McNeil et al. study, Plous (1993) concludes, "Thus, even in the case of life-and-death decisions made by highly trained specialists, framing can significantly influence the choices that are made" (p. 73). NDM researchers would argue against such a conclusion and point out the artificiality inherent in the type of task used in this experiment. Recent research by de Keyser and Nyssen (1998) indicates that the fidelity of the simulation used to study physicians' decision-making processes affects the results of the study.

NDM researchers are also concerned about the lack of an objective criterion for defining good decision making (e.g., Pliske et al., in press). Even in a domain such as weather forecasting, it is not clear how to define good performance. If a forecaster predicts rain for a certain city and it rains in only half of the city, was the forecaster right or wrong? This difficulty is not a limitation of NDM but is a general problem for working in field settings. It is more serious for NDM researchers because of their emphasis on working with experienced decision makers in natural environments. In many domains studied by NDM researchers, it is often difficult to specify the criteria that define true expertise. Typically, it is not merely a function of the number of years on the job, because years on the job do not necessarily equate to opportunities to experience many different situations. For example, an urban fire fighter may attend several calls a day and become an expert in only a few years, whereas a volunteer rural fire fighter may attend only one call a week and may never develop a high level of expertise. Although NDM researchers acknowledge the problems associated with using subject matter experts' performance as the criterion for good decision-making performance, they still contend that it is a better criterion than normative models such as Expected Utility Theory, which is irrelevant in many of the domains they study.

Research on behavioral decision making emerged from the mathematical proofs for Expected Utility Theory (e.g., Coombs, Dawes, & Tversky, 1970; Edwards, 1954; von Neumann & Morgenstern, 1947). These theorems provide a firm foundation for the subsequent work, a far more solid foundation than is found in other areas of behavioral science. Even though there have been few empirical demonstrations of the usefulness of this approach in naturalistic settings, research based on mathematical models has continued to be the dominant approach to studying decision makers and is frequently used as the basis for the development of decision-aiding techniques (e.g., Hammond, Keeney, & Raiffa, 1998). One reason for this persistence may be an underlying faith in mathematics, regardless of the demonstrated usefulness of this approach. When Simon (1957) contrasted optimizing with satisficing, he was describing a limitation to decision analysis. Optimization, the maximizing of expected utility, was beyond the reach of decision makers in many settings because of their limited computational capability. Therefore, Simon noted that decision makers have to rely on heuristics and strategies such as satisficing.

Klein (1999) has argued that the field of decision research was at a choice point following Simon's observations: to study the drawbacks of heuristics or to study their benefits. The path taken (Kahneman et al., 1982; Tversky & Kahneman, 1974) was the first one – to identify a wide range of heuristics and to show their limitations and distortions. An implication of this work was that decision makers are inherently flawed and in need of debiasing procedures (Hammond et al., 1998; Plous, 1993; Russo & Schoemaker, 1989). However, the debiasing methods offered have not generally been demonstrated to improve decision quality. Moreover, this approach seems inconsistent with Simon's assertion that heuristics are needed to circumvent computational limitations. If decision makers are pressed to abandon their heuristics, it is not clear how computational weaknesses are to be overcome.

The field of NDM has taken the second path – to examine the strengths of the heuristics and to study how expertise enabled decision makers to learn more powerful heuristics. As a result, NDM research has been linked to work in expertise, problem solving, ecological psychology, and cognitive science in a way that traditional decision research has not. Furthermore, NDM researchers are drawn to the messy configurations of ill-defined goals and ambiguous cues that traditional decision researchers have avoided. Clients interested in building computer aids and training systems to support decisions have by necessity worked within the constraints of natural settings. By avoiding these areas, traditional decision researchers created a vacuum. The need for decision support existed, but the community sidestepped it because the problems did not meet the requirements for applying the methodologies of decision analysis, multiattribute utility analysis, and so forth. The NDM framework was generated to fill this vacuum.

Conclusions

The NDM perspective has gained enthusiastic support from sponsors because it is able to provide timely solutions to applied problems. The results of NDM research projects have been used to design decision-centered training programs and to develop decision support systems. The NDM perspective was developed by practitioners, not academics; therefore, the focus of NDM researchers has not been on the development and validation of theories. These applied researchers have emphasized face validity (not internal validity) and user acceptance. However, many of the current applications developed by NDM researchers are broadly based on cognitive and social psychological theories (rather than the economic theories that have guided traditional research on decision making). The NDM approach could benefit from a clearer mapping of the links between these cognitive and social psychological theories and their applications to training and system design.

Theories from other areas of psychology may help decision researchers integrate findings from the NDM and traditional decision-making perspectives. Dual-process theories that propose that human behavior is guided by two parallel interacting systems may be particularly helpful to decision researchers interested in studying both intuitive and rational decision-making strategies. For example, Epstein and his colleagues have developed Cognitive-Experiential Self-Theory (e.g., Epstein, 1998; Epstein & Pacini, 1999), which describes two different modes of information processing: a slower, effortful system that is based on a person's understanding of logical rules of inference and a quicker, experience-based system for coping intuitively with situations faced in everyday life. Damasio and his colleagues (e.g., Bechara, Damasio,

Tranel & Damasio, 1997; Damasio, 1998) have established a biological basis for a separate intuitive, experience-based decision-making system.

Hopefully, the decision research in the next decade will benefit from past research from both the NDM and the traditional perspectives. The theories and methods that have been developed by NDM researcher/practitioners clearly need to be validated under more controlled conditions, such as realistic simulations (e.g., Driskell et al., 1994; Randel et al., 1994). Traditional decision researchers might also benefit from the success of the NDM perspective. More researchers may be motivated to study the value added by expert decision makers instead of how experts deviate from normative models. The success of the NDM perspective might also broaden the range of methods researchers use to include cognitive task analysis and to focus their efforts on solving applied problems.

References

Beach, L. R. (1990). *Image theory: Decision making in personal and organizational contexts*. West Sussex, U.K.: Wiley.

Beach, L. R. (Ed.). (1996). *Decision making in the workplace: A unified perspective*. Mahwah, NJ: LEA.

Beach, L. R., Chi, M., Klein, G., Smith, P., & Vicente, K. (1997). Naturalistic decision making and related research lines. In C. Zsambok & G. Klein (Eds.), *Naturalistic decision making* (pp. 29–36). Mahwah, NJ: LEA.

Bechara, A., Damasio, H., Tranel, D., & Damasio, A. R. (1997). Deciding advantageously before knowing the advantageous strategy. *Science, 275*, 1293–1295.

Cannon-Bowers, J. A., Salas, E., & Pruitt, J. S. (1996). Establishing the boundaries of a paradigm for decision making research. *Human Factors, 38*(2), 193–205.

Chi, M. T. H., Glaser, R., & Farr, M. J. (1988). *The nature of expertise*. Mahwah, NJ: LEA.

Cohen, M. S., Freeman, J. T., & Thompson, B. (1998). Critical thinking skills in tactical decision making: A model and a training strategy. In J. A. Cannon-Bowers & E. Salas (Eds.), *Making decisions under stress: Implications for individual and team training* (pp. 155–189). Washington, DC: American Psychological Association.

Cohen, M. S., Freeman, J. T., & Wolf, S. (1996). Meta-recognition in time-stressed decision making: Recognizing, critiquing, and correcting. *Proceedings of the 40th Human Factors and Ergonomics Society, 38*(2), 206–219.

Cook, R. I. (1998, May). Being bumpable. *Proceeding of the Fourth Conference on Naturalistic Decision Making*, Warrenton, VA: Klein Associates, Inc.

Cooke, N. J. (1994). Varieties of knowledge elicitation techniques. *International Journal of Human-Computer Studies, 41*, 801–849.

Coombs, C. H., Dawes, R. M., & Tversky, A. (1970). *Mathematical psychology*. Englewood Cliffs, NJ: Prentice-Hall.

Crandall, B., & Getchell-Reiter, K. (1993). Critical decision method: A technique for eliciting concrete assessment indicators from the "intuition" of NICU nurses. *Advances in Nursing Sciences, 16*(1), 42–51.

Damasio, A. R. (1998). Emotion and reason in the future of human life. In B. Cartledge (Ed.), *Mind, brain and the environment* (pp. 57–71). New York: Oxford University Press.

de Keyser, V., & Nyssen, A. (1998, May). *The management of temporal constraints in naturalistic decision making: The case of anesthesia.* Paper presented at the Fourth Conference on Naturalistic Decision Making, Warrenton, VA.

Dominguez, C. O., Flach, J. M., Lake, P. L., McKellar, D. P., & Dunn, M. (in press). The conversion decision in laparoscopic surgery: Knowing your limits and limiting your risks. In J. Shanteau, K. Smith, & P. Johnson (Eds.), *Psychological explorations of competence in decision making*. New York: Cambridge University Press.

Driskell, J. E., Salas, E., & Hall, J. K. (1994). *The effect of vigilant and hypervigilant decision training on performance*. Paper presented at the annual meeting of the Society of Industrial and Organizational Psychology, Nashville, TN.

Edwards, W. (1954). The theory of decision making. *Psychological Review, 51*, 380–417.

Endsley, M. R. (1990). Predictive utility of an objective measure of situation awareness. *Proceedings of the Human Factors Society, 34*, 41–45.

Endsley, M. R. (1995). Measurement of situation awareness in dynamic systems. *Human Factors, 37*(1), 65–84.

Epstein, S. (1998). Cognitive-Experiential Self-Theory. In D. Barone, M. Hersen, & V. Van Hasselt (Eds.), *Advanced Personality* (pp. 211–238). New York: Plenum Press.

Epstein, S., & Pacini, R. (1999). Some basic issues regarding dual-process theories from the perspective of Cognitive-Experiential Self-Theory. In S. Chaiken & Y. Trope (Eds.), *Dual-process theories in social psychology* (pp. 462–482). New York: Guilford Press.

Ericsson, K. A. (1996). The acquisition of expert performance: An introduction to some of the issues. In K. A. Ericsson (Ed.), *The road to excellence: The acquisition of expert performance in the arts and sciences, sports, and games* (pp. 1–50). Mahwah, NJ: LEA.

Ericsson, K. A., & Charness, N. (1994). Expert performance: Its structure and acquisition. *American Psychologist, 49*(8), 725–747.

Fallesen, J. J. (1995). *Overview of practical thinking instruction for battle command*. Research Report 1685. Leavenworth, KS: U.S. Army Research Institute for the Social and Behavioral Sciences.

Fallesen, J. J., Michel, R. R., Lussier, J. W., & Pounds, J. (1996). *Practical thinking: Innovation in battle command instruction*. Technical Report 1037. Leavenworth, KS: U.S. Army Research Institute for the Social and Behavioral Sciences.

Flin, R., Salas, E., Strub, M., & Martin, L. (Eds.). (1997). *Decision making under stress: Emerging themes and applications*. Aldershot: Ashgate.

Gettys, C. F., & Fisher, S. (1979). Hypothesis plausibility and hypothesis generation. *Organizational Behavior and Human Performance, 24*, 93–110.

Gettys, C. F., Pliske, R. M., Manning, C., & Casey, J. T. (1986). An evaluation of human act generation performance. *Organizational Behavior and Human Decision Processes, 39,* 23–51.

Gordon, S. E., & Gill, R. T. (1997). Cognitive task analysis. In C. E. Zsambok & G. Klein (Eds.), *Naturalistic decision making* (pp. 131–140). Mahwah, NJ: LEA.

Hammond, J. S., Keeney, R. L., & Raiffa, H. (1998). Even swaps: A rational method for making trade-offs. *Harvard Business Review, 76,* 137–150.

Hammond, K. R., Hamm, R. M., Grassia, J., & Pearson, T. (1987). Direct comparison of the efficacy of intuitive and analytical cognition in expert judgment. *IEEE Transactions on Systems, Man, and Cybernetics, 17*(5), 753–770.

Hammond, K. R., Stewart, T. R., Brehmer, B., & Steinmann, D. O. (1975). Social judgment theory. In M. Kaplan & S. Schwartz (Eds.), *Human judgment and decision processes* (pp. 271–312). New York: Academic Press.

Hancock, P., Flach, J., Caird, J., & Vicente, K. (Eds.) (1995). *Local applications of the ecological approach to human-machine system* (Vol. 2). Mahwah, NJ: LEA.

Hoffman, R. R., Crandall, B. W., & Shadbolt, N. R. (1998). Use of the Critical Decision Method to elicit expert knowledge: A case study in cognitive task analysis methodology. *Journal of Human Factors and Ergonomics Society, 40*(2), 254–276.

Jonassen, D. H., Tessmer, M., & Hannum, W. H. (1999). *Task analysis methods for instructional design.* Mahwah, NJ: LEA.

Kaempf, G. L., Klein, G. A., Thordsen, M. L., & Wolf, S. (1996). Decision making in complex command-and-control environments. *Human Factors and Ergonomics Society, 38*(2), 220–231.

Kahneman, D., Slovic, P., & Tversky, A. (Eds.). (1982). *Judgment under uncertainty: Heuristics and biases.* Cambridge, MA: Cambridge University Press.

Kahneman, D., & Tversky, A. (1972). Subjective probability: A judgment of representativeness. *Cognitive Psychology, 3,* 430–454.

Kanki, B. G., Lozito, S., & Foushee, H. C. (1989). Communication indices of crew coordination. *Aviation, Space, and Environmental Medicine, 60,* 56–60.

Klein, G. (1997). Developing expertise in decision making. *Thinking and Reasoning, 3,* 337–352.

Klein, G. (1998). *Sources of power: How people make decisions.* Cambridge, MA: MIT Press.

Klein, G. (1999). *The fiction of maximization.* Paper presented at the Dahlem Workshop on Bounded Rationality: The Adaptive Toolbox, Berlin.

Klein, G., Wolf, S., Militello, L., & Zsambok, C. (1995). Characteristics of skilled option generation in chess. *Organizational Behavior and Human Decision Processes, 62*(1), 63–69.

Klein, G. A., Calderwood, R., & Clinton-Cirocco, A. (1986). Rapid decision making on the fireground. *Proceedings of the 30th Annual Human Factors Society* (Vol. 1, pp. 576–580). Dayton, OH: Human Factors Society.

Klein, G. A., Orasanu, J., Calderwood, R., & Zsambok, C. E. (1993). *Decision making in action: Models and methods.* Norwood, NJ: Ablex.

Lipshitz, R. (1993). Converging themes in the study of decision making in realistic settings. In G. A. Klein, J. Orasanu, R. Calderwood, & C. E. Zsambok

(Eds.), *Decision making in action: Models and methods* (pp. 103–137). Norwood, NJ: Ablex.

McNeil, B. J., Pauker, S. G., Sox, H. C., & Tversky, A. (1982). On the elicitation of preferences for alternative therapies. *New England Journal of Medicine, 306,* 1259–1262.

Militello, L. G., & Hutton, R. J. B. (1998). Applied Cognitive Task Analysis (ACTA): A practitioner's toolkit for understanding cognitive task demands. *Ergonomics. Special Issue: Task Analysis, 41*(11), 1618–1641.

Militello, L., & Lim, L. (1994). *Early assessment of NEC in premature infants* (Final Progress Report Grant 1 R43 HD29905-01A1 for NIH/NICHD). Fairborn, OH: Klein Associates.

Miller, T. E., Kyne, M., & Lim, L. (1994). *Blood banking: The need for training and evaluation* (Contract No. 1 R43 HL49723-01 for the National Institutes of Health). Fairborn, OH: Klein Associates.

Montgomery, H. (1993). The search for a dominance structure in decision making: Examining the evidence. In G. A. Klein, J. Orasanu, R. Calderwood, & C. E. Zsambok (Eds.), *Decision making in action: Models and methods* (pp. 182–187). Norwood, NJ: Ablex.

Mosier, K. L. (1991). Expert decision making strategies. *Proceedings of the Sixth International Symposium on Aviation Psychology* (pp. 266–271). Columbus, OH:

Murphy, A. H., & Brown, B. G. (1984). A comparative evaluation of objective and subjective weather forecasts in the United States. *Journal of Forecasting, 3,* 369–393.

Murphy, A. H., & Winkler, R. L. (1974). Subjective probability forecasting experiments in meteorology: Some preliminary results. *Bulletin of the American Meteorologist Society, 55,* 1206–1216.

Murphy, A. H., & Winkler, R. L. (1977). Reliability of subjective probability forecasts of precipitation and temperature. *Applied Statistics, 26,* 41–47.

Orasanu, J., & Connolly, T. (1993). The reinvention of decision making. In G. A. Klein, J. Orasanu, R. Calderwood, & C. E. Zsambok (Eds.), *Decision making in action: Models and methods* (pp. 3–20). Norwood, NJ: Ablex.

Pascual, R., & Henderson, S. (1997). Evidence of naturalistic decision making in C^2. In C. Zsambok & G. Klein (Eds.), *Naturalistic decision making* (pp. 217–226). Mahwah, NJ: LEA.

Pennington, N., & Hastie, R. (1988). Explanation-based decision making: Effects of memory structure on judgment. *Journal of Experimental Psychology: Learning, Memory, & Cognition, 14*(3), 521–533.

Pitz, G., Sachs, N., & Heerboth, J. (1980). Procedures for eliciting choices in the analysis of individual decision. *Organizational Behavior and Human Performance, 26,* 396–408.

Pliske, R. M., Crandall, B., & Klein, G. (in press). Competence in weather forecasting. In J. Shanteau, P. Johnson, & K. Smith, (Eds.) *Psychological investigations of competent decision making.* New York: Cambridge University Press.

Pliske, R. M., McCloskey, M., & Klein, G. (2001). Decision skills training: Facilitating learning from experience. In E. Salas & G. Klein (Eds.), *Linking expertise and naturalistic decision making* (pp. 37–53). West Newton, MA: Argosy.

Plous, S. (1993). *The psychology of judgment and decision making.* Philadelphia: Temple University Press.

Randel, J. M., Pugh, H. L., Reed, S. K., Schuler, J. W., & Wyman, B. (1994). *Methods for analyzing cognitive skills for a technical task.* San Diego, CA: Navy Personnel Research and Development Center.

Rasmussen, J. (1983). Skill, rules and knowledge: Signals, signs, and symbols, and other distinctions in human performance models. *IEEE Transactions on Systems, Man and Cybernetics, 13*(3), 257–266.

Russo, J. E., & Schoemaker, P. J. H. (1989). *Decision traps: Ten barriers to brilliant decision making.* Garden City, NY: Doubleday.

Salas, E., & Klein, G. (Eds.). (2001). *Linking expertise and naturalistic decision making.* Mahwah, NJ: Erlbaum.

Sarter, N. B., & Woods, D. D. (1991). Situation awareness: A critical but ill-defined phenomenon. *The International Journal of Aviation Psychology, 1*(1), 45–57.

Shanteau, J. (1992). Competence in experts: The role of task characteristics. *Organizational Behavior and Human Decision Processes, 53,* 252–266.

Simon, H. A. (1957). *Models of man: Social and rational.* New York: Wiley.

Stewart, T. R., Heideman, K. F., Moninger, W. R., & Reagan-Cirincione, P. (1992). Effects of improved information on the components of skill in weather forecasting. Special Issue: *Experts and Expert Systems of Organizational Behavior & Human Decision Processes, 53*(2), 107–134.

Stewart, T. R., & Lusk, C. M. (1994). Seven components of judgmental forecasting skill: Implications for research and the improvement of forecasts. *Journal of Forecasting, 13,* 579–599.

Suchman, L. A. (1987). *Plans and situated actions: The problem of human–machine communication.* Cambridge: Cambridge University Press.

Tversky, A., & Kahneman, D. (1973). Availability: A heuristic for judging frequency and probability. *Cognitive Psychology, 4,* 207–232.

Tversky, A., & Kahneman, D. (1974). Judgment under uncertainty: Heuristics and biases. *Science, 185,* 1124–1131.

Tversky, A., & Kahneman, D. (1981). The framing of decisions and the psychology of choice, *Science, 211,* 453–458.

von Neumann, J., & Morgenstern, O. (1947). *Theory of games and economic behavior.* Princeton, NJ: Princeton University Press.

Wohl, J. C. (1981). Force management decision requirements for Air Force tactical command and control. *IEEE Transactions on Systems, Man, and Cybernetics, 11,* 618–639.

Woods, D. D. (1993). Process-tracing methods for the study of cognition outside of the experimental psychology laboratory. In G. A. Klein, J. Orasanu, R. Calderwood, & C. E. Zsambok (Eds.), *Decision making in action: Models and methods* (pp. 228–251). Norwood, NJ: Ablex.

Yates, J. F. (1998). *Observations on NDM – The phenomenon and the "framework."* Paper presented at the Fourth Conference on Naturalistic Decision Making, Warrenton, VA.

Zsambok, C. E. (1997). Naturalistic decision making: Where are we now? In C. Zsambok & G. Klein (Eds.), *Naturalistic decision making* (pp. 3–16). Mahwah, NJ: LEA.

Zsambok, C. E., & Klein, G. (Eds.). (1997). *Naturalistic decision making.* Mahwah, NJ: LEA.

18 Command Style and Team Performance in Dynamic Decision-Making Tasks

Julia M. Clancy, Glenn C. Elliott, Tobias Ley,
Mary M. Omodei, Alexander J. Wearing, Jim McLennan,
and Einar B. Thorsteinsson

ABSTRACT

Real-world tasks involving dynamic decision making are commonly distributed among a number of people, the organizational structure being typically hierarchical in nature. However, the optimal way to divide the responsibility for decision making among team members is not obvious. Should leaders make all decisions and communicate specific actions for subordinates to carry out? Or should decision-making responsibility be shared, with leaders communicating their intentions to subordinates, who then decide upon appropriate actions and carry these out? This is fundamentally an issue of the relative effectiveness of contrasting *command styles*. This chapter addresses this issue by reporting a study using teams of three persons (a leader and two subordinates) in a computer-simulated forest firefighting task. The results indicate a marked performance advantage for teams in which the leader is required to command by the communication of intentions rather than by the communication of orders for specific actions. An intention-based command style, which creates a more even distribution of decision-making responsibility across ranks, was found to result in a more equal distribution of the cognitive workload, to take greater advantage of subordinates' local knowledge, and to allow for greater overall team productivity.

CONTENTS

This research was funded under a Research Agreement with the Defence Science Technology Organization in Australia. The contribution of John Hansen of this organization is gratefully acknowledged. We also acknowledge programming support provided by Peter Taranto.

Dynamic decision making in real-life contexts, such as in firefighting and military combat, is often too complex for one individual to handle alone. As a consequence, several people are involved, commonly organized in hierarchical structures, with each individual assuming a particular role. This allows the activities that must be performed to control the task to be distributed in a systematic fashion. In such distributed dynamic decision-making (D3M) contexts, however, it is not clear how those cognitive activities that comprise the decision-making process should be distributed to allow for optimal performance. In particular, the optimal balance of responsibility for decision making among commanders and subordinates throughout a hierarchical organization is difficult to determine. An important question is, to what extent should specific actions be decided upon by the overall team leader (herein given the title of *commander*) and to what extent by subordinates? That is, should a commander exercise his or her command role primarily by communicating his or her general intent (formulated as goals to be achieved) or primarily by issuing orders for specific goal-directed actions to be carried out by subordinates?

The Fundamental Characteristics of D3M Environments

Most laboratory research on decision making has focused on single decisions, ranging from the relatively simple, such as choosing a gamble, to the relatively complex, such as a simulated decision to recall or not recall a possibly defective product. These studies usually see the decision maker as the one who chooses an action from an array of well-specified alternatives on the basis of some form of (a) subjective expected probability or (b) a utility-maximizing algorithm (Bobevski & McLennan, 1998). The bulk of this laboratory research has typically employed highly artificial tasks, and as such has yielded mostly trivial outcomes (Beach & Lipshitz, 1996; Orasanu & Connolly, 1993).

The single-decision tasks used in such laboratory research differ in important ways from dynamic decisions in naturalistic environments. In dynamic decision tasks, the goal is to control an environment through a sequence of related decisions rather than to make a single choice that will maximize a return. D3M occurs across a broad spectrum of task environments including medical emergencies, firefighting, search and rescue, military combat, manufacturing plant malfunction, and organizational crises. Researchers have only recently begun to study decision making in such D3M environments. A major reason for the limited research to date is that theoretical models developed to account for such single-decision behavior (most notably the classical decision-making model) have been found to be poorly suited to the kinds of situations that typically confront decision makers in D3M environments (Beach & Lipshitz, 1996).

The following key features characterize D3M tasks.

Main Aim Is to Exert Control

The overall aim of a decision maker in a D3M task is to gain control over the task environment through a sequence of related decisions rather than to make a single choice that will maximize the return. Rather than focusing on specific decisions, the decision maker's focus of concern is typically on achieving overall control of the situation. Interestingly, a decision maker's cognitive behavior in controlling the decision-making task appears to be an attempt to achieve and maintain a "compromise between the demands of the task and the need to conserve one's cognitive resources" (Brehmer, 2000).

Complex, Dynamic Environment with Action–Feedback Loops

The environment comprises many interrelated variables, usually interacting in complex ways. To exercise control over even one variable in such an environment requires not a single decision but a series of decisions. Typically, complex feedback loops operate, linking decision, action, and information about the effects of that particular action (Brehmer, 1992; Orasanu & Connolly, 1993).

Ill-Structured Problems with Multiple Goals

Problems are rarely well defined, at least initially, and the decision maker must struggle to identify the key features of the situation, generate hypotheses, and formulate options. Decision makers are usually driven by multiple goals. Moreover, the priorities of these goals may change as a situation develops, with some of these goals being mutually incompatible (Flin, 1996).

Uncertainty

Uncertainty has a complex meaning in a D3M environment. It may take the traditional meaning: the probability of an exogenous event. This notion may also be extended to refer to the probability of the "where" and "when" of an event and/or the likely outcomes of an intervention. In a dynamic environment, uncertainty often resides not in precise probabilities but in certain features of the probabilistic information. These features may include (a) the timeliness of the information – when, during the dynamic task, the information becomes available to the decision maker; (b) the accuracy of the information – whether the information is reliable and/or ambiguous and conflicting (Orasanu & Connolly, 1993; Schmitt & Klein, 1998); (c) the completeness of the information – whether some information is missing (Orasanu & Connolly, 1993; Schmitt & Klein, 1998); and (d) the complexity of the information – whether the decision maker is able to make practical sense of the information in the context of the current task (Lipshitz & Strauss, 1997; Schmitt & Klein, 1998).

Timeliness

Decisions must be made in real time. Situations may change regardless of any action or inaction of a decision maker, and often the timing of a decision action may be as important as its content. The onset of critical events in the environment is usually rapid, with little or no warning or preparation time (Flin, 1996). The rate of change of the task environment is also often rapid, so decision tasks often have a degree of time pressure such that decisions must be made rapidly, the decision process being constrained by the fact that time is a critical factor (Brehmer, 1992).

High Stakes

There is often an element of risk associated with the decision makers' actions (Orasanu & Connolly, 1993). For example, the incident in a D3M task could be directly threatening lives, as in the case of a house fire, or threatening the global economy, as in the case of a stock market crisis.

Multiple Decision Makers

Important real-world situations are rarely handled by just one person, either because there is too much information for any one person to handle or because others have too high a stake in the outcome to allow one person to have exclusive control (Orasanu & Salas, 1993). Often the organization of a D3M task is geographically distributed (for example, a large power plant control facility), which means that no single person has a complete view of the information necessary for effective control (Artman, 1998b). In D3M situations, information, knowledge, resources, roles, and responsibilities are all differentially distributed across team members, typically associated with some form of influence hierarchy.

Structuring of D3M Environments

Hierarchical Organizational Structure

As noted previously, many real-world high-stakes tasks are too large for one individual to handle, requiring several people to cooperate so as to reach common goals. Any one individual is usually limited with respect to the ability to perform the requisite actions, with events occurring over large geographical areas, with too much information for any one person to process (Brehmer, 2000). This raises the question: How, in a distributed environment with a given division of labor, do the component individuals work together and coordinate so that they can operate beyond the capabilities of any single individual? The answer is that the decision-making activities must be structured so that each individual has a physically and cognitively manageable role (Crecine & Salomone, 1989). It is most common to divide the tasks among participants in a systematic way by specifying roles that distribute *responsibility* for implementing tasks hierarchically. This is in contrast to adopting a *flat* distributional structure in which there is no systematic role differentiation.

A hierarchical command system imposes structure on a D3M environment in order to reduce its complexity and to make it understandable (Brehmer, 1991). The number of levels of such a hierarchy is entirely dependent on the individuals who create and impose the system (Brehmer, 1991). It is common in a hierarchical operational environment for one person (often referred to as a *commander*) to be assigned the responsibility for global decision making, with the other team members being responsible for localized areas of decision making. A hierarchical structure is particularly advantageous when large tasks can be decomposed into subtasks and the subtasks are stable subsystems that are self-maintaining. It must be noted, however, that a given hierarchical structure is advantageous only when the complexity of tasks at each level of the system does not exceed the capacity of the decision maker who controls the system on that level (Brehmer, 1991). A hierarchical structure is advantageous in that it requires less communication (Crecine & Salomone, 1989) and coordination, because the hierarchy acts to simplify the complex system. It acts to reduce the workload of each individual and aims to allow individuals to work within their physical and cognitive boundaries.

Time and Spatial Scales in a Hierarchical Structure

The nature of the situation at different levels of an organizational hierarchy varies with respect to the recency and adequacy of information available at the respective levels in the hierarchy. At lower levels of the organization, individuals have access to the situation at the hands-on level and thus have the most recent and immediate knowledge about the current state of the situation. In contrast, at higher levels, individuals have delayed access to information because information must be fed up the hierarchy from the lower to the higher levels. At lower levels of the hierarchy, individuals deal with specific operational information about a situation. At higher levels of the hierarchy, individuals deal with more global information about the situation as a whole (Brehmer, 1995a).

Persons located at different levels of a D3M environment therefore typically operate on different time scales and spatial scales (Brehmer, 1995a). Differences in *time scales* mean that at lower levels of the hierarchy, individuals have up-to-date information about the local problems of the task and are therefore able and required to act quickly. They essentially function on a short-term basis, meaning that the time scale they typically have to consider is quite small. On the other hand, individuals with higher levels of responsibility typically work on a longer time scale, their plans involving long-term coordination of action, taking into account time lags in the recency of their information (Brehmer, 1995a).

Differences in *spatial scales* reside in the fact that at higher levels of the decision hierarchy, individuals must consider events over a much larger (global) spatial area than do local subordinates. A real-world D3M example that illustrates such differences in time and spatial scales is that of a forest fire. Here we have individuals at different levels of a hierarchy operating on different time and spatial scales. The crews on the fireground operate on a very short time scale, reacting to their particular fire front, as it continually changes and demands immediate decisions and actions. These fire crews control only a small part of the whole fire, thereby acting on a small spatial scale. As one moves up the hierarchy to the fire management team, the time scales get longer (in deciding on the overall distribution of fire crews to the different parts of the fire front, or monitoring weather forecasts and deciding on changes in priorities of different fires). Also, the spatial scales get larger as one moves up the hierarchy, with the fire management team monitoring the whole region under threat.

A hierarchical command structure is therefore commonly implemented in an organization so as to achieve coordination more effectively across the different time and spatial scales that define the task environment. Thus, individuals at the highest level of a hierarchy do not always have information sufficiently up-to-date to be able to give specific commands to those at the lowest level. Thus lower-level individuals necessarily retain a degree of local control. However, individuals at the lowest level often do not have access to information about all aspects of the task environment, which limits the effectiveness of their decisions. Thus, some coordination of control must stem from the higher levels. With the constant flow of information both up and down a command chain that characterizes a D3M environment, such information is constantly transformed and reinterpreted in accordance with the level of abstraction relevant to each particular hierarchical level. This involves inescapable operational delays. Furthermore, the goals at each hierarchical level differ according to the corresponding time and spatial scales. Therefore, there may have to be tradeoffs in attempting to achieve goals that are locally relevant versus goals that are globally relevant (Artman, 1998a). Achieving cooperation among individuals operating on different time and spatial scales within a hierarchy is important. With adequate cooperation across levels, individuals operating at different time and spatial scales can compensate for each other's errors. For example, an individual operating at a lower level of the hierarchy is usually able to interpret the global commands of a commander according to specific details of the local situation. On the other hand, what a commander working on a long time scale and a global spatial scale lacks in specific details, he or she can compensate for in breadth (Artman, 1998a).

Shared Situation Awareness in a Hierarchical Structure

Despite any differences in time and spatial scales across levels of a command hierarchy, there remains the need for a shared understanding across such levels of (a) the present state of the environment to be controlled and (b) the goals to be achieved. As Brehmer and Dörner (1993) have argued, it is unlikely that the coordination and sharing of information and resources can be achieved in the absence of a shared understanding of the state of the system (i.e., a shared situation awareness). This shared situation awareness held by members of a hierarchically structured organization enables them to form accurate explanations and expectations of the task and therefore to coordinate their actions with, and adapt behavior toward, individuals at other levels of the hierarchy (Cannon-Bowers, Salas, & Converse, 1993).

The development of an adequate shared situation awareness is not possible, however, without appropriate *communication* among the members of a hierarchy. Communication is essential to allow information to filter up and down the hierarchy. Communication is necessary in "filling in the gaps" in each individual's representation of the current situation, as each decision maker has a limited window on the task as a whole (Brehmer, 1995b). Studies have shown that incomplete or interrupted communication leads to decreased situation awareness (Orasanu, 1995; Salas, Prince, Baker, & Shrestha, 1995). It has also been suggested that different communication structures and organizational arrangements have implications for the adequacy of the shared situation awareness of a team (Artman, 1999). This raises the question of the desirability of having all members achieve a totally shared situation awareness. Brehmer (1995b) suggests that it is not always necessary or beneficial for everyone in a distributed task environment to have exactly the same situation awareness. For example, subordinates have detailed information, which is not necessary for the commander to have. Further, it has been found that in some situations, local decision makers perform quite well on the basis of only localized information, without global information or input from a commander (Svenmark, 1998).

Distribution of Decision-Making Responsibility in a Hierarchical Structure

Obviously, the level of decision-making control must be distributed appropriately across a hierarchically structured organization to allow for optimal functioning. This raises the question of what constitutes an optimal balance in the distribution of decision-making control throughout a hierarchy. That is, how much of the decision-making responsibility should be centralized in a single commander and how much should be delegated to local subordinates? The discussion of the differences in time and spatial scales in D3M presented earlier indicates that commanders are usually the only team member with access to the "big picture," so it could be argued that most decision-making responsibility should reside with the commander. However, as subordinates have superior real-time access to local problem task information, it may be advantageous for subordinates to be given some decision-making power over their own resources (Brehmer, 1995a). These questions are central to the present study.

The traditional approach to the issue of distribution of decision-making responsibility in important D3M situations is to implement a command style in which one central individual (the commander) decides what actions need to take place and communicates these requirements to appropriate subordinates to implement. Therefore, in such a centralized structure, the commander is responsible for the cognitive work of situation assessment, intention generation, and action selection, and subordinates are responsible solely for action implementation. Such an organizational decision structure could be considered a *centralized* structure (Crecine & Salomone, 1989).

An alternative approach to the distribution of decision-making responsibility in D3M situations is for the commander to formulate intentions and, rather than proceed to action selection, to communicate these intentions directly to subordinates. By communicating intent, a commander communicates not only the goals to be achieved but also the reasons for pursuing these goals (purposes). It would then be left to subordinates to decide how goals are to be achieved locally and to plan actions accordingly. *Intent* has been defined as the general connotation of a specific aim or purpose (Pigeau & McCann, 1998). Commanders' intentions can thus guide subordinates' decisions in the absence of specific action orders. Such an intent command style represents a more decentralized organizational structure, as decision-making responsibility is not centered on one individual. A switch from a centralized to a more decentralized command style is found in the modern military command-and-control doctrine of *mission command* (Department of the Navy, 1995; Ministry of Defence, 1995).

According to the doctrine of mission command, command and control has been defined as "the establishment of shared intent and the transformation of common intent into coordinated action" (Pigeau & McCann, 1998, p. 3). How common intent is transformed into coordinated action hinges largely upon the commands of the commander.

For example, recommendations for a more decentralized military command style have been implemented in Sweden. These recommendations stemmed from the recognition that there are problems of differences in recency and complexity of information at different levels of a military command hierarchy (Brehmer, 1995a). As a result, the Swedish defense forces have addressed these recommendations by instructing commanders not to issue detailed orders about what should be *done* on a given level. Instead, all commands from a higher to a lower level should involve the communication of *goals* to the lower levels of the hierarchy. Decisions about how these goals should be achieved are left to individuals at lower levels, who are presumed to have superior knowledge about current local conditions at those levels (Brehmer, 1995b). However, despite these formal changes in command style being implemented in Swedish defense forces, the relative efficacy of such a change in command style was not evaluated prior to or since implementation.

The previously mentioned alternative approaches to the degree of delegation of decision-making responsibility in a hierarchical structure imply two contrasting command styles: an Action command style and an Intent command style. These command styles are summarized as follows:

1. In an Action command style, the commander not only assesses the situation and generates intentions, but also decides upon requisite actions and communicates these as specific action orders to subordinates. Subordinates then implement the actions as ordered.

2. In an Intent command style, the commander assesses the situation and then generates intentions, which are communicated to subordinates. The subordinates, in turn, exercise decision-making discretion in deciding which specific actions they should implement in order to give effect to their commander's intentions.

Implications for Cognitive Processing Demands: Strategic versus Tactical Thought

With respect to the nature of the cognitive demands placed on subordinates, these alternative command styles imply differences in cognitive processing demands. More specifically, there is a difference in the balance of strategic versus tactical thought that is required of both commanders and subordinates.

Concerning the distinction between strategic and tactical decision-making thought, there is the potential for confusion insofar as the terms *strategic* and *tactical* have somewhat different definitions in the formal systems implemented in military and emergency services contexts (such as firefighting) than they do in the theoretical literature on the nature of

Factors Favoring an Intent Command Style

The following three factors suggest that an Intent command style is likely to be more effective than an Action command style.

1. *The commander is less likely to be cognitively overloaded and thus to constitute a bottleneck.*

Structuring an organization in such a way that all decision-making responsibility lies with one individual (the commander) could mean that the amount of information that must be transmitted and assimilated may exceed a commander's cognitive capacity. Furthermore, as a result of recent developments in the speed and capacity of information technology (Schmitt & Klein, 1998), the amount of information potentially available to a commander is likely to increase dramatically. Therefore, the position of a commander may constitute a restrictive bottleneck leading to unnecessary delays in action implementation.

2. *The commander does not need to switch continually between time scales and between spatial scales.*

As indicated previously, different levels of a hierarchical organization operate on different time and spatial scales (Brehmer, 1995a). In making decisions about global factors such as resource distribution, commanders operate on a large time scale and a broad spatial scale. However, to make decisions at the level of specific actions, commanders must switch to operating on a smaller time scale and a narrower spatial scale. That is, to operate effectively, commanders who adopt an Action command style must continually oscillate between two time scales and between two spatial scales. As such, it may take more time for a commander than for a subordinate to accurately interpret and act on relatively low-level information (Artman, 1999). Furthermore, such oscillations between time and between spatial scales would impair a commander's ability to develop, and subsequently to maintain and revise, an overall understanding of the situation as a whole (i.e., an issue of adequacy of situational awareness).

3. *An Intent style takes maximum advantage of the local knowledge and expertise of subordinates.*

An Intent command style may be superior because an Action command style fails to exploit fully subordinates' local information and expertise. A commander is unlikely to have as detailed or as up-to-date knowledge of the local situation as do subordinates. Furthermore, subordinates are likely to have a better appreciation of the dynamic characteristics of a situation.

Regardless of the relative adequacy of subordinates' knowledge of the current local situation, any *decentralization* of decision-making responsibility, in principle, enables subordinates to exercise initiative when unexpected opportunities or problems arise. As suggested by Crecine and Salamone (1989), this gives the system the flexibility to adapt effectively to emerging situations.

In summary, the extent to which each of these factors might operate in a typical D3M environment is not at all clear. Furthermore, it is unclear whether any advantages of a decentralized (i.e., Intent) command structure outweigh any disadvantages of such a structure.

Computer-Simulated Decision Scenarios as a Research Platform

Laboratory-based decision-making tasks that have been developed for testing hypotheses about single and/or static decision making have not proved suitable for studying decision making in D3M environments. This is because the aim of laboratory experiments has generally been to reduce the complexity of real-world decisions and manipulate only a limited number of variables in order to reveal specific underlying relationships. To achieve the essential complexity of D3M environments, researchers to date have had to restrict their investigations to field studies as the only ecologically valid option. In field-based investigations, however, it has proved impossible to achieve the necessary experimental control required for unambiguous interpretation. It is impossible on practical, economic, political, or ethical grounds to implement explicit manipulations of adequate strength and/or to gather relevant data from participants (Ley, 1999).

Computer-generated scenarios have been proposed by several researchers as an appropriate platform for the controlled testing of hypotheses concerning psychological processes involved in multiperson decision environments (Ackerman & Kanfer, 1993; Brehmer & Dörner, 1993; Funke, 1991; Omodei & Wearing, 1995; Weaver, Bowers, Salas, & Cannon-Bowers, 1995). Such *microworlds* or *scaled worlds* simulate the essential (genotypic) features but not all the surface (phenotypic) details of a real-world D3M environment. According to Brehmer (2000), a task used to study dynamic decision making should meet the following conditions: (a) a series of decisions is required; (b) the decisions are not independent; (c) the state of the problem changes, both autonomously and as a result of the decision makers' actions; and (d) decisions have to be made in real time.

In the experiment reported here, we used the Networked Fire Chief (Omodei, Taranto, & Wearing, 1999) microworld generating program to create a complex forest firefighting task environment. Networked Fire Chief allows for detailed re-creation of landscapes of varying composition, flammability characteristics, and asset values. Participants are asked to control the spread of these simulated fires by dispatching fire trucks and helicopters to drop water on the fires and to refill with water at specified water locations. Although a wide range of scenarios can, in principle, be created with Networked Fire Chief, forest firefighting was selected as the specific microworld scenario, as we were able to recruit as participants persons who (although technically not experts) brought to the task a well-developed understanding of forest fire behavior and methods for its control.

Networked Fire Chief allows the experimenter to be primarily concerned with the creation of decision-making scenarios that embody the deep structure of command and control of emergency incidents rather than the more superficial surface structure of such incidents (thus we aim for psychological, as distinct from physical, fidelity). Although an optimal tradeoff between external (ecological) and internal validity is sought, we recognize the importance of keeping the microworld relatively simple so that we can be reasonably sure about what the results are telling us in terms of the generic aspects of a D3M task. We argue, therefore, that our findings are not limited to firefighting but can transfer to a range of time-pressured, high-stakes, multiparticipant D3M settings (such as military operations, transport control, plant operations, etc.).

Aims of the Study

The study to be reported compared the performance, in a computer-simulated D3M task, of teams whose commander employs an Intent command style with that of teams whose commander employs an Action command style.

Furthermore, participants' behaviour and experience were assessed in order to obtain evidence for the differential operation of factors favoring either an Action or an Intent command style (as described earlier). These assessments include (a) the overall quality of strategic thought,

(b) the amount of situation assessment, (c) the amount of tactical activity, and (d) the experienced workload.

Method

Participants

Forty 3-person teams were created from 120 second-year undergraduate psychology students ranging in age from 18 to 50 years. The majority (75%) were under 21 years of age. The 40 participants who occupied the role of commander were self-selected from the 120-participant pool, which presumably resulted in obtaining persons who desired a leadership role. Interestingly, of the 120 participants, approximately 40 volunteered for the commander role (referred to as the Incident Commander – IC), as distinct from the subordinate role (referred to as the Sector Controller – SC) role. The remaining 80 participants were then allocated randomly to Sector Controller roles to create 40 teams of 3 persons (1 IC plus 2 SCs).

Design

The design comprised a between-groups comparison. The independent variable was command style, with two conditions: Intent – IC command by communicating intention ($n = 18$ teams) and Action – IC command by communicating specific action orders ($n = 22$ teams). The major dependent variable of interest was team performance, operationalized as an objective score (automatically generated from the microworld) indicating the value of landscape assets saved from destruction by fire.

Materials

The Networked Fire Chief (Omodei et al., 1999) microworld generating program was used to create a dynamic forest firefighting decision-making task. The fundamental aim of this task is to limit the spread of fire in a designated area, which contains residential areas, vegetation areas, rivers and dams, by deploying fire trucks and helicopters. In order to provide research participants with adequate opportunities for strategic decision making, the simulated appliances were programmed to automatically locate and extinguish fires within a three-landscape-segment radius of their current position. Furthermore, if dispatched to fill with water, appliances automatically returned to resume firefighting in their original location. All scenarios were based on real-life priorities described in standard wildfire-fighting manuals, so that it was most important to save the residential areas from fire destruction in the following descending order: cities, dense housing, and then light housing. Vegetation areas were second in importance to residential areas, with the order of priority of vegetation areas being forest followed by grass and then clearing. Using the networking capabilities of the program, the current study implemented a three-person distributed environment, with the structure comprising one IC computer station linked to two SC computer stations.

Six training and two experimental firefighting scenarios were constructed. The training scenarios were graded so that they gradually become more difficult until they reached the level of difficulty of the experimental scenarios. Two experimental scenarios of identical difficulty were created by making one trial scenario a mirror image of the other (postexperimental debriefing indicated that participants did not detect any similarities between the mirror-imaged scenarios). These two almost identical scenarios were created to allow the reliability of the program-generated scores to be evaluated.

Each scenario could be operated simultaneously by three users, each at a separate computer station (thus distributing the opportunity to control the scenario across three computers). The IC's computer station presented a display of the total landscape area under the team's control. A vertical line down the center of the IC's map divided it into two sectors, which corresponded to the sectors visible to each subordinate. One subordinate, called the Left Sector Controller, was responsible for the left half of the map. The other subordinate, the Right Sector Controller, was responsible for the right half of the map. The sector controllers could only view their own sector, which was magnified (i.e., at a larger resolution) compared to the IC's view. This team structure simulates a typical command and control environment, in which an IC has the big picture at the expense of detail, whereas individual subordinates know the particular area under their responsibility in detail but lack information about the whole incident.

Although the IC computer station allowed firefighting appliances to be moved across sectors from base station to base station, it was not possible for the IC to undertake any firefighting activity directly. In addition to being able to deploy appliances from one SC base station to another, ICs were required to deploy helicopters (a total of eight) from a central base station (to which only ICs had access) to the SC's base station in order for the SC to use these helicopters. However, all direct firefighting by appliances could be carried out only from the two SC computer stations. Thus, all decisions made by the IC could be implemented only by communicating these to the appropriate SC, who then carried out the required action. Communications concerning locations on the fireground were in terms of the corresponding X- and Y-axis coordinates, as shown on the on-screen map of the simulated area. In accordance with typical fire management systems and procedures, the IC was analogous to an IC back at the control center who has an overview of the total area under his or her control displayed on a computer monitor. The SCs were analogous to local controllers on the fireground, responsible for several appliance crews. The SCs were therefore able to implement actions directly, but strictly under the overall command of the IC.

The communication system for each team comprised three sound-isolating aviation-style headsets with microphones, one for each team member. These were linked to a main operating switchboard, which was under the control of the IC. The IC could initiate communication with either subordinate through the switchboard, but there was no communication link between the two SCs, thus implementing a fully centralized communication structure.

Overview of Experimental Procedures

Three $1^{1}/_{2}$-hour sessions were scheduled at approximately weekly intervals. All 40 teams went through the following procedure: In the first session, participants were given detailed instructions about the nature of the task and the procedures for issuing commands to appliances, followed by several trials in which they practiced these techniques. In the second weekly session, teams were given graded trials of increasing difficulty, with the final trial being equivalent in difficulty to the experimental trials. In the final weekly session, teams were given a short warm-up trial to refamiliarize themselves with the task. They were then given the two mirror-imaged experimental trials. Immediately on completion of the second experimental trial, participants were asked to complete a questionnaire containing the measures outlined subsequently.

Command-Style Manipulation

Eighteen of the three-person teams were constrained to operate under the Intent command style condition, and 22 teams were constrained

Table 18.1. *Sample of IC Communication in the Intent and Action Command Style Conditions*

Intent Command Style	Action Command Style
IC: Left Sector, could you please fight the large fire front that has just broken out at 50-180. But your priority is still to protect the housing at 70-160. Also, make sure to protect the forest at 40-170	*IC*: Right Sector, please take one helicopter and two trucks from the fire at location 170-60, which is nearly extinguished, to the fire at location 120-90. Use the helicopter to fight the fire threatening the light housing and the two trucks to fight the fire in the forest area.

to operate under the Action command style condition. All teams were trained from the beginning in their appropriate condition. Command style was manipulated by giving different instructions to ICs on how to communicate to SCs.

ICs in the Intent command style condition were encouraged to communicate their *global* intentions about how best to control the incident environment and allow SCs to make lower-level decisions on how best to implement these intentions. They were given the rationale that due to the complexity of the task, it was preferable to give general commands rather than to be concerned with minor details such as exactly how to fight the fires. It was explained that a good way of stating their intentions was to talk in terms of their priorities and goals for extinguishing the fires while relying on the SCs to implement actions to best accomplish these goals.

ICs in the Action command style condition were encouraged to communicate explicit commands about specific actions to the SCs. ICs were given the rationale that because they alone had an overview of the entire map, they were in the best position to make specific decisions about what they wanted their SCs to do. They were told that a good way of issuing their commands was to talk in terms of how many trucks and helicopters to send to each fire and where these should be taken from. The SCs were not free to make any decisions about how and when to implement actions. They were completely reliant upon instructions from the IC. A sample of IC communication within each command style condition is presented in Table 18.1.

In both conditions, SCs were instructed to follow orders from the IC, and they were not permitted to implement any actions unless so instructed by the IC. However, they were told that they were responsible for refilling trucks and helicopters when they ran out of water.

Measures

Adequacy of the Manipulation of Command Style

Interpretation of experimental manipulation instructions. In order to assess participants' awareness of the intended manipulation, both ICs and SCs were asked to provide ratings on the following items (anchored by 1 = "not at all" and 9 = "very much"): (a) encouraged to give general orders; (b) actually gave general orders; and (3) felt it important to give general orders.

Relative amount of strategic versus tactical thought. The relative amount of time spent in various strategic and tactical cognitive activities was measured by asking participants (both ICs and SCs) to estimate how much time they spent doing each of the following (all anchored by 1 = "no time at all" and 9 = "most of my time").

> Strategic: (a) deciding which particular fire front to prioritize; (b) deciding which part of a particular fire to fight.
>
> Tactical: (a) deciding how many appliances were needed on a particular fire front; (b) deciding which particular appliances should be moved to a fire front.

Team Performance. The main outcome variable, Team Performance, was assessed in terms of the amount of landscape saved, weighted appropriately for the different priority values of the landscape types.

Quality of Strategic Decision Making. The quality of strategic decision making by the team was operationalized as the appropriateness of the priorities assigned to the different fires throughout the progression of the simulation trial. There is no simple Networked Fire Chief – generated indicator for the quality of strategic decisions because such decisions, by definition, always involve goal tradeoffs. Which goal tradeoff is more appropriate than another can be judged only by an expert in the task. Ratings of the appropriateness of such prioritization of fires was therefore obtained by having a person with expertise in the use of the Networked Fire Chief task independently review the replay of the final experimental trial for each team. At four times during the simulation trial, the expert judged the appropriateness of the priorities given to the fires in each sector on a scale from 1 ("completely inappropriate") to

4 ("completely appropriate"). The four times used for these ratings were selected as being critical times during the trial – for example, when several fires broke out simultaneously. Each team therefore received a total of eight expert ratings (four for each sector). The ratings were added to form a team score for the quality of strategic decision making, which could have values between 8 and 32.

Amount of Situation Assessment. The amount of situation assessment performed by participants was measured by asking participants (both ICs and SCs) to estimate how much time they spent doing each of the following (all anchored by 1 = "no time at all" and 9 = "most of my time"): (a) monitoring the current wind direction; (b) monitoring the forecast wind direction; (c) predicting the future developments of the fire.

Amount of Tactical Activity. The absolute amount of activity taken to limit the spread of fires (the outcome of tactical-level decision making) was assessed by the number of times appliances were commanded to be moved from one location to another. Amount of appliance movement is automatically generated by the Networked Fire Chief program, with subtotals being given for each team member. Note that as ICs could only move appliances between bases, the amount of movement of appliances to fires by SCs reflects tactical decision making not only by the SC but also by his or her IC.

Perceived Workload. Participants' experience of the workload was assessed by asking participants (both ICs and SCs) to indicate the extent to which they felt they had a heavy workload (anchored by 1 = "very light workload" and 9 = "very heavy workload").

Results and Discussion

In this section, the results of the study will be presented together with a brief discussion of the implications of each set of results. A general discussion section follows in which the implications of the pattern of findings overall are considered.

First of all, results concerning the adequacy of the experimental manipulations are presented. This is followed by results concerning the relative performance under an Intent versus Action command style. Finally, results that might bear on psychological processes underlying performance across alternative command styles are presented, namely,

Table 18.2. *Means (SD) for IC Responses on Manipulation Check Items Across Action (n = 22) and Intent (n = 18) Command Style Conditions*

Manipulation Check Item	Action	Intent	t-Value
Encouraged to give general orders	2.1 (1.8)	7.4 (1.8)	8.75**
Actually gave general orders	4.6 (1.7)	7.2 (1.4)	4.85**
Felt it important to give general orders	4.6 (2.4)	6.3 (1.7)	2.46*

Note: 9-point scales.
* $p < .05$, ** $p < .01$ (one-tailed).

(a) the overall quality of strategic thought, (b) the amount of situation assessment, (c) the amount of tactical activity, and (d) the experienced workload.

Adequacy of the Manipulation of Command Style

Interpretation of Experimental Manipulation Instructions. IC participants' responses to questions directly assessing their interpretation of experimental instructions are presented in Table 18.2. As the table shows, ICs in the Intent command style condition reported that they knew they were encouraged to give more general orders, that they actually did give more general orders, and that it was more important that they give general orders to achieve a high performance score. It can be concluded that the manipulation of command style was experienced as planned.

Relative Amount of Strategic versus Tactical Cognitive Activity. The experimental instructions given to participants concerning the level of specificity of commands were such that ICs adopting an Action command style should spend more time in tactically oriented thought than ICs adopting an Intent command style. Furthermore, when ICs adopt an Intent command style, their SCs should spend more time in strategically oriented thought.

Self-reported time spent in various strategic and tactical-level cognitive activities is presented in Table 18.3. First, it is clear that ICs in the Intent condition paid more attention to strategic activities and significantly less attention to tactical activities than did ICs in the Action condition. Second, SCs in the Intent condition not only spent significantly more time engaging in strategic activities, they also spent slightly *more* time engaging in tactical activities compared with SCs in the Action condition. That is, when ICs command by specification of intent, (a) strategic-level thought increased, not only in commanders but also in subordinates,

Table 18.3. *Means (SD) for Estimates of Time Spent in Task Activities Provided by ICs in Action (n = 22) and Intent (n = 18) Conditions and SCs in Action (n = 44) and Intent (n = 36) Conditions*

Activity	ICs			SCs		
	Action	Intent	*t*-Value	Action	Intent	*t*-Value
Tactical thought						
Deciding number of appliances needed	7.1 (1.6)	4.2 (2.1)	4.74**	4.8 (2.6)	6.8 (1.6)	3.94**
Deciding which appliance to use	6.8 (1.8)	4.3 (2.5)	3.46**	4.9 (2.6)	6.4 (1.5)	3.01**
Strategic thought						
Deciding which fire front to prioritize	7.5 (1.1)	7.9 (1.2)	1.13	4.9 (2.3)	6.2 (1.7)	2.73*
Deciding which part of a fire to fight	7.3 (1.5)	7.7 (1.4)	0.90	5.8 (2.5)	6.4 (1.6)	1.27
Situation assessment						
Monitoring current wind direction	6.2 (2.2)	6.8 (1.7)	0.88	3.8 (2.1)	4.8 (1.5)	2.24*
Monitoring forecast wind direction	5.7 (2.4)	7.1 (1.7)	2.01*	N/A	N/A	N/A
Predicting future developments of fires	6.8 (2.1)	7.9 (0.9)	2.15*	4.5 (2.5)	5.7 (1.6)	2.36*

Notes: N/A indicates that role delineation prevented SCs from performing these actions. All items scaled: 1 = "no time at all," 9 = "most of my time."
* $p < .05$, ** $p < .00$ (two tailed).

and (b) tactical-level thought decreased in commanders but increased in subordinates. This latter finding suggests that although the total amount of cognitive work engaged in by ICs did not change across experimental conditions, the total amount of cognitive work engaged in by SCs was significantly greater under a command by Intent style. This latter finding is considered in greater detail later when the data on reported workload are presented.

In summary, the overall pattern of findings suggests that the experimental manipulations were sufficiently strong to achieve the intended changes in cognitive activities required in both IC and SC roles.

Team Performance

Distribution and Reliability of Performance Scores. Scores of overall team performance (value of landscape assets saved) on each of the two experimental trials were found to be normally distributed. Scores on these two experimental trials were found to be of reasonably high reliability ($r = 0.73$, $p < 0.01$), indicating that teams performed consistently across the two trials. Only the scores for the final experimental trial are used in the subsequent analyses because self-report data were collected only after the second experimental trial (to avoid introducing reactivity into task performance).

Comparison of Performance Under Intent versus Action Command Styles. A one-way ANOVA was used to investigate the difference in team performance scores on the second experimental trial across command style conditions. Teams in the Intent condition ($M = 91.92$, $SD = 2.50$) performed significantly better on the Networked Fire Chief task than did teams in the Action condition ($M = 88.97$, $SD = 3.37$), with $F(1, 39) = 9.55$, $p < 0.005$. The effect size (d) was 0.97 ($CI_{95\%} = 0.31$–1.63), indicating that the magnitude of the effect was quite large. Before presenting a more general discussion of the implications of these findings, results that potentially bear on psychological processes underlying this difference in overall performance are presented.

Quality of Strategic Decision Making

As indicated in the Method section, the overall quality of strategic decision making by the team was operationalized as the appropriateness of the priorities assigned to the different fires throughout the progression of the second experimental trial. This was measured by viewing replays of the corresponding Networked Fire Chief replay file. Some replay files were not saved and so could not be analyzed. Therefore, 32 teams were analyzed (19 in the Action command style condition and 13 in the Intent command style condition).

Teams in the Intent condition ($M = 21.4$, $SD = 3.2$) were judged to have a significantly higher quality of strategic decision making than did teams in the Action condition ($M = 16.5$, $SD = 3.6$), with $F(1, 31) = 15.78$, $p < 0.01$. To test the assumed importance of quality of strategic decisions for overall decision performance, a correlation was performed between quality of strategic decisions and team performance ($r = 0.62$, $p < .01$).

Overall, teams in the Intent command style condition made better-quality strategic decisions. That is, not only did both ICs and SCs working under an Intent command style spend more time engaging in strategic thought (as discussed earlier), at the team performance level the actual quality of such thought was also superior. This suggests that the more equal distribution of strategic responsibilities that was implemented by an Intent command style resulted in an improvement in the strategic capability of the team as a whole. Furthermore, such increased strategic capability led to more effective tactical behaviors, which in turn led to superior control of the simulated fires.

Amount of Situation Assessment

The results for self-reported time spent in cognitive activities associated with situation assessment were presented in Table 18.3. Overall, both ICs and SCs reported spending more time engaged in situation assessment activities under the Intent than under the Action command style condition. This finding suggests that one of the factors responsible for the overall performance gains under an Intent command style resides in the superior situation awareness that is possible when an Intent command style is employed.

Amount of Tactical Activity

As indicated in the Method section, the absolute amount of activity taken to limit the spread of fires (the outcome of tactical-level decision making) was assessed by the number of times appliances were moved from one location to another. Note that regardless of command style, ICs could only move appliances between bases; the amount of movement of appliances to fires at SC computer stations reflects not only the tactical decisions taken by the SC in relation to firefighting actions, but also those tactical decisions communicated to him by his or her IC.

The quantity of output across command style conditions is presented separately for IC and SC computer stations (see Table 18.4).

First, with respect to appliance movements from IC computer stations, as can be seen in Table 18.4, there were significantly more appliance movements under the Intent command style than under the Action command style. This indicates that ICs made more appliance deployments across base stations under an Intent command style, although it should be noted that overall there was minimal redeployment of appliances by ICs. The distribution of the number of appliance deployments indicates

Table 18.4. *Means (SD) for Number of Appliance Movements at IC Computer Stations Under Action (n = 22) and Intent (n = 18) Command Styles and at SC Computer Stations Under Action (n = 44) and Intent (n = 36) Command Styles*

	Action	Intent	F value
IC	9 (2)	11 (2)	2.66*
SC	124 (28)	141 (26)	2.91*

* $p < .01$ (two-tailed).

that some ICs, regardless of command style condition, made fewer than eight movements of appliances. This indicates that they probably did not get all eight helicopters out of the central base station and into use. This lack of usage of all eight helicopters occurred more frequently in the Action command style condition. Such underutilization can be expected to impair performance. Underutilization of resources in dynamic tasks has been identified as an "error behavior" by Dörner and Pfeiffer (1993). In fact, Dörner and Pfeiffer, using a somewhat similar firefighting microworld task, showed that stressed participants (stress induced by noise) more frequently forgot to distribute their firefighting resources at the beginning of the trial.

With respect to appliance movements from SC computer stations, there also was significantly greater movement of appliances under the Intent command style, suggesting that the overall *quantity* of output was higher by teams as a whole operating under an Intent command style. In order to investigate whether the amount of tactical activity was associated with improved performance, correlations were obtained to estimate the relationship between the amount of tactical activity (number of appliance movements) and overall performance at SC computer stations. Significant positive relationships were obtained under both the Intent ($r = 0.40$, $p < .01$) and Action ($r = 0.52$, $p < .01$) command styles. This suggests that regardless of the amount and quality of strategic (goal-related) decisions, it is best to minimize the amount of time any one appliance is idle.

This overall pattern of findings with respect to appliance usage can be best interpreted as indicating higher *productivity* under an Intent command style. Possible reasons for this increased productivity under an Intent command style are further discussed in the subsequent General Discussion section.

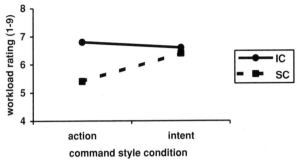

Figure 18.1 The effects of command style and team role on reported workload.

Perceived Workload

The distribution of self-reported workload across command style conditions for each role is presented in Figure 18.1. There was a trend toward an interaction between command style condition and team role with respect to reported workload ($F(1, 109) = 2.59$, $p = 0.11$), with SCs' ratings of workload being identical to ICs' ratings of workload in the Intent style condition, but with SCs' ratings of workload being lower than ratings of ICs in the Action command style condition.

SCs in the Action command style condition did not experience as high a workload as SCs in the Intent condition (Action: $M = 5.4$, $SD = 2.1$; Intent: $M = 6.4$, $SD = 2.0$; $t = 2.18$, $p < 0.05$). The most plausible account of why workload ratings may not have been as high for SCs in the Action command style condition as in the Intent condition is that in the Action condition SCs were restricted to simply implementing commands for specific actions (such as "Use the truck at coordinate 150-60 to put out the fire at 50-40"), with each such command requiring a *single* action. In contrast, SCs in the Intent command style condition, by being given the opportunity to translate any one Intent communication into subgoals (such as extinguish the fire centered around 50-40), were more likely to have to make a *series* of related actions.

It is apparent from the overall pattern in these results for cognitive workload that command style affects the distribution of workload among team members. It was somewhat unexpected that ICs failed to report a higher workload under an Action command style than under an Intent command style. In the Action command style condition ICs not only had to assess the situation and generate an intention, they also had to decide upon the appropriate action and then, finally, to communicate these actions to the appropriate SC (constituting a greater workload than merely having to communicate the intention itself). However, contrary to this expectation, ICs' mean workload ratings were *not* significantly different across command style conditions (Action: $M = 6.8$, $SD = 1.5$; Intent: $M = 6.6$, $SD = 1.3$; $t = 0.40$, ns).

The most plausible explanation for this overall pattern of findings with respect to workload is that under both command style conditions ICs were able to work to a preferred upper limit of cognitive workload, whereas SCs were able to perform at such a preferred upper limit of cognitive workload only under an Intent command style. As discussed further subsequently, this supports the interpretation that under an Action style condition, the cognitive capacities of subordinates were underutilized.

General Discussion

The major findings of this study are that under an Intent command style (a) overall performance is higher; (b) the quality of strategic thought is higher; (c) more time is spent on activities relating to the development and maintenance of situation awareness; (d) there is greater productivity at the tactical level; and (e) a higher level of cognitive workload can be assigned to subordinates.

In the introduction to this chapter, we discussed several factors that might confer an advantage on an Action command style and several factors that might confer an advantage on an Intent command style. The data obtained in this study can now be examined for evidence for the operation of each of these factors.

With respect to those factors that might confer an advantage on an Action command style, it was suggested that subordinates may misunderstand a commander's intent when commands are communicated in the form of intentions. The finding that the quality of strategic behavior of the team as a whole (adequacy of prioritization of fires) was higher under an Intent command style suggests that subordinates did not have difficulty interpreting the intentions communicated to them by their commander.

Another factor that was suggested as possibly conferring an advantage on an Action command style was that subordinates were likely to make errors in translating intentions into appropriate actions by not being fully informed about all aspects of the task (the big picture). Although we did not directly assess the level of overall understanding of the task, the following observations suggest that lack of such an understanding by subordinates did not constitute a source of error. First, under either an Action or an Intent command style, there was little advantage in subordinates (SCs) having detailed knowledge of the behavior of fires in the alternate sector. Second (and more importantly), subordinates under both command style conditions engaged in a substantial amount of situational assessment activity, and this was also higher under the Intent condition. From this one can conclude that (a) subordinates did seek some understanding of the big picture and (b) subordinates were more inclined to do so under an Intent than under an Action command style. From this we conclude that under an Intent command style, rather than making increased numbers of errors because of an inadequate understanding of the task as a whole, subordinates actually achieved a superior understanding of the overall task and accordingly made fewer errors.

With respect to those factors that were considered likely to confer an advantage on an Intent command style, the possibility was raised that in an Action style commanders are more likely to be cognitively overloaded and therefore represent a restrictive bottleneck with respect to the implementation of action. The pattern of findings suggests that commanders were in fact cognitively overloaded and did constitute a bottleneck. First, there is evidence that persons in the commander role were working to the limit of their cognitive capacity under both command style conditions, with the amount of tactical activity able to be delegated to subordinates (i.e., as appliance movements) being appreciably less under an Action command style. Secondly, there is evidence that under an Action command style, the full cognitive capacities of subordinates were underutilized, leading to the conclusion that the cognitive demands on commanders constituted a bottleneck. That is, command by communication of intent appeared to allow for a more equal distribution not only of responsibility for strategic input, but also of workload more generally.

A second factor that was discussed as being likely to confer an advantage on an Intent command style was that such a style allowed the commander to remain focused on events at a longer time scale and a more global spatial scale, without the inefficiencies that inevitably arise in having to oscillate continually between scale levels. Such oscillations between time scales and between spatial scales would impair a commander's ability to develop, and subsequently to maintain and revise, an overall understanding of the situation as a whole (i.e., an issue of adequacy of situation awareness). The pattern of findings with respect to activities involved in developing and maintaining overall situation awareness indicates that commanders were able to spend more time engaging in such global activity under an Intent than under an Action command style. As the quality of all decision-making activity, but especially strategic-level activity, is limited by the level of accuracy and adequacy of a commander's situational understanding, the performance advantage of an Intent style can in part be attributed to better overall situation awareness being achieved by commanders when they do not have to switch focus to a shorter time scale or to a smaller spatial scale.

The possibility was also raised that an Intent command style allows the expertise and local knowledge of subordinates to be more fully exploited. The increased quality of strategic decision making of the team as a whole, the greater involvement of subordinates in situation assessment activity, and the greater involvement of subordinates in strategic-level thought under an Intent command style suggest that subordinates did in fact have considerable expertise with respect to the overall demands of the task and that they exercised such expertise when given the opportunity to do so (i.e., under an Intent command style). This pattern of findings also suggests that under an Intent style, subordinates were able to exercise initiative as unexpected opportunities presented themselves or problems arose.

In summary, the overall pattern of findings indicates that an Intent-based command style affords substantial performance advantages over an Action-based command style with respect to a hierarchically structured team's ability to exercise control of a distributed D3M task. An Intent-based command style, by allowing for a more even distribution of decision-making responsibility across rank in the hierarchy, results in a more equal distribution of cognitive workload, leading to greater overall team productivity.

The different command styles investigated in our study were each created by the specific instructions given to participants in the role of commander in the two different experimental conditions. Such a situation is analogous to that brought about in real-world settings by commanders being indoctrinated in a particular approach to command through an organization's instruction and training programs. Presumably commanders exhibit individual differences in their preference for one command style rather than the other. The possible impact of such individual differences in command style preferences on commander effectiveness seems to be a topic for further investigation. Other important research questions include the extent to which command style is trainable and the extent to which the optimal command style depends on specific characteristics of the decision environment.

References

Ackerman, P. L., & Kanfer, R. (1993). Integrating laboratory and field study for improving selection: Development of a battery for predicting air traffic controller success. *Journal of Applied Psychology, 78*(3), 413–432.

Artman, H. (1998a). Co-operation and situation awareness within and between time-scales in dynamic decision making. In Y. Waern (Ed.), *Cooperative process management: Cognition and information technology* (pp. 117–130). London: Taylor & Francis.

Artman, H. (1998b). Team decision making and situation awareness in military command and control. In Y. Waern (Ed.), *Co-operative process management: Cognition and information technology* (pp. 55–68). London: Taylor & Francis.

Artman, H. (1999). Situation awareness and co-operation within and between hierarchical units in dynamic decision making. *Ergonomics, 42*(11), 1404–1417.

Beach, L. R., & Lipshitz, R. (1996). Why a new perspective on decision making is needed. In L. R. Beach (Ed.), *Decision making in the workplace: A unified perspective* (pp. 21–31). Mahwah, NJ: Erlbaum.

Bobevski, I., & McLennan, J. (1998). The telephone counseling interview as a complex, dynamic, decision process: A self-regulation model of counselor effectiveness. *Journal of Psychology, 132*(1), 47–60.

Brehmer, B. (1991). Organization for decision making in complex systems. In J. Rassmussen, B. Brehmer, & J. Leplat (Eds.), *Distributed decision making: Cognitive models for cooperative work* (pp. 335–347). Chichester, U.K.: Wiley.

Brehmer, B. (1992). Dynamic decision making: Human control of complex systems. *Acta Psychologica, 81*(3), 211–241.

Brehmer, B. (1995a). *Distributed decision making in dynamic environments.* Unpublished manuscript, Swedish Defence Research Institute.

Brehmer, B. (1995b). *Dynamic decision making: A paradigm for the study of problems of command and control.* Unpublished manuscript, Swedish Defence Research Institute.

Brehmer, B. (2000). Dynamic decision making in command and control. In C. McCann & R. Pigeau (Eds.), *The human in command: Exploring the modern military experience* (pp. 233–248). New York: Plenum.

Brehmer, B., & Dörner, D. (1993). Experiments with computer-simulated microworlds: Escaping both the narrow straits of the laboratory and the deep blue sea of the field study. *Computers in Human Behaviour, 9*(2–3), 171–184.

Cannon-Bowers, J. A., Salas, E., & Converse, S. (1993). Shared mental models in expert team decision making. In N. J. Castellan (Ed.), *Individual and group decision making: Current issues* (pp. 221–246). Hillsdale, NJ: Erlbaum.

Crecine, J. P., & Salomone, M. D. (1989). Organisation theory and C3. In S. E. Johnson & A. H. Levis (Eds.), *Science of command and control* (Vol. 2, pp. 45–57). Fairfax, VA: AFCEA International Press.

Department of the Navy (U.S.). (1995). *Naval command and control* (Naval Doctrine Publication 6). Washington, DC: Department of the Navy.

Dörner, D. (1991). The investigation of action regulation in uncertain and complex situations. In J. Rassmussen, B. Brehmer, & J. Leplat (Eds.), *Distributed decision making: Cognitive models for cooperative work* (pp. 349–355). Chichester, U.K.: Wiley.

Dörner, D., & Pfeiffer, E. (1993). Strategic thinking and stress. *Ergonomics, 36*(11), 1345–1360.

Flin, R. (1996). *Sitting in the hot seat: Leaders and teams for critical incident management.* Chichester, U.K.: Wiley.

Funke, J. (1991). Solving complex problems: Exploration and control of complex systems. In R. J. Sternberg & P. A. Frensch (Eds.), *Complex problem solving: Principles and mechanisms* (pp. 185–222). Hillsdale, NJ: Erlbaum.

Ley, T. (1999). *The leader's intent and strategic decision making in a distributed dynamic decision task.* Unpublished masters thesis, Technische Universitat Darmstadt, Germany.

Lipshitz, R., & Strauss, O. (1997). Coping with uncertainty: A naturalistic decision-making analysis. *Organisational Behaviour and Human Decision Processes, 69*(2), 149–163.

Luttwak, E. N. (1987). *Strategy: the logic of war and peace.* Cambridge, MA: Harvard University Press.

Ministry of Defence (U.K.). (1995). *Command* (Army Doctrine Publication Volume 2). London: Chief of the General Staff, Ministry of Defence.

Omodei, M. M., Taranto, P., & Wearing, A. J. (1999). *Networked Fire Chief* (Version 1.0) [computer program]. Melbourne: La Trobe University.

Omodei, M. M., & Wearing, A. J. (1995). The Fire Chief microworld generating program: An illustration of computer-simulated microworlds as an experimental paradigm for studying complex decision making behaviour. *Behaviour Research Methods, Instruments and Computers, 27*(3), 303–316.

Orasanu, J. (1995). *Evaluating team situation awareness through communication.* Paper presented at the international conference on experimental analysis and measurement of situation awareness, Daytona Beach, FL.

Orasanu, J., & Connolly, T. (1993). The reinvention of decision making. In G. A. Klein, J. Orasanu, R. Calderwood, & C. E. Zsambok (Eds.), *Decision making in action: Models and methods* (pp. 3–20). Norwood, NJ: Ablex.

Orasanu, J., & Salas, E. (1993). Team decision making in complex environments. In G. A. Klein & J. Orasanu (Eds.), *Decision making in action: Models and methods* (pp. 328–343). Norwood, NJ: Ablex.

Pigeau, R., & McCann, C. (1998). *Redefining command and control.* Paper presented at The Human in Command: NATO RTA Workshop, Kingston, Ontario, Canada.

Rasmussen, J. (1983). Skills, rules and knowledge; signals, signs and symbols and other distinctions in human performance models. *IEEE Transactions on Systems, Man and Cybernetics, 13*(3), 257–266.

Salas, E., Prince, C., Baker, D. P., & Shrestha, L. (1995). Situation awareness in team performance: Implications for measurement and training. Special Issue: Situation Awareness. *Human Factors, 37*(1), 123–136.

Schmitt, J. F., & Klein, G. A. (1998). Fighting in the fog: Dealing with battlefield uncertainty. *Human Performance in Extreme Environments, 3*(1), 57–63.

Svenmark, P. (1998). *Local coordination in dynamic environments: Theories and coordination support.* Linkoping, Sweden: Linkopings University.

Waern, Y. (1998). Background. In Y. Waern (Ed.), *Co-operative process management: cognition and information technology* (pp. 1–6). London: Taylor & Francis.

Weaver, J. L., Bowers, C. A., Salas, E., & Cannon-Bowers, J. A. (1995). Networked simulations: New paradigms for team performance research. *Behaviour Research Methods, Instruments, & Computers, 27*(1), 12–24.

19 How Can You Tell If Someone Is an Expert? Performance-Based Assessment of Expertise

James Shanteau, David J. Weiss, Rickey P. Thomas, and Julia Pounds

ABSTRACT

The definition of *expert performance* is obviously vital to any analysis of expertise. If external standards exist, then the definition is straightforward: The correct answers determine expert performance. Unfortunately, external standards seldom exist in domains requiring expertise; that is why experts are needed in the first place. The purposes of this chapter are (1) to review traditional methods for defining expert performance in the absence of external standards and (2) to present a promising new approach for assessing expert performance (labeled CWS for Cochran-Weiss-Shanteau). Eight traditional procedures are reviewed, along with discussions of their advantages and disadvantages. Then CWS is presented, along with a technical elaboration. The CWS approach is illustrated through reanalyses of three previous studies of experts. A study of physicians revealed that expert diagnostic skill was related to both discrimination and consistency – the two components of CWS. In a study of agricultural judges, the sensitivity of CWS was demonstrated by its ability to distinguish between livestock judges with different subspecialties. In a study of auditors, CWS correctly linked group differences in expertise (experts vs. novices) to information relevance. These reanalyses demonstrate that CWS offers new insights into the nature of expertise.

Preparation of this chapter was supported, in part, by Grant 96-12126 from the *National Science Foundation*, by Grant N00014-00-1-0769 from the *Office of Naval Research*, and by Grant 98-G-026 from the *Federal Aviation Administration* in the Department of Transportation.

Further information about the studies and analytic procedures described in this chapter can be found at the CWS website: www.ksu.edu/psych/edu

We wish to thank Ward Edwards, Brian Friel, Alice Isen, and Gary McClelland for their insightful comments on prior versions of the chapter. We also wish to acknowledge the feedback from various anonymous reviewers who have helped us clarify a number of concepts.

CONTENTS

Background

Although behavioral studies of expertise have been conducted for over a century (Shanteau, 1999), there remains an unanswered question: What is the definition of *expert performance?* If there are correct answers (a *gold standard*), the solution is straightforward – the correct answers define expert performance.

This validity-based approach is compelling in its simplicity. Unfortunately, it is problematic in its application. The problem is that experts are needed precisely in those domains where correct answers are least likely to exist (Gigerenzer, Todd, & the ABC Research Group, 1999; Shanteau, 1995). Indeed, if we have the correct answers, why do we need an expert?

The purpose of this chapter is to explore the application of a novel approach to assessing expert performance labeled CWS for *Cochran-Weiss-Shanteau*. The measure is based on the behavior of would-be experts, that is, their performance in the domain. In effect, the judgments of an individual are used to evaluate their expertise.

The chapter is organized into five sections: First, we review approaches used in previous research to define expert performance.

Second, we develop our proposed approach to evaluation of expert performance. Third, we apply this approach to several previous studies involving experts. Fourth, we describe some conditions that should be considered when applying CWS. Finally, we offer conclusions and final comments.

Previous Approaches

Investigators have used many approaches to define expert performance in previous studies. Eight of these traditional approaches are described here. We also consider the advantages and, more important, the disadvantages of each approach.

Experience

Many prior studies used number of years of job-relevant experience as a surrogate for expertise. That is, participants with more years of experience were classified as *experts*, whereas others with less experience were labeled as *novices*. In general, this approach seems reasonable. Presumably, no one can work as a professional for any length of time if he or she is incompetent.

Unfortunately, although experts normally have considerable experience, the converse may not be true. Many professionals with years of experience never become experts. Such individuals may work alongside top experts, but they never meet the standards required for true expertise.

In a study of grain judges, for instance, Trumbo, Adams, Milner, and Schipper (1962) reported that experience was uncorrelated with accuracy of wheat grading. Instead, they found a different trend: Judges with more experience overrated the quality of the grains – an early and interesting form of "grade inflation." Similarly, Goldberg (1968) asked clinical psychologists with varying amounts of experience to diagnose psychiatric patients. He found no relation between years of experience and accuracy; however, the confidence of clinicians in their diagnoses did increase with experience.

Although there are certainly instances of positive correlations between experience and expertise, there is little reason to expect this relation to apply universally. At best, experience is an uncertain predictor of degree of expertise. At worst, experience may reflect years on the job – and little more.

Accreditation

In many professions, individuals receive some form of accreditation or title as a certification of their skill. For instance, doctors may be *board-certified specialists* and university faculty may become *full professors*. It is safe to say that a certified specialist is more likely to perform as an expert than someone who is not certified.

The problem with accreditation is that it is often tied more to time on the job than to professional performance. This can be particularly true in structured bureaucracies such as the military. The rank of photo interpreters (PI), for instance, may range from sergeant to major. Yet, the performance of PIs is often unrelated to their rank (T. Levitt, personal communication, 1992).

Another example comes from the Israeli Air Force, where lead pilots in combat are identified by skill, not rank, that is, a general may be following a captain. This has been cited as one reason for the superiority of the Israelis against Arab Air Forces (where lead pilots are usually determined by rank, as they are in most countries). The Israelis recognized that skill is not always reflected by formal certification (R. Lipshitz, personal communication, 1995).

Another problem with accreditation is the *ratchet-up effect*: People often move up the certification ladder but seldom down. That is, once certified, the person is accredited for life. Even if his or her skill level suffers a serious decline, the title or rank remains. (Just ask students about the teaching ability of some full professors.)

Peer Identification

A method commonly used by many researchers (including the present authors) is to rely on identification of expert performers by those working in the field. That is, professionals are asked whom they would consider to be an expert. When there is some agreement on the identity of such individuals, they are labeled experts.

In a study of livestock judges, for example, Phelps (1977) asked professional animal scientists whom they considered to be the best. From their responses, she identified four livestock judges to be the experts in her investigation (this study is described further subsequently). Similarly, Nagy (1981) relied on peer identification to identify experts in her study of personnel selectors.

Absent other means of assessing expertise, peer identification is a good strategy to follow. It is unlikely that others working in a field will

Table 19.1. *Between-Expert Reliability Values*

Higher Levels of Performance		Lower Levels of Performance	
Aided Decisions	Competent	Restricted	Random
Weather Forecasters	Livestock Judges	Clinical Psychologists	Stockbrokers
$r = .95$	$r = .50$	$r = .40$	$r = .32$
Auditors	Grain Inspectors	Pathologists	Polygraphers
$r = .76$	$r = .60$	$r = .55$	$r = .33$

Note: The values cited in this table (from left to right) were drawn from the following studies: Stewart, Roebber, and Bosart (1997), Phelps and Shanteau (1978), Goldberg and Werts (1966), Slovic (1969), Kida (1980), Trumbo et al. (1962), Einhorn (1974), and Lykken (1979).

all identify the same wrong person as an expert. If they agree, it seems safe to assume that the agreed-upon person probably is an expert.

The problem with this approach is the *popularity effect*: Someone who is better known or more popular with his or her peers is likely to be identified as an expert. Meanwhile, someone outside the peer group is unlikely to be viewed as an expert – although that person may be on the cutting edge of new insights. Indeed, those who make new discoveries in a domain are frequently out of step with their peers at the time of their breakthroughs (Gardner, 1957). Thus, peer identification is more likely to identify yesterday's expertise than tomorrow's expertise.

Between-Expert Reliability

In seminal research on expertise, Einhorn (1972, 1974) argued that agreement between experts is a necessary condition. That is, experts should agree with each other (also see Ashton, 1985). If they do not, this suggests that some would-be experts are not what they claim to be.

To examine this argument, Table 19.1 lists between-expert correlations from eight published studies. The four categories correspond to a classification of task difficulty proposed by Shanteau (1999). Two domains are listed for each category, with the reliability values given as correlations. For example, the average correlation for weather forecasters (a decision-aided task) is quite high at .95, whereas the average *r* for stockbrokers (an unaided task) is low at .32. As predicted from Shanteau's classification, the correlations increase with more structured tasks.

To be sure, between-person reliability appears to be a compelling property for expertise. After all, we feel confused when two (or more)

Table 19.2. *Within-Expert Reliability Values*

Higher Levels of Performance		Lower Levels of Performance	
Aided Decisions	Competent	Restricted	Random
Weather Forecasters $r = .98$	Livestock Judges $r = .96$	Clinical Psychologists $r = .44$	Stockbrokers $r = < .40$
Auditors $r = .90$	Grain Inspectors $r = .62$	Pathologists $r = .50$	Polygraphers $r = .91$

Note: The values cited in this table (from left to right) were drawn from the following studies: Stewart, et al. (1997), Phelps and Shanteau (1978), Goldberg and Werts (1966), Slovic (1969), Kida (1980), Trumbo et al. (1962), Einhorn (1974), and Raskin and Podlesny (1979).

doctors disagree about a medical diagnosis. When doctors agree, on the other hand, we feel more comfortable with the agreed-upon diagnosis.

The problem with between-expert reliability is that agreement can result from artificial consensus, for example, groupthink (Janis, 1972). There are many historic cases where the best course of action was not identified by a group of experts because they focused initially on an inferior alternative, such as Bay of Pigs. Thus, a group of experts may agree – and they all may be wrong.

Within-Expert Reliability

Einhorn (1972, 1974) also argued that intraperson reliability is necessary for expertise. That is, an expert's judgments should be consistent from time to time. In contrast, inconsistency would be prima facie evidence that the person is not behaving as an expert.

To examine consistency, Table 19.2 lists within-person consistency values for the eight domains listed in Table 19.1. The average consistency r for weather forecasters is quite high at .98, whereas the average consistency for stockbrokers is low at less than .40.

As expected from the Shanteau (1989) classification, more structured tasks produce higher consistency values than unstructured tasks. To a first approximation, therefore, it appears that within-expert reliability provides a good correspondence to the performance levels of experts.

The shortcoming in this approach is that high consistency can be obtained by following a simple but incorrect rule. As long as the rule is followed precisely, a person's decisions will exhibit high consistency. By answering "yes" and "no" to alternating questions, for instance, one can be perfectly reliable. But such answers would generally be inappropriate. Thus, within-expert reliability is necessary – an expert could hardly behave randomly – but it is not sufficient.

Subject Matter Experts

In many fields, the decisions of one or more *superexperts* become(s) recognized as the equivalent of a gold standard. That is, the answers of these preidentified top experts become the de facto standard for evaluating the performance of others. In effect, the decisions of subject matter experts (SMEs) become the correct answer.

Not surprisingly, this approach is commonly used when no certifiably correct answers exist. For example, performance of air traffic controllers (ATCs) is evaluated by SMEs, that is, an ATC operator is certified based on how closely he or she matches the judgments of an SME. Similarly, in accounting, standard practice is established by a committee of SMEs.

Clearly, SMEs are often needed. For example, our empirical studies of experts have depended on input from SMEs in the planning and interpretation stages of research. Similarly, SMEs are essential for feedback on new procedures, equipment, and so on. There is an obvious circularity, however, in having one expert certify the performance of another expert. Among other problems, this can lead to gatekeeping, whereby senior SMEs keep out (demote) "young turks" who may have new ideas. Thus, SMEs can retard progress in a field, for example, by slowing adoption of new ideas.

Another difficulty is that reliance on SMEs confuses subjective and objective standards. One example occurs in food tasting panels, where trained tasters are often viewed as being "just as good as a machine." When the senior author questioned such claims, he was told that unreliability and lack of consensus are not issues with trained panelists. In effect, defining SMEs' judgments as the gold standard solved the problem of evaluating expertise. Clearly, such claims need to be tested.

Factual Knowledge

In many studies of skilled problem solving or game playing, expert performance has been identified using tests of factual knowledge. For example, Chi (1978) used knowledge about dinosaurs to separate children into experts and novices. Similarly, baseball experts have been identified using a test of knowledge about the rules of the game.

Knowledge of relevant facts is clearly necessary for expertise. Someone who does not know the facts about a domain will be unable to make competent decisions. Yet knowledge alone is seldom sufficient to establish that someone has expertise. For example, knowledge of the rules of baseball is not enough to know how to play a particular position, or to pitch a curve ball, or to manage a team in the bottom of the ninth inning. Each of these skills requires more than knowing what the facts are. They also require an understanding of what to do with the facts.

Another problem is knowing which facts to apply in a given situation. As one expert livestock judge put it, "Expertise lies in knowing when to follow the rules – and when not to." In most domains, that is the hard part for experts.

Creation of Experts

In certain special contexts, it is possible to create experts through extended training and practice. This approach has significant advantages, including the ability to study the development of expertise longitudinally. Moreover, the skills learned are under direct control of the researchers.

Chase used this approach to create a short-term memory *digit-span expert* (Chase & Ericsson, 1981). A student, who was a track athlete, learned to translate groups of digits into running times for various distances. When asked to retrieve the digits, the student recalled them in clusters tied to running. Based on such strategies, the student was able to break the old record for a digit span of 18. His new world record – over 80! (Other students have since pushed the record beyond 100.)

Expert performance can be created in this way for specific tasks, such as playing computer games or running a simulated microworld. Most realms of expertise, however, require a broad range of skills based on years of training and experience. For instance, it takes 15 to 20 years of practice to become a livestock judge. Obviously, this level of expertise cannot be simulated by working with students for a few months. Still, the creation of experts offers a promising approach that should be explored further.

The CWS Approach

As the preceding survey shows, many approaches have been used to define expertise. However, each of these approaches has one (or more) serious flaws; no generally acceptable technique exists at this time. To address this need, the two senior authors developed a novel approach for assessing expert performance. They combined two measures, each of which is a necessary but not sufficient condition for expertise, into a single index.

First, Weiss and Shanteau argued that *discrimination* is necessary for expertise (also see Hammond, 1996). The ability to differentiate between similar, but not identical, cases is a hallmark of expert performance; top experts make distinctions that novices miss. Second, they followed Einhorn's (1974) suggestion that within-person *consistency* is necessary for expertise; someone who cannot repeat his or her judgment of a case is not behaving as an expert.

Following a formulation used by Cochran (1943) in a different context, these two concepts are combined into an index using a ratio. The measure of *discrimination* (more is better) is divided by a measure of *inconsistency* (less is better). This ratio thus provides a descriptive index of degree of expertise, where bigger is better. The ratio has been labeled CWS (for Cochran-Weiss-Shanteau).

The CWS approach can be applied by asking would-be experts to judge a series of stimulus cases; this allows for assessment of their discrimination ability. In addition, at least some cases are repeated; this allows for assessment of their consistency. These two measures are combined by a ratio to yield the CWS value. The ratio can then be used to assess whether someone is behaving more (high value) or less (low value) like an expert.

Technical Issues

There are five technical issues involving CWS that deserve elaboration. For a more detailed discussion of these issues, see Weiss and Shanteau (submitted).

First, the CWS index could be computed in a variety of ways in addition to a ratio, for example, as a difference score. Alternatively, discrimination and consistency could be reported separately, without combining them into an index. The goal behind our approach was to summarize the tradeoff between two inconsistent entities, discrimination and consistency, in a rigorous quantitative fashion. Ratios are commonly used in such situations, such as price/quality ratio, speed/accuracy tradeoff, and cost/benefit ratio. We view CWS in a similar light. However, we also acknowledge that other analytic rules may have value in some settings.

Second, any measure of dispersion can be used to measure discrimination and consistency. There are three common measures of dispersion: variance (mean squares), standard deviation (square root of variance), and mean absolute deviation (MAD). Although any of these might work, we use variances as our default option. That is, we estimate discrimination as the variance between responses to different stimuli; larger variances imply greater discrimination. Similarly, we estimate consistency as the variance between responses to repeated stimuli; smaller variances imply greater consistency. Statisticians have traditionally used variances to evaluate the precision of measures (Grubbs, 1973). Further, a ratio of variances is an asymptotically efficient estimator (I. R. Goodman, personal communication, 1999). Another consideration is that the Schumann–Bradley (1959) procedure can be used to determine whether two CWS ratios are significantly different (see the example in the next section).

Third, computing CWS as a ratio of variances, of course, is parallel to the *F*-ratio commonly used in analysis of variance (ANOVA) for statistical tests. However, our use of a variance ratio is different in at least four respects: (1) CWS is a measurement instrument to evaluate individuals or conditions. We have no interest in using the variance ratio to test significance, for example, between treatments in an experiment. (2) The application of CWS is restricted to a particular set of stimuli in a specific domain. Thus, CWS cannot be used to compare responses of different stimuli sets or across different domains. In contrast, the *F*-test is designed to do both. (3) CWS makes no assumptions about the underlying distributions of responses or their properties. ANOVA, in contrast, rests on assumptions such as normality and independence of errors. (4) The concept of a CWS ratio (discrimination/consistency) can be extended to any level of response measure. For instance, CWS can be computed for categorical, classification, or nominal cases (Weiss & Shanteau, submitted).

Fourth, CWS is defined as a ratio with no other scaling required. There are conditions, however, in which a transformation of the ratio might be appropriate. When we applied CWS to response times for ATCs (Friel, Thomas, Raacke, & Shanteau, 2001), there was a strong correlation between means and variances. In such situations, the solution to the problem of homoscedasticity is to apply a square root transformation (Winer, 1971). This, of course, leaves the rank orders of the CWS scores unchanged. But it improves the distributional properties of the ratio.

Finally, although the correct gold standard answers are traditionally held up as the ultimate criteria, there may be circumstances in which CWS can actually outperform a gold standard. One example is ATC, where preventing airplanes from getting too close together (*separation errors*) is recognized as a gold standard. Although professional ATCs rarely commit such errors, there are still differences in performance in terms of efficiency, time, and so on. CWS has proved to be sensitive to these differences in performance, even when there were no errors. In other words, CWS is capable of assessing levels of expert performance beyond the point at which (because of ceiling/floor effects) gold standards are no longer useful (Friel et al., 2001).

Reanalyses of Previous Research

In this section, we illustrate CWS by applying the approach to three previous studies. The research in each case was designed to study a substantive problem involving experts. The use of CWS provides important supplementary information that advances the goals of each project.

Medical Diagnosis

Data from a study of medical diagnosis by Skånér, Strender, and Bring (1998) illustrates how CWS can be applied to evaluate expert performance. Twenty-seven Swedish general practitioners (GPs) judged the probability of heart failure in 45 case vignettes. Unknown to the GPs, five of the cases were presented twice. Based on real cases of chronic fatigue, they provided patient-specific information on age, gender, lung sounds, cardiac rhythm, heart rate, and heart/lung x-rays, and so on.

For each vignette, GPs rated the probability of heart failure using a graphic rating scale ranging from "totally unlikely" to "certain"; the responses were later converted to 0–100 values. The results of the original study revealed wide differences across GPs. Despite extensive analyses, the authors were unable to explain this large variation.

Graphical Analysis. The results for three GPs (identified by number) are graphed in Figure 19.1. The letters along the horizontal axis represent the five repeated cases. The open and filled points are the judgments for the two presentations. For instance, the first judgment of Case A by Doctor 12 is near 100; the second judgment is similar.

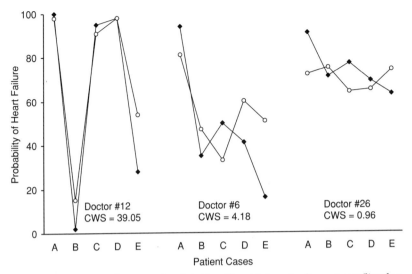

Figure 19.1 Judgments of probability of heart failure for five patients (listed as letters) by three GPs from Skånér et al. (1998). Open and closed points show judgments for two presentations. CWS values listed for each GP.

As can be seen, there is considerable variation among the three GPs. Still, each GP shows a distinctive pattern in terms of discrimination and reliability. Doctor 12 is highly discriminating (there are sizable differences among patients) and consistent (there is little difference between the first and second presentations). Doctor 6 shows some discrimination but lacks consistency (especially for patient E). Doctor 26 is more consistent but treats patients rather similarly; they are all viewed as having a moderately high chance of heart failure.

Based on these plots alone, we can gain considerable insight into the judgment abilities of the GPs. Doctors 12 and 26 are consistent, but one discriminates and the other does not. Doctors 12 and 6 show discrimination, but one is consistent and the other is not. We believe that without knowing anything further, most clients would prefer someone like Doctor 12, who makes clear discriminations in a consistent way. In effect, our proposed CWS measure quantifies this intuition.

CWS Analysis. The CWS ratios for the three doctors are given in Figure 19.1. To estimate discrimination, the variance between the means for the five patients was calculated; discrimination variances were 3377.60, 914.40, and 65.35 for Doctors 12, 6, and 26, respectively. To estimate consistency, the variance between the two responses for each case was calculated; consistency variances were 86.50, 218.80, and 68.30, respectively. When combined into a ratio, this led to CWS values of 39.05, 4.18, and .96, respectively, for the three GPs.

To compare two (or more) experts, CWS measures can be compared using a procedure developed by Schumann and Bradley (1959). This allows the researcher to determine whether one variance ratio is different from another (Weiss, 1985). This may be useful, for example, when CWS values vary widely and the goal is to determine if they are significantly different. For the three doctors in Figure 19.1, the Schumann–Bradley test revealed that the three GPs are significantly different from one another in two-tailed tests at the .05 level.

From these analyses, we can see that CWS analyses confirm the graphical analyses. That is, Doctor 12 appears to be a better diagnostician than Doctor 6, who in turn is better than Doctor 26. Moreover, we make these statements without any knowledge of the correct answers; in medicine, it is rare that gold standards exist at the time of initial diagnoses. That is why CWS is valuable: It provides a means of quantifying the observed patterns of behavior.

The results for the other 24 GPs can be categorized into three groups. Nine of the GPs had high discrimination and high consistency, as illustrated by Doctor 12. Thirteen of the GPs were discriminating but inconsistent, as illustrated by Doctor 6. The other five GPs revealed little discrimination, although they were fairly consistent, as illustrated by Doctor 26.

The latter pattern is particularly interesting, as it may illustrate a strategy of *defensive medicine*. By classifying all patients as needing further attention, GPs such as Doctor 26 may be trying to reduce false-negative diagnoses. The cost, of course, is an increase in the rate of false positives. The implications of this finding are presently being explored in collaboration with the original authors.

Caveats. Two caveats are necessary. First, these results are meaningful only if the five cases selected by Skånér et al. (1998) are representative real patients. We have no way of assessing this, although we have been assured that the cases are not atypical (Y. Skånér, personal communication, 2001). Thus, the usefulness of CWS depends on the selection of stimuli. Of course, the same applies to any other analytic procedure that might be used to examine expert performance.

Second, the CWS ratios are informative about rankings but should not be interpreted further. Specifically, we cannot say that Doctor 6 has four times the expertise of Doctor 26 or that the difference between Doctors 12 and 6 is greater than the difference between Doctors 6 and 26. What we can say is that the ordering of diagnostic ability for the three doctors is 12, 6, and 26.

Livestock Judging

The sensitivity of CWS was demonstrated in a reanalysis of a study of livestock judging. Phelps (1977) had four professional livestock judges evaluate 27 drawings of gilts (female pigs). An artist created the drawings to reflect a $3 \times 3 \times 3$ (Size $\times$ Breeding Potential $\times$ Meat Quality) factorial design. The judges independently made slaughter judgments (how good is the meat from the animal) and breeding judgments (how good is the animal for breeding) for each gilt. All stimuli were presented three times, although judges were not told about the repetition.

Two of the judges were nationally recognized swine experts and were quite familiar with gilts of the type shown in the drawings. The other two judges were nationally recognized cattle experts; they knew about swine judging but lacked day-to-day experience with gilts. The CWS ratio for each judge was computed separately and then averaged with that of the other similar judge. Based on the factorial structure of the stimuli, it was possible to compute CWS ratios for each of the three dimensions. The CWS values were computed separately for slaughter and breeding judgments.

The results appear in Figure 19.2. As can be seen, there is a substantial difference between the two sets of judges. For cattle judges, there is little difference in slaughter and breeding judgments; for both cases, meat quality dominated. For swine judges, meat quality also dominated for slaughter, but CWS values for breeding potential and meat quality are sizable for breeding judgments. This may reflect the unfamiliarity of breeding in swine by cattle judges. Swine judges, in contrast, focused on meat quality for slaughter judgments and breeding potential for breeding judgments.

It is worth emphasizing that the four judges were all highly skilled professionals. Nonetheless, the CWS approach proved sensitive to the differences between these two types of experts. This study also highlights the importance of examining task differences when evaluating expertise. In too many studies, the term expert is used generically, without reference to either the domain or the task within the domain. As illustrated in this study, even highly qualified (and highly paid) professionals

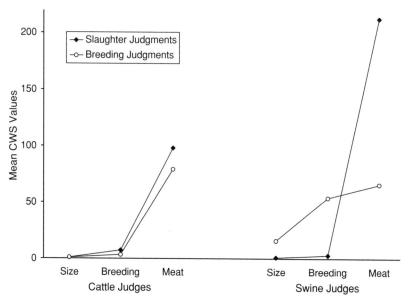

Figure 19.2 Mean CWS values for breeding and slaughter judgments of gilts (female pigs) by cattle specialists and swine specialists. Values are shown as a function of size, breeding potential, and meat quality. *Source*: Phelps (1977).

have skills that vary from task to task. Thus, we should not expect an expert on one task in one domain necessarily to behave expertly on another task.

Auditing Judgment

CWS has also proved sensitive to information relevance in distinguishing aggregate difference in expertise. Ettenson (1984; also see Ettenson, Shanteau, & Krogstad, 1987) had two groups of auditors evaluate a series of accounting cases described by a set of financial cues. One group of 15 expert auditors was recruited from Big Six accounting firms; they included audit seniors and partners with 4 to 25 years of experience. The other 15 novice auditors were advanced students in accounting.

For each case, participants were asked to make a Going Concern judgment. Based on feedback from a senior auditing associate, the financial cues were classified as either diagnostic (e.g., net income), *partially* diagnostic (aging of receivables), or nondiagnostic (prior audit results) for the Going Concern judgment. Discrimination was estimated from the mean-square variance for each financial cue. Consistency was estimated

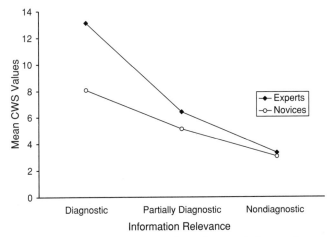

Figure 19.3 Mean CWS values for Going Concern judgments by expert and novice auditors as a function of three levels of relevance for financial information cues. *Source*: Ettenson, (1984).

from the average within-cell variance for each participant. In this way, separate CWS values could be estimated for the relevant, partially relevant, and irrelevant cues. The CWS values were then averaged for the two groups.

The results in Figure 19.3 show that CWS values for experts drop systematically as cue relevance declines. For novices, there is a similar but smaller decline. More important, the difference between experts and novices decreases as relevance drops. That is, the size of the difference between groups is smaller for less relevant cues. These results show that CWS can distinguish between levels of expertise for different groups – especially when cue information is highly relevant.

Comments

Six comments are appropriate concerning our use of CWS in these reanalyses. First, the stimuli in these studies were abstractions of real-world problems. In particular, the stimulus cues in each case were presented in static (nonchanging) formats, that is, there was no feedback or other dynamic changes over time. We are now applying CWS in real-time, dynamic environments. Thus far, the results are encouraging (see Friel et al., 2001).

Second, CWS was applied to individual performance in these studies. However, experts often work in teams. If teams are treated as decision-making units, then CWS can be used to evaluate each team. Preliminary efforts to apply CWS to team decision making have been positive.

Third, CWS assumes that there are real differences in the stimulus cases to be judged. If there are no such differences, then all judgments should be the same. If patients all have the same disease, for example, they presumably will all have the same diagnosis. The problem then is that it becomes impossible to distinguish between doctors with different diagnostic ability. Therefore, there must be differences in cases before CWS can evaluate expertise.

Fourth, it is possible for CWS to produce high values for a nonexpert who uses a consistent but incorrect rule. Suppose that all patients over age 70 receive one diagnosis and all patients under 70 receive another. Such a strategy would produce high CWS values, that is, consistent discriminations. But such a diagnostic strategy would clearly be inappropriate. One way around this "catch" is to ask judges to evaluate the same cases for different purposes, for example, diagnosis (what is it?) versus prognosis (what to do about it?). If the judgments in these two cases are the same, then the candidate is not behaving expertly – despite having a high CWS value.

Fifth, because CWS relies on repeated cases (to estimate consistency), it is necessary to take steps to prevent participants from memorizing responses and thus artificially inflating their consistency. This is potentially a problem if names or other unique identifiers are attached to the case descriptions. The solution, therefore, is to change such identifiers from replicate to replicate. Thus, a patient might be "Gerald" the first time, "William" the second time, and so forth. In our experience, such simple precautions effectively eliminate recall of previous responses.

Finally, it is important to emphasize that CWS does not determine which cues or responses to use in a study. As in any research, the dictates of good experimental design and sound methodology should guide the selection of independent and dependent variables. Once those decisions have been made, CWS can be applied to the data. However, the adage "garbage in, garbage out" applies.

Discussion

The present discussion of CWS leads to five conclusions: First, in our analyses, CWS has proved useful in evaluating expert performance.

If CWS continues to be successful, it may provide the answer to the long-standing question of how to evaluate expertise in the absence of an external standard.

Second, the success of CWS across different domains is noteworthy. Beyond medical diagnosis, livestock judging, and auditing, we have applied CWS to wine judging, personnel selection, food tasting, and ATC. To date, CWS has worked well in each domain.

Third, beyond evaluating expert performance, CWS has provided insights into the equipment and methods used by experts. In a simulation of ATC, for instance, we used CWS to track changes in operator performance as a function of monitor display sizes. In such cases, the purpose is to compare performance across conditions, not to evaluate expertise.

Fourth, by focusing on discrimination and consistency, CWS may have important implications for the selection and training of novices. It is an open question whether discrimination and consistency can be learned or whether novices should be preselected to already have these skills. Either way, CWS offers new perspectives on skill acquisition.

Finally, CWS outperforms existing approaches to evaluating expert performance. For instance, CWS and SME ratings were compared in a reanalysis of data from an ATC study conducted by the Federal Aviation Administration. SME ratings of ATC behavior were moderately sensitive to changes in the airspace environment. The effect sizes were considerably larger, however, when CWS was applied to the data (Thomas, Willems, Shanteau, Raacke, & Friel, 2001).

Conclusions

This chapter has shown that prior approaches to evaluating expertise have substantial flaws. The alternate CWS approach avoids most of these pitfalls. Reanalyses of previous studies demonstrated that (1) CWS can be applied to analyze the performance of experts in a variety of domains, (2) expert performance is tied to the two components of CWS – discrimination and consistency, (3) CWS is sensitive to task differences and to differences in subspecialty skills, and (4) differences between expert and novice performance can be distinguished by CWS – especially when cue relevance is taken into account. Some potential applications of CWS include evaluation of expert performance, selection and training of experts, and assessment of new methods/technologies. In summary, CWS is a promising new tool for studying expert behavior.

References

Ashton, A. H. (1985). Does consensus imply accuracy in accounting studies of decision making? *Accounting Review, 60,* 173–185.

Chase, W. G., & Ericsson, K. A. (1981). Skilled memory. In J. R. Anderson (Ed.), *Cognitive skills and their acquisition* (pp. 141–189). Hillsdale, NJ: Erlbaum.

Chi, M. T. H. (1978). Knowledge structures and memory development. In R. S. Siegler (Ed.), *Children's thinking: What develops?* (pp. 73–96). Hillsdale, NJ: Erlbaum.

Cochran, W. G., (1943). The comparison of different scales of measurement for experimental results. *Annals of Mathematical Statistics, 14,* 205–216.

Einhorn, H. J. (1972). Expert measurement and mechanical combination. *Organizational Behavior and Human Performance, 7,* 86–106.

Einhorn, H. J. (1974). Expert judgment: Some necessary conditions and an example. *Journal of Applied Psychology, 59,* 562–571.

Ettenson, R., (1984). *A schematic approach to the examination of the search for and use of information in expert decision making.* Doctoral dissertation, Kansas State University.

Ettenson, R., Shanteau, J., & Krogstad, J. (1987). Expert judgment: Is more information better? *Psychological Reports, 60,* 227–238.

Friel, B. M., Thomas, R. P., Raacke, J., & Shanteau, J. (2001). Utilitizing CWS to track the longitudinal development of expertise. In *2001 Proceedings of the Human Factors Society.* Minneapolis:.

Gardner, M. (1957). *Fads and fallacies in the name of science.* New York: Dover.

Gigerenzer, G., Todd, P. M., & the ABC Research Group. (1999). *Simple heuristics that make us smart.* New York: Oxford University Press.

Goldberg, L. R. (1968). Simple models or simple processes? Some research on clinical judgments. *American Psychologist, 23,* 482–496.

Goldberg, L. R., & Werts, C. E. (1966). The reliability of clinicians' judgments: A multitrait-multimethod approach. *Journal of Consulting Psychology, 30,* 199–206.

Grubbs, F. E. (1973). Errors of measurement, precision accuracy, and the statistical comparison of measuring instruments. *Technometrics, 15,* 53–66.

Hammond, K. R. (1996). *Human judgment and social policy.* New York: Oxford University Press.

Janis, I. L. (1972). *Victims of groupthink.* Boston: Houghton Mifflin.

Kida, T. (1980). An investigation into auditor's continuity and related qualification judgments. *Journal of Accounting Research, 22,* 145–152.

Lykken, D. T. (1979). The detection of deception. *Psychological Bulletin, 80,* 47–53.

Nagy, G. F. (1981). *How are personnel selection decisions made? An analysis of decision strategies in a simulated personnel selection task.* Doctoral dissertation, Kansas State University.

Phelps, R. H. (1977). *Expert livestock judgment: A descriptive analysis of the development of expertise.* Doctoral dissertation, Kansas State University.

Phelps, R. H., & Shanteau, J. (1978). Livestock judges: How much information can an expert use? *Organizational Behavior and Human Performance, 21,* 209–219.

Raskin, D. C., & Podlesny, J. A. (1979). Truth and deception: A reply to Lykken. *Psychological Bulletin, 86,* 54–59.

Schumann, D. E. W., & Bradley, R. A. (1959). The comparison of the sensitivities of similar experiments: Model II of the analysis of variance. *Biometrics, 15,* 405–416.

Shanteau, J. (1989). Psychological characteristics and strategies of expert decision makers. In B. Rohrmann, L. R. Beach, C. Vlek, & S. R. Watson (Eds.), *Advances in decision research* (pp. 203–215). Amsterdam: North Holland.

Shanteau, J. (1995). Expert judgment and financial decision making. In B. Green (Ed.), *Risky business* (pp. 16–32). Stockholm: University of Stockholm School of Business.

Shanteau, J. (1999). Decision making by experts: The GNAHM effect. In J. Shanteau, B. A. Mellers, & D. A. Schum (Eds.), *Decision science and technology: Reflections on the contributions of Ward Edwards* (pp. 105–130). Boston: Kluwer Academic.

Skånér, Y., Strender, L. E., & Bring, J. (1998). How do GPs use clinical information in their judgements of heart failure? A Clinical Judgment Analysis study. *Scandinavian Journal of Primary Health Care, 16,* 95–100.

Slovic, P. (1969). Analyzing the expert judge: A descriptive study of a stockbroker's decision processes. *Journal of Applied Psychology, 53,* 255–263.

Stewart, T. R., Roebber, P. J., & Bosart, L. F. (1997). The importance of the task in analyzing expert judgment. *Organizational Behavior and Human Decision Processes, 69,* 205–219.

Thomas, R. P., Willems, B., Shanteau, J., Raacke, J., & Friel, B. (2001). Measuring the performance of experts: An application to air traffic control. In *2001 Proceedings of Aviation Psychology*. Columbus, OH.

Trumbo, D., Adams, C., Milner, M., & Schipper, L. (1962). Reliability and accuracy in the inspection of hard red winter wheat. *Cereal Science Today, 7,* 62–71.

Weiss, D. J. (1985). SCHUBRAD: The comparison of the sensitivities of similar experiments. *Behavior Research Methods, Instrumentation, and Computers, 17,* 572.

Weiss, D. J., & Shanteau, J. (submitted). Performance-based assessment of expertise.

Winer, B. J. (1971). *Statistical principles in experimental design (second edition)*. New York: McGraw-Hill.

Part VI

Commentary

Michael E. Doherty

ABSTRACT

This commentary opens with a brief chronology of the major milestones in theory and research on judgment and decision making (JDM), followed by an expression of shared assumptions that characterize JDM researchers. Next comes a discussion of Jungermann's *The Two Camps on Rationality*, with an effort to see how the authors of the chapters in this book would fit into that dichotomy. After the characters and characteristics of the two opposing camps of *optimists* and *pessimists* are discussed, a third, over-arching category is proposed. I call that overarching category *realists*, that is, those who aspire to understand the nature of JDM processes, and I argue that *all* researchers in the JDM camp belong in that category. This commentary closes with what I see as seven themes coursing through the volume and through the field, and seven themes that I see as receiving sufficient emphasis neither in the volume nor in the field.

CONTENTS

In the late 1960s I conducted my first seminar in judgment and decision making, or JDM for short. The only appropriate source as a text was the 1967 Penguin paperback *Decision Making*, edited by Ward Edwards and Amos Tversky. The growth in the field can be measured by the explosion in the number and variety of JDM books in just a little over three decades. I could hardly list them here and have room for anything else!

This chapter is intended to set the chapters in the larger JDM context. It opens with a brief history of JDM, based in part on brief histories by Doherty (1993) and Hogarth (1993a) and on a longer one by Goldstein and Hogarth (1997). Next is a discussion of what I see as antithetic rhetorics and research styles that have characterized several major groups of researchers in the field. That discussion is an elaboration of Helmut Jungermann's 1983 work "The Two Camps on Rationality." The third major section of the chapter describes themes common to many chapters in the book, and briefly notes what I see as some topics that I believe should be investigated more widely in JDM.

A Brief History of JDM

The 1950s

One could begin the history of JDM in many places. The names Bernoulli, Savage, Thurstone, von Neumann and Morgenstern, Lewin, Swets, Tanner, and Birdsall come quickly to mind. They were important precursors, but it makes more sense to date the field to the middle 1950s, shortly *before* what is often cited as the inception of the *cognitive revolution* in 1956. The year 1954 was something of an *annus mirabilis* for JDM. It saw Ward Edwards's "The Theory of Decision Making," Paul Meehl's *Clinical versus Statistical Prediction,* and Savage's *The Foundations of Statistics.* Kenneth Hammond's "Probabilistic Functionalism and the Clinical Method" was published in 1955, as was Herbert Simon's "A Behavioral Model of Rational Choice." Hammond introduced what was to become Social Judgment Theory, and Simon introduced a concept that has remained of central importance across many areas in JDM, that is, *bounded rationality.* Duncan Luce and Howard Raiffa (1957) published

Games and Decisions: Introduction and Critical Survey, which has certainly had a profound impact on Decision Theory.

The 1960s

Researchers grappled with the relation between behavior and models of behavior, a problem that had been set by Edwards, Hammond, Meehl, and Simon for the JDM field in its first decade. The 1960s produced such widely cited works such as Clyde Coombs's (1964) *A Theory of Data*, Paul Hoffman's "The Paramorphic Representation of Clinical Judgment"(1960; for a retrospective on Hoffman's paper see Doherty & Brehmer, 1997) and Lewis Goldberg's (1968) "Simple Models or Simple Processes? Some Research on Clinical Judgments." The high watermark for the conceptualization of Decision Theory as a descriptive, as opposed to prescriptive, model of behavior, was Cam Peterson and Lee Beach's (1967) "Man as an Intuitive Statistician."

The 1970s

This decade saw both a coalescence of the field into what could legitimately be called JDM and a radical redirection of the field or even a paradigm shift (Kuhn, 1962). The paper "Comparison of Bayesian and Regression Approaches to the Study of Human Information Processing in Judgment" by Paul Slovic and Sarah Lichtenstein (1971) did the coalescing (with the J in Judgment provided by Hammond and the regression modelers and the DM by Edwards and the Decision Theorists). The radical redirection was initiated by a series of papers, including the 1974 "Judgment Under Uncertainty – Heuristics and Biases" by Amos Tversky and Daniel Kahneman. The ideas in that paper reverberated in the field even before it was published and continue to do so today. The recognition of community of purpose brought about by Slovic and Lichtenstein eventuated in the institutionalization of the field in the Society for Judgment and Decision Making. The founding in 1980 of this very active society was accomplished largely through the efforts of Jim Shanteau and Chuck Gettys. Five years later, The Brunswik Society joined the JDM Society as another home for some JDM researchers.

A significant book, *Decision Making: A Psychological Analysis of Conflict, Choice and Commitment,* by Irving Janis and Leon Mann (1977) never did become part of the JDM mainstream but has had considerable impact outside the field. Information Integration Theory (e.g., Anderson,

1970) came upon the scene at about the same time. All of these strains of research proceeded apace in the 1970s, but it is fair to say that the heuristics and biases program came to dominate JDM, especially in the eyes of those outside the field. The success of this program was capped off by Kahneman and Tversky's 1979 *Econometrica* paper "Prospect Theory: An Analysis of Decision Under Risk." Another significant event for the field came from the problem-solving literature, that is, Allen Newell and Herbert Simon's classic *Human Problem Solving* (1972). This book has heavily influenced both theory and methodology in JDM.

The 1980s

By the 1980s, then, JDM had become established and institutionalized. Hal Arkes and Ken Hammond (1986) could put together a compendium of dozens of papers exploring the impact of JDM on other areas of research and practice. Jim Naylor changed the name of what had become a major vehicle for JDM research from *Organizational Behavior and Human Performance* to *Organizational Behavior and Human Decision Processes*, and *The Journal of Behavioral Decision Making* was founded. Nisbett and Ross (1980) explored the implications of heuristics and biases for social psychology, and Detlof von Winterfeldt and Ward Edwards (1986) published a systematization of knowledge in the theory and application of decision analysis, expressing therein doubts about those very heuristics and biases.

The 1990s

This decade witnessed further broadening of JDM, but two major developments were to challenge the status quo. One was the emergence of Naturalistic Decision Making (NDM) under the auspices of Gary Klein and his collaborators (Klein, 1998; Klein, Orasanu, Calderwood, & Zsambok, 1993; Zsambok & Klein, 1997), an approach supported heavily by military funding agencies that wanted research on how people make decisions under duress in naturalistic situations rather than how they make decisions in the laboratory. The NDM approach was a challenge in the sense that one of its basic premises is that much laboratory research simply could not or did not address many important decision issues. The other challenge was directly to the generalizability of the conclusions of the heuristics and biases program. That was by Gerd Gigerenzer and his Adaptive Behavior and Cognition group (Gigerenzer, 1996, 2000;

Gigerenzer, Todd, & the ABC Research Group, 1999), who took the position that the biases explored by the heuristics and biases researchers were in the investigators, not in the people investigated.

Many interfield connections have been established in the past decade, and many more are being established. These interfield connections can be found in many of the chapters in this volume, and they provide one of the themes that will be explored subsequently. But perhaps the best way to summarize the decade of the 1990s and subsequent years is by noting the contents of the parts of this book, which range from foundations to applications:

Part I reflects the continuing concern with classic foundational issues; the chapter authors deal with issues such as criteria of rationality and the extent to which behavior coheres with models of rationality, as well as the nature of rationality itself.

Part II explores the burgeoning interest in ties between JDM and other areas in psychology; the chapter authors deal with explicit influences on decision making from research in developmental psychology, memory and other areas in cognitive psychology.

Part III explores the influence of affect on decision processes, and is dotted with terms not commonly found in early treatments of JDM, such as affect, mood, motivation, and goals.

Part IV deals with the impact of broader cultural issues, the chapter authors in this part calling attention to the obvious but too often ignored fact that decisions are taken in social contexts.

Part V describes a variety of ways in which JDM is reaching out to make a difference in the world; the authors deal with decisions made not solely for the purpose of being studied by decision researchers, but rather with decisions made to achieve some important purpose in reality.

Parts II to V of the book show clearly that the field can no longer be characterized as having shown a "relative neglect of emotional and social factors," an assessment that was made, I believe appropriately, by Daniel Kahneman in his 1991 *Psychological Science* paper. For a more detailed history of JDM, the reader might wish to see "Judgment and Decision Research: Some Historical Context," by Bill Goldstein and Robin Hogarth (1997).

The next major section of this chapter addresses two opposing positions that characterize two major groups of researchers in the field. This discussion will reprise Helmut Jungermann's 1983 paper "The Two Camps on Rationality" in light of the contributions in this volume. Before turning our attention to what appears to divide JDM, however, let's look at some *shared* assumptions that characterize JDM. For these shared assumptions I will adopt what Robin Hogarth (1993) saw as eight major ideas characterizing the field.

Shared Assumptions in JDM

- Judgment can be modeled. In elaborating on this, Hogarth wrote, "...the most amazing feature of our work is that we have been able to find ways of representing people's judgments and choices by different types of mathematical models" (1983a, p. 410).
- Rationality is bounded. While I will shortly explore Jungermann's dichotomy between JDMers, on the one hand, who believe that people are rational, and those, on the other, who believe that people are not, it is apparent that even the most ardent optimists see rationality as bounded.
- To understand decision making, understanding the task is more important than understanding the people.
- Decisions are taken with respect to levels of aspiration, or reference points.
- Decision makers use heuristic rules.
- Adding is important. That is, compared to unaided human judgment, simple linear models are remarkable at making good predictions, even better than the expert modeled.
- People search for confirmation in inference tasks.
- Thought is constructive; that is, in making decisions, people don't just consult preexisting tables of beliefs and probabilities.

Jungermann's Two Camps on Rationality Revisited

The research style and rhetoric of one camp focuses on success and what it is that makes human beings successful in their adaptation to the environment; those of the other camp focus on error and the use of error to gain insight into psychological process. Using the terminology of Jungermann (1983), we call the first camp the *optimists,* or the *efficiency* camp, the second the *pessimists,* or the *deficiency* camp. The catalyst that exacerbated the split was the publication of "Judgment Under Uncertainty – Heuristics and Biases" in *Science* (Tversky & Kahneman, 1974) and the subsequent book of the same name (Kahneman, Slovic, & Tversky, 1982). The heuristics and biases program introduced some radically new concepts into the field, concepts that were and still are resistant to full incorporation into formal models. The program has had a major impact on cognitive social psychology (Nisbett & Ross, 1980) and, of course, on behavioral economics (Hogarth & Reder, 1986). As Hammond (1990) noted in his paper in the memorial tribute to Hillel Einhorn (Hogarth, 1990), it has brought the whole field of JDM into much more prominence in psychology in general. This research showed clearly that formal decision theoretic models were of dubious validity as descriptive models, and that there were formidable measurement difficulties to be overcome when using decision analysis prescriptively, that is, as a decision aid. These messages were consonant with Herbert Simon's assessment of decision theory, which was stated forcefully in his 1983 *Reason in Human Affairs*.

Optimists: The Focus on Efficiency

Decision Theorists. Very early in his classic 1954 paper, Edwards noted that "the crucial fact about economic man is that he is rational" and that "economic man must make his choices in such a way as to maximize something" (p. 381). Over the almost five-decade course of the decision theoretic research program, the influences of economic theory, Bayesian statistical decision theory, and classical psychophysics, all of which were prominent in the 1954 paper, have been at the core of the enterprise.

A decision analysis can be usefully represented by either a decision tree or a payoff matrix; I choose the latter. There are four noteworthy aspects of Figure 20.1, given the purposes of this review.

1. The system is geared to result in action or choice. It is not aimed at judgment, or inference, or prediction, or problem structuring,

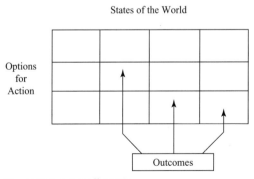

Figure 20.1 A payoff matrix.

or anything else except insofar as they play key roles in action selection.

2. The system requires the generation of a set of options.
3. The system requires prediction of possible world states. Those predictions typically involve the collection and aggregation of data.
4. The system requires the assessment of the degree to which the person or organization with a stake in the decision would like each outcome, should it occur.

Note that steps 2 and 3 require some creative activity on the part of the decision maker, and steps 2, 3, and 4 can all be characterized as requiring reasoning.

Where does rationality fit in the decision theory scheme? There are two places where criteria of rationality play a central role in decision theory. The first is in the prediction of possible states of the world. Note that in Figure 20.1 the word probability is associated with beliefs about states of the world. The idea is that the stakeholder must take the available data into account and aggregate those data such that a set of probabilities that conform to the rules of probability theory is associated with the anticipated states of the world. That is, the states must be mutually exclusive and exhaustive, and the probabilities of the states must sum to 1.0. Furthermore, the updating of the probabilities, given new data, must be in accord with Bayes's rule. Hence, the creation of the anticipated possible states of the world and the assessment of the probabilities thereof entail theoretical reasoning. The second place that a criterion of rationality is involved is in the choice of action. The criterion involves, as Edwards noted in 1954, maximization of some quantity. The most common criterion is that in order to be rational, the decision maker must maximize subjectively expected utility, which entails practical reasoning. Much of the technical apparatus of decision theoretic approaches is concerned with measurement of the probabilities and utilities.

Social Judgment Theorists. Whereas Decision Theory is beholden to economics, Bayesian statistics, and classical psychophysics, Social Judgment Theory has its roots in the probabilistic functionalism of Egon Brunswik and in correlational statistics. Brunswik's psychology had been most systematically applied to perception, his 1956 *Perception and the Representative Design of Psychological Experiments* being his best-known book in the United States. Hammond and his colleagues

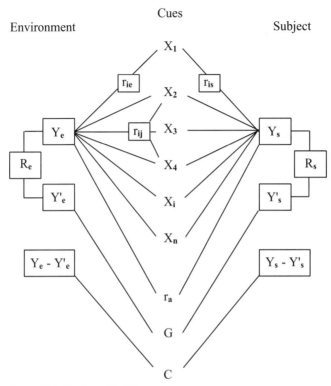

Figure 20.2 The Lens Model.

extended Brunswik's ideas first to clinical psychodiagnosis and subsequently to a wide variety of issues involving multiattribute judgment.

The "logo" of Social Judgment Theory is the Lens Model, presented in Figure 20.2. The lens model is an extremely useful device for structuring research and for guiding the analysis of research data. It is quite different in its essential function from a payoff matrix. It is a representation of the methodological implications of Social Judgment Theory rather than a guide to decision.

Note the structure of the model. The subject is on one side, the environment on the other. The lenslike aspect of the figure represents the idea that the subject's task is to come to terms with the environment in the sense of coming to know that environment. The Lens Model indicates that the environment is assumed to be knowable via the mediation of multiple intersubstitutable cues, and that the person is assumed to be aware of some of those cues and to be aggregating them by processes that can be represented in the same way as on the environmental side of the lens. The system used to capture the aggregation process has typically – almost exclusively until recently – been multiple regression, but as Hammond (1996) pointed out, that is not of the essence of the system. In fact, Slovic and Lichtenstein (1971) noted that the Lens Model could have been instantiated by Brunswik in terms of probability theory.

A brief description of how the Lens Model might be used is in order. Suppose that we are interested in assessing the diagnostic skills of a physician. Clearly, we cannot have a physician diagnose a single case and then make valid generalizations about his or her skill; there may be something unusual or even unique about that single case. Statistically speaking, were we to use the single case as a sample from which to draw statistical inferences about some population of cases, we would have 0 df for cases. We must observe the physician's behavior across an ensemble of cases that have been sampled from the domain of cases to which we wish to generalize. In this example thus far, we have turned the usual sampling asymmetry on its head; we have one subject and many situations! If we also wish to generalize across physicians, then we would sample a number of physicians, perform an idiographic-statistical analysis on each, and nomothetically aggregate the idiographic indices across physicians.

Consider the Lens Model as a framework for thinking about and analyzing the behavior of a single physician, who has made 100 diagnostic judgments (Y_s) with respect to the presence or absence of a particular disease on 100 cases, each case being represented by varying values on a set of n cues, in this example symptoms (X_i). Information subsequently becomes available on the true state (Y_e) for each case, perhaps via post-mortems or some gold standard. The judgments and the criteria can be binary yes/no judgments or they can be continuous. The number of cases is not represented in the figure; we could add another layer of subscripts to denote the number of cases.

Where does rationality fit in the scheme? There are a number of places where criteria of rationality play a central role in Social Judgment Theory. The fundamental one is how well the subject's perception, diagnosis, or whatever judgment is called for corresponds with the environment. This is called *achievement*, and it is reflected in the statistic r_a, the correlation between the person's responses and the ecological criterion values, in the example at hand between the diagnoses and the true states over the 100 cases.

There are other interrelated criteria for rationality, but all of them refer to characteristics that contribute to achievement. The multiple correlation R_s, which represents the degree to which the person's judgments are predictable assuming a linear, additive model, should ideally be 1.0 (assuming a stationary environment and, except in the case in which the subject is validly using nonlinearities of function form, nonadditivities in the integration rule, or cues that are available to the person making the judgments but not in the equation). The cue utilization coefficients (r_{is}) ought to match the ecological validities (r_{ie}), both of which are zero-order correlations. Typically, linearity of function forms is assumed, though it need not be. The G coefficient is the zero-order correlation between the predicted values of the two linear models, and can be interpreted as the validity of the person's knowledge of the linear additive components of the environment. The C index, the zero-order correlation between the residuals from the two models, reflects the extent to which the unmodeled aspects of the person's knowledge match unmodeled aspects of the environmental side of the lens. When applied to appropriate problems, lens model analyses provide hard-won insights, some of which are limited by the modeling assumptions, into the person's judgment policy.

Contributions to achievement. As implied by the very layout of the Lens Model, all of these indices are conceptually and statistically interrelated. The degrees to which r_{ie} and r_{is} are appropriate measures of relationship are influenced by whether we have specified the correct function form and by the real strength of relationship. The degree to which r_{ie} and r_{is} are similar determines G. R_e and R_s are determined by how predictable the environment and the person are and how well we have specified the true model of each. Achievement is influenced by all of these factors, as represented by the elegant formulation known as the Lens Model Equation (Tucker, 1964):

$$r_a = R_e * R_s * G + C\left[\left(1 - R_e^2\right) * \left(1 - R_s^2\right)\right]^{1/2}$$

which translates nicely into everyday speech as: *A person's ability to predict the world is completely determined by how well the world can be predicted from the available data (R_e), how consistently the person uses the available data (R_s), and how well the person understands the world (G and C).*

Other Players in the Efficiency Camp. There are many people in addition to Edwards and Hammond who are accentuating the positive, who readily admit that we humans are not perfect but who focus on cognitive success in a complex world. Perhaps the most extreme position is taken by L. J. Cohen (1981). It may be an unfair depiction of his position, but I'll summarize it by saying that it amounts to asserting that if people do it, then it must be rational because people are rational. Berndt Brehmer, of Uppsala, is a long-time contributor to the literature of Social Judgment Theory, now focusing on dynamic decision making. Gerd Gigerenzer (Gigerenzer, 2000; Gigerenzer, Todd, & the ABC Research Group, 1999) of the Max Planck Institute is a prominent proponent of a highly positive view of human cognitive abilities and a vocal critic of both the research methods and conclusions of the pessimists. Gigerenzer has proposed a process model in his theory of probabilistic mental models, or PMM theory, which is clearly Brunswikian in origin but not a derivative of Social Judgment Theory. This group is well represented in this volume in the chapter by Laura Martignon and Stefan Krauss.

Another prominent group in the efficiency camp is involved in the study of NDM, described in several recent books (Klein, 1998; Klein et al., 1993; Zsambok & Klein, 1997) and in the present volume in chapters by Rebecca Pliske and Gary Klein and by Jim Shanteau, David Weiss, Rick Thomas, and Julia Pounds. In the NDM group there are many others who place themselves explicitly and squarely in the efficiency camp, including Raanan Lipshitz, Terry Connolly, Lee Beach, Marvin Cohen, Jens Rasmussen, Henry Montgomery, Jay J. J. Christensen-Szalanski, and others. This group rejects the decision theoretic approach, even as they endorse the metatheoretical presupposition that decision making in action is highly adaptive. Herbert Simon might also be placed here, rejecting the subjective expected utility (SEU) model, as it requires perfect knowledge, infinite computing capacity, and Olympian wisdom, whereas he still sees human behavior as highly adaptive, seeking and obtaining not optimal outcomes but generally satisfactory ones. Jonathan Koehler's (1996) paper in *Behavioral and Brain Sciences* on the base rate places him here as well, but I do not draw the same conclusion as he does from the data that he presents. Jungermann also places Berkeley and Humphreys (1982), Einhorn and Hogarth (1981), and Phillips (1983) in with the optimists. I think that the pragmatic reasoning schema of Cheng and Holyoak (1985) marks them as optimists, too, as does the general tenor of the chapter by Yates, Veinott, and Patalano in this book. In that chapter, Yates et al. emphasize the fact that most people are pretty content with the outcomes of their major decisions.

It is more difficult to place people such as Duncan Luce and Michael Birnbaum, who are working on foundational issues, in one camp or another. Luce concluded that "What seems rational depends more on the formulation of the domain of study than we had previously acknowledged." This he said after presenting an alternative to SEU theory that he saw as equally rational from an axiomatic point of view, but that had different consequences for situations with mixed gains and losses, and asking whether there was some deeper sense of rationality that would select between alternative formalizations. It seems that there is some underlying commitment in such axiomatization to the idea that people are ultimately rational, and so I would tentatively place Luce in with the optimists. Conversely, it appears that Birnbaum fits better in the other camp.

As something of an aside, the same issue concerning two camps on rationality can be raised about what seems to me to be a potentially closely related field that is typically ignored in the JDM literature: thinking and reasoning. With all of the attention paid to reasoning errors in the thinking and reasoning literature, I was struck by the number of contributors in the Manktelow and Over (1993) volume who made statements to the effect that human beings are *inherently* rational and that errors are due to cognitive limitations. I take Jonathan Evans's position to be an endorsement of the proposition that human beings possess rationality$_1$ and the violations are of rationality$_2$ often in the service of rationality$_1$. In a similar vein, Keith Stanovich (1999) describes two systems of thought, one associative, holistic, automatic, fast, and acquired by exposure and experience, the other analytical, rule-based, controlled, and learned by more formal tuition. Although Stanovich's focus is on individual differences, the rhetoric of his work clearly places him in the optimists' camp.

Explanatory constructs proposed by the efficiency camp. How do the optimists provide explanations of success in a complex world? Here are some of the closely related ideas (some are so closely related as to be almost synonymous, but they're worth naming separately anyway) propounded by this camp:

- Ecological rationality – "a heuristic is ecologically rational to the degree that it is adapted to the structure of the environment" (Gigerenzer & Todd, 1999, p. 13)
- Satisficing
- Limited information search
- Fast and frugal reasoning
- The take-the-best algorithm, which is a case of one-reason decision making
- The recognition principle
- Recognition-primed decision making

Some books representative of the efficiency camp. The titles of some of the books that have come out of the Efficiency camp epitomize the attitudes of those in that camp:

- Gigerenzer (2000): *Adaptive Thinking: Rationality in the Real World.*
- Gigerenzer, Todd, and the ABC Research Group (1999): *Simple Heuristics That Make us Smart*
- Klein (1998): *Sources of Power: How People Make Decisions*

And if we broaden the definition of optimist a bit to include those who propose techniques to enhance decision making, then we can add

- Hogarth (2001): *Educating Intuition*

These titles are not as catchy as the titles from the Deficiency camp because it is easier to make up clever titles for bad thinking than for good thinking.

Characteristics of the Efficiency Camp. Obviously, the defining characteristic is that the investigators in this camp hold the human decision maker in relatively high regard. A distinction that Hammond has emphasized is especially relevant to the split, that is, the distinction between correspondence and coherence criteria of performance. *Correspondence criteria* are those that assess the goodness of decisions by how well they work in the world, that is, by their outcomes. *Coherence criteria* refer to how consistent the inference or decision process is with some formal model, such as SEU theory, formal logic, Bayes's theorem, and so on. The Efficiency camp, as should be clear from the preceding discussion, relies almost exclusively for its ultimate test of the goodness of judgments and decisions on correspondence of the decision with the outcomes in the world. Even though the formal criteria for decision theorists are Bayes's rule and utility maximization, the ultimate criterion for the practitioners of decision theory is how well, in their judgment, it works. I once spoke at a JDM meeting with Ward Edwards right after a presentation on pseudo-diagnosticity, that is, the tendency of people not to look for information in support of alternative hypotheses (see Doherty, Chadwick, Garavan, Barr, & Mynatt, 1996). He chided me for focusing on error rather than on how well people do in the world. Ken Hammond caught me in a hallway a few minutes later and did the same thing.

There are a number of attributes that are sort of fuzzy, characterizing the optimists' camp in general but not everyone in it. For reasons of space, I'll limit citations to just a few names after each attribute, with emphasis on founders and contributors to this volume.

- The research tends to focus both on action selection and on inferences and predictions about the world – Edwards, Hammond, Pliske, and Klein
- Adaptation, often with an evolutionary flavor, is emphasized – Gigerenzer and the ABC Group, Martignon and Krauss
- Idiographic research methodologies are often employed – Edwards, Hammond, Orasanu, Pliske, and Klein
- There is a strong tendency to apply the results to real problems – Edwards, Hammond, Orasanu, Yates, Pliske, and Klein
- There is a belief that the biases fondly talked about by the other camp are in the research rather than in the subjects – Gigerenzer and the ABC Group, Martignon and Krauss, Pliske and Klein
- There is a belief that if one considers all of the costs of deciding, then what may appear to be deficient at one level of analysis can be shown to be rational at another level – Gigerenzer and the ABC Group
- There is a belief that if one considers a different time horizon, then decisions that appear defective can often be shown to be highly adaptive – Schneider and Barnes, Clancy, Elliott, Ley, Omodei, Wearing, McLennan, and Thorsteinsson
- There is a predilection to study experts – Shanteau, Edwards, Hammond, Pliske, and Klein.

Before leaving the optimists' camp, I would like to make a comment about the optimists' charge that the pessimists have a serious criterion problem, that is, that it is not always clear what the appropriate criterion is, especially given time horizon problems, differences between experimenter and subject in the interpretation of the task, and so on. But it is not pointed out often enough that the optimists have just as great a criterion problem. I have read numerous times that people get along well in the world, but I have never seen anything remotely like good evidence for that statement. It is hand waving. It *may* be true that people, on the whole, get along well in the world, but I don't see serious scientific work to back that statement up; perhaps convincing evidence is not even possible, given the value-ladenness of the claim. Would it be germane for me to go through the litany of what one born in the middle of the Great Depression, a few years before the outbreak of World War II, has lived through? That would take up far too much space. Evans, Over, and Manktelow (1994, p. 169) say that "Our ability to solve problems and to achieve goals is self-evident." I think that the converse is equally true: Our *inability* to solve problems and to achieve goals is self-evident. In the words of Reyna, Lloyd, and Brainerd (in this volume), "One of the most important questions for anyone interested in improving human judgment and decision making . . . is why smart people, who often have the requisite competence, reason poorly or make stupid choices." The optimists, as scientists of reasoning, have precisely the same problem as clinical psychologists who attempt to do outcome research. What is an acceptable criterion for normal, healthy human behavior? What is an acceptable criterion for getting along well in the world?

Pessimists: The Focus on Deficiency

Heuristics and Biases Researchers. As we have noted, the catalyst that triggered the split into two camps was the 1974 publication of Tversky and Kahneman's "Judgment Under Uncertainty – Heuristics and Biases." That paper triggered an explosion of interest in JDM, with the explicit goal of using errors in inference and choice to gain insight into the cognitive processes involved. This tactic of focusing on error is a time-honored one, having been used by Freud in the study of unconscious motivation, Piaget in the study of cognitive development, and Bruner in the study of concept formation, as well as being at the heart of the theory of signal detectability. From the outset, the claim was that the "heuristics are highly economical and usually effective, but they lead to systematic and predictable errors" (Kahneman et al., 1982, p. 20). Nisbett and Ross (1980) made a similar disclaimer: "Specifically, we contend that people's inferential strategies are well adapted to deal with a wide range of problems, but that these same strategies become a liability when they are applied beyond that range" (p. xii). The problem, so the Efficiency camp argues, is that after making that concession in a sentence or two, the entire program of research is then devoted to the demonstration of errors (Christensen-Szalanski and Beach, 1984; Hammond, 1990). Considering the sheer volume of space devoted to error compared with that devoted to success, it is hard to counter that argument.

The Deficiency camp can also trace its parentage in part to Ward Edwards, but Ward would undoubtedly label the offspring as illegitimate. The heuristics and biases program was a reaction against the idea that the normative models of inference were, as Peterson and Beach had argued less than a decade before, also good descriptive models. Tversky and Kahneman's 1974 *Science* paper and the 1982 Kahneman et al. reader formed a set of demonstrations purporting to show that people

- were insensitive to base rates
- were insensitive to the implications of the central limit theorem
- were insensitive to the implications of regression to the mean
- saw patterns and correlations where there were none
- violated one of the most elementary and transparent rules of probability theory, the conjunction rule

This was surely a frontal attack on the assumption that people draw inferences in a rational fashion. In many subsequent papers, perhaps the best known of which was Kahneman and Tversky's 1979 paper on prospect theory, the assault on *Homo economicus* was broadened to include demonstrations that if one wanted to argue for rationality in choice, some of the principles of rationality had to undergo Procrustean operations to make them fit the data!

Explanatory constructs proposed by the Deficiency camp. In trying to build descriptive accounts of judgment and choice, the investigators in the Deficiency camp have proposed a number of explanatory constructs. These include

- representativeness
- availability
- anchoring and adjustment
- scenario thinking
- the valuation function of prospect theory
- the decision weight function of prospect theory

Other phenomena of nonoptimality have been identified, including framing effects that produce preference reversals, variance preferences, overconfidence, hindsight bias, and so on. The 1996 special issue of *Organizational Behavior and Human Decision Processes* edited by Gideon Keren is a rich source for debate about some of these issues.

Some books representative of the Deficiency camp. The titles of some of the books that have come out of the Deficiency camp epitomize the authors' attitudes:

- Baron (1998): *Judgment Misguided: Intuition and Error in Public Decision Making*
- Dawes (1994): *House of Cards: Psychology and Psychotherapy Built on Myth*

- Dawes (2001): *Everyday Irrationality: How Pseudo-Scientists, Lunatics, and the Rest of Us Systematically Fail to Think Rationally*
- Gilovich (1991): *How We Know What Isn't So: The Fallibility of Human Reason in Everyday Life*
- Nisbett and Ross (1980): *Human Inference: Strategies and Short-comings of Social Judgment*
- Piatelli-Palmarini (1994): *Inevitable Illusions: How Mistakes of Reason Rule Our Minds*

Other players in the Deficiency camp. There are many people in addition to Kahneman, Slovic, and Tversky who are focusing on error, who readily admit that we humans often make good judgments and decisions, but who focus on cognitive failures, generally in simple laboratory situations. One that must be mentioned is Sarah Lichtenstein, who has to count as one of the founders of the field of JDM. Jungermann locates Janis and Mann (1977) here in light of their emphasis on defective coping, bolstering, and other departures from what they call *vigilance*, their term for effective decision making. I do not feel comfortable putting some of the following into this camp, but at least some of their major contributions have been with respect to Deficiency. So Baruch Fischhoff is put here, given his work on hindsight bias and people's difficulties in the assessment of risk. Doerner, too, is placed here in light of the limitations he sees in people's dynamic decision making. Jonathan Baron (1998) has been investigating the differences between the impact of errors of commission and errors of omission.

The number of people investigating JDM from a heuristics and biases perspective is very, very large. In this volume, Birnbaum and Martin, in a chapter dealing with foundational issues, report that people violate stochastic dominance, a finding that most theorists would agree is inconsistent with canons of rationality. Birnbaum and Martin indicate that the result, obtained not only in the laboratory but also in Web-based investigations, "is not only upsetting to the view that people are rational, but also disproves descriptive theories that retain stochastic dominance." Haines and Moore cite a conclusion by Reyna and Brainerd (1995) that judgmental biases actually become more reliable with age. In their chapter, Reyna, Lloyd, and Brainerd accept that people perform less than rationally on some tasks, but it would be inappropriate to call them either optimists or pessimists. Lerner and Tetlock implicitly accept the existence of biases when they pose the question, Can accountability inoculate decision makers from commonly observed judgmental biases? However, they conclude their chapter by noting that "the political, institutional, and social settings of decisions may require us to rethink what counts as judgmental bias or error." This idea calls to mind some of the other questions about the generalizability of the heuristics and biases claims (e.g., Gigerenzer, 1996; Lopes, 1991).

Research programs that seek to find influences on decisions other than those implicated in rational models seem to me to be reason to place people tentatively in the pessimists' camp. For example, Kameda, Scott Tindale, and Davis explore some of the sources of "procedural manipulability of group outcomes." Clearly, if people accept voting procedures such that the outcome can be fixed by the order in which candidates are voted on, something is, from the perspective of one who believes that people are rational, amiss. Peterson, Miranda, Smith, and Haskell approach decision making from an even broader group context in that they are investigating cultural and organizational influences. In addressing the issue of rationality, Peterson et al. assert that "whereas researchers no longer assume that individuals involved in the process [of decision making] are motivated solely by economic rationality, they do assume that the overriding objective of decision making is to arrive at an economically viable or profitable solution for the organization." In exploring the purposes of decision making, they note that cultural differences might influence decision makers to regard the purpose of the decision as mainly to be rational, to socialize newcomers, to establish the legitimacy of premade choices, or to make sense of what is happening around the decision makers. These purposes do not lend themselves easily to rational models of choice!

Although I would not use the chapter by Rettinger and Hastie as grounds to call them pessimists, their evidence that content affects reasoning would lead some hard-line coherence theorists (see the preceding discussion of coherence vs. correspondence) to claim that such content effects violate abstract principles of rationality. A similar claim, one that I think would not, in the long run, be sustainable, could be made concerning the chapters by Finucane, Peters, and Slovic, by Svenson, by Lerner and Tetlock, or by most of the other chapters that are examining influences on the decision process other than those specified in models of rational inference or choice.

There are some who cross over from the JDM domain more into the thinking and reasoning literature, including myself and Mynatt, with our research program on the consequences of failing to attend to alternative hypotheses (Doherty et al., 1996). The influence of Peter Wason (1960, 1968) in that literature looms large.

Characteristics of the Deficiency camp. In many ways, the characteristics of this camp are the converse of those in the Efficiency camp. The dominant feature is the focus on errors, or cognitive illusions. Names were appended to the characteristics of the optimists' camp, but for this list I'll just let Kahneman, Slovic, and Tversky carry the burden. Let us look at some tendencies:

- The research tends to focus on inferences about the world rather than action selection.
- Artificial (i.e., human-made) problems are typical (N.B.: artificial does *not* mean unimportant).
- Large groups of subjects are typically run; the results are often frequency counts.
- There is a preference to stay in the laboratory, with problems designed to elicit error and in doing so, to reveal the psychological process.
- There is a belief that the high-quality behavior fondly talked about by the other camp is often due to focusing selectively on success and ignoring failure in the world.
- There is a belief that if the subject's behavior does not conform to a normative model, then attempts to rationalize the behavior are without warrant.
- There is a belief that if people cannot do simple, one-shot tasks in the laboratory, it is highly unlikely that they can do complex tasks outside.
- There is a tendency to study novices, or untutored subjects not allowed to use aids such as paper, pencil, calculators, or computer.

The distinction between optimists and pessimists is a useful one for appreciating research styles and rhetorics in the context of the recent history of JDM, but I believe that there is a superordinate category that more aptly characterizes *all* researchers in JDM. Let's call that category the *realists*.

Realists: The Focus on the Match Between Task and Cognition

Any group called realists is one in which I think most of us would want to claim membership. In spite of the two camps just described, I consider it self-evident that *all* of the JDM researchers previously cited are realists in a far deeper sense than they are either optimists or pessimists. I believe that every researcher in the JDM fold would agree with the generalization that we humans are highly efficient at some cognitive tasks but, in the absence of the appropriate tools such as measuring instruments, paper and pencil, computers, and the like, all of which evolved over the millennia of cultural evolution, very deficient at others. After all, these tools, including yardsticks, probability theory, calculators, and computers, were invented precisely to overcome human limitations. Whatever the complete set of characteristics distinguishing the tasks that we humans do well from those that we do badly may be, I do not pretend to know. It is not just complexity (see Reyna, Lloyd, and Brainerd's chapter on this point, where they conclude that the major phenomena of JDM are unrelated to computational capacity). Some of the tasks at which we are very good are highly complex, such as face recognition and speech comprehension. Some of the tasks at which we are very poor seem fairly simple, such as taking the base rate into account. Incidentally, I disagree with those who argue that there is no base rate neglect. In the first of many studies of pseudodiagnosticity that have been done in our laboratory (Doherty, Mynatt, Tweney, & Schiavo, 1979; see also Leach, 2001), the base rate was manipulated in a frequency format, which has a powerful effect in many tasks, but it had no effect on data selection or subsequent judgment.

The literature supports speculation about some of the task characteristics that influence whether cognition is successful or not. Those tasks toward the perceptual end of the cognitive spectrum are accomplished accurately, rapidly, and with little variation among people. Those somewhat closer to the cognitive end typically show less accuracy, slower solutions, and greater variability, but those cognitive tasks that reach back into the evolutionary past are accomplished rapidly and accurately. There are other tasks, incredibly important in 21st-century culture, that involve recent intellectual accomplishments, such as the use of probability theory and higher mathematics, that pose problems that are solved with vastly more difficulty and by relatively few people. The task matters. Several authors, including Rettinger and Hastie and Dougherty, Gronlund, and Gettys, argue that content effects on the decision process mean that theories of rationality would have to be supplemented by auxiliary theoretical principles. Rettinger and Hastie do not mention epicycles, secants, and deferents, but those images come to mind as I write this when I ponder *those* auxiliary principles!

Optimists Must Surely Recognize Deficiencies. Much of the rhetoric of decision theory is normative, but the *practice* of decision theory involves primarily what Baron (1994) calls *prescriptive decision theory.* When I laid out the decision matrix earlier, and commented on the role of creative forecasting of states and of classical psychophysics, it was primarily couched in the argot of prescriptive decision aiding. This use of decision theory seems highly relevant to the rationality debate in that the limitations of unaided cognition are *assumed,* and decision analytic techniques to overcome them are developed in the expectation that they will enable decision makers to make better decisions than they could make unaided.

Hammond's Cognitive Continuum Theory is especially apropos in this discussion. Hammond explicitly argues that people will perform well in decision tasks for which there is a match between the task and the form of cognition brought to bear on the decision, but will perform less well when there is a mismatch between task and cognitive mode. In addition, much of the early research in the social judgment theoretic tradition was directly concerned with cognitive limitations, including research on the lack of consistency in judgment policies and self-insight that sorely impeded conflict resolution (Balke, Hammond, & Meyer, 1973; Hammond & Adelman, 1976) and so forth.

Gigerenzer's work shows that alternative task construals can attenuate biases, but the construals that lead to the biases are also ones that are used in our everyday commerce with the world, which produces a bit of a paradox. If we tend to use construals that lead to biases outside the JDM laboratory, then those construals (e.g., Eddy, 1982) are worthy of investigation as a source of poor decisions. Furthermore, even in the extraordinarily interesting and scientifically productive program of research carried out under the aegis of the ABC Group, not all of the subjects "get it right" with the more effective task construals. For example, Hoffrage and Gigerenzer (1996) showed that a frequency format had a dramatic advantage over a probability format (46% to 10%) when physicians solved medical inference problems. But note that about half of the solutions were still incorrect.

Pessimists Must Surely Recognize Efficiencies. As we indicated in the preceding quotations, Kahneman, Slovic, and Tversky (1982) and Nisbett and Ross (1980) grant that people often make good decisions. In a similar vein, Plous (1993), in his afterword, concludes that "biases are not necessarily bad." In many of the demonstrations of biases, many of the subjects got it right in spite of the fact that the study was designed to elicit the bias in question. For example, in a classic paper on representativeness (Kahneman and Tversky, 1972, reprinted in Kahneman et al., 1982), 22 of 89 subjects correctly responded that a class with 55% boys was more likely to come from a program with 45% boys than one with 65% boys. The last sentence of Dawes's *Everyday Irrationality: How Pseudo-Scientists, Lunatics, and the Rest of Us Systematically Fail to Think Rationally* (2001) is "We can be rational." Perhaps most telling are the title and much of the content of a new (1999) book, *Well-Being: The Foundations of Hedonic Psychology*. It was edited by, among others, Daniel Kahneman, (Kahneman, Diener, & Schwarz, 1999). Kahneman's chapter in that book is called "Objective Happiness."

What Will the Shape of a Rapprochement Look Like? I believe that the heuristics and biases program inspired by Kahneman, Slovic, and Tversky and the adaptive behavior and cognition program inspired by Gigerenzer and his colleagues have both made great contributions to our understanding of inference, judgment, and choice. The programs may seem antithetical, but it is just a matter of time before some clever graduate student starts to sort out the task characteristics that lead to adaptive cognition and those that lead to maladaptive cognition.

I believe that the conflict inherent in the two camps recognized by Jungermann has started to dissipate, and this volume exemplifies that trend. In spite of the preceding references, there is very little in this book in the way of negative rhetoric. The chapter authors have simply gone about the job of exploring the foundations of the field, exploring the ties between JDM and other areas in psychology; examining influences on decision making from other areas in cognitive psychology, exploring the influence of affect and social/cultural issues on decision making, and describing how JDM is making a difference in the world. They were written by realists.

I think that the further coalescence of the field will be influenced by two related trends that are prominent in this book. One is the greater recognition of the importance of context and task, the other is an emerging consensus that there are dual modes of thinking. The investigation of contextual and task determinants so permeates this book that I will not try to identify individual authors. Just look again at the contents of each part of the book noted at the end of the first section of this chapter.

The second trend is the emerging consensus concerning (at least) two modes of thought, with the explicit idea that good decision performance will result if the mode is appropriate to the task and poor if there is a mismatch. Consider some of the terms used by the chapter authors to describe closely related types of thought (for reviews, see Hammond, 1996; Sloman, 1996):

- Finucane, Peters, and Slovic speak of *deliberative* and *nondeliberative* thought processes.
- Rettinger and Hastie speak of *evidence driven* and *verdict driven*, and of a continuum from *deliberate/analytical* to *automatic/intuitive*.
- Haines and Moore cite Brunswik's *perception* versus *thinking*, Hammond's *analysis* and *intuition*, and Piaget's "hypothesized development from qualitative and perceptual to formal operations (explicit, analytical reasoning)."
- Dougherty, Gronlund, and Gettys speak of two *complementary* models, one with complex processes operating on relatively simple representations, the other with simple processes operating on relatively complex representations. Their Figure 5.1 summarizes their position on the factors that determine the kinds of decision processes explored in several chapters of the book.
- Schneider and Barnes contrast relatively automatic decisions based on *routines* and carefully thought-out *policy decisions* that are critical for establishing those routines.
- Svenson distinguishes between *holistic differentiation* and *process differentiation*.
- Pliske and Klein conclude their chapter by noting that "dual-process theories that propose that human behavior is guided by two parallel, interacting systems may be particularly helpful to decision researchers interested in studying both intuitive and rational decision-making strategies." They cite Epstein's Cognitive-Experiential Self-Theory, which proposes a slow, effortful rule-based system and a fast, experience-based system.
- Reyna, Lloyd, and Brainerd present their dual process model, in which reasoning operates on either *gist* representations or detailed verbatim representations, as a central feature of their contribution. In examining the relations among JDM, memory, and task characteristics, Reyna et al. explore fuzzy-trace theory.

Let's focus on the approach taken in Reyna, Lloyd, and Brainerd's chapter. Their position concerning rationality is similar to the one just espoused: "This alternative conception of rationality characterizes judgment and decision making as neither irrational nor necessarily adaptive, but as exhibiting degrees of rationality, depending on the precise nature of the reasoning process." Reyna et al. posit that "reasoners encode multiple independent representations of the same information along a fuzzy-to-verbatim continuum, which ranges from verbatim surface details to vague gist that preserves the core meaning of inputs."

Fuzzy-trace theory, unlike many other approaches, assumes that the intuitive gist end of the scale is often involved in advanced reasoning, in that gist representations confer great cognitive flexibility and allow reasoners to treat superficially different problems as the same. Further, they propose that the preferred form of processing is toward the fuzzy end of the continuum. There is an important distinction between cognitive continuum theory and fuzzy-trace theory, if I understand them correctly. The former posits movement along the continuum, prompted by temporary failure of achievement, and the movement is along the continuum in the direction of the opposite pole. Thus, in Hammond's approach, a decision maker's judgment process is at one locus on the continuum, often involving what he calls *quasi-rational thinking*. By contrast, fuzzy-trace theory posits that both gist representations and verbatim representations might be brought to bear at essentially the same time on a given task, and that there might be interference from a representation that was inappropriate to the task. The points of agreement between the two, however, are great, the most important being the continuum from analytic to gist (to mix terms) and the explicit recognition of the relation between the task and the kind of thinking that the task calls for.

My speculation is that the answer to the question posed at the beginning of this section concerning the shape of a rapprochement will be a dual-process theory that integrates Hammond's and Reyna et al.'s approaches. Each is relevant to the explanation of both good and bad judgment and decision making. Such a dual-process approach, which Sloman (1996) traces to Aristotle and to William James, should be amenable to formal computational modeling and also, as Pliske and Klein imply, should be able to incorporate the sorts of phenomena that Gary Klein refers to as *recognition-primed* decision making.

Seven Other Themes in This Volume – and in the Field of JDM

It took some crunching of categories to get this section down to Miller's magical number. The seven themes that I see as currents coursing through the book are (1) concern for what constitute appropriate criteria for rationality, (2) recognition of the complexity of the phenomena under the JDM umbrella, (3) heterogeneity of JDM methodologies, (4) influences from outside of JDM, (5) the influence of affect, (6) interest in expert decision making, and (7) actual and potential applications of JDM findings. The seven themes are decidedly not independent; several are highly interrelated. I cannot possibly mention all of the places in which these themes are reflected, and the reader will undoubtedly see other chapters in which they are represented, as well as other themes that might have been selected for emphasis.

1. *What Are Appropriate Criteria for Rationality?* The first part of the book has foundational papers by Luce and by Birnbaum and Martin, for whom coherence, that is, the degree to which behavior agrees with some model, is important. For these authors, the essential criteria for rationality are the axioms that provide the standard for the assessment of behavior, much as probability theory provides the criteria for many in the pessimists' camp. The NDM and ABC groups rely, on the other hand, on correspondence with outcomes as the criterion, whereas Reyna, Lloyd, and Brainerd take the position that "ideal cognition satisfies both external correspondence with reality and internal coherence." It would be a considerable contribution to more unity of purpose in the field if it could be demonstrated that, for some important problems in the world outside the laboratory, the satisfaction of coherence criteria significantly improves correspondence. Reyna et al. also take the somewhat politically incorrect stance that people's goals may be called into question when assessing rationality, a position that makes a great deal of sense to me. Haines and Moore advance consistency across tasks as "one possible criterion of rationality" as they work through the idea that development in childhood and adolescence involves "improvement of performance toward an ideal state of rationality."

Yates, Veinott, and Patalano take a very different tack with regard to criteria for rationality in that they explore what people in general, rather than philosophers or decision theorists, consider good or bad decisions. Yates et al. show that laypeople regard the satisfactoriness of the outcome as the major criterion for the goodness of decisions, a conception that runs quite counter to that of decision theorists. Finally, Peterson, Miranda, Smith, and Haskell highlight the difficulty of the issue of rationality by introducing broad cultural considerations, especially with respect to the fact that members of different cultures may have fundamentally different conceptions of the very purposes of decision making.

2. *Judgment and Decision Tasks Are Characterized by Great Complexity.* A complete theory of decision making would have to account for many factors and for many cognitive processes. Classical decision theorists posit that the key determinants of decision making are the anticipated states and the probabilities thereof, the options for action, and the subjectively expected utility of each possible outcome. The reader is well aware of just how much complexity that "simple" set can produce. Judgment theorists worry about cue function forms and correlations, configurality, vicarious mediation, and so forth. As noted previously, the authors in this book are exploring the foundations of the field, the ties between JDM and other areas in psychology, and the many influences on decision making and trying to see how JDM is making a difference in the world. As a consequence, the book as a whole has pointed to many sources of complexity. Let's consider just a few.

Lerner and Tetlock explore the influences of different forms of accountability. Yates and his collaborators have shown the multidimensionality of the concept of decision quality, and Kameda, Tindale and Davis; Peterson, Miranda, Smith, and Haskell; and the NDM group have explored some of the complexities introduced by groups of various kinds, from small groups to entire cultures, and by procedural variations in group decision making. The NDM researchers are focusing on the special sorts of groups called *teams,* as these groups play specialized roles in our society. Schneider and Barnes note that the goals of the decision maker matter. The content of the decision matters. The degree of expertise matters. Whether the culture is individualistic or collective matters. How one assesses the quality of decision matters. Clancy, Elliott, Ley, Omodei, Wearing, McLennan, and Thorsteinsson list a whole set of additional factors that influence dynamic distributed decision-making (D3M) tasks, noting that such tasks are performed in "a complex, dynamic, opaque environment with action–feedback loops."

In short, the present volume powerfully demonstrates the breadth of influences on decision making.

3. *What Is an Appropriate Method in JDM Is Limited Only by the Creativity of the Investigator.* What JDM methods are reflected in this book? (For the sake of brevity, I'll let the reader fill in the names of the chapter authors in this paragraph.) Exploration of the implications of axiomatic systems. Asking students to list good decisions and bad decisions and say why they were good or bad. Connectionist modeling. Imagery. Having children perform tasks on computers. Gambles. Examining the effects of giving people candy or showing them film

clips of bloopers. Having people fight fires on computers. Interviewing fire chiefs who fight real fires. Riding a fire truck. Looking for age-related changes. Looking for within-person consistency across problem representations.

At a higher level of abstraction with respect to method, some of the investigators are using something similar to an idiographic approach, in the sense that a great deal of information is obtained about each individual subject, whereas others are using nomothetic methodologies. The former are illustrated by the NDM researchers, and the latter are illustrated by the work of Birnbaum and Martin, who rely on proportions, and by that of Martignon and Krauss, who do the same. A strategy that takes advantage of the strengths of both approaches is best illustrated by Shanteau, Weiss, Thomas, and Pounds in their development of the CWS measure of expertise.

The multiplicity of methods reflects the great complexity of human decision making just described. Such heterogeneity of methods is, I believe, a sign of the vitality of the JDM enterprise.

4. *Greater Recognition of Influences from Outside of JDM.* The chapters in this book show that JDM is now far less insular than it was in the past The traditional influences of philosophy, economics, statistical decision theory, and correlational statistics are still evident, but the insights of other fields, inside and outside of psychology, are being brought to bear on the understanding of judgment and decision processes.

The influence of neurophysiology is clearly felt in the chapters by Isen and Labroo and by Finucane, Peters, and Slovic, and the work of Antonio Damasio is cited in several places in the book. Rettinger and Hastie bring in work on psycholinguistics and text comprehension, especially the work of Walter Kintsch. They, and Haines and Moore, cite Wason's research on logical reasoning. Haines and Moore also bring the findings of developmental research to bear on JDM.

Mainstream cognitive psychology is clearly playing a larger role than before, with two chapters largely devoted to the implications of memory research and theory for JDM. Clearly, JDM processes involve operations on memory representations, and I think that theorizing and research such as that by Reyna, Lloyd, and Brainerd and by Dougherty, Gronlund, and Gettys will come to play a more and more central role in JDM. Reyna et al. show that memory limitations in particular and capacity limitations in general are not adequate explanations of biased processing, nor do such limitations explain the need for fast and frugal reasoning; Dougherty et al. point out that memory processes have been implicated in JDM from the early days in the explanations of availability and representativeness. The effects of memory representation in JDM processes are raised in too many chapters to mention.

The ties between JDM and social psychology, social cognition in particular, are long-standing, but the chapters by Svenson, by Eiser, and by Kameda, Tindale, and Davis reinforce and broaden those ties. Svenson briefly touches upon the history of the relation of social psychology to JDM, with allusions to Festinger, Lewin, and Janis and Mann. Eiser focuses on a particular phenomenon, the accentuation of characteristics that are associated with group membership, and Kameda, Tindale, and Davis describe the results of their research and that of others on group decision making. They strongly emphasize the importance of shared assumptions in effective group or team decision making.

One long-run effect of the influence of other areas on JDM will, I believe, be an inexorable march toward more process-oriented models. Dougherty, Gronlund, and Gettys note that "Perhaps the most striking difference between decision theorists and cognitive theorists is the focus of their theories and models. Decision theorists tend to focus on developing mathematical models that describe *data*. . . . In contrast, cognitive theorists develop quantitative models that describe *processes*" (italics in the original). The growing interest in process models is reflected in many places in this volume, including the chapters by Martignon and Krauss, Haines and Moore, Reyna, Lloyd, and Brainerd, Dougherty and his colleagues, Rettinger and Hastie, Finucane, Peters, and Slovic, Svenson, Isen and Labroo, Lerner and Tetlock, Eiser, and Pliske and Klein.

5. *Heightened Awareness of the Influence of Affect on JDM.* This issue could well have been addressed in the previous section, but it seems to me to be so important that it merits treatment as a separate theme. Historically, JDM took feelings, emotions, and affect of all stripes into account in the assessment of utilities, or alternatively, in Janis and Mann's (1977) work, in the categories of anticipated consequences. But this volume unpacks affect in very different ways. Isen and Labroo devote their chapter to the explication of the effects of affect as an independent variable in problem solving, creativity, and so forth. They also explore possible interrelations between affect and thought as determinants of decision. Rettinger and Hastie bring in affect by noting the importance to decision making of personal importance and moral relevance, and Schneider and Barnes implicate affect by bringing goals and motives into play. Perhaps the most dramatic treatment of affect, in addition to that of Isen

and Labroo, is in the chapter lyrically titled "Judgment and Decision Making: The Dance of Affect and Reason." In it, Finucane, Peters, and Slovic invoke Damasio's (1994) neurophysiological work and develop a theory of the interplay between affect and cognition, focusing primarily on evidence for the affective component.

A heightened awareness of the importance of affect for JDM can be found outside the pages of this volume, as well, for example in Risk as Feelings theory (Loewenstein, Weber, Hsee, & Welch, 2001) and Decision Affect Theory (Mellers, Schwartz, Ho, & Ritov, 1997).

6. *Maintaining a Long-standing JDM Concern with Experts.* This volume reflects the continuing concern in JDM with expert decision making. The chapter by Shanteau, Weiss, Thomas, and Pounds is all about how one can assess expertise, a task that they point out is easy in those uninteresting cases in which a gold standard is readily available but problematic in those domains in which expertise is most needed. Of course, Pliske and Klein's chapter deals, by the very nature of the NDM program, with the performance of experts. I would venture a guess that virtually all JDMers would prefer to run domain experts whenever such experts are available and resources permit. Reyna, Lloyd, and Brainerd report that class inclusion errors first studied in children were also found with expert cardiologists. Although their subjects were not experts in the usual sense, Birnbaum and Martin ran Web-based experiments to ensure that findings based on students in laboratory situations were generalizable.

7. *Application Is a Key Part of JDM.* Virtually every chapter either says something about potential applications or is devoted to applications. Lerner and Tetlock conclude their chapter with speculation about how an understanding of accountability effects will influence complex human interactions. The attempt to develop a means of assessing expertise by Shanteau and his colleagues has clear implications for practical applications; why else would we care about experts except as they implement that expertise in practice? The very thrust of the contribution by Yates, Veinott, and Patalano is concerned with decision making in everyday life rather than decision making in the laboratory. And, of course, the NDM program is driven by application and the need for good theory to enhance applications. The dynamic distributed decision-making research by Clancy and her colleagues is clearly intended to clarify the knotty issues involved in real dynamic environments. If we accept the adage that there is nothing so practical as a good theory, then every single chapter in this book has implications for application.

Seven Other Themes Neither in This Volume Nor Given Sufficient Emphasis in JDM

Let's briefly explore several ideas not found very much, if at all, in this volume. Again, these seven are not independent of one another.

1. *An Effort Toward Demarcation of JDM.* Our field is, as illustrated amply in this volume, highly heterogeneous. What is it that demarcates JDM from other fields? Yates, Veinott, and Patalano open the book with a definition of decision as "a commitment to a course of action that is intended to produce satisfying outcomes." This strikes me as a quite nice definition, but I do not know if all of the phenomena that are routinely studied under the JDM tent would be fit by it. The Linda problem concerns valid inference and is related only indirectly to a commitment to a course of action. Having a definition of the field is not crucial to good research and may even inadvertently limit it, but some explicit discussion of what JDM encompasses might be productive. The preceding definition has two necessary features: the commitment to action and the future orientation. The latter clearly demarcates JDM from learning, personality, and several other traditional research areas of psychological research.

2. *Some Effort to Develop a Taxonomy of Decisions.* Although this call may seem to identify me as a proponent of Aristotelian rather than Galilean science, I believe that a task taxonomy and a decision taxonomy, which may turn out to be the same thing, are crucial for the development of a cumulative science of JDM. We have many local taxonomies: static versus dynamic, individual versus group versus team, laboratory versus real world, hard versus easy, inference versus choice versus judgment, and so forth. Investigations yielding valid findings in one decision situation are often generalized to decision situations that appear to me to be fundamentally different, save for the label *decision.* This lament is clearly related to what Egon Brunswik called a *double standard in research,* whereby investigators study many subjects in one situation but then generalize over situations as well as over subjects. I believe that this tendency to overgeneralize across situations may be one of the sources of the dispute between the two camps on rationality.

Psychological researchers, and I assume people in general, have an urge toward classifications and taxonomies. In virtually every chapter of this volume, some effort is made to make distinctions and to classify responses or influences, but there is no effort at an overall taxonomy. This is obviously related to the demarcation problem.

3. *More Attention to Brunswik's Concept of Vicarious Functioning.* A key concept in Brunswik's (1952, 1956) probabilistic functionalism is *vicarious functioning*, or the ability of an organism to achieve some end by a variety of means. This is explicitly recognized in the work of the ABC group (e.g., Martignon and Krauss's chapter) and in that of the NDM group (e.g., the chapter by Pliske and Klein). But it is such a fundamental attribute of sentient organisms that I believe that it ought to have a more central place in JDM theorizing. Vicarious mediation is, of course, one of the building blocks of Social Judgment Theory as well as of the theorizing of the ABC group.

4. *Reporting Results in Terms of Effect Sizes.* Some results are reported intrinsically in terms of effect sizes such as correlation coefficients, frequencies, and differences between frequencies. But too often I read reports, especially in literature reviews, in which some effect is purported to be important but for which effect sizes are simply absent. This is not so much a criticism of JDM as it is of the entire field of psychology. But again and again in this book, I wondered just how generalizable some statements actually were.

5. *More Research on Data Search.* Here my own narrow interests come to the fore. In our investigations, we (e.g., Doherty et al., 1996) have repeatedly found that subjects from introductory psychology students to physicians, given information favoring a focal hypothesis, rarely select diagnostic data relevant to an alternative hypothesis when the diagnostic data are readily available. Unpublished data show the same effect for students in advanced mathematics classes, even immediately after the study of Bayes's theorem. Many tasks in our lives require us to seek out the data on which to base our inferences and decisions, yet the great bulk of JDM research involves situations in which the data are simply given to the subjects by the investigator.

6. *Some Explicit Attention to Decision Making in Science.* Another area in which I have a personal involvement is scientific inference (Tweney, Doherty, & Mynatt, 1981). The historian of science Butterfield (1957) wrote that the scientific revolution "reduces the Renaissance and Reformation to the rank of mere episodes.... It changed the character of men's habitual mental operations even in the conduct of the nonmaterial sciences, while transforming the whole diagram of the physical universe and the very texture of human life itself" (pp. 7–8). And that was written before the Human Genome Project! Yet, for some reason, the topic of scientific thinking is essentially ignored in JDM. There is a very small, active interdisciplinary group of researchers interested in what

has made science a unique endeavor in human history, but it is outside JDM and largely outside the mainstream of cognitive psychology.

7. *JDM Researchers Rarely Employ Imagery, Analogy, and Metaphor.* After noting the absence of interest among JDMers in scientific thinking, it is apropos to mention what I believe is the almost complete absence of the use of imagery, analogy, and metaphor in JDM. Historians and psychologists of science have emphasized the generativity of imagery, analogy, and metaphor in science, with well-known examples being Einstein's riding a light beam, Darwin's tangled bank, and Bohr's atom. JDM theorists and investigators may attribute imagery and analogy to their subjects, but the point here is that JDM theorists and investigators rarely report using these devices in their own thinking and theory development. An obvious exception to this generalization is the use of mathematical models, which one may consider a very special case of analogy. It may be easier to use imagery, analogy, and metaphor when the object of study is just that, an object with physical characteristics.

Conclusion

This volume nicely reflects the present state of theory and research in JDM. I'll conclude this commentary by paraphrasing an earlier sentence. This book explores the foundations of the field, explores the ties between JDM and other areas in psychology, examines influences on decision making from other areas in cognitive psychology, explores the influence of affect and social/cultural issues on decision making, and describes how JDM is making a difference in the world.

References

Anderson, N. H. (1970). Functional measurement and psychophysical judgment. *Psychological Review, 77*, 157–170.

Arkes, H. R., & Hammond, K. R. (1986). *Judgment and decision making: An interdisciplinary reader.* Cambridge: Cambridge University Press.

Balke, W. M., Hammond, K. R., & Meyer, G. D. (1973). An alternate approach to labor–management negotiations. *Administrative Science Quarterly, 18*, 311–327.

Baron, J. (1994). *Thinking and deciding.* Cambridge: Cambridge University Press.

Baron, J. (1998). *Judgment misguided: Intuition and error in public decision making.* New York: Oxford University Press.

Berkeley, D., & Humphreys, P. (1982). Structuring decision problems and the bias heuristic. *Acta Psychologica, 50*, 201–252.

Brunswik, E. (1952). The conceptual framework of psychology. In *International encyclopedia of unified science* (Vol. 1, No. 10). Chicago, IL: University of Chicago Press.

676 DOHERTY

Brunswik, E. (1956). *Perception and the representative design of psychological experiments*. Berkeley: University of California Press.

Butterfield, H. (1957). *The origins of modern science*. New York: Free Press.

Cheng, P. W., & Holyoak, K. J. (1985). Pragmatic reasoning schemas. *Cognitive Psychology, 17*, 391–416.

Christensen-Szalanski, J. J. J., & Beach, L. R. (1984). The citation bias: Fad and fashion in the judgment and decision literature. *American Psychologist, 39*, 75–78.

Cohen, L. J. (1981). Can human irrationality be experimentally demonstrated? *The Behavioral and Brain Sciences, 4*, 317–331.

Coombs, C. H. (1964). *A theory of data*. New York: Wiley.

Damasio, A. (1994). *Descartes' error: Emotion, reason, and the human brain*. New York: Putnam.

Dawes, R. M. (1994). *House of cards: Psychology and psychotherapy built on myth*. New York: Free Press.

Dawes, R. M. (2001). *Everyday irrationality: How pseudo-scientists, lunatics, and the rest of us systematically fail to think rationally*. Boulder, CO: Westview.

Doerner, D. (1996). *The logic of failure*. Reading, MA: Addison-Wesley.

Doherty, M. E. (1993). A laboratory scientist's view of naturalistic decision making. In G. Klein, J. Orasanu, E. Calderwood, & C. E. Zsambok (Eds), *Decision making in action: Models and methods* (pp. 362–388). Norwood, NJ: Ablex.

Doherty, M. E., & Brehmer, B. (1997). The Paramorphic representation of human judgment: A 30 year retrospective. In W. Goldstein & R. Hogarth (Eds.), *Judgment and decision making: Currents, connections and controversies* (pp. 537–551). Cambridge: Cambridge University Press.

Doherty, M. E., Chadwick, R., Garavan, H., Barr, D., & Mynatt, C. R. (1996). On people's understanding of the diagnostic implications of probabilistic data. *Memory & Cognition. 24*, 644–654.

Doherty, M. E., Mynatt, C. R., Tweney, R. D., & Schiavo, M. (1979). Pseudodiagnosticity. *Acta Psychologica. 43*, 111–121.

Eddy, D. M. (1982). Probabilistic reasoning in clinical medicine: Problems and opportunities. In D. Kahneman, P. Slovic, & A. Tversky (Eds.), *Judgment under uncertainty – heuristics and biases* (pp. 249–267). Cambridge: Cambridge University Press.

Edwards, W. (1954). The theory of decision making. *Psychological Bulletin, 51*, 380–417.

Edwards, W., & Tversky, A. (Eds.). (1957). *Decision making*. Harmondsworth, U.K.: Penguin Books.

Einhorn, H., & Hogarth, R. M. (1981). Behavioral decision theory: Processes of judgment and choice. *Annual Review of Psychology, 32*, 53–88.

Evans, J. St. B. T. (1993). Bias and rationality. In K. I. Manktelow & D. E. Over (Eds.), *Rationality: Psychological and philosophical perspectives* (pp. 6–30). London: Routledge.

Evans, J. St. B. T., Over, D. E., & Manktelow, K. I. (1994). Reasoning, decision making, and rationality. In P. N. Johnson-Laird & E. Shafir (Eds.), *Reasoning and decision making* (pp. 166–187). Cambridge, MA: Blackwell.

Gigerenzer, G. (1996). On content-blind norms and vague heuristics: A rebuttal to Kahneman and Tversky. *Psychological Review. 103*, 592–596.

Gigerenzer, G. (2000). *Adaptive thinking: Rationality in the real world*. New York: Oxford University Press.

Gigerenzer, G., & Todd, P. M. (1999). Fast and frugal heuristics: The adaptive toolbox. In G. Gigerenzer, P. M. Todd, & the ABC Research Group, *Simple heuristics that make us smart* (pp. 3–34). New York: Oxford University Press.

Gigerenzer, G., Todd, P. M., & the ABC Reseach Group. (1999). *Simple heuristics that make us smart*. New York: Oxford University Press.

Gilovich, T. (1991) *How we know what isn't so: The fallibility of human reason in everyday life*. New York: Free Press.

Goldberg, L. R. (1968). Simple models or simple processes? Some research on clinical judgments. *American Psychologist, 23*, 483–496.

Goldstein, W. M., & Hogarth, R. M. (1997). Judgment and decision research: Some historical context. In W. M. Goldstein & R. M. Hogarth (Eds.) *Judgment and decision making: Currents, connections and controversies* (pp. 3–65). Cambridge: Cambridge University Press.

Hammond, K. R. (1955). Probabilistic functionalism and the clinical method. *Psychological Review, 62*, 255–262.

Hammond, K. R. (1966). Probabilistic functionalism: Egon Brunswik's integration of the history, theory and methodology of psychology. In K. R. Hammond (Ed.), *The psychology of Egon Brunswik* (pp. 15–80). New York: Holt, Rinehart & Winston.

Hammond, K. R. (1990). Functionalism and illusionism: Can integration be usefully achieved? In R. M. Hogarth (Ed.), *Insights in decision making: A tribute to Hillel J. Einhorn.*(pp. 227–261). Chicago: University of Chicago Press.

Hammond, K. R. (1996). *Human judgment and social policy: Irreducible uncertainty, inevitable error, unavoidable injustice*. New York: Oxford University Press.

Hammond, K. R., & Adelman, L. (1976). Science, values, and human judgment. *Science, 194*, 389–396.

Hammond, K. R., Hursch , C. J., & Todd, F. J. (1964). Analyzing the components of clinical inference. *Psychological Review, 71*, 438–456.

Hoffman, P. J. (1960). The paramorphic representation of clinical judgment. *Psychological Bulletin, 57*, 116–131.

Hoffrage, U., & Gigerenzer, G. (1996). The impact of information representation on Bayesian reasoning. In G. Cotrell (Ed.), *Proceedings of the 18th annual Conference of the Cognitive Science Society* (pp. 126–130). Mahwah, NJ: Erlbaum.

Hogarth, R. M. (1990). *Insights in decision making: A tribute to Hillel J. Einhorn*. Chicago: University of Chicago Press.

Hogarth, R. M. (1993a). Accounting for decisions and decisions for accounting. *Accounting, Organizations and Society, 18*, 407–424.

Hogarth, R. M. (Ed.). (1993b). *Insights in decision making: A tribute to Hillel J. Einhorn*. Chicago: University of Chicago Press.

Hogarth, R. M., & Reder, M. (1986). The behavioral foundations of economic theory. *The Journal of Business, 59*, S181–S505.

Hogarth, R. M. (2001). *Educating intuition*. Chicago: University of Chicago Press.

Janis, I., & Mann, L. (1977). *Decision making: A psychological analysis of conflict, choice and commitment.* New York: Free Press.

Jungermann, H. (1983). The two camps on rationality. In R. W. Scholz (Ed.), *Decision making under uncertainty* (pp. 63–86). Amsterdam: Elsevier.

Kahneman, D. (1991). Judgment and decision making: A personal view. *Psychological Science. 2,* 142–145.

Kahneman, D., Diener, E., & Schwarz, N. (Eds.). (1999). *Well-being: The foundations of hedonic psychology.* New York: Russell Sage Foundation.

Kahneman, D., Slovic, P., & Tversky, A. (1982). *Judgment under uncertainty – heuristics and biases.* Cambridge: Cambridge University Press.

Kahneman, D., & Tversky, A. (1972). Subjective probability: A judgment of representativeness. *Cognitive Psychology, 3,* 430–454.

Kahneman, D., & Tversky, A. (1979). Prospect theory: An analysis of decision under risk. *Econometrica, 47,* 263–291.

Kahneman, D., & Tversky, A. (1996). On the reality of cognitive illusions: A reply to Gigerenzer's critique. *Psychological Review, 103,* 582–591.

Klein, G. (1998). *Sources of power: How people make decisions.* Cambridge, MA: MIT Press.

Klein, G. A., Orasanu, J., Calderwood, R., & Zsambok, C. E. (1993). *Decision making in action: Models and methods.* Norwood, NJ: Ablex.

Koehler, J. J. (1996). The base rate fallacy reconsidered: Descriptive, normative, and methodological challenges. *Behavioral and Brain Sciences, 13,* 1–17.

Kuhn, T. (1962). *The structure of scientific revolutions.* Chicago: University Press of Chicago.

Leach, J. R. (2001). *Information selection in a simulated medical diagnosis task: The effects of external representations and completely natural sampling.* Unpublished doctoral dissertation, Bowling Green State University.

Loewenstein, G. F., Weber, E. U., Hsee, C. K., & Welch, E. S. (2001). Risk as feelings. *Psychological Bulletin, 127,* 267–286.

Lopes, L. L. (1991). The rhetoric of irrationality. *Theory and Psychology, 1,* 65–82.

Luce, R. D., & Raiffa, H. (1957). *Games and decisions: Introduction and critical survey.* New York: Wiley.

Manktelow, K. I., & Over, D. E. (1993). *Rationality: Psychological and philosophical perspectives.* London: Routledge.

Meehl, P. E. (1954). *Clinical versus statistical prediction: A theoretical analysis and a review of the evidence.* Minneapolis: University of Minnesota Press.

Mellers, B. A., Schwartz, A., Ho, K., & Ritov, I. (1997). Decision affect theory: Emotional reactions to the outcomes of risky options. *Psychological Science, 8,* 423–429.

Newell, A., & Simon, H. A. (1972). *Human problem solving.* Englewood Cliffs, NJ: Prentice Hall.

Nisbett, R., & Ross, L. (1980). *Human inference: Strategies and shortcomings of social judgment.* Englewood-Cliffs, NJ: Prentice Hall.

Payne, J. W. (1976). Task complexity and contingent processing in decision making: An information search and protocol analysis. *Organizational Behavior and Human Performance, 16,* 366–387.

Peterson, C. R., & Beach, L. R.(1967). Man as an intuitive statistician. *Psychological Bulletin, 68*, 29–46.

Phillips, L. D. (1983). A theoretical perspective on heuristics and biases in probabilistic thinking. In P. C. Humphreys, O, Svenson & A. Vari (Eds.) *Analyzing and aiding decision processes.*(pp. 525–543). Amsterdam: North-Holland.

Piatelli-Palmarini, M. (1994). *Inevitable illusions: How mistakes of reason rule our minds.* New York: Wiley.

Plous, S. (1993). *The psychology of judgment and decision making.* New York: McGraw-Hill.

Reyna, V. F., & Brainerd, C. J. (1995). Fuzzy trace theory: An interim synthesis. *Learning and Individual Differences, 7*, 1–75.

Savage, L. J. (1954). *The foundations of statistics.* New York: Wiley.

Simon, H. A. (1955). A behavioral model of rational choice. *Quarterly Journal of Economics, 69*, 99–118.

Sloman, S. A. (1996). The empirical case for two systems of reasoning. *Psychological Bulletin, 119*, 3–22.

Slovic, P., & Lichtenstein, S. (1971). Comparison of Bayesian and regression approaches to the study of human information processing in judgment. *Organizational Behavior and Human Performance, 6*, 649–744.

Stanovich, K. (1999).*Who is rational? Studies of individual differences in reasoning.* Mahwah, NJ: Erlbaum.

Tucker, L. R. (1964). A suggested alternative formulation in the developments by Hursch, Hammond and Hursch, and by Hammond, Hursch and Todd. *Psychological Review, 71*, 528–530.

Tversky, A., & Kahneman, D. (1974). Judgment under uncertainty – heuristics and biases. *Science, 185*, 1124–1131.

Tweney, R. D., Doherty, M. E., & Mynatt, C. R. (1981). *On scientific thinking.* New York: Columbia University Press.

von Winterfeldt, D., & Edwards, W. (1986). *Decision analysis and behavioral research.* Cambridge: Cambridge University Press.

Wason, P. C. (1960). On the failure to eliminate hypotheses in a conceptual task. *Quarterly Journal of Experimental Psychology, 12*, 129–140.

Wason, P. C. (1968). Reasoning about a rule. *Quarterly Journal of Experimental Psychology, 20*, 273–281.

Zsambok, C. E., & Klein, G. (Eds.). (1997). *Naturalistic decision making.* Mahwah, NJ: Erlbaum.

Author Index

Subject Index